Renault 19
Service and Repair Manual

Steve Rendle

Models covered

All Renault 19 models with petrol engines, including Chamade, Cabriolet, 16-valve and special/limited editions
1237 cc, 1390 cc, 1397 cc, 1721 cc, 1764 cc & 1794 cc

Does not cover Diesel engine

(1646-1AF4-320)

ABCDE
FGHIJ
KLMNO
PQRST
2

© Haynes Publishing 2002

A book in the **Haynes Service and Repair Manual Series**

ISBN **1 85960 932 5**

British Library Cataloguing in Publication Data
A catalogue record for this book is available from the British Library.

Printed in the USA

Haynes Publishing
Sparkford, Yeovil, Somerset BA22 7JJ, England

Haynes North America, Inc
861 Lawrence Drive, Newbury Park, California 91320, USA

Editions Haynes
4, Rue de l'Arreuvoir, 924

Haynes Publishing Nord
Box 1504, 751 45 Uppsa

Contents

LIVING WITH YOUR RENAULT 19

Roadside Repairs

MOT Test Checks

General Repair Procedures

MAINTENANCE

Routine Maintenance and Servicing

Contents

Introduction

Introduction to the Renault 19

The Renault 19 was first introduced in France, in September 1988, in Hatchback form. The Renault 19 Hatchback became available in the UK in February 1989, and was followed by the Chamade Saloon version in November 1989.

Since introduction, the model range has expanded to include 3- and 5-door Hatchback models, 4-door Saloon models (known originally as the Chamade), and 2-door Cabriolet models. Utility models based on the Hatchback are also available in some territories. In mid-1992, the "Phase 2" models were introduced, with a revised engine range, and revised body styling. At the same time, engines with catalytic converters became standard for all models.

The car follows conventional front-wheel-drive design practice, with a transverse engine and transmission unit accommodated within a subframe.

All engines are of four-cylinder in-line type. Originally, the car was available with 1237 cc and 1397 cc overhead valve engines, and 1390 cc and 1721 cc overhead camshaft engines (not all of these engines have been available in all territories). In early 1991, the 16-valve (double overhead camshaft) engine was introduced to the range. When the "Phase 2" models were introduced in 1992, the 1721 cc engine was superseded by an improved 1794 cc version. A 1390 cc overhead valve engine is also available in the more basic models in some territories.

Four- and five-speed manual gearboxes are available in addition to three- and four-speed automatic transmissions.

Renault 19 TXE 5-door Hatchback ("Phase 1")

Renault 19 RN ("Phase 2")

Renault 19 16V Cabriolet ("Phase 2")

The front suspension is of MacPherson type, and the torsion bar rear suspension is of either tubular (enclosed-bar) or four-bar (open-bar) type.

A wide range of standard and optional equipment is available across the model range, including power steering, anti-lock braking, electric windows, central locking, etc.

The car is quite conventional in design, and the DIY home mechanic should find most work straightforward.

General dimensions and weights

Note: *All figures are approximate, and may vary according to model. Refer to manufacturer's data for exact figures.*

Dimensions

Overall length:	
Hatchback and Cabriolet models	4150 to 4160 mm
Saloon models	4250 to 4260 mm
Overall width	1680 to 1700 mm
Overall height (unladen):	
All except Cabriolet models	1400 to 1410 mm
Cabriolet models	1340 mm
Wheelbase	2540 mm
Front and rear track	1400 to 1430 mm

Weights

Kerb weight:	
"Phase 1" models:	
3-door Hatchback	900 to 1060 kg
5-door Hatchback	920 to 1080 kg
4-door Saloon	920 to 1080 kg
Cabriolet	1125 to 1180 kg
"Phase 2" models:	
3-door Hatchback	930 to 1115 kg
5-door Hatchback	950 to 1135 kg
4-door Saloon	950 to 1135 kg
Cabriolet	1135 to 1190 kg
Maximum gross vehicle weight:	
"Phase 1" models:	
3-door Hatchback	1350 to 1505 kg
5-door Hatchback	1370 to 1525 kg
4-door Saloon	1370 to 1525 kg
Cabriolet	1500 to 1550 kg
"Phase 2" models:	
3-door Hatchback	1385 to 1580 kg
5-door Hatchback	1405 to 1600 kg
4-door Saloon	1405 to 1600 kg
Cabriolet	1500 to 1530 kg
Maximum roof rack load	70 kg
Maximum towing weight:	
Braked trailer:	
1237 cc, 1390 cc and 1397 cc engines	800 to 900 kg
1721 cc, 1764 cc and 1794 cc engines	900 to 1000 kg
Unbraked trailer:	
1237 cc, 1390 cc and 1397 cc engines	450 to 480 kg
1721 cc, 1764 cc and 1794 cc engines	470 to 595 kg

Acknowledgements

Thanks are due to Champion Spark Plug, who supplied spark plug information. Certain illustrations are the copyright of Renault (UK) Ltd, and are used with their permission. Thanks are also due to Kings of Taunton Ltd, who provided technical assistance, to Draper Tools Limited, who provided some of the workshop tools, and to all those people at Sparkford who helped in the production of this manual.

Working on your car can be dangerous. This page shows just some of the potential risks and hazards, with the aim of creating a safety-conscious attitude.

General hazards

Scalding

• Don't remove the radiator or expansion tank cap while the engine is hot.
• Engine oil, automatic transmission fluid or power steering fluid may also be dangerously hot if the engine has recently been running.

Burning

• Beware of burns from the exhaust system and from any part of the engine. Brake discs and drums can also be extremely hot immediately after use.

Crushing

• When working under or near a raised vehicle, always supplement the jack with axle stands, or use drive-on ramps. *Never venture under a car which is only supported by a jack.*

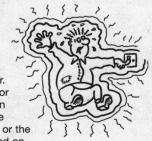

• Take care if loosening or tightening high-torque nuts when the vehicle is on stands. Initial loosening and final tightening should be done with the wheels on the ground.

Fire

• Fuel is highly flammable; fuel vapour is explosive.
• Don't let fuel spill onto a hot engine.
• Do not smoke or allow naked lights (including pilot lights) anywhere near a vehicle being worked on. Also beware of creating sparks (electrically or by use of tools).
• Fuel vapour is heavier than air, so don't work on the fuel system with the vehicle over an inspection pit.
• Another cause of fire is an electrical overload or short-circuit. Take care when repairing or modifying the vehicle wiring.
• Keep a fire extinguisher handy, of a type suitable for use on fuel and electrical fires.

Electric shock

• Ignition HT voltage can be dangerous, especially to people with heart problems or a pacemaker. Don't work on or near the ignition system with the engine running or the ignition switched on.

• Mains voltage is also dangerous. Make sure that any mains-operated equipment is correctly earthed. Mains power points should be protected by a residual current device (RCD) circuit breaker.

Fume or gas intoxication

• Exhaust fumes are poisonous; they often contain carbon monoxide, which is rapidly fatal if inhaled. Never run the engine in a confined space such as a garage with the doors shut.
• Fuel vapour is also poisonous, as are the vapours from some cleaning solvents and paint thinners.

Poisonous or irritant substances

• Avoid skin contact with battery acid and with any fuel, fluid or lubricant, especially antifreeze, brake hydraulic fluid and Diesel fuel. Don't syphon them by mouth. If such a substance is swallowed or gets into the eyes, seek medical advice.
• Prolonged contact with used engine oil can cause skin cancer. Wear gloves or use a barrier cream if necessary. Change out of oil-soaked clothes and do not keep oily rags in your pocket.
• Air conditioning refrigerant forms a poisonous gas if exposed to a naked flame (including a cigarette). It can also cause skin burns on contact.

Asbestos

• Asbestos dust can cause cancer if inhaled or swallowed. Asbestos may be found in gaskets and in brake and clutch linings. When dealing with such components it is safest to assume that they contain asbestos.

Special hazards

Hydrofluoric acid

• This extremely corrosive acid is formed when certain types of synthetic rubber, found in some O-rings, oil seals, fuel hoses etc, are exposed to temperatures above 400°C. The rubber changes into a charred or sticky substance containing the acid. *Once formed, the acid remains dangerous for years. If it gets onto the skin, it may be necessary to amputate the limb concerned.*
• When dealing with a vehicle which has suffered a fire, or with components salvaged from such a vehicle, wear protective gloves and discard them after use.

The battery

• Batteries contain sulphuric acid, which attacks clothing, eyes and skin. Take care when topping-up or carrying the battery.
• The hydrogen gas given off by the battery is highly explosive. Never cause a spark or allow a naked light nearby. Be careful when connecting and disconnecting battery chargers or jump leads.

Air bags

• Air bags can cause injury if they go off accidentally. Take care when removing the steering wheel and/or facia. Special storage instructions may apply.

Diesel injection equipment

• Diesel injection pumps supply fuel at very high pressure. Take care when working on the fuel injectors and fuel pipes.

⚠️ *Warning: Never expose the hands, face or any other part of the body to injector spray; the fuel can penetrate the skin with potentially fatal results.*

Remember...

DO

• Do use eye protection when using power tools, and when working under the vehicle.

• Do wear gloves or use barrier cream to protect your hands when necessary.

• Do get someone to check periodically that all is well when working alone on the vehicle.

• Do keep loose clothing and long hair well out of the way of moving mechanical parts.

• Do remove rings, wristwatch etc, before working on the vehicle – especially the electrical system.

• Do ensure that any lifting or jacking equipment has a safe working load rating adequate for the job.

DON'T

• Don't attempt to lift a heavy component which may be beyond your capability – get assistance.

• Don't rush to finish a job, or take unverified short cuts.

• Don't use ill-fitting tools which may slip and cause injury.

• Don't leave tools or parts lying around where someone can trip over them. Mop up oil and fuel spills at once.

• Don't allow children or pets to play in or near a vehicle being worked on.

Roadside Repairs

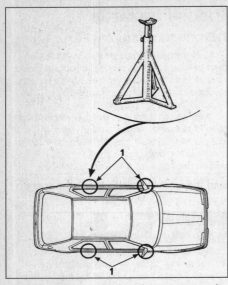

Jacking points (1) for use with vehicle jack and axle stands

Jacking

The jack supplied with the vehicle tool kit should only be used for changing the roadwheels - see "Wheel changing" later in this Section. When carrying out any other kind of work, raise the vehicle using a hydraulic jack, and always supplement the jack with axle stands positioned under the vehicle jacking points.

When using a hydraulic jack or axle stands, always position the jack head or axle stand head under one of the relevant jacking points (note that the jacking points for use with a hydraulic jack are different to those for use with the vehicle jack and axle stands) **(see illustrations)**. Do not jack the vehicle under the sump, or under any of the steering or suspension components. Never work under, around, or near a raised vehicle, unless it is adequately supported in at least two places.

Note the following when using a hydraulic jack:

(a) When raising the side of the vehicle, ensure that the load is taken by the raised jacking plates on the sill panels (refer to the accompanying illustration) - do not jack under the body panel behind the sill panels.

(b) When raising the front of the vehicle, use a suitable metal or strong wooden bar and wooden spacer blocks under the front suspension subframe (refer to the accompanying illustration).

(c) When raising the rear of the vehicle, position the jack or axle stands under the rear jacking plates on the sill panels. DO NOT place a jack or axle stands under the rear axle components.

Towing

Towing eyes are fitted to the front and rear of the vehicle for attachment of a tow rope. The towing eyes can be accessed through slots in the bumpers **(see illustrations)**. Always turn the ignition key to position "M" when the vehicle is being towed, so that the steering lock is released and the direction indicator and brake lights are operational.

Before being towed, release the handbrake and place the gear lever in neutral on manual transmission models, or "N" on automatic transmission models. Note that greater-than-usual pedal pressure will be required to operate the brakes, since the vacuum servo unit is only operational with the engine running. Similarly, on models with power

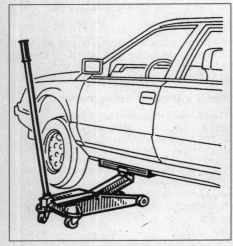

Jacking up the side of the car using a hydraulic jack

Front towing eye – "Phase 1" model

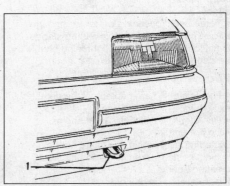

Front towing eye (1) (alternative location) – "Phase 1" model

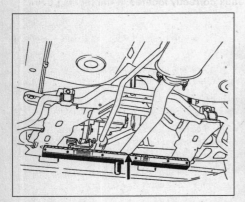

Beam for raising the front of the car – cut where shown (arrowed) if necessary to clear exhaust system

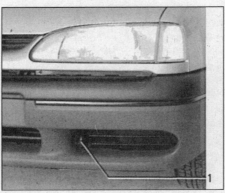

Front towing eye (1) – "Phase 2" model

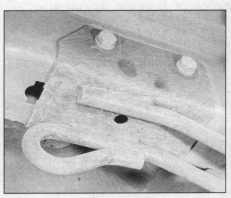

Rear towing eye

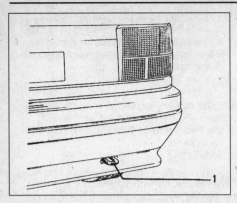

Rear towing eye (1) – alternative location

steering, greater-than-usual steering effort will be required.

Where possible, models with automatic transmission should ideally be towed with the front wheels off the ground, particularly if a transmission fault is suspected. If the vehicle is to be towed with its front wheels on the ground, the following precautions must be observed, according to transmission type.

MB1 and MB3 (3-speed) transmissions

The vehicle can be towed with all four wheels on the ground, if the following precautions are observed:

(a) Add 2.0 litres of the appropriate transmission fluid (see "Lubricants, fluids and capacities").
(b) Do not tow the vehicle faster than 18 mph (30 km/h).
(c) Do not tow the vehicle over a distance of more than 30 miles (50 km).
(d) Remove the additional fluid immediately after towing.

AD4 (4-speed) transmission

The vehicle can be towed with all four wheels on the ground, or with the front wheels on the ground and the rear wheels raised by a maximum of 150 mm, using the towing eye, if the following precautions are observed:

(a) Do not tow the vehicle faster than 25 mph (40 km/h).
(b) Do not tow the vehicle over a distance of more than 15 miles (25 km).

Wheel changing

The spare wheel is located in a cradle under the rear of the vehicle. The cradle is lowered by turning the cradle retaining screw, located at the rear of the luggage compartment near the tailgate/boot lid lock striker. The cradle retaining screw can be turned by engaging the end of the wheel brace (located in clips on the side of the luggage compartment) with the slot in the screw. Lift the cradle to release the retaining catch, then lower for access to the spare wheel. The jack is located in clips on the side of the luggage compartment. Note that on Cabriolet models, the jack is stowed behind a cover on the left-hand side of the luggage compartment (above the wheel brace), which must be unclipped for access to the jack **(see illustrations)**.

To change a wheel, remove the spare wheel and jack (as described previously), and apply the handbrake. Place chocks at the front and rear of the wheel diagonally opposite the one to be changed. On automatic transmission models, place the selector lever in position "P". Make sure that the vehicle is located on firm level ground, and then slightly loosen the wheel bolts with the brace provided (where applicable, remove the wheel trim first). Locate the jack head in the jacking point on the relevant side of the vehicle to be raised, and raise the jack by turning the screw using the wheel brace. When the wheel is clear of the ground, remove the bolts and lift off the wheel. Fit the spare wheel, and moderately tighten the bolts. Lower the vehicle, and then tighten the bolts fully. Refit the wheel trim where applicable. If possible, check the tyre pressure on the spare wheel. Remove the chocks, and stow the jack, tools, and the damaged wheel. Have the damaged tyre or wheel repaired, or renew it as soon as possible.

Using the wheel brace to lower the spare wheel

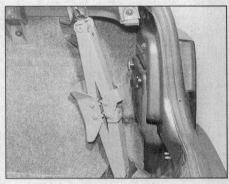

Jack location in luggage compartment

Jack correctly located in the jacking point

Roadside Repairs

Jump starting will get you out of trouble, but you must correct whatever made the battery go flat in the first place. There are three possibilities:

1 *The battery has been drained by repeated attempts to start, or by leaving the lights on.*

2 *The charging system is not working properly (alternator drivebelt slack or broken, alternator wiring fault or alternator itself faulty).*

3 *The battery itself is at fault (electrolyte low, or battery worn out).*

When jump-starting a car using a booster battery, observe the following precautions:

✔ Before connecting the booster battery, make sure that the ignition is switched off.

✔ Ensure that all electrical equipment (lights, heater, wipers, etc) is switched off.

✔ Take note of any special precautions printed on the battery case.

Jump starting

✔ Make sure that the booster battery is the same voltage as the discharged one in the vehicle.

✔ If the battery is being jump-started from the battery in another vehicle, the two vehicles MUST NOT TOUCH each other.

✔ Make sure that the transmission is in neutral (or PARK, in the case of automatic transmission).

1 Connect one end of the red jump lead to the positive (+) terminal of the flat battery

2 Connect the other end of the red lead to the positive (+) terminal of the booster battery.

3 Connect one end of the black jump lead to the negative (-) terminal of the booster battery

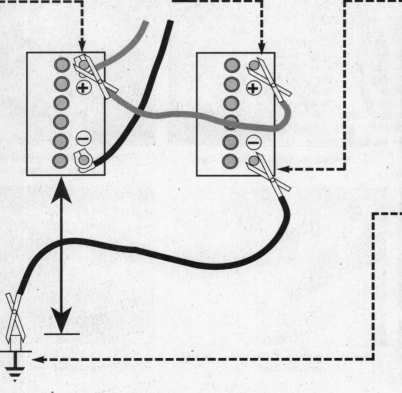

4 Connect the other end of the black jump lead to a bolt or bracket on the engine block, well away from the battery, on the vehicle to be started.

5 Make sure that the jump leads will not come into contact with the fan, drivebelts or other moving parts of the engine.

6 Start the engine using the booster battery and run it at idle speed. Switch on the lights, rear window demister and heater blower motor, then disconnect the jump leads in the reverse order of connection. Turn off the lights etc.

Identifying leaks

 Warning: Most automotive oils and fluids are poisonous. Wash them off skin, and change out of contaminated clothing, without delay.

Puddles on the garage floor or drive, or obvious wetness under the bonnet or underneath the car, suggest a leak that needs investigating. It can sometimes be difficult to decide where the leak is coming from, especially if the engine bay is very dirty already. Leaking oil or fluid can also be blown rearwards by the passage of air under the car, giving a false impression of where the problem lies.

 The smell of a fluid leaking from the car may provide a clue to what's leaking. Some fluids are distictively coloured. It may help to clean the car carefully and to park it over some clean paper overnight as an aid to locating the source of the leak.
Remember that some leaks may only occur while the engine is running.

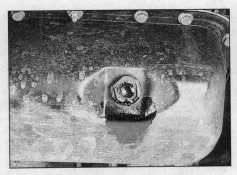

Engine oil may leak from the drain plug...

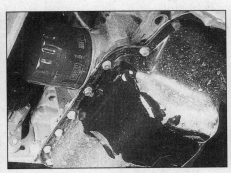

...or from the base of the oil filter

Leaking antifreeze often leaves a crystalline deposit like this

Gearbox oil can leak from the seals at the inboard ends of the driveshafts

A leak occurring at a wheel is almost certainly brake fluid

Power steering fluid may leak from the pipe connectors on the steering rack

MOT Test Checks

This is a guide to getting your vehicle through the MOT test. Obviously it will not be possible to examine the vehicle to the same standard as the professional MOT tester. However, working through the following checks will enable you to identify any problem areas before submitting the vehicle for the test.

Where a testable component is in borderline condition, the tester has discretion in deciding whether to pass or fail it. The basis of such discretion is whether the tester would be happy for a close relative or friend to use the vehicle with the component in that condition. If the vehicle presented is clean and evidently well cared for, the tester may be more inclined to pass a borderline component than if the vehicle is scruffy and apparently neglected.

It has only been possible to summarise the test requirements here, based on the regulations in force at the time of printing. Test standards are becoming increasingly stringent, although there are some exemptions for older vehicles.

An assistant will be needed to help carry out some of these checks.

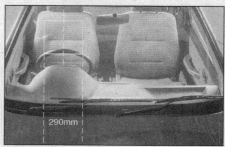

The checks have been sub-divided into four categories, as follows:

1 Checks carried out **FROM THE DRIVER'S SEAT**

2 Checks carried out **WITH THE VEHICLE ON THE GROUND**

3 Checks carried out **WITH THE VEHICLE RAISED AND THE WHEELS FREE TO TURN**

4 Checks carried out on **YOUR VEHICLE'S EXHAUST EMISSION SYSTEM**

---

1 Checks carried out **FROM THE DRIVER'S SEAT**

Handbrake

☐ Test the operation of the handbrake. Excessive travel (too many clicks) indicates incorrect brake or cable adjustment.

☐ Check that the handbrake cannot be released by tapping the lever sideways. Check the security of the lever mountings.

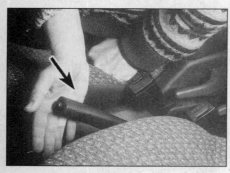

Footbrake

☐ Depress the brake pedal and check that it does not creep down to the floor, indicating a master cylinder fault. Release the pedal, wait a few seconds, then depress it again. If the pedal travels nearly to the floor before firm resistance is felt, brake adjustment or repair is necessary. If the pedal feels spongy, there is air in the hydraulic system which must be removed by bleeding.

☐ Check that the brake pedal is secure and in good condition. Check also for signs of fluid leaks on the pedal, floor or carpets, which would indicate failed seals in the brake master cylinder.

☐ Check the servo unit (when applicable) by operating the brake pedal several times, then keeping the pedal depressed and starting the engine. As the engine starts, the pedal will move down slightly. If not, the vacuum hose or the servo itself may be faulty.

Steering wheel and column

☐ Examine the steering wheel for fractures or looseness of the hub, spokes or rim.

☐ Move the steering wheel from side to side and then up and down. Check that the steering wheel is not loose on the column, indicating wear or a loose retaining nut. Continue moving the steering wheel as before, but also turn it slightly from left to right.

☐ Check that the steering wheel is not loose on the column, and that there is no abnormal

movement of the steering wheel, indicating wear in the column support bearings or couplings.

Windscreen, mirrors and sunvisor

☐ The windscreen must be free of cracks or other significant damage within the driver's field of view. (Small stone chips are acceptable.) Rear view mirrors must be secure, intact, and capable of being adjusted.

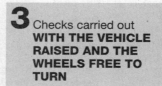

☐ The driver's sunvisor must be capable of being stored in the "up" position.

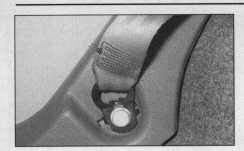

Seat belts and seats

Note: *The following checks are applicable to all seat belts, front and rear.*

☐ Examine the webbing of all the belts (including rear belts if fitted) for cuts, serious fraying or deterioration. Fasten and unfasten each belt to check the buckles. If applicable, check the retracting mechanism. Check the security of all seat belt mountings accessible from inside the vehicle.

☐ Seat belts with pre-tensioners, once activated, have a "flag" or similar showing on the seat belt stalk. This, in itself, is not a reason for test failure.

☐ The front seats themselves must be securely attached and the backrests must lock in the upright position.

Doors

☐ Both front doors must be able to be opened and closed from outside and inside, and must latch securely when closed.

2 Checks carried out WITH THE VEHICLE ON THE GROUND

Vehicle identification

☐ Number plates must be in good condition, secure and legible, with letters and numbers correctly spaced – spacing at (A) should be at least twice that at (B).

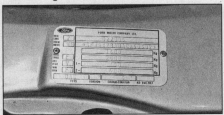

☐ The VIN plate and/or homologation plate must be legible.

Electrical equipment

☐ Switch on the ignition and check the operation of the horn.

☐ Check the windscreen washers and wipers, examining the wiper blades; renew damaged or perished blades. Also check the operation of the stop-lights.

☐ Check the operation of the sidelights and number plate lights. The lenses and reflectors must be secure, clean and undamaged.

☐ Check the operation and alignment of the headlights. The headlight reflectors must not be tarnished and the lenses must be undamaged.

☐ Switch on the ignition and check the operation of the direction indicators (including the instrument panel tell-tale) and the hazard warning lights. Operation of the sidelights and stop-lights must not affect the indicators - if it does, the cause is usually a bad earth at the rear light cluster.

☐ Check the operation of the rear foglight(s), including the warning light on the instrument panel or in the switch.

☐ The ABS warning light must illuminate in accordance with the manufacturers' design. For most vehicles, the ABS warning light should illuminate when the ignition is switched on, and (if the system is operating properly) extinguish after a few seconds. Refer to the owner's handbook.

Footbrake

☐ Examine the master cylinder, brake pipes and servo unit for leaks, loose mountings, corrosion or other damage.

☐ The fluid reservoir must be secure and the fluid level must be between the upper (A) and lower (B) markings.

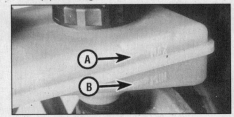

☐ Inspect both front brake flexible hoses for cracks or deterioration of the rubber. Turn the steering from lock to lock, and ensure that the hoses do not contact the wheel, tyre, or any part of the steering or suspension mechanism. With the brake pedal firmly depressed, check the hoses for bulges or leaks under pressure.

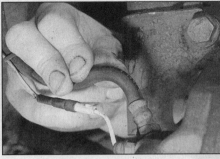

Steering and suspension

☐ Have your assistant turn the steering wheel from side to side slightly, up to the point where the steering gear just begins to transmit this movement to the roadwheels. Check for excessive free play between the steering wheel and the steering gear, indicating wear or insecurity of the steering column joints, the column-to-steering gear coupling, or the steering gear itself.

☐ Have your assistant turn the steering wheel more vigorously in each direction, so that the roadwheels just begin to turn. As this is done, examine all the steering joints, linkages, fittings and attachments. Renew any component that shows signs of wear or damage. On vehicles with power steering, check the security and condition of the steering pump, drivebelt and hoses.

☐ Check that the vehicle is standing level, and at approximately the correct ride height.

Shock absorbers

☐ Depress each corner of the vehicle in turn, then release it. The vehicle should rise and then settle in its normal position. If the vehicle continues to rise and fall, the shock absorber is defective. A shock absorber which has seized will also cause the vehicle to fail.

MOT Test Checks

Exhaust system

☐ Start the engine. With your assistant holding a rag over the tailpipe, check the entire system for leaks. Repair or renew leaking sections.

3 Checks carried out **WITH THE VEHICLE RAISED AND THE WHEELS FREE TO TURN**

Jack up the front and rear of the vehicle, and securely support it on axle stands. Position the stands clear of the suspension assemblies. Ensure that the wheels are clear of the ground and that the steering can be turned from lock to lock.

Steering mechanism

☐ Have your assistant turn the steering from lock to lock. Check that the steering turns smoothly, and that no part of the steering mechanism, including a wheel or tyre, fouls any brake hose or pipe or any part of the body structure.

☐ Examine the steering rack rubber gaiters for damage or insecurity of the retaining clips. If power steering is fitted, check for signs of damage or leakage of the fluid hoses, pipes or connections. Also check for excessive stiffness or binding of the steering, a missing split pin or locking device, or severe corrosion of the body structure within 30 cm of any steering component attachment point.

Front and rear suspension and wheel bearings

☐ Starting at the front right-hand side, grasp the roadwheel at the 3 o'clock and 9 o'clock positions and rock gently but firmly. Check for free play or insecurity at the wheel bearings, suspension balljoints, or suspension mountings, pivots and attachments.

☐ Now grasp the wheel at the 12 o'clock and 6 o'clock positions and repeat the previous inspection. Spin the wheel, and check for roughness or tightness of the front wheel bearing.

☐ If excess free play is suspected at a component pivot point, this can be confirmed by using a large screwdriver or similar tool and levering between the mounting and the component attachment. This will confirm whether the wear is in the pivot bush, its retaining bolt, or in the mounting itself (the bolt holes can often become elongated).

☐ Carry out all the above checks at the other front wheel, and then at both rear wheels.

Springs and shock absorbers

☐ Examine the suspension struts (when applicable) for serious fluid leakage, corrosion, or damage to the casing. Also check the security of the mounting points.

☐ If coil springs are fitted, check that the spring ends locate in their seats, and that the spring is not corroded, cracked or broken.

☐ If leaf springs are fitted, check that all leaves are intact, that the axle is securely attached to each spring, and that there is no deterioration of the spring eye mountings, bushes, and shackles.

☐ The same general checks apply to vehicles fitted with other suspension types, such as torsion bars, hydraulic displacer units, etc. Ensure that all mountings and attachments are secure, that there are no signs of excessive wear, corrosion or damage, and (on hydraulic types) that there are no fluid leaks or damaged pipes.

☐ Inspect the shock absorbers for signs of serious fluid leakage. Check for wear of the mounting bushes or attachments, or damage to the body of the unit.

Driveshafts (fwd vehicles only)

☐ Rotate each front wheel in turn and inspect the constant velocity joint gaiters for splits or damage. Also check that each driveshaft is straight and undamaged.

Braking system

☐ If possible without dismantling, check brake pad wear and disc condition. Ensure that the friction lining material has not worn excessively, (A) and that the discs are not fractured, pitted, scored or badly worn (B).

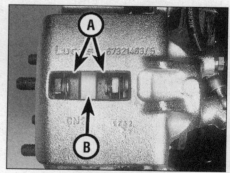

☐ Examine all the rigid brake pipes underneath the vehicle, and the flexible hose(s) at the rear. Look for corrosion, chafing or insecurity of the pipes, and for signs of bulging under pressure, chafing, splits or deterioration of the flexible hoses.

☐ Look for signs of fluid leaks at the brake calipers or on the brake backplates. Repair or renew leaking components.

☐ Slowly spin each wheel, while your assistant depresses and releases the footbrake. Ensure that each brake is operating and does not bind when the pedal is released.

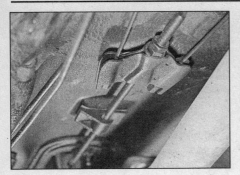

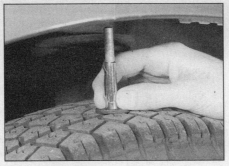

□ Examine the handbrake mechanism, checking for frayed or broken cables, excessive corrosion, or wear or insecurity of the linkage. Check that the mechanism works on each relevant wheel, and releases fully, without binding.

□ It is not possible to test brake efficiency without special equipment, but a road test can be carried out later to check that the vehicle pulls up in a straight line.

Fuel and exhaust systems

□ Inspect the fuel tank (including the filler cap), fuel pipes, hoses and unions. All components must be secure and free from leaks.

□ Examine the exhaust system over its entire length, checking for any damaged, broken or missing mountings, security of the retaining clamps and rust or corrosion.

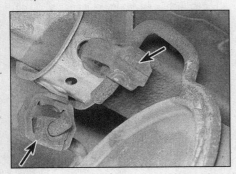

Wheels and tyres

□ Examine the sidewalls and tread area of each tyre in turn. Check for cuts, tears, lumps, bulges, separation of the tread, and exposure of the ply or cord due to wear or damage. Check that the tyre bead is correctly seated on the wheel rim, that the valve is sound and properly seated, and that the wheel is not distorted or damaged.

□ Check that the tyres are of the correct size for the vehicle, that they are of the same size and type on each axle, and that the pressures are correct.

□ Check the tyre tread depth. The legal minimum at the time of writing is 1.6 mm over at least three-quarters of the tread width. Abnormal tread wear may indicate incorrect front wheel alignment.

Body corrosion

□ Check the condition of the entire vehicle structure for signs of corrosion in load-bearing areas. (These include chassis box sections, side sills, cross-members, pillars, and all suspension, steering, braking system and seat belt mountings and anchorages.) Any corrosion which has seriously reduced the thickness of a load-bearing area is likely to cause the vehicle to fail. In this case professional repairs are likely to be needed.

□ Damage or corrosion which causes sharp or otherwise dangerous edges to be exposed will also cause the vehicle to fail.

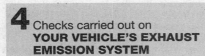

4 Checks carried out on YOUR VEHICLE'S EXHAUST EMISSION SYSTEM

Petrol models

□ Have the engine at normal operating temperature, and make sure that it is in good tune (ignition system in good order, air filter element clean, etc).

□ Before any measurements are carried out, raise the engine speed to around 2500 rpm, and hold it at this speed for 20 seconds. Allow the engine speed to return to idle, and watch for smoke emissions from the exhaust tailpipe. If the idle speed is obviously much too high, or if dense blue or clearly-visible black smoke comes from the tailpipe for more than 5 seconds, the vehicle will fail. As a rule of thumb, blue smoke signifies oil being burnt (engine wear) while black smoke signifies unburnt fuel (dirty air cleaner element, or other carburettor or fuel system fault).

□ An exhaust gas analyser capable of measuring carbon monoxide (CO) and hydrocarbons (HC) is now needed. If such an instrument cannot be hired or borrowed, a local garage may agree to perform the check for a small fee.

CO emissions (mixture)

□ At the time of writing, for vehicles first used between 1st August 1975 and 31st July 1986 (P to C registration), the CO level must not exceed 4.5% by volume. For vehicles first used between 1st August 1986 and 31st July 1992 (D to J registration), the CO level must not exceed 3.5% by volume. Vehicles first

used after 1st August 1992 (K registration) must conform to the manufacturer's specification. The MOT tester has access to a DOT database or emissions handbook, which lists the CO and HC limits for each make and model of vehicle. The CO level is measured with the engine at idle speed, and at "fast idle". The following limits are given as a general guide:

At idle speed -
    CO level no more than 0.5%
At "fast idle" (2500 to 3000 rpm) -
    CO level no more than 0.3%
    (Minimum oil temperature 60°C)

□ If the CO level cannot be reduced far enough to pass the test (and the fuel and ignition systems are otherwise in good condition) then the carburettor is badly worn, or there is some problem in the fuel injection system or catalytic converter (as applicable).

HC emissions

□ With the CO within limits, HC emissions for vehicles first used between 1st August 1975 and 31st July 1992 (P to J registration) must not exceed 1200 ppm. Vehicles first used after 1st August 1992 (K registration) must conform to the manufacturer's specification. The MOT tester has access to a DOT database or emissions handbook, which lists the CO and HC limits for each make and model of vehicle. The HC level is measured with the engine at "fast idle". The following is given as a general guide:

At "fast idle" (2500 to 3000 rpm) -
    HC level no more than 200 ppm
    (Minimum oil temperature 60°C)

□ Excessive HC emissions are caused by incomplete combustion, the causes of which can include oil being burnt, mechanical wear and ignition/fuel system malfunction.

Diesel models

□ The only emission test applicable to Diesel engines is the measuring of exhaust smoke density. The test involves accelerating the engine several times to its maximum unloaded speed.

Note: *It is of the utmost importance that the engine timing belt is in good condition before the test is carried out.*

□ The limits for Diesel engine exhaust smoke, introduced in September 1995 are:
Vehicles first used before 1st August 1979:
    Exempt from metered smoke testing, but must not emit "dense blue or clearly visible black smoke for a period of more than 5 seconds at idle" or "dense blue or clearly visible black smoke during acceleration which would obscure the view of other road users".
Non-turbocharged vehicles first used after 1st August 1979: 2.5m-1
Turbocharged vehicles first used after 1st August 1979: 3.0m-1

□ Excessive smoke can be caused by a dirty air cleaner element. Otherwise, professional advice may be needed to find the cause.

General Repair Procedures

Whenever servicing, repair or overhaul work is carried out on the car or its components, observe the following procedures and instructions. This will assist in carrying out the operation efficiently and to a professional standard of workmanship.

Joint mating faces and gaskets

When separating components at their mating faces, never insert screwdrivers or similar implements into the joint between the faces in order to prise them apart. This can cause severe damage which results in oil leaks, coolant leaks, etc upon reassembly. Separation is usually achieved by tapping along the joint with a soft-faced hammer in order to break the seal. However, note that this method may not be suitable where dowels are used for component location.

Where a gasket is used between the mating faces of two components, a new one must be fitted on reassembly; fit it dry unless otherwise stated in the repair procedure. Make sure that the mating faces are clean and dry, with all traces of old gasket removed. When cleaning a joint face, use a tool which is unlikely to score or damage the face, and remove any burrs or nicks with an oilstone or fine file.

Make sure that tapped holes are cleaned with a pipe cleaner, and keep them free of jointing compound, if this is being used, unless specifically instructed otherwise.

Ensure that all orifices, channels or pipes are clear, and blow through them, preferably using compressed air.

Oil seals

Oil seals can be removed by levering them out with a wide flat-bladed screwdriver or similar implement. Alternatively, a number of self-tapping screws may be screwed into the seal, and these used as a purchase for pliers or some similar device in order to pull the seal free.

Whenever an oil seal is removed from its working location, either individually or as part of an assembly, it should be renewed.

The very fine sealing lip of the seal is easily damaged, and will not seal if the surface it contacts is not completely clean and free from scratches, nicks or grooves. If the original sealing surface of the component cannot be restored, and the manufacturer has not made provision for slight relocation of the seal relative to the sealing surface, the component should be renewed.

Protect the lips of the seal from any surface which may damage them in the course of fitting. Use tape or a conical sleeve where possible. Lubricate the seal lips with oil before fitting and, on dual-lipped seals, fill the space between the lips with grease.

Unless otherwise stated, oil seals must be fitted with their sealing lips toward the lubricant to be sealed.

Use a tubular drift or block of wood of the appropriate size to install the seal and, if the seal housing is shouldered, drive the seal down to the shoulder. If the seal housing is unshouldered, the seal should be fitted with its face flush with the housing top face (unless otherwise instructed).

Screw threads and fastenings

Seized nuts, bolts and screws are quite a common occurrence where corrosion has set in, and the use of penetrating oil or releasing fluid will often overcome this problem if the offending item is soaked for a while before attempting to release it. The use of an impact driver may also provide a means of releasing such stubborn fastening devices, when used in conjunction with the appropriate screwdriver bit or socket. If none of these methods works, it may be necessary to resort to the careful application of heat, or the use of a hacksaw or nut splitter device.

Studs are usually removed by locking two nuts together on the threaded part, and then using a spanner on the lower nut to unscrew the stud. Studs or bolts which have broken off below the surface of the component in which they are mounted can sometimes be removed using a stud extractor. Always ensure that a blind tapped hole is completely free from oil, grease, water or other fluid before installing the bolt or stud. Failure to do this could cause the housing to crack due to the hydraulic action of the bolt or stud as it is screwed in.

When tightening a castellated nut to accept a split pin, tighten the nut to the specified torque, where applicable, and then tighten further to the next split pin hole. Never slacken the nut to align the split pin hole, unless stated in the repair procedure.

When checking or retightening a nut or bolt to a specified torque setting, slacken the nut or bolt by a quarter of a turn, and then retighten to the specified setting. However, this should not be attempted where angular tightening has been used.

For some screw fastenings, notably cylinder head bolts or nuts, torque wrench settings are no longer specified for the latter stages of tightening, "angle-tightening" being called up instead. Typically, a fairly low torque wrench setting will be applied to the bolts/nuts in the correct sequence, followed by one or more stages of tightening through specified angles.

Locknuts, locktabs and washers

Any fastening which will rotate against a component or housing during tightening should always have a washer between it and the relevant component or housing.

Spring or split washers should always be renewed when they are used to lock a critical component such as a big-end bearing retaining bolt or nut. Locktabs which are folded over to retain a nut or bolt should always be renewed.

Self-locking nuts can be re-used in non-critical areas, providing resistance can be felt when the locking portion passes over the bolt or stud thread. However, it should be noted that self-locking stiffnuts tend to lose their effectiveness after long periods of use, and should then be renewed as a matter of course.

Split pins must always be replaced with new ones of the correct size for the hole.

When thread-locking compound is found on the threads of a fastener which is to be re-used, it should be cleaned off with a wire brush and solvent, and fresh compound applied on reassembly.

Special tools

Some repair procedures in this manual entail the use of special tools such as a press, two or three-legged pullers, spring compressors, etc. Wherever possible, suitable readily-available alternatives to the manufacturer's special tools are described, and are shown in use. In some instances, where no alternative is possible, it has been necessary to resort to the use of a manufacturer's tool, and this has been done for reasons of safety as well as the efficient completion of the repair operation. Unless you are highly-skilled and have a thorough understanding of the procedures described, never attempt to bypass the use of any special tool when the procedure described specifies its use. Not only is there a very great risk of personal injury, but expensive damage could be caused to the components involved.

Environmental considerations

When disposing of used engine oil, brake fluid, antifreeze, etc, give due consideration to any detrimental environmental effects. Do not, for instance, pour any of the above liquids down drains into the general sewage system, or onto the ground to soak away. Many local council refuse tips provide a facility for waste oil disposal, as do some garages. If none of these facilities are available, consult your local Environmental Health Department, or the National Rivers Authority, for further advice.

With the universal tightening-up of legislation regarding the emission of environmentally-harmful substances from motor vehicles, most vehicles have tamperproof devices fitted to the main adjustment points of the fuel system. These devices are primarily designed to prevent unqualified persons from adjusting the fuel/air mixture, with the chance of a consequent increase in toxic emissions. If such devices are found during servicing or overhaul, they should, wherever possible, be renewed or refitted in accordance with the manufacturer's requirements or current legislation.

OIL CARE
FOLLOW THE CODE

OIL BANK LINE
0800 66 33 66
www.oilbankline.org.uk

Note: It is antisocial and illegal to dump oil down the drain. To find the location of your local oil recycling bank, call this number free.

Chapter 1 Routine maintenance and servicing

Contents

Degrees of difficulty

Easy, suitable for novice with little experience

Fairly easy, suitable for beginner with some experience

Fairly difficult, suitable for competent DIY mechanic

Difficult, suitable for experienced DIY mechanic

Very difficult, suitable for expert DIY or professional

Maintenance Schedule

Renault 19 maintenance schedule

The maintenance intervals in this manual are provided with the assumption that you, not the dealer, will be carrying out the work. These are the minimum maintenance intervals recommended by the manufacturer for vehicles driven daily. If you wish to keep your vehicle in peak condition at all times, you may wish to perform some of these procedures more often. We encourage frequent maintenance because it enhances the efficiency, performance and resale value of your vehicle. If the vehicle is driven in dusty areas, used to tow a trailer, or driven frequently at slow speeds (idling in traffic) or on short journeys, more frequent maintenance intervals are recommended.

No time intervals are specified by the manufacturer. It is suggested that, for vehicles covering less than 12 000 miles (20 000 km) per year, the 6000-mile service be carried out every 6 months, the 12 000-mile service every 12 months, and so on.

When the vehicle is new, it should be serviced by a factory-authorised dealer service department, in order to preserve the factory warranty.

Every 250 miles (400 km) or weekly

☐ Check the engine oil level (Section 3)
☐ Check the engine coolant level (Section 3)
☐ Check the washer fluid level (Section 3)
☐ Check the condition of the battery (Section 4)
☐ Visually examine the tyres for tread depth, and for wear or damage (Section 5)
☐ Check and adjust the tyre pressures (Section 5)

Every 6000 miles (10 000 km)

In addition to all the items listed above, carry out the following:

☐ Renew the engine oil (Section 6)*
☐ Check the brake fluid level (Section 7)
☐ Check the power steering fluid level (Section 7)
☐ Check the manual gearbox oil level (Section 7)
☐ Check the automatic transmission fluid level (Section 7)
☐ Check all underbonnet components and hoses for fluid leaks (Section 8)
☐ Check the condition of the auxiliary drivebelt(s), and renew if necessary (Section 9)
☐ Check the condition of the ignition HT leads, distributor cap and rotor arm, and renew if necessary (Section 10)
☐ Check the condition of the spark plugs, and renew if necessary (Section 11)
☐ Check the condition of the contact breaker points, and renew if necessary - 1397 cc (C1J) engine (Section 12)
☐ Check the ignition timing, and adjust if necessary - 1397 cc (C1J) engine only (Section 13)
☐ Check the idle speed and mixture (where possible), and adjust if necessary (Section 14)
☐ Check the operation of the air cleaner air temperature control system – carburettor and single-point fuel injection models (Section 15)
☐ Check the operation of the horn, all lights, and the wipers and washers (Section 16)
☐ Check the operation of the heating and (where applicable) the air conditioning system (Section 17)
☐ Check the condition of the air conditioning system refrigerant - where applicable (see Section 17)
☐ Check the headlight beam alignment (Section 18)
☐ Check the condition of the wiper blades (Section 19)
☐ Check the condition of the front brake pads, and renew if necessary (Section 20)

☐ Check the suspension and steering components for condition and security (Section 21)
☐ Check the condition of the driveshafts (Section 22)
☐ Check for damage and corrosion (Section 23)
☐ Check the condition of the exhaust (Section 24)

*Note: *The engine oil filter should also be renewed at the first 6000-mile (10 000 km) service, and then at every 12 000 miles (20 000 km) thereafter.*

Every 12 000 (20 000 km)

In addition to all the items listed above, carry out the following:

☐ Renew the engine oil filter (Section 6)
☐ Renew the air filter (Section 25)
☐ Renew the spark plugs (Section 26)
☐ Carry out a road test (Section 27)

Every 30 000 miles (50 000 km)

In addition to all the items listed above, carry out the following:

☐ Renew the fuel filter (where applicable) (Section 28)
☐ Check the operation of the clutch mechanism, where applicable (Section 29)
☐ Check the operation of the handbrake mechanism, and adjust if necessary (Section 30)
☐ Check the condition of the rear brake shoes, and renew if necessary - rear drum brake models (Section 31)
☐ Check the condition of the rear disc brake pads, and renew if necessary - rear disc brake models (Section 32)
☐ Check the front wheel alignment, and adjust (Section 33)
☐ Renew the brake fluid (Section 34)
☐ Renew the automatic transmission fluid and filter (Section 35)

Every 72 000 miles (120 000 km)

In addition to all the items listed above, carry out the following:

☐ Renew the timing belt - all engines except C-type (Section 36)

Every 2 years

In addition to all the items listed above, carry out the following:

☐ Renew the coolant (Section 37)

Maintenance and Servicing

1•3

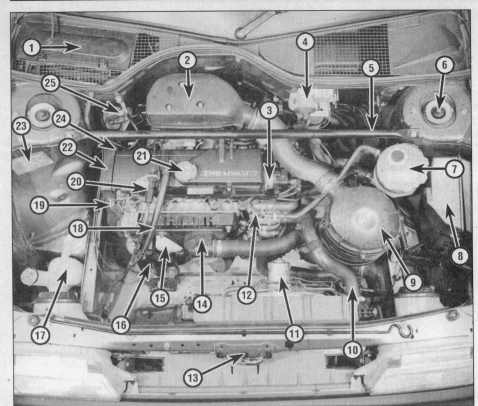

View of the engine compartment - Renault 19 TSE with 1390 cc (E6J) carburettor engine

1 Battery compartment
2 Air inlet duct to carburettor
3 Distributor and cap
4 Ignition module
5 Strengthening bar
6 Front suspension strut upper mounting
7 Coolant expansion tank
8 Auxiliary fuse/relay box
9 Air cleaner assembly
10 Radiator top hose
11 Electric cooling fan
12 Engine oil level dipstick
13 Bonnet lock
14 Exhaust manifold hot air shroud
15 Oil filter
16 Right-hand front engine mounting
17 Washer fluid reservoir
18 Choke cable
19 Engine lifting eye
20 Accelerator cable
21 Engine oil filler cap
22 Alternator (hidden from view)
23 Vehicle identification (VIN) plate
24 Timing belt cover
25 Brake fluid reservoir

View of the front underside - Renault 19 TSE with 1390 cc (E6J) carburettor engine

1 Front towing eyes
2 Subframe
3 Driveshaft
4 Engine oil drain plug
5 Exhaust front section
6 Gearbox oil drain plug
7 Gearbox
8 Front suspension lower arm
9 Steering track rod
10 Front anti-roll bar
11 Brake fluid pipes
12 Gearchange link rod
13 Exhaust expansion box
14 Steering gear
15 Fuel pipes
16 Subframe mounting

Maintenance and Servicing

View of the rear underside - Renault 19 TSE with 1390 cc (E6J) carburettor engine

1 Exhaust silencer
2 Spare wheel
3 Fuel tank
4 Fuel tank filler pipe
5 Rear shock absorber
6 Rear anti-roll bar
7 Rear axle
8 Fuel pipes
9 Exhaust rear section
10 Handbrake cables

View of the engine compartment - Renault 19 TXE with 1721 cc (F2N) carburettor engine

1 Brake fluid reservoir
2 Fuel filter
3 Air inlet duct to carburettor
4 Distributor
5 Ignition module
6 Strengthening bar
7 Front suspension strut upper mounting
8 Coolant expansion tank
9 Auxiliary fuse/relay box
10 Air cleaner assembly
11 Engine lifting eye
12 Electric cooling fan
13 Carburettor cooling air duct (anti-percolation system)
14 Radiator
15 Oil filter
16 Engine oil level dipstick
17 Oil pressure switch
18 Power steering fluid reservoir
19 Alternator
20 Auxiliary drivebelt
21 Washer fluid reservoir
22 Choke cable
23 Accelerator cable
24 Fuel flowmeter
25 Engine oil filler cap
26 Battery compartment

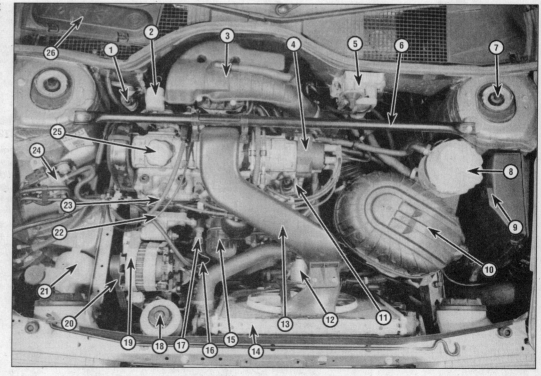

View of the front underside - Renault 19 TXE with 1721 cc (F2N) carburettor engine

1 Front suspension lower arm
2 Gearchange link rod
3 Steering track rod
4 Subframe mounting
5 Brake pipes
6 Exhaust intermediate section
7 Exhaust front section
8 Front anti-roll bar
9 Driveshaft
10 Engine oil drain plug
11 Gearbox oil drain plug
12 Radiator bottom hose

View of the rear underside - Renault 19 TXE with 1721 cc (F2N) carburettor engine

1 Fuel tank filler pipe
2 Fuel tank
3 Brake fluid pipes
4 Fuel pipes
5 Handbrake cables
6 Exhaust expansion box
7 Rear axle side mounting bracket
8 Rear axle
9 Rear shock absorber
10 Exhaust silencer
11 Spare wheel

Maintenance and Servicing

View of engine compartment - Renault 19 TXE with 1721 cc (F3N) multi-point fuel injection engine

1 Battery compartment
2 Air inlet ducting to fuel rail (anti-percolat ion system)
3 Air inlet plenum chamber
4 Ignition module/coil
5 Manifold absolute pressure (MAP) sensor
6 Front suspension strut upper mounting
7 Coolant expansion tank
8 Auxiliary fuse/relay box
9 Air cleaner assembly
10 Inlet air temperature sensor
11 Distributor
12 Idle speed control valve
13 Fuel rail cooling air duct (anti-percolation system)
14 Electric cooling fan
15 Radiator
16 Engine oil level dipstick (hidden from view)
17 Oil filter
18 Power steering fluid reservoir
19 Alternator
20 Vehicle identification number (VIN) plate
21 Washer fluid reservoir
22 Fuel injection computer
23 Accelerator cable
24 Timing belt cover
25 Engine oil filler cap
26 Throttle housing

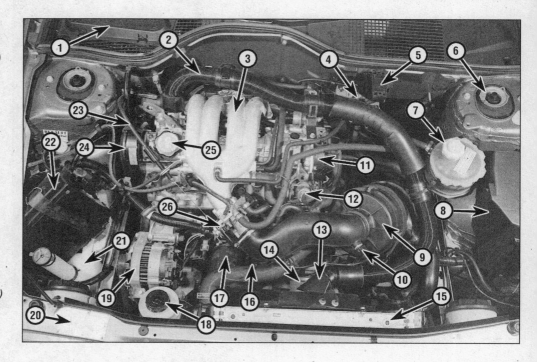

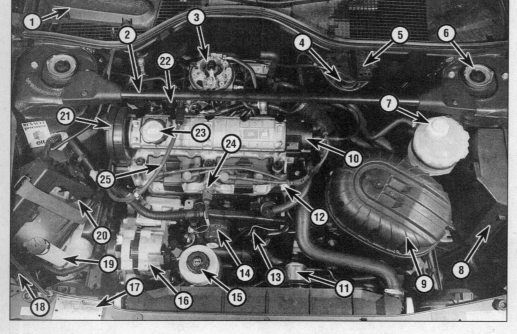

View of engine compartment (throttle housing air duct removed) - Renault 19 RT with 1794 cc (F3P) single-point fuel injection engine

1 Battery compartment
2 Strengthening bar
3 Throttle housing
4 Ignition module/coil
5 Manifold absolute pressure (MAP) sensor
6 Front suspension strut upper mounting
7 Coolant expansion tank
8 Auxiliary fuse/relay box
9 Air cleaner
10 Distributor cap
11 Electric cooling fan
12 Coolant temperature sensor
13 Engine oil level dipstick
14 Oil filter
15 Power steering fluid reservoir
16 Alternator
17 Vehicle identification number (VIN) plate
18 Charcoal canister
19 Washer fluid reservoir
20 Fuel injection computer
21 Timing belt cover
22 Charcoal canister solenoid valve
23 Engine oil filler cap
24 Knock sensor
25 Accelerator cable

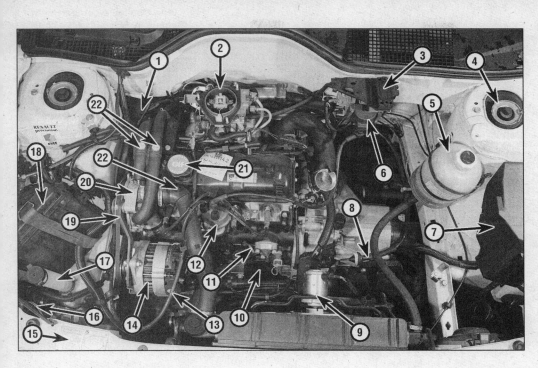

View of the engine compartment (air cleaner removed) - Renault 19 RL Prima with 1390 cc (C3J) fuel injection engine

1 Brake fluid reservoir
2 Throttle housing
3 Manifold absolute pressure (MAP) sensor
4 Front suspension strut upper mounting
5 Coolant expansion tank
6 Ignition module/coil
7 Auxiliary fuse/relay box
8 Clutch cable
9 Electric cooling fan
10 Oil filter
11 Engine oil level dipstick
12 Distributor
13 Accelerator cable
14 Alternator
15 Vehicle identification number (VIN) plate
16 Charcoal canister
17 Washer fluid reservoir
18 Fuel injection computer
19 Auxiliary drivebelt
20 Coolant pump
21 Engine oil filler cap
22 Coolant bleed screws

1

View of the engine compartment (air cleaner removed) - Renault 19 RT with 1390 cc (E7J) engine

1 Brake fluid reservoir
2 Charcoal canister solenoid valve
3 Throttle housing
4 Distributor
5 Ignition module/coil
6 Manifold absolute pressure (MAP) sensor
7 Coolant expansion tank
8 Coolant bleed screw
9 Electric cooling fan
10 Engine oil level dipstick
11 Exhaust manifold hot air shroud
12 Oil filter
13 Power steering fluid reservoir
14 Power steering pump
15 Vehicle identification number (VIN) plate
16 Charcoal canister
17 Washer fluid reservoir
18 Power steering pump drivebelt
19 Fuel injection computer
20 Timing belt cover
21 Engine oil filler cap
22 Accelerator cable
23 Front suspension strut upper mounting

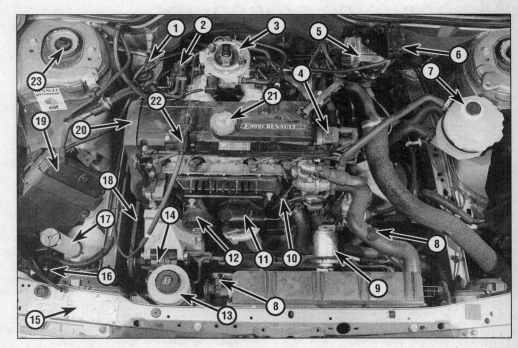

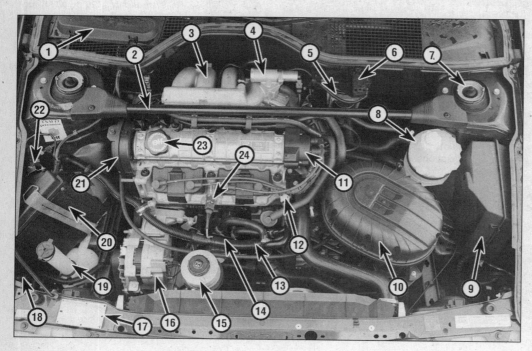

View of engine compartment -
Renault 19 RSi with 1794 cc (F3P)
multi-point fuel injection engine

1   Battery compartment
2   Strengthening bar
3   Inlet manifold
4   Idle speed control valve
5   Ignition module/coil
6   Manifold absolute pressure
    (MAP) sensor
7   Front suspension strut upper
    mounting
8   Coolant expansion tank
9   Auxiliary fuse/relay box
10 Air cleaner
11 Distributor cap
12 Coolant temperature sensor
13 Engine oil level dipstick (hidden
    from view)
14 Oil filter and cooler (hidden
    beneath hose)
15 Power steering fluid reservoir
16 Alternator
17 Vehicle identification number
    (VIN) plate
18 Charcoal canister
19 Washer fluid reservoir
20 Fuel injection computer
21 Timing belt cover
22 Charcoal canister solenoid valve
23 Engine oil filler cap
24 Knock sensor

Maintenance procedures

1 Introduction

This Chapter is designed to help the home mechanic maintain his/her vehicle for safety, economy, long life and peak performance.

The Chapter contains a master maintenance schedule, followed by Sections dealing specifically with each task on the schedule. Visual checks, adjustments, component renewal and other helpful items are included. Refer to the accompanying illustrations of the engine compartment and the underside of the vehicle for the locations of the various components.

Servicing of your vehicle in accordance with the mileage/time maintenance schedule and the following Sections will provide a planned maintenance programme, which should result in a long and reliable service life. This is a comprehensive plan, so maintaining some items but not others at the specified service intervals will not produce the same results.

As you service your vehicle, you will discover that many of the procedures can - and should - be grouped together because of

the particular procedure being performed, or because of the close proximity of two otherwise-unrelated components to one another. For example, if the vehicle is raised for any reason, the exhaust can be inspected at the same time as the suspension and steering components.

The first step in this maintenance programme is to prepare yourself before the actual work begins. Read through all the Sections relevant to the work to be carried out, then make a list and gather together all the parts and tools required. If a problem is encountered, seek advice from a parts specialist, or a dealer service department.

Engine identification

Throughout this Chapter, engines are referred to by type, or type code, as follows:
  C-type: 1237 cc (C1G), 1390 cc (C3J) and
    1397 cc (C1J and C2J)
  E-type: 1390 cc (E6J and E7J)
  F-type: 1721 cc (F2N and F3N), 1764 cc
    (F7P) and 1794 cc (F3P)
For further details of engine identification, refer to *"Buying spare parts and vehicle identification numbers"*.

2 Intensive maintenance

If, from the time the vehicle is new, the routine maintenance schedule is followed closely, and frequent checks are made of fluid levels and high-wear items, as suggested throughout this manual, the engine will be kept in relatively good running condition, and the need for additional work will be minimised.

It is possible that there will be times when the engine is running poorly due to the lack of regular maintenance. This is even more likely if a used vehicle, which has not received regular and frequent maintenance checks, is purchased. In such cases, additional work may need to be carried out, outside of the regular maintenance intervals.

If engine wear is suspected, a compression test (Chapter 2A, 2B or 2C) will provide valuable information regarding the overall performance of the main internal components. Such a test can be used as a basis to decide on the extent of the work to be carried out. If, for example, a compression test indicates serious internal engine wear, conventional maintenance as described in this Chapter will not greatly improve the performance of the engine, and may prove a waste of time and money, unless extensive overhaul work (Chapter 2D) is carried out first.

The following series of operations are those most often required to improve the performance of a generally poor-running engine.

Primary operations

Clean, inspect and test the battery (Section 4)
Check all the engine-related fluids (Section 3)

Check the condition and tension of the auxiliary drivebelt(s) (Section 9)
Renew the spark plugs (Section 26)
Inspect the distributor cap and rotor arm (Section 10)
Inspect the ignition HT leads (Section 10)
Check and if necessary adjust the idle speed (where applicable) (Section 14)
Check the condition of the air filter, and renew if necessary (Section 25)
Check the condition of all hoses, and check for fluid leaks (Section 8)

If the above operations no not prove fully effective, carry out the following secondary operations.

Secondary operations

All items listed under "Primary operations", plus the following:

Check the ignition system (Chapter 5B or 5C, as applicable)
Check the charging system (Chapter 5A)
Check the fuel system (Chapter 4A or 4B, as applicable)
Renew the air filter (Section 25)
Renew the distributor cap and rotor arm (Section 10)
Renew the ignition HT leads (Section 10)

Weekly checks

3 Fluid level checks

Note: *Refer to Section 1 for details of engine identification.*

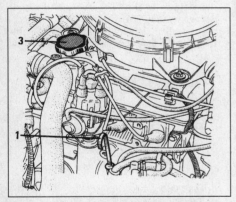

3.1a Engine oil level dipstick (1) and oil filler cap (3) - C-type engines

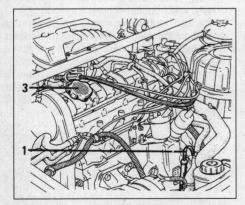

3.1c Engine oil level dipstick (1) and oil filler cap (3) - 1721 cc (F2N and F3N single-point fuel injection) and 1794 cc (F3P) engines

Engine oil

1 The engine oil level is checked with a dipstick that extends through a tube and into the sump at the bottom of the engine. The dipstick is located towards the front of the engine **(see illustrations)**. On models equipped with an oil level gauge, the check can be made by switching on the ignition - the

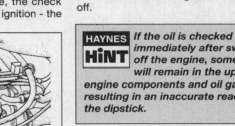

3.1b Engine oil level dipstick (1) and oil filler cap (3) - E-type engines

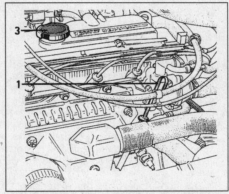

3.1d Engine oil level dipstick (1) an oil filler cap (3) - 1721 cc (F3N) multi-point fuel injection engine

upper and lower limits on the gauge correspond to the upper and lower marks on the dipstick.

2 The oil level should be checked with the vehicle standing on level ground. Check the level before starting the engine, or wait at least 5 minutes after the engine has been switched off.

> **HAYNES HiNT** *If the oil is checked immediately after switching off the engine, some of the oil will remain in the upper engine components and oil galleries, resulting in an inaccurate reading on the dipstick.*

3 Withdraw the dipstick from the tube, and wipe all the oil from the end with a clean rag or paper towel. Insert the clean dipstick back into the tube as far as it will go, then withdraw it once more. Check that the oil level is between the upper ("MAX") and lower ("MIN") marks/notches on the dipstick. If the level is towards the lower ("MIN") mark/notch, unscrew the oil filler cap on the valve cover, and add fresh oil until the level is on the upper

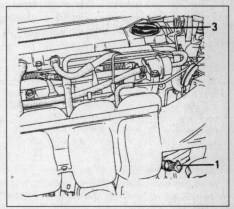

3.1e Engine oil level dipstick (1) and oil filler cap (3) - 1764 cc (F7P) engine

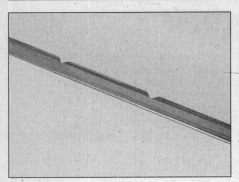

3.3a **Engine oil level dipstick "MIN" and "MAX" level notches**

3.3b **Oil is added through the filler on the valve cover**

3.9 **Adding coolant to the expansion tank**

3.12 **Topping-up the washer fluid level**

4.2 **Lifting the cover for access to the battery**

("MAX") mark/notch **(see illustrations)**. Note that the difference between the minimum and maximum marks/notches on the dipstick corresponds to 1.0 litre on C-type engines, 1.5 litres on E-type engines, 2.0 litres on 1721 cc and 1794 cc F-type engines, and 0.6 litre on 1764 cc F-type engines.

4 Always maintain the level between the two dipstick marks/notches. If the level is allowed to fall below the lower mark/notch, oil starvation may result, which could lead to severe engine damage. If the engine is overfilled by adding too much oil, this may result in oil-fouled spark plugs, oil leaks or oil seal failures.

5 An oil can spout or funnel may help to reduce spillage when adding oil to the engine. Always use the correct grade and type of oil, as shown in "Lubricants, fluids and capacities".

Coolant

 Warning: DO NOT attempt to remove the expansion tank pressure cap when the engine is hot, as there is a very great risk of scalding.

6 All vehicles covered by this manual are equipped with a pressurised cooling system. An expansion tank is located on the left-hand side of the engine compartment. On the C-type engines, the expansion tank has only one hose which is connected directly to the radiator. As engine temperature increases, the

coolant expands and travels through the hose to the expansion tank. As the engine cools, the coolant is automatically drawn back into the system to maintain the correct level. On the E-type and F-type engines, the expansion tank has a continual flow of coolant, in order to purge air from the cooling system. Hoses are connected to the tank from the top of the cylinder head, and from the tank to the water pump inlet.

7 The coolant level in the expansion tank should be checked regularly. The level in the tank varies with the temperature of the engine. When the engine is cold, the coolant level should be up to the maximum ("MAX") level mark on the side of the tank. When the engine is hot, the level will be slightly above the mark.

8 If topping-up is necessary, wait until the engine is cold, then slowly unscrew the pressure cap on the expansion tank. Allow any remaining pressure to escape, then fully unscrew the cap.

9 Add a mixture of water and antifreeze (see below) through the expansion tank filler neck until the coolant is up to the maximum ("MAX") level mark **(see illustration)**. Refit and tighten the pressure cap.

10 With a sealed type cooling system such as this, the addition of coolant should only be necessary at very infrequent intervals. If frequent topping-up is required, it is likely there is a leak in the system. Check the radiator, and all hoses and joint faces, for any sign of staining or actual wetness, and rectify as necessary. If no leaks can be found, it is

advisable to have the pressure cap and the entire system pressure-tested by a dealer or suitably-equipped garage, as this will often show up a small leak not previously visible.

Washer fluid

11 The windscreen/rear window/headlight washer fluid reservoir is located at the right-hand front corner of the engine compartment.

12 Check that the fluid level is at least up to the bottom of the filler neck, and top-up if necessary **(see illustration)**. When topping-up the reservoir, a screen wash additive should be added in the recommended quantities.

4 Battery check

 Caution: Before carrying out any work on the vehicle battery, read through the precautions given in "Safety first!" at the beginning of this manual.

1 The battery is located on the right-hand side of the engine compartment, on the bulkhead.

2 Prise up the plastic battery cover for access to the top of the battery **(see illustration)**.

3 The exterior of the battery should be inspected for damage such as a cracked case or cover.

4 Check the tightness of the battery cable clamp nuts to ensure good electrical connections, and check the entire length of each cable for cracks and frayed conductors.

5 If corrosion (visible as white, fluffy deposits) is evident, remove the cables from the battery terminals, clean them with a small wire brush, then refit them. Corrosion can be kept to a minimum by applying a thin layer of petroleum jelly to the clamps and terminals after they have been reconnected.

6 Make sure that the battery tray is in good condition, and that the retaining clamp is tight.

7 Corrosion on the tray, retaining clamp and the battery itself can be removed with a solution of water and baking soda. Thoroughly rinse all cleaned areas with plain water. Dry the battery and its surroundings with rags or tissues - these should then be discarded.

8 Any metal parts damaged by corrosion

4.13 Topping-up the battery electrolyte level

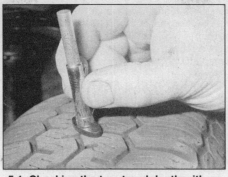

5.1 Checking the tyre tread depth with an indicator gauge

5.3 Checking the tyre pressures with a tyre pressure gauge

should be covered with a zinc-based primer, then painted.

9 Most models are fitted with a "maintenance-free" battery, which does not require topping-up. If this is the case, the battery will be sealed, and it will not be possible to remove the cell covers.

10 On models fitted with a low-maintenance or a conventional battery, the electrolyte level should be checked periodically as follows.

11 Pull out the cell covers from the top of the battery.

12 Check that the level of electrolyte is approximately 15 mm above the tops of the cell plates.

13 If necessary top-up the level, using only distilled or demineralised water **(see illustration)**.

14 Refit the cell covers.

15 Further information on the battery, charging and jump-starting can be found in Chapter 12, and in the preliminary Sections of this manual.

5 Tyre checks

1 The original tyres on this car are equipped with tread wear safety bands, which will appear when the tread depth reaches approximately 1.6 mm (0.063in). Tread wear can be monitored with a simple, inexpensive device known as a tread depth indicator gauge **(see illustration)**.

2 Wheels and tyres should give no real problems in use, provided that a close eye is kept on them with regard to excessive wear or damage. To this end, the following points should be noted.

3 Ensure that tyre pressures are checked regularly and maintained correctly. Checking should be carried out with the tyres cold, and not immediately after the vehicle has been in use **(see illustration)**. If the pressures are checked with the tyres hot, an apparently-high

Tyre Tread Wear Patterns

Shoulder Wear

Underinflation (wear on both sides)
Check and adjust pressures

Incorrect wheel camber (wear on one side)
Repair or renew suspension parts

Hard cornering
Reduce speed!

Centre Wear

Overinflation
Check and adjust pressures

If you sometimes have to inflate your car's tyres to the higher pressures specified for maximum load or sustained high speed, don't forget to reduce the pressures to normal afterwards.

Toe Wear

Incorrect toe setting
Adjust front wheel alignment

Note: The feathered edge of the tread which characterises toe wear is best checked by feel.

Uneven Wear

Incorrect camber or castor
Repair or renew suspension parts

Malfunctioning suspension
Repair or renew suspension parts

Unbalanced wheel
Balance tyres

Out-of-round brake disc/drum
Machine or renew

reading will be obtained, owing to heat expansion. *Under no circumstances* should an attempt be made to reduce the pressures to the quoted cold reading in this instance, or effective under-inflation will result.

4 Note any abnormal tread wear. Tread pattern irregularities such as feathering, flat spots, and more wear on one side than the other, are indications of front wheel alignment and/or balance problems. If any of these conditions is noted, the problem should be rectified as soon as possible.

5 Under-inflation will cause overheating of the tyre, owing to excessive flexing of the casing; also, the tread will not sit correctly on the road surface. This will cause a consequent loss of adhesion and excessive wear, not to mention the danger of sudden tyre failure due to heat build-up.

6 Over-inflation will cause rapid wear of the centre part of the tyre tread, coupled with reduced adhesion, harsher ride, and the danger of shock damage occurring in the tyre casing.

7 Regularly check the tyres for damage in the form of cuts or bulges, especially in the sidewalls. Remove any nails or stones embedded in the tread before they penetrate the tyre to cause deflation. If removal of a nail reveals that the tyre has been punctured, refit the nail, so that its point of penetration is marked. Immediately change the wheel, and have the tyre repaired by a tyre dealer. Do not drive on a tyre in such a condition. If in any doubt as to the possible consequences of any damage found, consult your local tyre dealer for advice.

8 Periodically remove the wheels, and clean any dirt or mud from the inside and outside surfaces. Examine the wheel rims for signs of rusting, corrosion or other damage. Light alloy wheels are easily damaged by "kerbing" whilst parking, and similarly, steel wheels may become dented or buckled. Renewal of the wheel is very often the only course of remedial action possible.

9 The balance of each wheel and tyre assembly should be maintained to avoid excessive wear, not only to the tyres but also to the steering and suspension components. Wheel imbalance is normally signified by vibration through the vehicle's bodyshell, although in many cases it is particularly noticeable through the steering wheel. Conversely, it should be noted that wear or damage in suspension or steering components may cause excessive tyre wear. Out-of-round or out-of-true tyres, damaged wheels, and wheel bearing wear/maladjustment also fall into this category. Balancing will not usually cure vibration caused by such wear.

10 Wheel balancing may be carried out with the wheel either on or off the vehicle. If balanced on the vehicle, ensure that the wheel-to-hub relationship is marked in some way prior to subsequent wheel removal, so that it may be refitted in its original position.

11 General tyre wear is influenced to a large degree by driving style - harsh braking and acceleration, or fast cornering, will all produce more rapid tyre wear. Interchanging of tyres may result in more even wear. However, it is worth bearing in mind that if this is completely effective, the added expense is incurred of replacing a complete set of tyres at the same time, which may prove financially restrictive for many owners.

12 Front tyres may wear unevenly as a result of wheel misalignment. The front wheels should always be correctly aligned according to the settings specified by the vehicle manufacturer (see Chapter 10).

13 Legal restrictions apply to many aspects of tyre fitting and usage. In the UK, this information is contained in the Motor Vehicle Construction and Use Regulations. It is suggested that a copy of these regulations is obtained from your local police if in doubt as to current legal requirements with regard to tyre type and condition, minimum tread depth, etc.

Every 6000 miles/10 000 km

6 Engine oil and filter renewal

Note: *The filter should be renewed at the first 6000-mile (10 000 km) service, then at every 12 000 miles (20 000 km) thereafter.*

1 Frequent oil and filter changes are the most important preventative maintenance procedures that can be undertaken by the DIY owner. As engine oil ages, it becomes diluted and contaminated, which leads to premature engine wear.

2 Before starting this procedure, gather together all the necessary tools and materials **(see illustration)**. Also make sure that you have plenty of clean rags and newspapers handy, to mop up any spills. Ideally, the engine oil should be warm, as it will drain better, and more built-up sludge will be removed with it. Take care, however, not to touch the exhaust or any other hot parts of the engine when working under the vehicle. Access to the underside of the vehicle will be greatly improved if it can be raised on a lift, driven onto ramps, or jacked up and supported on axle stands (see *"Jacking, towing and wheel changing"*). Whichever method is chosen, make sure that the car remains as level as possible, to enable the oil to drain fully.

HAYNES HiNT *To avoid any possibility of scalding, and to protect yourself from possible skin irritants and other harmful contaminants in used engine oils, it is advisable to wear rubber gloves when carrying out this work*

3 Remove the oil filler cap from the valve cover, then position a suitable container beneath the sump. Where applicable, remove the cover from the engine/transmission splash shield, then clean the drain plug and the area

6.2 Tools and materials necessary for engine oil change and filter renewal

around it. Slacken the drain plug half a turn using a special drain plug key (8 mm square) **(see illustrations)**. If possible, try to keep the plug pressed into the sump while unscrewing it by hand the last couple of turns. As the plug releases from the threads, move it away sharply so the stream of oil issuing from the sump runs into the container, not up your sleeve!

4 Allow some time for the old oil to drain, noting that it may be necessary to reposition the container as the oil flow slows to a trickle.

5 After all the oil has drained, wipe off the drain plug with a clean rag, and fit a new sealing washer. Clean the area around the drain plug opening, then refit and tighten the plug to the specified torque setting.

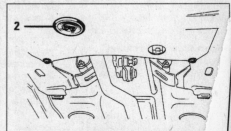

6.3a Sump drain plug cover (2) - not fi[tted] to all models

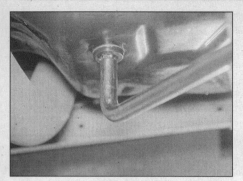

6.3b Using the special drain plug key to unscrew the sump drain plug

6.3c Sump drain plug (arrowed) - 1764 cc (F7P) 16-valve engine with aluminium sump

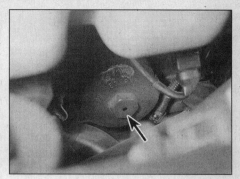

6.7 Hexagon (arrowed) to aid oil filter removal - 1764 cc (F7P) 16-valve engine

1

6 If applicable at this service, move the container into position under the oil filter, located on the front of the cylinder block.

7 Using an oil filter removal tool, slacken the filter initially (on certain filters, a hexagon is provided on the end of the filter to enable the use of a spanner or socket - **see illustration**)). Loosely wrap some rags around the oil filter, then unscrew it and immediately turn its open end uppermost to prevent further spillage of oil. Remove the oil filter from the engine compartment, and empty the oil into the container.

8 Use a clean rag to remove all oil, dirt and sludge from the filter sealing area on the engine. Check the old filter to make sure that the rubber sealing ring hasn't stuck to the engine. If it has, carefully remove it.

9 Apply a light coating of clean oil to the sealing ring on the new filter, then screw it into position on the engine **(see illustration)**. Tighten the filter firmly by hand only - do not use any tools. Wipe clean the exterior of the oil filter.

10 Remove the old oil and all tools from under the car, then (if applicable) lower the car to the ground.

11 Fill the engine with the specified quantity and grade of oil, as described earlier in this Section. Pour the oil in slowly, otherwise it may overflow from the top of the valve cover. Check that the oil level is up to the maximum mark on the dipstick, then refit and tighten the oil filler cap.

12 Start the engine and run it for a few minutes, checking that there are no leaks around the oil filter seal and the sump drain plug. Note that, when the engine is first started, there will be a delay of a few seconds before the oil pressure warning light goes out while the new filter fills with oil. Do not race the engine while the warning light is on.

13 Switch off the engine, and wait a few minutes for the oil to settle in the sump once more. With the new oil circulated and the filter now completely full, recheck the level on the dipstick, and add more oil if necessary.

14 Dispose of the used engine oil safely, with reference to "General repair procedures" in the Reference Sections of this manual.

7 Fluid level checks

Brake fluid

1 The location of the brake fluid reservoir varies according to model. On models without ABS, the brake fluid reservoir is located on the top of the brake master cylinder which is attached to the front of the vacuum servo unit. Alternatively, on certain models, the reservoir may be remotely-mounted on the bulkhead,

with hoses supplying the master cylinder. On models with ABS, the brake fluid reservoir is located on top of the ABS hydraulic unit attached to the bulkhead. The maximum and minimum marks are indicated on the side of the reservoir, and the fluid level should be maintained between these marks at all times **(see illustrations)**.

2 On models with ABS, first switch on the ignition, then depress the brake pedal several times in order to activate the electric hydraulic pump on the ABS unit. Leave the ignition switched on during the check.

3 The brake fluid inside the reservoir is readily visible. With the car on level ground, the level should be above the "MIN" (Danger) mark, and preferably on or near the "MAX" mark. Note that wear of the brake pads or brake shoe linings causes the level of the brake fluid to gradually fall, so that when the brake pads are renewed, the original level of the fluid is restored. It is not therefore necessary to top-up the level to compensate for this minimal drop. However, the level must never be allowed to fall below the minimum mark.

4 If topping-up is necessary, first wipe the area around the filler cap with a clean rag before removing the cap. When adding fluid, pour it carefully into the reservoir to avoid

6.9 Applying a light coating of oil to the oil filter sealing ring

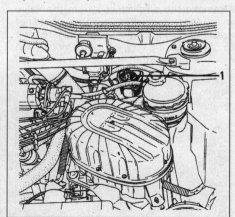

7.1a Brake fluid reservoir (1) - left-hand-drive non-ABS model (some right-hand-drive models have a remotely-mounted reservoir in the same location)

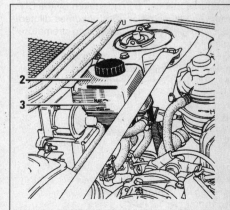

7.1b Brake fluid reservoir (2) and level markings (3) - left-hand-drive ABS model

Every 6000 miles / 10 000 km

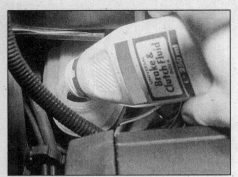

7.4 Topping-up the brake fluid level - right-hand-drive non-ABS model

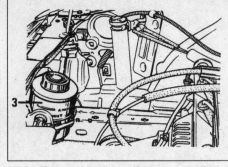

7.8a Remotely-mounted power steering fluid reservoir (3)

7.8b Pump-mounted power steering fluid reservoir (4)

5 Dipstick   A and B Level markings

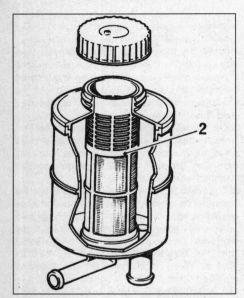

7.10a Early-type power steering fluid reservoir, showing level shoulder (2) on filler neck

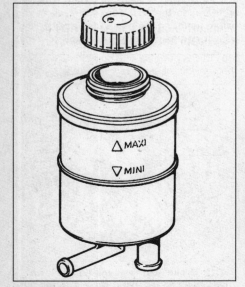

7.10b Later-type power steering fluid reservoir

spilling it on surrounding painted surfaces **(see illustration)**. Be sure to use only the specified brake hydraulic fluid, since mixing different types of fluid can cause damage to the system. See *"Lubricants, fluids and capacities"* at the end of this Chapter.

⚠️ *Warning: Brake hydraulic fluid can harm your eyes, and will damage painted surfaces, so use extreme caution when handling and pouring it. Do not use fluid that has been standing open for some time, as it absorbs moisture from the air. Excess moisture in the fluid can cause a dangerous loss of braking effectiveness.*

5 When adding fluid, it is a good idea to inspect the reservoir for contamination. The system should be drained and refilled if deposits, dirt particles or contamination are seen in the fluid.

6 After filling the reservoir to the proper level, make sure that the cap is refitted securely, to avoid leaks and the entry of foreign matter. On models with ABS, switch off the ignition.

7 If the reservoir requires repeated replenishing to maintain the proper level, this is an indication of a hydraulic leak somewhere in the system, which should be investigated immediately.

Power steering fluid

8 The power steering fluid reservoir may be located at the front of the engine compartment, or attached to the power

7.12 Topping-up the power steering fluid reservoir

steering pump, depending on model **(see illustrations)**.

9 For the check, the front wheels should be pointing straight-ahead, and the engine should be stopped and cold. The car should be positioned on level ground.

10 Level markings vary according to model. On models fitted with a remotely-mounted reservoir, there are two types of reservoir fitted. On the first type, the fluid should be on the shoulder of the filter screen, and on the later type, the fluid should be between the "MIN" and "MAX" level marks **(see illustrations)**. On models with a reservoir mounted on the power steering pump, the level should be between the maximum and minimum marks on the dipstick.

11 Before removing the filler cap, use a clean rag to wipe the cap and the surrounding area, to prevent any foreign matter from entering the reservoir. Unscrew and remove the filler cap.

12 Top-up if necessary with the specified grade of fluid **(see illustration)**. Be careful not to introduce dirt into the system, and do not overfill. Frequent topping-up indicates a leak, which should be investigated and rectified.

Manual gearbox oil

13 Position the car over an inspection pit, on car ramps, or jack it up and support it (see *"Jacking, towing and wheel changing"*), but make sure that it is level. Where applicable, remove the engine/gearbox splash shield.

14 Unscrew the filler plug from the front-facing side of the gearbox **(see illustration)**.

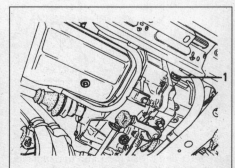

7.14 Manual gearbox filler plug location (1)

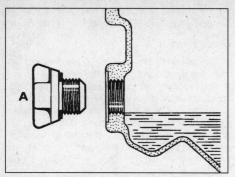

7.15 Manual gearbox filler plug (A) - correct oil level shown

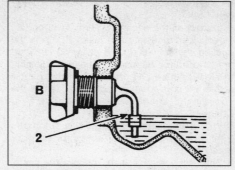

7.16 Alternative type of manual gearbox filler plug (B) and oil level collar (2)

7.17 Topping-up the manual gearbox oil level

15 Where a steel filler plug is fitted, the oil level should be up to the lower edge of the filler hole. Insert a finger to check the level **(see illustration)**.

16 Where a plastic filler plug is fitted, wipe clean the dipstick part of the plug, then check the level by inserting the shouldered end of the plug through the hole without engaging the threads. Position the plug so that the outer arrow is pointing upwards and the inner dipstick is pointing downwards. On removal of the plug, the level should be at the top of the collar on the dipstick. The bottom of the collar indicates the minimum level **(see illustration)**.

17 Where necessary, top-up the level using the correct grade of oil, then refit and tighten the filler plug **(see illustration)**.

18 If the gearbox requires frequent topping-up, check it for leakage, especially around the driveshaft oil seals, and repair as necessary.

19 Where applicable, refit the engine/gearbox splash shield, and lower the car to the ground.

Automatic transmission fluid

MB1 and MB3 (3-speed) automatic transmissions

20 Check the fluid level when the car has been standing for some time and the fluid is cold.

21 Position the car on level ground, then apply the handbrake and select "P" with the selector lever. Start the engine, and allow it to run for a few minutes.

22 With the engine still idling, withdraw the dipstick from the front of the transmission housing, wipe it on a clean cloth, and insert it again. Withdraw it once more and read off the level **(see illustration)**. Ideally, the level should be in the centre of the mark on the dipstick. The fluid must never be allowed to fall below the bottom of the mark, otherwise there is a risk of damaging the transmission. The transmission must never be overfilled so that the level is above the top of the mark, otherwise there is a risk of overheating.

23 If topping-up is necessary, add a quantity of the specified fluid to the transmission through the dipstick tube. Use a clean funnel with a fine-mesh screen, to avoid spillage, and to ensure that any foreign matter is not introduced into the transmission.

24 After topping-up, recheck the level again, as described above. Refit the dipstick and switch off the engine.

AD4 (4-speed) automatic transmission

Note: *The fluid level checking procedure on the AD4 automatic transmission is particularly complicated, and the home mechanic would be well-advised to take the car to a Renault dealer to have the work carried out, as special test equipment is necessary to carry out the check. However, the following procedure is given for those who may have access to this equipment. Note that the final drive oil level is not checked as a routine maintenance task, as it is sealed for life.*

25 First add 0.5 litre (1 pint) of the specified fluid to the transmission by removing the vent from the top of the filler tube and using a clean funnel with a fine-mesh filter **(see illustration)**. Refit the vent.

26 Position the car on a ramp, or jack it up and support on axle stands.

27 Connect the Renault XR25 test meter to the diagnostic socket, and enter "DO4" then number "04". With the selector lever in "Park", run the engine at idle speed until the temperature reaches 60°C.

28 With the engine still running, unscrew the topping-up plug on the transmission **(see illustration)**. Allow the excess fluid to run out into a calibrated container for 20 seconds, then refit the plug. The amount of fluid should be more than 0.1 litre (about a fifth of a pint); if it is not, the fluid level in the transmission is incorrect.

29 If fluid is to be added, pour 1 litre (nearly 2 pints) of the specified fluid through the filler tube, after removing the vent. Allow the transmission to cool down, then repeat the checking procedure again as described in the previous paragraphs.

Final drive oil level check - AD4 (4-speed) automatic transmission

30 This is not a routine operation, but it may be considered necessary if there is reason to

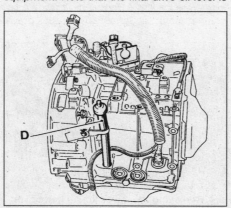

7.22 MB1 and MB3 automatic transmission fluid level dipstick location (1)

A Minimum cold level marking
B Maximum cold level marking

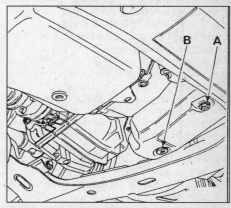

7.25 AD4 automatic transmission fluid filler tube (D) and vent

7.28 AD4 automatic transmission topping-up plug (A) and drain plug (B)

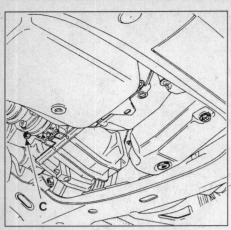

7.32 AD4 automatic transmission final drive level plug (C)

suspect that the oil level is incorrect - for instance if there has been an oil leak.

31 Position the vehicle on ramps, or jack it up and support securely on axle stands (see *"Jacking, towing and wheel changing"*). Make sure that the vehicle is level.

32 Unscrew the final drive level plug located behind the right-hand driveshaft on the right-hand side of the transmission **(see illustration)**.

33 Check that the level of the oil is up to the bottom of the plug hole. If not, inject oil of the correct grade into the hole until if overflows.

34 Wipe clean the level plug, then refit and tighten it.

35 Lower the vehicle to the ground.

8 Hose and fluid leak check

1 Visually inspect the engine joint faces, gaskets and seals for any signs of water or oil leaks. Pay particular attention to the areas around the valve cover, cylinder head, oil filter, and sump joint faces. Bear in mind that over a period of time, some very slight seepage from these areas is to be expected; what you are really looking for is any indication of a serious leak. Should a leak be found, renew the offending gasket or oil seal by referring to the appropriate Chapters in this manual.

2 Also check the security and condition of all the engine-related pipes and hoses. Ensure that all cable ties or securing clips are in place and in good condition. Clips which are broken or missing can lead to chafing of the hoses, pipes, or wiring, which could cause more serious problems in the future.

3 Carefully check the radiator hoses and heater hoses along their entire length. Renew any hose which is cracked, swollen or deteriorated. Cracks will show up better if the hose is squeezed. Pay close attention to the hose clips that secure the hoses to the cooling system components. Hose clips can pinch and puncture hoses, resulting in cooling system leaks. If wire type hose clips are used, it may

be a good idea to replace them with screw-type clips.

4 Inspect all the cooling system components (hoses, joint faces etc.) for leaks. A leak in the cooling system will usually show up as white or rust-coloured deposits on the area adjoining the leak. Where any problems of this nature are found on system components, renew the component or gasket with reference to Chapter 3.

5 Where applicable, inspect the automatic transmission fluid cooler hoses for leaks or deterioration.

6 With the vehicle raised, inspect the petrol tank and filler neck for punctures, cracks and other damage. The connection between the filler neck and tank is especially critical. Sometimes, a rubber filler neck or connecting hose will leak due to loose retaining clamps or deteriorated rubber.

7 Carefully check all rubber hoses and metal fuel lines leading away from the petrol tank. Check for loose connections, deteriorated hoses, crimped lines, and other damage. Pay particular attention to the vent pipes and hoses, which often loop up around the filler neck, and can become blocked or crimped. Follow the lines to the front of the vehicle carefully, inspecting them all the way. Renew damaged sections as necessary.

8 From within the engine compartment, check the security of all fuel hose attachments and pipe unions, and inspect the fuel hoses and vacuum hoses for kinks, chafing and deterioration.

9 Where applicable, check the condition of the power steering fluid hoses and pipes.

9 Auxiliary drivebelt checking and renewal

Note: *The auxiliary drivebelt configuration varies considerably depending on model. Removal and refitting should be self-explanatory with reference to the accompanying illustrations, which show the most common configurations likely to be encountered. For models with drivebelt configurations not shown in the accompanying illustrations, consult a Renault dealer for advice*

9.4 Removing the lower timing belt cover for access to the auxiliary drivebelt - 1764 cc (F7P) 16-valve engine model

on the correct tensioning procedure. Refer to Section 1 for details of engine identification.

Checking

1 The auxiliary drivebelt(s) is/are located on the front right-hand side of the engine.

2 The number and configuration of drivebelts fitted varies considerably depending on model, and whether or not the vehicle is equipped with power steering and/or air conditioning.

3 Due to their function and material makeup, drivebelts are prone to failure after a period of time. They should therefore be inspected, and if necessary adjusted, periodically.

4 Since the drivebelt(s) is/are located very close to the right-hand side of the engine compartment, it is possible to gain better access by raising the front of the vehicle and removing the right-hand wheel, then removing the splash shield from inside the wheelarch. On models with the 1764 cc (F7P) 16-valve engine, improved access can be gained by removing the right-hand headlight (see alternator removal procedure in Chapter 5A). It will also be necessary to remove the lower timing belt cover for access to the drivebelt **(see illustration)**.

5 With the engine switched off, inspect the full length of the drivebelt(s) for cracks and separation of the belt plies. It will be necessary to turn the engine in order to move the belt(s) from the pulleys so that the belt(s) can be inspected thoroughly. Twist the belt(s) between the pulleys so that both sides can be viewed. Also check for fraying, and glazing, which gives the belt(s) a shiny appearance. Check the pulleys for nicks, cracks, distortion and corrosion.

Tensioning

6 The tension of the belt(s) is checked by pushing midway between the pulleys at the

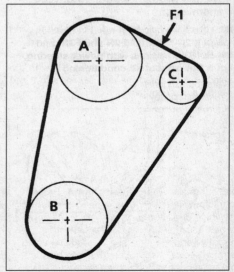

9.6a Auxiliary drivebelt tension checking point (F1) - C-type engines

A Water pump pulley   C Alternator pulley
B Crankshaft pulley   F1 = 4.0 mm

Every 6000 miles / 10 000 km 1•17

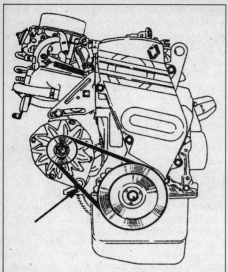

9.6b Alternator drivebelt tension checking point (arrowed) - E-type engines

Deflection (arrowed) = 3.0 mm

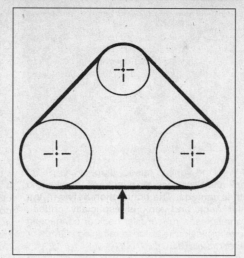

9.6c Air conditioning compressor drivebelt checking point (arrowed) - E-type engine without power steering

Deflection (arrowed) = 4.0 mm

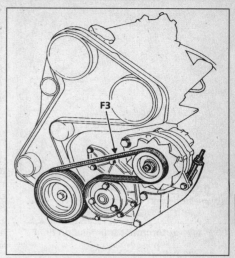

9.6d Auxiliary drivebelt tension checking point (F3) - 1721 cc (F2N and F3N) and 1794 cc (F3P) engines without power steering or air conditioning

F3 = 2.5 to 3.5 mm cold/3.5 to 4.5 mm hot

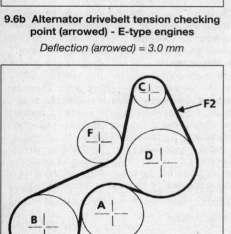

9.6e Auxiliary drivebelt tension checking point (F2) - 1721 cc (F2N and F3N) and 1794 cc (F3P) engines with power steering, but without air conditioning

A Water pump pulley
B Crankshaft pulley
C Alternator pulley
D Power steering pump pulley
F Tensioner pulley
F2 = 3.5 to 4.5 mm cold/5.5 to 7.0 mm warm

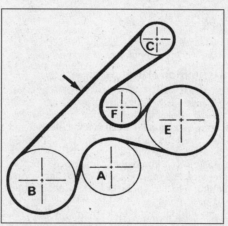

9.6f Auxiliary drivebelt tension checking point (arrowed) - 1721 cc (F2N and F3N) and 1794 cc (F3P) engines with air conditioning, but without power steering

A Water pump pulley
B Crankshaft pulley
C Alternator pulley
E Air conditioning compressor pulley
F Tensioner pulley
Deflection (arrowed) = 4.0 to 5.0 mm

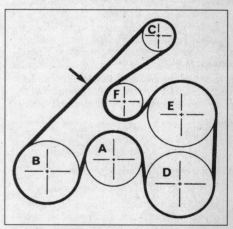

9.6g Auxiliary drivebelt tension checking point (arrowed) - 1721 cc (F2N and F3N) and 1794 cc (F3P) engines with power steering and air conditioning

A Water pump pulley
B Crankshaft pulley
C Alternator pulley
D Power steering pump pulley
E Air conditioning compressor pulley
F Tensioner pulley
Deflection (arrowed) = 4.0 to 5.0 mm

point indicated **(see illustrations)**. Renault technicians use a special spring-tensioned tool which applies a force of 30 N (6.75 lbf) to the belt and then measures the deflection. An alternative arrangement can be made by using a straight-edge, steel rule and spring balance. Hold the straight-edge across the two pulleys, then position the steel rule on the belt, apply the force with the spring balance, and measure the deflection. The same arrangement is shown in Chapter 2A and 2C for the adjustment of the timing belt.

7 If adjustment is necessary, loosen the alternator/power steering pump/air conditioning compressor pivot bolt first, then loosen the adjustment bolt (if applicable). Alternatively, on models equipped with a separate belt tensioner/adjuster mechanism, loosen the tensioner bolt(s) and move or turn the tensioner (as applicable) to relieve the tension in the belt **(see illustrations)**.
8 To apply tension to the belt, on models without a separate belt tensioner/adjuster mechanism, insert a lever between the pulley

end of the alternator/power steering pump/air conditioning compressor (as applicable), and move the relevant component to tension the belt. Tighten the adjustment bolt and the pivot bolt.
9 To apply tension to the belt, on models with a separate belt tensioner/adjuster mechanism, turn or reposition the tensioner (as applicable) to achieve the correct belt tension.
10 Run the engine for about 5 minutes, then recheck the tension.

9.7a Alternator drivebelt tension adjustment bolt (A) and alternator pivot bolt (B) - 1390 cc (C3J) engine

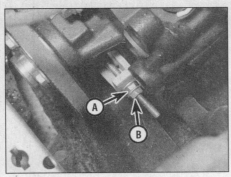

9.7b Power steering pump drivebelt tension adjustment nut (A) and locknut (B) - 1390 cc (E7J) engine

9.7c Auxiliary drivebelt tension adjustment bolt (arrowed) - 1721 cc (F3N) engine with power steering but without air conditioning

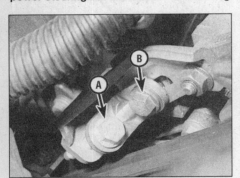

9.7d Auxiliary drivebelt tension adjustment bolt (A) and lockbolt (B) - 1764 cc (F7P) 16-valve engine

Removal and refitting

11 To remove a belt, slacken the belt tension fully as described previously. Slip the belt off the pulleys, then fit the new belt, ensuring that it is routed correctly. Note that on models with two drivebelts, it will be necessary to remove the front drivebelt for access to the rear belt.
12 With the belt in position, adjust the tension as previously described.

10 Ignition HT leads, distributor cap and rotor arm – checking and renewal

1 The spark plug HT leads should be checked whenever the spark plugs are checked (Section 11).
2 Ensure that the leads are numbered before removing them, to avoid confusion when refitting (No 1 cylinder is at the transmission end of the engine). Pull one HT lead from its plug by gripping the end fitting, not the lead, otherwise the lead connection may be fractured. Note that, on models with the 1764 cc (F7P) 16-valve engine, it is necessary to remove the engine top cover (secured by two screws) for access to the spark plug HT leads **(see illustrations)**.
3 Check inside the end fitting for signs of corrosion, which will look like a white crusty

powder. Scrape out such deposits using a small screwdriver. Push the end fitting back onto the spark plug, ensuring that it is a tight fit on the plug. If not, remove the lead again, and use pliers to carefully crimp the metal connector inside the end fitting until it fits securely on the end of the spark plug.
4 Using a clean rag, wipe the entire length of the lead to remove any built-up dirt and grease. Once the lead is clean, check for burns, cracks and other damage. Do not bend the lead excessively, or pull the lead lengthwise - the conductor inside might break.
5 Disconnect the other end of the lead from the distributor cap. Again, pull only on the end fitting. Check for corrosion and a tight fit in the same manner as the spark plug end. If an ohmmeter is available, check the continuity of the HT lead by connecting the meter between the spark plug end of the lead and the segment inside the distributor cap **(see illustration)**. (Resistive leads are commonly fitted, giving an ohmmeter reading of several hundred or thousand ohms per lead.) Refit the lead securely on completion.
6 Check the remaining HT leads one at a time, in the same way.
7 If new HT leads are required, purchase a set suitable for your specific vehicle and engine.
8 Remove the distributor cap (secured by clips or screws), wipe it clean, and carefully inspect it inside and out for signs of cracks, carbon tracks (tracking) and worn, burned or loose contacts. Also inspect the condition of the carbon brush in the centre of the cap. Similarly inspect the rotor arm **(see illustrations)**. Renew these components if any defects are found (see Chapter 5B or 5C, as applicable). It is common practice to renew the cap and rotor arm whenever new HT leads are fitted. When fitting a new cap, remove the HT leads from the old cap one at a time, and fit them to the new cap in the exact same location - do not simultaneously remove all the leads from the old cap, or firing-order confusion may occur.
9 Even with the ignition system in first-class condition, some engines may still occasionally experience poor starting, attributable to damp ignition components.

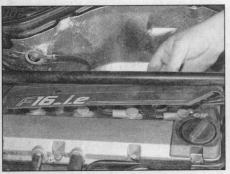

10.2a Removing the engine top cover . . .

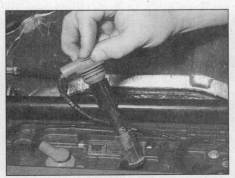

10.2b . . . for access to the spark plug HT leads - 1764 cc (F7P) 16-valve engine

10.5 Checking the resistance of an HT lead with a digital ohmmeter

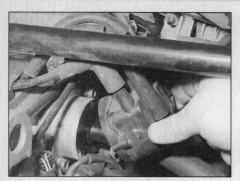

10.8a Removing the distributor cap . . .

10.8b . . . and the rotor arm - 1764 cc (F7P) 16-valve engine

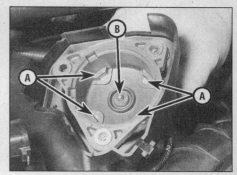

10.8c Inspect the distributor cap contacts (A) and the carbon brush (B) - 1794 cc (F3P) engine shown

1

11 Spark plug check

1 The correct functioning of the spark plugs is vital for the correct running and efficiency of the engine. It is essential that the plugs fitted are appropriate for the engine, the suitable type being specified at the end of this Chapter. If the correct type of plug is used and the engine is in good condition, the spark plugs should not need attention between scheduled renewal intervals, except for adjustment of their gaps. Spark plug cleaning is rarely necessary, and should not be attempted unless specialised equipment is available, as damage can easily be caused to the firing ends.

2 To remove the plugs, first open the bonnet. On models with the 1764 cc (F7P) 16-valve engine, remove the engine top cover, which is secured by two screws.

3 On all models, check that the HT leads are marked one to four, to correspond to the appropriate cylinder number (No 1 cylinder is at the transmission end of the engine). Failure to do this may result in confusion when refitting, if all the HT leads are disconnected at the same time. Pull the HT leads from the plugs; grip the end fitting, not the lead, otherwise the lead connection may be fractured **(see illustration)**.

4 On models with 1794 cc (F3P) engines, if desired, unclip the plastic covers from the cylinder head for improved access to the spark plugs, and to enable cleaning of the spark plug recesses **(see illustration)**.

5 It is advisable to remove any dirt from the spark plug recesses using a clean brush, a vacuum cleaner or compressed air before removing the plugs, to prevent the dirt dropping into the cylinders.

6 Unscrew the plugs using a spark plug spanner, suitable box spanner or a deep socket and extension bar **(see illustrations)**. Keep the socket in alignment with the spark plug, otherwise if it is forcibly moved to either side, the ceramic top of the spark plug may be broken off. As each plug is removed, examine it as follows.

7 Examination of the spark plugs will give a good indication of the condition of the engine. If the insulator nose of the spark plug is clean and white, with no deposits, this is indicative of a weak fuel/air mixture or too hot a plug (a hot plug transfers heat away from the electrode slowly, a cold plug transfers heat away quickly).

8 If the tip and insulator nose are covered with hard black-looking deposits, then this is indicative that the mixture is too rich. Should the plug be black and oily, then it is likely that the engine is fairly worn, as well as the mixture being too rich.

9 If the insulator nose is covered with light tan to greyish-brown deposits, then the mixture is correct, and it is likely that the engine is in good condition.

10 If the spark plug has only completed 6000 miles (10 000 km) in accordance with the routine maintenance schedule, it should still be serviceable until the 12 000 mile (20 000 km) service, when it is renewed. However, it is recommended that it be re-gapped in order to maintain peak engine efficiency, and to allow for the slow increase in gap (approximately 0.025 mm per 1000 miles) which occurs in normal operation. If, due to engine condition, the spark plug is not serviceable, or if poor starting has been experienced, it should be renewed.

11 The spark plug gap is of considerable importance as, if it is too large or too small, the size of the spark and its efficiency will be seriously impaired. For best results, the spark

11.3 Disconnecting a spark plug HT lead - 1794 cc (F3P) engine

11.4 Removing a spark plug cover - 1794 cc (F3P) engine

11.6a Tools required for spark plug removal, gap adjustment and refitting

11.6b Removing a spark plug - 1764 cc (F7P) 16-valve engine

11.12 Measuring a spark plug gap with a feeler blade

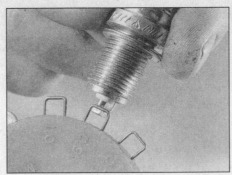

11.13a Measuring the spark plug gap with a wire gauge . . .

11.13b . . . and adjusting the gap using a special adjusting tool

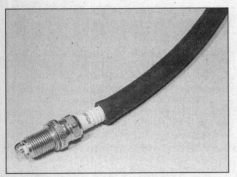

11.15 Using a short length of rubber hose to insert a spark plug

plug gap should be set in accordance with the Specifications at the end of this Chapter.

12 To set it, measure the gap with a feeler blade, and then bend open, or closed, the outer plug electrode until the correct gap is achieved **(see illustration)**. The centre electrode should never be bent, as this may crack the insulation and cause plug failure, if nothing worse.

13 Special spark plug electrode gap measuring and adjusting tools are available from most motor accessory shops **(see illustrations)**.

14 Before fitting the spark plugs, check that the threaded connector sleeves are tight, and that the plug exterior surfaces and threads are

clean. Apply a little anti-seize compound to the threads.

15 It is very often difficult to insert spark plugs into their holes without cross-threading them. To avoid this possibility, fit a short length of rubber or plastic hose over the end of the spark plug **(see illustration)**. The flexible hose acts as a universal joint to help align the plug with the plug hole. Should the plug begin to cross-thread, the hose will slip on the spark plug, preventing thread damage to the cylinder head.

16 Remove the hose (if used) and tighten the plug to the specified torque using the spark plug socket and a torque wrench. Refit the remaining spark plugs in the same manner.

17 Wipe clean the HT leads, then reconnect them in their correct order.

12 Contact breaker points check - 1397 cc (C1J) engine

1 Release the two spring clips and lift off the distributor cap. Pull the rotor arm off the shaft, and remove the plastic shield **(see illustration)**.

2 With the ignition switched off, use a screwdriver to open the contact breaker points, then visually check the points surfaces for pitting, roughness and discoloration. If the points have been arcing, there will be a build-up of metal on the moving contact, and a corresponding hole in the fixed contact; if this

is the case, the points should be renewed.

3 Another method of checking the contact breaker points is by using a test meter available from most car accessory shops. Rotate the engine if necessary until the points are fully shut. Connect the meter between the distributor LT wiring terminal and earth, and read off the condition of the points.

4 To remove the points, first unscrew the adjusting nut on the side of the distributor body, and then unscrew the two baseplate retaining screws **(see illustration)**.

5 Unhook the end of the adjustment rod from the fixed contact, and slide the rod and spring out of the distributor body **(see illustration)**.

6 Prise out the small plug and then remove the retaining clip, noting that the hole in the clip is uppermost **(see illustrations)**.

7 Slacken the LT terminal nut and detach the lead **(see illustration)**.

8 Remove the spring retaining clip from the top of the moving contact pivot post, and take off the fibre insulating washer **(see illustration)**.

9 Ease the spring blade away from its nylon support, and lift the moving contact upwards and off the pivot post **(see illustration)**.

10 Unscrew the retaining screw, and remove the fixed contact from the baseplate **(see illustration)**.

11 The purpose of the condenser (located externally on the side of the distributor body) is

12.1 Removing the rotor arm from the contact breaker distributor

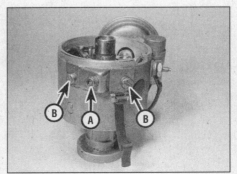

12.4 Contact breaker points adjusting nut (A) and baseplate retaining screw (B)

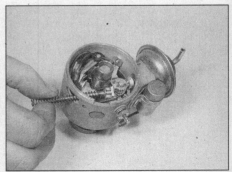

12.5 Removing the adjustment rod and spring

12.6a Prise out the plastic plug . . .

12.6b . . . to gain access to the retaining clip (arrowed) . . .

12.6c . . . which can then be removed with pliers. Note which way up it is fitted

1

to ensure that when the contact breaker points open, there is no sparking across them, which would cause wear of their faces and prevent the rapid collapse of the magnetic field in the coil. Failure of the condenser would cause a reduction in coil HT voltage, and ultimately lead to engine misfire.

12 If the engine becomes very difficult to start, or begins to miss after several miles of running, and the contact breaker points show signs of excessive burning, the condition of the condenser must be suspect. A further test can be made by separating the points by hand with the ignition switched on. If this is accompanied by a strong bright flash, it is indicative that the condenser has failed.

13 Without special test equipment, the only sure way to diagnose condenser trouble is to fit a new one, and note if there is any improvement.

14 To remove the condenser, unscrew the nut at the LT terminal post, and slip off the lead. Unscrew the condenser retaining screw and remove the unit from the side of the distributor body.

15 Refitting of the condenser is a reversal of the removal procedure.

16 To fit the new contact breaker points, first check if there is any greasy deposit on them, and if necessary clean them using methylated spirit.

17 Fit the points using a reversal of the removal procedure, then adjust them as

follows. Turn the engine over using a socket or spanner on the crankshaft pulley bolt, until the heel of the contact breaker arm is on the peak of one of the four cam lobes.

18 With the points fully open, a clean feeler blade equal to the contact breaker points gap, as given in the Specifications, should now just fit between the contact faces **(see illustration)**.

19 If the gap is too large or too small, turn the adjusting nut on the side of the distributor body using a small spanner until the specified gap is obtained.

20 With the points correctly adjusted, refit the plastic shield, rotor arm and distributor cap. Check the ignition timing as described later in this Section.

21 If a dwell meter is available, a far more accurate method of setting the contact breaker points is by measuring and setting the distributor dwell angle.

22 The dwell angle is the number of degrees of distributor shaft rotation during which the contact breaker points are closed (ie the period from when the points close after being opened by one cam lobe until they are opened again by the next cam lobe). The advantages of setting the points by this method are that any wear of the distributor shaft or cam lobes is taken into account, and also the inaccuracies of using a feeler gauge are eliminated.

23 To check and adjust the dwell angle,

12.7 Slacken the LT terminal nut (A) and detach the lead (B) from the connector

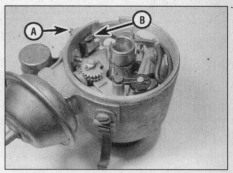

12.8 Remove the retaining clip and the fibre washer from the pivot post

12.9 Withdraw the moving contact from the pivot post

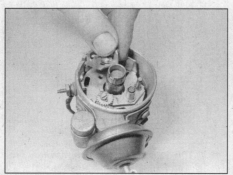

12.10 Removing the fixed contact from the baseplate

12.18 Measuring the points gap using a feeler blade. Adjust if necessary by turning nut (A)

connect one lead of the meter to the ignition coil + terminal and the other lead to the coil - terminal, or in accordance with the meter maker's instructions.

24 Start the engine, allow it to idle, and observe the reading on the dwell meter scale. If the dwell angle is not as specified, turn the adjusting nut on the side of the distributor body as necessary to obtain the correct setting. **Note:** *Owing to machining tolerances, or wear in the distributor shaft or bushes, it is not uncommon for a contact breaker points gap correctly set with feeler gauges, to give a dwell angle outside the specified tolerances. If this is the case, the dwell angle should be regarded as the preferred setting.*

25 After completing the adjustment, switch off the engine and disconnect the dwell meter. Check the ignition timing as described in the following Section.

13 Ignition timing check - 1397 cc (C1J) engine

1 In order that the engine can run efficiently, it is necessary for a spark to occur at the spark plug and ignite the fuel/air mixture at the instant just before the piston on the compression stroke reaches the top of its travel. The precise instant at which the spark occurs is determined by the ignition timing, and this is quoted in degrees Before Top Dead Centre (BTDC).

2 The timing may be checked and adjusted in one of two ways, either by using a test bulb to obtain a static setting (with the engine stationary), or by using a stroboscopic timing light to obtain a dynamic setting (with the engine running).

3 Before checking or adjusting the ignition timing, make sure that the contact breaker points are in good condition and correctly adjusted, as described previously.

Static setting

4 Refer to the Specifications at the end of this Chapter, and note the specified setting for static ignition timing. This value will also be found stamped on a clip fastened to one of the HT leads **(see illustration)**.

5 Pull off the HT lead and remove No 1 spark plug (nearest the transmission end of the engine).

6 Place a finger over the plug hole, and turn the engine in the normal direction of rotation (clockwise from the crankshaft pulley end) until pressure is felt in No 1 cylinder. This indicates that the piston is commencing its compression stroke. The engine can be turned using a socket or spanner on the crankshaft pulley bolt, or by engaging a gear and pushing the car along.

7 Continue turning the engine until the mark on the flywheel is aligned with the appropriate notch on the clutch bellhousing **(see illustration)**.

8 Remove the distributor cap, and check that the rotor arm is pointing towards the No 1 spark plug HT lead segment in the cap.

9 Connect a 12-volt test light and leads between a good earth point and the LT terminal nut on the side of the distributor body.

10 Slacken the distributor clamp retaining nut, and then switch on the ignition.

11 If the test light is on, this shows that the points are open. Turn the distributor slightly clockwise until the light goes out, showing that the points have closed.

12 Now turn the distributor anti-clockwise until the test light just comes on. Hold the distributor in this position, and tighten the clamp retaining nut.

13 Test the setting by turning the engine two complete revolutions, observing when the light comes on in relation to the timing marks.

14 Switch off the ignition and remove the test light. Refit No 1 spark plug, the distributor cap and HT lead.

Dynamic setting

15 Refer to the Specifications at the end of this Chapter, and note the setting for ignition timing at idle. This initial value will also be found stamped on a clip fastened to one of the HT leads.

> **HAYNES HINT** *To make subsequent operations easier, it is advisable to highlight the mark on the flywheel and the appropriate notch on the clutch bellhousing with white paint (typist's correction fluid is ideal) or chalk.*

16 Connect the timing light in accordance with the equipment manufacturer's instructions (usually interposed between the end of No 1 spark plug HT lead and No 1 spark plug terminal).

17 Disconnect the vacuum advance pipe from the distributor vacuum unit, and plug its end.

18 Start the engine and leave it idling at the specified speed (refer to the Specifications).

19 Point the timing light at the timing marks. They should appear to be stationary, with the mark on the flywheel aligned with the appropriate notch on the clutch bellhousing **(see illustration)**.

20 If adjustment is necessary (ie the flywheel mark does not line up with the appropriate notch), slacken the distributor clamp retaining nut, and turn the distributor body either anti-clockwise to advance the timing, or clockwise to retard it. Tighten the clamp nut when the setting is correct.

21 Gradually increase the engine speed while still pointing the timing light at the marks. The mark on the flywheel should appear to advance further, indicating that the distributor centrifugal advance mechanism is functioning. If the mark remains stationary or moves in a jerky, erratic fashion, the advance mechanism must be suspect.

22 Reconnect the vacuum pipe to the distributor, and check that the advance alters when the pipe is connected. If not, the vacuum unit on the distributor may be faulty.

23 After completing the checks and adjustments, switch off the engine and disconnect the timing light.

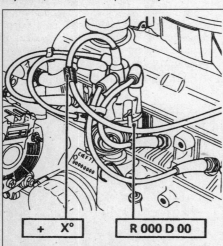

13.4 Ignition timing setting (X° BTDC) is stamped on clip - 1397 cc (C1J) engine only

13.7 Timing marks (notch on flywheel rim and scale on bellhousing) - 1397 cc (C1J) engine only

O = TDC

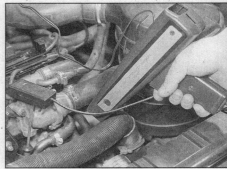

13.19 Checking the ignition timing with a stroboscopic timing light

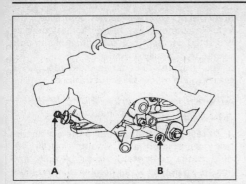

14.1a Carburettor adjustment screws - Solex 32 BIS 936 (1237 cc/C1G engine)

A Idle speed   B Idle mixture (CO)

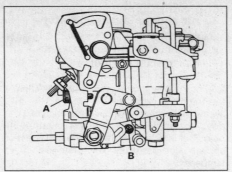

14.1b Carburettor adjustment screws - Zenith 32 IF2 (1397 cc/C1J engine)

A Idle speed   B Idle mixture (CO)

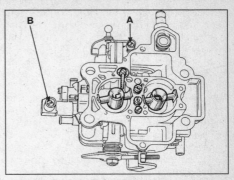

14.1c Carburettor adjustment screws - Weber 32 DRT (1397 cc/C2J engine)

A Idle speed   B Idle mixture (CO)

14 Idle speed and mixture check

Note: *A suitable tachometer and an exhaust gas analyser (CO meter) will be required for this task.*

Carburettor models

1 The procedure for idle speed and CO content adjustment is the same regardless of which carburettor type may be fitted. Before proceeding, identify the carburettor type fitted and the adjustment screw locations (see also Chapter 4A) **(see illustrations)**.

2 Before carrying out the following adjustments, ensure that the spark plugs are in good condition and correctly gapped. On the 1397 cc (C1J) engine, also ensure that the contact breaker points and ignition timing settings are correct.

3 Make sure that all electrical components are switched off during the following procedure. If the electric cooling fan operates, wait until it has stopped before continuing.

4 Connect a tachometer to the engine in accordance with its manufacturer's instructions. The use of an exhaust gas analyser (CO meter) is also recommended to obtain an accurate setting.

5 Remove the tamperproof cap (where fitted) from the mixture adjustment screw by hooking it out with a scriber or small screwdriver.

6 Run the engine at a fast idle speed until it reaches normal operating temperature. Increase the engine speed to 2000 rpm for 30 seconds, and repeat this at three-minute intervals during the adjustment procedure. This will ensure that any excess fuel is cleared from the inlet manifold.

7 With the engine idling, turn the idle speed screw until the engine is idling at the specified speed **(see illustrations)**.

8 Turn the mixture adjustment screw clockwise to weaken the mixture or anticlockwise to richen it, until the CO reading is as given in the Specifications. If a CO meter is not being used, weaken the mixture as described, then richen it until the maximum

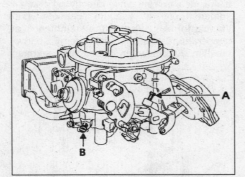

14.1d Carburettor adjustment screws - Weber 32 TLDR (1390 cc/E6J engine)

A Idle speed   B Idle mixture (CO)

engine speed is obtained, consistent with even running.

9 If necessary, re-adjust the idle speed, then check the CO reading again. Repeat as necessary until both the idle speed and CO reading are correct.

10 Where required by law, fit a new tamperproof cap to the mixture adjustment screw.

Fuel injection models

11 The idle speed on all fuel injection models is electronically-controlled by the computer, via the idle speed control motor, and no adjustment is possible.

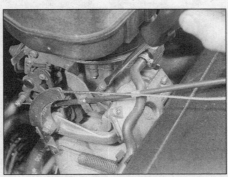

14.7a Adjusting the idle speed - Weber 32 TLDR (1390 cc/E6J engine)

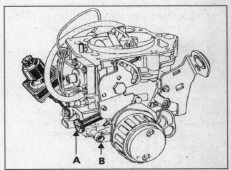

14.1e Carburettor adjustment screws - Solex 32 x 34 Z13 (1721 cc/F2N engine)

A Idle speed   B Idle mixture (CO)

12 The CO content is also electronically-controlled on all models with a catalytic converter (see Chapter 4C). This means that the only engines on which adjustment is possible (models without a catalytic converter) are the 1721 cc (F3N 746) and the 1764 cc (F7P 700).

13 Adjustment is carried out by turning the screw on the CO adjustment potentiometer located next to the MAP sensor on the engine compartment bulkhead **(see illustration)**. Accurate adjustment can only be carried out by using an exhaust gas analyser (CO meter) in accordance with its manufacturer's instructions.

14.7b Idle speed adjustment screw (arrowed) - Solex 32 x 34 Z13 (1721 cc/F2N engine)

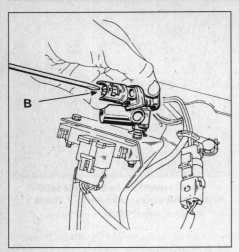

14.13 CO adjustment potentiometer (B) - 1764 cc (F7P-700) engine

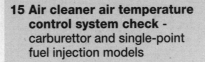

15 Air cleaner air temperature control system check - carburettor and single-point fuel injection models

1 In order for the engine to operate efficiently, the temperature of the air entering the inlet system is controlled within certain limits. (This does not apply to models fitted with multi-point fuel injection, on which the fuel injection system compensates for changes in air temperature.)

2 The air cleaner has two sources of air, one direct from the outside of the engine compartment (cold air), and the other from a shroud on the exhaust manifold (warm air). A wax capsule thermostat controls a flap inside the air cleaner inlet, either directly or under the influence of a vacuum capsule **(see illustrations)**. When the ambient air temperature is below the predetermined level, the flap directs warm air from the exhaust manifold shroud. As the temperature of the incoming (ambient) air rises, the flap opens to admit colder air from outside the car until eventually it is fully open.

3 The temperature control system fitted varies according to model **(see illustrations)**.

All engines except 1721 cc (F3N) and 1794 cc (F3P)

4 To test the system, remove the air cleaner body as described in Chapter 4A or 4B, detach the temperature control unit, and immerse it in cold water (temperature no more than 20°C). After a maximum of 5 minutes, the flap should shut off the cold air inlet. Now increase the temperature of the water to 40°C, and check that the flap shuts off the hot air inlet. If the flap does not operate correctly, check first that it is not seized. No adjustment is possible; the unit should be renewed if faulty.

1721 cc (F3N) and 1794 cc (F3P) single-point injection engines

5 This system is different in that the position of the flap is determined not only by

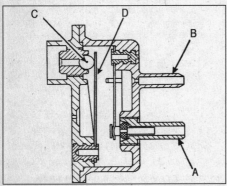

15.2a Detail of thermostatic vacuum valve

A To vacuum capsule   C Ball valve
B From inlet manifold   D Bi-metallic strip

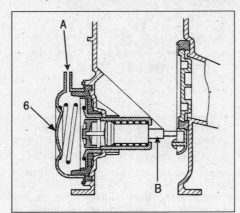

15.2b Detail of thermostat/vacuum capsule unit (6)

A From vacuum valve   B Thermostat

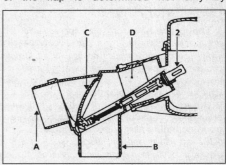

15.3a Air cleaner air temperature control system fitted to C-type and some E-type engines

A Cold air inlet   B Hot air inlet   C Flap
D Air to the carburettor/throttle housing
2 Wax-controlled thermostatic valve

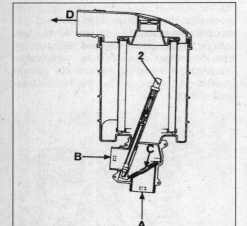

15.3b Alternative air cleaner air temperature control system fitted to E-type engines

A Cold air inlet   B Hot air inlet   C Flap
D Air to the carburettor/throttle housing
2 Wax-controlled thermostatic valve

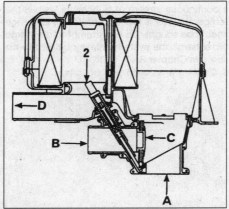

15.3c Air cleaner air temperature control system fitted to the 1721 cc (F2N) engine

A Cold air inlet   B Hot air inlet   C Flap
D Air to the carburettor
2 Wax-controlled thermostatic valve

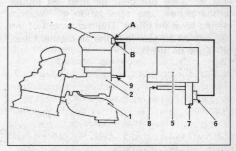

15.3d Air cleaner air temperature control system fitted to the 1721 cc (F3N) and 1794 cc (F3P) engines

A To vacuum capsule   6 Thermostat/vacuum
B From inlet manifold   capsule
1 Exhaust manifold   7 Cold air inlet
2 Inlet manifold   8 Hot air inlet
3 Air inlet cover   9 Manifold vacuum
5 Air cleaner   connection

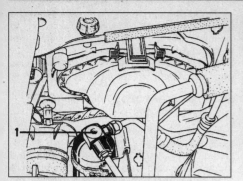

17.2 Air conditioning refrigerant sight glass (1) on top of dehydration unit

18.1a Headlight beam vertical (height) adjustment screw (arrowed) - "Phase 1" models

18.1b Headlight beam horizontal adjustment screw (arrowed) - "Phase 1" models

1

temperature but also by inlet manifold vacuum. The combined thermostat and vacuum capsule in the air cleaner inlet shuts off the cold air inlet at temperatures below - 10°C, and shuts off the hot air inlet at temperatures above +20°C. However, a high manifold vacuum (in excess of 200 mbars) will cause the cold air inlet to be closed again at temperatures up to 35°C. Above 35°C, the vacuum feed to the capsule is cut off by a thermostatic valve located in the air intake cover, and the hot air inlet is closed.

6 Checking of this system for the DIY mechanic is more difficult; begin by making sure that all the vacuum hoses are sound.

7 The combined thermostat and vacuum capsule can be checked as described for the directly-operated system, but place the unit in a freezer to check low temperature operation. Warm the unit gently (for instance with a hairdryer) to check high temperature operation.

8 To check the operation of the thermostatic valve, disconnect the hose from the manifold side of the valve. Connect a length of plastic or rubber hose to the valve, and suck through the hose, or apply vacuum using a hand pump if available. At valve temperatures below 35°C, the application of vacuum should move the flap to close the cold air inlet. At higher temperatures, the application of vacuum should have no effect. The movement of the flap cannot be seen with the air cleaner fitted, but it can be heard.

16 Electrical system check

1 Check the operation of all the electrical equipment, ie lights, direction indicators, horn etc. Refer to the appropriate Sections of Chapter 12 for details if any of the circuits are found to be inoperative.

2 Note that stop-light switch adjustment is described in Chapter 9.

3 Visually check all accessible wiring connectors, harnesses and retaining clips for security, and for signs of chafing or damage. Rectify any faults found.

17 Heating/air conditioning system check

1 Check that the heating system operates correctly. See Chapter 3, Section 12.

2 On models with air conditioning, check that the system operates correctly. Run the engine, and switch the air conditioning on to its maximum setting. After it has been operating for a few minutes, inspect the sight glass on top of the dehydration unit (see illustration). If a continuous stream of bubbles is visible, the refrigerant level is low, and professional advice should be sought. Do not attempt to discharge or recharge the system unless qualified to do so - see Chapter 3.

3 Check the tension and condition of the air

conditioning compressor drivebelt. Refer to the auxiliary drivebelt checking procedure in Section 9 of this Chapter for details.

4 During the Winter period, it is advisable to run the air conditioning system occasionally (for 10 minutes or so once a month) in order to ensure correct functioning of the compressor and distribution of the oil within the system.

18 Headlight beam alignment check

1 Accurate adjustment of the headlight beam is only possible using optical beam-setting equipment, and this work should therefore be carried out by a Renault dealer or service station with the necessary facilities. For reference, the location of the beam adjusting screws are as shown (see illustrations).

2 On all models, it is possible to adjust the headlight beam to compensate for the load being carried. An adjustment knob is located on the rear of each headlight on some models. On other models, a five-position knob is located on the facia panel inside the car (which operates an electric motor to adjust the headlights). In the latter case, position "0" should be selected for an unladen vehicle, and position "5" should be selected for maximum load. On models with electrically-adjustable headlights, a screw is provided for manual adjustment on the rear of the motor (see illustration).

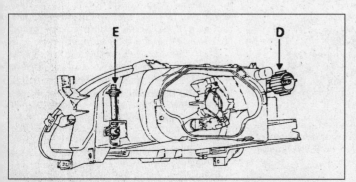

18.1c Headlight beam adjustment screws - "Phase 2" models

D Vertical (height) adjustment   E Horizontal adjustment

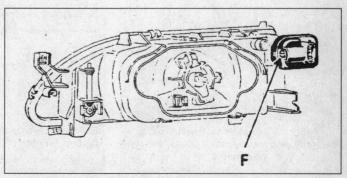

18.2 Headlight beam vertical (height) adjustment screw (F) - "Phase 2" models with electrically-adjustable headlights

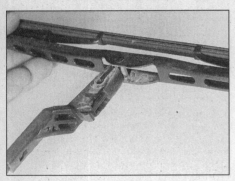

19.3 Removing a wiper blade from the arm fork

19.6 Hinged cover lifted on the tailgate wiper arm

19.8 Unscrewing the wiper arm retaining nut from the spindle

19 Wiper blade check

1 The wiper blades should be renewed when they are deteriorated, cracked, or when they no longer clean the windscreen or rear window glass effectively.
2 Lift the wiper arm away from the glass.
3 Release the catch on the arm, turn the blade through 90° and withdraw the blade from the arm fork **(see illustration)**.
4 Insert the new blade into the arm, making sure that it locates securely.
5 Check the wiper arms for worn hinges and weak springs, and renew as necessary.

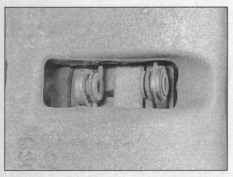

20.3 Brake pad thickness viewing aperture on Girling caliper

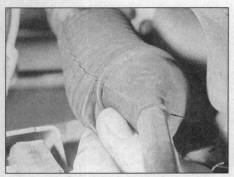

21.2 Checking the condition of a steering rack rubber gaiter

6 If working on the rear window wiper, lift the hinged cover for access to the retaining nut **(see illustration)**.

> **HAYNES HiNT** *Mark the wiper blade position for correct refitting by sticking masking tape to the glass.*

7 Make sure that the wiper is in its rest ("parked") position. If necessary, switch the wipers on and off in order to allow them to return to the "parked" position.
8 Unscrew the retaining nut, and pull the arm from the spindle **(see illustration)**. If necessary, use a screwdriver to prise off the arm, being careful not to damage the paintwork. On the tailgate wiper, it will help if the arm is moved to its fully-raised position before removing it from the spindle.
9 Fit the new arm using a reversal of the removal procedure.
10 At the same time, take the opportunity to check the washer jets for blockages. Blockages can be removed with a pin, which can also be used to adjust the aim of the jets, if necessary.

20 Front brake disc pad check

1 Apply the handbrake, then jack up the front of the car and support on axle stands (see *"Jacking, towing and wheel changing"*).

21.4 Checking for wear in the front suspension hub bearings

2 For better access to the front brake calipers, remove both front wheels.
3 Using a steel rule, check that the thickness of the brake pad linings and backing plates is not less than the minimum thickness given in the Specifications. On the Girling caliper, it will only be possible to view the centre area of the pads through the small aperture **(see illustration)**, but on the Bendix type, all of the pad area is visible.
4 If any one pad thickness is less than the minimum amount, renew *all* the front pads with reference to Chapter 9.

21 Suspension and steering check

Front suspension and steering check

1 Raise the front of the vehicle, and securely support it on axle stands (see *"Jacking, towing and wheel changing"*).
2 Visually inspect the balljoint dust covers and the steering rack-and-pinion gaiters for splits, chafing or deterioration **(see illustration)**. Any wear of these components will cause loss of lubricant, together with dirt and water entry, resulting in rapid deterioration of the balljoints or steering gear.
3 On vehicles equipped with power-assisted steering, check the fluid hoses for chafing or deterioration, and the pipe and hose unions for fluid leaks. Also check for signs of fluid leakage under pressure from the steering gear rubber gaiters, which would indicate failed fluid seals within the steering gear.
4 Grasp the roadwheel at the 12 o'clock and 6 o'clock positions, and try to rock it **(see illustration)**. Very slight free play may be felt, but if the movement is appreciable, further investigation is necessary to determine the source. Continue rocking the wheel while an assistant depresses the footbrake. If the movement is now eliminated or significantly reduced, it is likely that the hub bearings are at fault. If the free play is still evident with the footbrake depressed, then there is wear in the suspension joints or mountings.
5 Now grasp the wheel at the 9 o'clock and

3 o'clock positions, and try to rock it as before. Any movement felt now may again be caused by wear in the hub bearings or the steering track-rod balljoints. If the outer balljoint is worn, the visual movement will be obvious. If the inner joint is suspect, it can be felt by placing a hand over the rack-and-pinion rubber gaiter and gripping the track-rod. If the wheel is now rocked, movement will be felt at the inner joint if wear has taken place.

6 Using a large screwdriver or flat bar, check for wear in the suspension mounting bushes by levering between the relevant suspension component and its attachment point. Some movement is to be expected, as the mountings are made of rubber, but excessive wear should be obvious. Also check the condition of any visible rubber bushes, looking for splits, cracks or contamination of the rubber.

7 With the car standing on its wheels, have an assistant turn the steering wheel back and forth about an eighth of a turn each way. There should be very little, if any, lost movement between the steering wheel and roadwheels. If this is not the case, closely observe the joints and mountings previously described. In addition, check the steering column universal joints for wear, and also check the rack-and-pinion steering gear itself.

Rear suspension check

8 Chock the front wheels, then jack up the rear of the car and support it securely on axle stands (see *"Jacking, towing and wheel changing"*).

9 Working as described previously for the front suspension, check the rear hub bearings, the suspension bushes and the shock absorber mountings for wear.

22 Driveshaft check

1 With the vehicle raised and securely supported on stands (see *"Jacking, towing and wheel changing"*), turn the steering onto full-lock, then slowly rotate the roadwheel. Inspect the condition of the outer constant velocity (CV) joint rubber gaiters, while squeezing the gaiters to open out the folds **(see illustration)**. Check for signs of cracking, splits or deterioration of the rubber, which may allow the escape of grease, and lead to the ingress of water and grit into the joint. Also check the security and condition of the retaining clips. Repeat these checks on the inner CV joints. If any damage or deterioration is found, the gaiters should be renewed as described in Chapter 8.

2 At the same time, check the general condition of the outer CV joints themselves, by first holding the driveshaft and attempting to rotate the wheels. Repeat this check on the right-hand inner joint by holding the inner joint yoke and attempting to rotate the driveshaft. On models with a manual gearbox or MB1 automatic transmission, the left-hand inner joint is concealed by a rubber gaiter which is bolted to the transmission casing, and it is not possible to hold the joint since the yoke is an integral part of the differential sunwheel. However, on manual gearbox models, one way to get round this problem is to have an assistant hold the right-hand wheel stationary with 4th gear selected, and then to attempt to rotate the left-hand driveshaft. If this method is used, beware of confusing wear in the left-hand CV joint with general wear in the transmission.

3 Any appreciable movement in the CV joint indicates wear in the joint, wear in the driveshaft splines, or a loose driveshaft retaining nut.

23 Bodywork and underframe check

1 With the car raised and supported on axle stands or over an inspection pit, thoroughly inspect the underbody and wheelarches for signs of damage and corrosion. In particular, examine the bottom of the side sills and concealed areas where mud can collect. Where corrosion and rust is evident, press firmly on the panel by hand and check for possible repairs. If the panel is not seriously corroded, clean away the rust and apply a new coating of underseal. Refer to Chapter 11 for more details of body repairs.

2 Check all external body panels for damage, and rectify where necessary.

24 Exhaust system check

1 With the engine cold (at least an hour after the vehicle has been driven), check the complete exhaust system from the engine to the end of the tailpipe. Ideally, the inspection should be carried out with the vehicle on a hoist to permit unrestricted access, but if a hoist is not available, raise and support the vehicle safely on axle stands (see *"Jacking, towing and wheel changing"*).

2 Check the exhaust pipes and connections for evidence of leaks, severe corrosion and damage. Make sure that all brackets and mountings are in good condition and tight. Leakage at any of the joints or in other parts of the system will usually show up as a black sooty stain in the vicinity of the leak.

3 Where applicable (on models fitted with a catalytic converter), check the oxygen sensor wiring for damage. Refer to Chapter 4C for details.

4 Rattles and other noises can often be traced to the exhaust system, especially the brackets and mountings **(see illustration)**. Try to move the pipes and silencers. If the components can come into contact with the body or suspension parts, secure the system with new mountings or if possible, separate the joints and twist the pipes as necessary to provide additional clearance.

5 Run the engine at idle speed, then temporarily place a cloth rag over the rear end of the exhaust pipe and listen for any escape of exhaust gases that would indicate a leak.

6 On completion, lower the car to the ground.

7 The inside of the exhaust tailpipe can be an indication of the running condition of the engine. The exhaust deposits here are an indication of the engine's state-of-tune. If the pipe is black and sooty, the engine is in need of a tune-up, including a thorough fuel system inspection and adjustment.

22.1 Checking the condition of a driveshaft outer constant velocity (CV) joint rubber gaiter

24.4 Exhaust rubber mounting (arrowed)

25.1a Air cleaner cover securing nut (arrowed) - 1390 cc (C3J) engine

25.1b Unscrewing an air cleaner cover securing screw - 1390 cc (E7J) engine. Note cover retaining clip (arrowed)

25.2 Lifting off the air cleaner cover . . .

Every 12 000 miles / 20 000 km

25 Air filter renewal

Carburettor/throttle housing-mounted air cleaner

1 Remove the securing screw(s) or nut(s), as applicable, securing the cover to the air cleaner casing **(see illustrations)**.
2 Where applicable, release the air cleaner cover spring clips, then lift the cover from the air cleaner **(see illustration)**.

3 Lift the filter element from the air cleaner casing **(see illustration)**.
4 Clean the inside of the air cleaner casing and the cover, and fit a new filter element.
5 Refit the cover and secure with the screw(s), nut(s) and spring clips, as applicable.

Remotely-mounted air cleaner

6 On models where the air inlet trunking is attached to the air cleaner cover, where applicable, disconnect the battery negative lead, then disconnect the wiring plug from the

inlet air temperature sensor, located in the air inlet trunking **(see illustration)**. Loosen the clamp screw, and disconnect the air inlet trunking from the throttle housing or the air cleaner cover, as desired.
7 Where applicable, disconnect the breather hose(s) leading to the air inlet trunking.
8 Remove the securing screws and/or release the spring clips, and lift the cover from the air cleaner **(see illustrations)**.
9 Lift the filter element from the air cleaner casing **(see illustrations)**.
10 Clean the inside of the air cleaner

25.3 . . . for access to the air filter element - 1390 cc (C3J) engine

25.6 Disconnecting the wiring plug from the inlet air temperature sensor - 1721 cc (F3N) engine

25.8a Remove the centre . . .

25.8b . . . and lower securing screws . . .

25.8c . . . and lift the cover from the air cleaner - 1794 cc (F3P) engine

25.8d Lifting the cover from the air cleaner - 1721 cc (F3N) engine

**25.9a Lifting out the air filter element -
1390 cc (E6J) engine**

**25.9b Lifting out the air filter element -
1721 cc (F2N) engine**

**25.9c Lifting out the air filter element -
1721 cc (F3N) engine**

1

casing and the cover, and fit a new filter element.
11 Refit the cover using a reversal of the removal procedure. Ensure that all hoses are securely reconnected.

26 Spark plug renewal

To renew the spark plugs, refer to the procedure given in Section 11 for the spark plug check. Fit new plugs, and set their gaps as described.

27 Road test

Instruments and electrical equipment

1 Check the operation of all instruments and electrical equipment.
2 Make sure that all instruments read correctly, and switch on all electrical equipment in turn to check that it functions properly.

Steering and suspension

3 Check for any abnormalities in the steering, suspension, handling or road "feel".
4 Drive the vehicle, and check that there are

no unusual vibrations or noises.
5 Check that the steering feels positive, with no excessive "sloppiness", or roughness, and check for any suspension noises when cornering and driving over bumps.

Drivetrain

6 Check the performance of the engine, clutch (where applicable), transmission and driveshafts.
7 Listen for any unusual noises from the engine, clutch and transmission.
8 Make sure that the engine runs smoothly when idling, and that there is no hesitation when accelerating.
9 Check that, where applicable, the clutch action is smooth and progressive, that the drive is taken up smoothly, and that the pedal travel is not excessive. Also listen for any noises when the clutch pedal is depressed.
10 On manual transmission models, check that all gears can be engaged smoothly without noise, and that the gear lever action is not abnormally vague or "notchy".
11 On automatic transmission models, make sure that all gearchanges occur smoothly without snatching, and without an increase in engine speed between changes. Check that all the gear positions can be selected with the vehicle at rest. If any problems are found, they should be referred to a Renault dealer.
12 Listen for a metallic clicking sound from

the front of the vehicle as the vehicle is driven slowly in a circle with the steering on full-lock. Carry out this check in both directions. If a clicking noise is heard, this indicates wear in a driveshaft joint, in which case renew the joint if necessary.

Check the operation and performance of the braking system

13 Make sure that the vehicle does not pull to one side when braking, and that the wheels do not lock prematurely when braking hard.
14 Check that there is no vibration through the steering when braking.
15 Check that the handbrake operates correctly without excessive movement of the lever, and that it holds the vehicle stationary on a slope.
16 Test the operation of the brake servo unit as follows. Depress the footbrake four or five times to exhaust the vacuum, then start the engine. As the engine starts, there should be a noticeable "give" in the brake pedal as vacuum builds up. Allow the engine to run for at least two minutes, and then switch it off. If the brake pedal is now depressed again, it should be possible to detect a hiss from the servo as the pedal is depressed. After about four or five applications, no further hissing should be heard, and the pedal should feel considerably harder.

Every 30 000 miles / 50 000 km

28 Fuel filter renewal

Carburettor models

1 An in-line fuel filter is provided in the fuel pump outlet line **(see illustration)**. To remove it, release the clips (if fitted) and pull the filter from the hoses.
2 Fit the new filter, making sure that the fuel direction arrow is pointing away from the fuel pump side. If crimped type clips were used to secure the hoses, these should be replaced with worm-drive alternatives.

**28.1 Typical in-line fuel filter fitted to
carburettor models**

**28.3 Typical fuel filter fitted to fuel injection
models - clamp screw arrowed**

28.7 Removing the fuel filter from its clamp. Note flow direction arrow on filter body

Fuel injection models

3 The fuel filter is located under the rear right-hand side of the vehicle **(see illustration)**. Raise and support the rear of the vehicle (see "Jacking, towing and wheel changing").
4 Depressurise the fuel system as described in Chapter 4B.
5 Clamp the hose on the tank side of the filter.
6 Remove the screw from the filter securing clamp, and slacken the hose clips. If crimped-type hose clips are fitted, cut them off and obtain worm drive clips for reassembly.
7 Remove the filter and dispose of it safely. Where applicable, note the flow direction markings on the filter body **(see illustration)**.
8 Fit the new filter, making sure that the flow direction marking is pointing in the direction of fuel flow (from the tank towards the engine).
9 Reconnect the hoses, then tighten the hose clips and the filter securing clamp.
10 Release the hose clamp and check that there are no leaks, then lower the vehicle to the ground.

29 Clutch mechanism check

Note: The following check is not specified by Renault, but is included by the author.
1 Check that the clutch pedal moves smoothly and easily through its full travel, and that the clutch itself functions correctly, with no trace of slip or drag. If the movement is uneven or stiff in places, check that the cable is routed correctly, with no sharp turns.
2 Inspect the ends of the clutch inner cable, both at the gearbox end and inside the vehicle, for signs of wear and fraying.

30 Handbrake checking and adjustment

1 The handbrake should be capable of holding the parked vehicle stationary, even on steep slopes, when applied with moderate force. The mechanism should be firm and positive in feel, with no trace of stiffness or sponginess from the cables, and should release immediately the handbrake lever is released. If the mechanism is faulty in any of

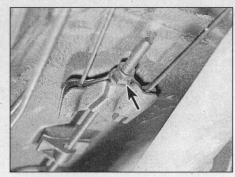

30.3 Handbrake cable adjuster locknut and adjuster nut (arrowed)

these respects, it must be checked immediately as follows. **Note:** On models with rear drum brakes, if the handbrake is not functioning correctly or is incorrectly adjusted, the rear brake self-adjust mechanism will not function. This will lead to the brake pedal travel becoming excessive as the shoe linings wear. Under no circumstances should the handbrake cables be tightened in an attempt to compensate for excessive brake pedal travel.
2 Chock the front wheels and release the handbrake. Jack up the rear of the vehicle, and support it securely on axle stands (see "Jacking, towing and wheel changing"). On models with a catalytic converter, where applicable, undo the heat shield retaining nut(s), and lower the rear of the heat shield to gain access to the handbrake cable adjuster nut.
3 Slacken the locknut, then fully slacken the cable adjuster nut **(see illustration)**.

Models with rear drum brakes

4 Remove both the rear brake drums as described in Chapter 9.
5 Check that the knurled adjuster wheel on the adjuster strut is free to rotate in both directions. If it is seized, the brake shoes and strut must be removed and overhauled as described in Chapter 9.
6 If all is well, back off the adjuster wheel by five or six teeth, so that the diameter of the brake shoes is slightly reduced.
7 Check that the handbrake cables slide freely by pulling on their front ends. Also check that the operating levers on the rear brake trailing shoes return to their correct positions, with their stop-pegs in contact with the edge of the trailing shoe web.
8 With the aid of an assistant, tighten the adjuster nut on the handbrake lever operating rod so that the lever on each rear brake assembly starts to move as the handbrake is moved between the first and second notch (click) of its ratchet mechanism. This is the case when the stop-pegs are still in contact with the shoes when the handbrake is on the first notch of the ratchet, but no longer contact the shoes when the handbrake is on the second notch. Once the adjustment is correct, hold the adjuster nut and securely tighten the locknut. Where necessary, refit the catalytic converter heat shield retaining nuts.

9 Refit the brake drums as described in Chapter 9, then lower the vehicle to the ground.
10 With the vehicle standing on its wheels, repeatedly depress the footbrake to adjust the shoe-to-drum clearance. Whilst depressing the pedal, have an assistant listen to the rear drums to check that the adjuster strut mechanism is functioning; if this is so, a clicking sound will be heard from the adjuster strut as the pedal is depressed.

Models with rear disc brakes

11 Check that the handbrake cables slide freely by pulling on their front ends, and check that the operating levers on the rear brake calipers move smoothly.
12 Move both of the caliper operating levers as far rearwards as possible, then tighten the adjuster nut on the handbrake lever operating rod until all free play is removed from both cables. With the aid of an assistant, from this point adjust the nut so that the operating lever on each rear brake caliper starts to move as the handbrake lever is moved between the first and second notch (click) of its ratchet mechanism. Once the handbrake adjustment is correct, hold the adjuster nut and securely tighten the locknut.
13 Refit the catalytic converter heat shield retaining nuts (where necessary), then lower the vehicle to the ground.

31 Rear brake shoe lining check - models with rear drum brakes

1 Remove the rear brake drums with reference to Chapter 9.
2 Check that each brake shoe lining thickness (including the shoe) is not less than the thickness given in the Specifications.
3 If any one lining thickness is less than the minimum amount, renew *all* of the rear brake shoes, as described in Chapter 9.

32 Rear brake disc pad check - models with rear disc brakes

1 Chock the front wheels, then jack up the rear of the vehicle, and support securely on axle stands (see "Jacking, towing and wheel changing").
2 For improved access to the rear brake calipers, remove both rear wheels.
3 Using a steel rule, check that the thickness of the brake pad linings and backing plate is not less than the minimum thickness given in the Specifications.
4 If any one pad thickness is less than the minimum amount, renew *all* the rear pads with reference to Chapter 9.

33 Front wheel alignment check

Refer to the information given in Chapter 10.

34 Brake fluid renewal

Note: *When carrying out this procedure, do not allow the brake fluid level in the reservoir to fall below the "MIN" mark, otherwise air may be drawn into the system, necessitating further bleeding.*

1 The procedure is similar to that for the bleeding of the hydraulic system described in Chapter 9. Before starting, remove as much old brake fluid as possible (down to the "MIN" mark) from the reservoir by syphoning, using a clean poultry baster or similar. Refill the reservoir with fresh fluid.

2 Working as described in Chapter 9, open the first bleed nipple in the sequence, and pump the brake pedal gently until the fluid level is down to the "MIN" mark. Top-up to the "MAX" mark with new fluid, and continue pumping until only the new fluid remains in the reservoir, and new fluid can be seen emerging from the bleed nipple. Old hydraulic fluid is invariably much darker in colour than the new, making it easy to distinguish the two.

3 Tighten the nipple, and top the reservoir level up to the "MAX" mark.

4 Work through all the remaining nipples in the sequence until new fluid can be seen at all of them. Be careful to keep the master cylinder reservoir topped-up to above the "MIN" level at all times, or air may enter the system and greatly increase the length of the task.

5 When the operation is complete, check that all nipples are securely tightened, and that their dust caps are refitted. Wash off all traces of spilt fluid, and recheck the master cylinder reservoir fluid level.

6 Check the operation of the brakes before taking the vehicle on the road.

35 Automatic transmission fluid and filter renewal

MB1 and MB3 (3-speed) automatic transmissions

1 The automatic transmission fluid should only be changed when cold.

2 Raise the vehicle on car ramps, or jack it up (see *"Jacking, towing and wheel changing"*), but make sure that it is level. Where applicable, remove the engine/transmission splash shield.

3 Place a suitable container beneath the drain plug on the transmission sump pan, and at the base of the transmission housing.

4 Remove the dipstick to speed up the draining operation. Unscrew the two drain plugs, and allow the fluid to drain **(see illustration)**.

5 When all the fluid has drained (this may take quite some time), clean the drain plugs. Refit them, together with new seals, and tighten them securely.

6 Unbolt and remove the sump pan and

gasket. It may be necessary to raise the transmission to allow sufficient clearance to remove the sump pan. If this is necessary, proceed as described in paragraphs 15 to 19 for the AD4 (4-speed) transmission **(see illustration)**.

7 Unscrew the filter retaining bolts, and remove the filter and sealing ring. Note which way round the filter is fitted.

8 Fit the new filter into position, ensuring it is the correct way round. Tighten the bolts to the specified torque.

9 Clean the sump pan, and check that the filter magnets are correctly positioned **(see illustration)**, with their ribbed sides against the plate. Refit the sump pan, ensuring that the new gasket is correctly located. Tighten the bolts to the specified torque.

10 Place a funnel with fine-mesh screen in the dipstick tube, and fill the transmission with the specified type of fluid. Depending on the extent to which the fluid was allowed to drain, refilling will only require approximately 2.0 litres (3.5 pints). Add about half this amount, and then check the level on the dipstick. When the level approaches the correct mark, place the selector lever in position "P", start the engine and allow it to run for approximately 2 minutes. Now check the level and complete the final topping-up as described previously.

AD4 (4-speed) automatic transmission

Note: *On completion of fluid renewal, the fluid level checking procedure on the AD4 automatic transmission is particularly complicated (see Section 7), and the home mechanic would be well-advised to take the car to a Renault dealer to have the work carried out, as special test equipment is necessary to carry out the check. However, the following procedure is given for those who may have access to this equipment. Note that the final drive oil level is not renewed as a routine maintenance task, as it is sealed for life.*

11 The automatic transmission fluid should only be changed when cold.

12 Raise the vehicle on car ramps, or jack it up (see *"Jacking, towing and wheel changing"*), but make sure that it is level. Where applicable, remove the engine/transmission splash shield.

13 Place a suitable container beneath the drain plug on the transmission sump pan, and at the base of the transmission housing (see illustration 7.28 for drain plug location).

14 Unscrew the drain plug, and allow the fluid to drain.

15 To gain access, move the coolant expansion tank to one side, and, on models with a remotely-mounted air cleaner assembly, remove the air cleaner with reference to Chapter 4A or 4B.

16 Remove the two upper transmission mounting bolts, and loosen the two lower bolts without removing them **(see illustration)**.

17 Where applicable, unscrew the nut securing the ABS electric pump unit to the body panel **(see illustration)**.

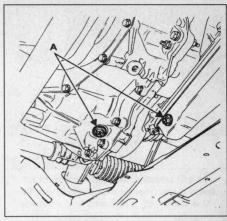

35.4 Automatic transmission fluid drain plug locations (A) - MB1 and MB3 (3-speed) automatic transmissions

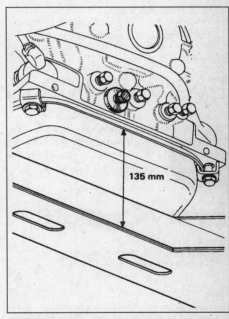

135 mm

35.6 Raise the transmission as shown before removing the sump pan - MB1 and MB3 (3-speed) automatic transmissions

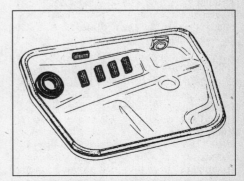

35.9 Filter magnet locations in the automatic transmission sump - MB1 and MB3 (3-speed) automatic transmissions

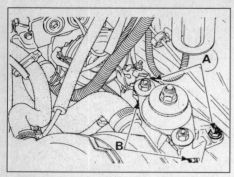

35.16 Transmission upper mounting bolts (A) and lower mounting bolts (B) - AD4 (4-speed) automatic transmission

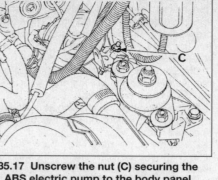

35.17 Unscrew the nut (C) securing the ABS electric pump to the body panel

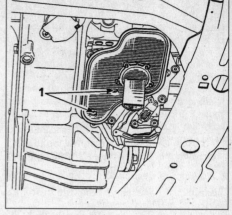

35.21 AD4 (4-speed) automatic transmission filter retaining bolts (1)

18 Remove the front left-hand wheel and the wheel arch shield.
19 Using a trolley jack and a block of wood, raise the transmission sufficiently to permit removal of the sump pan.
20 Unbolt the sump pan from the bottom of the transmission, and remove the gasket.
21 Unbolt the filter and its seal **(see illustration)**.

22 Clean the pan and its sediment magnet. Examine the pan gasket and the drain and topping-up plugs, and renew them if necessary. Renew the plug seals, where applicable, as a matter of course.
23 Fit the new filter, together with its seal, and tighten the bolts.
24 Fit the pan, together with a new gasket, and tighten the bolts.

25 The remaining procedure is a reversal of removal, but finally refill the transmission with fluid as described in Section 7.

Every 72 000 miles / 120 000 km

36 Timing belt renewal -
all engines except C-type

Proceed as described in Chapter 2A, or 2C, as applicable.

⚠️ *Caution: If this operation is neglected, and the timing belt breaks in service, extensive engine damage may result. The author recommends that consideration is given to renewing the timing belt at around 50 000 miles (80 000 km), in order to err on the side of safety.*

Every 2 years

37 Coolant renewal

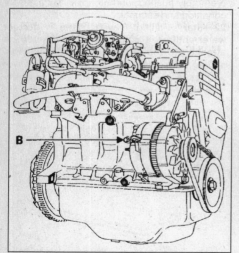

37.4a Coolant drain plug location (B) on the rear of the cylinder block - E-type engines

Coolant draining

⚠️ *Warning: Wait until the engine is cold before starting this procedure. Do not allow antifreeze to come in contact with your skin, or with the painted surfaces of the vehicle. Rinse off spills immediately with plenty of water.*

37.4b Coolant drain plug location (arrowed) on the rear of the cylinder block - F-type engines (viewed with engine removed from vehicle)

1 If the engine is cold, unscrew and remove the pressure cap from the expansion tank. If it is not possible to wait until the engine is cold, place a cloth over the pressure cap of the expansion tank, and *slowly* unscrew the cap. Wait until all pressure has escaped, then remove the cap.
2 Place a suitable container beneath the bottom hose connection to the radiator.
3 Loosen the clip, then disconnect the bottom hose and allow the coolant to drain into the container. The hose clips fitted as original equipment are released by squeezing the tags together with pliers.
4 Move the container beneath the cylinder block drain plug. On the C-type engines (see *Section 1* for details of engine identification), the drain plug is located at the crankshaft pulley end of the engine, below the water pump. On the other engines, it is located at the rear right-hand side of the cylinder block **(see illustrations)**.
5 Unscrew the plug, and drain the coolant into the container.
6 Flush the system if necessary as described in the following paragraphs, then refit the drain plug and secure the bottom hose. Use a new

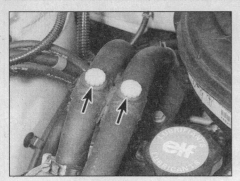

37.14a Coolant bleed screw locations (arrowed) in heater hoses - 1390 cc (C3J) engine

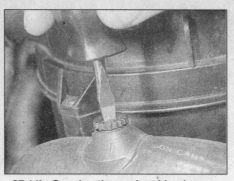

37.14b Opening the coolant bleed screw located in the top radiator hose - 1390 cc (E6J) engine

37.14c Coolant bleed screw location (arrowed) in radiator - 1390 cc (E6J) engine

hose clip if necessary. Refill the system as described later in this Section.

System flushing

7 With time, the cooling system may gradually lose its efficiency if the radiator matrix becomes choked with rust and scale deposits. If this is the case, the system must be flushed as follows. First drain the coolant as already described.

8 Loosen the clip and disconnect the top hose from the radiator. Insert a garden hose in the radiator top hose connection stub, and allow the water to circulate through the radiator until it runs clear from the bottom outlet.

9 To flush the engine and the remainder of the system, disconnect the top hose at the water pump on C-type engines, or remove the thermostat as described in Chapter 3 on the other engines. Insert the garden hose, and allow the water to circulate through the engine until it runs clear from the bottom hose.

10 In severe cases of contamination, the radiator should be reverse-flushed. To do this, first remove it from the vehicle, as described in Chapter 3, invert it and insert a hose in the bottom outlet. Continue flushing until clear water runs from the top hose outlet.

11 If, after a reasonable period, the water still does not run clear, the radiator should be flushed with a good proprietary cleaning agent.

12 Regular renewal of the antifreeze mixture as specified should prevent severe contamination of the system. Note that, as the radiator is made of aluminium, it is important not to use caustic soda or alkaline compounds to clean it. See Chapter 3 for more details.

Coolant filling

13 Refit the cylinder block drain plug, radiator bottom hose, and any other hoses removed if the system has just been flushed.

14 Open the coolant bleed screws. On C-type engines, there are three bleed screws - one each on the heater supply and return hoses, and one in the top hose next to the thermostat. On E-type engines, there are two bleed screws, one in the top radiator hose, and one at the top right-hand side of the radiator. On F-type engines, there is only one, situated on one side of the radiator towards the top **(see illustrations)**.

15 Pour the appropriate mixture of water and antifreeze into the expansion tank, and close each bleed screw in turn as soon as a continuous flow of bubble-free coolant can be seen flowing from it. Continue to fill the expansion tank until the coolant is at the maximum level.

16 Start the engine, and run it at 1500 rpm (ie a fast idle speed) for approximately 4 minutes. Keep the expansion tank topped-up to the maximum level during this period.

17 Refit the pressure cap to the expansion tank, and run the engine at 1500 rpm for approximately 10 minutes until the electric cooling fan cuts in. During this period, the coolant will circulate around the engine, and any remaining air will be purged to the expansion tank.

18 Switch off the engine and allow it to cool, then check the coolant level as described in Section 3, and top-up if necessary.

Antifreeze mixture

19 The antifreeze should always be renewed at the specified intervals. This is necessary not

37.14d Coolant bleed screw location (arrowed) in radiator - 1794 cc (F3P) engine

only to maintain the antifreeze properties, but also to prevent corrosion which would otherwise occur as the corrosion inhibitors become progressively less effective.

20 Always use an ethylene-glycol-based antifreeze which is suitable for use in mixed-metal cooling systems. The proportion of antifreeze and levels of protection afforded are indicated in the Specifications.

21 Before adding antifreeze, the cooling system should be completely drained, preferably flushed, and all hoses checked for condition and security.

22 After filling with the correct water/antifreeze mixture, a label should be attached to the radiator or expansion tank, stating the type and concentration of antifreeze used, and the date installed. Any subsequent topping-up should be made with the same type and concentration of antifreeze.

23 Do not use engine antifreeze in the screen washer system, as it will cause damage to the vehicle paintwork.

Specifications

Note: Refer to Section 1 of this Chapter, and to "Buying spare parts and vehicle identification numbers" for details of engine identification

Engine

Oil filter type:
C-type and E-type engines	Champion F101
1721 cc (F2N and F3N) and 1794 cc (F3P) engines	Champion F103
1764 cc (F7P) engine	Champion F120

Cooling system

Coolant pump drivebelt tension (C-type and F-type engines)	See Section 9 of this Chapter	
Air conditioning compressor drivebelt tension	See Section 9 of this Chapter	

Antifreeze mixtures:

	Antifreeze	**Water**
Protection to -23°C	35%	65%
Protection to -40°C	50%	50%

Fuel octane requirements

Carburettor models:
1237 cc (C1G) engine	97 RON (4-star) leaded
1390 cc (E6J) engine except for "Utility" models	95 RON (Premium) or 98 RON (Super) unleaded 97 RON (4-star) leaded
1390 cc (E6J) engine for "Utility" models	97 RON (4-star) leaded
1397 cc (C1J) engine	95 RON (Premium) or 98 RON (Super) unleaded or 97 RON (4-star) leaded
1397 cc (C2J) engine	89 RON (2-star) or 97 RON (4-star) leaded
1721 cc (F2N) engine except for "Utility" models	95 RON (Premium) or 98 RON (Super) unleaded or 97 RON (4-star) leaded
1721 cc (F2N) engine for "Utility" models	97 RON (4-star) leaded

Fuel injection models:
1390 cc (C3J) engine	91 RON (Regular), 95 RON (Premium) or 98 RON (Super) unleaded
1390 cc (E7J) engine	95 RON (Premium) or 98 RON (Super) unleaded
1721 cc (F3N 740 and F3N 741) engines	91 RON (Regular), 95 RON (Premium) or 98 RON (Super) unleaded
1721 cc (F3N 742 and F3N 743) engines	95 RON (Premium) or 98 RON (Super) unleaded
1721 cc (F3N 746) engine	95 RON (Premium) or 98 RON (Super) unleaded, or 97 RON (4-star) leaded
1764 cc (F7P 700) engine	95 RON (Premium) unleaded or 97 RON (4-star) leaded
1764 cc (F7P 704) engine	95 RON (Premium) or 98 RON (Super) unleaded
1794 cc (F3P) engines (all codes)	95 RON (Premium) or 98 RON (Super) unleaded

Carburettor fuel system

Air filter element type*:
1397 cc (C1J) and 1390 cc (E6J) engines	Champion W145 (flat) or W115 (canister), depending on model
1721 cc (F2N) engine	Champion W212
Fuel filter type	Champion L101

Idle speed:
1237 cc (C1G) engine - Solex 32 BIS 936 carburettor	700 ± 50 rpm
1390 cc (E6J) engine - Weber 32 TLDR carburettor	750 ± 50 rpm
1397 cc (C1J) engine - Zenith 32 IF2 carburettor	700 ± 50 rpm
1397 cc (C2J) engine - Weber 32 DRT carburettor	700 ± 50 rpm
1721 cc (F2N) engine - Solex 32 x 34 Z13 carburettor	800 ± 50 rpm
Idle mixture CO content	1.5 ± 0.5%

* The air filter recommendations are the latest available at the time of writing, and may be suject to change during the production run of the vehicle.

Fuel injection systems

Air filter element type*:
1764 cc (F7P) and 1794 cc (F3P) engines	Champion W212
1721 cc (F3N) engines	Champion W230
Fuel filter type	Champion L206
Idle speed	Not adjustable

Idle mixture:
All except 1721 cc (F3N 746) and 1764 cc (F7P 700) engines	Not adjustable (0.5% maximum)
1721 cc (F3N 746) and 1764 cc (F7P 700) engines	1.5 ± 0.5%

* The air filter recommendations are the latest available at the time of writing, and may be suject to change during the production run of the vehicle.

Ignition system - general

Firing order	1-3-4-2
Location of No 1 cylinder	Transmission end of engine

Transistor-assisted contact breaker ignition system - 1397 cc (C1J) engine only

Contact breaker points gap	0.4 mm
Dwell angle	57° ± 3° (63 ± 3%)
Ignition timing:	
Static	5° ± 2°BTDC
Dynamic at idling speed:	
Vacuum hose disconnected	5° ± 2°BTDC
Vacuum hose connected	10° ± 1°BTDC
Spark plugs:	
Type	Champion RN9YCC or N281YC
Electrode gap*	0.8 mm

* The spark plug gap quoted is that recommended by Champion for their specified plugs listed above. If spark plugs of any other type are to be fitted, refer to their manufacturer's spark plug gap recommendations.

Electronic ignition system

Ignition timing	Non-adjustable, computer-controlled
Spark plugs:	
Type:	
1390 cc (E6J) engine	Champion C9YC or RC9YCC
1721 cc (F2N and F3N) non-catalyst engines	Champion N7YCC or N279YC
1721 cc (F3N) engine with single-point fuel injection	Champion RN7YCC or N7YCC
1721 cc (F3N) engine with catalyst and multi-point fuel injection	Champion RN6YCC or N6YCC
1764 cc (F7P) catalyst engine	Champion C7BMC
Electrode gap*	0.8 mm

* The spark plug gap quoted is that recommended by Champion for their specified plugs listed above. If spark plugs of any other type are to be fitted, refer to their manufacturer's spark plug gap recommendations.

Braking system

Minimum front brake disc pad thickness (including backplate)	6.0 mm
Minimum rear brake disc pad thickness (including backplate)	5.0 mm
Minimum rear brake shoe lining thickness (including shoe)	2.5 mm

Suspension and steering

	Front	Rear
Power steering pump drivebelt tension	See Section 9 of this Chapter	
Tyre pressures (tyres cold):		
Manual gearbox (except 16-valve) models	2.0 bars (29 psi)	2.2 bars (32 psi)
Manual gearbox 16-valve models	2.2 bars (32 psi)	2.2 bars (32 psi)
Automatic transmission (except 16-valve) models	2.1 bars (31 psi)	2.2 bars (32 psi)
Automatic transmission 16-valve models	2.3 bars (33 psi)	2.2 bars (32 psi)

Note: Recommended tyre pressures are marked on a label attached to the driver's door edge or frame. Pressures apply only to original-equipment tyres, and may vary if any other make or type of tyre is fitted; check with the tyre manufacturer or supplier for correct pressures if necessary.

Electrical system

Alternator drivebelt tension	See Section 9 of this Chapter
Wiper blade type:	
Windscreen	Champion X-5103
Rear window (Saloon)	Champion X-4503
Tailgate (Hatchback)	Champion X-5103

Torque wrench settings

	Nm	lbf ft
Engine sump drain plug	15 to 25	11 to 18
Spark plugs	24 to 30	18 to 22
Automatic transmission gauze filter	5	4
Automatic transmission sump pan:		
MB1 and MB3 (3-speed) transmissions	6	4
AD4 (4-speed) transmission	10	7
Roadwheel bolts	80	59

Lubricants, fluids and capacities

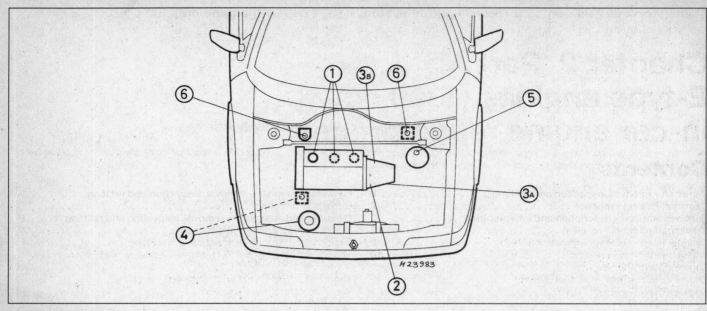

Lubricants and fluids

Component or system	Lubricant type/specification
1 Engine	Multigrade engine oil, viscosity 15W/40 to 20W/50, to CCMC G2, API SG, or better
2 Manual transmission	Tranself TRX 80W
3A Automatic transmission (not AD4 final drive - see below)	Elf Renaultmatic D2
3B AD4 (four-speed) automatic transmission final drive	Tranself TRX 80X 140
4 Power steering	Elf Renaultmatic D2
5 Cooling system	Soft water, and antifreeze (ethylene glycol-based, suitable for use in mixed-metal cooling systems)
6 Braking system	Hydraulic fluid to SAE J1703, DOT 3 or DOT 4

Capacities

Engine oil

Sump capacity (for oil change, excluding filter):
C-type engines	3.0 litres
E-type engines	3.5 litres
1721 cc (F2N and F3N) engines	4.7 litres
1764 cc (F7P) engines (tin sump)	4.0 litres
1764 cc (F7P) engines (aluminium sump)	4.2 litres
1794 cc (F3P) engines	5.5 litres

Oil filter:
All except 1764 cc (F7P) engine	0.5 litre
1764 cc (F7P) engine	0.25 litre

Difference between "MAX" and "MIN" dipstick marks:
C-type engines	1.0 litre
E-type engines	1.5 litres
1721 cc (F2N and F3N) and 1794 cc (F3P) engines	2.0 litres
1764 cc (F7P) engine	0.6 litre

Coolant (approximate capacities)

C-type engines	5.4 litres
E-type engines	5.2 litres

1721 cc (F2N and F3N) engines	6.0 litres
1764 cc (F7P) engine	7.0 litres
1794 cc (F3P) single-point fuel injection engine	6.5 litres
1794 cc (F3P) multi-point fuel injection engine	6.1 litres

Manual gearbox

Four-speed:
JB0 type gearbox	3.25 litres
JB4 type gearbox	2.75 litres

Five-speed:
JB1 and JB3 type gearboxes	3.4 litres
JB5 type gearbox	2.9 litres

Automatic transmission

MB1 and MB3 (3-speed) transmissions:
Total capacity	4.5 litres
Drain and refill	2.0 litres

AD4 (4-speed) transmission:
Main section total capacity	5.7 litres
Main section drain and refill	3.5 litres
Final drive section	1.0 litre

Fuel tank . . . . 55.0 litres

Chapter 2 Part A:
E-type engines (1390 cc) -
in-car engine repair procedures

Contents

2A

Degrees of difficulty

| Easy, suitable for novice with little experience | | Fairly easy, suitable for beginner with some experience | | Fairly difficult, suitable for competent DIY mechanic | | Difficult, suitable for experienced DIY mechanic | | Very difficult, suitable for expert DIY or professional | |

Specifications

General

Type	Four-cylinder, in-line, overhead camshaft
Designation:	
Carburettor engine	E6J
Fuel injection engine	E7J
Bore	75.8 mm
Stroke	77.0 mm
Capacity	1390 cc
Firing order	1-3-4-2 (No 1 cylinder at transmission end of engine)
Direction of crankshaft rotation	Clockwise viewed from timing belt end
Compression ratio	9.5:1
Maximum power output (typical)	58 kW (80 bhp) at 5750 rpm
Maximum torque (typical)	107 Nm (79 lbf ft) at 3500 rpm

Camshaft

Drive	Toothed belt
Number of bearings	5
Camshaft endfloat	0.06 to 0.15 mm

Valve clearances (cold)

Inlet	0.10 mm
Exhaust	0.25 mm

Lubrication system

System pressure:	
At idle	1.0 bar
At 4000 rpm	3.0 bars
Oil pump type	Two-gear
Oil pump clearances:	
Gear-to-body (minimum)	0.110 mm
Gear-to-body (maximum)	0.249 mm
Gear endfloat (minimum)	0.020 mm
Gear endfloat (maximum)	0.086 mm

Torque wrench settings

	Nm	lbf ft
Camshaft sprocket bolt	50 to 60	37 to 44
Crankshaft pulley/sprocket bolt	80 to 90	59 to 66
Rocker shaft bolts	21 to 25	16 to 18
Flywheel/driveplate bolts	50 to 55	37 to 41
Exhaust manifold	23 to 28	17 to 21
Inlet manifold	23 to 28	17 to 21
Main bearing cap bolts	60 to 67	44 to 50
Connecting rod (big-end) cap bolts (oiled):		
Stage 1	10	7
Stage 2	45	33
Sump bolts	7 to 9	4 to 7
Oil drain plug	15 to 25	11 to 19
Cylinder head bolts:		
Stage 1	30	22
Stage 2	60	44
Alternative Stage 1	20	15
Alternative Stage 2	Angle-tighten all bolts by 97° ± 2°	
Stage 3	Wait for at least 3 minutes	
Stage 4	Slacken bolts 1 and 2 fully	
Stage 5	Tighten bolts 1 and 2 to:	
	20	15
Stage 6	Angle-tighten bolts 1 and 2 by 97° ± 2°	
Stage 7	Slacken bolts 3, 4, 5 and 6 fully	
Stage 8	Tighten bolts 3, 4, 5 and 6 to:	
	20	15
Stage 9	Angle-tighten bolts 3, 4, 5 and 6 by 97° ± 2°	
Stage 10	Slacken bolts 7, 8, 9 and 10 fully	
Stage 11	Tighten bolts 7, 8, 9 and 10 to:	
	20	15
Stage 12	Angle-tighten bolts 7, 8, 9 and 10 by 97° ± 2°	

1 General information

How to use this Chapter

This Part of Chapter 2 is devoted to in-car repair procedures for the E-type engines. Similar information covering the C-type engines will be found in Chapter 2B, and information for F-type engines will be found in Chapter 2C. All procedures concerning engine removal and refitting, and engine block/cylinder head overhaul for all engine types can be found in Chapter 2D.

Note that as well as the E-type 1390 cc (E6J and E7J) engine, there is also a C-type 1390 cc (C3J) engine, details of which can be found in Chapter 2B. Refer to the *"Buying spare parts and vehicle identification numbers"* Section at the beginning of this manual for details of engine code locations.

Most of the operations included in Chapter 2A are based on the assumption that the engine is still installed in the vehicle. Therefore, if this information is being used during a complete engine overhaul, with the engine already removed, many of the steps included here will not apply.

Engine description

The engine is of four-cylinder, in-line, overhead camshaft type, mounted transversely in the front of the car and inclined 12° rearwards (see illustration).

The cast-iron cylinder block is of the replaceable wet-liner type. The crankshaft is supported within the cylinder block on five shell-type main bearings. Thrustwashers are fitted at the centre main bearing, to control crankshaft endfloat.

The connecting rods are attached to the crankshaft by horizontally-split shell-type big-end bearings, and to the pistons by interference-fit gudgeon pins. The aluminium alloy pistons are of the slipper type, and are fitted with three piston rings - two com-

1.4 Cutaway view of the 1390 cc (E6J) engine

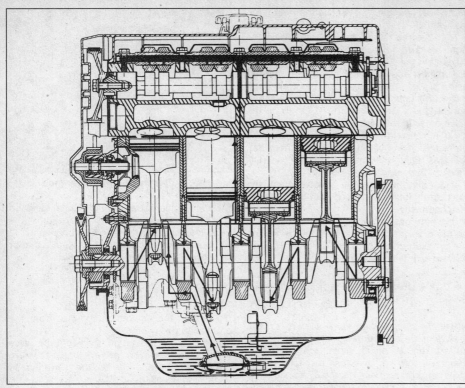

1.8 Lubrication circuit of the 1390 cc (E6J) engine

2.5 Compression gauge in use

2A

pression rings and a scraper-type oil control ring.

The overhead camshaft is mounted directly in the cylinder head. The camshaft is driven by the crankshaft, via a toothed rubber timing belt which also drives the water pump. The camshaft operates the valves via rocker arms, located on a rocker shaft bolted to the top of the cylinder head.

A semi-enclosed crankcase ventilation system is employed.

Lubrication is by pressure feed from a gear-type oil pump, which is chain-driven direct from the crankshaft **(see illustration)**. Certain models are fitted with an oil cooler, mounted between the oil filter and the cylinder block.

The distributor rotor is driven direct from the rear end of the camshaft, and on carburettor models, the fuel pump is also operated by the camshaft via an eccentric and lever. On fuel injection models, an electric fuel pump is fitted.

Repair operations possible with the engine in the vehicle

The following operations can be carried out without having to remove the engine from the vehicle:

(a) Removal and refitting of the cylinder head.
(b) Removal and refitting of the timing belt and sprockets.
(c) Removal and refitting of the camshaft.
(d) Removal and refitting of the sump.
(e) Removal and refitting of the connecting rods, pistons and liners*.

(f) Removal and refitting of the oil pump.
(g) Renewal of the engine mountings.
(h) Removal and refitting of the flywheel (manual gearbox models only).
(i) Renewal of the crankshaft oil seals.

* Although the pistons and liners can be removed and refitted with the engine in the vehicle after removal of the sump, it is better to carry this work out with the engine removed, in the interests of cleanliness and improved access. Refer to Chapter 2D for details.

2 Compression test - description and interpretation

Note: A suitable compression gauge will be required for this test.

1 A compression check will tell you what mechanical condition the upper end (pistons, rings, valves, head gaskets) of the engine is in. Specifically, it can tell you if the compression is down due to leakage caused by worn piston rings, defective valves and seats, or a blown head gasket. **Note:** The engine must be at normal operating temperature, and the battery fully charged, for this check.

2 Begin by cleaning the area around the spark plugs before you remove them (compressed air should be used, if available; otherwise, a small brush or even a bicycle tyre pump will work). The idea is to prevent dirt from getting into the cylinders as the compression check is being done.

3 Remove all of the spark plugs from the engine (see Chapter 1).

4 Disconnect the coil HT lead from the centre of the distributor cap, and earth it on the cylinder block. Use a jumper lead or similar wire to make a good connection.

5 Fit the compression gauge into the No 1 spark plug hole **(see illustration)**. No 1 cylinder is at the transmission end of the engine.

6 Have your assistant hold the accelerator pedal fully depressed to the floor, while at the same time cranking the engine over several times on the starter motor. Observe the compression gauge, noting that the compression should build up quickly in a healthy engine. Low compression on the first stroke, followed by gradually-increasing pressure on successive strokes, indicates worn piston rings. A low compression reading on the first stroke, which does not build up during successive strokes, indicates leaking valves or a blown head gasket (a cracked head could also be the cause). Deposits on the undersides of the valve heads can also cause low compression. Record the highest gauge reading obtained, then repeat the procedure for the remaining cylinders.

7 Add some engine oil (about three squirts from a plunger-type oil can) to each cylinder, through the spark plug hole, and repeat the test.

8 If the compression increases after the oil is added, the piston rings are definitely worn. If the compression does not increase significantly, the leakage is occurring at the valves or head gasket. Leakage past the valves may be caused by burned valve seats and/or faces or warped, cracked or bent valves.

9 If two adjacent cylinders have equally low compression, there is a strong possibility that the head gasket between them is blown. The appearance of coolant in the combustion chambers or the crankcase (visible on the engine oil dipstick) would verify this condition.

10 If one cylinder is about 20 percent lower than the other, and the engine has a slightly rough idle, a worn lobe on the camshaft could be the cause.

11 If the compression is unusually high, the combustion chambers are probably coated with carbon deposits. If this is the case, the

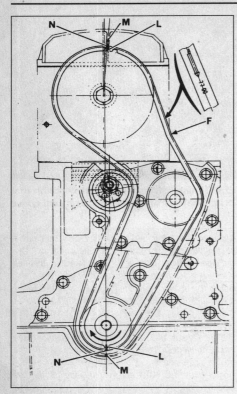

3.6 Timing belt and timing marks

F *Belt tension checking point*
L *Timing marks on the camshaft and crankshaft sprockets*
M *Fixed timing marks*
N *Timing bands on the belt*

cylinder head should be removed and decarbonised.

12 Actual compression pressures for the engines covered by this manual are not specified by the manufacturer. However, bearing in mind the information given in the preceding paragraphs, the results obtained should give a good indication of engine condition and what, if any, course of action to take. Consult a Renault dealer or engine reconditioning specialist for further advice.

3 Top dead centre (TDC) for No 1 piston - locating

1 Top dead centre (TDC) is the highest point in the cylinder that each piston reaches as the crankshaft turns. Each piston reaches TDC at the end of the compression stroke, and again at the end of the exhaust stroke. However, for the purpose of timing the engine, TDC refers to the position of No 1 piston at the end of its compression stroke. On all engines in this manual, No 1 piston and cylinder is at the transmission end of the engine.
2 Disconnect both battery leads.
3 Unscrew the bolts and remove the upper timing cover.
4 Apply the handbrake, then jack up the front right-hand side of the vehicle and support it securely on axle stands (see *"Jacking, towing*

and wheel changing"). Remove the right-hand roadwheel.
5 Remove the plastic cover from within the right-hand wheelarch, to gain access to the crankshaft pulley bolt.
6 Turn the engine in a clockwise direction, using a socket or spanner on the crankshaft pulley bolt, until the TDC mark on the camshaft sprocket is aligned with the TDC tab on the valve cover **(see illustration)**.
7 Look through the aperture at the transmission end of the engine, and check that the TDC timing mark is aligned with the TDC mark on the gearbox bellhousing.
8 If the distributor cap is now removed, the rotor arm should be aligned with the No 1 HT lead segment.
9 It is not possible to check the timing marks on the crankshaft sprocket without removing the crankshaft pulley first. The pulley is not marked with timing marks.

4 Valve clearances - adjustment

Note: *This operation is not part of the maintenance schedule. It should be undertaken if noise from the valvegear becomes evident, or if loss of performance gives cause to suspect that the clearances may be incorrect. A new valve cover gasket may be required on refitting.*

1 Remove the air cleaner and, on carburettor models, disconnect the choke cable as described in Chapter 4A.
2 On fuel injection models, disconnect the accelerator cable from the lever on the throttle housing, with reference to Chapter 4B.
3 Unscrew the bolts and remove the valve cover and gasket. Disconnect the crankcase ventilation hoses from the cover.
4 Remove the spark plugs (Chapter 1) in order to make turning the engine easier.
5 Draw the valve positions on a piece of paper, numbering them 1 to 4 inlet and exhaust according to their cylinders, from the transmission (left-hand) end of the engine (ie 1I, 1E, 2I, 2E, 3E, 3I, 4E, 4I). As the valve clearances are adjusted, cross them off. Inlet and exhaust valves can be distinguished by the positions of the inlet and exhaust manifolds.
6 Using a socket or spanner on the crankshaft pulley bolt, turn the engine in a clockwise direction until No 1 exhaust valve is completely open (ie the valve spring is completely compressed).
7 Insert a feeler blade of the correct thickness between the No 3 cylinder inlet valve stem and the end of the rocker arm. It should be a firm sliding fit. If adjustment is necessary, loosen the locknut on the rocker arm using a ring spanner and turn the adjustment screw with a BA spanner until the fit is correct **(see illustration)**. Tighten the locknut and recheck the adjustment, then repeat the adjustment procedure on No 4 cylinder exhaust valve.
8 Turn the engine in a clockwise direction until No 3 exhaust valve is completely open. Adjust

4.7 Adjusting a valve clearance

the valve clearances on No 4 inlet, and on No 2 exhaust valves. Continue to adjust the valve clearances in the following sequence:

Exhaust valve fully open	Adjust inlet valve	Adjust exhaust valve
1E	3I	4E
3E	4I	2E
4E	2I	1E
2E	1I	3E

9 Remove the socket or spanner from the crankshaft pulley bolt.
10 Refit the spark plugs, then refit the valve cover together with a new gasket where necessary. Reconnect the crankcase ventilation hoses.
11 Refit the air cleaner, and on carburettor models, re-connect the choke cable as described in Chapter 4A.
12 On fuel injection models, reconnect the accelerator cable with reference to Chapter 4B.

5 Timing belt - removal, inspection and refitting

Note: *A suitable tool will be required to check the timing belt tension on completion of refitting - see text.*

> ⚠ **Caution: If the timing belt breaks or slips in service, extensive engine damage may result. Renew the belt at the intervals specified in Chapter 1, or earlier if its condition is at all doubtful.**

Removal

1 Disconnect both the battery leads.
2 Remove the auxiliary drivebelt(s), as described in Chapter 1.
3 Unscrew the bolts and remove the upper timing cover **(see illustration)**.
4 Apply the handbrake, then jack up the front right-hand side of the vehicle and support securely on axle stands (see *"Jacking, towing and wheel changing"*). Remove the roadwheel.
5 Remove the plastic cover from within the right-hand wheelarch, to gain access to the crankshaft pulley.
6 Turn the engine in a clockwise direction, using a socket on the crankshaft pulley bolt, until the TDC mark on the camshaft sprocket is aligned with the TDC tab on the valve cover.

5.3 Removing the upper timing cover

5.7 Unscrewing the crankshaft pulley bolt

5.9 Timing marks aligned (arrowed) on the crankshaft sprocket and front oil seal cover

7 Unscrew the crankshaft pulley bolt while holding the crankshaft stationary **(see illustration)**. To do this, have an assistant insert a screwdriver in the starter ring gear teeth through the access hole in the top of the gearbox bellhousing. Take care not to damage the engine speed/position sensor.

8 Remove the crankshaft pulley from the nose of the crankshaft. If it is tight, use a puller.

9 Note that the timing mark on the crankshaft sprocket is aligned with the mark on the front oil seal cover **(see illustration)**.

10 Loosen the nut securing the timing belt tensioner, then move the tensioner outwards to release the tension from the belt; re-tighten the nut.

11 Check if the belt is marked with arrows to indicate its running direction, and if necessary, mark it. Release the belt from the camshaft sprocket, water pump sprocket, and crankshaft sprocket, and remove it from the engine.

12 Clean the sprockets and tensioner, and wipe them dry. Also clean the front of the cylinder head and block.

Inspection

13 Examine the timing belt carefully for any signs of cracking, fraying or general wear, particularly at the roots of the teeth. Renew the belt if there is any sign of deterioration of this nature, or if there is any oil or grease contamination. The belt must, of course, be renewed if it has completed the maximum mileage given in Chapter 1.

Refitting

14 Check the directional mark and timing bands on the back of the timing belt, then locate the belt on the crankshaft sprocket so that one of the timing bands is aligned with the marks on the sprocket and cover. The other timing band should be positioned so that it will locate on the camshaft sprocket in alignment with the other timing mark. After engaging the belt with the crankshaft sprocket, pull it taut over the water pump sprocket and onto the camshaft sprocket, then position it over the tensioner wheel **(see illustrations)**.

15 With the belt fully engaged with the sprockets, unscrew the tensioner nut and tension the belt, then tighten the nut. The tensioner is not spring-loaded, so it will have to be rotated manually to tension the belt; a screwdriver can be used as a lever between bolts in the holes in the tensioner hub, or use a tool like the one in illustration 6.2.

16 The belt deflection must now be checked. To do this, first make a mark on the front engine lifting bracket in line with the timing belt, mid-way between the camshaft and water pump sprockets. A force of 30 N (7 lbf) must now be applied to the timing belt, and its deflection should be 6 ± 0.5 mm (0. 236 ± 0.02 in). Renault technicians use a special tool to do this, but an alternative arrangement can be made by using a spring balance and steel rule. Apply the force with the spring balance, and read off the deflection on the steel rule **(see illustrations)**.

5.14a Fitting the timing belt over the camshaft sprocket

5.14b Timing mark on the belt aligned with the mark on the camshaft sprocket (arrowed)

5.14c Timing belt correctly located over water pump sprocket and tensioner wheel

5.16a Timing belt deflection mark (arrowed) made on the front engine lifting bracket

5.16b Checking the timing belt tension using a spring balance and steel rule

17 If the adjustment is incorrect, the tensioner hub will have to be repositioned.

18 Refit the crankshaft pulley to the nose of the crankshaft, then screw in the bolt. Tighten the bolt while holding the crankshaft stationary using the same method as described in paragraph 7.

19 Using a socket on the crankshaft pulley bolt, turn the engine through two complete revolutions, then recheck the timing belt tension and make sure that the timing marks are still in alignment.

20 The tensioner nut must be tightened securely - if it were to come loose, considerable engine damage would result.

21 Refit the plastic cover inside the right-hand wheelarch.

22 Refit the roadwheel, and lower the vehicle to the ground.

23 Refit the upper timing belt cover.

24 Refit and tension the auxiliary drivebelt(s) with reference to Chapter 1.

25 Reconnect the battery leads.

6 Timing belt sprockets and tensioner - removal, inspection and refitting

Removal

1 Remove the timing belt as described in Section 5.

2 To remove the camshaft sprocket, hold the sprocket stationary using a metal bar with two bolts tightened onto it, inserted into the holes in the sprocket, then unscrew the bolt. Renault

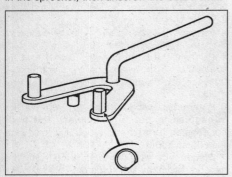

6.2 Renault tool for holding the camshaft sprocket stationary

6.6 Removing the timing belt tensioner

use a special tool for this purpose **(see illustration)**.

3 Remove the sprocket from the end of the camshaft. Note that it has a tab on its inner face, which locates in a slot in the end of the camshaft.

4 A puller may be necessary to remove the crankshaft sprocket. However, it is a simple matter to make up a puller using two bolts, a metal bar and the existing crankshaft pulley bolt **(see illustration)**. By unscrewing the crankshaft pulley bolt, the sprocket is pulled from the end of the crankshaft.

5 If necessary, remove the Woodruff key from the slot in the crankshaft.

6 Unscrew the nut and withdraw the timing belt tensioner from the stud on the front cover **(see illustration)**.

Inspection

7 Inspect the teeth of the sprockets for signs of nicks and damage. Also examine the water pump sprocket teeth. The teeth are not prone to wear, and should normally last the life of the engine.

8 Spin the tensioner by hand, and check it for any roughness or tightness. Do not attempt to clean it with solvent, as this may enter the bearing. If wear is evident, renew the tensioner.

Refitting

9 Locate the tensioner on the stud on the front cover, then refit the nut, and tighten it finger-tight at this stage.

10 Fit the Woodruff key in its slot in the crankshaft, making sure that it is level, to

6.4 Using a home-made puller to remove the crankshaft sprocket

7.4 Fitting a new camshaft oil seal

ensure engagement with the sprocket.

11 Slide the sprocket fully onto the crankshaft; use a metal tube if necessary to tap it into position.

12 Locate the sprocket on the end of the camshaft, making sure that the tab locates in the special slot, then screw in the bolt. Tighten the bolt to the specified torque, while holding the sprocket stationary using the method described in paragraph 2.

13 Refit the timing belt as described in Section 5.

7 Camshaft oil seal - renewal

1 Remove the camshaft sprocket as described in Section 6.

2 To ensure correct fitting, note the fitted position and depth of the old oil seal. Using a small screwdriver, prise out the oil seal from the cylinder head.

3 Wipe clean the seating in the cylinder head.

4 Smear a little oil on the outer surface of the new oil seal, then locate it squarely in the cylinder head, and drive it into position. Use a metal tube which has an external diameter slightly less than that of the cylinder head **(see illustration)**. Make sure that the oil seal is the correct way round, with its sealed face outwards.

5 Refit the camshaft sprocket as described in Section 6.

8 Camshaft - removal, inspection and refitting

Removal

1 Remove the cylinder head as described in Section 9, and place it on the workbench.

2 Progressively unscrew the bolts holding the rocker shaft and retaining plate to the cylinder head, and withdraw the shaft. Note that the bolts are different, and should be identified for position before removal. Nos 2 and 4 bolts have solid shanks, whereas the other bolts have hollow shanks. Their heads are coloured as shown **(see illustrations)**.

3 Hold the camshaft stationary using a spanner on the special flats provided on the camshaft, then unscrew the bolt and withdraw the sprocket **(see illustration)**.

4 Using a Torx key, unscrew the two bolts holding the distributor on the cylinder head, and remove the distributor. There is no need to mark the distributor, as it is not possible to adjust its position. Although there is an elongated slot for one of the bolts, the other bolt locates in a single hole.

5 Using a dial gauge, measure the endfloat of the camshaft, and compare with that given in the Specifications **(see illustration)**. This will give an indication of the amount of wear in the thrust plate.

6 Unscrew the two bolts, and lift the thrust plate out from the slot in the camshaft **(see illustration)**.

8.2a Two of the rocker shaft mounting bolts (arrowed)

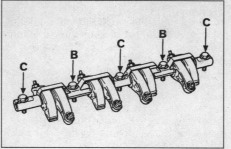

8.2b Rocker shaft bolt identification

B Solid bolts coloured yellow
C Hollow bolts coloured black

8.3 Holding the camshaft stationary while unscrewing the camshaft sprocket bolt

2A

7 Carefully withdraw the camshaft from the sprocket end of the cylinder head, taking care not to damage the bearing surfaces **(see illustration)**.

Inspection

8 Examine the camshaft bearing surfaces, cam lobes and fuel pump eccentric for wear ridges and scoring. Renew the camshaft if any of these conditions are apparent.
9 Examine the condition of the bearing surfaces both on the camshaft and in the cylinder head. If the head bearing surfaces are worn excessively, the cylinder head will need to be renewed.

Refitting

10 Lubricate the bearing surfaces in the cylinder head and the camshaft journals, then insert the camshaft into the head.
11 Refit the thrust plate, then insert and tighten the bolts.
12 Measure the endfloat as described in paragraph 5, and make sure that it is within the limits given in the Specifications.
13 Refit the distributor, and tighten the two bolts using a Torx key.
14 Refit the camshaft sprocket, making sure that the tab engages with the cut-out in the end of the camshaft. Hold the camshaft stationary with a spanner on the special flats, then insert the sprocket bolt and tighten it to the specified torque **(see illustration)**.
15 Refit the rocker shaft and retaining plate, then insert the bolts in their original positions and tighten them to the specified torque.

16 Refit the cylinder head as described in Section 9.

9 Cylinder head - removal and refitting

Note: *A new cylinder head gasket and a new valve cover gasket must be used on refitting.*

Removal

1 Disconnect both battery leads.
2 Drain the cooling system, including the cylinder block, with reference to Chapter 1. The block drain plug is located on the right-hand rear face of the engine, beneath the inlet manifold. It is important to drain the block as, if the wet cylinder liners are disturbed, the coolant will drain into the sump.
3 Drain the engine oil with reference to Chapter 1.
4 Remove the timing belt with reference to Section 5 of this Chapter.
5 Remove the complete air cleaner and air inlet duct with reference to Chapter 4A (carburettor models) or 4B (fuel injection models).
6 Where applicable, unbolt and remove the strengthening bar from between the front suspension turrets, and place it to one side **(see illustration)**.
7 Disconnect all electrical wiring from the sensors, switches and actuators located in the cylinder head, carburettor/throttle housing (as

8.5 Measuring the camshaft endfloat with a dial gauge

8.6 Lifting out the camshaft thrust plate

8.7 Withdrawing the camshaft from the cylinder head

8.14 Tightening the camshaft sprocket bolt

9.6 Removing a strengthening bar securing bolt from a front suspension turret

9.12a Remove the valve cover . . .

9.12b . . . and the gasket

9.15a Lift the cylinder head from the block . . .

applicable), and inlet manifold. Identify each wire with adhesive tags if necessary, to ensure correct refitting.

8 Similarly, loosen the clips, where applicable, and disconnect all coolant, vacuum and breather hoses from the cylinder head, carburettor/throttle housing and inlet manifold. Again, identify each hose to ensure correct refitting. Disconnect the fuel hoses from the carburettor/throttle housing, with reference to Chapter 4, identifying each hose to ensure correct refitting. Plug the open ends of the hoses and the carburettor/throttle housing, to prevent dirt ingress and fuel spillage.

 Warning: On fuel injection models, the fuel system should be depressurised as described in Chapter 4B before attempting to disconnect the fuel hoses.

9 Disconnect the accelerator cable and choke cable (carburettor models) from the carburettor/throttle housing and valve cover brackets, and position them to one side. Refer to Chapter 4A (carburettor models) or 4B (fuel injection models) for details.

10 Remove the inlet and exhaust manifolds with reference to Chapter 4A (carburettor models) or 4B (fuel injection models).

11 Disconnect the HT leads from the spark plugs, and pull them carefully from the HT lead holder on the valve cover. Unbolt and remove the holder.

12 Unbolt the valve cover from the cylinder head, and remove the gasket **(see illustrations)**.

13 Progressively unscrew the cylinder head bolts in the reverse order to that shown in illustration 9.26a, then remove them all except the bolt positioned on the front right-hand corner, which should be unscrewed by only three or four threads.

14 The joint between the cylinder head, gasket and cylinder block must now be broken without disturbing the wet liners. To do this, pull the distributor end of the cylinder head forward so as to swivel it around the single bolt still fitted, then locate the head back in its original position. If this procedure is not followed, there is a possibility of the wet liners moving and their bottom seals being disturbed, causing leakage after refitting the head.

15 Remove the remaining bolt, and lift the head from the cylinder block followed by the gasket. Note the location dowel on the front right-hand corner of the block **(see illustrations)**.

16 Note that the crankshaft *must not* be rotated with the cylinder head removed, otherwise the wet liners will be displaced. If it is necessary to turn the engine (eg to clean the piston crowns), clamp the liners using suitable bolts and washers, or make up some retaining clamps out of flat metal bar, held in place with bolts screwed into the block **(see illustration)**.

Refitting

17 The mating faces of the cylinder head and block must be perfectly clean before refitting the head. Use a scraper to remove all traces of gasket and carbon, and also clean the tops of

the pistons (clamp the cylinder liners before turning the engine). Take particular care with the aluminium cylinder head, as the soft metal is damaged easily. Also, make sure that the carbon is not allowed to enter the oil and water channels - this is particularly important for the oil circuit, as carbon could block the oil supply to the camshaft and rocker arms, or to the crankshaft main and big-end bearings. Using adhesive tape and paper, seal the water, oil and bolt holes in the cylinder block. Clean the piston crowns in the same way.

> **HAYNES HiNT** *To prevent carbon entering the gap between the pistons and bores, smear a little grease in the gap. After cleaning the piston, rotate the crankshaft so that the piston moves down the bore, then wipe out the grease and carbon with a cloth rag.*

18 Check the block and head for nicks, deep scratches and other damage. If slight, they may be removed carefully with a file; however, if excessive, machining may be the only alternative.

19 If warpage of the cylinder head is suspected, use a straight-edge to check it for distortion. Refer to Chapter 2D if necessary.

20 Clean out all the bolt holes in the block using a cloth rag and screwdriver **(see illustration)**. Make sure that all oil is removed, otherwise there is a possibility of the block

9.15b . . . and recover the gasket

9.16 Clamps (arrowed) holding the liners in place

9.20 Cleaning the cylinder head bolt holes in the cylinder block

9.23 Cylinder head locating dowel (arrowed)

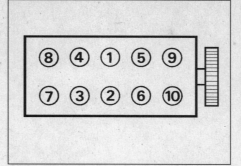

9.26a Cylinder head bolt tightening sequence - E-type engines

9.26b Tighten the cylinder head bolts to the specified torque . . .

2A

9.26c . . . and then through the specified angle

being cracked by hydraulic pressure when the bolts are tightened.

21 Examine the bolt threads and the threads in the cylinder block for damage. If necessary, use the correct-size tap to chase out the threads in the block. Use a die to clean the threads on the bolts.

22 Position No 1 piston at TDC, then remove the cylinder liner clamps or washers as applicable, and wipe clean the faces of the head and block.

23 Check that the location dowel is in position on the front right-hand corner of the block **(see illustration)**.

24 Position the new gasket on the block and over the dowel. It can only be fitted one way round.

25 Lower the cylinder head onto the block, then insert the bolts and initially screw them in finger-tight.

26 Tighten the cylinder head bolts to the specified torques in the sequence shown, and in the stages given in the Specifications at the beginning of this Chapter. The first two stages pre-compress the gasket, and the remaining stages are the main tightening procedure **(see illustrations)**.

27 If the cylinder head has been overhauled, it is worthwhile checking the valve clearances at this stage, to prevent any possibility of the valves touching the pistons when the timing belt is being fitted. Use a socket on the camshaft sprocket to turn the camshaft, but before doing this, turn the crankshaft so that the pistons in Nos 1 and 4 cylinders are *not* at TDC.

28 Refit the timing belt with reference to Section 5 of this Chapter.

29 Adjust the valve clearances as described in Section 4 of this Chapter.

30 Refit the valve cover together with a new gasket, and tighten the bolts progressively.

31 Refit the spark plugs if removed.

32 Refit the HT lead holder, then connect the HT leads to the spark plugs, and insert the leads in the holder.

33 Reconnect all coolant, vacuum and breather hoses, ensuring that they are correctly connected as noted before removal. Where applicable, tighten the securing clips. Reconnect the fuel hoses, ensuring that they

are securely refitted to their correct locations as noted before removal.

34 Refit the inlet and exhaust manifolds with reference to Chapter 4A (carburettor models) or 4B (fuel injection models).

35 Reconnect the accelerator and choke cables, as applicable, and if necessary adjust them with reference to Chapter 4A or 4B, as applicable.

36 Reconnect all wiring, using the tags fitted before removal to ensure that each wire is correctly positioned.

37 Where applicable, refit the strengthening bar between the front suspension turrets, and tighten the bolts.

38 Refit the air cleaner and air inlet duct with reference to Chapter 4A or 4B.

39 Refill the engine with oil with reference to Chapter 1.

40 Reconnect both battery leads.

41 Refill and bleed the cooling system with reference to Chapter 1.

10 Sump - removal and refitting

Note: *An engine lifting hoist is required during this procedure. A new sump gasket must be used on refitting.*

Removal

1 Disconnect the battery leads.

2 Drain the engine oil as described in Chapter 1, then refit and tighten the drain plug to the specified torque setting.

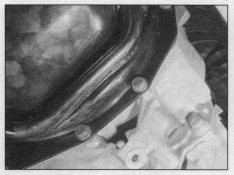

10.7a Unscrew the bolts . . .

3 Apply the handbrake, then jack up the front right-hand side of the vehicle, and support securely on axle stands (see *"Jacking, towing and wheel changing"*). Remove the roadwheel.

4 Remove the plastic cover from inside the wheelarch for access to the engine.

5 Unscrew the nuts securing the exhaust front pipe to the exhaust manifold, and remove the springs.

6 Working under the vehicle, disconnect the front exhaust pipe from the rear system by unscrewing the clamp bolts. Remove the front pipe.

7 Unscrew the bolts securing the tie-bar and cover assembly to the gearbox bellhousing and engine block, and lower it from the sump **(see illustrations)**.

8 The engine must now be raised by

10.7b . . . and remove the tie-bar and cover assembly

10.8 Right-hand engine mounting nut

10.10 Lowering the sump from the engine

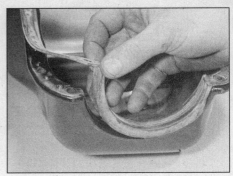

10.12 Fitting a new gasket to the sump

11.3 Removing the Woodruff key (arrowed) from the crankshaft

11.4 Removing the front cover from the cylinder block

approximately 75 to 100 mm (3 to 4 in) before the sump can be removed. To do this, first unscrew the right-hand engine mounting nut from under the vehicle, and remove the bracket plate (see illustration). Attach a hoist to the engine lifting eye next to the timing cover, and raise the engine.

9 Unscrew the bolts securing the sump to the cylinder block.

10 Break the joint by striking the sump with the palm of your hand, then lower the sump over the oil pump and withdraw it (see illustration).

Refitting

11 Clean all traces of gasket from the cylinder block and sump, and wipe them dry.

12 Locate a new gasket on the sump, making sure that it is correctly positioned on the curved sections (see illustration).

13 Offer the sump to the cylinder block, and insert the bolts. Progressively tighten the bolts in diagonal sequence to the specified torque.

14 Lower the engine, and refit the right-hand engine mounting plate and nut. Remove the hoist.

15 Refit the tie-bar and cover assembly to the gearbox bellhousing and engine block.

16 Refit the front exhaust pipe, and tighten the bolts (see Chapter 4A, or 4B).

17 Refit the plastic cover to the inside of the wheelarch.

18 Refit the roadwheel, and lower the vehicle to the ground.

19 Refill the engine with oil, with reference to Chapter 1.

20 Reconnect the battery leads.

11 Oil pump and sprockets - removal, inspection and refitting

Note: A new crankshaft front oil seal should be used on refitting, and suitable sealant will be required when refitting the front cover to the cylinder block.

Removal

1 Remove the timing belt and crankshaft sprocket with reference to Sections 5 and 6.

2 Remove the sump as described in Section 10.

3 Remove the Woodruff key from its slot in the crankshaft (see illustration).

4 Unbolt the front cover from the cylinder block (see illustration).

5 Slide off the oil seal spacer.

6 Unscrew the bolts securing the sprocket to the oil pump hub. Use a screwdriver through one of the holes in the sprocket to hold it stationary (see illustration).

7 Remove the oil pump sprocket, and release the chain from the crankshaft sprocket.

8 Slide the sprocket from the crankshaft.

9 Unscrew the two mounting bolts, and withdraw the oil pump from the crankcase (see illustration). If the two locating dowels are displaced, refit them in the crankcase.

11.6 Unscrewing the oil pump sprocket bolts

11.9 Oil pump mounting bolts (arrowed)

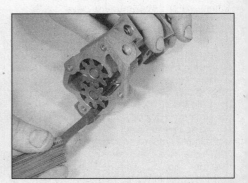

11.11 Checking the clearance between the oil pump gears and body

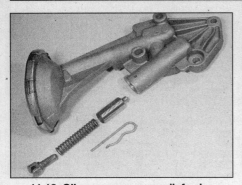

11.12 Oil pump pressure relief valve components

11.21a Removing the oil seal from the front cover

11.21b Driving the new oil seal into the front cover

Inspection

10 Unscrew the four retaining bolts, and lift off the pump cover and pick-up tube.

11 Using a feeler gauge, check the clearance between each of the gears and the oil pump body. Also check the clearance (endfloat) between the gears and the cover joint face **(see illustration)**. If any clearance is outside the tolerances given in the Specifications, the oil pump must be renewed.

12 Mount the cover in a vice, then depress the relief valve end stop, and extract the spring clip. Release the end stop, and remove the spring and piston **(see illustration)**.

13 Examine the relief valve piston and seat for signs of wear and damage. If evident, renew the oil pump complete.

14 If the components are serviceable, clean them, and reassemble in the reverse order to dismantling. Before refitting the cover, fill the pump with fresh engine oil, to assist circulation when the engine is first started.

15 Examine the chain for excessive wear, and renew it if necessary. Similarly check the sprockets.

Refitting

16 Wipe clean the oil pump and crankcase mating surfaces.

17 Check that the two locating dowels are fitted in the crankcase, then position the oil pump on them, and insert the two mounting bolts. Tighten the bolts securely.

18 Slide the sprocket onto the crankshaft.

19 Engage the oil pump sprocket with the chain, then engage the chain with the

crankshaft sprocket, and locate the sprocket on the oil pump hub.

20 Align the holes, then insert the sprocket bolts and tighten them securely, while holding the sprocket stationary with a screwdriver.

21 The oil seal in the front cover should be renewed whenever the cover is removed. Note the fitted position of the old seal, then prise it out with a screwdriver and wipe clean the seating. Smear the outer perimeter of the new seal with fresh engine oil, and locate it squarely on the cover, with its closed side facing outwards. Place the cover on a block of wood, then use a socket or metal tube to drive in the oil seal **(see illustrations)**.

22 Clean all traces of sealant from the front cover and block mating faces. Apply a 0.6 to 1.0 mm diameter bead of sealant around the perimeter of the front cover, then refit it to the cylinder block and tighten the bolts securely **(see illustration)**.

23 Smear the oil seal with a little engine oil, then slide the spacer onto the front of the crankshaft **(see illustration)**. Turn it slightly as it enters the oil seal, to prevent damage to the seal lip. If the spacer is worn excessively where the old oil seal contacted it, it may be turned around so that the new oil seal contacts the unworn area.

24 Refit the Woodruff key to its slot in the crankshaft.

25 Refit the sump with reference to Section 10.

26 Refit the crankshaft sprocket and timing belt with reference to Sections 5 and 6.

12 Crankshaft oil seals - renewal

Front/right-hand oil seal

1 The renewal procedure is included in the procedure for the removal and refitting of the oil pump in Section 11 of this Chapter.

Rear/left-hand oil seal

2 Remove the flywheel/driveplate as described in Section 13.

3 Prise out the old oil seal using a small screwdriver, taking care not to damage the surface on the crankshaft.

> **HAYNES HINT** *Alternatively, the oil seal can be removed by drilling two small holes diagonally opposite each other, and inserting self-tapping screws in them. A pair of grips can then be used to pull out the oil seal, by pulling on each screw in turn.*

4 Inspect the seal rubbing surface on the crankshaft. If it is grooved or rough in the area where the old seal was fitted, the new seal should be fitted slightly less deeply, so that it rubs on an unworn part of the surface.

5 Wipe clean the oil seal seating. Dip the new seal in fresh engine oil, and locate it over the crankshaft, with its closed side facing outwards. Make sure that the oil seal lip is not damaged as it is located on the crankshaft.

6 Using a metal tube, drive the oil seal squarely into the bore until flush. A block of wood cut to pass over the end of the crankshaft may be used instead.

7 Refit the flywheel/driveplate with reference to Section 13.

13 Flywheel/driveplate - removal, inspection and refitting

Note: *On models with automatic transmission, the engine and transmission must be removed as an assembly (see Chapter 2D) before the driveplate can be removed. Suitable thread-locking compound must be used when refitting the flywheel bolts.*

2A

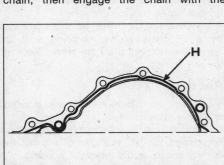

11.22 Sealant bead application (H) around the front cover

11.23 Sliding the spacer onto the front of the crankshaft

13.5 Flywheel mounting bolts

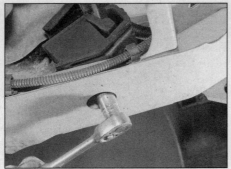

14.7 Unscrewing the engine front left-hand mounting lower nut

14.12 Unscrewing the engine rear mounting through-bolt

Removal

1 Remove the gearbox (manual gearbox models - see Chapter 7A) or the engine/transmission assembly (automatic transmission models - see Chapter 2D), as applicable.
2 On manual gearbox models, remove the clutch (Chapter 6).
3 Mark the flywheel or driveplate in relation to the crankshaft.
4 The flywheel/driveplate must now be held stationary while the bolts are loosened. To do this, locate a long bolt in one of the transmission mounting bolt holes, and either insert a wide-bladed screwdriver in the starter ring gear, or use a piece of bent metal bar engaged with the ring gear.
5 Unscrew the mounting bolts and withdraw the flywheel/driveplate from the crankshaft **(see illustration)**.

Inspection

6 On manual gearbox models, examine the flywheel for scoring of the clutch face, and for wear or chipping of the ring gear teeth. If the clutch face is scored, the flywheel may be machined until flat, but renewal is preferable.
7 On automatic transmission models, check the torque converter driveplate carefully for signs of distortion. Also look for any hairline cracks around the bolt holes, or radiating outwards from the centre.
8 If the ring gear is worn or damaged, it may be possible to renew it separately, but this job is best left to a Renault dealer or engineering works. The temperature to which the new ring gear must be heated for installation is critical and, if not done accurately, the hardness of the teeth will be destroyed.

Refitting

9 Clean the flywheel/driveplate and crankshaft faces, then coat the locating face on the crankshaft with Loctite Autoform, or an equivalent compound.
10 Locate the flywheel/driveplate on the crankshaft, making sure that any previously-made marks are aligned.

11 Apply a few drops of thread-locking fluid to the mounting bolt threads, fit the bolts and tighten them in a diagonal sequence to the specified torque.
12 On manual gearbox models, refit the clutch (Chapter 6).
13 Refit the gearbox (Chapter 7A) or the engine/transmission assembly (Chapter 2D), as applicable.

14 Engine mountings - renewal

1 Apply the handbrake, then jack up the front of the vehicle, and support it securely on axle stands (see *"Jacking, towing and wheel changing"*).

Front right-hand mounting

2 Unscrew the nut, and remove the plate from under the front subframe.
3 Using a hoist, raise the right-hand side of the engine 50 to 75 mm (2 to 3 in).
4 Unscrew the nuts and remove the mounting from the bracket.
5 If necessary, unbolt the bracket from the cylinder block.
6 Fit the new mounting using a reversal of the removal procedure.

Front left-hand mounting

7 Using a socket through the hole in the subframe, unscrew the lower mounting nut **(see illustration)**.
8 Take the weight of the transmission with a trolley jack, then unscrew the upper nut and withdraw the mounting from the engine compartment. If necessary, the mounting bracket can be unbolted from the cylinder block.
9 Fit the new mounting using a reversal of the removal procedure.

Rear mounting

10 Apply the handbrake, then jack up the front of the vehicle and support it securely on

axle stands (see *"Jacking, towing and wheel changing"*).
11 Support the weight of the engine/transmission using a hoist or trolley jack.
12 Unscrew and remove the through-bolt **(see illustration)**.
13 Fit the new mounting using a reversal of the removal procedure.

Transmission mounting

14 Apply the handbrake, then jack up the front of the vehicle and support it securely on axle stands (see *"Jacking, towing and wheel changing"*).
15 Take the weight of the transmission with a trolley jack, then unscrew the nuts/bolts and withdraw the mounting from the transmission.
16 Fit the new mounting using a reverse of the removal procedure.

15 Engine oil cooler - removal and refitting

Removal

1 Drain the cooling system as described in Chapter 1.
2 Position a suitable container beneath the oil filter. Unscrew the filter (using an oil filter removal tool if necessary), and drain the oil into the container.
3 Release the hose clips, and disconnect the coolant hoses from the oil cooler.
4 Unscrew the oil cooler from the cylinder block, or unscrew the mounting stud, as applicable, and withdraw the cooler. Recover the sealing ring.

Refitting

5 Examine the condition of the sealing ring, and renew if necessary.
6 Refitting is a reversal of removal, but on completion, top-up the engine oil and refill the cooling system as described in Chapter 1.

Chapter 2 Part B:
C-type engines (1237 cc, 1390 cc and 1397 cc) – in-car engine repair procedures

Contents

2B

Degrees of difficulty

Easy, suitable for novice with little experience	Fairly easy, suitable for beginner with some experience	Fairly difficult, suitable for competent DIY mechanic	Difficult, suitable for experienced DIY mechanic	Very difficult, suitable for expert DIY or professional

Specifications

General

Type	Four-cylinder, in-line, overhead valve
Designation:	
1237 cc engine	C1G
1390 cc engine	C3J
1397 cc engine (Zenith carburettor - see Chapter 4A)	C1J
1397 cc engine (Weber carburettor - see Chapter 4A)	C2J
Bore:	
1237 cc (C1G) engine	71.5 mm
1390 cc (C3J) engine	75.8 mm
1397 cc (C1J and C2J) engines	76.0 mm
Stroke (all engines)	77.0 mm
Firing order	1-3-4-2 (No 1 cylinder at transmission end of engine)
Direction of crankshaft rotation	Clockwise viewed from timing belt end
Compression ratio:	
1237 cc (C1G) engine	9.2:1
1390 cc (C3J) engine	9.0:1
1397 cc (C1J) engine	9.0:1
1397 cc (C2J) engine	9.25:1
Maximum power output (typical):	
1237 cc (C1G) engine	No information at time of writing
1390 cc (C3J) engine	43 kW (60 bhp) at 4750 rpm
1397 cc (C1J and C2J) engines	43 kW (60 bhp) at 5250 rpm
Maximum torque (typical):	
1237 cc engine	No information at time of writing
1390 cc (C3J) engine	100 Nm (74 lbf ft) at 3000 rpm
1397 cc (C1J and C2J) engines	105 Nm (79 lbf ft) at 2750 rpm

Camshaft

Drive	Chain
Number of bearings	4
Camshaft endfloat	0.05 to 0.12 mm

Valve clearances (cold)

Inlet	0.15 mm
Exhaust	0.20 mm

Lubrication system

System pressure:	
At idle	0.7 bars
At 4000 rpm	3.5 bars
Oil pump type	Two-gear or bi-rotor
Oil pump clearances:	
Two-gear:	
Gear-to-body (maximum)	0.20 mm
Bi-rotor:	
Inner-to-outer rotors (at centre of peaks)	0.04 to 0.29 mm

Torque wrench settings

	Nm	lbf ft
Rocker shaft nuts and bolts	15 to 20	11 to 15
Camshaft sprocket bolt	30	22
Crankshaft sprocket/pulley bolt:		
Bolt 40 mm long	80	59
Bolt 45 mm long	110	81
Connecting rod (big-end) cap bolts		
1237 cc (C1G) engine	35	26
1390 cc (C3J) engine	45	33
1397 cc (C1J and C2J) engines	45	33
Main bearing cap bolts	55 to 65	41 to 48
Flywheel bolts*	50	37
Cylinder head bolts:		
Stage 1	55 to 65	41 to 48
Stage 2	Run the engine for 20 minutes, then allow to cool for 2½ hours	
Stage 3	Loosen bolt 1 fully, then tighten to:	
	55 to 65	41 to 48
Stage 4	Loosen and tighten remaining bolts to Stage 3 setting	

*Note: *Use new bolts and thread-locking compound.*

1 General information

How to use this Chapter

This Part of Chapter 2 is devoted to in-car repair procedures for the C-type engines. Similar information covering the E-type engines will be found in Chapter 2A, and information for F-type engines will be found in Chapter 2C. All procedures concerning engine removal and refitting, and engine block/cylinder head overhaul for all engine types can be found in Chapter 2D.

Note that as well as the C-type 1390 cc (C3J) engine, there is also an E-type 1390 cc (E6J and E7J) engine, details of which can be found in Chapter 2A. Refer to the *"Buying spare parts and vehicle identification numbers"* Section at the beginning of this manual for details of engine code locations.

Most of the operations included in Chapter 2B are based on the assumption that the engine is still installed in the vehicle. Therefore, if this information is being used during a complete engine overhaul, with the engine already removed, many of the steps included here will not apply.

1.4 1397 cc (C1J) engine

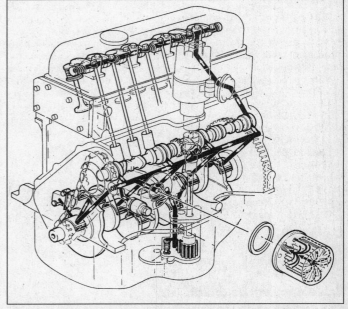

1.9 Lubrication circuit of the 1397 cc (C1J) engine

Engine description

The engine is of four-cylinder, in-line, overhead valve type, mounted transversely in the front of the vehicle (see illustration).

The cast-iron cylinder block is of the replaceable wet-liner type. The crankshaft is supported within the cylinder block on five shell-type main bearings. Thrustwashers are fitted at the centre main bearing, to control crankshaft endfloat.

The connecting rods are attached to the crankshaft by horizontally-split shell-type big-end bearings, and to the pistons by interference-fit gudgeon pins. The aluminium alloy pistons are of the slipper type, and are fitted with three piston rings - two compression rings and a scraper-type oil control ring.

The camshaft is chain-driven from the crankshaft, and operates the rocker arms via pushrods. The inlet and exhaust valves are each closed by a single valve spring, and operate in guides pressed into the cylinder head. The valves are actuated directly by the rocker arms.

A semi-closed crankcase ventilation system is employed; crankcase gases are drawn from the rocker cover via a hose to the air cleaner and inlet manifold.

Lubrication is provided by a gear-type oil pump, driven from the camshaft and located in the crankcase. Engine oil is fed through an externally-mounted full-flow filter to the engine oil gallery, and then to the crankshaft, camshaft and rocker shaft bearings (see illustration). A pressure relief valve is incorporated in the oil pump.

Repair operations possible with the engine in the vehicle

The following operations can be carried out without having to remove the engine from the vehicle:

(a) Removal and refitting of the cylinder head.
(b) Removal and refitting of the timing cover, chain and gears.
(c) Removal and refitting of the sump.
(d) Removal and refitting of the connecting rods, pistons and liners*.
(e) Removal, overhaul and refitting of the oil pump.

(f) Renewal of the engine mountings.
(g) Removal and refitting of the flywheel.
(h) Renewal of the crankshaft oil seals.

* Although the pistons and liners can be removed and refitted with the engine in the vehicle after removal of the sump, it is better to carry this work out with the engine removed, in the interests of cleanliness and improved access. Refer to Chapter 2D for details.

2 Compression test - description and interpretation

Refer to Chapter 2A.

3 Top dead centre (TDC) for No 1 piston - locating

1 Top dead centre (TDC) is the highest point in the cylinder that each piston reaches as the crankshaft turns. Each piston reaches TDC at the end of the compression stroke, and again at the end of the exhaust stroke. However, for the purpose of timing the engine, TDC refers to the position of No 1 piston at the end of its compression stroke. No 1 piston is at the transmission end of the engine.
2 Disconnect both battery leads.
3 Apply the handbrake, then jack up the front right-hand side of the vehicle and support it securely on axle stands (see "Jacking, towing and wheel changing"). Remove the right-hand roadwheel.
4 Remove the plastic cover from within the right-hand wheel arch, to gain access to the crankshaft pulley bolt.
5 Remove the spark plugs as described in Chapter 1.
6 Place a finger over the No 1 spark plug hole in the cylinder head (No 1 is at the transmission end of the engine). Turn the engine in a clockwise direction, using a socket or spanner on the crankshaft pulley bolt, until pressure is felt in the No 1 cylinder. This indicates that No 1 piston is rising on its compression stroke.
7 Look through the aperture at the flywheel end of the engine, and continue turning the crankshaft until the timing mark on the

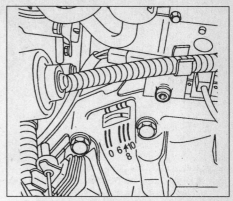

3.7 Timing marks (notch on flywheel rim and scale on bellhousing)
TDC position indicated by "0"

flywheel is aligned with the TDC ("0") mark on the gearbox bellhousing (see illustration).
8 If the distributor cap is now removed, the rotor arm should be aligned with the No 1 HT lead segment.

4 Valve clearances - adjustment

Note: A new valve cover gasket may be required on refitting.
1 Remove the air cleaner and, on carburettor models, disconnect the choke cable, as described in Chapter 4A, or 4B, as applicable.
2 Where applicable, disconnect the accelerator cable from the carburettor/throttle housing (refer to Chapter 4A for carburettor models, and 4B for fuel injection models), and move it to one side, clear of the valve cover. On fuel injection models, also disconnect the throttle return spring from the bracket on the valve cover (see illustration).
3 Where applicable, unclip the HT lead(s) from the valve cover.
4 Unscrew the nuts, and remove the valve cover and gasket. Disconnect the crankcase ventilation hose from the cover.
5 Remove the spark plugs (Chapter 1) in order to make turning the engine easier.
6 Draw the valve positions on a piece of paper, numbering them 1 to 4 inlet and exhaust according to their cylinders, from the transmission (left-hand) end of the engine (ie 1E, 1I, 2I, 2E, 3E, 3I, 4I, 4E). As the valve clearances are adjusted, cross them off.
7 Using a socket or spanner on the crankshaft pulley bolt, turn the engine in a clockwise direction until No 1 exhaust valve is completely open (ie the valve spring is completely compressed).
8 Insert a feeler blade of the correct thickness between the No 3 cylinder inlet valve stem and the end of the rocker arm. It should be a firm sliding fit. If adjustment is necessary, loosen the locknut on the rocker arm using a ring spanner and turn the adjustment screw with a screwdriver or a BA spanner (as applicable) until the fit is correct (see illustration). Tighten the locknut and recheck the adjustment, then

4.2 Disconnect the throttle return spring from the valve cover bracket (arrowed)

4.8 Adjusting a valve clearance

2B

5.5 A puller may be needed to remove the crankshaft pulley hub

repeat the adjustment procedure on No 4 cylinder exhaust valve.

9 Turn the engine in a clockwise direction until No 3 exhaust valve is completely open. Adjust the valve clearances on No 4 inlet, and No 2 exhaust valves. Continue to adjust the valve clearances in the following sequence:

Exhaust valve fully open	Adjust inlet valve	Adjust exhaust valve
1E	3I	4E
3E	4I	2E
4E	2I	1E
2E	1I	3E

10 Remove the socket or spanner from the crankshaft pulley bolt.

11 Refit the spark plugs with reference to Chapter 1, then refit the valve cover, together with a new gasket where necessary. Reconnect the crankshaft ventilation hose.

12 Refit the air cleaner and, on carburettor models, re-connect the choke cable as described in Chapter 4A or 4B, as applicable.

13 Where applicable, reconnect the accelerator cable, with reference to Chapter 4, and reconnect the throttle return spring to the bracket on the valve cover.

14 Where applicable, clip the HT lead(s) into position on the valve cover.

5 Timing cover, chain and gears -
removal, inspection and refitting

Note: *A new timing cover oil seal must be used on refitting, and suitable sealing compound may be required when refitting the timing cover - see text.*

Removal

1 Remove the auxiliary drivebelt with reference to Chapter 1.

2 Remove the sump with reference to Section 7.

3 Refer to Section 3, and bring the engine to TDC, No 1 firing.

4 Lock the starter ring gear to prevent the engine turning, by using a wide-bladed screwdriver inserted between the ring gear teeth and the crankcase. Alternatively, engage 4th gear and have an assistant depress the footbrake pedal. With the engine locked, use a

socket or spanner to unscrew the crankshaft pulley retaining bolt.

5 With the bolt removed, lift off the pulley and withdraw the pulley hub. If the hub is tight, carefully lever it off using two screwdrivers, or use a two- or three-legged puller **(see illustration)**.

6 Unscrew the nuts and bolts securing the timing cover to the cylinder block, and carefully prise the timing cover off using a screwdriver to release it. Remove the gasket where fitted.

7 Observe the components of the timing chain tensioner, noting that one of two types may be fitted. The mechanical tensioner is identified by its coil tensioning spring and single mounting bolt, and the automatic hydraulic tensioner by its piston plunger and two mounting bolts **(see illustrations)**.

8 To remove the mechanical-type tensioner, Renault technicians use a special tubular tool which locates over the tensioner and spring, and holds all the components together until the assembly is refitted **(see illustration)**. If the tool is not available, simply unscrew the retaining bolt using an Allen key, hold the tensioner slipper and spring end together, and withdraw the assembly from the cylinder block.

9 If a hydraulic tensioner is fitted, lock the plunger with locking wire tied around the body. Unscrew the mounting bolts and withdraw the tensioner from the block. Extract the gauze filter from the hole in the cylinder block.

10 Bend back the locktab, then unscrew and remove the camshaft sprocket retaining bolt. Remove the washer. Withdraw the camshaft sprocket and chain from the camshaft, then release the chain from the crankshaft sprocket **(see illustration)**. Use two screwdrivers or a puller to remove the sprocket from the crankshaft.

11 With the sprockets and chain removed, check that the Woodruff key in the nose of the crankshaft is a tight fit in its slot. If not, remove it now and store it safely, to avoid the risk of it dropping out and getting lost.

Inspection

12 Examine all the teeth on the camshaft and crankshaft sprockets. If these are "hooked" in appearance, renew the sprockets.

13 If a mechanical-type chain tensioner is fitted, examine the chain contact pad, and renew the tensioner assembly if the pad is heavily scored.

14 If a hydraulic-type chain tensioner is fitted, dismantle it by releasing the slipper piston with a 3 mm Allen key. Examine the piston, spring, sleeve and tensioner body bore for signs of scoring, and renew if evident. Also renew the tensioner if the chain contact pad is heavily scored.

15 If the hydraulic tensioner is serviceable, lubricate the components, and reassemble. Lock the sleeve in the slipper piston first by turning it clockwise with an Allen key, then slide this assembly into the tensioner body. Avoid pressing the slipper now, or the sleeve

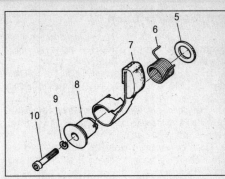

5.7a Mechanical timing chain tensioner components

5 Washer	8 Collar
6 Spring	9 Washer
7 Slipper arm	10 Retaining bolt

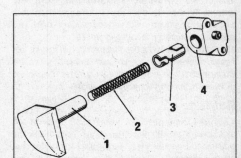

5.7b Hydraulic timing chain tensioner components

1 Piston with tensioner slipper	3 Sleeve
2 Spring	4 Tensioner body

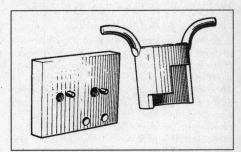

5.8 Renault tool for holding the mechanical tensioner together

5.10 Removing the timing chain and sprockets

5.16 Use a socket or tube to renew the timing cover oil seal

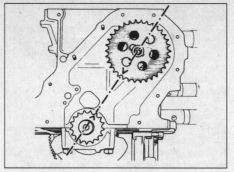

5.19 Correct alignment of crankshaft and camshaft sprocket timing marks

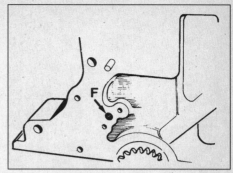

5.23 Location (F) of gauze filter in the cylinder block for the hydraulic tensioner

2B

will be released and the whole assembly will fly apart. New hydraulic tensioners are supplied with a 2 mm thick safety spacer inserted between the pad and the tensioner body to prevent the assembly flying apart.

16 Renew the oil seal in the timing cover by first driving out the old seal using a suitable drift. Install the new seal using a large socket or block of wood **(see illustration)**.

Refitting

17 Refit the Woodruff key to the crankshaft slot, and then tap the crankshaft sprocket into position. Ensure that the timing mark on the sprocket is on the side facing away from the engine.

18 Turn the crankshaft if necessary until the timing notch on the flywheel is in line with the TDC ("0") mark on the bellhousing timing scale.

19 Temporarily place the camshaft sprocket in position. Turn the camshaft so that the timing marks on the sprocket faces are facing each other, coinciding with an imaginary line joining the crankshaft and camshaft centres, then remove the camshaft sprocket **(see illustration)**.

20 Fit the timing chain to the camshaft sprocket, position the sprocket in its approximate fitted position, and locate the chain over the crankshaft sprocket. Position the camshaft sprocket on the camshaft, and check that the marks are still aligned when there is an equal amount of slack on both sides of the chain.

21 Refit the camshaft sprocket retaining bolt using a new locktab, and tighten the bolt to the specified torque. Bend up the locktabs to retain the bolt.

22 If a mechanical-type tensioner is fitted, place it in position, and locate the spring ends in the block and over the slipper arm. Refit the retaining bolt, and tighten it securely using an Allen key.

23 If a hydraulic-type tensioner is fitted, first insert the gauze filter in the cylinder block **(see illustration)**. Remove the safety spacer (if fitting a new tensioner), and locate the tensioner on the cylinder block. Insert the bolts and tighten them. Push the slipper fully inwards, then release it. The piston should spring out automatically under spring pressure.

24 Oil the chain, sprockets and tensioner.

25 Ensure that the mating faces of the timing cover are clean and dry, with all traces of old sealant removed. A new oil seal must be in place in the timing cover.

26 If there are no locating dowels for the timing cover, a gasket must be fitted. Locate the gasket on the cylinder block, retaining it with a smear of grease. Fit the timing cover, and finger-tighten the nuts and bolts. Oil the pulley hub, and temporarily fit it on the end of the crankshaft so that the timing cover is positioned correctly, then tighten the cover nuts and bolts.

27 Where locating dowels are fitted, apply a bead of CAF 4/60 THIXO paste to the timing

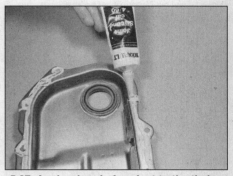

5.27 Apply a bead of sealant to the timing cover face

cover joint face, then position the cover over the dowels and the two studs **(see illustration)**. Refit the nuts and retaining bolts, then progressively tighten them in a diagonal sequence.

28 Lubricate the crankshaft pulley hub, and carefully slide it onto the end of the crankshaft **(see illustration)**.

29 Place the pulley in position, refit the retaining bolt and washer, and tighten the bolt to the specified torque **(see illustrations)**. Hold the crankshaft stationary using the method described in paragraph 4.

30 Refit the sump with reference to Section 7.

31 Refit and tension the auxiliary drivebelt with reference to Chapter 1.

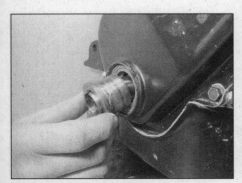

5.28 Refit the crankshaft pulley hub . . .

5.29a . . . followed by the pulley . . .

5.29b . . . and retaining bolt

6.6 Disconnecting the water temperature sender lead

6.7a Slacken the alternator mountings, and slip the drivebelt off the pulleys

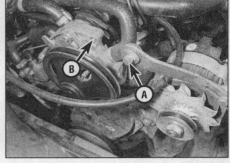

6.7b Unscrew the bolt (A) and remove the alternator adjustment arm from the pump at (B)

6 Cylinder head - removal and refitting

Note: A new cylinder head gasket and a new valve cover gasket must be used on refitting.

Removal

1 Disconnect both battery leads, referring to Chapter 12 if necessary.
2 Drain the cooling system, including the cylinder block, with reference to Chapter 1. The block drain plug is located on the crankshaft pulley end of the engine, beneath the water pump. It is important to drain the block as, if the wet cylinder liners are disturbed, the coolant will drain into the sump.

6.14 Removing the cable-and-hose guide

3 Drain the engine oil with reference to Chapter 1.
4 Remove the air cleaner with reference to Chapter 4.
5 Disconnect the HT leads at the spark plugs, release the distributor cap retaining clips or screws, and remove the cap and leads.
6 Disconnect the wiring at the water temperature gauge sender on the water pump (see illustration). Label the wire, to ensure correct refitting.
7 Slacken the alternator mountings and adjustment arm bolt, push the alternator in towards the engine, and slip the drivebelt off the pulleys. Unscrew the bolt securing the alternator adjustment arm to the water pump, and swing the alternator clear of the engine (see illustrations).
8 Release the hose clips, and disconnect the coolant hoses from the water pump, noting their locations. Also remove the support bracket from the valve cover, where applicable.
9 Disconnect the accelerator cable and (on carburettor models) the choke cable, with reference to Chapter 4 if necessary.
10 Disconnect all electrical wiring from the sensors, switches and actuators located in the cylinder head, carburettor/throttle housing (as applicable), and inlet manifold. Identify each wire with adhesive tags if necessary, to ensure correct refitting.
11 Similarly, loosen the clips, where applicable, and disconnect all coolant, vacuum and breather hoses from the cylinder

head, carburettor/throttle housing and inlet manifold. Again, identify each hose to ensure correct refitting. Disconnect the fuel hoses from the carburettor/throttle housing, with reference to Chapter 4. Plug the open ends of the hoses and the carburettor/throttle housing, to prevent dirt ingress and fuel spillage.

⚠️ Warning: On fuel injection models, the fuel system should be depressurised as described in Chapter 4B before attempting to disconnect the fuel hoses.

12 Unscrew the nut and washer on the inlet manifold and on the cylinder block, and lift off the heat shield, where fitted.
13 Disconnect the distributor wiring.
14 Unscrew the bolt, and release the retaining clip securing the cable-and-hose guide to the side of the cylinder head (see illustration).
15 Unscrew the two bolts, and withdraw the tension springs securing the exhaust front section to the manifold.
16 Unscrew the nuts and remove the valve cover, complete with gasket, from the cylinder head (see illustration).
17 Progressively unscrew the two bolts and two nuts securing the rocker shaft pedestals to the cylinder head. Lift the rocker shaft assembly upwards and off the two studs (see illustration).
18 Lift out each of the pushrods in turn, using a twisting action to release them from their cam followers (see illustration). Keep them in strict order of removal by inserting them in a

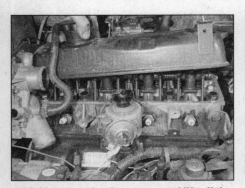

6.16 Unscrew the three nuts and lift off the valve cover

6.17 Unscrew the two nuts and two bolts (arrowed) and withdraw the rocker shaft

6.18 Take out the pushrods, and keep them in order

6.21 Free the cylinder head from the gasket, then lift the head, complete with manifolds and water pump, off the engine

6.27 Place the cylinder head gasket in position

6.28a Lower the cylinder head onto the gasket and . . .

strip of cardboard having eight numbered holes punched in it. Note that No 1 should be the pushrod nearest the transmission end of the engine.

19 Slacken all the cylinder head retaining bolts half a turn at a time, in the reverse order to that shown in illustration 6.28c. When the tension has been relieved, remove all the bolts, with the exception of the centre bolt on the distributor side.

20 Using a hide or plastic mallet, tap each end of the cylinder head so as to pivot the head around the remaining locating bolt and unstick the gasket. *Do not* attempt to lift the head until the gasket has been unstuck, otherwise the seal at the base of each cylinder liner will be broken, allowing water and foreign matter to enter the sump.

21 After unsticking the cylinder head from the gasket, remove the remaining bolt and lift the head, complete with water pump, manifolds and carburettor/throttle housing, off the engine **(see illustration)**. Note: *The crankshaft must not be rotated with the head removed, otherwise the liners will be displaced. If it is necessary to turn the engine (eg to clean the piston crowns), use liner clamps (or suitable bolts and washers) screwed into the top of the block to retain the liners. If the condition of the liner seals is in any doubt, they must be renewed with reference to Chapter 2D.*

Inspection

22 The mating faces of the cylinder head and block must be perfectly clean before refitting

the head. Use a scraper to remove all traces of gasket and carbon, and also clean the tops of the pistons (clamp the cylinder liners before turning the engine). Take particular care with the aluminium cylinder head, as the soft metal is damaged easily. Also, make sure that the carbon is not allowed to enter the oil and water channels - this is particularly important for the oil circuit, as carbon could block the oil supply to the camshaft, rocker shaft, rocker arms or crankshaft bearings. Using adhesive tape and paper, seal the water, oil and bolt holes in the cylinder block.Clean the piston crowns in the same way.

> **HAYNES HINT** *To prevent carbon entering the gap between the pistons and bores, smear a little grease in the gap. After cleaning the piston, rotate the crankshaft so that the piston moves down the bore, then wipe out the grease and carbon with a cloth rag.*

23 Check the block and head for nicks, deep scratches and other damage. If slight, they may be removed carefully with a file; however, if excessive, machining may be the only alternative.

24 If warpage of the cylinder head is suspected, use a straight-edge to check it for distortion. Refer to Chapter 2D if necessary.

25 Clean out all the bolt holes in the block using pipe cleaners or a rag and a screwdriver. Make sure that all oil is removed, otherwise there is a possibility of the block being cracked

by hydraulic pressure when the bolts are tightened.

26 Examine the bolt threads and the threads in the cylinder block for damage. If necessary, use the correct-size tap to chase out the threads in the block. Use a die to clean the threads on the bolts.

Refitting

27 Remove the cylinder liner clamps or washers, and make sure that the faces of the cylinder head and the cylinder block are perfectly clean. Lay a new gasket on the cylinder block with the words "Haut-Top" uppermost. Do not use any kind of jointing compound **(see illustration)**.

28 Lower the cylinder head into position. Insert the cylinder head bolts, and tighten them progressively to the Stage 1 specified torque in the sequence shown **(see illustrations)**.

29 Install the pushrods in their original locations.

30 Lower the rocker shaft assembly onto the cylinder head, making sure that the adjusting ball-ends locate in the pushrods **(see illustration)**. Install the spring washers (convex side uppermost), nuts and bolts, and tighten them progressively to the specified torque.

31 Adjust the valve clearances as described in Section 4.

32 Refit the valve cover using a new gasket, and tighten the nuts.

33 Connect the exhaust front section to the

6.28b . . . fit the retaining bolts; tighten in the correct sequence to the specified torque

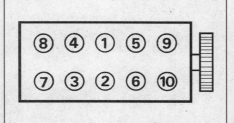

6.28c Cylinder head bolt tightening sequence - C-type engines

6.30 Refit the rocker shaft assembly

manifold, then refit the tension springs and tighten the bolts. Refer to Chapter 4 if necessary.

34 Refit the cable-and-hose guide to the side of the cylinder head, and retain with the clip and bolt.

35 Reconnect the distributor wiring.

36 Reconnect all coolant, vacuum and breather hoses, ensuring that they are correctly connected as noted before removal. Where applicable, tighten the securing clips.

37 Reconnect the fuel hoses, ensuring that they are refitted to their correct locations as noted before removal.

38 Reconnect all wiring, using the tags fitted before removal to ensure that each wire is correctly positioned.

39 Refit the heat shield (where fitted) and tighten the nut.

40 Reconnect the accelerator cable and (on carburettor models) the choke cable, with reference to Chapter 4.

41 Reconnect the radiator top hose to the water pump, and tighten the clip.

42 Fit the support bracket to the valve cover, then reconnect the two heater hoses to the water pump and tighten the clips.

43 Refit the alternator and drivebelt, and adjust the drivebelt tension with reference to Chapter 1.

44 Reconnect the lead to the water temperature gauge sender on the water pump.

45 Refit the distributor cap and leads, and connect the HT leads to the spark plugs.

46 Refit the air cleaner with reference to Chapter 4.

47 Refill the engine with oil with reference to Chapter 1.

48 Refit the cylinder block drain plug, if removed. Refill the cooling system with reference to Chapter 1.

49 Reconnect the battery leads. Run the engine for 20 minutes, then switch off and allow it to cool for at least two and a half hours. Remove the valve cover.

50 Slacken and retighten each cylinder head bolt in turn to the torque wrench setting given in the Specifications.

51 Recheck the valve clearances, and adjust if necessary. Finally, refit the valve cover.

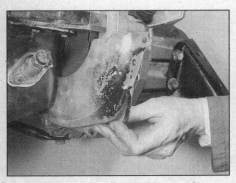

7.5 Remove the flywheel cover plate

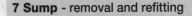

7 Sump - removal and refitting

Note: *A new sump gasket or suitable sealing compound will be required when refitting - see text.*

Removal

1 Disconnect the battery negative and positive leads.

2 Apply the handbrake, then jack up the front of the vehicle and support it securely on axle stands (see *"Jacking, towing and wheel changing"*).

3 Where fitted, remove the splash shield, then unscrew the two bolts, noting the position of the spacer, and remove the engine steady rod.

4 Drain the engine oil as described in Chapter 1, then refit and tighten the drain plug, using a new washer.

5 Unscrew the bolts, and remove the flywheel cover plate from the bellhousing **(see illustration)**.

6 Where fitted, disconnect the two wires at the oil level sensor on the front face of the sump.

7 Unscrew and remove the bolts securing the sump to the cylinder block **(see illustration)**.

8 Tap the sump with a hide or plastic mallet to break the seal between the sump flange, crankcase and timing cover. Lower the sump, and remove the gaskets and rubber seals (where fitted). On some models, a gasket is not used, only a sealing compound.

Refitting

9 Check that the mating faces of the sump, timing cover and cylinder block are perfectly clean and dry.

10 Where gaskets are fitted, first locate the rubber seals in the curved sections of the sump. These seals locate on the front timing cover and rear main bearing cap. Apply a little CAF 4/60 THIXO paste to the ends of the side gaskets, then locate them on the sump so that their ends are over the rubber seals.

11 Where gaskets are not used, apply a 3 mm diameter bead of CAF 4/60 THIXO paste on the sump as shown, adding an extra amount

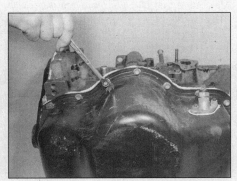

7.7 Unscrew the retaining bolts and remove the sump

at each of the four corners **(see illustration)**. Where a rubber seal is fitted instead of the previous cork type, do not apply the paste in the hatched area. Do not apply excessive paste, otherwise it may find its way into the lubrication circuit and cause damage to the engine.

12 If no gaskets are fitted, it is important that the sump is positioned correctly on refitting, and not moved around after the paste has touched the crankcase. Long bolts or dowel rods may be fitted temporarily to help achieve this.

13 To prevent oil dripping from the oil pump and crankcase, wipe these areas clean before refitting the sump.

14 Lift the sump into position, then insert the bolts and tighten them progressively until they are secure.

15 Reconnect the two wires at the oil level sensor on the front face of the sump, where applicable.

16 Refit the flywheel/driveplate cover plate to the bellhousing, and tighten the bolts.

17 Fill the engine with oil, with reference to Chapter 1.

18 Refit the engine steady rod and splash shield, and tighten the bolts.

19 Lower the vehicle to the ground.

20 Reconnect the battery.

8 Oil pump - removal, inspection and refitting

Removal

1 Remove the sump as described in Section 7.

2 Unscrew the mounting bolts, and withdraw the oil pump from the crankcase and drivegear **(see illustration)**.

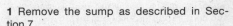

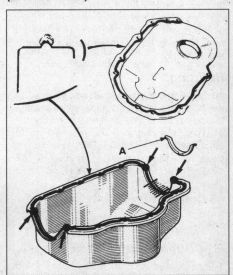

7.11 Sealing paste application diagram for the sump and timing cover

A Alternative rubber seal - if used, do not apply sealing paste to the hatched area shown

8.2 Unscrew the retaining bolts and withdraw the oil pump

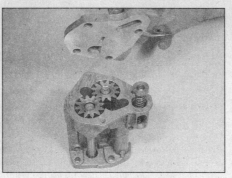

8.4 Lift off the oil pump cover

8.5a Remove the pressure relief valve ball seat and ball (arrowed) . . .

Inspection

3 Clean the exterior of the oil pump.
4 Unscrew the four retaining bolts and lift off the pump cover, taking care not to lose the oil pressure relief valve components, which may be ejected under the action of the spring **(see illustration)**.
5 Remove the pressure relief valve ball seat, ball, spring and spring seat from the pump body **(see illustrations)**.
6 Lift out the idler gear, and the drivegear and shaft (gear-type pump) or the drivegear and rotors (bi-rotor type pump).
7 Clean the components, and carefully examine them for any signs of scoring or wear. Renew the pump if these conditions are apparent. The only spares available are those for the pressure relief valve.
8 If the components appear serviceable, use a feeler blade to measure the clearance between the pump body and the gears, or between the inner and outer rotors **(see illustration)**. If the clearance exceeds the specified amount, the pump must be renewed.
9 If the pump is satisfactory, reassemble the components in the reverse order of removal, fill the pump with oil, and refit the cover. If a new pump is being fitted, prime it with oil before fitting.

Refitting

10 Enter the oil pump shaft into its location in the cylinder block, and engage the shaft with the distributor drivegear **(see illustration)**.
11 Push the pump up into contact with the block, then refit and tighten the three mounting bolts. Note that a gasket is not used.
12 Refit the sump with reference to Section 7.

9 Crankshaft oil seals - renewal

Front/right-hand oil seal

1 This procedure is included in the removal and refitting of the timing cover. Refer to Section 5.

8.5b . . . followed by the spring and spring seat

2 Before refitting the pulley hub, inspect the seal rubbing surface. If it is grooved or rough, renew the hub.

Rear/left-hand oil seal

3 Remove the flywheel as described in Section 10.
4 Prise out the old oil seal using a small screwdriver, taking care not to damage the surface of the crankshaft. Alternatively, the oil seal can be removed by drilling two small holes diagonally opposite each other and inserting self-tapping screws in them. A pair of grips can then be used to pull out the oil seal, by pulling on each screw in turn.
5 Inspect the seal rubbing surface on the crankshaft. If it is grooved or rough in the area where the old seal was fitted, the new seal should be fitted approximately 2 mm less deep, so that it rubs on an unworn part of the surface.
6 Wipe clean the oil seal seating, then dip the new seal in fresh engine oil. Locate it over the crankshaft, with its closed side facing outwards. Make sure that the oil seal lip is not damaged as it is located on the crankshaft.
7 Using a metal tube, drive the oil seal squarely into the bore until flush. A block of wood cut to pass over the end of the crankshaft may be used instead.
8 Refit the flywheel with reference to Section 10.

8.8 Check the gear-to-body clearance using feeler blades

8.10 Refitting the oil pump

10 Flywheel - removal, inspection and refitting

Refer to Chapter 2A, but note that the flywheel securing bolts must be renewed on refitting.

11 Engine mountings - renewal

Refer to Chapter 2A.

2B

Notes

Chapter 2 Part C:
F-type engines (1721 cc, 1764 cc and 1794 cc) – in-car engine repair procedures

Contents

2C

Degrees of difficulty

Easy, suitable for novice with little experience	Fairly easy, suitable for beginner with some experience	Fairly difficult, suitable for competent DIY mechanic	Difficult, suitable for experienced DIY mechanic	Very difficult, suitable for expert DIY or professional

Specifications

General

Type	Four-cylinder, in-line, single (8-valve) or double (16-valve) overhead camshaft
Designation:	
1721 cc carburettor engine	F2N
1721 cc fuel injection engine	F3N
1764 cc (16-valve) engine	F7P
1794 cc engine	F3P
Bore:	
1721 cc (F2N and F3N engines)	81.0 mm
1764 cc (F7P) engine	82.0 mm
1794 cc (F3P) engine	82.7 mm
Stroke (all engines)	83.5 mm
Firing order	1-3-4-2 (No 1 cylinder at transmission end of engine)
Direction of crankshaft rotation	Clockwise, viewed from timing belt end
Compression ratio:	
1721 cc (F2N and F3N engines)	9.5:1
1764 cc (F7P) engine	10.0:1
1794 cc (F3P) engine	
Single-point fuel injection	9.7:1
Multi-point fuel injection	9.8:1
Maximum power output (typical):	
1721 cc (F2N) engine	66.5 kW (92 bhp) at 5750 rpm
1721 cc (F3N) engine	70.0 kW (95 bhp) at 5750 rpm
1764 cc (F7P) engine	102 kW (137 bhp) at 6500 rpm
1794 cc (F3P) engine:	
Single-point fuel injection	68.5 kW (95 bhp) at 5750 rpm
Multi-point fuel injection	81.0 kW (113 bhp) at 5500 rpm

Maximum torque (typical):

1721 cc (F2N) engine	135 Nm (100 lbf ft) at 3000 rpm
1721 cc (F3N) engine	No information available at time of writing
1764 cc (F7P) engine	158 Nm (116 lbf ft) at 4250 rpm
1794 cc (F3P) engine:	
Single-point fuel injection	142 Nm (105 lbf ft) at 2750 rpm
Multi-point fuel injection	160 Nm (118 lbf ft) at 4250 rpm

Camshaft

Drive	Toothed belt
Number of bearings	5
Camshaft endfloat:	
All engines except 1764 cc (F7P)	0.048 to 0.133 mm
1764 cc (F7P) engine	Not stated

Valve clearances

All engines except 1764 cc (F7P):	
Inlet	0.20 mm
Exhaust	0.40 mm
1764 cc (F7P) engine	Not adjustable (hydraulic tappets)

Auxiliary shaft

Endfloat	0.07 to 0.15 mm

Lubrication system

System pressure:	
At 1000 rpm	2.0 bars
At 3000 rpm	3.5 bars
Oil pump type	Two-gear
Oil pump clearances:	
Gear-to-body (minimum)	0.10 mm
Gear-to-body (maximum)	0.24 mm
Gear endfloat (minimum)	0.02 mm
Gear endfloat (maximum)	0.085 mm

Torque wrench settings

	Nm	lbf ft
Camshaft sprocket	50	37
Camshaft bearing caps:		
8 mm diameter bolts (all except 1764 cc/F7P engine)	20	15
8 mm diameter bolts (1764 cc/F7P engine)	24	18
6 mm diameter bolts	10	7
Timing belt idler wheel bolts	20	15
Timing belt tensioner roller nut:		
All except 1764 cc/F7P engines	40	30
1764 cc/F7P engine	48	35
Auxiliary shaft sprocket bolt	50	37
Crankshaft pulley bolt:		
All except 1764 cc/F7P engines	90 to 100	66 to 74
1764 cc/F7P engine	90	66
Oil pump cover:		
6 mm diameter bolts	10	7
8 mm diameter bolts	20 to 25	15 to 18
Connecting rod (big-end) caps	45 to 50	33 to 37
Sump bolts	12 to 15	9 to 11
Flywheel/driveplate bolts*	50 to 55	37 to 41
Valve cover nuts/bolts	3 to 6	2 to 4
Main bearing caps	60 to 65	44 to 48
Cylinder head bolts:		
All except 1764 cc/F7P engine:		
Stage 1	30	22
Stage 2	70	52
Stage 3	Wait for 3 minutes minimum	
Stage 4	Loosen all the bolts completely	
Stage 5	20	15
Stage 6	Angle-tighten by 123° ± 2°	
1764 cc/F7P engine:		
Stage 1	30	22
Stage 2	50	37
Stage 3	Wait for 3 minutes minimum	
Stage 4	Loosen all the bolts completely	
Stage 5	25	18
Stage 6	Angle-tighten by 107° ± 2°	

*Note: Use new bolts.

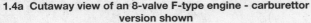

1.4a Cutaway view of an 8-valve F-type engine - carburettor version shown

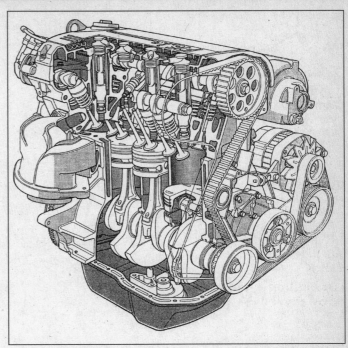

1.4b Cutaway view of the 16-valve F-type engine

2C

1 General information

How to use this Chapter

This Part of Chapter 2 is devoted to in-car repair procedures for the F-type engines. Similar information covering the E-type engines will be found in Chapter 2A, and information for C-type engines will be found in Chapter 2B. All procedures concerning engine removal and refitting, and engine block/cylinder head overhaul for all engine types can be found in Chapter 2D.

Refer to the *"Buying spare parts and vehicle identification numbers"* Section at the beginning of this manual for details of engine code locations.

Most of the operations included in Chapter 2C are based on the assumption that the engine is still installed in the car. Therefore, if this information is being used during a complete engine overhaul, with the engine already removed, many of the steps included here will not apply.

Engine description

The engine is of four-cylinder, in-line, single overhead camshaft (8-valve) or double overhead camshaft (16-valve) type, mounted transversely at the front of the vehicle **(see illustrations)**.

The crankshaft is supported in five shell-type main bearings. Thrustwashers are fitted to No 2 main bearing to control crankshaft endfloat.

The connecting rods are attached to the crankshaft by horizontally-split shell-type big-end bearings, and to the pistons by gudgeon pins. The gudgeon pins are a press fit in the connecting rods on all engines except the 1764 cc (F7P/16-valve) engine. On the 1764 cc (F7P/16-valve) engine, the gudgeon pins are fully-floating and are retained by circlips. The aluminium alloy pistons are of the slipper type, and are fitted with three piston rings - two compression rings and a scraper-type oil control ring.

The single overhead camshaft (8-valve engines) or double overhead camshafts (16-valve engine) are mounted directly in the cylinder head, and are driven by the crankshaft via a toothed timing belt.

On the 8-valve engines, the camshaft operates the valves via inverted bucket-type tappets, which operate in bores machined directly in the cylinder head. Valve clearance adjustment is by shims located externally between the tappet bucket and the cam lobe. The inlet and exhaust valves are mounted vertically in the cylinder head, and are each closed by a single valve spring.

On the 16-valve engine, the camshafts operate the valves via hydraulic tappets, which operate in bores machined directly in the cylinder head. Valve clearances are adjusted automatically. The inlet valves are inclined to the front of the engine, and are operated by the front (inlet) camshaft. The exhaust valves are inclined to the rear of the engine, and are operated by the rear (exhaust) camshaft. Each cylinder has four valves, two inlet and two exhaust, and each pair of valves operates simultaneously.

An auxiliary shaft located alongside the crankshaft is also driven by the timing belt, and actuates the oil pump via a skew gear.

A semi-closed crankcase ventilation system is employed; crankcase fumes are drawn from an oil separator on the cylinder block, and passed via a hose to the inlet manifold.

Engine lubrication is by pressure feed from a gear-type oil pump located beneath the crankshaft. Engine oil is fed through an externally-mounted oil filter to the main oil gallery feeding the crankshaft, auxiliary shaft and camshaft(s). On the 16-valve engine, oil jets at the bottom of the cylinders spray cooling oil into the pistons. Certain models are fitted with an oil cooler mounted between the oil filter and the cylinder block **(see illustrations)**.

The distributor rotor is driven directly from the left-hand end of the camshaft (rear/exhaust camshaft on 16-valve engines). On carburettor models, the fuel pump is driven by an eccentric and plunger from the camshaft. On fuel injection models, an electric fuel pump is used.

Repair operations possible with the engine in the vehicle

The following operations can be carried out without having to remove the engine from the vehicle:

(a) Removal and refitting of the cylinder head.
(b) Removal and refitting of the timing belt and sprockets.
(c) Renewal of the camshaft oil seal(s).
(d) Removal and refitting of the camshaft(s).

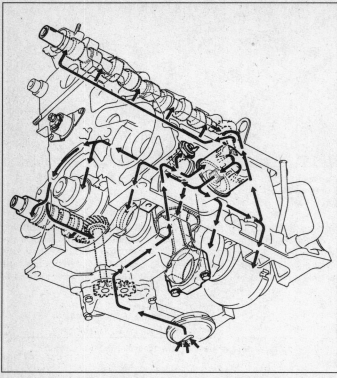

1.12a Lubrication circuit on an 8-valve F-type engine

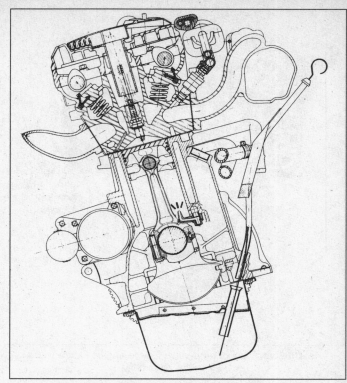

1.12b Lubrication circuit on a 16-valve F-type engine

(e) Removal and refitting of the sump.
(f) Removal and refitting of the connecting rods and pistons*.
(g) Removal and refitting of the oil pump.
(h) Renewal of the crankshaft oil seals.
(i) Renewal of the engine mountings.
(j) Removal and refitting of the flywheel.
(k) Removal and refitting of the auxiliary shaft (on certain models, this may not be possible with the engine in the vehicle, due to limited access).

* Although the operation marked with an asterisk can be carried out with the engine in the car after removal of the sump, it is better for the engine to be removed, in the interests of cleanliness and improved access. For this reason, the procedure is described in Chapter 2D.

2 Compression test - description and interpretation

Refer to Chapter 2A.

3 Top dead centre (TDC) for No 1 piston - locating

1 Top dead centre (TDC) is the highest point in the cylinder that each piston reaches as the crankshaft turns. Each piston reaches TDC at the end of the compression stroke and again at the end of the exhaust stroke. However, for the purpose of timing the engine, TDC refers to the position of No 1 piston at the end of its compression stroke. On all engines in this manual, No 1 piston (and cylinder) is at the transmission end of the engine.

Basic procedure

2 Disconnect both battery leads.
3 Apply the handbrake, then jack up the front right-hand side of the vehicle and support it securely on axle stands (see "Jacking, towing and wheel changing"). Remove the right-hand roadwheel.
4 Remove the plastic cover from within the right-hand wheel arch, to gain access to the crankshaft pulley bolt. On the 16-valve engine, unbolt and remove the lower timing cover, as this covers the pulley completely.
5 Remove the spark plugs with reference to Chapter 1.

3.9a Releasing a timing cover clip - 1721 cc (F2N) carburettor engine

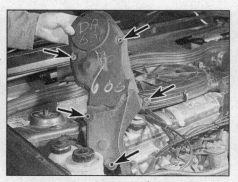

3.9b Removing the timing cover - 1721 cc (F2N) carburettor engine (securing bolt locations arrowed)

3.9c Camshaft sprocket mark aligned with TDC pointer on outer timing belt cover

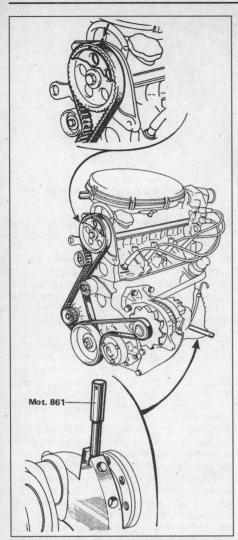

3.10c Timing mark on camshaft sprocket (A) aligned with mark on valve cover (B) - 16-valve F-type engine

4.5 Removing the valve cover

2C

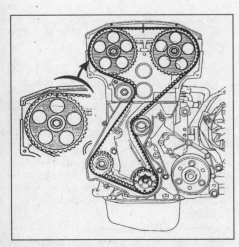

3.10a TDC setting on the 8-valve F-type engine

Mot 861 TDC setting rod - see text

3.10b TDC setting on the 16-valve F-type engine

Mot. 861

6 Place a finger over the No 1 spark plug hole (No 1 is at the transmission end of the engine) in the cylinder head. Turn the engine in a clockwise direction, using a socket on the crankshaft pulley bolt, until pressure is felt in the No 1 cylinder. This indicates that No 1 piston is rising on its compression stroke. On the 16-valve engine, due to the deep recess of the spark plugs in the cylinder head, it will not be possible to place a finger over the spark plug hole; a length of wooden dowel rounded at one end may be used instead, or the spark plug held loosely over the spark plug hole.

7 Remove the air cleaner assembly as described in Chapter 4.

8 Look through the aperture at the transmission end of the engine, and continue turning the crankshaft until the timing mark on the flywheel/driveplate is aligned with the TDC mark on the transmission bellhousing.

Camshaft sprocket timing marks

9 To view the camshaft sprocket timing marks on most later models, it is necessary to unscrew the securing bolts and release the clips (where applicable), and remove the outer timing belt cover. Note that on some early models, it may be possible to align the sprocket mark with a pointer on the outer timing belt cover **(see illustrations)**.

10 Check that the TDC mark(s) on the camshaft sprocket(s) are aligned with the TDC mark on the outer or rear timing belt cover, or the end of the valve cover, as applicable **(see illustrations)**.

11 If the distributor cap is now removed, the rotor arm should be in alignment with the No 1 HT lead segment.

TDC setting plug

12 It is possible to lock the crankshaft in the TDC position as follows.

13 Remove the plug on the lower front-facing side of the engine, at the transmission end, and obtain a metal rod which is a snug fit in the plug hole. Turn the crankshaft slightly if necessary to the TDC position, then push the rod through the hole to locate in the slot in the crankshaft web. Make sure that the crankshaft is exactly at TDC for No 1 piston (transmission end) by aligning the timing notch on the

flywheel/driveplate with the corresponding mark on the transmission bellhousing. If the crankshaft is not positioned accurately, it is possible to engage the rod with a balance hole in the crankshaft web by mistake, instead of the TDC slot (see illustration 3.10a).

4 Valve clearances (8-valve engines only) - adjustment

Note: *This operation is not part of the maintenance schedule. It should be undertaken if noise from the valvegear becomes evident, or if loss of performance gives cause to suspect that the clearances may be incorrect. A new valve cover gasket may be required on refitting.*

1 On carburettor models, remove the air cleaner as described in Chapter 4. Also unbolt the fuel vapour separator from the front of the engine, but leave the hoses connected.

2 On 1721 cc (F3N) engines with multi-point fuel injection, remove the air inlet plenum chamber as described in Chapter 4B.

3 Where applicable, disconnect the crankcase ventilation hose from the valve cover. Also, where applicable, disconnect the air ducting from the cooling fan shroud and the carburettor/throttle body/fuel rail assembly (as applicable).

4 If desired, for improved access on certain models, disconnect the accelerator cable from the throttle housing, and move the cable to one side, clear of the cylinder head.

5 Unscrew the nuts from the valve cover, and withdraw the cover from the engine **(see illustration)**. Where applicable, lift the fuel pipe cluster slightly before removing the cover. Remove the gasket.

6 Remove the spark plugs with reference to Chapter 1, in order to make turning the engine easier.

7 Draw the valve positions on a piece of paper, numbering them 1 to 8 from the transmission end of the engine. Identify them as inlet or exhaust (ie 1E, 2I, 3E, 4I, 5I, 6E, 7I, 8E) **(see illustration)**.

8 Using a socket or spanner on the crankshaft pulley bolt, turn the engine until the valves of No 1 cylinder (transmission end) are "rocking". The exhaust valve will be closing, and the inlet

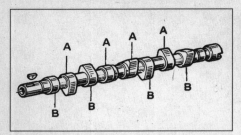

4.7 Cam lobe identification on the 8-valve engine

A Inlet   B Exhaust

4.9 Measuring a valve clearance

4.11 Shim thickness engraved on the underside

valve will be opening. The piston of No 4 cylinder will be at the top of its compression stroke, with both valves fully closed. The clearances for both valves of No 4 cylinder may be checked at the same time.

9 Insert a feeler blade of the correct thickness (see Specifications) between the cam lobe and the shim on the top of the tappet bucket, and check that it is a firm sliding fit **(see illustration)**. If it is not, use the feeler blades to ascertain the exact clearance, and record this for use when calculating the new shim thickness required. Note that the inlet and exhaust valve clearances are different (see Specifications).

10 With No 4 cylinder valve clearances checked, turn the engine through half a turn so that No 3 valves are "rocking", then check the valve clearances of No 2 cylinder in the same way. Similarly check the remaining valve clearances in the following sequence:

Valves rocking on cylinder	Check clearances on cylinder
1	4
3	2
4	1
2	3

11 Where a valve clearance differs from the specified value, then the shim for that valve must be replaced with a thinner or thicker shim accordingly. The shim size is stamped on the bottom face of the shim **(see illustration)**; however, it is prudent to use a micrometer to measure the true thickness of any shim removed, as it may have been reduced by wear.

12 The size of shim required is calculated as follows. If the measured clearance is less than specified, subtract the measured clearance from the specified clearance, and deduct the result from the thickness of the existing shim. For example:

Sample calculation - clearance too small
Clearance measured (A) = 0.15 mm
Desired clearance (B) = 0.20 mm
Difference (B - A) = 0.05 mm
Shim thickness fitted = 3.70 mm
Shim thickness required = 3.70 - 0.05 = 3.65 mm

13 If the measured clearance is greater than specified, subtract the specified clearance from the measured clearance, and add the result to the thickness of the existing shim. For example:

Sample calculation - clearance too big
Clearance measured (A) = 0.50 mm
Desired clearance (B) = 0.40 mm
Difference (A - B) = 0.10 mm
Shim thickness fitted = 3.45 mm
Shim thickness required = 3.45 + 0.10 = 3.55 mm

14 The shims can be removed from their locations on top of the tappet buckets without removing the camshaft if the Renault tool shown can be borrowed, or a suitable alternative fabricated **(see illustration)**. On carburettor models, the fuel pump must also be removed if the tool is being used.

15 To remove the shim, the tappet bucket has to be pressed down against valve spring pressure, just far enough to allow the shim to be slid out. Theoretically, this could be done by levering against the camshaft between the cam lobes with a suitable pad to push the bucket down, but this is not recommended by the manufacturers.

16 An arrangement similar to the Renault tool can be made by bolting a bar to the camshaft bearing studs, and levering down against this with a stout screwdriver. The contact pad should be a triangular-shaped metal block, with a lip filed along each side to contact the

edge of the buckets. Levering down against this will open the valve and allow the shim to be withdrawn.

17 Make sure that the cam lobe peaks are uppermost when depressing a tappet, and rotate the buckets so that the notches are at right-angles to the camshaft centre-line. When refitting the shims, ensure that the size markings face the tappet buckets (ie face downwards).

18 If the Renault tool cannot be borrowed or a suitable alternative made up, then it will be necessary to remove the camshaft to gain access to the shims, as described in Section 9.

19 Remove the socket or spanner from the crankshaft pulley bolt.

20 Refit the spark plugs with reference to Chapter 1, then refit the valve cover, together with a new gasket where necessary.

21 On 1721 cc (F3N) engines with multi-point fuel injection, refit the air inlet plenum chamber with reference to Chapter 4.

22 Where applicable, reconnect the accelerator cable to the throttle housing.

23 Reconnect the crankcase ventilation hose and fuel pipe cluster (where fitted). Refit the fuel vapour separator, air cleaner and air ducting, as applicable.

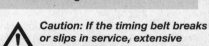

5 Timing belt (8-valve engines) - removal, inspection and refitting

⚠️ *Caution: If the timing belt breaks or slips in service, extensive engine damage may result. Renew the belt at the intervals specified in Chapter 1, or earlier if its condition is at all doubtful.*

Note: *A suitable tool will be required to check the timing belt tension on completion of refitting - see text. A suitable puller may be required to remove the crankshaft pulley.*

Removal

1 Disconnect both battery leads.

2 Remove the auxiliary drivebelt(s) as described in Chapter 1.

3 Remove the securing screws, and where

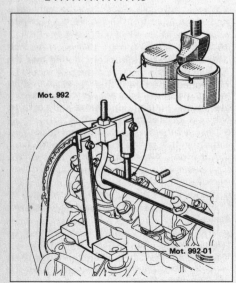

4.14 Renault tool for compressing tappet buckets to change tappet shims

Fit with notches (A) at right-angles to the camshaft

5.12a Timing belt, viewed with the engine removed from the car

5.12b Arrows on timing belt show running direction

5.19 Timing belt run on the 8-valve engine, showing alignment of lines on belt with camshaft and crankshaft sprocket backplate marks

1 *Crankshaft pulley*
2 *Auxiliary shaft sprocket*
3 *Camshaft sprocket*
A *Arrows showing belt running direction*
B *Point to check timing belt tension*

2C

applicable release the spring clips, and lift off the timing belt cover.

4 Apply the handbrake, then jack up the front right-hand side of the vehicle and support it securely on axle stands (see *"Jacking, towing and wheel changing"*). Remove the roadwheel.

5 Remove the plastic cover from within the right-hand wheelarch, to gain access to the crankshaft pulley.

6 Turn the engine in a clockwise direction, using a socket on the crankshaft pulley bolt, until the TDC mark on the camshaft sprocket is uppermost, and in line with the corresponding mark or notch on the rear timing belt cover or the valve cover (as applicable). Note that on some early models, it may be possible to align the sprocket mark with a pointer on the outer timing belt cover.

7 For improved access on fuel injection models, remove the air cleaner assembly, as described in Chapter 4.

8 Unscrew the crankshaft pulley bolt while holding the crankshaft stationary. To do this, have an assistant insert a screwdriver in the starter ring gear teeth through the access hole in the top of the transmission bellhousing. Take care not to damage the engine speed/position sensor.

9 Remove the crankshaft pulley from the nose of the crankshaft. If it is tight, use a suitable puller.

10 Remove the plug on the lower front-facing side of the engine, at the transmission end, and obtain a metal rod which is a snug fit in the plug hole. Turn the crankshaft slightly as necessary to the TDC position, then push the rod through the hole to locate in the slot in the

crankshaft web. Make sure that the crankshaft is exactly at TDC for No 1 piston (transmission end) by aligning the timing notch on the flywheel/driveplate with the corresponding mark on the transmission bellhousing. If the crankshaft is not positioned accurately, it is possible to engage the rod with a balance hole in the crankshaft web, which is not the TDC slot.

11 Double-check that the camshaft sprocket timing mark is aligned with the corresponding mark on the timing belt rear cover, or the valve cover (as applicable).

12 Check if the belt is marked with arrows to indicate its running direction, and if necessary, mark it **(see illustrations)**.

13 Loosen the nut, turn the timing belt tensioner clockwise to relieve the tension from the belt, and re-tighten the nut.

14 Release the belt from the camshaft sprocket, idler wheel, auxiliary shaft sprocket and crankshaft sprocket, and remove it from the engine.

15 Clean the sprockets and tensioners, and wipe them dry. Do not apply excessive amounts of solvent to the tensioner wheels, otherwise the bearing lubricant may be contaminated. Also clean the front of the cylinder head and block.

Inspection

16 Examine the timing belt carefully for any signs of cracking, fraying or general wear, particularly at the roots of the teeth. Renew the belt if there is any sign of deterioration of this nature, or if there is any oil or grease contamination. The belt must, of course, be

renewed if it has completed the maximum mileage given in Chapter 1.

Refitting

17 Check that the crankshaft is at the TDC position for No 1 cylinder, and that the crankshaft is locked in this position using the metal rod through the hole in the crankcase, as described previously.

18 Check that the timing mark on the camshaft sprocket is in line with the corresponding mark on the timing belt rear cover or the valve cover, as applicable.

19 Align the timing mark bands on the belt with those on the sprockets, noting that the running direction arrows on the belt should be positioned between the auxiliary shaft sprocket and the idler pulley. The crankshaft sprocket mark is in the form of a notch in its rear guide perimeter. The auxiliary shaft sprocket has no timing mark. Fit the timing belt over the crankshaft sprocket first, then the auxiliary shaft sprocket, followed by the camshaft sprocket **(see illustration)**.

20 Check that all the timing marks are still aligned, then temporarily tension the belt by turning the tensioner pulley anti-clockwise and tightening the retaining nut. As a rough guide to the correct tension, it should just be possible to turn the belt through 90° using a finger and thumb placed approximately midway between the auxiliary shaft sprocket and the idler wheel.

21 Remove the TDC locating rod from the slot in the crankshaft.

22 Refit the crankshaft pulley and the retaining bolt. Prevent the crankshaft turning using the method described previously, and tighten the bolt to the specified torque.

23 Using a socket or spanner on the crankshaft pulley bolt, turn the crankshaft two complete turns in the normal direction of rotation. Return it to the TDC position with No 1 cylinder on compression, and insert the TDC locating rod again.

24 Check that the timing marks are still aligned.

25 The belt deflection must now be checked. To do this, first make a mark on the front of the engine, in line with the outer surface of the timing belt, midway between the auxiliary shaft sprocket and idler wheel. A force of 30 N (7 lbf) must now be applied to the timing belt, and its deflection should be 7.5 mm (0.3 in) with the engine cold. Should the deflection be checked with the engine hot, the deflection should be 5.5 mm (0.22 in). Renault technicians use a special tool to do this, but an alternative arrangement can be made by using a spring balance and steel rule. Apply the force with the spring balance, and read off the deflection on the steel rule (see illustration 5.16b in Chapter 2A).

26 If the tension is incorrect, adjust the tensioner as necessary, then re-tighten the nut to the specified torque. This torque is critical, since if the nut were to come loose, considerable engine damage would result.

27 Remove the TDC locating rod, and refit the plug.

28 Refit the plastic cover to the right-hand wheelarch.

29 Refit the roadwheel, and lower the vehicle to the ground.

30 Refit the timing belt cover, and tighten the bolts. Refit the spring clips, where applicable.

31 Refit and tension the auxiliary drivebelts, with reference to Chapter 1.

32 Where applicable, refit the air cleaner assembly, with reference to Chapter 4.

33 Reconnect both battery leads.

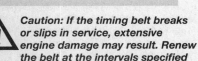

6 Timing belt (16-valve engines) - removal, inspection and refitting

⚠️ *Caution: If the timing belt breaks or slips in service, extensive engine damage may result. Renew the belt at the intervals specified in Chapter 1, or earlier if its condition is at all doubtful.*

Note: *A suitable tool will be required to check the timing belt tension on completion of refitting - see text. A suitable puller may be required to remove the crankshaft pulley.*

Removal

1 Disconnect both battery leads.

2 For improved access, unbolt the strengthening bar from the suspension turrets in the engine compartment.

3 Apply the handbrake, then jack up the front of the vehicle and support it securely on axle stands (see *"Jacking, towing and wheel changing"*). Remove the right-hand roadwheel,

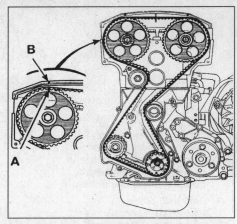

6.7 TDC marks (A) on camshaft sprockets aligned with marks (B) on valve cover - 16-valve engine

and remove the lower plastic cover from the wheel arch for access to the crankshaft pulley.

4 Remove the auxiliary drivebelt with reference to Chapter 1.

5 Slacken the crankshaft pulley bolt while holding the crankshaft stationary. To do this, have an assistant insert a screwdriver in the starter ring gear teeth, through the access hole in the top of the gearbox bellhousing. Take care not to damage the engine speed/position sensor.

6 Where applicable, unclip the hoses from the brackets on the timing belt cover, then unscrew the securing bolts and remove the timing belt cover.

7 Turn the engine in a clockwise direction, using a socket on the crankshaft pulley bolt, until the TDC marks on the camshaft sprockets are uppermost, and in line with the corresponding marks or notches on the valve cover **(see illustration)**.

8 Remove the plug on the lower front-facing side of the engine, at the transmission end, and obtain a metal rod which is a snug fit in the plug hole. Turn the crankshaft slightly as necessary to the TDC position, then push the rod through the hole to locate in the slot in the crankshaft web. Make sure that the crankshaft is exactly at TDC for No 1 piston (transmission end) by aligning the timing notch on the flywheel with the corresponding mark on the gearbox bellhousing. If the crankshaft is not positioned accurately, it is possible to engage the rod with a balance hole in the crankshaft web, which is not the TDC slot.

9 Fully unscrew the crankshaft pulley bolt, and remove the crankshaft pulley from the nose of the crankshaft. If it is tight, use a puller.

10 Double-check that the camshaft sprocket timing marks are aligned with the corresponding marks on the valve cover.

11 Check if the belt is marked with arrows to indicate its running direction; mark it if necessary.

12 Loosen the nut, move the timing belt tensioner bracket out to release the tension from the belt, then retighten the nut **(see illustration)**.

6.12 Timing belt tensioner nut (arrowed) - 16-valve engine

13 Release the belt from the camshaft sprockets, idler wheel, auxiliary shaft sprocket and crankshaft sprocket, and remove it from the engine. Be careful not to kink or otherwise damage it, if it is to be re-used.

14 Clean the sprockets and tensioner wheels, and wipe them dry. Do not apply excessive amounts of solvent to the tensioner wheels, otherwise the bearing lubricant may be contaminated. Also clean the cylinder head and block behind the belt running area. **Note:** *It is advisable not to turn the crankshaft or the camshafts with the timing belt removed, as there may be a risk of the valves contacting the pistons.*

Inspection

15 Refer to paragraph 16 of the previous Section.

Refitting

16 Check that the crankshaft is still at the TDC position for No 1 cylinder, and locked in this position using the metal rod through the hole in the cylinder block.

17 Check that the timing marks on the camshaft sprockets are in line with the corresponding marks or notches on the valve cover.

18 Align the timing mark bands on the belt with those on the sprockets. The crankshaft sprocket mark is in the form of a notch in its rear guide perimeter. The auxiliary shaft sprocket has no timing mark. Fit the timing belt over the crankshaft sprocket first, then the auxiliary shaft sprocket, followed by the camshaft sprockets.

19 Check that all the timing marks are still aligned, then temporarily tension the belt by pivoting the tensioner pulley on its bracket and tightening the retaining nut. As a rough guide to the correct tension, it should just be possible to turn the belt through 90°, using a finger and thumb placed approximately midway between the auxiliary shaft sprocket and the tensioner pulley. The tensioner bracket position may be adjusted using a bolt (diameter 6 mm, length 45 mm) through the special hole next to the tensioner **(see illustration)**.

20 Remove the TDC locating rod from the cylinder block.

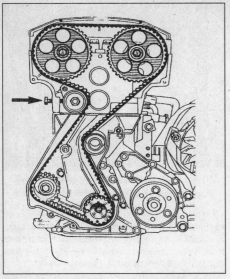

6.19 Using a bolt (arrowed) to adjust the position of the timing belt tensioner bracket - 16-valve engine

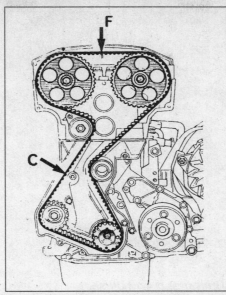

6.24 Checking the timing belt tension - 16-valve engine

C Apply a force of 100 N (22.5 lbf) here
F Deflection at this point should be
3.0 ± 0.5 mm (0.12 ± 0.2 in)

21 Refit the crankshaft pulley and retaining bolt, but do not fully tighten the bolt at this stage.

22 Using a socket or spanner on the crankshaft pulley bolt, turn the crankshaft two complete turns in the normal direction of rotation. On regaining the TDC position with No 1 cylinder on compression, insert the TDC locating rod again.

23 Check that all the timing marks are still aligned.

24 The belt deflection must now be checked. To do this, first make a mark on the valve cover in line with the outer surface of the timing belt, midway between the two camshaft sprockets. Apply a force of approximately 100 N (22.5 lbf) to the timing belt, at the midpoint of the belt run between the auxiliary shaft sprocket and the tensioner pulley; this must produce a deflection of 3.0 mm ± 0.5 mm (0.12 in ± 0.02 in) midway between the camshaft sprockets, with the engine cold (see illustration). Renault technicians use a special tool to do this, but an alternative arrangement

can be made by using a spring balance and steel rule. Apply the force with the spring balance, and read off the deflection on the steel rule.

25 If the tension is incorrect, adjust the tensioner as necessary, then re-tighten the nut to the specified torque. This torque is critical, since if the nut were to come loose, considerable engine damage would result.

26 If the tensioner has been adjusted, repeat the procedure described in paragraphs 21 to 24 inclusive until the correct tension is achieved.

27 Remove the TDC locating rod from the cylinder block, and refit the plug.

28 Prevent the crankshaft from turning as described previously, and tighten the crankshaft pulley bolt to the specified torque.

29 Refit the timing belt cover, and tighten the bolts. Where applicable, clip the hoses into position in the timing belt cover brackets.

30 Refit and tension the auxiliary drivebelt with reference to Chapter 1.

31 Refit the plastic cover inside the wheel arch, then refit the roadwheel and lower the vehicle to the ground.

32 Refit the strengthening bar to the suspension turrets in the engine compartment.

33 Reconnect the battery leads.

7 Timing belt sprockets and tensioners - removal, inspection and refitting

Removal

1 Remove the timing belt as described in Section 5 or 6, as applicable (see illustration).

2 To remove a camshaft sprocket, hold the sprocket stationary using a metal bar with two bolts tightened onto it, inserted into the holes in the sprocket, then unscrew the bolt. Alternatively, an old timing belt may be wrapped around the sprocket and held firm with a pair of grips to hold the sprocket stationary, or a special gear-holding tool may be used (see illustration). Do not allow the camshaft to turn while unscrewing the bolt, or the valves may contact the pistons.

3 Pull the sprocket from the end of the camshaft, if necessary using two levers or screwdrivers. Where applicable, check whether the Woodruff key is likely to drop out of its slot in the camshaft; if so, remove it and store it safely. (There are no keys on the 1764 cc/16-valve engine, as the sprocket incorporates a tab to engage with the camshaft.)

4 The sprocket can be removed from the auxiliary shaft in the same manner (see illustration). Again, check that the Woodruff key is firmly located in the slot in the shaft.

5 A puller may be necessary to remove the crankshaft sprocket. It is a simple matter to make up a puller using two bolts, a metal bar and the existing crankshaft pulley bolt. By unscrewing the crankshaft pulley bolt, the

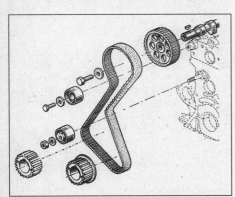

7.1 Timing belt and sprockets - 8-valve engine

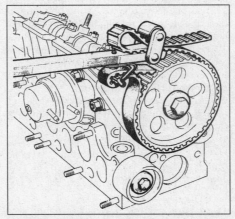

7.2 Method of using an old timing belt to hold the camshaft sprocket stationary while the bolt is being loosened

7.4 Removing the bolt from the auxiliary shaft

7.5 Removing the crankshaft sprocket

7.7 Removing the timing belt lower idler wheel assembly - 8-valve engine

7.14 Using a special tool to hold the auxiliary shaft sprocket stationary while tightening the bolt

sprocket is pulled from the end of the crankshaft. If necessary, remove the Woodruff key from the slot in the crankshaft **(see illustration)**.

6 Unscrew the nut or bolt, and remove the timing belt upper idler wheel or tensioner, as applicable. If necessary, the rear timing belt cover(s) may be unbolted at this stage.

7 Unscrew the nut or bolts, and remove the timing belt lower idler wheel or tensioner as applicable **(see illustration)**.

Inspection

8 Inspect the teeth of the sprockets for signs of nicks and damage. The teeth are not prone to wear, and should normally last the life of the engine.

9 Spin the tensioner and idler wheel by hand, and check for any roughness or tightness. Do not attempt to clean them with solvent, as this may enter the bearings. If wear is evident, renew the tensioner and/or idler wheel as necessary.

Refitting

10 Refit the timing belt idler wheel, and tighten the nut or bolt to the specified torque.

11 Refit the tensioner, but do not tighten the nut at this stage.

12 Where applicable, refit the timing belt rear cover(s), and tighten the bolts.

13 Check that the Woodruff key is located in the crankshaft slot, then slide on the sprocket. Use a suitable piece of metal tube to tap it fully home.

14 Check that the Woodruff key is located in the auxiliary shaft slot, then slide on the sprocket. Again, use a metal tube to tap it home, if necessary. Apply a little locking fluid to the bolt threads. Fit the bolt and washer, and tighten the bolt to the specified torque, holding the sprocket using one of the methods described in paragraph 2 **(see illustration)**.

15 Fit and secure the camshaft sprocket(s) in the same way (make sure that the Woodruff key is in place in the camshaft slot, where applicable), being careful not to allow the camshaft to turn while tightening the bolt.

16 Refit the timing belt as described in Section 5 or 6, as applicable.

8 Camshaft oil seals - renewal

Timing belt end oil seal

1 Remove the camshaft sprocket with reference to Section 7.

2 If necessary for improved access, unbolt the rear timing belt cover.

3 Note the fitted depth of the oil seal, then prise it out using a small screwdriver. Be careful not to damage the seating or the camshaft seal rubbing surface.

4 Wipe clean the seating in the cylinder head.

5 Smear a little fresh oil on the outer surface of the new oil seal. Locate the seal squarely in the cylinder head, then drive it into position, using a metal tube of diameter slightly less than that of the bore in the cylinder head. Make sure that the oil seal is the correct way round, with the lips facing inwards.

6 Where applicable, refit the rear timing belt cover.

7 Refit the camshaft sprocket with reference to Section 7.

Distributor end oil seal

8 Remove the distributor cap and rotor arm (Chapter 5). Where applicable, remove the rotor arm shield to expose the oil seal.

9 Prise out the old seal. Fit the new one as described previously for the timing belt end seal.

10 Refit the rotor arm shield (where applicable), rotor arm and distributor cap.

9 Camshaft and tappets (8-valve engines) - removal, inspection and refitting

Note: *New camshaft oil seals, and a new valve cover gasket, must be used on refitting. Suitable sealant will be required for the camshaft bearing caps and the bearing cap bolts.*

Removal

1 On carburettor models, remove the air cleaner as described in Chapter 4A. Also unbolt the fuel vapour separator from the front

of the engine, but leave the hoses connected.

2 On 1721 cc (F3N) engines with multi-point fuel injection, remove the air inlet plenum chamber as described in Chapter 4B.

3 Where applicable, disconnect the crankcase ventilation hose from the valve cover. Also, where applicable, disconnect the air ducting from the cooling fan shroud and the carburettor/throttle body/fuel rail assembly (as applicable).

4 If desired, for improved access on certain models, disconnect the accelerator cable from the throttle housing, and move the cable to one side, clear of the cylinder head.

5 Unscrew the nuts from the valve cover, and withdraw the cover from the engine. Where applicable, lift the fuel pipe cluster slightly before removing the cover. Remove the gasket.

6 Remove the timing belt as described in Section 5.

7 Disconnect the HT leads, and remove the distributor cap and rotor arm (Chapter 5). Where applicable, also remove the rotor arm shield.

8 On carburettor models, remove the fuel pump, as described in Chapter 4A.

9 Remove the camshaft sprocket with reference to Section 7.

10 If necessary for improved access, unbolt the rear timing belt cover.

11 Using a dial gauge, measure the camshaft endfloat, and compare with the value given in the Specifications. This will give an indication of the amount of wear present on the thrust surfaces.

12 Make identifying marks on the camshaft bearing caps, so that they can be refitted in the same positions and the same way round.

13 Progressively slacken the bearing cap bolts until the valve spring pressure is relieved. Remove the bolts, and the bearing caps themselves **(see illustrations)**.

14 Note the position of the cam lobes. The lobes for No 1 cylinder (transmission end) will be pointing upwards. Lift out the camshaft, together with the oil seals.

15 Remove the tappets, keeping each with its shim **(see illustration)**. Place them in a compartmented box, or on a sheet of card marked into eight sections, so that they may be refitted to their original locations. Write

9.13a Camshaft bearing cap and bolts (arrowed)

9.13b Removing the No 1 (flywheel end) camshaft bearing cap

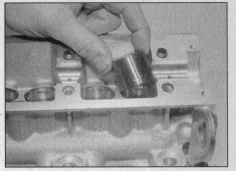
9.15 Removing a tappet

2C

down the shim thicknesses - they will be needed later if any of the valve clearances are incorrect. The shim size is stamped on the bottom face of the shim, but it is prudent to use a micrometer to measure the true thickness of any shim removed, as it may have been reduced by wear.

Inspection

16 Examine the camshaft bearing surfaces, cam lobes (and the fuel pump eccentric, on carburettor engines) for wear ridges, pitting or scoring. Renew the camshaft if evident.

17 Renew the oil seals at the ends of the camshaft as a matter of course. Lubricate the lips of the new seals before fitting them, and store the camshaft so that its weight is not resting on the seals.

18 Examine the camshaft bearing surfaces in the cylinder head and bearing caps. Deep scoring or other damage means that the cylinder head must be renewed.

19 Inspect the tappet buckets and shims for scoring, pitting and wear ridges. Renew as necessary.

Refitting

20 Oil the tappets, and fit them to the bores from which they were removed. Fit the correct shim, numbered side downwards, to each tappet.

21 Oil the camshaft bearings. Place the camshaft with its oil seals onto the cylinder head. The oil seals must be positioned so that they are flush with the cylinder head faces. The cam lobes must be positioned as noted before removal (paragraph 14).

 Caution: If the cam lobes are not positioned correctly, the valves may be forced into the pistons when the bearing caps are tightened.

22 Refit the camshaft bearing caps to their original locations, applying a little sealant to the end caps where they meet the cylinder head.

23 Apply sealant to the threads of the bearing cap bolts. Fit the bolts and tighten them progressively to the specified torque.

24 If a new camshaft has been fitted,

measure the endfloat using a dial gauge, and check that it is within the specified limits.

25 Where applicable, refit the rear timing belt cover.

26 Refit the camshaft sprocket with reference to Section 7.

27 On carburettor models, refit the fuel pump (Chapter 4A).

28 Refit the timing belt with reference to Section 5.

29 Check and adjust the valve clearances as described in Section 4.

30 Refit the valve cover, using a new gasket, and tighten the nuts.

31 Where applicable, reconnect the crankcase ventilation hose to the valve cover, and reconnect the air ducting.

32 On carburettor models, refit the fuel vapour separator to the front of the engine, tighten the bolts, and refit the air cleaner.

33 Where applicable, reconnect the accelerator cable, and adjust it if necessary (Chapter 4).

34 Refit the rotor arm shield (where applicable), rotor arm and distributor cap, with reference to Chapter 5.

35 On 1721 cc (F3N) engines with multi-point fuel injection, refit the air inlet plenum chamber as described in Chapter 4B.

36 Reconnect the HT leads.

10 Camshafts and tappets (16-valve engines) - removal, inspection and refitting

Removal

1 Remove the timing belt as described in Section 6.

2 For improved access, unbolt the strengthening bar from the suspension turrets in the engine compartment.

3 Remove the spark plugs and distributor, with reference to Chapters 1 and 5 respectively.

4 Unbolt the spark plug tube housing from the top of the valve cover.

5 Disconnect the crankcase ventilation hoses, then unbolt the valve cover from the cylinder

head. Remove the double gasket (this may be in two sections, or joined).

6 Remove both camshaft sprockets with reference to Section 7.

7 Using a dial gauge, measure the endfloat of the camshafts. No values were specified at the time of writing, but it is suggested that the value given in the Specifications for the 8-valve engines be used as a guide. This will give an indication of the amount of wear present on the thrust surfaces.

8 Progressively slacken the camshaft bearing housing bolts on both housings until the valve spring pressure is relieved. Remove the bolts and the housings.

9 Note the position of the cam lobes; the lobes for No 1 cylinder (transmission end) will be pointing upwards. Remove the camshafts from the cylinder head, together with the oil seals. It is not necessary to identify them, as the exhaust camshaft has a slot in its end to drive the distributor. Recover the inlet camshaft plug from the cylinder head.

10 Remove the hydraulic tappets, noting which way round they are fitted, and place them in a compartmented box, or on a sheet of card marked into sixteen sections, so that they may be refitted to their original locations. Ideally, they should be placed in a compartmented box filled with engine oil, to prevent the oil draining from them.

Inspection

11 Examine the camshaft bearing surfaces and cam lobes for wear ridges, pitting or scoring. Renew the camshafts if evident.

12 Renew the camshaft oil seals as a matter of course. Lubricate the lips of the new seals before fitting them, and store the camshaft so that its weight is not resting on the seals.

13 Examine the camshaft bearing surfaces in the cylinder head and bearing housings. Deep scoring or other damage means that the cylinder head and bearing housings must be renewed.

14 Examine the hydraulic tappets for scoring, pitting and wear ridges. The tappets should be renewed if they are obviously worn, or if they have been excessively noisy in operation.

15 If new hydraulic tappets are being fitted, or if the old ones have been allowed to drain,

prime them with fresh engine oil before fitting them, as follows. Immerse each tappet in oil with the hole uppermost, and use flat-nosed pliers to move them up and down until all the air is forced out.

Refitting

16 Fit the hydraulic tappets to the bores from which they were removed.

17 Oil the camshaft bearings. Place both camshafts, together with oil seals, onto the cylinder head. The oil seals must be positioned so that they are flush with the cylinder head faces. The cam lobes must be positioned as noted before removal (paragraph 9).

 Caution: If the cam lobes are not positioned correctly, the valves may be forced into the pistons when the bearing caps are tightened.

18 Apply a bead of sealing compound to the housing contact faces on the cylinder head. Also apply the compound to the inlet camshaft end plug, and locate it on the cylinder head.

19 Refit the camshaft bearing housings to their original locations, then insert the bolts and progressively tighten them to the specified torque. Note that the torque is different for 6 mm and 8 mm bolts.

20 If new camshafts have been fitted, measure the endfloat using a dial gauge (see paragraph 7).

21 Refit both camshaft sprockets with reference to Section 7.

22 Refit the valve cover together with new gaskets, and tighten the bolts to the specified torque.

23 Reconnect the crankcase ventilation hoses.

24 Refit the spark plug tube housing to the top of the valve cover, and tighten the bolts.

25 Refit the spark plugs and distributor with reference to Chapters 1 and 5 respectively.

26 Refit the strengthening bar to the suspension turrets.

27 Refit the timing belt with reference to Section 6.

11 Cylinder head (8-valve engines) - removal, inspection and refitting

Removal

1 Disconnect both battery leads.

2 Drain the cooling system with reference to Chapter 1. Also drain the cylinder block by unscrewing the drain plug located on the right-hand rear face of the engine. Refit the plug after draining.

3 Where applicable, remove the air cleaner assembly (carburettor models) or the air box (single-point fuel injection models) from the carburettor or throttle housing.

4 Remove the timing belt with reference to Section 5.

5 Remove the camshaft sprocket with reference to Section 7.

6 Unbolt the rear timing belt cover from the cylinder head.

7 Disconnect the accelerator cable (and on carburettor models, the choke cable) and position them to one side (Chapter 4).

8 Disconnect the exhaust downpipe from the manifold (Chapter 4).

9 If wished, the inlet and exhaust manifolds can be removed at this stage. Otherwise, disconnect the various vacuum and coolant hoses, and electrical feeds from the carburettor or throttle body, and from the inlet manifold (see Chapter 4). Label all hoses and wires before disconnecting them, to avoid confusion when refitting.

10 Similarly, disconnect the fuel hoses from the carburettor, throttle housing, or fuel rail, as applicable.

Warning: On fuel injection models, the fuel system should be depressurised as described in Chapter 4 before attempting to disconnect the fuel hoses. Plug the open ends of the hoses and the unions, to prevent dirt ingress and fuel spillage.

11 Remove the spark plugs and distributor cap, with reference to Chapters 1 and 5 respectively.

12 On carburettor models, unbolt the fuel vapour separator from the front of the engine, leaving the hoses connected.

13 Unscrew the nuts from the valve cover, and withdraw the cover from the cylinder head **(see illustration)**. Where applicable, lift the fuel pipe cluster slightly before removing the cover. Remove the gasket.

14 Disconnect the wiring from all sensors located in the cylinder head, labelling them to avoid confusion when refitting.

15 On carburettor models, disconnect the fuel feed and return pipes at the fuel pump, and plug their ends.

16 Disconnect the heater hoses, and the

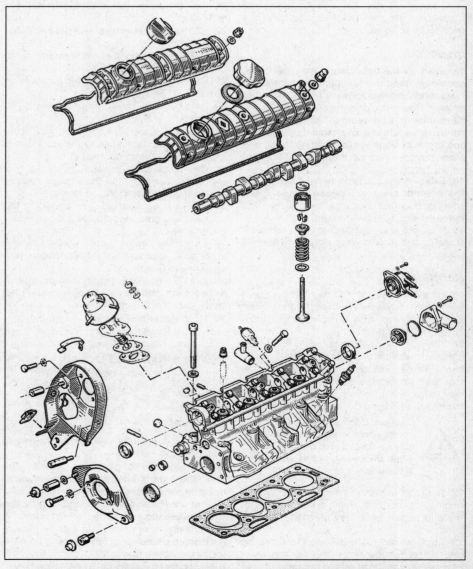

11.13 Exploded view of the cylinder head on the 8-valve engine

crankcase ventilation hoses. Also remove the two nuts securing the support plate to the rear-facing side of the cylinder head, where applicable. Label all hoses, to avoid confusion when refitting.

17 Disconnect the radiator top hose from the thermostat housing.

18 Using a suitable hexagon-headed socket bit, progressively slacken the cylinder head retaining bolts half a turn at a time, in the reverse order to that shown in illustration 11.30. When the tension has been relieved, remove all the bolts.

19 Lift the cylinder head upwards and off the cylinder block. If it is stuck, tap it upwards using a hammer and block of wood. *Do not* try to turn it (it is located by two dowels), nor attempt to prise it free using a screwdriver inserted between the block and head faces.

Inspection

20 The mating faces of the cylinder head and block must be perfectly clean before refitting the head. Use a scraper to remove all traces of gasket and carbon, and also clean the tops of the pistons. Take particular care with the aluminium cylinder head, as the soft metal is damaged easily. Also, make sure that debris is not allowed to enter the oil and water channels - this is particularly important for the oil circuit, as carbon could block the oil supply to the camshaft or crankshaft bearings. Using adhesive tape and paper, seal the water, oil and bolt holes in the cylinder block. Clean the piston crowns in the same way.

 HAYNES HINT *To prevent carbon entering the gap between the pistons and bores, smear a little grease in the gap. After cleaning the piston, rotate the crankshaft so that the piston moves down the bore, then wipe out the grease and carbon with a cloth rag*

21 Check the block and head for nicks, deep scratches and other damage. If slight, they may be removed carefully with a file. More serious damage may be repaired by machining, but this is a specialist job.

22 If warpage of the cylinder head is suspected, use a straight-edge to check it for distortion. Refer to Chapter 2D if necessary.

23 Clean out the bolt holes in the block using a pipe cleaner, or a rag and screwdriver. Make sure that all oil is removed, otherwise there is a possibility of the block being cracked by hydraulic pressure when the bolts are tightened.

24 Examine the bolt threads and the threads in the cylinder block for damage. If necessary, use the correct-size tap to chase out the threads in the block, and use a die to clean the threads on the bolts.

Refitting

25 Ensure that the mating faces of the cylinder block and head are spotlessly clean,

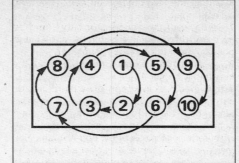

11.30 Cylinder head bolt tightening sequence - 8-valve and 16-valve F-type engines

that the retaining bolt threads are also clean and dry, and that they screw easily in and out of their locations.

26 Check that No 1 piston is still at TDC, and that the camshaft is in the correct position (No 1 cylinder cam lobes pointing upwards).

 Caution: If the camshaft position is wrong, there is a risk of valves being forced into pistons.

27 Fit a new cylinder head gasket to the block, locating it over the dowels. Make sure it is the right way up.

28 Lower the cylinder head onto the block, engaging it over the dowels.

29 Lightly oil the cylinder head bolts, both on their threads and under their heads. Insert the bolts, and tighten them finger-tight.

30 Following the sequence shown **(see illustration)**, tighten the bolts to the torque specified for Stage 1. In the same sequence, tighten to the torque specified for Stage 2.

31 Wait three minutes, then progressively slacken all the bolts in the reverse of the tightening sequence until completely loose (these are Stages 3 and 4).

32 Again following the tightening sequence, tighten the bolts to the torque specified for Stage 5.

33 Final tightening is carried out by turning each bolt through the angle specified for Stage 6. Measure the angle using a commercially-available gauge, or make up a cardboard template cut to the angle required **(see illustration)**. There is no need for retightening after warm-up.

34 Reconnect the radiator top hose to the thermostat housing, and tighten the clip.

35 Reconnect the heater hoses and crankcase ventilation hoses. Also refit the support plate to the rear facing side of the cylinder head, where applicable.

36 On carburettor models, reconnect the fuel feed and return pipes at the fuel pump.

37 Reconnect the wiring to all cylinder-head mounted sensors.

38 Refit the valve cover, using a new gasket, and tighten the nuts.

39 On carburettor models, refit the fuel vapour separator, and tighten the bolts.

40 Refit the spark plugs and distributor cap,

11.33 Angle-tightening the cylinder head bolts

with reference to Chapters 1 and 5 respectively.

41 If they were removed, refit the inlet and exhaust manifolds, with reference to Chapter 4. Otherwise, reconnect the various hoses and wires to the inlet manifold, and to the carburettor or throttle body, as applicable.

42 Reconnect the exhaust downpipe, using a new sealing ring (see Chapter 4).

43 Reconnect the choke cable (when applicable) and the accelerator cable, with reference to Chapter 4.

44 Refit the rear timing belt cover to the cylinder head.

45 Refit the camshaft sprocket with reference to Section 7.

46 Refit the timing belt as described in Section 5.

47 Check the valve clearances if necessary (Section 4).

48 Refit the air cleaner or air box, where applicable.

49 Refill the cooling system with reference to Chapter 1.

50 Reconnect the battery leads.

12 Cylinder head (16-valve engines) - removal, inspection and refitting

Note: *At the time of writing, it was not possible to obtain a vehicle on which to carry out detailed work. It is therefore possible that some differences to the sequence of work described in the following paragraphs may be noted on certain models. It is recommended that notes and, where necessary, sketches are made during removal, where any differences to procedures are noted. A new cylinder head gasket and new valve cover gaskets must be used on refitting.*

Removal

1 Disconnect both battery leads.

2 Drain the cooling system, including the cylinder block, with reference to Chapter 1. The block drain plug is located on the right-hand rear face of the engine.

3 Remove the timing belt as described in Section 6.

2C

12.5 Crankcase ventilation hose connections on the valve cover

4 Disconnect the exhaust downpipe from the manifold (Chapter 4).

5 Disconnect the crankcase ventilation hoses from the valve cover **(see illustration)**.

6 Disconnect the accelerator cable from the throttle housing and the bracket on the end of the cylinder head, and place it to one side. Refer to Chapter 4B if necessary.

7 Remove the spark plugs and distributor cap with reference to Chapters 1 and 5 respectively.

8 If desired, to improve access to the inlet manifold, and to avoid the risk of damage to the radiator matrix, the radiator can be removed as described in Chapter 3.

9 Similarly, if desired, unscrew the mounting screw, and move the power steering fluid reservoir clear of the manifold.

10 If wished, the inlet and exhaust manifolds can be removed at this stage. Otherwise, disconnect the various vacuum, breather and coolant hoses, and electrical feeds from the throttle body, and from the inlet manifold (see Chapter 4). Label all hoses and wires before disconnecting them, to avoid confusion when refitting.

 Warning: The fuel system should be depressurised as described in Chapter 4B before attempting to disconnect the fuel hoses. Plug the open ends of the hoses and unions, to prevent dirt ingress and fuel spillage.

12 Disconnect the wiring from all relevant sensors located in the cylinder head. Again, label all the wires to avoid confusion when refitting.

13 Unbolt the alternator mounting bracket from the inlet manifold.

14 Unbolt the exhaust manifold heat shield.

15 Where applicable, unbolt the starter motor mounting bracket from the exhaust manifold.

16 Where applicable, unbolt the two bracing struts from the bottom of the inlet manifold.

17 Unbolt the spark plug tube housing from the top of the valve cover.

18 Unbolt the valve cover from the cylinder head, and remove the two gaskets **(see illustration)**.

19 Make a final check to ensure that all relevant hoses and wires have been disconnected to facilitate cylinder head

removal. If necessary, disconnect any remaining hoses and wires, labelling them to avoid confusion when refitting.

20 Using a T55 Torx key, progressively unscrew the cylinder head bolts half a turn at a time, in the reverse order to that shown in illustration 11.31. When the tension has been relieved, remove all the bolts.

21 Lift the cylinder head upwards and off the cylinder block. If it is stuck, tap it upwards using a hammer and block of wood. *Do not* try to turn it (it is located by two dowels), nor attempt to prise it free using a screwdriver inserted between the block and head faces.

Inspection

22 Refer to paragraphs 20 to 24 of the previous Section.

Refitting

23 Ensure that the mating faces of the

cylinder block and head are spotlessly clean. The retaining bolt threads should also be clean and dry, and they should screw easily in and out of their locations.

24 Check that No 1 piston is still at TDC (see Section 3). Temporarily refit the valve cover, and align the timing marks on the camshaft sprockets with the marks on the cover.

 Caution: If the camshafts are wrongly positioned, the valves may be forced into the pistons.

25 Fit a new cylinder head gasket to the block, locating it over the dowels. Make sure it is the right way up.

26 Lower the cylinder head onto the block, engaging it over the dowels.

27 Lightly oil the cylinder head bolts, both on their threads and under their heads. Insert the bolts, and tighten them finger-tight.

28 Following the sequence shown in

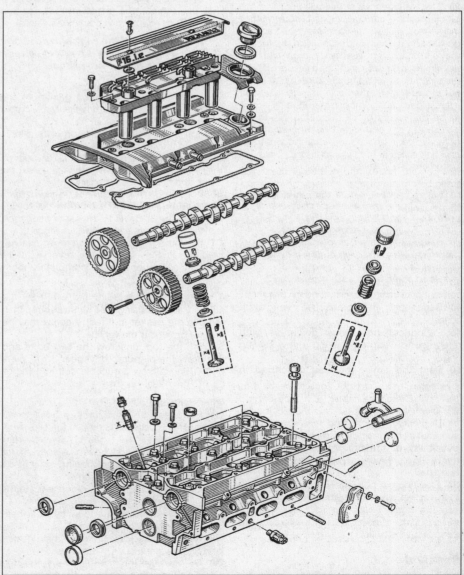

12.18 Exploded view of the cylinder head on the 16-valve engine F-type engine

illustration 11.31, tighten the bolts to the torque specified for Stage 1. Repeat the sequence by tightening to the torque specified for Stage 2.

29 Wait three minutes, then progressively slacken all the bolts in the reverse of the tightening sequence until completely loose (this is Stage 3 and Stage 4).

30 Again following the tightening sequence, tighten the bolts to the torque specified for Stage 5.

31 Final tightening is carried out by turning each bolt through the angle specified for Stage 6. Measure the angle using a commercially-available gauge, or make up a cardboard template cut to the angle required. No retightening after warm-up is required.

32 Refit the valve cover, together with new gaskets, and tighten the bolts to the specified torque.

33 Refit the spark plug tube housing to the valve cover, and tighten the bolts.

34 Where applicable, secure the bracing struts to the inlet manifold.

35 Where applicable, secure the starter motor mounting bracket to the exhaust manifold.

36 Refit the exhaust manifold heat shield.

37 Refit the alternator mounting bracket.

38 Reconnect the wiring to all sensors located in the cylinder head, ensuring that all wires are correctly reconnected as noted before removal.

39 Where applicable, refit the manifolds, and/or reconnect all relevant vacuum, breather and coolant hoses and electrical feeds, as noted before removal.

40 Where applicable, refit the power steering fluid reservoir.

41 Where applicable, refit the radiator, but do not fill the cooling system at this stage.

42 Refit the spark plugs and distributor cap with reference to Chapters 1 and 5 respectively.

43 Reconnect the accelerator cable and adjust if necessary, as described in Chapter 4.

44 Reconnect the crankcase ventilation hoses.

45 Reconnect the exhaust downpipe, with reference to Chapter 4, using a new sealing ring.

46 Refit the timing belt as described in Section 6.

47 Refill the cooling system with reference to Chapter 1.

48 Reconnect the battery leads.

13 Auxiliary shaft - removal, inspection and refitting

Note: *On certain models, this job may not be possible with the engine in the car, due to limited access. A new auxiliary shaft oil seal, and a new housing gasket, or suitable sealant (as applicable) must be used on refitting.*

Removal

1 Remove the timing belt as described in Section 5 or 6, as applicable.

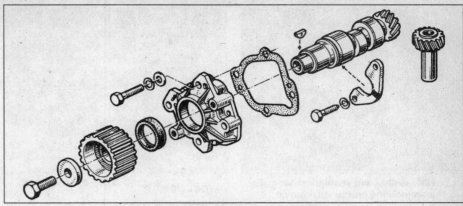

13.4a Auxiliary shaft components

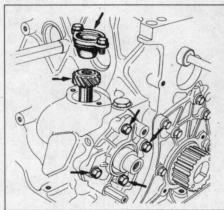

13.4b Auxiliary shaft housing retaining bolt locations, oil pump driveshaft and cover plate

2 Remove the auxiliary shaft sprocket with reference to Section 7.

3 Where applicable, unbolt the timing belt rear lower cover from the cylinder block.

4 Unscrew the four bolts and withdraw the auxiliary shaft housing **(see illustrations)**, then remove the gasket (if fitted). Access may be easier from under the vehicle.

5 From the top, unscrew the two bolts and withdraw the oil pump drivegear cover plate and O-ring. Screw a suitable bolt into the oil pump drivegear, or use a tapered wooden

13.4c Removing the auxiliary shaft housing

shaft, and withdraw the drivegear from its location **(see illustrations)**.

6 Unscrew the two bolts and washers, and lift out the auxiliary shaft thrustplate and the auxiliary shaft **(see illustrations)**.

Inspection

7 Examine the auxiliary shaft and oil pump driveshaft for pitting, scoring or wear ridges on the bearing journals, and for chipping or wear of the gear teeth. Renew as necessary. Check the auxiliary shaft bearings in the cylinder block for wear and, if worn, have these renewed by your Renault dealer or suitably-equipped engineering works. Wipe them clean if they are still serviceable.

8 Temporarily fit the thrustplate to its position

13.5a Removing the oil pump drivegear cover plate . . .

13.5b . . . and drivegear

2C

13.6a Removing the auxiliary shaft thrust plate . . .

13.6b . . . and the auxiliary shaft itself

13.9a Prising the auxiliary shaft oil seal from the housing

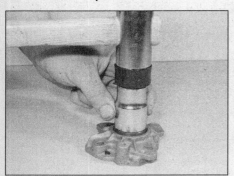

13.9b Driving in the new oil seal

13.12 Auxiliary shaft housing gasket positioned on the dowels

on the auxiliary shaft, and use a feeler gauge to check that the endfloat is as given in the Specifications. If it is greater than the upper tolerance, a new thrustplate should be obtained, but first check the thrust surfaces on the shaft to ascertain if wear has occurred here.

Refitting

9 Clean off all traces of the old gasket or sealant from the auxiliary shaft housing, and prise out the oil seal with a screwdriver. Install the new oil seal using a block of wood, and tap it in until it is flush with the outer face of the housing. The open side of the seal must be towards the engine **(see illustrations)**.
10 Liberally lubricate the auxiliary shaft, and slide it into its bearings.
11 Place the thrustplate in position with its curved edge away from the crankshaft, and refit the two retaining bolts, tightening them securely.
12 Place a new housing gasket in position over the dowels of the cylinder block **(see illustration)**. If a gasket was not used previously, apply a bead of CAF 4/60 THIXO paste to the housing mating face.
13 Liberally lubricate the oil seal lips, and then locate the housing in place. Refit and tighten the housing retaining bolts progressively in a diagonal sequence.
14 Lubricate the oil pump drivegear, and lower the gear into its location.
15 Where applicable, refit the rear lower timing belt cover to the cylinder block, and tighten the bolts.

16 Position a new O-ring seal on the drivegear cover plate, fit the plate and secure with the two retaining bolts.
17 Refit the auxiliary shaft sprocket with reference to Section 7.
18 Refit the timing belt as described in Section 5 or 6, as applicable.

14 Sump (8-valve engines) - removal and refitting

Note: *A new sump gasket or suitable sealant (as applicable) must be used on refitting.*

Removal

1 Apply the handbrake, then jack up the front of the vehicle and support it securely on axle stands (see *"Jacking, towing and wheel changing"*).
2 Drain the engine oil as described in Chapter 1, then refit and tighten the drain plug.
3 Unscrew the bolts and remove the flywheel/driveplate cover plate.
4 Where applicable, disconnect any electrical wiring from the sump sensors.
5 Unscrew and remove the bolts securing the sump to the crankcase. Tap the sump with a hide or plastic mallet to break the seal, then remove the sump.
6 Remove the gasket where fitted.

Refitting

7 Clean all traces of gasket or sealing compound from the mating faces of the sump and crankcase.

8 Where fitted, locate a new gasket on the sump, otherwise apply a bead of CAF 4/60 THIXO paste to the sump face.
9 If a gasket is not fitted, it is important when refitting that the sump is positioned correctly the first time, and not moved around after the paste has touched the crankcase. Temporary long bolts or dowel rods may be used to help achieve this.
10 To prevent oil dripping from the oil pump and crankcase, wipe these areas clean before refitting the sump.
11 Lift the sump into position, then insert the bolts and tighten them progressively to the specified torque.
12 Reconnect the electrical wiring to the sump sensors, where applicable.
13 Lower the vehicle to the ground.
14 Fill the engine with fresh oil, with reference to Chapter 1.

15 Sump (16-valve engines) - removal and refitting

Note: *An engine lifting hoist is required during this procedure.*

Models with tin (pressed) sump

1 Proceed as described in Section 14 for the 8-valve engines, noting that the flywheel/driveplate cover plate is integral with a tie-bar, which joins the engine to the gearbox/transmission.
2 Before the sump can be removed, the bolts securing the tie-bar and cover assembly to the gearbox/transmission bellhousing and engine must be unscrewed, and the tie-bar and cover assembly must be lowered from the sump.

Models with aluminium (cast) sump

Note: *At the time of writing, it was not possible to obtain a vehicle on which to carry out detailed work. It is therefore possible that some differences to the sequence of work described in the following paragraphs may be noted. It is recommended that notes and, where necessary, sketches are made during removal, where any differences to procedures are noted.*

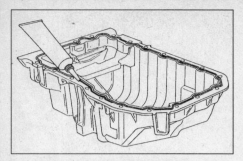

15.10 Applying a bead of sealant to the sump mating faces - 16-valve engine

16.2 Removing the oil pump from the crankcase

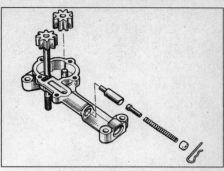

16.4 Exploded view of the oil pump

Removal

3 Disconnect the battery leads.

4 Drain the engine oil as described in Chapter 1. Refit and tighten the drain plug, using a new washer.

5 Jack up the front of the vehicle and support it securely on axle stands (see *"Jacking, towing and wheel changing"*).

6 Unscrew the bolts securing the sump to the cylinder block, but leave two bolts finger-tight at this stage.

7 Unscrew the nuts and remove the four studs attaching the sump to the gearbox. Use two nuts tightened against each other to remove the studs.

8 Remove the two remaining bolts, then break the joint by striking the sump with the palm of your hand. Lower the sump over the oil pump, and withdraw it.

Refitting

9 Clean all traces of sealing compound from the mating faces of the sump and crankcase.

10 Apply a bead of CAF 4/60 THIXO paste to the sump mating faces **(see illustration)**.

11 It is important when refitting that the sump is positioned correctly the first time, and not moved around after the paste has touched the crankcase. Long bolts or dowel rods may be fitted temporarily to help achieve this.

12 To prevent oil dripping from the oil pump and crankcase, wipe these areas clean before refitting the sump.

13 Lift the sump into position, then insert two diagonally-opposite bolts, and finger-tighten them at this stage.

14 Insert and tighten the four studs attaching the sump to the gearbox. Use two nuts tightened against each other to tighten the studs.

15 Insert the remaining sump bolts, and tighten them progressively to the specified torque.

16 Fit the four nuts to the studs, and tighten them to the specified torque.

17 Fill the engine with fresh oil, with reference to Chapter 1.

18 Reconnect the battery leads.

16 Oil pump - removal, inspection and refitting

Removal

1 Remove the sump as described in Section 14 or 15, as applicable.

2 Unscrew the four retaining bolts at the ends of the pump body, and withdraw the pump from the crankcase and drivegear **(see illustration)**.

Inspection

3 Unscrew the retaining bolts, and lift off the pump cover.

4 Withdraw the idler gear and the drivegear/shaft. Mark the idler gear so that it can be refitted in its same position **(see illustration)**.

5 Extract the retaining clip, and remove the oil pressure relief valve spring retainer, spring, spring seat and plunger.

6 Clean the components, and carefully examine the gears, pump body and relief valve plunger for any signs of scoring or wear. Renew the pump complete if excessive wear is evident.

7 If the components appear serviceable, measure the clearance between the pump body and the gears using feeler blades. Also measure the gear endfloat, and check the flatness of the end cover **(see illustrations)**. If the clearances exceed the specified tolerances, the pump must be renewed.

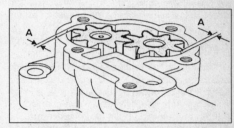

16.7a Oil pump gear-to-body clearance measurement points (A)

16.7b Checking the clearance between the oil pump gears and the body

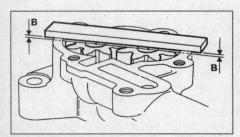

16.7c Oil pump gear endfloat measurement points (B)

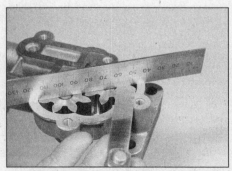

16.7d Checking the endfloat of the oil pump gears

16.7e Checking the flatness of the oil pump cover

2C

16.8 Tightening the oil pump cover bolts

16.10 Tightening the oil pump mounting bolts

17.3 Removing the front plate and oil seal

8 If the pump is satisfactory, reassemble the components in the reverse order of removal. Fill the pump with oil, then refit the cover and tighten the bolts securely **(see illustration)**. (A new pump should also be primed with oil.) Where applicable, check that the locating dowel is in position where the driveshaft enters the oil pump body.

Refitting

9 Wipe clean the mating faces of the oil pump and crankcase.
10 Lift the oil pump into position with its shaft engaged with the drivegear. Insert and fully tighten the retaining bolts **(see illustration)**.
11 Refit the sump as described in Section 14 or 15.

17 Crankshaft oil seals - renewal

Right-hand (pulley end) oil seal

Note: *Suitable sealant will be required for the cylinder block front plate on refitting.*
1 Remove the timing belt and crankshaft sprocket with reference to Sections 5, 6 and 7 (as applicable).
2 Remove the sump as described in Section 14 or 15.
3 Unscrew the bolts securing the front plate to the cylinder block. Withdraw the plate, noting that it is located by dowels in the two lower bolt hole locations **(see illustration)**.

4 Clean the front plate, and scrape off all traces of sealant from the plate and cylinder block.
5 Prise out the old oil seal, and clean the seating.
6 Fit a new seal so that it is flush with the outer face of the front plate, using a block of wood. Ensure that the open side of the seal is fitted towards the engine.
7 Lubricate the oil seal lips. Apply a bead of CAF 4/60 THIXO paste to the mating face of the front plate, making sure that the oilway cavity is not blocked.
8 Refit the front plate and insert the retaining bolts. The two bolts around the oil seal opening at the 2 o'clock and 8 o'clock positions should also have a small quantity of the sealant paste applied to their threads, as they protrude into the crankcase. Progressively tighten the retaining bolts in a diagonal sequence.
9 Refit the sump as described in Section 14 or 15.
10 Refit the crankshaft sprocket and timing belt with reference to Sections 5, 6 and 7.

Left-hand (transmission end) oil seal

11 Remove the flywheel/driveplate as described in Section 18.
12 Prise out the old oil seal using a small screwdriver, taking care not to damage the surface of the crankshaft. Alternatively, the oil seal can be removed by drilling two small holes diagonally opposite each other, and inserting self-tapping screws in them. A pair of

grips can then be used to pull out the oil seal, by pulling on each screw in turn.
13 Inspect the seal rubbing surface on the crankshaft. If it is grooved or rough in the area where the old seal was fitted, the new seal should be fitted slightly less deeply, so that it rubs on an unworn part of the surface.
14 Wipe clean the oil seal seating, then dip the new seal in fresh engine oil. Locate it over the crankshaft, with its closed side facing outwards. Make sure that the oil seal lip is not damaged as it is located on the crankshaft.
15 Using a metal tube, drive the oil seal squarely into the bore until flush. A block of wood cut to pass over the end of the crankshaft may be used instead.
16 Refit the flywheel/driveplate with reference to Section 18.

18 Flywheel/driveplate - removal, inspection and refitting

Refer to Chapter 2A.

19 Engine mountings - renewal

Refer to Chapter 2A.

20 Engine oil cooler - removal and refitting

Refer to Chapter 2A.

Chapter 2 Part D: Engine removal and general engine overhaul procedures

Contents

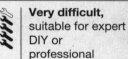

Degrees of difficulty

Easy, suitable for novice with little experience		Fairly easy, suitable for beginner with some experience		Fairly difficult, suitable for competent DIY mechanic		Difficult, suitable for experienced DIY mechanic		Very difficult, suitable for expert DIY or professional	

Specifications

Note: Throughout these Specifications, engines are identified by type as follows:

E-type . . . . 1390 cc (E6J and E7J)
C-type . . . . 1237 cc (C1G), 1390 cc (C3J) and 1397 cc (C1J and C2J)
F-type . . . . 1721 cc (F2N and F3N), 1764 cc (F7P) and 1794 cc (F3P)

Cylinder block - E-type engines

Material . . . . Cast-iron
Liner bore diameter . . . . 75.8 mm + 0.03 mm - 0.00 mm
Liner height:
  Total . . . . 130.0 mm
  From shoulder to top . . . . 91.5 mm + 0.035 mm+ 0.005 mm
Cylinder block depth (from top to liner locating shoulder) . . . . 91.5 mm - 0.015 mm - 0.055 mm
Liner protrusion without O-ring . . . . 0.02 to 0.09 mm
Maximum difference in protrusion between adjacent liners . . . . 0.05 mm

Cylinder block - C-type engines

Material . . . . Cast-iron
Liner bore diameter:
  1237 cc (C1G) engine . . . . 71.5 mm
  1390 cc (C3J) engine . . . . 75.8 mm
  1397 cc (C1J and C2J) engines . . . . 76.0 mm
Liner height (from shoulder to top) . . . . 95.005 to 95.035 mm
Cylinder block depth (from top to liner locating shoulder) . . . . 94.945 to 94.985 mm
Liner protrusion . . . . 0.04 to 0.12 mm
Maximum difference in protrusion between adjacent liners . . . . 0.04 mm
Liner base seal thickness:
  Blue . . . . 0.08 mm
  Red . . . . 0.10 mm
  Green . . . . 0.12 mm

Cylinder block - F-type engines

Material	Cast-iron
Cylinder bore diameter:	
Class A or 1	81.000 to 81.010 mm
Class B or 2	81.010 to 81.020 mm
Class C or 3	81.020 to 81.030 mm
Class U or 4	81.250 to 81.260 mm
Class V or 5	81.225 to 81.270 mm
Class W or 6	81.235 to 81.245 mm

Crankshaft

Number of main bearings	5
Main bearing journal diameter:	
Standard	54.795 ± 0.01 mm
1st undersize	54.545 ± 0.01 mm
Main bearing running clearance	0.020 to 0.058 mm
Crankpin (big-end) journal diameter:	
E-type and C-type engines:	
Standard	43.980 + 0.00 mm - 0.02 mm
1st undersize	43.730 + 0.00 mm - 0.02 mm
F-type engines:	
Standard	48.0 mm
1st undersize	47.75 mm + 0.02 mm - 0.00 mm
Big-end bearing running clearance	0.014 to 0.053 mm
Big-end cap side play:	
E-type C-type engines	0.310 to 0.572 mm
F-type engines	0.220 to 0.400 mm
Crankshaft endfloat	
E-type and C-type engines	0.050 to 0.230 mm
F-type engines	0.070 to 0.230 mm

Pistons and piston rings

Piston ring end gaps	Rings supplied pre-set
Piston ring thickness:	
E-type engines:	
Top compression ring	1.5 mm
Second compression ring	1.75 mm
Oil control ring	3.0 mm
C-type engines:	
Top compression ring	1.75 mm
Second compression ring	2.0 mm
Oil control ring	4.0 mm
F-type engines:	
Top compression ring	1.75 mm
Second compression ring	2.0 mm
Oil control ring	3.0 mm
Piston clearance in liner:	
E-type and C-type engines	0.045 to 0.065 mm (suggested values)
F-type engines:	
1721 cc (F2N and F3N) engines with de Colmar piston	0.025 to 0.045 mm
1721 cc (F2N and F3N) engines with SMM normal piston	0.040 to 0.060 mm
1721 cc (F2N and F3N) engines with SMM reduced-clearance piston	0.035 to 0.055 mm
1764 cc (F7P) engine	0.025 to 0.045 mm
1794 cc (F3P) engine	0.025 to 0.050 mm (suggested values)

Gudgeon pins

E-type engines:	
Length	60.0 mm
Outside diameter	19.0 mm
Bore	11.0 mm
C-type engines:	
Length	59.0 mm
Outside diameter	18.0 mm
Bore	11.0 mm
F-type engines:	
Fit in connecting rod:	
1721 cc (F2N and F3N) and 1794 cc (F3P) engines	Interference
1764 cc (F7P) engine	Floating

Connecting rods

Big-end side play:
  E-type and C-type engines .... 0.310 to 0.572 mm (suggested values)
  F-type engines .... 0.220 to 0.400 mm (suggested values)
Small-end side play:
  E-type and C-type engines .... 0.310 to 0.572 mm (suggested values)
  F-type engines .... 0.220 to 0.400 mm (suggested values)

Cylinder head

Material .... Aluminium
Height:
  E-type engines .... 113.0 ± 0.05 mm
  C-type engines:
    Nominal .... 70.15 mm
    Repair .... 69.65 mm
  F-type engines:
    1721 cc (F2N and F3N) and 1794 cc (F3P) engines .... 169.5 mm ± 0.2 mm
    1764 cc (F7P) engine .... 136.5 mm ± 0.05 mm
Maximum acceptable gasket face distortion .... 0.05 mm

Valve seat angle:	Inlet	Exhaust
E-type engines	120°	90°
C-type engines	90°	90°
F-type engines:		
1721 cc (F2N and F3N) and 1794 cc (F3P) engines	120°	90°
1764 cc (F7P) engine	90°	90°

Valve seat width:
  E-type engines .... 1.7 mm
  C-type engines .... 1.1 to 1.5 mm
  F-type engines:
    1721 cc (F2N and F3N) and 1794 cc (F3P) engines .... 1.7 ± 0.2 mm

	Inlet	Exhaust
1764 cc (F7P) engine	1.4 mm	1.7 mm

Valves

Head diameter:	Inlet	Exhaust
E-type engines	37.5 mm	33.5 mm
C-type engines	33.5 mm	30.3 mm (1st model)
		29.0 mm (2nd model)
F-type engines:		
1721 cc (F2N and F3N) and 1794 cc (F3P) engines	38.1 mm	32.5 mm
1764 cc (F7P) engine	30.0 mm	28.5 mm

Stem diameter:
  E-type and C-type engines .... 7.0 mm
  F-type engines:
    1721 cc (F2N and F3N) and 1794 cc (F3P) engines .... 8.0 mm
    1764 cc (F7P) engine .... 7.0 mm
Valve spring free length:
  E-type engines:
    1st type .... 46.64 mm
    2nd type .... 44.93 mm
  C-type engines:
    1st type .... 42.2 mm
    2nd type .... 46.9 mm
  F-type engines:
    1721 cc (F2N and F3N) and 1794 cc (F3P) engines .... 44.9 mm
    1764 cc (F7P) engine .... Not stated

Pushrods - C-type engines

Length .... 172.3 mm (1st model), 176.3 mm (2nd model) or
                                                                     173.5 mm (3rd model)

Tappets - C-type engines

External diameter:
  Standard .... 19.0 mm
  Oversize .... 19.2 mm

Torque wrench settings

Refer to Specifications for Part A, B, or C, as applicable

2D

1 General information

General

Included in this part of Chapter 2 are the general overhaul procedures for the cylinder head, cylinder block/crankcase and internal engine components.

The information ranges from advice concerning preparation for an overhaul and the purchase of replacement parts, to detailed step-by-step procedures covering removal, inspection, renovation and refitting of internal engine parts.

The following Sections have been compiled based on the assumption that the engine has been removed from the car. For information concerning in-car engine repair, as well as the removal and refitting of the external components necessary for the overhaul, refer to Chapter 2A (E-type engine), 2B (C-type engines), or 2C (F-type engines) of this Chapter and to Section 7 of this Chapter.

Engine identification

1237 cc (C1G), 1390 cc (C3J), and 1397 cc (C1J and C2J) engines are referred to throughout this Chapter as C-type engines. All C-type engines are of the overhead valve type. Note that there is also an E-type 1390 cc engine.

1390 cc (E6J and E7J) engines are referred to throughout this Chapter as E-type engines. E-type engines are of the overhead camshaft type. Note that there is also a C-type 1390 cc engine (see previous paragraph).

1721 cc (F2N and F3N), 1764 cc (F7P) and 1794 cc (F3P) engines are referred to throughout this Chapter as F-type engines. F-type engines are of the single overhead camshaft (1721 cc and 1794 cc engines) or double overhead camshaft (1764 cc) type.

Refer to the *"Buying spare parts and vehicle identification numbers"* Section at the beginning of this manual for details of engine code locations.

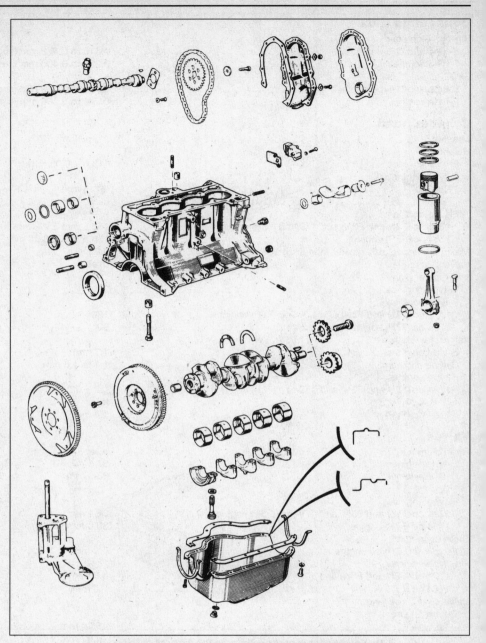

1.1a Lower engine components on the 1397 cc (C1J) engine

2 Engine overhaul - general information

It is not always easy to determine when, or if, an engine should be completely overhauled, as a number of factors must be considered.

High mileage is not necessarily an indication that an overhaul is needed, while low mileage does not preclude the need for an overhaul. Frequency of servicing is probably the most important consideration. An engine which has had regular and frequent oil and filter changes, as well as other required maintenance, will most likely give many thousands of miles of reliable service. Conversely, a neglected engine may require an overhaul very early in its life.

Excessive oil consumption is an indication that piston rings, valve seals and/or valve guides are in need of attention. Make sure that oil leaks are not responsible before deciding that the rings and/or guides are bad. Perform a cylinder compression check to determine the extent of the work required.

Check the oil pressure with a gauge fitted in place of the oil pressure sender, and compare it with the Specifications. If it is extremely low, the main and big-end bearings and/or the oil pump are probably worn out.

Loss of power, rough running, knocking or metallic engine noises, excessive valve gear noise, and high fuel consumption, may also point to the need for an overhaul, especially if they are all present at the same time. If a complete tune-up does not remedy the situation, major mechanical work is the only solution.

An engine overhaul involves restoring the internal parts to the specifications of a new engine. During an overhaul, the pistons and rings are replaced and the cylinder bores are reconditioned. New main bearings, connecting rod (big-end) bearings and camshaft bearings are generally fitted, and if necessary, the crankshaft may be reground to restore the journals. The valves are also serviced as well, since they are usually in less-than-perfect condition at this point. While the engine is being overhauled, other components, such as the distributor, starter and alternator, can be overhauled as well. The end result should be a like-new engine that will give many trouble-

Since the condition of the block will be the major factor to consider when determining whether to overhaul the original engine or buy a reconditioned unit, do not purchase parts or have overhaul work done on other components until the block has been thoroughly inspected. As a general rule, time is the primary cost of an overhaul, so it does not pay to fit worn or sub-standard parts.

As a final note, to ensure maximum life and minimum trouble from a reconditioned engine, everything must be assembled with care, in a spotlessly-clean environment.

3 Engine removal - methods and precautions

If you have decided that an engine must be removed for overhaul or major repair work, several preliminary steps should be taken.

Locating a suitable place to work is extremely important. Adequate work space, along with storage space for the vehicle, will be needed. If a garage is not available, at the very least a flat, level, clean work surface is required.

Cleaning the engine compartment and engine before beginning the removal procedure will help keep tools clean and organized.

An engine hoist or A-frame will also be necessary. Make sure the equipment is rated in excess of the combined weight of the engine and transmission. Safety is of primary importance, considering the potential hazards involved in lifting the engine out of the vehicle.

Particularly if this is the first time you have removed an engine, an assistant should be available. Advice and aid from someone more experienced would also be helpful. There are many instances when one person cannot simultaneously perform all of the operations required when lifting the engine out of the vehicle.

Plan the operation ahead of time. Arrange for, or obtain, all of the tools and equipment you will need, prior to beginning the job. Some of the equipment necessary to perform engine removal and installation safely and with relative ease are (in addition to an engine hoist) a heavy-duty floor jack, complete sets of spanners and sockets as described at the front of this manual, wooden blocks, and plenty of rags and cleaning solvent for mopping up spilled oil, coolant and fuel. If the hoist must be hired, make sure that you arrange for it in advance, and perform all of the operations possible without it beforehand. This will save you money and time.

Plan for the vehicle to be out of use for quite a while. An engineering works will be required to perform some of the work which the do-it-yourselfer cannot accomplish without special equipment. These places often have a busy schedule, so it would be a good idea to consult them before removing the engine, in order to accurately estimate the amount of time required to rebuild or repair components that may need work.

2D

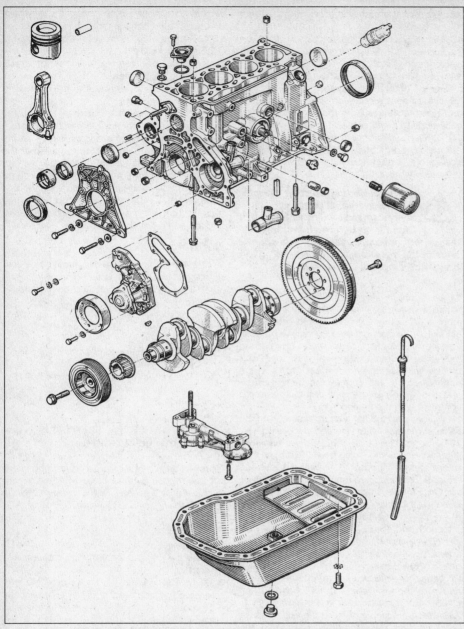

1.1b Lower engine components on the 1721 cc (F2N) engine

free miles. **Note:** *Critical cooling system components such as the hoses, drivebelts, thermostat and water pump MUST be renewed when an engine is overhauled. The radiator should be checked carefully, to ensure that it is not clogged or leaking. Also, it is a good idea to renew the oil pump whenever the engine is overhauled.*

Before beginning the engine overhaul, read through the entire procedure to familiarise yourself with the scope and requirements of the job. Overhauling an engine is not difficult if you follow all of the instructions carefully, have the necessary tools and equipment, and pay close attention to all specifications; however, it can be time-consuming. Plan on the vehicle being tied up for a minimum of two weeks,

especially if parts must be taken to an engineering works for repair or reconditioning. Check on the availability of parts, and make sure that any necessary special tools and equipment are obtained in advance. Most work can be done with typical hand tools, although a number of precision measuring tools are required for inspecting parts to determine if they must be renewed. Often the engineering works will handle the inspection of parts, and offer advice concerning reconditioning and renewal. **Note:** *Always wait until the engine has been completely disassembled, and all components, especially the engine block, have been inspected, before deciding what service and repair operations must be performed by an engineering works.*

Always be extremely careful when removing and refitting the engine. Serious injury can result from careless actions. Plan ahead, take your time, and you will find that a job of this nature, although major, can be accomplished successfully.

4 Engine (C-type) - removal and refitting (without transmission)

Note: *Only the C-type engines may be removed on their own, leaving the transmission in situ. The engines may also be removed together with the gearbox as described in Section 5. An engine hoist and suitable lifting tackle will be required for this operation.*

Removal

1 Disconnect both battery leads.
2 Remove the bonnet as described in Chapter 11.
3 Where applicable, unbolt and remove the strengthening bar from between the front suspension unit turrets.
4 Remove the radiator with reference to Chapter 3.
5 Remove the auxiliary drivebelt(s) with reference to Chapter 1.
6 Apply the handbrake, then jack up the front of the vehicle and support it securely on axle stands (see *"Jacking, towing and wheel changing"*). Remove both front wheels.
7 Unbolt and remove the engine-to-gearbox tie-bar.
8 Unbolt and remove the cover from the bottom of the gearbox.
9 Turn the engine until No 1 piston is at TDC on the compression stroke, as described in Chapter 2B, Section 3.
10 Using a socket or spanner, unscrew the crankshaft pulley retaining bolt. Lock the starter ring gear to prevent the engine turning by using a wide-bladed screwdriver inserted between the ring gear teeth and the crankcase. Alternatively, apply the handbrake and engage top gear.
11 With the bolt removed, lift off the pulley and withdraw the pulley hub. If the hub is tight, carefully lever it off using two screwdrivers, or use a two- or three-legged puller. Take care not to lose the Woodruff key from the nose of the crankshaft.

12 Remove the starter motor with reference to Chapter 5A.
13 Disconnect the accelerator cable (and, on carburettor models, the choke cable) with reference to Chapter 4.
14 Refer to Chapter 4 and remove the air cleaner unit and its mounting.
15 Disconnect all relevant coolant, vacuum and breather hoses from the engine, labelling each hose to avoid confusion when refitting.
16 Similarly, disconnect the fuel hoses from the fuel pump/carburettor/throttle housing, as applicable, again labelling them to avoid confusion when refitting.

> ⚠ **Warning: On fuel injection models, the fuel system should be depressurised as described in Chapter 4B before attempting to disconnect the fuel hoses. Plug the open ends of the hoses and the unions, to prevent dirt ingress and fuel spillage.**

17 Disconnect all relevant wiring from the sensors, switches and actuators on the engine, labelling all wires to aid refitting. If necessary, disconnect the main wiring harness connector blocks. Note that on certain models, if the main wiring harness connector blocks are disconnected, most of the wiring connections to the engine can be left intact, and the wiring harnesses can be removed complete with the engine.
18 Disconnect the exhaust front pipe from the exhaust manifold with reference to Chapter 4.
19 On models fitted with power-assisted steering, unbolt the pump from the engine with reference to Chapter 10. Leave the hose attached, and position the pump to one side.
20 On models fitted with air conditioning, unbolt the compressor from the engine with reference to Chapter 3. Leave the hose attached, and position the pump to one side.
21 Where applicable, unbolt the engine speed/position sensor from the top of the gearbox bellhousing.
22 Make a final check to ensure that all relevant hoses and wires have been disconnected to facilitate engine removal.
23 Attach a suitable hoist to the engine lifting brackets, then raise the hoist to just take the weight of the engine.
24 Position a trolley jack under the gearbox,

with an interposed block of wood, and just take the weight if the engine.
25 Unscrew and remove the gearbox-to-engine nuts and bolts.
26 Unscrew and remove the location studs shown **(see illustration)**.
27 Unscrew the lower nut from the right-hand front engine mounting.
28 Separate the engine from the gearbox until the gearbox input shaft is clear of the clutch.
29 With the help of an assistant, slowly lift the engine, and at the same time, check that the right-hand driveshaft is not dislocated.
30 Lift the engine from the engine compartment, taking care not to damage any components on the surrounding panels. When high enough, lift it over the front body panel, and lower the unit to the ground.

Refitting

31 Refitting is a reversal of removal, however note the following additional points:
   (a) Apply a little high melting-point grease to the splines of the gearbox input shaft.
   (b) Tighten all nuts and bolts to the specified torque.
   (c) Refer to the applicable Chapters and Sections as for removal.
   (d) Ensure that all hoses and wires are correctly reconnected, as noted before removal.

5 Engine - removal and refitting (with manual gearbox)

Note: *An engine hoist and suitable lifting tackle will be required for this operation. New roll pins and suitable sealant will be required when refitting the right-hand driveshaft.*

Removal

1 Disconnect both battery leads.
2 Drain the cooling system with reference to Chapter 1.
3 Drain the engine and gearbox oil with reference to Chapters 1 and 7A, as applicable.
4 Remove the bonnet with reference to Chapter 11.
5 Unbolt and remove the strengthening bar from between the front suspension unit turrets.
6 Remove the radiator with reference to Chapter 3. Also disconnect the bottom hose from the cylinder block inlet elbow **(see illustration)**.
7 Apply the handbrake, then jack up the front of the vehicle and support it securely on axle stands (see *"Jacking, towing and wheel changing"*). Remove both front wheels.
8 Working beneath the right-hand side of the vehicle, use a parallel pin punch to drive out the double roll pin securing the right-hand driveshaft to the gearbox differential sunwheel stub shaft.
9 Unscrew and remove the two nuts and bolts securing the right-hand stub axle carrier to the suspension strut. Note that the nuts are on the rear side of the strut.

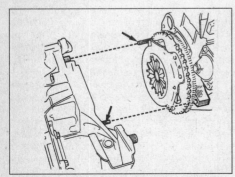

4.26 Location studs (arrowed) on the gearbox and engine - C-type engine

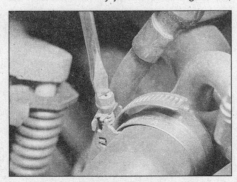

5.6 Disconnecting the bottom hose

5.19a Oil pressure switch (arrowed) on the front of the cylinder block - E-type engine

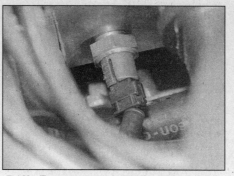

5.19b Temperature sender on the cylinder head - E-type engine

5.19c Main wiring harness connector blocks

10 Pull the top of the stub axle carrier outwards until the inner end of the driveshaft is released from the stub shaft.

11 Working on the left-hand side, unbolt the front brake caliper with reference to Chapter 9, but leave the hydraulic hose connected. Tie the caliper to the front suspension coil spring with wire or string, taking care not to strain the hose.

12 Disconnect the steering track rod end from the left-hand stub axle carrier, with reference to Chapter 10.

13 Unscrew the three bolts securing the driveshaft rubber gaiter retaining plate to the left-hand side of the gearbox.

14 Unscrew and remove the two nuts and bolts securing the left-hand stub axle carrier to the suspension strut. Note that the nuts are on the rear side of the strut.

15 Pull the top of the left-hand stub axle carrier outwards until the inner end of the driveshaft is released from the yoke. There may be some loss of oil from the gearbox, so position a small container on the floor to catch it.

16 Refer to Chapter 4, and remove the air cleaner unit and its mounting. Also disconnect the air ducting from the carburettor/throttle housing/fuel rail, where applicable.

17 Disconnect all relevant coolant, vacuum and breather hoses from the engine, labelling each hose to avoid confusion when refitting.

18 Similarly, disconnect the fuel hoses from the fuel pump/carburettor/throttle housing/fuel rail, as applicable, again labelling them to avoid confusion when refitting.

> ⚠ Warning: On fuel injection models, the fuel system should be depressurised as described in Chapter 4B before attempting to disconnect the fuel hoses. Plug the open ends of the hoses and the unions, to prevent dirt ingress and fuel spillage.

19 Disconnect all relevant wiring from the sensors, switches and actuators on the engine, labelling all wires to aid refitting. If necessary, disconnect the main wiring harness connector blocks. Note that on certain models, if the main wiring harness connector blocks are disconnected, most of the wiring

connections to the engine can be left intact, and the wiring harnesses can be removed complete with the engine (see illustrations).

20 Disconnect the accelerator cable (and, on carburettor models, the choke cable) with reference to Chapter 4.

21 Disconnect the speedometer cable with reference to Chapter 12.

22 Disconnect the engine earthing straps as applicable.

23 Disconnect the gearchange linkage from the transmission, with reference to Chapter 7A.

24 Disconnect the clutch cable with reference to Chapter 6.

25 Disconnect the exhaust front pipe from the exhaust manifold, with reference to Chapter 4. On the E-type engine, remove the front exhaust pipe completely.

26 On models fitted with power-assisted steering, unbolt the pump with reference to Chapter 10. Leave the hose attached, and position the pump to one side.

27 On models fitted with air conditioning, unbolt the compressor with reference to Chapter 3. Leave the hose attached, and position the pump to one side.

28 Make a final check to ensure that all relevant hoses and wires have been disconnected to facilitate engine removal.

29 Attach a suitable hoist to the engine lifting brackets, then raise the hoist to just take the weight of the engine.

30 Disconnect the engine mountings with reference to Chapter 2A.

31 With the help of an assistant, slowly lift the engine/gearbox assembly from the engine compartment, taking care not to damage any components on the surrounding panels (see illustration). When high enough, lift it over the front body panel, and lower the unit to the ground.

32 To separate the gearbox from the engine, proceed as follows.

33 Support the engine and gearbox on blocks of wood.

34 Where applicable, unscrew the bolts securing the engine-to-gearbox tie-rod bracket to the engine and gearbox, and remove the tie-rod. Note that the tie-rod is fixed to the gearbox bellhousing cover plate.

35 Where applicable, if not already done,

unbolt and remove the engine speed/position sensor from the aperture at the top of the clutch bellhousing.

36 Unbolt and remove the gearbox bellhousing cover plate.

37 Unscrew and remove the engine-to-gearbox nuts and bolts from around the gearbox, and from the starter motor. There is no need to remove the starter motor. Note the locations of any brackets which may be secured by the bolts and nuts.

38 Ensure that the engine and gearbox are adequately supported, then carefully withdraw the gearbox from the engine, ensuring that the weight of the gearbox is not allowed to hang on the input shaft while it is engaged with the clutch friction disc.

Refitting

39 Refitting is a reversal of removal, however note the following additional points:
  (a) Enure that, where applicable, any brackets are refitted to their locations on the engine-to-gearbox bolts and nuts.
  (b) Refer to the applicable Chapters and Sections as for removal.
  (c) Fit new roll pins to the right-hand driveshaft, and seal the ends using a suitable sealant.
  (d) Refit and tighten the brake caliper mounting bolts with reference to Chapter 9.
  (e) Tighten all nuts and bolts to the specified torque.

5.31 Lifting the engine/manual gearbox assembly from the engine compartment

(f) Refill the engine and gearbox with oil, with reference to Chapters 1 and 7.

(g) Refill the cooling system, with reference to Chapter 1.

(h) Ensure that all hoses and wires are correctly reconnected, as noted before removal.

6 Engine - removal and refitting (with automatic transmission)

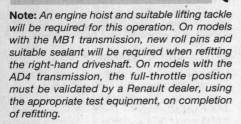

Note: *An engine hoist and suitable lifting tackle will be required for this operation. On models with the MB1 transmission, new roll pins and suitable sealant will be required when refitting the right-hand driveshaft. On models with the AD4 transmission, the full-throttle position must be validated by a Renault dealer, using the appropriate test equipment, on completion of refitting.*

Removal

1 Disconnect both battery leads.
2 Drain the cooling system with reference to Chapter 1.
3 Drain the engine oil and transmission fluid with reference to Chapter 1.
4 Remove the bonnet with reference to Chapter 11.
5 Unbolt and remove the strengthening bar from between the front suspension unit turrets.
6 Remove the radiator with reference to Chapter 3. Also disconnect the bottom hose from the cylinder block inlet elbow.
7 Apply the handbrake, then jack up the front of the vehicle and support it securely on axle stands (see *"Jacking, towing and wheel changing"*). Remove both front wheels.

Models with MB1 automatic transmission

8 Working beneath the right-hand side of the vehicle, use a parallel pin punch to drive out the double roll pin securing the right-hand driveshaft to the differential sunwheel stub shaft.
9 Unscrew and remove the two nuts and bolts securing the right-hand stub axle carrier to the suspension strut. Note that the nuts are on the rear side of the strut.
10 Pull the top of the stub axle carrier outwards until the inner end of the driveshaft is released from the stub shaft.
11 Working on the left-hand side, unbolt the front brake caliper with reference to Chapter 9, but leave the hydraulic hose connected. Tie the caliper to the front suspension coil spring with wire or string, taking care not to strain the hose.
12 Disconnect the steering track rod end from the left-hand stub axle carrier, with reference to Chapter 10.
13 Unscrew the three bolts securing the driveshaft rubber gaiter retaining plate to the left-hand side of the transmission.
14 Unscrew and remove the two nuts and bolts securing the left-hand stub axle carrier to the suspension strut. Note that the nuts are on the rear side of the strut.

15 Pull the top of the left-hand stub axle carrier outwards until the inner end of the driveshaft is released from the yoke. There may be some loss of fluid from the transmission, so position a small container on the floor to catch it.

Models with AD4 automatic transmission

16 On models with ABS, the hydraulic valve block must be removed (see Chapter 9). Where necessary, also disconnect any relevant brake fluid lines, and move them to one side to leave sufficient clearance to enable removal of the engine/transmission assembly.
17 Working on one side of the vehicle, unbolt the front brake caliper with reference to Chapter 9, but leave the hydraulic hose connected. Tie the caliper to the front suspension coil spring with wire or string, taking care not to strain the hose.
18 Disconnect the steering track rod end from the stub axle carrier, with reference to Chapter 10.
19 Unscrew the six bolts securing the driveshafts to the transmission flanges. An Allen key or 12-sided socket will be required for this. Rotate the driveshafts for access to each bolt in turn.
20 Unscrew and remove the two nuts and bolts securing the stub axle carrier to the suspension strut. Note that the nuts are on the rear side of the strut.
21 Pull the top of the stub axle carrier outwards until the inner end of the driveshaft is released from the drive flange.
22 Repeat the procedure given in paragraphs 17 to 21 on the other side of the vehicle.

All models

23 Refer to Chapter 4, and remove the air cleaner unit and its mounting. Also disconnect the air ducting from the carburettor/throttle housing/fuel rail, where applicable.
24 Disconnect all relevant coolant, vacuum and breather hoses from the engine and transmission, labelling each hose to avoid confusion when refitting.
25 Similarly, disconnect the fuel hoses from the fuel pump/carburettor/throttle housing/fuel rail, as applicable, again labelling them to avoid confusion when refitting.

⚠️ **Warning: On fuel injection models, the fuel system should be depressurised as described in Chapter 4B before attempting to disconnect the fuel hoses. Plug the open ends of the hoses and the unions, to prevent dirt ingress and fuel spillage.**

26 Disconnect all relevant wiring from the sensors, switches and actuators on the engine and transmission, labelling all wires to aid refitting. If necessary, disconnect the main wiring harness connector blocks. Note that on certain models, if the main wiring harness connector blocks are disconnected, most of the wiring connections to the engine can be left intact, and the wiring harnesses can be

removed complete with the engine/transmission assembly.
27 Disconnect the accelerator cable (and, on carburettor models, the choke cable) with reference to Chapter 4.
28 Disconnect the speedometer cable with reference to Chapter 12.
29 Disconnect the engine/transmission earthing straps as applicable.
30 Disconnect the transmission selector mechanism from the transmission with reference to Chapter 7B.
31 Disconnect the exhaust front pipe from the exhaust manifold, with reference to Chapter 4. On the E-type engine, remove the front exhaust pipe completely.
32 On models fitted with power-assisted steering, unbolt the pump with reference to Chapter 10. Leave the hose attached, and position the pump to one side.
33 On models fitted with air conditioning, unbolt the compressor with reference to Chapter 3. Leave the hose attached, and position the pump to one side.
34 Make a final check to ensure that all relevant hoses and wires have been disconnected to facilitate removal of the engine/transmission assembly.
35 Attach a suitable hoist to the engine lifting brackets, then raise the hoist to just take the weight of the engine and transmission.
36 Disconnect the engine and transmission mountings with reference to Chapter 2A.
37 With the help of an assistant, slowly lift the engine/transmission assembly from the engine compartment, taking care not to damage any components on the surrounding panels. When high enough, lift it over the front body panel, and lower the unit to the ground.
38 To separate the transmission from the engine, proceed as follows.
39 Remove the starter motor, with reference to Chapter 5A.
40 Support the engine and transmission on blocks of wood.
41 Unbolt the protection plate from the bottom of the transmission.
42 Unscrew and remove the bolts securing the driveplate to the torque converter, while holding the starter ring gear stationary with a wide-bladed screwdriver engaged with the ring gear teeth. Turn the ring gear as required to bring each of the bolts into view.
43 Make up a suitable plate to retain the torque converter in position while pulling the transmission from the engine, and attach it to the transmission using one of the starter motor bolts **(see illustration)**. This is important, because the torque converter could be seriously damaged if it is dropped. The retaining plate will also be necessary when reconnecting the transmission to the engine, in order to keep the torque converter engaged with the transmission pump.
44 Unscrew and remove the transmission-to-engine nuts and bolts, and withdraw the transmission from the engine.
45 If necessary, unbolt the fluid cooler from the transmission, with reference to Chapter 7B.

Refitting

46 Refitting is a reversal of removal, however note the following additional points.

(a) Make sure that the torque converter is fully engaged with the transmission pump before reconnecting the transmission to the engine.

(b) Refer to the applicable Chapters and Sections as for removal.

(c) On models with the MB1 transmission, fit new roll pins to the right-hand driveshaft, and seal the ends using a suitable sealant.

(d) Refit and tighten the brake caliper mounting bolts with reference to Chapter 9.

(e) Tighten all nuts and bolts to the specified torque.

(f) Refill the engine and transmission with oil and fluid respectively, with reference to Chapter 1. On the AD4 transmission, also check that the final drive section of the transmission is filled with the correct quantity and grade of oil.

(g) Refill the cooling system, with reference to Chapter 1.

(h) Ensure that all hoses and wires are correctly reconnected, as noted before removal.

(i) If necessary, adjust the selector cable as described in Chapter 7B.

(j) On the AD4 transmission, on completion of refitting, the full-throttle position must be validated by a Renault dealer, using the appropriate test equipment.

(k) Reconnect the accelerator and (where applicable) choke cables, and adjust as described in Chapter 4.

7 Engine overhaul - dismantling sequence

1 It is much easier to dismantle and work on the engine if it is mounted on a portable engine stand. These stands can often be hired from a tool hire shop. Before the engine is mounted on a stand, the flywheel/driveplate should be removed from the engine, so that the engine stand bolts can be tightened into the end of the cylinder block.

2 If a stand is not available, it is possible to dismantle the engine with it blocked up on a sturdy workbench or on the floor. Be extra-careful not to tip or drop the engine when working without a stand.

3 If you are going to obtain a reconditioned engine, all the external components must come off first, in order to be transferred to the replacement engine (just as they will if you are doing a complete engine overhaul yourself). Check with the engine supplier for details. Normally these components include:

(a) Alternator and brackets.

(b) Distributor components, HT leads and spark plugs.

(c) Thermostat and cover.

(d) Carburettor or fuel injection equipment.

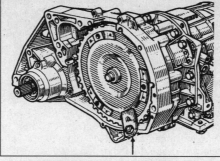

6.43 Torque converter retaining plate (arrowed) attached to MB1 type transmission

(e) Inlet and exhaust manifolds.

(f) Oil filter.

(g) Fuel pump (carburettor models).

(h) Engine mountings.

(i) Flywheel/driveplate.

(j) Ancillary brackets (power steering pump, air conditioning compressor, etc).

Note: *When removing the external components from the engine, pay close attention to details that may be helpful or important during refitting. Note the fitted position of gaskets, seals, spacers, pins, washers, bolts and other small items.*

4 If you are obtaining a "short" motor (which, when available, consists of the engine cylinder block, crankshaft, pistons and connecting rods all assembled), then the cylinder head, sump, oil pump, and timing belt (where applicable) will have to be removed also.

5 If you are planning a complete overhaul, the engine can be disassembled and the internal components removed in the following order:

(a) Inlet and exhaust manifolds.

(b) Timing belt/chain and sprockets.

(c) Cylinder head.

(d) Flywheel/driveplate.

(e) Sump.

(f) Oil pump.

(g) Pistons.

(h) Crankshaft.

6 Before beginning the disassembly and overhaul procedures, make sure that you have all of the correct tools necessary. Refer to the introductory pages at the beginning of this manual for further information.

8 Cylinder head - dismantling

Note: *New and reconditioned cylinder heads are available from the manufacturers, and from engine overhaul specialists. Due to the fact that some specialist tools are required for the dismantling and inspection procedures, and new components may not be readily available, it may be more practical and economical for the home mechanic to purchase a reconditioned head, rather than dismantle, inspect and recondition the original head.*

C-type and E-type engines

1 Remove the rocker shaft and retaining plate, if not already done.

1721 cc (F2N and F3N) and 1794 cc (F3P) engines

2 Withdraw the tappet buckets (if not already done), complete with shims, from their bores in the head. Place them on a sheet of cardboard numbered 1 to 8 (No 1 at the transmission end of the engine). It is a good idea to write the shim thickness size on the card alongside each bucket, in case the shims are accidentally knocked off their buckets and mixed up. The size is etched on the shim bottom face.

1764 cc (F7P) engine

3 Remove the hydraulic tappets (if not already done), noting which way round they are fitted. Place them in a compartmented box, or on a sheet of card marked into sixteen sections, so that they may be refitted to their original locations. Ideally, they should be placed in a compartmented box filled with engine oil, to prevent the oil draining from them.

All engines

4 Using a valve spring compressor, compress each valve spring in turn until the split collets can be removed. Release the compressor and lift off the cap, spring(s) and spring seat **(see illustrations)**. If, when the valve spring compressor is screwed down, the valve spring cap refuses to free and expose the split collets, gently tap the top of the tool, directly

8.4a Removing the split collets

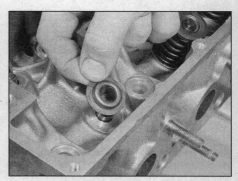

8.4b Removing a valve spring seat

8.5 Removing the oil seal from the top of the valve guide

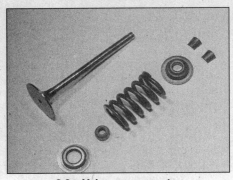

8.6a Valve components

8.6b Store the valve components in a polythene bag after removal

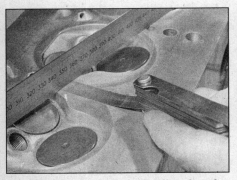

9.6 Checking the cylinder head surface for distortion

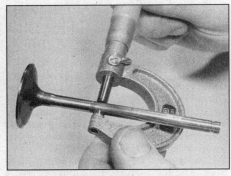

9.9 Measuring the valve stem diameter

over the cap, with a light hammer. This will free the cap.

5 Withdraw the oil seal from the top of the valve guide **(see illustration)**, then remove the valve through the combustion chamber.

6 It is essential that the valves and associated components are kept in their correct sequence, unless they are so badly worn that they are to be renewed. If they are going to be kept and used again, place them in labelled polythene bags, or in a compartmented box **(see illustrations)**.

9 Cylinder head and valves - cleaning, inspection and renovation

1 Thorough cleaning of the cylinder head and valve components, followed by a detailed inspection, will enable you to decide how much valve service work must be carried out during the engine overhaul.

Cleaning

2 Scrape away all traces of old gasket material and sealing compound from the cylinder head.

3 Scrape away the carbon from the combustion chambers and ports, then wash the cylinder head thoroughly with paraffin or a suitable solvent.

4 Scrape off any heavy carbon deposits that may have formed on the valves, then use a power-operated wire brush to remove deposits from the valve heads and stems.

Inspection and renovation

Note: *Be sure to perform all the following inspection procedures before concluding that the services of an engine overhaul specialist are required. Make a list of all items that require attention.*

Cylinder head

5 Inspect the head very carefully for cracks, evidence of coolant leakage, and other damage. If cracks are found, a new cylinder head should be obtained.

6 Use a straight-edge and feeler blade to check that the cylinder head surface is not distorted **(see illustration)**. If it is, it may be possible to have it resurfaced ("skimmed") on C-type engines. The manufacturers do not allow resurfacing on the other engine types.

7 Examine the valve seats in each of the combustion chambers. If they are severely pitted, cracked or burned, then they will need to be renewed or recut by an engine overhaul specialist. If they are only slightly pitted, this can be removed by grinding the valve heads and seats together with coarse, then fine, grinding paste as described in the following paragraphs.

8 If the valve guides are worn, indicated by a side-to-side motion of the valve in the guide, new guides must be fitted. A dial gauge may be used to determine the amount of side play of the valve. Recheck the fit using a new valve

if in doubt, to decide whether it is the valve or the guide which is worn. If new guides are to be fitted, the valves must be renewed in any case. Valve guides may be renewed using a press and a suitable mandrel, making sure that they are at the correct height. The work is best carried out by an engine overhaul specialist, since if it is not done skilfully, there is a risk of damaging the cylinder head.

Valves

⚠️ *Warning: The exhaust valves on the 16-valve 1764 cc (F7P) engine are filled with sodium, and must be disposed of carefully. Ideally, they should be cut in half and then immersed in water (approximately 10 litres for four exhaust valves). It is important to take adequate safety precautions during this operation by wearing goggles and suitable clothing, since the sodium reacts violently when it contacts the water. When the reaction has subsided, the water will contain sodium hydroxide (caustic soda), which must itself be disposed of safely.*

9 Examine the heads of each valve for pitting, burning, cracks and general wear, and check the valve stem for scoring and wear ridges. Rotate the valve, and check for any obvious indication that it is bent. Look for pits and excessive wear on the end of each valve stem. If the valve appears satisfactory at this stage, measure the valve stem diameter at several points using a micrometer **(see illustration)**. Any significant difference in the readings obtained indicates wear of the valve stem. Should any of these conditions be apparent, the valve(s) must be renewed. If the valves are in satisfactory condition, or if new valves are being fitted, they should be ground (lapped) into their respective seats to ensure a smooth gas-tight seal.

10 Valve grinding is carried out as follows. Place the cylinder head upside-down on a bench, with a block of wood at each end to give clearance for the valve stems.

11 Smear a trace of coarse carborundum paste on the seat face, and press a suction grinding tool onto the valve head. With a semi-rotary action, grind the valve head to its seat, lifting the valve occasionally to redistribute the

9.11 Grinding-in the valves

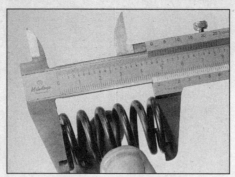

9.12 Checking the valve spring free length

9.15 Priming the hydraulic tappets with oil

grinding paste **(see illustration)**. When a dull-matt even surface is produced on both the valve seat and the valve, wipe off the paste and repeat the process with fine carborundum paste. A light spring placed under the valve head will greatly ease this operation. When a smooth unbroken ring of light grey matt finish is produced on both the valve and seat, the grinding operation is complete. Be sure to remove all traces of grinding paste, using paraffin or a suitable solvent, before reassembly of the cylinder head.

Valve components

12 Examine the valve springs for signs of damage and discoloration, and also measure their free length using vernier calipers **(see**

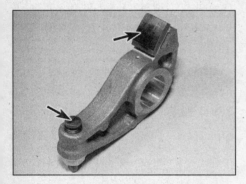

9.16a Check the rocker arm contact surfaces (arrowed) for wear

illustration) or by comparing the existing spring with a new component.
13 Stand each spring on a flat surface, and check it for squareness. If any of the springs are damaged, distorted or have lost their tension, obtain a complete new set of springs. It is normal to renew the springs as a matter of course during a major overhaul.
14 On the 1721 cc (F2N and F3N) and 1794 cc (F3P) engines, inspect the tappet buckets and their shims for scoring, pitting (especially on the shims), and wear ridges. Renew any components as necessary. Note that some scuffing is to be expected, and is acceptable provided that the tappets are not scored.
15 On the 1764 cc (F7P) engine, examine the hydraulic tappets for scoring, pitting and wear ridges. Renew as necessary. If new hydraulic tappets are being fitted, or if the old ones have been allowed to drain, prime them with fresh engine oil before fitting them, as follows. Immerse each tappet in oil with the hole uppermost, and use flat-nosed pliers to move them up and down until all air is forced out **(see illustration)**.

Rocker arm components - C-type and E-type engines

16 Check the rocker arm contact surfaces for pitting, wear, score marks, or any indication that the surface-hardening has worn through. Dismantle the rocker shaft, and check the rocker arm and rocker shaft pivot and contact

areas in the same way. Measure the internal diameter of each rocker, and check their fit on the shaft. Clean out the oil spill holes in each rocker using a length of wire **(see illustrations)**. Renew the rocker arm or the rocker shaft itself if any are suspect.
17 On the C-type engines, inspect the pushrod ends for scuffing and excessive wear. Roll each pushrod on a flat surface, such as a piece of plate glass, and check for straightness.

Valve stem oil seals

18 The valve stem oil seals should be renewed as a matter of course.

2D

10 Cylinder head - reassembly

Note: *New valve stem oil seals should be fitted on reassembly.*
1 Lubricate the stems of the valves, and insert them into their original locations. If new valves are being fitted, insert them into the locations to which they have been ground.
2 Working on the first valve, dip the new oil seal in engine oil, then carefully locate it over the valve and onto the guide. Take care not to damage the seal as it is passed over the valve stem. Use a suitable socket or metal tube to press the seal firmly onto the guide **(see illustration)**.
3 Locate the spring seat on the guide,

9.16b Checking the internal diameter of the rocker arms

9.16c Clean the oil spill holes using a length of wire

10.2 Pressing a valve seal onto its guide

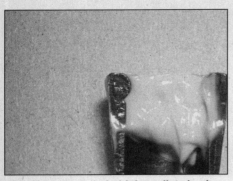

10.4 Use grease to hold the collets in place on reassembly

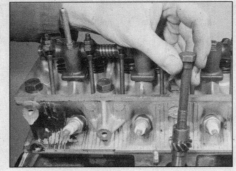

11.15 Fit the distributor drivegear . . .

11.16 . . . so that the slot is at right-angles to the crankshaft centre-line, with its larger offset side facing the flywheel when fitted

followed by the spring(s) and cap. Where applicable, the spring should be fitted with its closest coils towards the head.

4 Compress the valve spring, and locate the split collets in the recess in the valve stem. Use a little grease to hold the collets in place **(see illustration)**. Note that on the C-type engines, the collets are different for the inlet and exhaust valves, that latter type having two curved collars. Release the compressor, then repeat the procedure on the remaining valves.

5 With all the valves installed, place the cylinder head flat on the bench and, using a hammer and interposed block of wood, tap the end of each valve stem to settle the components.

6 On the 1764 cc (F7P) engine, fit the hydraulic tappets to the bores from which they were removed.

7 On the 1721 cc (F2N and F3N) and 1794 cc (F3P) engines, lubricate the tappet buckets, and insert them into their respective locations, as noted during removal. Make sure that each bucket has its correct tappet shim in place on its upper face, and that the shim is installed with its etched size number facing downwards.

11 Camshaft and followers (C-type engines) - removal, inspection and refitting

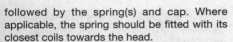

Removal

1 Remove the cylinder head, timing chain and camshaft sprocket with reference to Chapter 2B.

2 Remove the distributor with reference to Chapter 5.

3 Using a suitable bolt screwed into the distributor drivegear, or a length of tapered dowel rod, extract the drivegear from the distributor aperture.

4 Withdraw the camshaft followers from the top of the cylinder block, keeping them in strict order of removal.

5 Unscrew and remove the two bolts securing the camshaft retaining plate to the cylinder block, and carefully withdraw the camshaft from its location.

Inspection

6 Examine the camshaft bearing surfaces, cam lobes and skew gear for wear ridges, pitting, scoring or chipping of the gear teeth. Renew the camshaft if any of these conditions are apparent.

7 If the camshaft is serviceable, temporarily refit the sprocket, and secure with the retaining bolt. Using a feeler blade, measure the clearance between the camshaft retaining plate and the outer face of the bearing journal. If the clearance (endfloat) exceeds the specified dimension, renew the retaining plate. To do this, remove the sprocket, and draw off the plate and retaining collar using a suitable puller. Fit the new plate and a new collar, using a hammer and tube to drive the collar into position.

8 Examine the condition of the camshaft bearings. If renewal is necessary, have this work carried out by a Renault dealer or engineering works.

9 Inspect the cam followers for wear ridges and pitting of their camshaft lobe contact faces, and for scoring on the sides of the follower body. Light scuff marks are normal, but there should be no signs of scoring or ridges. If the followers show signs of wear, renew them. Note that they must all be renewed if a new camshaft is being fitted.

Refitting

10 Lubricate the camshaft bearings, and carefully insert the camshaft from the timing gear end of the engine.

11 Refit the retaining plate, then insert and tighten the bolts securely. Check that the camshaft rotates smoothly.

12 Lubricate the cam followers, and insert them into their original bores in the cylinder block.

13 Refit the camshaft sprocket and timing chain, and the cylinder head, with reference to Chapter 2B.

14 Using a ring spanner on the crankshaft pulley bolt, turn the crankshaft until No 1 piston (flywheel end) is at the top of its compression stroke. This position can be established by placing a finger over No 1 plug hole and rotating the crankshaft until compression can be felt; continue turning the crankshaft until the piston reaches the top of its stroke. Use a screwdriver through the plug hole to feel the movement of the piston, but be careful not to damage the piston crown or the plug threads in the cylinder head.

15 Without moving the crankshaft, position the drivegear so that its slots are at the 2 o'clock and 8 o'clock positions, with the larger offset side facing away from the engine **(see illustration)**.

16 Now lower the drivegear into mesh with the camshaft and oil pump driveshaft. As the gear meshes with the camshaft, it will rotate anti-clockwise; it should end up with its slot at right-angles to the crankshaft centre-line, and with the larger offset towards the flywheel. It will probably be a tooth out on the first attempt, and will take two or three attempts to get it just right **(see illustration)**.

17 Refit the distributor with reference to Chapter 5.

12 Piston/connecting rod assemblies - removal

1 With the cylinder head, sump and oil pump removed, proceed as follows.

2 Rotate the crankshaft so that No 1 big-end cap (nearest the flywheel position) is at the lowest point of its travel. If the big-end cap and rod are not already numbered, mark them with a centre-punch **(see illustration)**. Mark both cap and rod to identify the cylinder they operate in, noting that No 1 is nearest the flywheel end of the engine.

3 Before removing the big-end caps, use a feeler blade to check the amount of side play between the caps and the crankshaft webs **(see illustration)**.

4 Unscrew and remove the big-end bearing cap nuts (C-type and E-type engines) or bolts (F-type engines). Withdraw the cap, complete with shell bearing, from the connecting rod. Strike the cap with a wooden or copper mallet if it is stuck.

5 If only the bearing shells are being attended to, push the connecting rod up and off the crankpin, and remove the upper bearing shell. Keep the bearing shells and cap together in their correct sequence if they are to be refitted.

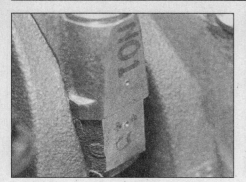

12.2 Big-end caps marked with a centre-punch

12.3 Checking the big-end cap side play

13.2 Checking the crankshaft endfloat with a dial gauge

C-type and E-type engines

6 Remove the liner clamps and withdraw each liner, together with piston and connecting rod, from the top of the cylinder block. Mark the liners using masking tape, so that they may be refitted in their original locations.

7 Withdraw the piston from the bottom of the liner. Keep each piston with its respective liner if they are to be re-used.

F-type engines

8 Push the connecting rod up, and remove the piston and rod from the bore. Note that if there is a pronounced wear ridge at the top of the bore, there is a risk of damaging the piston as the rings foul the ridge. However, it is reasonable to assume that a rebore and new pistons will be required in any case if the ridge is so pronounced.

---

13 Crankshaft - removal

---

1 With the timing belt/chain, rear timing cover and front plate (E-type and F-type engines), flywheel/driveplate and pistons removed, proceed as follows.

2 Before the crankshaft is removed, check the endfloat using a dial gauge in contact with the end of the crankshaft **(see illustration)**. Push the crankshaft fully one way, and then zero the gauge. Push the crankshaft fully the other way,

and check the endfloat. The result can be compared with the specified amount, and will give an indication as to whether new thrustwashers are required.

3 If a dial gauge is not available, feeler blades can be used. First push the crankshaft fully towards the flywheel end of the engine, then slip the feeler blade between the web of No 2 crankpin and the thrustwasher of the centre main bearing (C-type and E-type engines) **(see illustration)**, or between the web of No 1 crankpin and the thrustwasher of No 2 main bearing (F-type engines).

4 Identification numbers should already be cast onto the base of each main bearing cap. If not, number the cap and crankcase using a centre-punch, as was done for the connecting rods and caps **(see illustration)**.

5 Unscrew and remove the main bearing cap retaining bolts, and withdraw the caps, complete with bearing shells **(see illustration)**. Tap the caps with a wooden or copper mallet if they are stuck.

6 Carefully lift the crankshaft from the crankcase.

7 Remove the thrustwashers at each side of the centre main bearing (C-type and E-type engines) or No 2 main bearing (F-type engines), then remove the bearing shell upper halves from the crankcase **(see illustrations)**. Place each shell with its respective bearing cap.

8 Remove the oil seal from the rear of the crankshaft.

13.3 Checking the crankshaft endfloat with a feeler blade - C- and E-type engines

13.4 Identification numbers (arrowed) on the main bearings

13.5 Removing No 1 main bearing cap

13.7a Removing the thrustwashers . . .

13.7b . . . and main bearing shell upper halves

2D

14.1a Removing the coolant pipe from the cylinder block (E-type engine)

14.1b Oil pressure switch location (arrowed) on the cylinder block (F-type engine)

14.1c Oil sprayer location on the bottom of the bore

14 Cylinder block/crankcase - cleaning and inspection

Note: *On C-type and E-type engines, new base seals/O-rings will be required for the cylinder liners on refitting.*

Cleaning

1 For complete cleaning, the core plugs should be removed. Drill a small hole in them, then insert a self-tapping screw, and pull out the plugs using a pair of grips or a slide-hammer. Also remove all external components and senders, and where applicable, unbolt the drivebelt tensioner bracket from the cylinder block. Where applicable, on F-type engines, unbolt the coolant pipe, oil cooler and alternator drivebelt tensioner bracket. Remove the oil sprayers (when fitted) from the bottom of each bore by unscrewing the retaining bolts **(see illustrations)**.

2 Scrape all traces of gasket from the cylinder block, taking care not to damage the head and sump mating faces.

3 Remove all oil gallery plugs. The plugs are usually very tight - they may have to be drilled out and the holes re-tapped. Use new plugs when the engine is reassembled.

4 If the block is extremely dirty, it should be steam-cleaned.

5 After the block has been steam-cleaned, clean all oil holes and oil galleries one more time. Flush all internal passages with warm water until the water runs clear, dry the block thoroughly, and wipe all machined surfaces with a light rust-preventative oil. If you have access to compressed air, use it to speed up the drying process, and to blow out all the oil holes and galleries.

 Warning: Wear eye protection when using compressed air!

6 If the block is not very dirty, you can do an adequate cleaning job with hot soapy water and a stiff brush. Take plenty of time, and do a thorough job. Regardless of the cleaning method used, be sure to clean all oil holes and galleries very thoroughly, dry the block completely, and coat all machined surfaces with light oil.

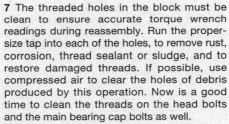

14.1d Removing the oil level sender from the cylinder block

7 The threaded holes in the block must be clean to ensure accurate torque wrench readings during reassembly. Run the proper-size tap into each of the holes, to remove rust, corrosion, thread sealant or sludge, and to restore damaged threads. If possible, use compressed air to clear the holes of debris produced by this operation. Now is a good time to clean the threads on the head bolts and the main bearing cap bolts as well.

8 Refit the main bearing caps, and tighten the bolts finger-tight.

9 After coating the mating surfaces of the new core plugs with suitable sealant, refit them in the cylinder block. Make sure that they are driven in straight and seated properly, or leakage could result.

 HAYNES HiNT *Special tools are available to fit core plugs, but a large socket, with an outside diameter that will just slip into the core plug, will work just as well.*

10 Apply suitable sealant to the new oil gallery plugs, and insert them into the holes in the block. Tighten them securely.

11 If the engine is not going to be reassembled right away, cover it with a large plastic bag, to keep it clean and prevent it rusting.

Inspection

12 Visually check the block for cracks, rust and corrosion. Look for stripped threads in the

14.1e Coolant pipe and mounting bolt - F-type engine

threaded holes. If there has been any history of internal water leakage, it may be worthwhile having an engine overhaul specialist check the block with special equipment. If defects are found, have the block repaired, if possible, or renewed.

13 Check the cylinder bores/liners for scuffing and scoring. Normally, bore wear will be evident in the form of a wear ridge at the top of the bore. This ridge marks the limit of piston travel.

14 Measure the diameter of each cylinder at the top (just under the ridge area), centre and bottom of the cylinder bore, parallel to the crankshaft axis.

15 Next measure each cylinder's diameter at the same three locations across the crankshaft axis. If the difference between any of the measurements is greater than 0.20 mm, indicating that the cylinder is excessively out-of-round or tapered, then remedial action must be considered.

16 Repeat this procedure for the remaining cylinders.

17 If the cylinder walls are badly scuffed or scored, or if they are excessively out-of-round or tapered, have the cylinder block rebored (F-type engines) or obtain new cylinder liners (C-type and E-type engines). New pistons (oversize in the case of a rebore) will also be required.

18 If the cylinders are in reasonably good condition, then it may only be necessary to renew the piston rings.

19 If this is the case, the bores should be

honed, in order to allow the new rings to bed-in correctly and provide the best possible seal. The conventional type of hone has spring-loaded stones, and is used with a power drill. You will also need some paraffin or honing oil, and rags. The hone should be moved up and down the cylinder to produce a crosshatch pattern, and plenty of honing oil should be used. Ideally, the crosshatch lines should intersect at approximately a 60° angle. Do not take off more material than is necessary to produce the required finish. If new pistons or rings are being fitted, their manufacturers may specify a finish with a different angle, so their instructions should be followed. Do not withdraw the hone from the cylinder while it is still being turned, but stop it first. After honing a cylinder, wipe out all traces of the honing oil. If equipment of this type is not available, or if you are not sure whether you are competent to undertake the task yourself, an engine overhaul specialist will carry out the work at a moderate cost.

20 Before refitting the cylinder liners, their protrusions must be checked as follows, and new base seals/O-rings fitted. On the C-type engines, the seals are a flat ring-type gasket of special material. The seals are available in three thickn0esses, colour-coded blue, red and green. On the E-type engines, the seals are in the form of a rubber O-ring.

21 Place the liner with a blue base seal (C-type engines) or without a base O-ring (E-type engines) in the cylinder block, and press down to make sure that it is seated correctly. Using a dial gauge or straight-edge and feeler blade, check that the protrusion of the liner above the upper surface of the cylinder block is within the specified limits **(see illustrations)**. Check all of the liners in the same manner, and record the protrusions. If the protrusions are incorrect on the C-type engines, try again using a red or green seal instead of the blue one. Note that there is also a limit specified for the difference of protrusion between two adjacent liners. If new liners are being fitted, it is permitted to interchange them to bring this difference within limits. The protrusions may be stepped upwards or downwards from the flywheel end of the engine.

22 Refit all external components and senders.

14.21a Checking the liner protrusion with a dial gauge . . .

14.21b . . . and with feeler blades

15 Piston/connecting rod assemblies - inspection and reassembly

Inspection

1 Before the inspection process can begin, the piston/connecting rod assemblies must be cleaned, and the original piston rings removed from the pistons.

2 Carefully expand the old rings over the top of the pistons. The use of two or three old feeler blades will be helpful in preventing the rings dropping into empty grooves **(see illustration)**. Take care, as piston rings are sharp.

3 Scrape away all traces of carbon from the top of the piston. A hand-held wire brush or a piece of fine emery cloth can be used once the majority of the deposits have been scraped away.

4 Remove the carbon from the ring grooves in the piston by cleaning them using an old ring. Break the ring in half to do this. Be very careful to remove only the carbon deposits; do not remove any metal, nor nick or scratch the sides of the ring grooves. Protect your fingers - piston rings are sharp.

5 Once the deposits have been removed, clean the piston/connecting rod assembly with paraffin or a suitable solvent, and dry thoroughly. Make sure the oil return holes in the back sides of the ring grooves are clear.

6 If the pistons and cylinder bores are not damaged or worn excessively, and if the cylinder block does not need to be rebored, the original pistons can be re-used. Normal piston wear appears as even vertical wear on the piston thrust surfaces, and slight looseness of the top ring in its groove. New piston rings, however, should always be used when the engine is reassembled.

7 Carefully inspect each piston for cracks around the skirt, at the gudgeon pin bosses, and at the piston ring lands (between the piston ring grooves).

8 Look for scoring and scuffing on the sides of the skirt, holes in the piston crown, and burned areas at the edge of the crown. If the skirt is scored or scuffed, the engine may have been

suffering from overheating and/or abnormal combustion, which caused excessively-high operating temperatures. The cooling and lubricating systems should be checked thoroughly. A hole in the piston crown is an indication that abnormal combustion (pre-ignition) was occurring. Burned areas at the edge of the piston crown are usually evidence of knocking (detonation). If any of the above problems exist, the causes must be corrected, or the damage will occur again. The causes may include inlet air leaks, incorrect fuel/air mixture, or (when applicable) incorrect ignition timing.

9 Corrosion of the piston, in the form of small pits, indicates that coolant is leaking into the combustion chamber and/or the crankcase. Again, the cause must be corrected, or the problem may persist in the rebuilt engine.

10 If new rings are being fitted to old pistons, measure the piston ring-to-groove clearance by placing a new piston ring in each ring groove and measuring the clearance with a feeler blade **(see illustration)**. Check the clearance at three or four places around each groove. No values are specified, but if the measured clearance is excessive - say greater than 0.10 mm - new pistons will be required. If the new ring is excessively tight, the most likely cause is dirt remaining in the groove.

11 Check the piston-to-bore/liner clearance by measuring the cylinder bore/liner (see Section 14) and the piston diameter. Measure the piston across the skirt, at a 90° angle to

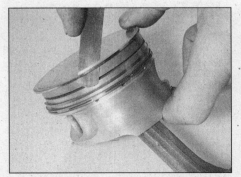

15.2 Using an old feeler blade to remove the piston rings

15.10 Measuring the piston ring-to-groove clearance

2D

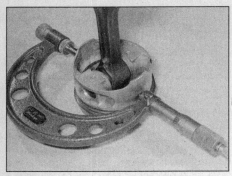

15.11 Measuring the pistons for ovality

15.13 Measuring the piston ring end gap

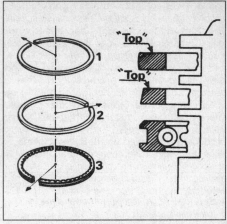

15.14 Piston ring identification on the E-type engine

the gudgeon pin, approximately halfway down the skirt **(see illustration)**. Subtract the piston diameter from the bore/liner diameter to obtain the clearance. On F-type engines, if this is greater than the figures given in the Specifications, the block will have to be rebored and new pistons and rings fitted. On C- and E-type engines, new pistons and liners are supplied in matched pairs.

12 Check the fit of the gudgeon pin by twisting the piston and connecting rod in opposite directions. Any noticeable play indicates excessive wear, which must be corrected. If the pistons or connecting rods are to be renewed, the work should be carried out by a Renault garage or engine overhaul specialist. (In the case of the 1764 cc/F7P engine, the gudgeon pins are secured by circlips, so the pistons and connecting rods can be separated without difficulty. Note the position of the piston relative to the rod before dismantling, and use new circlips on reassembly.)

13 Before refitting the rings to the pistons, check their end gaps by inserting each of them in their cylinder bores **(see illustration)**. Use the piston to make sure that they are square. No values are specified, but typical gaps would be of the order of 0.50 mm for compression rings, perhaps somewhat greater for the oil control rings. Renault rings are supplied pre-gapped; no attempt should be made to adjust the gaps by filing.

Reassembly

14 Install the new rings by fitting them over the top of the piston, starting with the oil control scraper ring. Use feeler blades or strips of tin in the same way as when removing the old rings. Note that the second compression ring is tapered. Both compression rings must be fitted with the word "TOP" uppermost **(see illustration)**. Be careful when handling the compression rings; they will break if they are handled roughly or expanded too far.

15 With all the rings in position, space the ring gaps at 120° to each other.

16 Note that, if new piston and liner assemblies have been obtained, each piston is matched to its respective liner, and they must not be interchanged.

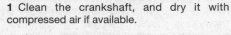

16 Crankshaft - inspection

1 Clean the crankshaft, and dry it with compressed air if available.

 Warning: Wear eye protection when using compressed air! Be sure to clean the oil holes with a pipe cleaner or similar probe.

2 Check the main and big-end bearing journals for uneven wear, scoring, pitting and cracking.

3 Check the bearing journals for roughness by running a finger lightly over the bearing surface. Any roughness (which will be accompanied by obvious bearing wear) indicates the that the crankshaft requires regrinding.

4 Remove all burrs from the crankshaft oil holes with a stone, file or scraper.

5 Using a micrometer, measure the diameter of the main bearing and connecting rod journals, and compare the results with the Specifications at the beginning of this Chapter **(see illustration)**. By measuring the diameter at a number of points around each journal's circumference, you will be able to determine whether or not the journal is out-of-round. Take the measurement at each end of the journal, near the webs, to determine if the journal is tapered. If any of the measurements vary by more than 0.025 mm, the crankshaft

16.5 Using a micrometer to check the crankshaft journals

will have to be reground, and undersize bearings fitted.

6 Check the oil seal journals as applicable at each end of the crankshaft for wear and damage. If the seal has worn an excessive groove in the journal, consult an engine overhaul specialist, who will be able to advise if a repair is possible, or whether a new crankshaft is necessary.

17 Main and big-end bearings - inspection

1 Even though the main and big-end bearings should be renewed during the engine overhaul, the old bearings should be retained for close examination, as they may reveal valuable information about the condition of the engine. The size of the bearing shells is stamped on the back metal **(see illustration)**, and this information should be given to the supplier of the new shells.

2 Bearing failure occurs because of lack of lubrication, the presence of dirt or other foreign particles, overloading the engine, and corrosion. Regardless of the cause of bearing failure, it must be corrected before the engine is reassembled, to prevent it from happening again.

3 When examining the bearings, remove them

17.1 Typical marking on the back metal of a bearing shell

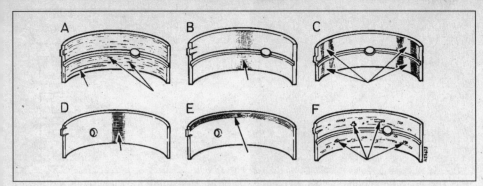

17.2 Typical bearing failures

A Scratched by dirt; dirt embedded into
   bearing material
B Lack of oil; overlay wiped out
C Improper seating; bright (polished) sections

D Tapered journal; overlay gone from entire
   surface
E Radius ride
F Fatigue failure; craters or pockets

from the engine block, the main bearing caps, the connecting rods and the rod caps, and lay them out on a clean surface in the same general position as their location in the engine. This will enable you to match any bearing problems with the corresponding crankshaft journal.

4 Dirt and other foreign particles get into the engine in a variety of ways. Dirt may be left in the engine during assembly, or it may pass through filters or the crankcase ventilation system. It may get into the oil, and from there into the bearings. Metal chips from machining operations and normal engine wear are often present. Abrasives are sometimes left in engine components after reconditioning, especially when parts are not thoroughly cleaned using the proper cleaning methods. Whatever the source, these foreign objects often end up embedded in the soft bearing material, and are easily recognized. Large particles will not embed in the bearing, and will score or gouge the bearing and journal. The best prevention for this cause of bearing failure is to clean all parts thoroughly, and keep everything spotlessly-clean during engine assembly. Frequent and regular engine oil and filter changes are also recommended.

5 Lack of lubrication (or lubrication breakdown) has a number of interrelated causes. Excessive heat (which thins the oil), overloading (which squeezes the oil from the bearing face) and oil leakage (from excessive bearing clearances, worn oil pump or high engine speeds) all contribute to lubrication breakdown. Blocked oil passages, which usually are the result of misaligned oil holes in a bearing shell, will also oil-starve a bearing and destroy it. When lack of lubrication is the cause of bearing failure, the bearing material is wiped or extruded from the steel backing of the bearing. Temperatures may increase to the point where the steel backing turns blue from overheating.

6 Driving habits can have a definite effect on bearing life. Full-throttle, low-speed operation (labouring the engine) puts very high loads on bearings, which tends to squeeze out the oil film. These loads cause the bearings to flex,

which produces fine cracks in the bearing face (fatigue failure). Eventually, the bearing material will loosen in pieces, and tear away from the steel backing. Short-trip driving leads to corrosion of bearings, because insufficient engine heat is produced to drive off the condensed water and corrosive gases. These products collect in the engine oil, forming acid and sludge. As the oil is carried to the engine bearings, the acid attacks and corrodes the bearing material.

7 Incorrect bearing installation during engine assembly will lead to bearing failure as well. Tight-fitting bearings leave insufficient bearing oil clearance, and will result in oil starvation. Dirt or foreign particles trapped behind a bearing shell result in high spots on the bearing which lead to failure.

18 Engine overhaul - reassembly sequence

1 Before reassembly begins, ensure that all new parts have been obtained, and that all necessary tools are available. Read through the entire procedure to familiarise yourself with the work involved, and to ensure that all items necessary for reassembly of the engine are at hand. In addition to all normal tools and materials, a thread-locking compound will be needed. A tube of RTV sealing compound will also be required for the joint faces that are fitted without gaskets; it is recommended that CAF 4/60 THIXO paste (obtainable from Renault dealers) is used, as it is specially-formulated for this purpose.

2 In order to save time and avoid problems, engine reassembly can be carried out in the following order.
(a) Crankshaft.
(b) Pistons/connecting rod assemblies.
(c) Oil pump.
(d) Sump.
(e) Flywheel/driveplate.
(f) Cylinder head.
(g) Timing chain/belt and sprockets.
(h) Engine external components.

19 Crankshaft - refitting and main bearing running clearance check

Note: *Suitable seals or suitable sealant, and on certain engines suitable hardener, will be required when refitting No 1 main bearing cap - see text. New crankshaft oil seals should be used on refitting.*

1 Before fitting the crankshaft and main bearings on F-type engines, a decision has to be made on the method to be used to seal the No 1 main bearing cap. Two types of bearing cap may be fitted. The earlier type has sealing grooves in the sides of the cap, and in the lower mating face of the cylinder block. The later type of bearing cap has sealing grooves in the sides of the cap, which extend onto the upper cylinder block mating face of the cap; there are no grooves in the lower cylinder block mating face. The earlier type of bearing cap can be sealed using butyl seals or silicone sealant. The later type of bearing cap must be sealed using silicone sealant. If butyl seals are to be used to seal an early-type bearing cap, it is necessary to determine the correct thickness of the seals to obtain from Renault, as follows:
(a) Place the bearing cap in position without any seals, and secure it with the two retaining bolts.

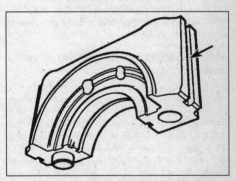

19.1a Early-type No 1 main bearing cap with sealing grooves (arrowed) in side of cap

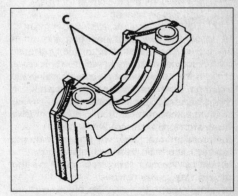

19.1b Later-type No 1 main bearing cap with sealing grooves (C) extending into cylinder block mating face of cap

2D

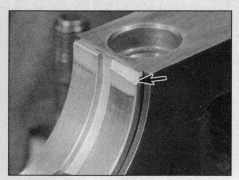

19.4 Oil pump lubricating chamfer (arrowed) on No 5 upper main bearing shell on the E-type engine

19.7 Thread of Plastigage (arrowed) placed on a crankshaft main journal

19.11 Measuring the Plastigage width with the special gauge

(b) Locate a twist drill, dowel rod or any other suitable implement which will just fit in the side seal groove.

(c) Now measure the implement - this dimension is the side seal groove size. If the dimension is less than or equal to 5 mm, a 5.10 mm thick side seal is needed. If the dimension is more than 5 mm, a 5.4 mm thick side seal is required.

(d) Having determined the side seal size and obtained the necessary seals, proceed as follows for the other types of engine as well. Note that silicone sealant is used instead of side seals when the engine is originally assembled at the factory.

Main bearing running clearance check

2 Clean the backs of the bearing shells and the bearing recesses in both the cylinder block and main bearing caps.

3 Press the bearing shells without oil holes into the caps, ensuring that the tag on the shell engages in the notch in the cap.

4 Press the bearing shells with the oil holes/grooves into the recesses in the cylinder block. Note the following points:

(a) On C-type engines, the upper shells for Nos 1 and 3 main bearings are identical, as are the shells for Nos 2, 4 and 5 main bearings.

(b) On E-type engines, No 5 upper main bearing shell is different from the rest, in that it has an oil pump pinion lubricating chamfer which must face the timing belt end of the crankshaft (see illustration).

(c) On all engines, if the original main bearing shells are being re-   used, these must be refitted to their original locations in the block and caps.

5 Before the crankshaft can be permanently installed, the main bearing running clearance should be checked; this can be done in either of two ways. One method is to fit the main bearing caps to the cylinder block, with the bearing shells in place. With the cap retaining bolts tightened to the specified torque, measure the internal diameter of each

assembled pair of bearing shells using a vernier dial indicator or internal micrometer. If the diameter of each corresponding crankshaft journal is measured and then subtracted from the bearing internal diameter, the result will be the main bearing running clearance. The second (and more accurate) method is to use an American product known as "Plastigage". This consists of a fine thread of perfectly-round plastic, which is compressed between the bearing cap and the journal. When the cap is removed, the deformation of the plastic thread is measured with a special card gauge supplied with the kit. The running clearance is determined from this gauge. Plastigage is sometimes difficult to obtain in the UK, but enquiries at one of the larger specialist chains of quality motor factors should produce the name of a stockist in your area. The procedure for using Plastigage is as follows.

6 With the upper main bearing shells in place, carefully lay the crankshaft in position. Do not use any lubricant; the crankshaft journals and bearing shells must be perfectly clean and dry.

7 Cut several pieces of the appropriate-size Plastigage (they should be slightly shorter than the width of the main bearings), and place one piece on each crankshaft journal axis (see illustration).

8 With the bearing shells in position in the caps, fit the caps to their numbered or previously-noted locations. Take care not to disturb the Plastigage.

9 Starting with the centre main bearing and working outward, tighten the main bearing cap bolts progressively to their specified torque setting. Don't rotate the crankshaft at any time during this operation.

10 Remove the bolts and carefully lift off the main bearing caps, keeping them in order. Don't disturb the Plastigage or rotate the crankshaft. If any of the bearing caps are difficult to remove, tap them from side-to-side with a soft-faced mallet.

11 Compare the width of the crushed Plastigage on each journal to the scale printed on the Plastigage envelope, to obtain the main bearing running clearance (see illustration).

12 If the clearance is not as specified, the bearing shells may be the wrong size (or

19.17 Rear oil seal located on the crankshaft

excessively-worn, if the original shells are being re-used). Before deciding that different-size shells are needed, make sure that no dirt or oil was trapped between the bearing shells and the caps or block when the clearance was measured. If the Plastigage was wider at one end than at the other, the journal may be tapered.

13 Carefully scrape away all traces of the Plastigage material from the crankshaft and bearing shells, using your fingernail or something which is unlikely to score the shells.

Final refitting

14 Carefully lift the crankshaft out of the cylinder block once more.

15 Using a little grease, stick the thrustwashers to each side of the centre main bearing (C- and E-type engines) or No 2 main bearing (F-type engine). Ensure that the oilway grooves on each thrustwasher face outwards from the bearing.

16 Lubricate the lips of the new crankshaft rear oil seal, and carefully slip it over the crankshaft rear journal. Do this carefully, as the seal lips are very delicate. Ensure that the open side of the seal faces the engine.

17 Liberally lubricate each bearing shell in the cylinder block, and lower the crankshaft into position. Check that the rear oil seal is positioned correctly (see illustration).

18 Lubricate the bearing shells, then fit the bearing caps in their numbered or previously-

19.18a Applying sealant to No 1 main bearing cap on the E-type engine

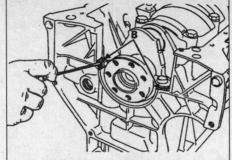

19.18b Coating the lower faces of the cylinder block (B) with sealant - early-type No 1 main bearing cap on F-type engine

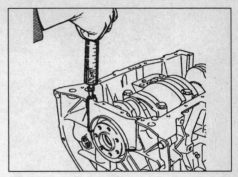

19.21a Injecting sealant into No 1 main bearing cap grooves - early-type No 1 main bearing cap on F-type engine

2D

noted locations. Note the following points (see illustrations):

(a) On C-type engines, apply Loctite Frenetanch to the bearing faces of No 1 main bearing cap.

(b) On E-type engines, apply a thin coating of CAF 4/60 THIXO sealant to the outer corners of No 1 main bearing cap, as shown (see illustration).

(c) When fitting the butyl seals to the early-type No 1 main bearing cap on the F-type engine (see paragraph 1), fit the seals with their grooves facing outwards. Position the seals so that approximately 0.2 mm (0.008 in) of seal protrudes at the bottom-facing side (the side towards the crankcase). Lubricate the seals with a little oil, and apply a little CAF 4/60 THIXO sealant to the bottom corners of the cap prior to fitting it. When the cap is being fitted, use the bolts as a guide by just starting them in their threads, then pressing the cap firmly into position.

(d) Where silicone sealant is to be used on the early-type No 1 main bearing on the F-type engine (see paragraph 1), clean all the mating faces of the cylinder block and bearing cap using a degreasing agent, then allow the cleaned areas to dry. Lightly coat the lower faces of the cylinder block with CAF 4/60 THIXO sealant, but do not block the oil retention grooves.

19 Fit the main bearing cap bolts, and tighten them progressively to the specified torque.

20 Where butyl seals have been fitted on the F-type engine, trim the protruding ends flush with the surface of the crankcase.

21 Where silicone sealant is being used on an early-type No 1 main bearing cap on the F-type engine (see paragraph 1), mix 45 ml of CAF 4/60 THIXO sealant with half the contents of the tube of hardener supplied, to obtain a homogenous mixture which is slightly pink in colour. Inject the mixture into the bearing cap grooves, allowing the mixture to flow out slightly either side of the grooves to ensure that the grooves are completely filled. Using a cloth, wipe away the surplus mixture both inside and outside the cylinder block, and at

the areas "A" shown (see illustration). Pass a length of steel wire through the lubrication oilways to check that they are not blocked. Alternatively, blow through the oilways with compressed air.

⚠️ **Warning: Always wear eye protection when using compressed air! Allow the assembly to dry for a few minutes, then cut away surplus sealant from the joint face.**

22 Where silicone sealant is being used on a later-type No 1 main bearing cap on the F-type engine (see paragraph 1), follow the procedure described previously in paragraph 21, noting the following differences:

(a) Fit the crankshaft oil seals before the silicone is injected.

(b) Allow the sealant to escape via the bearing cap sealing grooves (see illustration).

23 Check that the crankshaft is free to turn. Some stiffness is normal if new components have been fitted, but there must be no jamming or tight spots.

24 Check the crankshaft endfloat with reference to Section 13.

20 Piston/connecting rod assemblies - refitting and big-end bearing running clearance check

Note: A piston ring compressor tool will be required for this operation.

1 Clean the backs of the big-end bearing shells, and the recesses in the connecting rods and big-end caps. If new shells are being fitted, ensure that all traces of the protective grease are cleaned off using paraffin. Wipe the shells and connecting rods dry with a lint-free cloth.

2 Press the big-end bearing shells into the connecting rods and caps, in their correct positions. Make sure that the location tabs are engaged with the cut-outs in the connecting rods (see illustration).

19.21b Using a cloth, wipe away the surplus sealant mixture from the areas (A) shown - early-type No 1 main bearing cap on F-type engine

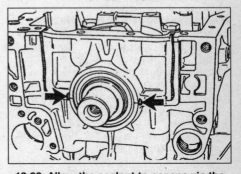

19.22 Allow the sealant to escape via the bearing cap sealing grooves - later-type No 1 main bearing cap on the F-type engine

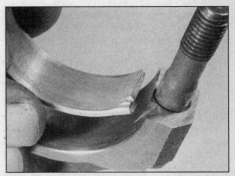

20.2 Engaging the shell tab with the cut-out in the connecting rod

20.3 Fitting a liner base O-ring - E-type engine

20.6a Use a piston ring compressor when inserting the pistons in the liners

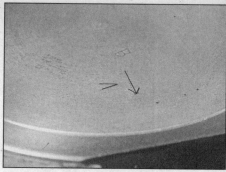

20.6b The arrow on the piston crown must be facing the flywheel end of the engine

C-type and E-type engines

Big-end bearing running clearance check

3 Place the four liners face down in a row on the bench, in their correct order. Turn them as necessary so that the flats on the edges of liners 1 and 2 are towards each other, and the flats on liners 3 and 4 are towards each other also. Fit the previously-selected base seals (C-type engine) or O-rings (E-type engine) to the base of each liner **(see illustration)**.

4 Lubricate the pistons and piston rings, then place each piston and connecting rod assembly with its respective liner.

5 Starting with assembly No 1, make sure that the piston ring gaps are still spaced at 120° to each other. Clamp the piston rings using a piston ring compressor.

6 Insert the piston and connecting rod assembly into the bottom of the liner, ensuring that the arrow on the piston crown will be facing the flywheel/driveplate end of the engine **(see illustrations)**. Using a block of wood or a hammer handle against the end of the connecting rod, tap the piston into the liner until the top of the piston is approximately 25 mm away from the top of the liner.

7 Repeat the procedure for the remaining three piston-and-liner assemblies.

8 Turn the crankshaft so that No 1 crankpin is at the bottom of its travel.

9 With the liner seal/O-ring in position, place

No 1 liner, piston and connecting rod assembly into its location in the cylinder block. Ensure that the arrow on the piston crown faces the flywheel/driveplate end of the engine, and that the flat on the liner is positioned as described previously.

10 To measure the big-end bearing running clearance, refer to the information provided in Section 19; the same general procedures apply. If the Plastigage method is being used, ensure that the crankpin journal and the big-end bearing shells are clean and dry, then pull the connecting rod down and engage it with the crankpin. Place the Plastigage strip on the crankpin, check that the marks made on the cap and rod during removal are next to each other, then refit the cap and retaining nuts. Tighten the nuts to the specified torque. Do not rotate the crankshaft during this operation. Remove the cap, and check the running clearance by measuring the Plastigage as previously described.

11 With the liner/piston assembly installed, retain the liner with a bolt and washer screwed into the cylinder head bolt holes, or by using liner clamps **(see illustration)**.

12 Repeat the above procedures for the remaining piston-and-liner assemblies.

Final refitting

13 Having checked the running clearance of all the crankpin journals, and taken any corrective action necessary, clean off all traces

of Plastigage from the bearing shells and crankpin.

14 Liberally lubricate the crankpin journals and big-end bearing shells. Refit the bearing caps once more, ensuring correct positioning as previously described. Tighten the bearing cap nuts to the specified torque, and turn the crankshaft each time to make sure that it is free before moving on to the next assembly. On completion, check that all the liners are positioned relative to each other, so that a 0.1 mm feeler blade can pass freely through the gaps between the liners **(see illustration)**. If this is not the case, it may be necessary to interchange one or more of the complete piston/liner assemblies to achieve this clearance.

F-type engines

Big-end bearing running clearance check

15 Lubricate No 1 piston and piston rings, and check that the ring gaps are spaced at 120° intervals to each other.

16 Fit a ring compressor to No 1 piston, then insert the piston and connecting rod into No 1 cylinder. With No 1 crankpin at its lowest point, drive the piston carefully into the cylinder with the wooden handle of a hammer **(see illustration)**, at the same time guiding the connecting rod onto the crankpin. Make sure that the arrow on the piston crown faces the flywheel end of the engine.

20.11 Liner clamp to hold the liners in place

20.14 Checking the gap between the liners

20.16 Using a hammer handle to drive the piston into the cylinder (F-type engine)

20.20 Tightening the big-end bearing cap bolts

17 To measure the big-end bearing running clearance, refer to the information contained in Section 19; the same general procedures apply. If the Plastigage method is being used, ensure that the crankpin journal and the big-end bearing shells are clean and dry, then engage the connecting rod with the crankpin. Place the Plastigage strip on the crankpin, fit the bearing cap in its previously-noted position, then tighten the bolts to the specified torque. Do not rotate the crankshaft during this operation. Remove the cap, and check the

running clearance by measuring the Plastigage as previously described.
18 Repeat the above procedures on the remaining piston/connecting rod assemblies.

Final refitting

19 Having checked the running clearance of all the crankpin journals, and taken any corrective action necessary, clean off all traces of Plastigage from the bearing shells and crankpin.
20 Liberally lubricate the crankpin journals and big-end bearing shells. Refit the bearing caps once more, ensuring correct positioning as previously described. Tighten the bearing cap bolts to the specified torque, and turn the crankshaft each time to make sure that it is free before moving on to the next assembly **(see illustration)**.

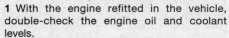

**21 Engine -
  initial start-up after overhaul**

1 With the engine refitted in the vehicle, double-check the engine oil and coolant levels.
2 With the spark plugs removed, and the ignition system disabled by connecting the coil HT lead to ground with a jumper lead, crank

the engine on the starter motor until the oil pressure light goes out.
3 Refit the spark plugs, and connect all the HT leads.
4 Start the engine, noting that this may take a little longer than usual, due to the fuel pump and carburettor (where applicable) being empty.
5 While the engine is idling, check for fuel, water and oil leaks. Do not be alarmed if there are some odd smells and smoke from parts getting hot and burning off oil deposits.
6 Keep the engine idling until hot water is felt circulating through the top hose, then switch it off.
7 After a few minutes, recheck the oil and water levels, and top-up as necessary.
8 There is no requirement to retighten the cylinder head bolts on E- and F-type engines. On the C-type engine, the bolts must be retightened as described in Chapter 2B, Section 6.
9 If new pistons, rings or crankshaft bearings have been fitted, the engine must be run-in for the first 500 miles (800 km). Do not operate the engine at full-throttle, nor allow it to labour in any gear during this period. It is recommended that the oil and filter be changed at the end of this period.

2D

Notes

Chapter 3 Cooling, heating and air conditioning systems

Contents

3

Degrees of difficulty

Easy, suitable for novice with little experience | **Fairly easy,** suitable for beginner with some experience | **Fairly difficult,** suitable for competent DIY mechanic | **Difficult,** suitable for experienced DIY mechanic | **Very difficult,** suitable for expert DIY or professional

Specifications

General

Cooling system type . . . . Pressurised, with belt-driven pump, front-mounted radiator and electric cooling fan
Coolant type . . . . See Chapter 1 (*"Lubricants, fluids and capacities"*)
Coolant capacity . . . . See Chapter 1 (*"Lubricants, fluids and capacities"*)
System pressure:
  Brown cap . . . . 1.2 bars
  Blue cap . . . . 1.6 bars

Thermostat

Type . . . . Wax

	Starts to open	Fully open
Opening temperatures:		
C-type (1237 cc/C1G, 1390 cc/C3J and 1397 cc/C1J/C3J) and E-type (1390 cc/E6J/E7J) engines	86°C	98°C
F-type (1721 cc/F2N/F3N, 1764 cc/F7P and 1794 cc/F3P) engines	89°C	101°C

Travel (closed to fully-open) . . . . 7.5 mm

Temperature gauge/warning light sender unit

Resistance values (typical):
  20°C . . . . 3550 ± 500 ohms
  80°C . . . . 335 ± 35 ohms
  90°C . . . . 240 ± 30 ohms

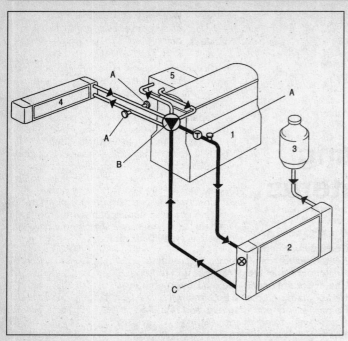

1.1a Cooling system schematic view - C-type engines

1 Cylinder block	A Bleed screws
2 Radiator	B Water pump
3 Expansion tank	C Cooling fan switch
4 Heater matrix	T Thermostat
5 Inlet manifold	

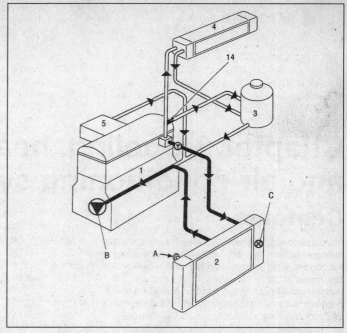

1.1b Cooling system schematic view - E-type engines

1 Cylinder block	14 Restrictor
2 Radiator	A Bleed screw
3 Expansion tank	B Water pump
4 Heater matrix	C Cooling fan switch
5 Inlet manifold	T Thermostat

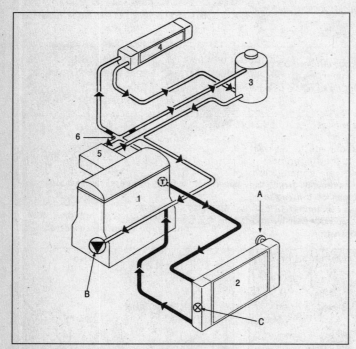

1.1c Cooling system schematic view - 1721 cc (F2N and F3N) and 1794 cc (F3P) engines

1 Cylinder block	6 Restrictors
2 Radiator	A Bleed screw
3 Expansion tank	B Water pump
4 Heater matrix	C Cooling fan switch
5 Inlet manifold	T Thermostat

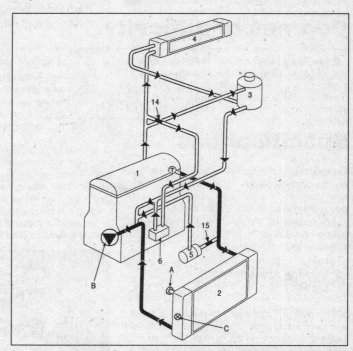

1.1d Cooling system schematic view - 1764 cc (F7P) engine

1 Cylinder block	14 Restrictor
2 Radiator	15 Restrictor
3 Expansion tank	A Bleed screw
4 Heater matrix	B Water pump
5 Auxiliary water pump	C Cooling fan switch
6 Engine oil cooler	T Thermostat

1 General information

The cooling system is of the pressurised type. The main components are a belt-driven pump, an aluminium crossflow radiator, an expansion tank, an electric cooling fan, a thermostat, and the associated hoses (see illustrations).

The system functions as follows. When the engine is cold, coolant is pumped around the cylinder block and head passages. After cooling the cylinder bores, combustion surfaces and valve seats, the coolant passes through the heater and inlet manifold, and is returned to the water pump.

When the coolant reaches a predetermined temperature, the thermostat opens, and the hot coolant passes through the top hose to the radiator. As the coolant circulates through the radiator, it is cooled by the inrush of air when the vehicle is in motion. The airflow is supplemented by the action of the electric cooling fan when necessary. Upon reaching the bottom of the radiator, the coolant returns to the pump via the radiator bottom hose, and the cycle is repeated.

As the coolant warms up, it expands; the increased volume is accommodated in an expansion tank. On the C-type (1237 cc/C1G, 1390 cc/C3J and 1397 cc/C1J/C2J) engine models, the expansion tank is "cold", simply receiving a small volume of coolant as the temperature increases, and returning it to the system as it cools down. On all other models, the tank is "hot", coolant circulating through the tank all the time that the engine is running.

The electric cooling fan, mounted behind the radiator, is controlled by a thermostatic switch located in the side of the radiator. At a predetermined coolant temperature, the switch contacts close, actuating the fan via a relay.

On certain models, an engine oil cooler is fitted, mounted between the oil filter and the cylinder block.

The cooling system on 16-valve models has an auxiliary electric water pump, which operates in conjunction with the anti-percolation system (see Chapter 4C).

For details of the air conditioning system (when fitted) and the precautions associated with it, refer to Section 19.

2 Cooling system hoses - renewal

1 The number, routing and pattern of hoses will vary according to model, but the same basic procedure applies. Before commencing work, make sure that the new hoses are to hand, along with new hose clips if needed. It is good practice to renew the hose clips at the same time as the hoses.
2 Drain the cooling system, saving the coolant if it is fit for re-use (Chapter 1). Squirt a little penetrating oil onto the hose clips if they are rusty.

3 Release the hose clips from the hose concerned. Three types of clip are used: worm-drive, spring and "sardine-can". The worm-drive clip is released by turning its screw anti-clockwise. The spring clip is released by squeezing its tags together with pliers, at the same time working the clip away from the hose stub. The "sardine-can" clip is not re-usable, and is best cut off with snips or side cutters.
4 Unclip any wires, cables or other hoses which may be attached to the hose being removed. Make notes for reference when reassembling if necessary.
5 Release the hose from its stubs with a twisting motion. Be careful not to damage the stubs on delicate components such as the radiator. If the hose is stuck fast, the best course is often to cut it off using a sharp knife, but again be careful not to damage the stubs.
6 Before fitting the new hose, smear the stubs with washing-up liquid or a suitable rubber lubricant to aid fitting. Do not use oil or grease, which may attack the rubber.
7 Fit the hose clips over the ends of the hose, then fit the hose over its stubs. Work the hose into position. When satisfied, locate and tighten the hose clips.
8 Refill the cooling system (Chapter 1). Run the engine, and check that there are no leaks.
9 Recheck the tightness of the hose clips on any new hoses after a few hundred miles.
10 Top-up the coolant level if necessary.

3 Radiator - removal, inspection, cleaning and refitting

Removal

Note: If the radiator is being removed because it is leaking, note that minor leaks can be repaired without removing the radiator, using a radiator sealant.
1 Disconnect the battery leads.
2 Drain the cooling system as described in Chapter 1.
3 Where applicable, disconnect the air duct leading from the radiator to the carburettor.
4 On models fitted with air conditioning, unbolt the condenser assembly from the radiator, and move it clear of the radiator, leaving the refrigerant lines connected.
5 Loosen the clip and disconnect the top hose from the radiator (see illustration).

3.9a Unscrew the mounting bolts . . .

Warning: Do not under any circumstances attempt to disconnect the refrigerant lines (see Section 19).

6 Disconnect the wiring from the thermostatic switch, located on the side of the radiator. The switch may be on the left- or the right-hand side of the radiator, depending on model.
7 Separate the two halves of the cooling fan wiring connector, and release the connector from the plastic clip (see illustration).
8 On automatic transmission models, place a container beneath the radiator to catch any spilled fluid, then unscrew the fluid cooling pipe unions. Plug the ends of the pipes.
9 Unscrew the two mounting bolts from the engine compartment cross panel. Move the radiator to the rear, and remove the mounting brackets (see illustrations).

3.5 Disconnecting the top hose from the radiator

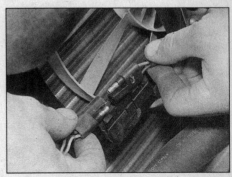
3.7 Separating the two halves of the cooling fan wiring connector

3.9b . . . and remove the radiator mounting brackets

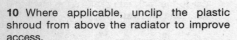
3.11a Lift the radiator from the lower locating rubber bushes . . .

3.11b . . . and withdraw it from the engine compartment

5.1 Cylinder head outlet elbow (arrowed) housing the thermostat on the E-type engines

10 Where applicable, unclip the plastic shroud from above the radiator to improve access.

11 Lift the radiator up from the lower locating rubber bushes, then withdraw it from the engine compartment **(see illustrations)**.

Inspection and cleaning

12 Radiator repair is best left to a specialist, but minor leaks may be sealed using a radiator sealant. Clear the radiator matrix of flies and small leaves with a soft brush, or by hosing.

13 If the radiator is to be left out of the vehicle for more than 48 hours, special precautions must be taken to prevent the brazing flux used during manufacture from reacting with the chloride elements remaining from the coolant.

This reaction could cause the aluminium core to oxidize, causing leakage. To prevent this, either flush the radiator thoroughly with clean water, dry with compressed air and seal all outlets, or refill the radiator with coolant and temporarily plug all outlets.

Refitting

14 Refitting is a reversal of removal, but check the condition of the mounting bushes, and if necessary renew them. Refill the cooling system with reference to Chapter 1. On automatic transmission models, check and if necessary top-up the automatic transmission fluid level.

4 Expansion tank -
removal, inspection and refitting

Removal

1 With the engine cold, drain some coolant from the system until the expansion tank is empty.

2 Release the strap or the clip (as applicable) which secures the tank. Disconnect the hose (or hoses) and remove the tank.

Inspection

3 Clean the tank, and inspect it for cracks and other damage. Renew it if necessary. Also inspect the cap; if there is evidence that coolant has been vented through the cap, renew it.

Refitting

4 Refit by reversing the removal operations. Refill and bleed the cooling system as described in Chapter 1.

5 Thermostat -
removal, testing and refitting

1 On the E-type (1390 cc/E6J/E7J) engines, the thermostat is located in the cylinder head outlet elbow on the left-hand side of the engine **(see illustration)**.

2 On the C-type (1237 cc/C1G, 1390 cc/C3J and 1397 cc/C1J/C2J) engines, the thermostat is located in the end of the radiator top hose at the water pump, and is retained by a hose clip.

3 On the F-type (1721 cc/F2N/F3N, 1764 cc/F7P and 1794 cc/F3P) engines, the thermostat is located in a housing bolted to the left-hand side of the cylinder head, beneath the distributor cap. Access can be improved by removing the distributor cap and the air cleaner or air inlet trunking.

Removal

4 Partially drain the cooling system, so that the coolant level is below the thermostat location.

5 Loosen the clip and disconnect the hose.

6 On the C-type engines, withdraw the thermostat from inside the hose. On other engines, unbolt the cover and remove the thermostat, then remove the sealing ring **(see illustrations)**.

Testing

7 To test whether the unit is serviceable, suspend it on a string in a saucepan of cold water, together with a thermometer. Heat the water, and note the temperature at which the thermostat begins to open. Continue heating the water until the thermostat is fully open, and then remove it from the water.

8 The temperature at which the thermostat should start to open is stamped on the unit. If the thermostat does not start to open at the specified temperature, does not fully open in boiling water, or does not fully close when removed from the water, then it must be discarded and a new one fitted.

5.6a Removing the thermostat on a C-type (1397 cc/C1J) engine

5.6b Removing the thermostat on an E-type (1390 cc/E6J) engine

5.6c Removing the thermostat on an F-type (1721 cc/F2N) engine

Refitting

9 Refitting is a reversal of removal, but where applicable renew the sealing ring. On the C-type engines, make sure that the thermostat bleed hole is in the slot on the end of the water pump outlet. Refill the cooling system as described in Chapter 1.

6 Electric cooling fan assembly - removal and refitting

Removal

1 Remove the radiator as described in Section 3.

2 Remove the shroud/fan bracket from the radiator by unscrewing the bolts, or where necessary by drilling the heads off the rivets **(see illustration)**.

3 Unscrew the nut or extract the retaining clip, and slide the fan off the motor shaft.

4 The motor can now be removed by drilling out the retaining rivets.

Refitting

5 Refitting is a reversal of removal. Where applicable, new rivets are obtainable from Renault parts stockists.

7 Electric cooling fan thermostatic switch - testing, removal and refitting

Testing

1 The thermostatic switch is located in the side of the radiator. The switch may be on the left- or the right-hand side of the radiator, depending on model. If it develops a fault, it is most likely to fail open-circuit. This will result in the fan motor remaining stationary even though the coolant temperature exceeds the switch-on point. The coolant may even reach boiling point.

2 To test for a faulty thermostatic switch, disconnect the two switch wires, and join them together with a suitable length of wire. If the fan now operates with the ignition switched

6.2 Electric cooling fan mounting bolts (arrowed) on the radiator

on, the thermostatic switch is proved faulty and must be renewed. If the fan is still inoperative, this proves that there is a fault in the fan motor or associated wiring.

Removal

3 To remove the switch, disconnect the battery negative terminal and drain the cooling system, as described in Chapter 1.

4 Separate the two halves of the wiring connector, then unscrew the switch from the radiator **(see illustration)**. Remove the sealing washer.

Refitting

5 Refitting is a reversal of removal, but fit a new sealing washer and fully tighten the switch.

6 On completion, refill the cooling system as described in Chapter 1.

8 Temperature gauge/warning light sender unit - testing, removal and refitting

Note: *Suitable sealant will be required when refitting.*

1 The location of the temperature gauge/warning light sender unit varies according to model. On the C-type (1237 cc/ C1G, 1390 cc/C3J and 1397 cc/C1J/C2J) engines, it is on top of the water pump. On the

7.4 Separating the two halves of the electric cooling fan thermostatic switch wiring connector

1764 cc (F7P) engine, it is screwed into the thermostat housing, or the left-hand end of the cylinder head (depending on model) **(see illustrations)**. On the other engines, it is located on the front of the cylinder head, at the left-hand end. In all cases, the procedures are the same.

Testing

2 Disconnect the multi-plug from the sender unit **(see illustration)**. Using an ohmmeter, measure the resistance of the sender, and compare it with the values given in the Specifications. If the value obtained is greatly different from that specified, the sender is probably defective.

3 For accurate testing across the temperature range, the sender unit will have to be removed.

Removal

4 Drain the cooling system (Chapter 1). Alternatively, remove the expansion tank cap to depressurise the system, and have the new sender unit or a suitable bung to hand.

5 Disconnect the multi-plug and unscrew the sender unit.

Refitting

6 Apply a little sealant to the sender threads, and screw it into position. Reconnect the multi-plug.

7 Top-up or refill the cooling system as necessary.

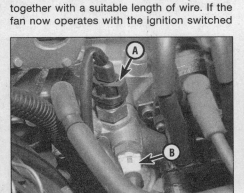

8.1a Temperature gauge/warning light sender unit (A) and coolant temperature sensor (B) located in thermostat housing - 1764 cc (F7P) engine

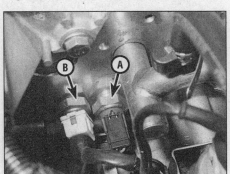

8.1b Alternative locations for temperature gauge/warning light sender unit (A) and coolant temperature sensor (B) in cylinder head - 1764 cc (F7P) engine

8.2 Disconnecting the multi-plug from the temperature gauge/warning light sender unit - 1794 cc (F3P) engine

3

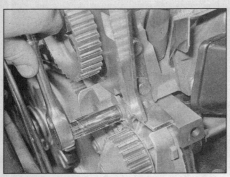

9.3a Unscrew the mounting bolts . . .

9.3b . . . and remove the water pump - E-type (1390 cc/E6J) engine

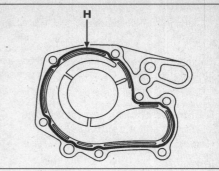

9.4 Apply a bead of sealant (H) as shown when refitting the water pump on an E-type engine

9 Water pump - removal and refitting

E-type (1390 cc/E6J/E7J) engine

Note: *Suitable sealant will be required on refitting.*

Removal

1 Disconnect the battery leads, then drain the cooling system with reference to Chapter 1.
2 Remove the timing belt with reference to Chapter 2A.
3 Unbolt the water pump from the front of the cylinder block (see illustrations).

9.13 Work through the holes in the pulley for access to one of the water pump bolts - C-type engine

Refitting

4 Clean the mating faces of the water pump and cylinder block, then apply a bead of sealant 0.6 to 1.0 mm wide around the inner perimeter of the water pump sealing face on the water pump (see illustration).
5 Locate the water pump on the cylinder block, then insert the bolts and tighten them evenly.
6 Refit the timing belt with reference to Chapter 2A.
7 Refill the cooling system with reference to Chapter 1, and re-connect the battery leads.

C-type (1237 cc/C1G, 1390 cc/C3J and 1397 cc/C1J/C2J) engines

Note: *New gaskets must be used on refitting.*

Removal

8 Disconnect the battery leads, and then refer to Chapter 1 and drain the cooling system.
9 Refer to Chapter 1, and remove the auxiliary drivebelt.
10 Unscrew the bolt securing the alternator adjusting arm to the pump body, remove the bolt, and swing the arm clear.
11 Slacken the hose clips and disconnect the hoses from the pump.
12 Disconnect the lead from the coolant temperature gauge sender unit on top of the pump body.
13 Unscrew and remove the bolts securing the water pump to the cylinder head. Access

to the bolt behind the pulley can be gained by inserting a socket and extension bar through the holes in the pulley (see illustration).
14 With all the bolts removed, withdraw the pump from the cylinder head (see illustration). If it is stuck, strike it sharply with a plastic or hide mallet.

Refitting

15 Refitting is a reversal of removal, but use new gaskets. Adjust the drivebelt tension and refill the cooling system as described in Chapter 1.

F-type (1721 cc/F2N/F3N, 1764 cc/ F7P and 1794 cc/F3P) engines

Note: *A new gasket must be used on refitting.*

Removal

16 Disconnect the battery leads, then refer to Chapter 1 and drain the cooling system.
17 Remove the auxiliary drivebelt with reference to Chapter 1.
18 Unscrew the three bolts and remove the pump pulley (see illustration).
19 Unscrew the bolts securing the water pump to the cylinder block, and withdraw the pump from its location (see illustrations). If it is stuck, strike it sharply with a plastic or hide mallet. Remove the gasket.

Refitting

20 Clean the mating faces of the water pump and cylinder block.

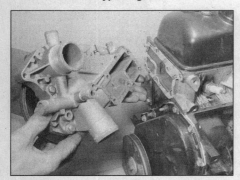

9.14 Withdrawing the water pump from the cylinder head - C-type engine

9.18 Water pump pulley securing bolts (arrowed) - F-type engine

9.19 Withdrawing the water pump from the cylinder block - F-type engine

21 Locate the water pump on the cylinder block, together with a new gasket, and insert the bolts. Tighten the bolts.
22 Refit the pump pulley and tighten the bolts.
23 Refit and tension the auxiliary drivebelt, with reference to Chapter 1.
24 Refill the cooling system (Chapter 1) then re-connect the battery leads.

10 Auxiliary water pump (16-valve models) - general

The auxiliary water pump fitted to 16-valve models is electrically-operated. It forms part of the anti-percolation system, which is designed to reduce under-bonnet temperatures when the vehicle is stopped after a run. This system is described in Chapter 4B.

11 Auxiliary water pump (16-valve models) - removal and refitting

Removal

1 Disconnect the battery negative lead.
2 Drain the cooling system as described in Chapter 1.
3 The pump is located on the left-hand side of the engine compartment, in front of the gearbox. Access is obtained from underneath the vehicle **(see illustration)**.
4 Apply the handbrake, then jack up the front of the vehicle and support securely on axle stands (see *"Jacking, towing and wheel changing"*).
5 Disconnect the pump wiring plug.
6 Loosen the securing clips, and disconnect the two coolant hoses from the pump.
7 Release the pump from its mounting, and withdraw it from under the vehicle.

Refitting

8 Refitting is a reversal of removal. Refill the cooling system as described in Chapter 1.

12 Heating system - general information and checks

General information

The heater and fresh air ventilation unit works on the principle of mixing hot and cold air in the proportions selected by means of the central (temperature) control knob. Coolant flows through the heater matrix all the time that the engine is running, regardless of the temperature selected.

Air distribution is selected by the left-hand control knob. Additional control is possible by opening, closing or redirecting individual vents in the facia panel.

A three-speed blower is controlled by the right-hand knob.

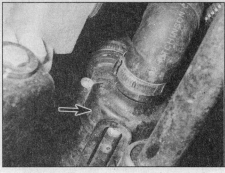

11.3 Auxiliary water pump (arrowed) viewed from underneath vehicle - 16-valve model

For details of the air conditioning system fitted to some models, refer to Section 19.

Checks

Periodically check that all the controls operate as intended. Problems related to the temperature and air distribution controls may be due to cables being broken or disconnected (Section 18).

If the blower does not operate at all, check the fuse and the blower multi-plug before condemning the motor. If one or two speeds do not work, the fault is almost certainly in the resistor unit (Section 16).

Check the condition and security of the coolant hoses which feed the heater matrix. The matrix-to-hose joints are at the bulkhead under the bonnet. If water leaks inside the vehicle seem to be coming from the heater, establish whether the leak is of coolant (indicating a leaking heater matrix) or of rainwater (indicating a defective scuttle seal). Cooling system antifreeze has a distinctive sweet smell.

13 Heater unit - removal and refitting

Removal

1 Disconnect the battery leads with reference to Chapter 5.
2 Remove the complete facia panel with reference to Chapter 11.
3 Remove the upper seal from the scuttle to the rear of the engine compartment. Also remove the external air inlet grilles.
4 Disconnect the wiring from the heater blower motor.
5 Remove the heater blower unit with reference to Section 14.
6 Drain the cooling system with reference to Chapter 1.
7 Loosen the two clips and disconnect the hoses from the heater matrix.
8 Unbolt the heater unit and remove it from inside the vehicle **(see illustration)**.

Refitting

9 Check that the seals are in good condition, then locate the unit on the bulkhead.

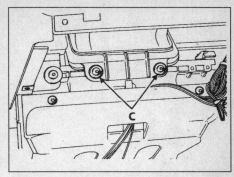

13.8 Heater unit-to-facia bracket securing bolts (arrowed)

10 Position the blower motor over the heater, and insert the bolts finger-tight. Also insert the heater mounting bolts.
11 Check and if necessary adjust the heater control cables (Section 18).
12 Connect the hoses to the heater unit and tighten the clips.
13 Tighten the heater and blower motor mounting bolts, then reconnect the wiring to the blower motor.
14 Refit the upper seal to the scuttle, and also refit the external air inlet grilles.
15 Refit the facia panel with reference to Chapter 11.
16 Refill the cooling system with reference to Chapter 1.
17 Reconnect the battery leads with reference to Chapter 5.

14 Heater blower unit - removal and refitting

Removal

1 Remove the scuttle upper seal and the external air inlet grille.
2 Disconnect the wiring from the blower unit **(see illustration)**.
3 Unscrew the two mounting bolts, then remove the unit from the left-hand side of the bulkhead **(see illustration)**. It is necessary to turn the unit on its side to do this.
4 Release the clips, then separate the two

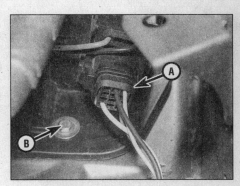

14.2 Heater blower unit wiring (A) and mounting bolt (B)

3

14.3 Removing the heater blower unit

14.4a Release the securing clips . . .

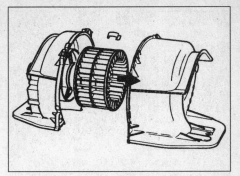

14.4b . . . and separate the two half-casings for access to the motor assembly

half-casings of the unit, and remove the motor assembly **(see illustrations)**. If the unit has not previously been separated from new, the two casings will be hot-crimped together, and it will be necessary to split them apart with a knife.

Refitting

5 Locate the motor assembly in the two half-casings, making sure that the wiring connector can be fitted without stress.
6 Fit the casings together, and secure with clips which are available in a kit from Renault dealers. The kit also contains a new seal for fitting to the unit. Do not refit the original seal, since if it does not seal correctly, there is a risk of water entry into the passenger compartment.

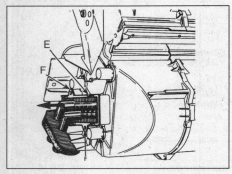

15.2 Removing the heater matrix

E Retaining clips F Mounting screw locations

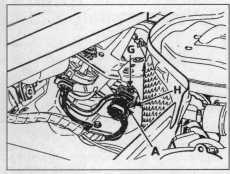

16.3 Heater resistor unit location

A Wiring connector H Securing clip
G Mounting screw

7 Refit the unit and tighten the mounting bolts.
8 Reconnect the wiring to the blower unit.
9 Refit the external air inlet grille and the water box upper seal.

15 Heater matrix - removal and refitting

Removal

1 Remove the heater unit with reference to Section 13.
2 Prise out the retaining clips, then pull out the matrix **(see illustration)**. Take care not to damage the air control flaps.

Refitting

3 Check that the sealing foam is in good condition, then insert the matrix and retain with the clips **(see illustration)**. If the clips have been broken during removal, fit two screws instead (see illustration 15.2).
4 Refit the heater unit with reference to Section 13.

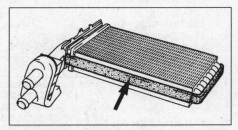

15.3 Heater matrix sealing foam (arrowed)

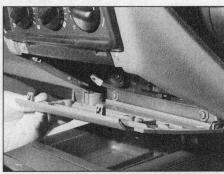

17.1 Removing the lower heater cover

16 Heater resistor unit - removal and refitting

Removal

1 Remove the scuttle upper seal and external air inlet grille.
2 Unplug the wiring connector, then unscrew the two mounting screws.
3 Pull the clips apart and remove the resistor unit **(see illustration)**.

Refitting

4 If the resistor unit is being removed because it has been damaged, check that the heater fan motor turns freely before refitting it.
5 Refitting is a reversal of removal.

17 Heater control panel - removal and refitting

Removal

1 Unscrew the two screws securing the central lower cover beneath the heater control panel. Remove the cover **(see illustration)**.
2 Unscrew the two mounting screws, then remove the control panel by releasing it at the bottom and removing the four clips **(see illustrations)**.
3 Disconnect the cables by releasing the clips.
4 If desired, the trim panel can be removed from the control panel by releasing the four securing clips **(see illustration)**.

Refitting

5 Refitting is a reversal of removal.

18 Heater control cables - removal and refitting

Removal

1 Remove the control panel as described in Section 17.
2 Remove the air deflector (two screws) **(see illustration)**.

17.2a Heater control panel mounting screw (arrowed)

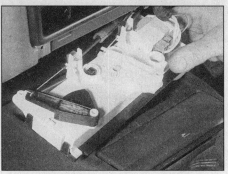

17.2b Removing the heater control panel

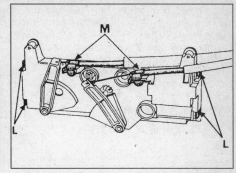

17.4 Heater control panel trim securing clips (L) and control cable clips (M)

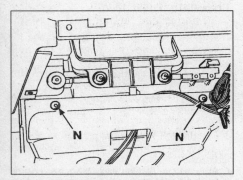

18.2 Air deflector securing screws (N)

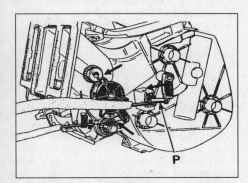

18.8 Heater unit mixer flap return spring location (P)

3 Release the relevant cable from the flap control lever by releasing the clip and turning it through a quarter-turn.

Refitting

4 Refit the cable so that it is flush with the sheath stop.
5 Turn the control knobs to the "ventilation" and "cold" positions.
6 Refit the control panel.
7 Place the control flaps in the "ventilation" and "cold" positions, then align the marks on the flap control sections.
8 Refit the mixer flap return spring (air mixer control), then the air deflector and lower cover **(see illustration)**. Note that the control cables are of different lengths - the longer one controls the mixer flap.

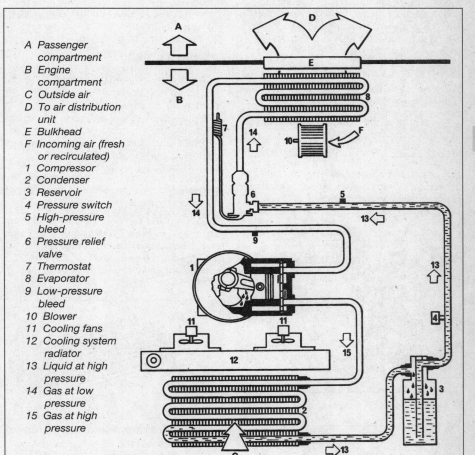

A Passenger compartment
B Engine compartment
C Outside air
D To air distribution unit
E Bulkhead
F Incoming air (fresh or recirculated)
1 Compressor
2 Condenser
3 Reservoir
4 Pressure switch
5 High-pressure bleed
6 Pressure relief valve
7 Thermostat
8 Evaporator
9 Low-pressure bleed
10 Blower
11 Cooling fans
12 Cooling system radiator
13 Liquid at high pressure
14 Gas at low pressure
15 Gas at high pressure

19.1 Air conditioning system components

19 Air conditioning system - general information and precautions

General information

1 An air conditioning system is available on some models. It enables the temperature of incoming air to be lowered; it also dehumidifies the air, which makes for rapid demisting and increased comfort **(see illustration)**.
2 The cooling side of the system works in the same way as a domestic refrigerator. Refrigerant gas is drawn into a belt-driven compressor, and passes into a condenser in front of the radiator, where it loses heat and becomes liquid. The liquid passes through an expansion valve to an evaporator, where it changes from liquid under high pressure to

gas under low pressure. This change is accompanied by a drop in temperature, which cools the evaporator. The refrigerant returns to the compressor and the cycle begins again.

3 Air blown through the evaporator passes to the air distribution unit, where it is mixed with hot air blown through the heater matrix, to achieve the desired temperature in the passenger compartment.

21.4 Three of the scuttle bulkhead cover securing screws (A)

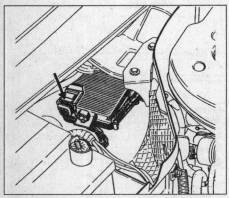

21.5 Air conditioning control unit wiring plug (arrowed)

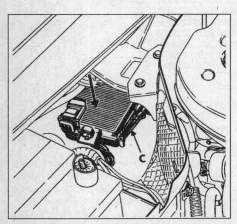

21.8 Remove the control unit assembly (arrowed) for access to the ventilation unit mounting bolt (C)

4 The heating side of the system is identical to that for models without air conditioning.

Precautions

5 The refrigerant (Freon R12) is potentially dangerous, and should only be handled by qualified persons. If it is splashed onto the skin, it can cause frostbite. It is not itself poisonous, but in the presence of a naked flame (and particularly if inhaled through a lighted cigarette) it forms a poisonous gas.

6 Uncontrolled discharging of the refrigerant is dangerous, and potentially damaging to the environment. It follows that any work on the air conditioning system which involves opening the refrigerant circuit must only be carried out by a Renault dealer or an air conditioning specialist.

7 Do not operate the air conditioning system if it is known to be short of refrigerant; the compressor may be damaged.

20 Air conditioning system - checking and maintenance

1 Routine maintenance is limited to checking the tension and condition of the compressor drivebelt, and checking the refrigerant sight glass for bubbles. Refer to Chapter 1.

2 Periodic recharging of the system will be required, since there is inevitably a slow loss of refrigerant. It is suggested that the system is inspected by a specialist every 2 years, or at once if a loss of performance is noticed.

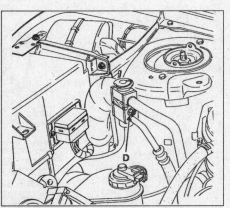

21.6 Disconnect the refrigerant pipes from the pressure relief valve (D)

21 Air conditioning system components - removal and refitting

⚠ *Warning: The system should be professionally discharged before carrying out any of the following work. Cap or plug the pipe lines as soon as they are disconnected, to prevent the entry of moisture. Refer to the precautions given in Section 19 before proceeding.*

Blower unit and fan motor

Removal

1 Disconnect the battery leads.

2 Where applicable, unbolt and remove the strengthening bar from between the front suspension turrets.

3 Remove the ignition module from the bulkhead.

4 Remove the five securing screws, and withdraw the scuttle bulkhead cover (see illustration).

5 Disconnect the wiring plug from the air conditioning control unit assembly (see illustration).

6 Refer to the warning at the beginning of this Section, then disconnect the refrigerant pipes from the pressure relief valve (see illustration). Plug or cover the ends of the pipes, to prevent dirt ingress.

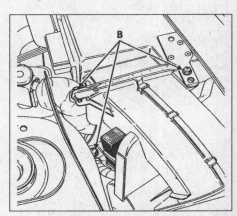

21.7 Three bolts (B) securing the blower unit assembly to the ventilation unit body

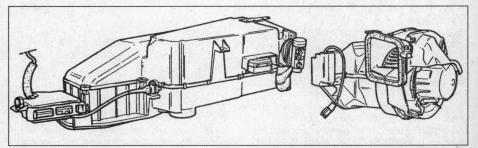

21.9 Blower unit assembly and ventilation unit removed from vehicle

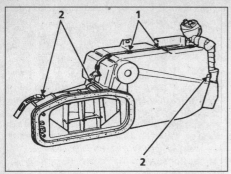
21.16 Clips (1) and screws (2) securing the ventilation unit half-casings together

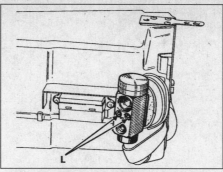
21.17 Pressure relief valve securing bolts (L)

7 Unscrew the three bolts, and separate the blower unit assembly from the ventilation unit body **(see illustration)**.
8 Release the retaining strap, and remove the control unit assembly from the scuttle for access to the ventilation unit mounting bolt **(see illustration)**. Remove the mounting bolt.
9 Working inside the vehicle, unscrew the two ventilation unit mounting bolts from under the left-hand side of the facia panel, then withdraw the ventilation unit and the blower unit assembly separately **(see illustration)**.
10 To remove the fan motor, proceed as follows.
11 Pull the rubber cover from the blower unit, then unsolder the wiring.
12 Prise off the clips and separate the two half-casings.
13 Using a screwdriver, push back the rubber beads holding the motor in the casing. Pull the fan motor directly from the casings.

Refitting

14 Refitting is a reversal of removal, but make sure that the foam seals are in good condition, and renew them if necessary. Have the system recharged by a Renault dealer or refrigeration specialist.

Evaporator
Removal

15 Remove the blower unit as described previously.
16 Remove the clips and the three screws securing the two ventilation unit half-casings together **(see illustration)**.
17 Unscrew the two securing bolts, and remove the pressure relief valve from the ventilation unit **(see illustration)**.
18 Withdraw the evaporator.

Refitting

19 Refitting is a reversal of removal, but make sure that the foam seals are in good condition, and renew them if necessary. Have the system recharged by a Renault dealer or refrigeration specialist.

Compressor - E-type (1390 cc/E6J/E7J) engines
Removal

20 Disconnect the battery leads.
21 Slacken the two drivebelt tensioner securing bolts, and back off the tensioner bolt until the drivebelt can be removed **(see illustration)**.
22 Disconnect the wiring from the compressor.
23 Refer to the warning at the beginning of this Section, then disconnect the refrigerant pipes from the compressor. Plug or cover the ends of the pipes, to prevent dirt ingress.
24 Apply the handbrake, then jack up the

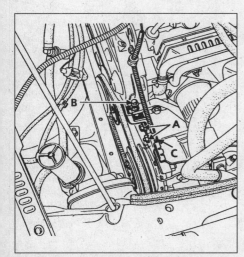
21.21 Compressor drivebelt tensioner securing bolts (A), tensioner bolt (B) and wiring connection (C) - E-type engines

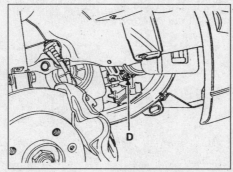
21.25 Lower compressor mounting bolt (D) - E-type engines

front of the vehicle and support it securely on axle stands (see *"Jacking, towing and wheel changing"*). Remove the right-hand front roadwheel.
25 Working under the wheel arch, remove the lower compressor mounting bolt **(see illustration)**.
26 Remove the oil filter, with reference to Chapter 1.
27 Unscrew the nut, and remove the spring and washers from the compressor side of the exhaust downpipe-to-manifold joint (see Chapter 4).
28 Remove the compressor upper mounting bolt, then withdraw the compressor.

Refitting

29 Refitting is a reversal of removal, bearing in mind the following points:
(a) Before refitting the compressor, the oil level should be checked by a Renault dealer.
(b) Check that all seals and pipes are in good condition, and renew any which are not, as necessary.
(c) Refit the exhaust downpipe-to-manifold spring and nut, with reference to Chapter 4.
(d) Refit the oil filter, and top-up the oil level with reference to Chapter 1.
(e) On completion, have the system recharged by a Renault dealer or air conditioning specialist.

Compressor - F-type (1721 cc/F2N/F3N, 1764 cc/F7P and 1794 cc/F3P) engines
Removal

30 Disconnect the battery leads.
31 Remove the lower compressor mounting bracket securing nut and stud **(see illustration)**.
32 Remove the alternator as described in Chapter 5.
33 Unbolt the alternator mounting bracket from the engine.
34 Disconnect the wiring from the compressor.

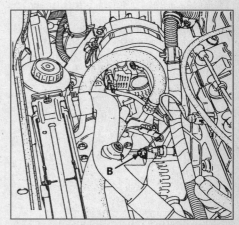
21.31 Lower compressor mounting bracket securing nut and stud (B) - F-type engines

3

21.35 Remove the bolt (C) securing the refrigerant pipes to the compressor - F-type engines

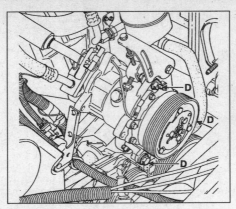

21.36 Three of the compressor mounting bolts (D) - F-type engines

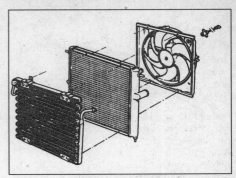

21.43 Air conditioning condenser, radiator and electric cooling fan

35 Remove the bolt securing the refrigerant pipes to the compressor **(see illustration)**.
36 Remove the four securing bolts (noting that one of the bolts is located behind the compressor), and withdraw the compressor **(see illustration)**.

Refitting

37 Refitting is a reversal of removal, bearing in mind the following points:
   a) Before refitting the compressor, the oil level should be checked by a Renault dealer.
   b) Check that all seals and pipes are in good condition, and renew any which are not, as necessary.
   c) On completion, have the system recharged by a Renault dealer or air conditioning specialist.

Condenser
Removal

38 Drain the cooling system with reference to Chapter 1.
39 Disconnect the refrigerant lines from the condenser, while counterholding the unions with a further spanner.
40 Disconnect the wiring from the cooling fan motor.
41 Remove the radiator upper mounting bolts.
42 Lift the radiator and condenser assembly upwards from the engine compartment.
43 Remove the screws, and separate the condenser from the radiator **(see illustration)**.

Refitting

44 Refitting is a reversal of removal. When reconnecting the lines to the condenser, oil them, and hold the unions with a spanner to prevent any damage to the condenser.

Fan control module
Removal

45 Remove the five securing screws, and withdraw the scuttle bulkhead cover.
46 Remove the two bolts securing the module to the control unit assembly, and withdraw the module **(see illustration)**.

Refitting

47 Refitting is a reversal of removal.

Temperature sensor
Removal

48 Remove the five securing screws, and withdraw the scuttle bulkhead cover.
49 The sensor is located in the side of the air conditioning control unit assembly **(see illustration)**.
50 Disconnect the sensor wiring plug.
51 Release the locating tab, and turn the sensor 90° clockwise to remove it from the control unit.

Refitting

52 Refitting is a reversal of removal.

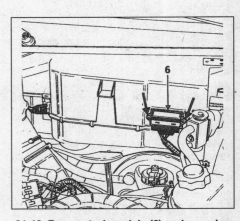

21.46 Fan control module (6) and securing bolts (arrowed)

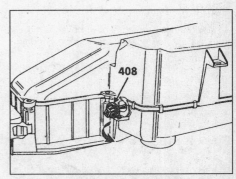

21.49 Air conditioning temperature sensor (408)

Chapter 4 Part A: Carburettor fuel system

Contents

Degrees of difficulty

Easy, suitable for novice with little experience	**Fairly easy,** suitable for beginner with some experience	**Fairly difficult,** suitable for competent DIY mechanic	**Difficult,** suitable for experienced DIY mechanic	**Very difficult,** suitable for expert DIY or professional

4A

Specifications

Note: The engine code appears on a plate attached to the engine. Refer to *"Buying spare parts and vehicle identification numbers"* for further details.

General

Fuel octane requirement	Refer to *Chapter 1 Specifications*
Carburettor type	Single- or twin-choke downdraught
Choke type	Manual
Carburettor application:	
1237 cc (C1G) engine	Solex 32 BIS 936
1390 cc (E6J) engine	Weber 32 TLDR
1397 cc (C1J) engine	Zenith 32 IF2
1397 cc (C2J) engine	Weber 32 DRT
1721 cc (F2N) engine	Solex 32 x 34 Z13

Fuel pump

Type	Mechanical, operated by eccentric on camshaft
Delivery pressure (static, with engine idling):	
Minimum	0.170 bars
Maximum	0.325 bars

Solex 32 BIS 936 carburettor data

Idle speed	700 ± 50 rpm
Idle speed mixture CO content	1.5 ± 0.5%
Needle valve	1.3 mm
Float level	Not adjustable
Positive throttle opening	0.7 mm (20°30')
Degassing valve travel	3.0 ± 0.5 mm
Choke tube	24
Main jet	120
Idling jet	42
Air correction jet	130
Pneumatic enrichener	40
Accelerator pump injector	40
Choke flap opening after starting	2.4 mm

Weber 32 TLDR carburettor data

Idle speed .... 750 ± 50 rpm
Idle mixture CO content .... 1.5 ± 0.5%
Needle valve .... 1.75 mm
Float level .... 31 mm
Accelerator pump injector 55
Positive throttle opening .... 0.65 mm (18°)
Pneumatic initial opening at 290 mbars .... 3.0 ± 0.5 mm
Mechanical initial opening .... 4.5 ± 0.5 mm

	Primary	Secondary
Choke tube	23	24
Main jet	122	160
Air correction jet	175	210
Idling jet	50	40
Auxiliary venturi	3.5R	3.5R
Emulsion tube	F3	F56
Enrichener	60	40

Zenith 32 IF2 carburettor data

Idle speed .... 700 ± 50 rpm
Idle mixture CO content .... 1.5 ± 0.5%
Choke tube 24
Main jet 130
Idling jet 53
Air correction jet .... 90 x 160
Pneumatic enrichener 74
Accelerator pump travel .... 28.3 mm
Accelerator pump injector 50
Accelerator pump tube height .... 60 mm
Needle valve .... 1.25 mm
Float level .... 13.65 ± 0.1 mm
Auxiliary jet 110
Auxiliary tube height .... 0.6 mm
Degassing valve dimension .... 2.0 mm minimum
Positive throttle opening .... 0.9 mm
Pneumatic opening (upper choke opening after starting) ..... 2.6 mm

Weber 32 DRT carburettor data

Idle speed .... 700 ± 50 rpm
Idle mixture CO content .... 1.5 ± 0.5 %
Fast idling speed .... 900 ± 50 rpm
Needle valve 175
Float level .... 8.0 mm
Accelerator pump injector 50
Positive throttle opening .... 0.75 mm
Pneumatic opening (part-open) .... 3.5 mm
Throttle opening with degassing valve closed .... 0.3 mm

	Primary	Secondary
Choke tube	23	24
Main jet	110	105
Idling jet	55	70
Air correction jet	230	135
Emulsion tube	F58	F56
Auxiliary venturi	4	4R
Enrichener	60	50

Solex 32 x 34 Z13 carburettor data

Idle speed .... 800 ± 50 rpm
Idle mixture CO content .... 1.5 ± 0.5%
Fast idling speed:
  Models with power-assisted steering (PAS):
    Front wheels straight-ahead .... 975 ± 50 rpm
    Front wheels on full-lock .... 700 to 730 rpm
  Models with air conditioning (A/C) or PAS and A/C .... 950 rpm
Needle valve .... 1.8 mm
Float level .... 33.5 ± 0.5 mm
Positive throttle opening .... 0.75 mm (22°30')
Mechanical initial opening .... 3.5 mm
Degassing valve dimension .... 0.3 mm

Solex 32 x 34 Z13 carburettor data (cont.)

	Primary	Secondary
Choke tube	24	27
Main jet	115	137.5
Air correction jet	165	190
Idling jet	43	50
Econostat	-	120
Enrichener	50	-
Accelerator pump injector	40	35
Fast idle throttle valve setting:		
Power steering or air conditioning	11°15'	
Power steering and air conditioning	13°	

1 General information and precautions

The fuel system consists of a fuel tank mounted under the rear of the vehicle, a mechanical fuel pump, and a single- or twin-choke downdraught carburettor. The mechanical fuel pump is operated by an eccentric on the camshaft. The pump is mounted on the forward side of the cylinder block on 1237 cc (C1G) and 1397 cc (C1J and C2J) engines, or on the rear side of the cylinder head on 1390 cc (E6J) and 1721 cc (F2N) engines. A degassing chamber is located on the fuel line on the 1721 cc (F2N) engine (see illustration). The air cleaner contains a disposable paper filter element, and incorporates a flap valve air temperature control system. This system allows cold air from the outside of the vehicle, and warm air from the exhaust manifold, to enter the air cleaner in the correct proportions, according to ambient air temperatures. The flap is controlled automatically by a temperature-sensitive wax capsule.

Carburettors may be of Zenith, Solex or Weber manufacture, according to model. The Zenith carburettor incorporates a water-heated lower body, to improve fuel atomisation, particularly when the engine is cold. On engines fitted with the Solex and Weber carburettors, the inlet manifold is heated by the cooling system coolant. Mixture enrichment for cold starting is by a manually-operated choke control on all models.

The exhaust system is in three sections; the front downpipe (attached to the exhaust manifold by a spring-tensioned flange), the

intermediate section and resonator (attached to the downpipe by a clamped flange), and the tailpipe and silencer (attached to the intermediate section by a clamped flange). The system is suspended throughout its entire length by rubber mountings.

⚠️ **Warning: Many of the procedures in this Chapter require the removal of fuel lines and connections, which may result in some fuel spillage. Before carrying out any operation on the fuel system, refer to the precautions given in "Safety first!" at the beginning of this manual, and follow them implicitly. Petrol is a highly-dangerous and volatile liquid, and the precautions necessary when handling it cannot be overstressed.**

2 Air cleaner housing assembly - removal and refitting

1237 cc (C1G) and 1397 cc (C1J and C2J) engines

Removal

1 Remove the air cleaner filter element as described in Chapter 1.
2 Disconnect the air inlet hose and hot-air hose from the air cleaner inlet.
3 Unscrew and remove the mounting bolts, noting the arrangement of the rubber spacers, washers and sleeves.
4 Withdraw the air cleaner body from the engine.

Refitting

5 Refitting is a reversal of removal.

1.1 De-gassing chamber (arrowed) on the 1721 cc (F2N) engine

1390 cc (E6J) engine

Removal

6 Remove the air cleaner filter element as described in Chapter 1.
7 Using a screwdriver, loosen the clip securing the air cleaner body to the support bracket (see illustration). Remove the clip.
8 Loosen the clip, and remove the air inlet hose from the duct on the carburettor (see illustration).
9 Disconnect the hot-air hose and elbow from the side of the air cleaner body (see illustration).
10 Disconnect the fresh-air hose from the inlet elbow on the front left-hand corner of the engine compartment, below the rear of the headlight (see illustration).
11 Withdraw the air cleaner body from the support bracket (see illustration).

Refitting

12 Refitting is a reversal of removal.

4A

2.7 Removing the air cleaner housing securing clip - 1390 cc (E6J) engine

2.8 Removing the air inlet hose - 1390 cc (E6J) engine

2.9 Removing the hot-air hose and elbow - 1390 cc (E6J) engine

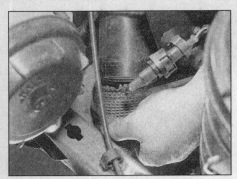

2.10 Disconnecting fresh air hose from the inlet elbow - 1390 cc (E6J) engine

2.11 Withdrawing the air cleaner body - 1390 cc (E6J) engine

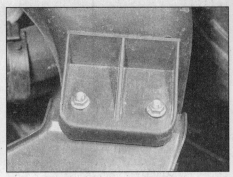

2.14a Carburettor cooling duct attachment to the radiator support . . .

2.14b . . . and the engine compartment strengthening bar - 1721 cc (F2N) engine

2.15 Disconnecting the hot-air hose from the air cleaner housing and exhaust manifold shroud - 1721 cc (F2N) engine

2.17 Disconnecting the crankcase ventilation hose from the T-piece - 1721 cc (F2N) engine

1721 cc (F2N) engine

Removal

13 Remove the air cleaner filter element as described in Chapter 1.

14 For better access, unbolt the carburettor cooling duct from the radiator support and from the engine compartment strengthening bar **(see illustrations)**.

15 Loosen the clips and disconnect the hot-air hose from the air cleaner body, and from the shroud on the exhaust manifold **(see illustration)**.

16 Disconnect the fresh-air hose from the bottom of the air cleaner, and from the front left-hand corner of the engine compartment.

17 Disconnect the crankcase ventilation hose from the air cleaner, and from the T-piece near the bulkhead **(see illustration)**.

18 Unscrew the mounting nuts, and withdraw the air cleaner body from the engine compartment **(see illustrations)**.

19 Check the condition of the rubber mountings where applicable, and renew them as necessary **(see illustration)**. Also check the hoses and hose clips for condition.

Refitting

20 Refitting is a reversal of removal.

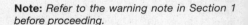

3 Fuel pump -
testing, removal and refitting

Note: *Refer to the warning note in Section 1 before proceeding.*

Testing

1 To test the fuel pump on the engine, temporarily disconnect the outlet pipe which leads to the carburettor, and hold a wad of rag over the pump outlet while an assistant spins the engine on the starter. Keep your hands

2.18a Air cleaner body mounting - 1721 cc (F2N) engine

2.18b Removing the air cleaner body - 1721 cc (F2N) engine

2.19 Air cleaner body rubber mounting (arrowed) - 1721 cc (F2N) engine

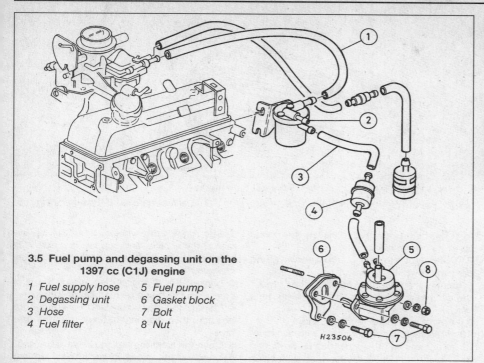

3.5 Fuel pump and degassing unit on the 1397 cc (C1J) engine

1 Fuel supply hose	5 Fuel pump
2 Degassing unit	6 Gasket block
3 Hose	7 Bolt
4 Fuel filter	8 Nut

4.2 Fuel gauge sender unit and connections

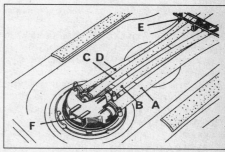

4.4 Fuel gauge sender unit hose connections

A Degassing pipe	D Fuel return pipe
B Vent pipe	E Hose retaining clip
C Fuel feed pipe	F Wiring connector

4A

away from the electric cooling fan. Regular spurts of fuel should be ejected as the engine turns.

2 The pump can also be tested by removing it. With the pump outlet pipe disconnected, but the inlet pipe still connected, hold the wad of rag by the outlet. Operate the pump lever by hand; if the pump is in a satisfactory condition, a strong jet of fuel should be ejected. On 1237 cc (C1G), 1390 cc (E6J) and 1397 cc (C1J and C2J) engines, the pump lever should be moved up and down; on the 1721 cc (F2N) engine, the plunger should be pushed in and out.

3 If a suitable pressure gauge is available, a more accurate test may be carried out. Before connecting the gauge to the fuel system, run the engine at idling speed for several minutes, in order to completely fill the carburettor float chamber. With the engine switched off, disconnect the fuel supply pipe at the carburettor end, and then connect the pressure gauge to it. The gauge connection pipe should be transparent and short. Using a hose clamp, pinch the return pipe leading to the fuel tank. Hold the gauge as high as possible with the pipe vertical, then start the engine and allow it to idle. Lower the gauge until the level of fuel in the transparent pipe is level with the fuel pump diaphragm, then check that the pump static pressure is as given in the Specifications (note that the engine must be idling, but there is no fuel movement as the gauge is connected to the outlet). Check the return pipe for obstruction by removing the clamp from the return hose and checking that the pressure then drops to between 0.01 and 0.02 bars - if the pressure is higher than this, blow through the return hose to clear the obstruction.

Removal

4 Disconnect the battery negative lead.
5 Identify the fuel pump inlet and outlet hoses for position, then disconnect and plug them **(see illustration)**.
6 Unscrew the nuts/bolts securing the pump to the cylinder block (1237 cc/C1G and 1397 cc/C1J/C2J engines) or cylinder head (1390 cc/E6J and 1721 cc/F2N engines), and remove the washers.
7 Withdraw the fuel pump from the engine, and remove the gasket block. On the 1721 cc (F2N) engine, note the number and location of the gaskets.

Refitting

8 Refitting is a reversal of removal, but clean the mating surfaces, and fit a new gasket block. Tighten the securing nuts/bolts securely.

4 Fuel gauge sender unit - removal and refitting

Note: Refer to the warning note in Section 1 before proceeding.

Removal

1 Disconnect the battery negative lead.
2 Working in the rear luggage compartment, lift the carpet, and prise out the rubber cover to gain access to the fuel gauge sender unit **(see illustration)**.
3 Disconnect the wiring connector from the sender unit, and secure it in the luggage compartment, to prevent it from falling out of reach beneath the rear floor.
4 Identify the hoses for position, then loosen the clips, where applicable, and disconnect

them from the sender unit **(see illustration)**. Tie the hoses and wiring connector together, and move them to one side.
5 Unscrew the plastic ring nut. To do this, it is recommended that a removal tool is made out of a U-shaped piece of metal which will engage with the serrations in the plastic ring nut.
6 With the ring nut removed, withdraw the sender unit from the fuel tank, followed by the special gasket. Be prepared for fuel spillage.

Refitting

7 Refitting is a reversal of removal, but use a new gasket if the old one is damaged or shows signs of deterioration.

5 Fuel tank - removal and refitting

Note: Refer to the warning note in Section 1 before proceeding.

Removal

1 A drain plug is not provided on the fuel tank, and it is therefore preferable to carry out the removal operation when the tank is nearly empty. Before proceeding, disconnect the battery negative lead, and then syphon or hand-pump the remaining fuel from the tank.
2 Chock the front wheels, then jack up the rear of the vehicle and support it securely on

5.5 Fuel tank mounting bolt (arrowed)

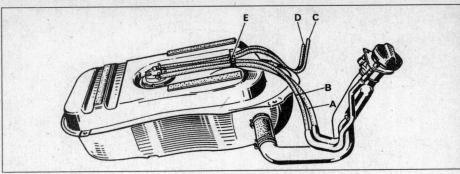

5.6 Fuel tank hoses

A Degassing pipe   B Vent pipe   C Fuel feed pipe   D Fuel return pipe   E Pipe retaining clip

axle stands (see *"Jacking, towing and wheel changing"*).

3 Remove the spare wheel, then unbolt the spare wheel carrier from the underbody.

4 Loosen the clip(s) and disconnect the filler hose from the fuel tank.

5 Take the weight of the fuel tank, using a trolley jack together with an interposed block of wood. Unscrew and remove the fuel tank mounting bolts **(see illustration)**.

6 Lower the fuel tank sufficiently to gain access to the hose connections on the fuel gauge sender unit **(see illustration)**. As the

tank is being lowered, release the hose retaining clip on the top of the tank.

7 Disconnect the fuel gauge sender wiring connector.

8 Identify the hoses for position, then loosen the clips and disconnect them from the tank unit.

9 Lower the fuel tank to the ground.

10 If the tank is contaminated with sediment or water, remove the sender unit as described in Section 4 and swill the tank out with clean fuel. If the tank is damaged, or if leaks are apparent, it should be repaired by a specialist, or alternatively, renewed.

Refitting

11 Refitting is a reversal of removal, but make sure that the hoses are not trapped as the tank is lifted into place.

6 Fuel tank filler pipe - removal and refitting

Note: *Refer to the warning note in Section 1 before proceeding.*

Removal

1 A drain plug is not provided on the fuel tank, and it is therefore preferable to carry out the removal operation when the tank is nearly empty. Before proceeding, disconnect the battery negative lead, and then syphon or hand-pump the remaining fuel from the tank.

2 Chock the front wheels, then jack up the rear of the vehicle, and support it securely on axle stands (see *"Jacking, towing and wheel changing"*).

3 Loosen the clip and disconnect the filler hose from the filler pipe **(see illustration)**.

4 Identify the degassing and vent pipes for position, then disconnect them from the filler pipe.

5 Open the fuel filler flap and remove the cap.

6 Unscrew the cross-head screws located inside the filler flap recess, and remove the filler pipe assembly.

Refitting

7 Refitting is a reversal of removal.

7 Accelerator cable - removal, refitting and adjustment

Removal

1 Remove the air cleaner assembly (1237 cc/ C1G and 1397 cc/C1J/C2J engines) or the air duct (1390 cc/E6J and 1721 cc/F2N engines) from the carburettor.

2 Working inside the vehicle, release the cable end fitting, which is a push fit in the accelerator pedal rod **(see illustration)**.

3 At the carburettor, open the throttle and unhook the end of the accelerator cable from the sector arm **(see illustrations)**.

4 Pull the adjustment ferrule from the bracket

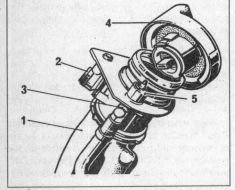

6.3 Fuel tank filler pipe

1 Filler pipe
2 Safety valve
3 Filling limiter
4 Cap
5 Plunger

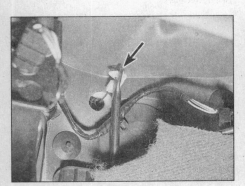

7.2 Accelerator cable end fitting (arrowed) at accelerator pedal

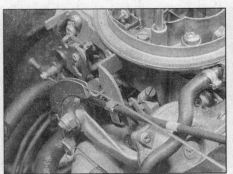

7.3a Accelerator cable connection to sector arm on the carburettor

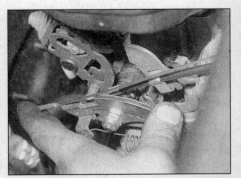

7.3b Unhooking the accelerator cable from the sector arm

7.4 Accelerator cable adjustment ferrule on the valve cover

9.3 Disconnecting the choke cable from the lever on the carburettor

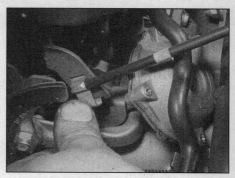

9.4 Prising out the choke outer cable securing clip

on the valve cover, and feed the cable through the bracket **(see illustration)**.

5 Release the cable from the cable ties/support clips, and withdraw it through the bulkhead into the engine compartment.

Refitting and adjustment

6 Refitting is a reversal of removal, but if necessary adjust it as follows.

7 With the pedal fully released, check that there is a small amount of slack in the cable with the throttle sector on its stop. Have an assistant fully depress the accelerator pedal, then check that the throttle sector is in its fully-open position. If adjustment is required, remove the spring clip from the adjustment ferrule, reposition the ferrule as necessary, then insert the clip in the next free groove on the ferrule.

8 Accelerator pedal - removal and refitting

Removal

1 Working inside the vehicle, release the accelerator cable end fitting, which is a push fit in the pedal rod.

2 Unscrew the bolt securing the pedal assembly to the bulkhead, and withdraw it from inside the vehicle.

Refitting

3 Refitting is a reversal of removal, but check the accelerator
cable adjustment as described in Section 7.

9 Choke cable - removal, refitting and adjustment

Removal

1 Disconnect the battery negative lead.

2 Remove the carburettor inlet air duct.

3 Using a screwdriver or pair of pliers, disconnect the coiled end of the choke cable from the lever on the carburettor **(see illustration)**.

4 Prise out the clip securing the choke outer cable to the bracket on the side of the carburettor **(see illustration)**.

5 Working inside the vehicle, remove the screw and withdraw the choke control knob panel from the facia **(see illustrations)**.

6 Disconnect the warning light wiring from the knob **(see illustration)**.

7 Release the cable from the cable ties/support clips in the engine compartment, then withdraw it through the bulkhead into the vehicle interior.

Refitting and adjustment

8 Refitting is a reversal of removal, but adjust the cable as follows.

9 With the control knob pulled out approximately 2.0 mm, and the choke lever on the carburettor in its rest position (ie choke valve fully-open), fit the clip over the outer cable, and attach it to the support bracket. Check that the choke control lever is in its rest

position with the knob pushed home, and fully-closed (ie choke valve shut) with the knob pulled out.

10 Unleaded petrol - general information and usage

Refer to Chapter 1 Specifications for details of unleaded petrol usage. Note that certain engines must not be operated on unleaded petrol, and must use leaded petrol at all times.

For engines which can be operated on either unleaded or leaded petrol, no adjustments to the ignition timing are required.

11 Carburettor - general information

The carburettors may be of Weber, Zenith or Solex manufacture, according to model. All are of downdraught design, and of single-choke type on the 1237 cc (C1G) and 1397 cc (C1J) engines; twin-choke units are fitted on other engines. On certain engines, the carburettor may be fitted with an idle step-up solenoid valve, in order to increase the engine speed when the power-assisted steering pump or air conditioning compressor is operating, and prevent stalling.

4A

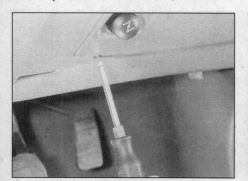

9.5a Remove the screw . . .

9.5b . . . and withdraw the choke control knob panel from the facia

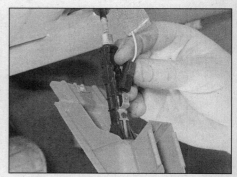

9.6 Disconnecting the warning light wiring from the choke control knob

12.3a Carburettor air inlet duct securing nuts - 1390 cc (E6J) engine

12.3b Unscrew the nuts . . .

12.3c . . . and remove the air inlet duct . . .

12.3d . . . and gasket from the carburettor - 1721 cc (F2N) engine

12 Carburettor - removal and refitting

Removal

1 Where applicable, unbolt the strengthening bar from between the front suspension strut turrets. Where applicable, also remove the air duct which runs from the cooling fan shroud to the carburettor.

2 Where applicable, drain the cooling system as described in Chapter 1, then disconnect the coolant hoses from the carburettor.

3 Remove the air cleaner or inlet duct from the top of the carburettor, and place to one side. Remove the gasket (see illustrations).

4 Disconnect the accelerator and choke cables from the carburettor, as described in the relevant Sections of this Chapter.

5 Disconnect the fuel inlet hose, and plug its end (see illustrations).

6 On 1390 cc (E6J) and 1721 cc (F2N) engines, disconnect the crankcase ventilation hose (see illustration).

7 On the 1721 cc (F2N) engine, disconnect the wiring for the anti-run-on solenoid and, where applicable, the idle step-up valve, carburettor temperature sender and carburettor heater (see illustrations).

8 Unscrew the mounting nuts/bolts, remove the washers and withdraw the carburettor from the inlet manifold. On 1390 cc (E6J) and 1721 cc (F2N) engines, a Torx key will be

12.5a Fuel inlet hose (arrowed) - 1390 cc (E6J) engine

12.5b Disconnecting the fuel inlet hose - 1721 cc (F2N) engine

12.6 Disconnecting the crankcase ventilation hose - 1721 cc (F2N) engine

12.7a Disconnecting the wiring from the anti-run-on solenoid - 1721 cc (F2N) engine

12.7b Disconnecting the idle step-up valve wiring connector - 1721 cc (F2N) engine

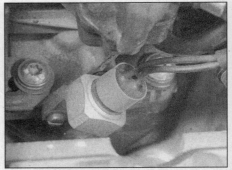

12.7c Carburettor temperature sender - 1721 cc (F2N) engine

12.8a Carburettor mounting bolts (arrowed) - 1390 cc (E6J) engine

12.8b Removing the carburettor - 1390 cc (E6J) engine

13.3 Choke pull-off vacuum hose (arrowed) - Weber 32 TLDR carburettor

required to unscrew the bolts **(see illustrations)**. Recover the set of gaskets and, where applicable, the heat shield.

Refitting

9 Refitting is a reversal of removal, bearing in mind the following points:

  (a) Make sure that the mating surfaces of the carburettor and inlet manifold are clean, and fit a new set of gaskets.
  (b) Adjust the accelerator and choke cables as described in Sections 7 and 9.
  (c) Where applicable, refill the cooling system as described in Chapter 1.
  (d) On completion, adjust the idle speed and mixture with reference to Chapter 1.

13 Carburettor - fault diagnosis, overhaul and adjustments

Fault diagnosis

1 Faults with the carburettor are usually associated with dirt entering the float chamber and blocking the jets, causing a weak mixture or power failure within a certain engine speed range. If this is the case, then a thorough clean will normally cure the problem. If the carburettor is well-worn, uneven running may be caused by air entering through the throttle valve spindle bearings. All the carburettors

fitted to the Renault 19 are fitted with manually-operated chokes, which do not normally cause any problems.

Overhaul and adjustments

2 The following paragraphs describe cleaning and adjustment procedures which can be carried out by the home mechanic, after the carburettor has been removed from the inlet manifold. If the carburettor is worn or damaged, it should either be renewed or overhauled by a specialist, who will be able to restore the carburettor to its original calibration.

Weber 32 TLDR and 32 DRT

3 Disconnect the vacuum hose from the choke pull-off vacuum capsule **(see illustration)**.

4 Unscrew and remove the slotted screws from the top of the carburettor cover, and lift the cover from the main body **(see illustration)**. Remove the gasket from the cover.

5 Note the locations of the various jets **(see illustrations)**. Each jet should be removed and identified for position, then the float chamber

can be cleaned of any sediment. Clean the main body and the cover thoroughly with fuel, and blow through the carburettor internal channels and jets, using air from an air line or foot pump.

6 With the jets refitted and a new gasket located on the cover, check the float level setting as follows. Hold the cover vertical, so that the floats hang down and close the needle valve, without causing the valve ball to be depressed. Measure the distance between the gasket and the nearest point of the float, and compare with the dimension given in the Specifications. If adjustment is necessary, bend the tag on the float arm, and make the check again.

7 Reassembly is a reversal of dismantling.

Zenith 32 IF2

8 Unscrew and remove the screws, and lift the cover off the main body. Remove the gasket.

9 Note the locations of the various jets **(see illustration)**. Remove each jet, and identify it for position. Using fuel, thoroughly clean the float chamber, main body and cover. Blow through the carburettor internal channels and jets, using air from an air line or foot pump.

10 To check the float level setting, turn the

4A

13.4 Carburettor cover securing screws (arrowed) - Weber 32 TLDR carburettor

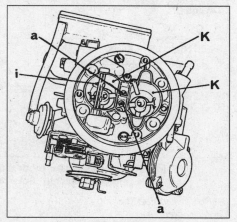

13.5a Weber 32 TLDR carburettor main body components

a Air correction jet
i Accelerator pump injector
K Venturi ("choke tube")

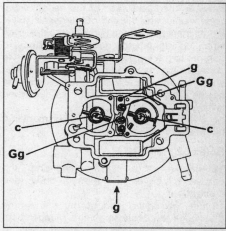

13.5b Weber 32 TLDR carburettor cover components

c Auxiliary venturi   Gg Main jet
g Idling jet

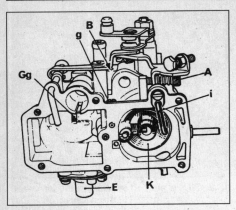

13.9 Zenith 32 IF2 carburettor main body components

A Idling speed air screw
B Idling speed mixture screw
E Pneumatic richener
g Idling jet
Gg Main jet
i Accelerator pump jet
K Venturi ("choke tube")

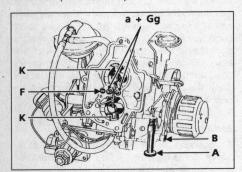

13.14 Solex 32 x 34 Z13 carburettor main body components

a Air correction jet
A Idle volume screw
B Idle mixture screw
F Idle fuel circuit filter
Gg Main jet
K Venturi ("choke tube")

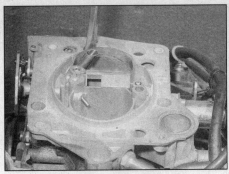

13.12 Removing the carburettor cover securing screws - Solex 32 x 34 Z13 carburettor

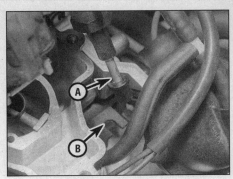

13.13 Disengaging the degassing valve plunger (A) from the operating lever (B) - Solex 32 x 34 Z13 carburettor

13.15 Float arm fulcrum pin (arrowed) - Solex 32 x 34 Z13 carburettor

13.16 Measuring the float level setting - Solex 32 x 34 Z13 carburettor

cover upside-down. Measure the distance between the upper face of the needle valve body washer and the end of the needle valve. If the measured dimension is greater than specified, tighten the needle valve body to compress the washer until the dimension is correct. If the measured dimension is less than specified, renew the washer, and tighten the needle valve body until the correct dimension is obtained.

11 Reassembly is a reversal of dismantling, but fit a new gasket.

Solex 32 x 34 Z13

12 Remove the screws securing the carburettor cover to the main body (see illustration).

13 Lift the cover, and at the same time disengage the degassing valve plunger from the operating lever (see illustration).

14 Note the locations of the various jets (see illustration). Remove each jet, and identify it for location. Using fuel, thoroughly clean the float chamber, main body and cover. Blow

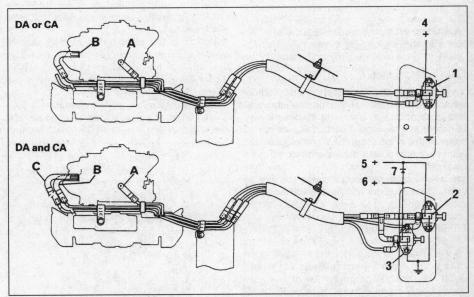

13.18 Idle step-up system for models fitted with power-assisted steering or air conditioning - Solex 32 x 34 Z13 carburettor

DA Power-assisted steering
CA Air conditioning
A Carburettor connection (red ring)
B Actuator connection (blue ring) on DA or CA models
C Connection on actuator (grey ring) on CA and DA + CA models

1 DA or CA solenoid valve
2 DA solenoid valve
3 CA solenoid valve
4 DA pressure switch or CA compressor
5 DA pressure switch
6 CA compressor
7 Diode

13.19a Adjustment screw (arrowed) for idle step-up actuator - Solex 32 x 34 Z13 carburettor model with power steering

through the carburettor internal channels and jets, using air from an air line or foot pump.

15 Note how the needle valve is attached to the float arm, then push out the fulcrum pin, remove the float assembly and valve, and remove the gasket (see illustration). Renew the gasket, and refit the float assembly.

16 To check the float level setting, hold the cover vertical so that the floats hang down. The needle valve should be closed, but the spring-tensioned ball in the end of the valve should not be depressed. Measure the distance between the gasket and the floats, and compare with the dimension given in the Specifications (see illustration). If adjustment is necessary, bend the tag on the float arm and make the check again.

17 Reassembly is a reversal of dismantling.

18 Models fitted with this carburettor may be equipped with power-assisted steering, air conditioning, or both. On these models, an idle step-up system is fitted, to compensate for the extra load of the power-assisted steering pump and/or air conditioning compressor (see illustration). The fast idle speed checking procedure is as follows. The normal idle speed adjustment should be made as described in Chapter 1. The engine must be at its normal operating temperature, and any adjustments must be made with the electric cooling fan stopped.

19 On models with power-assisted steering, make sure that the front wheels are pointing straight-ahead, then apply a vacuum of 600 mbars (or manifold vacuum) to the idle step-up actuator (blue ring) on the carburettor. The engine speed should be as given in the Specifications at the beginning of this Chapter. If not, turn the adjustment screw. On models with air conditioning, switch on the air conditioner to its maximum position before making the adjustment. On models with both power-assisted steering and air conditioning, carry out the power steering adjustment as described, then carry out the air conditioning adjustment, in that order (see illustrations).

Solex 32 BIS 936

20 The procedure is the same as that described for the Solex 32 x 34 Z13 carburettor in paragraphs 12 to 17 (see illustration). Note that it is not possible to

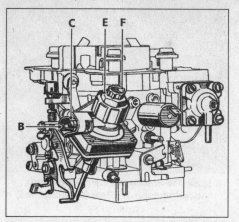

13.19b Idle step-up system for models with power-assisted steering and air conditioning - Solex 32 x 34 Z13 carburettor

B Actuator vacuum connection (blue ring) for models with power steering or air conditioning (single stage)
C Actuator arm connection (grey ring) for models with air conditioning and power steering (double stage)
E Power steering adjusting screw
F Air conditioning adjusting screw

adjust the float level; if the thickness of the washer beneath the needle valve body is 1 mm, the adjustment is correct. Renew the washer if necessary.

14 Anti-percolation system - general

1 The anti-percolation system is fitted to most carburettor models. Its purpose is to reduce carburettor temperature when the vehicle is stopped after a run. This prevents fuel percolation (vaporisation due to excess heat) occurring in the carburettor, so avoiding hot-start problems and excess fuel vapour emissions.

2 The main components of the system are an electric fan, air ducts leading to the carburettor, and the control circuitry. A combined temperature switch/timer unit actuates the fan for a set period after switch-off, if the temperature exceeds a certain value.

3 No specific testing or repair procedures for the anti-percolation system were available at the time of writing.

15 Inlet manifold pre-heater (1721 cc engine) - removal and refitting

Removal

1 Unbolt the strengthening bar from between the front suspension strut turrets. It will also be necessary to remove the carburettor cooling duct.

2 Remove the air inlet duct from the top of the carburettor, and move it to one side.

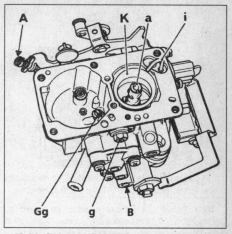

13.20 Solex 32 BIS 936 carburettor main body components

A Idle speed screw
B Idle speed mixture screw
K Venturi ("choke tube")
a Air correction jet
g Idling jet
Gg Main jet
i Accelerator pump jet

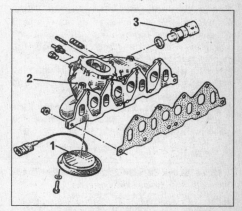

15.4 Inlet/exhaust manifolds, and pre-heater on the 1721 cc (F2N) engine

1 Pre-heater
2 Inlet/exhaust manifold
3 Temperature switch

3 Separate the two halves of the connector which connects the main wiring harness to the pre-heater wiring.

4 Unbolt the pre-heater from the bottom of the inlet manifold, and lower it down through the aperture in the exhaust manifold (see illustration).

Refitting

5 Refitting is a reversal of removal.

16 Inlet and exhaust manifold assembly (1237 cc/C1G and 1397 cc/C1J engines) - removal and refitting

Removal

1 Remove the carburettor as described in Section 12.

4A

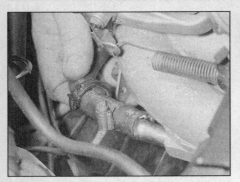

18.2 Disconnecting the coolant hoses from the inlet manifold - 1390 cc (E6J) engine

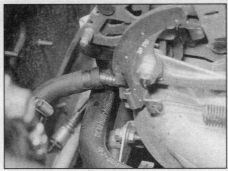

18.3 Disconnecting the brake servo vacuum hose - 1390 cc (E6J) engine

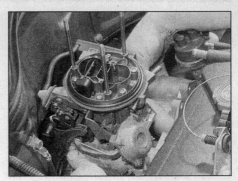

18.4a Withdrawing the inlet manifold complete with the carburettor . . .

2 Disconnect the brake servo vacuum hose and the crankcase ventilation hose from the inlet manifold.
3 Unbolt and remove the starter motor protective shield.
4 Remove the hot-air ducting, then unbolt the metal tube and air cleaner support bracket.
5 Unscrew the nut and withdraw the heat shield from the exhaust manifold.
6 Unscrew and remove the two nuts, then remove the washers, tension springs and sleeves securing the exhaust front pipe to the manifold. Slide the flange plate off the manifold studs, and separate the joint.
7 Progressively unscrew the nuts securing the manifold assembly to the cylinder head, and remove the washers.
8 Withdraw the manifold assembly from the studs on the cylinder head, then remove the gasket.

Refitting

9 Refitting is a reversal of removal, bearing in mind the following points:
  (a) Ensure that the cylinder head and manifold mating faces are clean, and use a new gasket.
  (b) Reconnect the exhaust front pipe to the manifold with reference to Section 20.
  (c) Refit the carburettor with reference to Section 12.

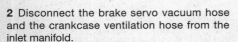

17 Inlet and exhaust manifolds (1721 cc/F2N engine) - removal and refitting

Removal

1 Remove the carburettor as described in Section 12.
2 Drain the cooling system as described in Chapter 1, then disconnect the coolant hoses from the inlet manifold.
3 Disconnect the brake servo vacuum hose from the inlet manifold.
4 Unscrew and remove the two nuts, then remove the washers, tension springs and sleeves securing the exhaust front pipe to the manifold. Slide the flange plate off the manifold studs, and separate the joint.
5 Unscrew the nuts securing the hot-air

18.4b . . . and recovering the gasket - 1390 cc (E6J) engine

shroud to the manifold, and remove the shroud.
6 Unbolt and remove the manifold support brackets.
7 Progressively unscrew the nuts and bolts securing the inlet and exhaust manifolds, and withdraw them from the cylinder head. Although the manifolds are separate, they are retained by the same bolts, since the bolt holes are split between the manifold flanges. Recover the manifold gasket.

Refitting

8 Refitting is a reversal of removal, bearing in mind the following points:
  (a) Ensure that the cylinder head and manifold mating faces are clean, and use a new gasket.
  (b) Reconnect the exhaust front pipe to the manifold with reference to Section 20.
  (c) Refit the carburettor with reference to Section 12.
  (d) Refill the cooling system with reference to Chapter 1.

18 Inlet manifold (1390 cc/E6J engine) - removal and refitting

Removal

1 Remove the carburettor as described in Section 12. Alternatively, the inlet manifold may be removed together with the carburettor,

19.1 Unscrewing the exhaust front pipe-to-manifold nuts - 1390 cc (E6J) engine

but if this method is used, it will still be necessary to disconnect the accelerator and choke cables, and the various hoses.
2 Drain the cooling system as described in Chapter 1, then disconnect the coolant hoses from the inlet manifold (see illustration).
3 Disconnect the brake servo vacuum hose (see illustration).
4 Progressively unscrew the nuts, then withdraw the inlet manifold from the studs on the cylinder head. Remove the gasket (see illustrations).

Refitting

5 Refitting is a reversal of removal, bearing in mind the following points:
  (a) Ensure that the cylinder head and manifold mating faces are clean, and use a new gasket.
  (b) Where applicable, refit the carburettor with reference to Section 12.
  (c) Refill the cooling system with reference to Chapter 1.

19 Exhaust manifold (1390 cc/E6J engine) - removal and refitting

Removal

1 Unscrew and remove the two nuts, then remove the washers, tension springs and sleeves securing the exhaust front pipe to the manifold (see illustration). Slide the flange plate

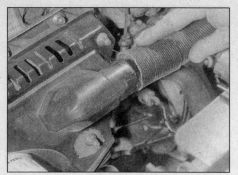

19.2 Disconnecting the hot-air hose from the manifold hot-air shroud - 1390 cc (E6J) engine

19.3 Removing the hot-air shroud from the manifold - 1390 cc (E6J) engine

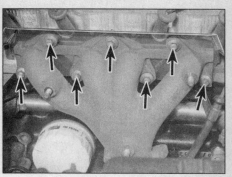

19.4a Unscrew the nuts (arrowed) . . .

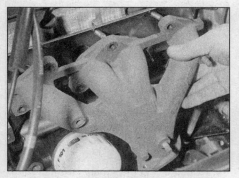

19.4b . . . and withdraw the exhaust manifold . . .

19.4c . . . and gasket

off the manifold studs, and separate the joint.
2 Loosen the clip, and disconnect the hot-air hose for the air cleaner from the exhaust manifold hot-air shroud **(see illustration)**.
3 Unscrew the nuts and remove the hot-air

shroud from the manifold **(see illustration)**.
4 Progressively unscrew the nuts securing the exhaust manifold, then withdraw it from the cylinder head. Recover the manifold gasket **(see illustrations)**.

Refitting

5 Refitting is a reversal of removal. Ensure that the cylinder head and manifold mating faces are clean, and use a new gasket. Reconnect the exhaust front pipe to the manifold with reference to Section 20.

20 Exhaust system - general information and component renewal

General information

1 The exhaust system consists of three sections, the sections varying in detail depending on model **(see illustrations)**. Note that the centre section may contain one or two silencers, depending on model. Both the front pipe and tail pipe can be removed

4A

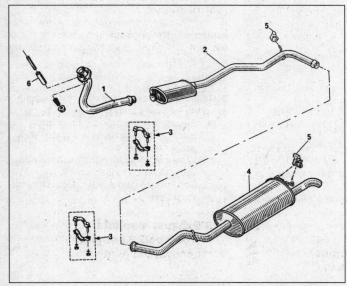

20.1a Typical exhaust system components for the 1397 cc (C1J) engine

1 *Front pipe*
2 *Intermediate pipe and resonator*
3 *Connecting clamp*
4 *Tailpipe and silencer*
5 *Exhaust rubber mounting*
6 *Spacer to limit tightening of front pipe nut*

20.1b Typical exhaust system components for the 1721 cc (F2N) engine

1 *Front pipe*
2 *Spherical joint*
3 *Intermediate pipe and expansion chamber*
4 *Tailpipe and silencer*
5 *Exhaust rubber mounting*
6 *Front pipe-to-intermediate pipe connecting clamp*
7 *Spacer to limit tightening of front pipe nut*

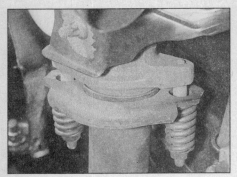

20.3 Exhaust front pipe-to-manifold joint - 1390 cc (E6J) engine

20.4 Exhaust front pipe-to-intermediate section joint - 1390 cc (E6J) engine

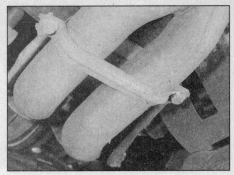

20.5 Heat shield and bracket - 1721 cc (F2N) engine

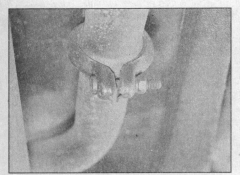

20.7 Tailpipe-to-intermediate section clamp - 1390 cc (E6J) engine

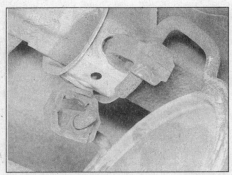

20.8 Tailpipe rear rubber mountings - 1390 cc (E6J) engine

20.13 Exhaust intermediate section rubber mounting - 1390 cc (E6J) engine

20.14 Strengthening bracket fitted to the exhaust intermediate section - 1390 cc (E6J) engine

independently, leaving the remaining exhaust system in position. To remove the intermediate section, it is recommended that the tail pipe is removed first, before disconnecting the intermediate section from the front pipe.

Component renewal

2 To remove the system or part of the system, first jack up the front or rear of the vehicle, as

applicable, and support it securely on axle stands (see *"Jacking, towing and wheel changing"*). Alternatively, position the vehicle on car ramps.

Front pipe

3 To remove the front pipe, unscrew and remove the two nuts, then remove the washers, tension springs and sleeves securing the exhaust front pipe to the manifold **(see illustration)**. Slide the flange plate off the manifold studs, and separate the joint.
4 Unscrew the nuts and remove the clamp securing the front pipe to the intermediate section **(see illustration)**. Pull the front pipe from the intermediate section.
5 On the 1721 cc (F2N) engine, unbolt the heat shield if necessary **(see illustration)**.
6 Refitting is a reversal of removal, but tighten the nuts securely.

Tailpipe

7 To remove the tailpipe, unscrew the nuts and remove the clamp securing the tailpipe to the intermediate section **(see illustration)**.
8 Slide the rubber mountings off the bars, and if necessary remove them from the underbody

by turning them through 90° **(see illustration)**. Separate the tailpipe from the intermediate section.
9 On the 1721 cc (F2N) engine, unbolt the heat shield if necessary. 10 Refitting is a reversal of removal, but tighten the clamp nuts securely, and renew the rubber mountings if necessary.

Intermediate section

11 To remove the intermediate section, first remove the tailpipe as described previously.
12 Unscrew the nuts and remove the clamp securing the front pipe to the intermediate section.
13 Slide the rubber mountings off the bars, and if necessary remove them from the underbody by turning them through 90° **(see illustration)**.
14 Separate the intermediate section from the front pipe, and if necessary unbolt the strengthening bracket **(see illustration)**.
15 On the 1721 cc (F2N) engine, unbolt the heat shield if necessary.
16 Refitting is a reversal of removal, but tighten the clamp nuts securely, and renew the rubber mountings if necessary.

Chapter 4 Part B: Fuel injection systems

Contents

Degrees of difficulty

Easy, suitable for novice with little experience	Fairly easy, suitable for beginner with some experience	Fairly difficult, suitable for competent DIY mechanic	Difficult, suitable for experienced DIY mechanic	Very difficult, suitable for expert DIY or professional

Specifications

Note: The engine code appears on a plate attached to the engine. Refer to *"Buying spare parts and vehicle identification numbers"* for further details.

General

System type:
1390 cc (C3J) engine	Single-point with catalyst
1390 cc (E7J) engine	Single-point with catalyst
1721 cc (F3N 740 and F3N 741) engines	Single-point with catalyst
1721 cc (F3N 746) engine	Multi-point non-catalyst
1721 cc (F3N 742 and F3N 743)engines	Multi-point with catalyst
1764 cc (F7P 700) engine	Multi-point non-catalyst
1764 cc (F7P 704) engine	Multi-point with catalyst
1794 cc (F3P 704, F3P 705, F3P 706 and F3P 707) engines	Single-point with catalyst
1794 cc (F3P 700) engine	Multi-point with catalyst
Fuel octane requirement	Refer to *Chapter 1 Specifications*

Fuel pump

Type	Electric, immersed in fuel tank

Delivery:
Single-point system	0.83 litres per minute
Multi-point system	1.08 litres per 30 seconds

Fuel pressure

Regulated:
Single-point injection:
1390 cc (C3J) engine	1.00 ± 0.2 bar
1390 cc (E7J) engine	1.06 ± 0.1 bars
1721 cc (F3N) engines	1.20 ± 0.2 bars
1794 cc (F3P) engines	1.06 ± 0.2 bars

Multi-point injection:
All except 1721 cc (F3N 746) engine	2.5 ± 0.2 bars
1721 cc (F3N 746) engine	3.0 ± 0.2 bars

Unregulated:
All except 1721 cc (F3N 746) engine	3.0 ± 0.2 bars
1721 cc (F3N 746) engine	3.5 ± 0.2 bars

4B

Fuel injectors

Operating voltage	12 volts

Resistance:

Single-point injection:

1390 cc (C3J) engine	1.4 ohms (approx)
1390 cc (E7J) engine	1.2 ohms (approx)
1721 cc (F3N) engines	1.4 ohms (approx)
1794 cc (F3P) engine	1.2 ohms (approx)

Multi-point injection:

1721 cc (F3N 742 and F3N 743) engines	2.5 ± 0.5 ohms
1721 cc (F3N 746) engine	14.5 ohms (approx)
1764 cc (F7P) engines	2.5 ± 0.5 ohms
1794 cc (F3P) engine	14.5 ohms (approx)

Inlet air temperature sensor

Resistance:

Single-point injection:

	20°C	70°C
1390 cc (C3J) engine	3400 ohms	450 ohms
	20°C	40°C
1390 cc (E7J) engine	2400 to 2600 ohms	1300 to 1100 ohms
	20°C	70°C
1721 cc (F3N) engines	3400 ohms	450 ohms
	20°C	40°C
1794 cc (F3P) engines	2400 to 2600 ohms	1300 to 1100 ohms
	20°C	40°C
Multi-point injection (all engines)	3060 to 4050 ohms	1290 to 1650 ohms

Coolant temperature sensor

Resistance:

Single-point injection:

	20°C	70°C
1390 cc (C3J) engine	3400 ohms	450 ohms
	40°C	80°C
1390 cc (E7J) engine	1310 to 1600 ohms	300 to 370 ohms
	20°C	70°C
1721 cc (F3N) engine	3400 ohms	450 ohms
	40°C	80°C
1794 cc (F3P) engine	1310 to 1600 ohms	300 to 370 ohms
	20°C	80°C
Multi-point injection (all engines)	3060 to 4050 ohms	300 to 370 ohms

1 General information and precautions

This part of Chapter 4 deals with the fuel injection systems and associated components fitted to the Renault 19. There are two basic types of fuel injection system: a single-point system, and a multi-point system. Refer to the Specifications for details of the system type applicable to each engine. The systems are described in detail in Section 6.

The fuel pump on all fuel injection models is electric; it is located inside the fuel tank. As with the carburettor models, fuel circulates continuously when the pump is operating, excess fuel being returned to the tank.

The exhaust system is conventional. On most models, it incorporates a catalytic converter, to reduce emissions of toxic gases. The catalytic converter and other emission control components are described in Chapter 4C.

⚠️ *Warning: Many of the procedures in this Chapter require the removal of fuel lines and connections, which may result in some fuel spillage (refer to Section 7, and depressurise the fuel system before disconnecting any fuel lines or hoses). Before carrying out any operation on the fuel system, refer to the precautions given in "Safety first!" at the beginning of this manual, and follow them implicitly. Petrol is a highly-dangerous and volatile liquid, and the precautions necessary when handling it cannot be overstressed.*

2 Air cleaner housing assembly - removal and refitting

1390 cc (C3J) engine

Removal

1 Remove the air cleaner filter element as described in Chapter 1.

2 Disconnect the air inlet hose and hot-air hose from the air cleaner inlet **(see illustration)**. Where applicable, also disconnect the breather hose.

3 Unscrew and remove the mounting bolt and nuts, noting the arrangement of the rubber

2.2 Disconnecting the hot-air hose from the air cleaner inlet - 1390 cc (C3J) engine

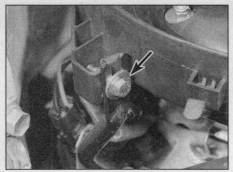

2.3a Remove the right-hand mounting bolt (arrowed) . . .

2.3b . . . front mounting nut (arrowed) . . .

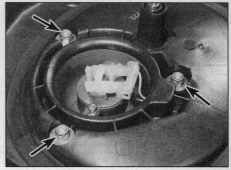

2.3c . . . and top mounting nuts (arrowed) - 1390 cc (C3J) engine

spacers, washers and sleeves **(see illustrations)**.
4 Withdraw the air cleaner body from the engine.

Refitting

5 Refitting is a reversal of removal.

1390 cc (E7J) engine
Removal

6 Remove the bolts securing the air cleaner to the throttle housing.
7 Loosen the securing clips, and disconnect the hot-air hose and the air intake hoses from the air cleaner body **(see illustration)**.
8 Release the strap which secures the casing to the bracket on the cylinder head **(see illustration)**.
9 Lift the air cleaner assembly from the throttle housing, and disconnect the breather hose from the camshaft cover **(see illustration)**.

Refitting

10 Refitting is a reversal of removal.

1721 cc, 1764 cc and 1794 cc (F-type) engines
Removal

11 Where applicable, release the securing clip, and disconnect the wiring plug from the air temperature sensor located in the air

trunking between the air cleaner and the throttle housing.
12 Loosen the securing clip, and disconnect the air trunking from the throttle housing or air duct, as applicable.
13 Where possible, loosen the securing clip, and disconnect the air intake hose from the air cleaner.
14 Unhook the retaining strap(s), or remove the securing screws and/or nuts, as applicable, and lift the assembly from the mounting bracket **(see illustrations)**.
15 Disconnect any remaining hoses from the assembly, noting their locations and routing.

Refitting

16 Refitting is a reversal of removal, ensuring that all hoses are correctly reconnected.

3 Accelerator cable - removal, refitting and adjustment

1 The procedure is as described for carburettor models in Chapter 4A, noting the following points **(see illustration)**.
2 Ignore any references to a carburettor.
3 On single-point fuel injection models, to improve access where necessary, remove the air cleaner assembly or the air duct, as applicable, from the top of the throttle housing.

2.7 Disconnecting the air intake hose from the air cleaner - 1390 cc (E7J) engine

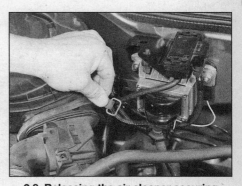

2.8 Releasing the air cleaner securing strap - 1390 cc (E7J) engine

2.9 Disconnecting the breather hose from the camshaft cover - 1390 cc (E7J) engine

2.14a Unhooking the air cleaner retaining strap - 1721 cc (F3N) engine

2.14b Air cleaner securing nut (arrowed) - 1794 cc (F3P) engine

4B

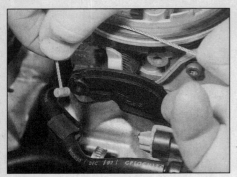

3.1 Disconnecting the throttle cable from the throttle quadrant - 1794 cc (F3P) single-point injection engine

3.4 Accelerator cable end securing clip (1) and adjustment ferrule (2) - 1390 cc (C3J) engine

3.5 Throttle cable adjustment ferrule (arrowed) - 1794 cc (F3P) single-point injection engine

4 On certain models, the end of the cable may be secured to the throttle sector arm by a clip. It may also be necessary to remove the locknut before sliding the adjustment ferrule from its bracket (see illustration).

5 The bracket retaining the adjustment ferrule may be attached to the throttle housing or manifold (see illustration).

6 Note that on models with single-point injection, there will be more free-play in the cable with the engine stopped, than when the engine is idling. This is because when the engine stops, the idle speed control motor closes the throttle, then partially opens it ready for the next start. For this reason, it is wise to re-check the cable free-play with the engine idling.

4 Accelerator pedal - removal and refitting

The procedure is as described for carburettor models in Chapter 4A.

5 Unleaded petrol - general information and usage

Refer to Chapter 1 Specifications for details of unleaded petrol usage. Note that, with the exception of the 1721 cc (F3N 746) and 1764 cc (F7P 700) engines, all fuel injection engines must be operated on unleaded petrol at all times; leaded petrol *must not* be used, as it will damage the catalytic converter. 1721 cc

(F3N 746) and 1764 cc (F7P 700) engines can be operated on unleaded or leaded petrol.

Note that there is no requirement to adjust the ignition timing when operating the engine on different types of petrol.

6 Fuel injection systems - general information

Single-point system

This system is fitted to certain models with the 1390 cc (C3J and E7J), 1721 cc (F3N) and 1794 cc (F3P) engines. Refer to the Specifications for details of applicable engine codes, noting that 1721 cc and 1794 cc engines are also available with multi-point injection. The system is fundamentally the same on all three engine sizes; detail differences are given in the Specifications. Note that the components used in the single-point injection system may be sourced from a number of different manufacturers, including Bosch, Weber, GM and Renix. Although the components may differ in appearance and location, the basic information given in this Section applies to all models (see illustration).

The system can be considered as a halfway stage between a conventional fixed-jet carburettor and an electronically-controlled multi-point injection system. As with a carburettor, fuel metering and vaporisation take place in one unit (the throttle housing), and the fuel/air mixture is then distributed to the cylinders via the inlet manifold. As with any modern petrol injection system, fuel metering is controlled electronically by a computer, which receives information from various sensors. The computer also controls the idle speed, and manages the emission control and ignition systems.

The main advantage of single-point injection over a carburettor is that the injection system allows much more precise control over the air-fuel ratio (mixture) under all operating conditions. This control is necessary to keep exhaust emissions to a minimum, and for the correct operation and long life of the catalytic converter. Additional benefits from the driver's point of view are improved fuel economy

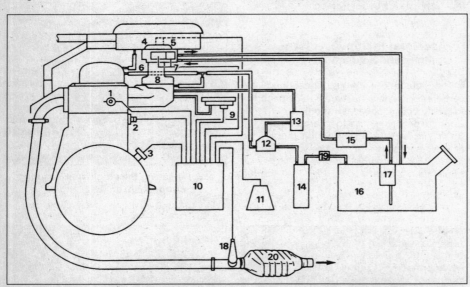

6.1 Single-point fuel injection system component layout - 1390 cc (E7J) engine with Bosch system shown, other systems similar

1 Coolant temperature sensor	8 Throttle housing	14 Charcoal canister
2 Knock sensor	9 Manifold absolute pressure	15 Fuel filter
3 Engine speed/position	(MAP) sensor	16 Fuel tank
sensor	10 Computer	17 Fuel pump
4 Fuel injector	11 Ignition module	18 Oxygen sensor
5 Inlet air temperature sensor	12 Vacuum bleed valve	19 Non-return valve
6 Throttle position sensor	13 Fuel vapour recirculation	20 Catalytic converter
7 Idle speed control motor	solenoid	

under all operating conditions, and better driveability when cold.

The system is best understood if considered in two parts: the fuel supply and the control sub-systems.

Fuel supply

The fuel supply sub-system consists of an electric fuel pump immersed in the tank, a fuel filter, a fuel pressure regulator and a fuel injector. These last two items are located in the throttle housing.

Fuel passes from the pump through the filter to the throttle housing, where it enters the fuel pressure regulator. The pressure regulator maintains a constant fuel pressure at the injector, relative to the pressure in the throttle body upstream of the throttle plate. Excess fuel is returned to the tank. Fuel is therefore circulating all the time that the pump is running, which ensures a constant supply of cool fuel, and reduces problems with vapour-locks.

The fuel injector consists of a needle valve, which is opened by an electromagnet and closed by a spring. The electromagnet is controlled by the injection computer. When the valve is open, fuel is sprayed from the injector onto the throttle plate. Because the relative fuel pressure is constant, the quantity of fuel injected varies directly according to the opening time.

The electrical feed to the fuel pump is via a relay controlled by the injection computer. The pump is only energised when the engine is running, or when the starter motor is operating. Some procedures in this Chapter require the pump to be running when the engine is stopped; this is achieved by bridging two terminals in the relay socket (see Section 9).

Control

The injection control sub-system consists of the injection computer and its associated sensors and actuators. As mentioned previously, the computer also controls the emission control and ignition systems; there is some overlap between these functions.

The computer is located at the front right-hand corner of the engine compartment. (On certain models fitted with air conditioning, the computer may be located inside the vehicle, beneath the glovebox). It receives signals from sensors which monitor the following functions:

Coolant temperature.
Inlet manifold pressure (MAP sensor).
Engine speed (flywheel sensor).
Throttle position/full-load/no-load (throttle switch/sensor).
Inlet air temperature.
Exhaust gas oxygen content (oxygen sensor).
Knock sensor - not all models.
Road speed (speedometer cable sensor) - not on all models.

Where a knock sensor is fitted, this works in conjunction with the ignition side of the system, and further details are given in

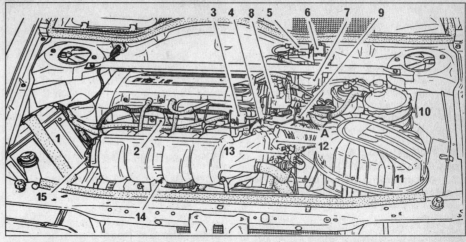

6.16 Multi-point fuel injection system component layout - 1764 cc (F7P) engine models

1 Computer	*6 Manifold absolute pressure*	*12 Throttle housing*
2 Fuel rail and injectors	*(MAP) sensor*	*13 Throttle position sensor*
3 Fuel pressure regulator	*7 Ignition module*	*14 Knock sensor*
4 Coolant temperature sensor	*8 Distributor*	*15 Inlet air temperature*
5 Mixture adjustment	*9 Idle speed control valve*	*sensor*
potentiometer (non-catalyst	*10 Relay*	*A Bypass airflow adjusting*
models only)	*11 Air filter*	*screw*

Chapter 5C. The oxygen sensor is properly part of the emission control system, and further details are given in Chapter 4C. The engine speed/position sensor is covered in Chapter 5C.

Outputs from the computer control the operation of the following components:
Fuel pump (via the fuel pump relay).
Fuel injector.
Idle speed control motor.
Evaporative emission control solenoid valve.
Ignition power module.

The computer processes the information from the various sensors, to determine the quantity of fuel which must be injected to suit operating conditions at any given moment. For this purpose, the volume of inlet air is calculated from the engine speed and throttle position signals, with a correction being made for inlet air temperature. Extra enrichment is provided at full-load and during warm-up. Compensation is also made for the effect of changes in battery voltage.

In the no-load condition (throttle in idle position), the computer cuts off injection at engine speeds above idle. At idle, the engine speed is controlled by the computer sending signals to the idle speed control motor incorporated in the throttle housing. The motor opens or closes the throttle butterfly, to maintain a constant idle speed regardless of engine temperature or additional loads (alternator, power steering pump, etc). There is no need for periodic adjustment of idle speed or mixture, even to compensate for long-term factors such as engine wear. The system is also self-correcting for changes in altitude.

When stopping the engine, the idle speed control motor first closes the throttle completely, then opens it again in readiness for the next start. This means that, with the

engine stopped, there will be more slack in the accelerator cable than with the engine idling.

Multi-point system

This system is fitted to certain models with the 1721 cc (F3N), 1764 cc (F7P) and 1794 cc (F3P) engines. Refer to the Specifications for details of applicable engine codes, noting that 1721 cc and 1794 cc engines are also available with single-point injection. The system is fundamentally the same on all engine types, although there are detailed differences, particularly relating to the type and location of sensors and actuators used (see illustration). Most models are fitted with a catalytic converter, although some earlier engines were available without. On models without a catalytic converter, adjustment of the exhaust gas CO content (mixture) is possible. Refer to Chapter 1 for details.

In many respects, the multi-point system is similar to the single-point system just described. The major differences are as follows.

Fuel supply

Four fuel injectors, one per cylinder, are used. The injectors are located in the inlet manifold, downstream of the throttle valve. On 1764 cc (F7P) engines, a single additional cold start injector provides extra fuel when the starter motor is operating and the coolant temperature is below 20°C. The other engines do not use a separate cold start injector, cold start enrichment being provided by the main injectors. All the injectors are fed from a common fuel rail (except for the cold start injector, where applicable, which is located in the underside of the inlet manifold), which also carries the fuel pressure regulator. As with the

4B

single-point system, excess fuel is returned to the tank.

Control

The computer receives information from various sensors, as detailed for the single-point system.

The idle speed regulation system is slightly different. An idle speed control valve opens or closes an auxiliary air circuit, bypassing the throttle valve. There is no idle switch.

Fault diagnosis - all systems

Note: *Refer to the precautions given in Chapter 5C for models equipped with electronic control units before attempting to carry out any fault diagnosis.*

In the event of a fault developing, the amount of diagnostic work possible for the home mechanic is limited. Renault technicians use dedicated test equipment, which can find a fault quickly and precisely. Initial fault-finding checks should concentrate on external factors such as a blocked fuel filter, loose or corroded electrical connections, and loose or damaged vacuum hoses. Remember also that incorrect adjustment of the accelerator cable can affect operation of the fuel injection system, especially at idle.

If it appears that the fault is in one of the sensors or in the computer, it will probably be more satisfactory to consult a Renault dealer or other specialist, rather than to embark on a hit-and-miss programme of component renewal.

7 Fuel system - depressurisation

Note: *Refer to the warning at the end of Section 1 before proceeding.*
1 Fuel lines may contain fuel under pressure, even though the engine is not running. Depressurisation of the fuel system is therefore necessary before undertaking any work which will involve opening a fuel line or

union, otherwise fuel under pressure could spray out onto hot engine components.
2 Remove the fuel pump fuse, which is the 30 amp fuse located in the under-bonnet (auxiliary) fusebox (see Chapter 12).
3 Try to start the engine. It may run briefly and die, or it may not start at all. Operate the starter motor a couple more times, to ensure that all fuel pressure has been relieved.
4 Switch off the ignition, and refit the fuel pump fuse.

8 Fuel system - pressure check

Note: *Refer to the warning at the end of Section 22 before proceeding.*
1 Depressurise the fuel system (Section 7), remembering to refit the fuel pump fuse.

Single-point system

2 Remove the air cleaner or air duct, as applicable, from the top of the throttle housing.
3 Connect a pressure gauge (range 0 to 3 bars) into the fuel feed pipe where it enters the throttle housing, using a T-piece **(see illustration)**.
4 Make the fuel pump run by bridging terminals 3 and 5 of the fuel pump relay (located in the computer case or in the auxiliary fusebox in the engine compartment - see Chapter 12) **(see illustration)**. The fuel pump relay can be distinguished by the thick leads connected to terminals 3 (red or red/white lead) and 5 (brown or white lead).
5 Note the pressure shown on the gauge. It should correspond to the regulated fuel pressure given in the Specifications.
6 Momentarily pinch the fuel return pipe. Note the pressure registered on the gauge: this must correspond to the unregulated pressure given in the Specifications.

Multi-point system

7 Connect a pressure gauge (range 0 to 6 bars) into the fuel feed pipe where it joins the injector rail, using a T-piece **(see illustration)**.

8 Make the fuel pump run by bridging terminals 3 and 5 of the fuel pump relay (located in the computer case or in the auxiliary fusebox in the engine compartment - see Chapter 12). The fuel pump relay can be distinguished by the thick leads connected to terminals 3 (red or red/white lead) and 5 (brown or white lead) (see illustration 8.4).
9 Note the pressure shown on the gauge. It should correspond to the regulated fuel pressure given in the Specifications.
10 Momentarily pinch the fuel return pipe. Note the pressure registered on the gauge: this must correspond to the unregulated pressure given in the Specifications.
11 If a vacuum pump and gauge are available, disconnect the vacuum hose from the pressure regulator. Apply vacuum of approximately 500 mbars to the pressure regulator, and check that the fuel pressure drops by the same amount.

All systems

12 If the pressure readings are low, check the pump delivery (Section 9) to see whether the fault is in the pump or the pressure regulator. Also check the fuel filter(s). If the readings are high, the fault can only be in the pressure regulator.
13 Remove the bridge from the fuel pump relay. Depressurise the fuel system (see Section 7) and disconnect the pressure gauge, then remake the original connections.

9 Fuel pump - testing, removal and refitting

Note: *Refer to the warning at the end of Section 1 before proceeding.*

Testing

1 Carry out a pressure check as described in the previous Section.
2 Disconnect the fuel return pipe from the throttle housing or injector rail, as applicable. Connect a length of flexible hose to the return union, and place the other end of the hose in a measuring jar (capacity 2 litres approx).

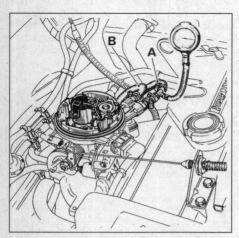

8.3 Fuel system pressure check - single-point injection

A Fuel feed pipe B Fuel return pipe

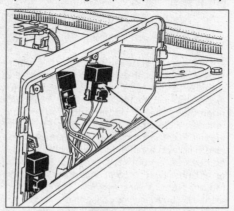

8.4 Fuel pump relay location (arrowed) in auxiliary fusebox

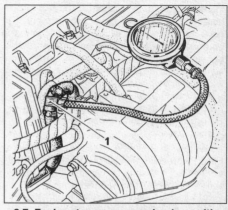

8.7 Fuel system pressure check - multi-point injection (1764 cc/F7P engine shown)

1 T-piece

3 Make the fuel pump run by bridging terminals 3 and 5 of the fuel pump relay as described in the previous Section.

4 Note the quantity of fuel delivered in exactly one minute (single-point system) or 30 seconds (multi-point system). Correct values are given in the Specifications.

5 Remove the bridge from the fuel pump relay. Return the pumped fuel to the tank, or put it in a suitable sealed container.

6 If delivery is low, check that full battery voltage is available at the pump relay contacts, and at the pump itself. (Refer to the pump removal procedure for details of the pump wiring connector location). A 1 volt drop in supply voltage will result in a drop of approximately 10% in delivery.

7 If the supply voltage is correct, but delivery is still low, there are two possible reasons. Either there is a blockage somewhere in the supply line (including the main fuel filter and the pump pick-up filter), or the pump is defective. If the pump is defective, it must be renewed.

8 On completion, remake the original fuel pipe connections.

Removal

Underbody-mounted pump

9 Depressurise the fuel system as described in Section 7.

10 Disconnect the battery negative lead.

11 Chock the front wheels, then jack up the rear of the vehicle, and support securely on axle stands (see "Jacking, towing and wheel changing").

12 Working under the rear of the vehicle, clamp the fuel hoses on either side of the pump.

13 Loosen the clips, and disconnect the fuel hoses, noting their locations. Be prepared for fuel spillage.

14 Disconnect the wiring plug(s) from the pump.

15 Loosen the clamp screw, then withdraw the pump from its mounting clamp (see illustration).

Fuel tank-mounted pump (separate fuel gauge sender unit)

16 Remove the fuel tank (Section 11).

17 Disconnect the fuel hoses from the top of the pump, noting their locations (see illustration).

18 Disconnect the wiring plug from the pump.

19 Using a suitable tool, unscrew the ring nut from the top of the pump unit. The tool must fit the slots snugly, to avoid damage. Remove the ring nut and withdraw the pump assembly. Recover the seal.

20 The pump motor can be removed from the assembly as follows. Release the retaining clips. Note which way round the wires are connected, then disconnect them and remove the pump motor (see illustration).

Fuel tank-mounted pump (integral with fuel gauge sender unit)

21 Depressurise the fuel system as described in Section 7.

22 Proceed as described in Chapter 4A for the fuel gauge sender unit on carburettor models.

Refitting

Underbody-mounted pump

23 Refitting is a reversal of removal, ensuring that the fuel hoses are correctly reconnected.

Fuel tank-mounted pump (separate fuel gauge sender unit)

24 Refit the pump to the tank using a reversal of the removal procedure. Use a new seal, and ensure that the wires and fuel hoses are correctly reconnected.

25 Refit the fuel tank with reference to Section 11.

Fuel tank-mounted pump (integral with fuel gauge sender unit)

26 Refit the unit as described for the fuel gauge sender unit in Chapter 4A, ensuring that the fuel hoses are correctly reconnected.

10 Fuel gauge sender unit - removal and refitting

Refer to the procedure given in Chapter 4A for removal and refitting of the sender unit on carburettor models, noting that the hose and wiring connections may differ. Note also that on certain models, the fuel pump is integral with the gauge sender unit.

11 Fuel tank - removal and refitting

Refer to Chapter 4A, but note that on certain models, the hoses and wiring must be disconnected from the fuel pump (see Section 9) before the tank can be removed.

12 Fuel tank filler pipe - removal and refitting

Refer to Chapter 4A.

13 Single-point fuel injection system - component testing

1 Renault dealers use dedicated test equipment (test box XR25) which plugs into the diagnostic socket provided on the main fuse/relay box in the facia. This equipment provides a rapid and comprehensive diagnosis of the complete system. It is the only means of checking the operation of the computer.

2 Limited testing of individual components is still possible. The information in the following paragraphs is given as a guide to the owner who wishes to carry out preliminary checks if a fault develops. However, it may still be necessary to enlist the help of a Renault dealer or other specialist for positive diagnosis of a fault.

3 Where the use of an electrical multi-meter is

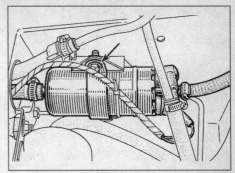

9.15 Fuel pump clamp screw (arrowed) - underbody-mounted pump

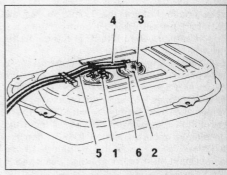

9.17 Fuel pump mounting details

1 Fuel gauge sender unit   *4 Fuel outlet pipe*
2 Fuel pump   *5 Fuel return pipe*
3 Wiring connector

4B

9.20 Fuel pump assembly

6 Hose clip *7 Wire* *8 Wire* *9 Fuel hose*

called for, this should be a modern digital type, with an internal resistance of at least 10 megohms. *Do not* use analogue (moving pointer) meters, which may have an unacceptably-low internal resistance.

4 No meaningful testing is possible on the idle

13.9a Inlet air temperature sensor wiring plug (arrowed) - Weber-type throttle housing

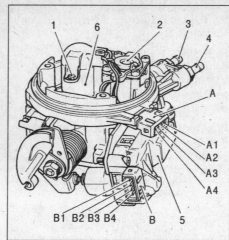

13.9b Terminal and component identification - Bosch-type single-point throttle housing

1 Inlet air temperature sensor
2 Fuel pressure regulator
3 Fuel return connection
4 Fuel feed connection
5 Idle speed control motor
6 Fuel injector
A Inlet air temperature sensor/fuel injector wiring connector
A1 Inlet air temperature sensor
A2 Injector +
A3 Injector -
A4 Inlet air temperature sensor
B Idle speed motor/idle switch connector
B1 Motor feed
B2 Motor feed
B3 Idle switch
B4 Idle switch

speed control motor, the throttle sensor, the manifold pressure (MAP) sensor, the road speed sensor (when fitted), or the computer itself.

5 Before testing individual components, make sure that all system electrical connections are clean and secure, and that all fuel, air and vacuum hoses are in good condition. Also remember that problems with idle speed regulation may simply be due to incorrect accelerator cable adjustment (see Section 3).

6 Where a component is found to be defective, it must be renewed as described in the following Section.

Inlet air temperature sensor

7 Refer to Section 14 for details of the sensor location.

8 Where applicable, for access, remove the air cleaner or the air duct from the top of the throttle housing.

9 Disconnect the sensor wiring plug **(see illustrations)**.

10 Use an ohmmeter across the sensor terminals to measure the resistance of the sensor. Typical values which can be expected are given in the Specifications.

11 Use a hairdryer or a fan heater to raise the temperature of the sensor, and check that the resistance of the sensor falls as it warms up.

Coolant temperature sensor

12 Refer to Section 14 for details of the sensor location.

13 Disconnect the multi-plug from the sensor unit.

14 Using an ohmmeter, measure the resistance of the sensor, and compare it with the typical values given in the Specifications. If the value obtained is greatly different from that specified, the sensor is probably defective.

Fuel injector

15 Refer to Section 14 for details of access to the injector.

16 The resistance of the injector winding can be checked at the injector wiring connector, using an ohmmeter between the appropriate terminals (see illustration 13.9b for Bosch-type throttle housing).

17 Typical values for the resistance are given in the Specifications. If the resistance is significantly different from that specified,

remove the plug from the top of the sensor, and repeat the measurement at the terminals of the injector itself.

18 If the resistance is now correct, there was a fault in the wiring between the wiring connector and the injector. If the resistance is still incorrect, the injector is defective.

19 If it is suspected that dirt or gum in the injector is impairing performance, the use of a proprietary cleaning additive in the fuel tank may be effective.

Fuel pressure regulator

20 Testing of the fuel pressure regulator is included in the fuel pressure check (Section 8).

14 Single-point fuel injection system - component removal and refitting

Note: *Special test equipment may be required for initial setting-up after renewal of some components described in this Section. Read through the procedures carefully before starting work, to see what is involved. Also refer to the warning note at the end of Section 1. A number of different types of throttle housing may be fitted, including Bosch, Weber, and GM. Although the components differ in detail, the general procedures given below can be used for all types* **(see illustrations)**.

14.a Top view of Bosch-type throttle housing (air cleaner removed)

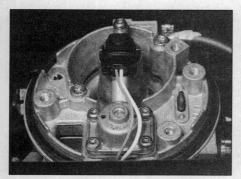

14.b Top view of Weber-type throttle housing (air duct removed)

14.c Top view of GM-type throttle housing (air cleaner removed)

14.d Top view of the throttle housing on 1390 cc (C3J) engine

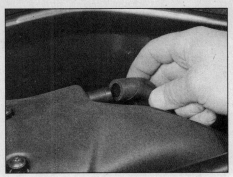

14.2 Disconnecting a hose from the air duct - 1794 cc (F3P) engine

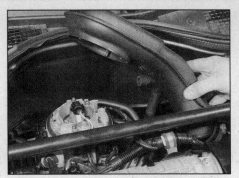

14.4 Lifting the air duct from the throttle housing - 1794 cc (F3P) engine

14.9a Fuel supply line connection (arrowed) - Weber-type throttle housing

14.9b Fuel supply and return hose connections (arrowed) - 1390 cc (C3J) engine

14.9c Fuel supply (1) and return (2) hose connections - Bosch-type throttle housing. Note flow direction arrows on throttle housing

14.12a Throttle housing securing nuts (arrowed) - GM-type throttle housing

4B

Air duct

Removal

1 Certain models have an air duct fitted to the top of the throttle housing, which is connected to the main air cleaner via the inlet air trunking.
2 Disconnect the hoses from the air duct, noting their locations to aid refitting (see illustration).
3 Loosen the hose clip, and disconnect the inlet air trunking from the air duct.
4 Remove the screws securing the air duct to the throttle housing, then lift off the air duct and recover the gasket (see illustration).

Refitting

5 Refit by reversing the removal operations, making sure that the hoses are connected

correctly. Use a new gasket if necessary on the top of the throttle housing.

Throttle housing

Note: *A number of different types of throttle housing may be fitted, including Bosch, Weber, and GM. Although the components differ in detail, the general procedures given below can be used for all types.*

Removal

6 Depressurise the fuel system as described in Section 7, then disconnect the battery negative lead.
7 Remove the air cleaner or the air duct, as applicable, from the top of the throttle housing.

8 Disconnect all relevant wiring plugs (throttle position sensor, fuel injector, idle speed control motor) from the throttle housing.
9 Disconnect the fuel supply and return lines, making identification marks for reference when refitting (see illustrations). Be prepared for fuel spillage.
10 Where applicable, disconnect any vacuum and breather hoses from the throttle housing, noting their locations.
11 Disconnect the accelerator cable (see Section 3).
12 Remove the securing screws or nuts (as applicable), and lift the throttle housing from the inlet manifold (see illustrations). Recover the gasket.
13 On models fitted with the Bosch-type

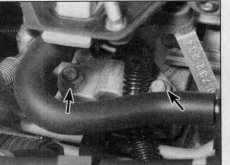

14.12b Two of the throttle housing securing nuts (arrowed) - 1390 cc (C3J) engine

14.13a Release the studs by squeezing them with pliers . . .

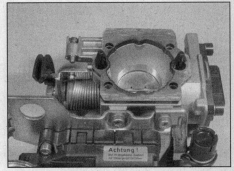

14.13b . . . to separate the two halves of the throttle housing - Bosch-type throttle housing

14.14 Throttle housing upper-to-lower section securing screws (arrowed) - GM-type throttle housing

14.15 Fitting a new gasket to the top of the Bosch-type throttle housing

14.21 Disconnecting the inlet air temperature sensor/fuel injector multi-plug - Bosch-type throttle housing

throttle housing, the two halves of the housing can be separated if necessary, after releasing the press-stud fastenings which hold the halves together (see illustrations). Renew the seals between the housing halves when reassembling.

14 On models fitted with the GM-type throttle housing, the two halves of the housing can be separated by removing the two securing screws (see illustration).

Refitting

15 Refit by reversing the removal operations, using new gaskets (see illustration).

16 Ensure that all wiring plugs and hoses are correctly reconnected.

14.22 Removing the fuel injector wiring plug securing screw - Bosch-type throttle housing

17 On Bosch-type throttle housings, if the lower half of the throttle housing has been renewed, the initial setting of the throttle sensor must be verified using Renault test box XR25.

Inlet air temperature sensor

Bosch-type throttle housing

18 The sensor is integral with the fuel injector wiring plug.

19 Disconnect the battery negative lead.

20 Remove the air cleaner housing or the air duct, as applicable.

21 Disconnect the sensor/fuel injector multi-plug, located on the side of the throttle housing (see illustration).

22 Remove the single securing screw, and free the fuel injector wiring plug (see illustration).

23 Lift the rubber seal from the throttle housing, and unclip the multi-plug from the side of the throttle housing.

24 Free the connector lugs, and withdraw the wiring plug/sensor together with the cover, wiring and connector (see illustration).

25 Refit by reversing the removal operations.

GM-type throttle housing

26 The sensor is screwed into the top of the inlet manifold.

27 Disconnect the battery negative lead.

28 Disconnect the sensor wiring plug (see illustration).

29 Unscrew the sensor, and withdraw it from the manifold.

30 Refitting is a reversal of removal.

Weber-type throttle housing

31 The sensor is located in the upper section of the throttle housing (see illustration).

32 To gain access to the sensor securing screws, it is necessary to remove the throttle housing as described previously in this Section.

33 Working under the throttle housing, remove the securing screws, then withdraw the sensor.

34 Refitting is a reversal of removal.

1390 cc (C3J) and 1721 cc (F3N) engines

35 The sensor is screwed into the top of the inlet manifold.

36 Disconnect the battery negative lead.

37 Unclip the sensor wiring connector from its bracket, and separate the two halves of the connector.

38 Unscrew the sensor, and withdraw it from the manifold.

39 Refitting is a reversal of removal.

Coolant temperature sensor

Removal

40 The location of the coolant temperature sensor varies according to model. On 1390 cc

14.24 Removing the fuel injector wiring plug/inlet air temperature sensor - Bosch-type throttle housing

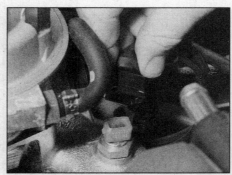

14.28 Disconnecting the inlet air temperature sensor wiring plug - GM-type throttle housing

14.31 Inlet air temperature sensor (arrowed) - Weber-type throttle housing

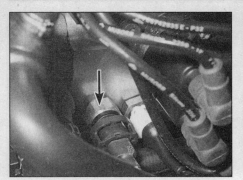

14.40a Coolant temperature sensor (arrowed) - 1390 cc (E7J) engine

14.40b Coolant temperature sensor (arrowed) located on rear of cylinder block - 1794 cc (F3P) engine

14.47 Removing the fuel injector - Bosch-type throttle housing

(C3J and E7J) engines, it is located on the left-hand end of the cylinder head. On 1721 cc (F3N) and 1794 cc (F3P) engines, it is located on the rear of the cylinder block (see illustrations).

41 Drain the cooling system with reference to Chapter 1. Alternatively, remove the expansion tank cap to depressurise the system, and have the new sensor or a suitable bung to hand.

42 Disconnect the multi-plug and unscrew the sensor.

Refitting

43 Apply a little sealant to the sensor threads, and screw it into position. Reconnect the multi-plug.

44 Top-up or refill the cooling system as necessary.

Fuel injector

Bosch-type throttle housing

45 Depressurise the fuel system as described in Section 7.

46 Remove the inlet air temperature sensor as described previously in this Section.

47 Note the fitted position of the injector, then withdraw it (see illustration).

48 Refit by reversing the removal operations, but fit new seals to the injector, and lubricate them with silicone grease.

GM-type throttle housing

49 Depressurise the fuel system as described in Section 7.

50 Remove the air cleaner or the air duct, as

applicable, from the top of the throttle body.

51 Disconnect the battery negative lead.

52 Squeeze the securing lugs, and disconnect the wiring plug from the fuel injector.

53 Remove the Torx-type securing screw, and withdraw the injector clamp bracket (see illustrations).

54 Carefully withdraw the injector from the throttle housing (see illustration).

55 Refitting is a reversal of removal, bearing in mind the following points:

(a) Use new injector seals.

(b) The injector wiring socket should point towards the clamp bracket screw hole.

(c) Ensure that the clamp bracket engages with the slot below the wiring socket in the injector.

(d) Coat the threads of the clamp bracket screw with thread-locking compound.

Weber-type throttle housing

56 Proceed as described previously for the GM-type throttle housing, but when refitting, note that the wiring plug should point away from the clamp bracket screw hole (see illustration).

1390 cc (C3J) and 1721 cc (F3N) engines

57 Proceed as described previously for the GM-type throttle housing, noting the following points:

(a) The injector clamp bracket is secured by two screws (see illustration).

14.53a Remove the securing screw . . .

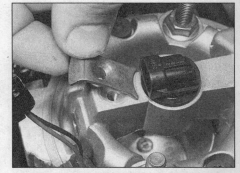

14.53b . . . and withdraw the injector clamp bracket - GM-type throttle housing

14.54 Removing the fuel injector. Note O-rings (arrowed) - GM-type throttle housing

14.56 Disconnecting the fuel injector wiring plug - Weber-type throttle housing

14.57 Fuel injector clamp bracket screws (arrowed) - 1390 cc (C3J) engine

14.60 Disconnecting the wiring plug (arrowed) from the idle speed control motor - Bosch-type throttle housing

14.61 Idle speed control motor securing screws (arrowed) - Bosch-type throttle housing

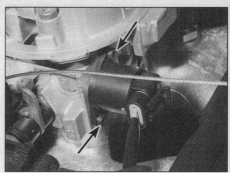

14.69 Idle speed control motor securing screws (arrowed) - GM-type throttle housing

(b) Note the location of the collar below the clamp bracket.
(c) When refitting, ignore the references to the orientation of the wiring socket.

Idle speed control motor
Bosch-type throttle housing

58 Remove the air cleaner or the air duct, as applicable.
59 Where necessary, for improved access to the motor securing screws, remove the securing screws and lift the throttle housing.
60 Disconnect the motor wiring plug (see illustration).
61 Remove the securing screws and withdraw the motor (see illustration).

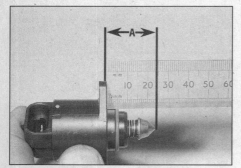

14.70 Measure the distance (A) between the end of the idle speed control motor piston and the end face of the motor body flange - GM-type throttle housing

62 Refitting is a reversal of removal, but on completion, the initial position of the throttle must be set as follows.
63 Using a suitable shim or feeler blades, bridge the gap between the throttle lever and the motor plunger.
64 Switch the ignition on for a few seconds, then switch it off again. Remove the shim or blades, then switch on and off again.
65 Run the engine and check that the idle speed and quality are satisfactory.

GM-type throttle housing

66 Remove the air cleaner or the air duct, as applicable.
67 Where necessary, for improved access to the motor securing screws, remove the securing screws and lift the throttle housing.
68 Disconnect the motor wiring plug.
69 Remove the securing screws or nuts (as applicable) and withdraw the motor (see illustration).
70 Refitting is a reversal of removal, bearing in mind the following points:
(a) To avoid damage to the housing during refitting, the distance between the end of the motor piston and the end face of the motor body flange should not be greater than 28.0 mm (see illustration). Measure the distance, and if greater than specified, carefully push the piston back into the motor body as far its stop.
(b) Refit the motor using a new O-ring seal.

(c) Coat the threads of the motor securing screws with suitable thread-locking compound before fitting.

Weber-type throttle housing

71 Proceed as described previously for the GM-type throttle housing, but ignore the reference to setting the motor piston (see illustrations).

1390 cc (C3J) and 1721 cc (F3N) engines

72 Proceed as described previously for the Bosch-type throttle housing, but note that the motor is secured to its mounting bracket by four nuts (see illustration).

Fuel pressure regulator
Bosch-type throttle housing

73 The fuel pressure regulator is an integral part of the upper half of the throttle housing. If it is defective, the upper half of the housing must be renewed.

GM-type and Weber-type throttle housings

74 Depressurise the fuel system as described in Section 7.
75 Disconnect the battery negative lead.
76 Remove the air cleaner or the air duct, as applicable, from the top of the throttle housing.

14.71a Idle speed control motor wiring plug (arrowed) - Weber-type throttle housing

14.71b One of the idle speed control motor securing screws (arrowed) - Weber-type throttle housing

14.72 Two of the idle speed control motor securing nuts (arrowed) - 1390 cc (C3J) engine

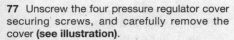

14.77a Removing the fuel pressure regulator cover - GM-type throttle housing

14.77b Fuel pressure regulator cover securing screws (arrowed) - Weber-type throttle housing

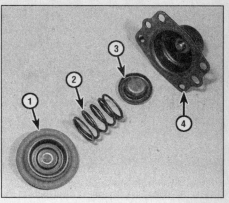

14.78 Fuel pressure regulator components - GM-type throttle housing

1 Diaphragm 3 Spring seat
2 Spring   4 Cover

77 Unscrew the four pressure regulator cover securing screws, and carefully remove the cover (see illustration).
78 Recover the spring seat and spring assembly, and lift out the diaphragm (see illustration).
79 Refitting is a reversal of removal, but ensure that the diaphragm is correctly located in the groove in the throttle housing, and coat the threads of the cover securing screws with suitable thread-locking compound before fitting.

1390 cc (C3J) and 1721 cc (F3N) engines

80 The pressure regulator is located under the left-hand side of the throttle housing.
81 Proceed as described previously for the GM-type and Weber-type throttle housings, noting the following points:
(a) The regulator cover is secured by three screws.
(b) Note that the regulator components differ from those described previously (see illustration). Note the location of all components during removal, to ensure correct refitting.

Throttle position sensor
Bosch-type throttle housing

82 The throttle position sensor is an integral part of the lower part of the throttle housing. If it is defective, the lower half of the housing must be renewed. The idle speed control

motor can be transferred from the old half-housing to the new one.
83 After renewal, the initial setting of the sensor must be verified using Renault test box XR25.

GM-type and Weber-type throttle housings

84 Disconnect the battery negative lead.
85 Remove the air cleaner or the air duct, as applicable, from the top of the throttle housing.
86 Disconnect the wiring plug from the sensor.
87 Remove the two securing screws, and withdraw the sensor from its housing (see illustration).
88 Refitting is a reversal of removal, but ensure that the throttle valve is closed before refitting the sensor, and make sure that the sensor arm is correctly engaged with the throttle shaft. Coat the sensor securing screws with suitable thread-locking compound before fitting.

1390 cc (C3J) and 1721 cc (F3N) engines

89 To gain access, remove the idle speed control motor, as described previously in this Section.
90 Release the sensor wiring connector from its bracket, and separate the two halves of the connector.
91 Remove the two securing screws, and withdraw the sensor from its bracket (see illustration).

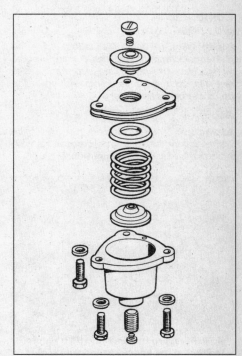

14.81 Fuel pressure regulator components - 1390 cc (C3J) and 1721 cc (F3N) engines

14.87a Throttle position sensor wiring plug (1) and securing screws (2) - GM-type throttle housing

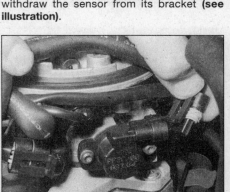

14.87b Disconnecting the throttle position sensor wiring plug - Weber-type throttle housing

14.91 Throttle position sensor (arrowed) - 1390 cc (C3J) engine

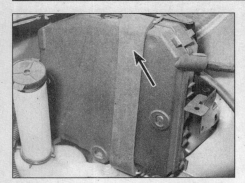

14.95a Computer retaining strap (arrowed) - 1390 cc (E7J) engine model

14.95b Unclipping the computer retaining strap - 1794 cc (F3P) engine model

14.96a Unclipping the computer casing cover . . .

92 Refitting is a reversal of removal, but refit the idle speed control motor as described previously in this Section.

Computer

Note: *On certain models fitted with air conditioning, the computer is located in the passenger compartment, below the glovebox. At the time of writing, no information was available for the removal and refitting of the computer on these models.*

Removal

93 The computer is located in a protective plastic casing in the engine compartment, in front of the right-hand suspension turret.

14.96b . . . for access to the wiring plug - 1794 cc (F3P) engine

94 Disconnect the battery negative lead.
95 Unclip the retaining strap, then remove the casing from its location **(see illustrations)**.
96 Where applicable, unclip the casing cover, then disconnect the computer wiring plug **(see illustrations)**.
97 Where applicable, remove the securing bolts, and withdraw the computer from the casing.

Refitting

98 Refitting is a reversal of removal, ensuring that the wiring plug is securely reconnected.

Manifold absolute pressure (MAP) sensor

Removal

99 Unclip the MAP sensor from its bracket on the bulkhead, then disconnect the multi-plug and the vacuum hose **(see illustrations)**.

Refitting

100 Refit by reversing the removal operations.

Road speed sensor

101 The road speed sensor is an integral part of the speedometer cable. For cable renewal procedures, see Chapter 12 **(see illustration)**.

Engine speed/position sensor

102 Refer to Chapter 5C for details.

15 Multi-point fuel injection system - component testing

General

1 Refer to the information given in Section 13, paragraphs 1 to 6.
2 Refer to Section 16 for details of component locations.
3 *Do not* attempt to adjust the stop screw on the throttle housing in an attempt to correct idle speed problems, or for any other reason. Note that idle speed problems on this system may be caused by erroneous or missing signals from the road speed sensor, where applicable.

Inlet air temperature sensor

4 Refer to the procedure given for single-point injection models in Section 13. Refer to Section 16 for details of the sensor location.

Coolant temperature sensor

5 Refer to the procedure given for single-point injection models in Section 13. Refer to Section 16 for details of the sensor location.

Fuel injectors

6 Refer to Section 16, and withdraw the fuel rail complete with injectors, but without disconnecting the fuel hoses (there is no need to depressurise the fuel system).

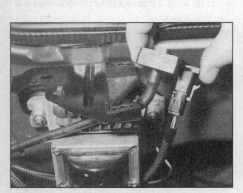

14.99a Unclip the MAP sensor from its bracket . . .

14.99b . . . and disconnect the wiring plug. Vacuum hose arrowed

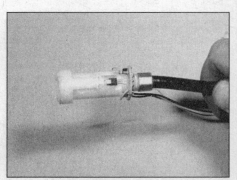

14.101 Road speed sensor located in speedometer cable - details may differ from those shown

7 Position each injector in a clean glass jar. Run the fuel pump (see Section 9), and check that no fuel drips from any injector.
8 With the fuel pump still running, apply 12 volts to the terminals of each injector in turn.
9 With voltage applied, the injector must spray fuel into the glass jar.

Cold start injector

10 The cold start injector is tested in the same way as described previously for the main injectors. Refer to Section 16 for details of the sensor location.

Idle speed control valve

11 A quick check of the idle speed control valve can be made by pinching or plugging the air hose on the inlet side of the valve while the engine is idling. The idle speed should drop, perhaps to the point where the engine stalls. When the airflow is restored, the idle speed should rise and then stabilise. Refer to Section 16 for details of the sensor location.

Fuel pressure regulator

12 Testing of the fuel pressure regulator is included in the fuel pressure check (Section 8).

16 Multi-point fuel injection system - component removal and refitting

Note: *Special test equipment may be required for initial setting-up after renewal of some components described in this Section. Read through the procedures carefully before starting work, to see what is involved. Also refer to the warning note at the end of Section 1.*

Air inlet plenum chamber - 1721 cc (F3N) engines only
Removal

1 Disconnect the battery negative lead.
2 Disconnect the accelerator cable (Section 3), the electrical wiring plugs, and all breather and vacuum hoses, from the throttle housing and the plenum chamber. Note the locations of all hoses and wires to aid refitting **(see illustration)**.
3 On models fitted with an anti-percolation

16.2 Accelerator cable bracket (arrowed) on air inlet plenum chamber - 1721 cc (F3N) engine

system, disconnect the air ducting from the fuel rail.
4 Unscrew the bolt securing the front of the plenum chamber to the bracket on the cylinder head.
5 Unscrew the three bolts and two nuts securing the plenum chamber to the inlet manifold, then lift the plenum chamber, complete with throttle housing, from the inlet manifold **(see illustration)**. Recover the gasket.

Refitting

6 Refitting is a reversal of removal, but ensure that all hoses and wires are correctly reconnected, and use a new gasket between the plenum chamber and the inlet manifold.

Throttle housing
Removal

7 Disconnect the battery negative lead.
8 Disconnect the accelerator cable (Section 3), the electrical wiring plugs, and any breather or vacuum hoses, as applicable, from the throttle housing.
9 Loosen the clamp screw, and disconnect the air inlet trunking from the throttle housing.
10 Remove the securing nuts, or bolts, as applicable, and withdraw the throttle housing from the inlet manifold or plenum chamber (1721 cc/F3N engines) **(see illustration)**.

Refitting

11 Refit by reversing the removal operations.

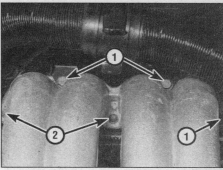

16.5 Air inlet plenum chamber securing bolts (1) and nuts (2) - 1721 cc (F3N) engine

Inlet air temperature sensor
Removal

12 On 1721 cc (F3N) engine models, the sensor is located in the air inlet trunking just downstream of the air cleaner (between the air cleaner and the throttle housing). On 1764 cc (F3P) engine models, the sensor is located in the right-hand end of the inlet manifold. On 1794 cc (F3P) engine models, the sensor is located in the air inlet trunking, just upstream of the throttle housing (between the air cleaner and the throttle housing) **(see illustrations)**.
13 To remove the sensor, first disconnect the battery negative lead, then disconnect the wiring plug from the sensor **(see illustration)**.
14 Unscrew the sensor from its location, and where applicable, recover the sealing ring.

4B

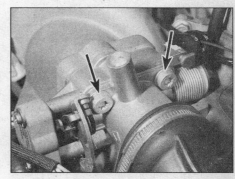

16.10 Two of the throttle housing securing bolts (arrowed) - 1764 cc (F7P) engine

16.12a Inlet air temperature sensor (arrowed) - 1721 cc (F3N) engine

16.12b Inlet air sensor (arrowed) - 1794 cc (F3P) engine

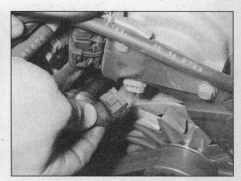

16.13 Disconnecting the wiring plug from the inlet air temperature sensor - 1764 cc

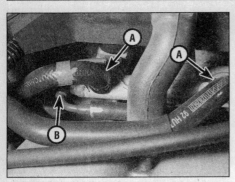

16.28 Fuel supply and return pipes (A) and cold start injector fuel supply pipe (B) connection at fuel rail - 1764 cc (F7P) engine

16.31 Fuel rail securing nuts (arrowed) - 1764 cc (F7P) engine

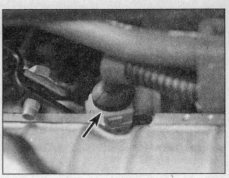

16.38 Fuel injector wiring plug (arrowed) - 1794 cc (F3P) engine

Refitting

15 Refitting is a reversal of removal, but where applicable, use a new sealing ring.

Coolant temperature sensor

16 On 1721 cc (F3N) and 1794 cc (F3P) engines, the sensor is located on the rear of the cylinder block (see illustration 14.40b). On the 1764 cc (F7P) engine, the sensor is located in the thermostat housing, or in the left-hand end of the cylinder head (depending on model - see Chapter 3).

17 Removal and refitting procedures are as described in Section 14 for models with single-point injection.

Fuel injectors

1721 cc (F3N) engine

18 Depressurise the fuel system as described in Section 7, then disconnect the battery negative lead.

19 For access to the fuel rail, remove the air inlet plenum chamber as described previously in this Section.

20 Disconnect the fuel feed and return hoses from the injector rail. Be prepared for fuel spillage. Plug or clamp the hoses.

21 Unplug the electrical connectors from the injectors. (If preferred, this can be done as the injector rail is withdrawn.)

22 Remove the two bolts securing the fuel rail to the inlet manifold, noting the locations of any brackets which may be secured by the bolts.

23 Withdraw the fuel rail and the injectors.

24 The injectors can be separated from the rail after removing the retaining clips. Recover the sealing rings.

25 Refit by reversing the removal operations. Use new injector sealing rings if necessary. Apply a little silicone grease (or a similar lubricant) to the sealing rings.

26 Check that there are no fuel leaks on completion.

1764 cc (F7P) engine

27 Depressurise the fuel system as described in Section 7, then disconnect the battery negative lead.

28 Disconnect the fuel feed and return hoses from the injector rail, noting their locations. Be prepared for fuel spillage. Plug or clamp the hoses. Also disconnect the cold start injector fuel supply union from the end of the fuel rail (see illustration).

29 Remove the breather hoses and pipes which run from the engine valve cover across the injector rail. Also disconnect the vacuum hose from the fuel pressure regulator.

30 Unplug the electrical connectors from the injectors. (If preferred, this can be done as the injector rail is withdrawn.)

31 Remove the securing nuts, and withdraw the rail and the injectors (see illustration).

32 The injectors can be separated from the rail after removing the retaining clips. Recover the sealing rings.

33 Refit by reversing the removal operations. Use new injector sealing rings if necessary.

Apply a little silicone grease (or a similar lubricant) to the sealing rings.

34 Check that there are no fuel leaks on completion.

1794 cc (F3P) engine

35 Depressurise the fuel system as described in Section 7, then disconnect the battery negative lead.

36 To improve access, unbolt and remove the strengthening bar from between the front suspension unit turrets.

37 Disconnect the fuel feed and return hoses from the injector rail. Be prepared for fuel spillage. Plug or clamp the hoses. Also disconnect the vacuum hose from the fuel pressure regulator.

38 Unplug the electrical connectors from the injectors (see illustration). (If preferred, this can be done as the injector rail is withdrawn.)

39 Unclip any wires, or hoses, as applicable, from the brackets attached to the fuel rail.

40 Remove the two extended bolts securing the fuel rail to the inlet manifold (see illustration).

41 Manipulate the fuel rail, complete with injectors, from the inlet manifold.

42 The injectors can be removed from the fuel rail after unscrewing the securing screws, and withdrawing the injector clamp plates from the top of the fuel rail. Note the locations of the injector clamp plates, as they differ in shape (see illustration).

43 Refit by reversing the removal operations. Use new injector sealing rings if necessary. Apply a little silicone grease (or a similar lubricant) to the sealing rings.

44 Check that there are no fuel leaks on completion.

Cold start injector - 1764 cc (F7P) engine

Removal

45 It is possible (but difficult) to gain access to the cold start injector by reaching up under the inlet manifold (see illustration). If desired for improved access, the radiator can be removed or tilted forwards, with reference to Chapter 3.

46 Depressurise the fuel system as described

16.40 Fuel rail securing bolt (arrowed) - 1794 cc (F3P) engine

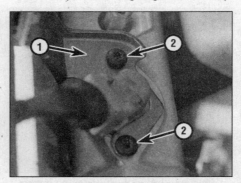

16.42 Fuel injector clamp plate (1) and securing screws (2) viewed with fuel rail in place - 1794 cc (F3P) engine

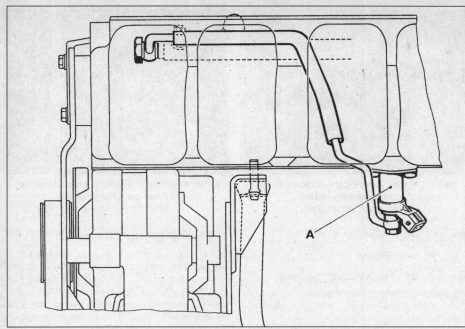

16.45 Location of the cold start injector (A) on the underside of the inlet manifold - 1764 cc (F7P) engine

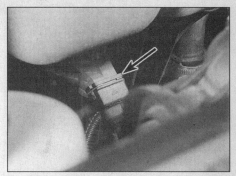

16.47 Cold start injector wiring plug (arrowed) - 1764 cc (F7P) engine

in Section 7, then disconnect the battery negative lead.

47 Disconnect the wiring plug from the cold start injector (see illustration).

48 Disconnect the fuel line from the injector. Be prepared for fuel spillage, and recover the union seals, where applicable.

49 Unscrew the two securing bolts, and withdraw the injector from the inlet manifold. Recover the sealing ring.

Refitting

50 Refitting is a reversal of removal, using a new injector seal, and new fuel union sealing rings, where applicable. On completion, check for fuel leaks.

Idle speed control valve

1721 cc (F3N) and 1764 cc (F7P) engines

51 The valve is located on a bracket attached to the left-hand end of the cylinder head, or on

certain 1721 cc (F3N) engines, on the front of the air inlet plenum chamber (see illustrations).

52 Disconnect the battery negative lead.

53 Disconnect the multi-plug from the top of the valve.

54 Remove the clamp which secures the valve. Disconnect the air hoses and withdraw the valve.

55 Refit by reversing the removal operations.

1794 cc (F3P) engine

56 The valve is located at the left-hand end of the inlet manifold.

57 Disconnect the battery negative lead.

58 Disconnect the wiring plug from the valve, and disconnect the air hose.

59 Unscrew the two securing screws, and withdraw the valve from the inlet manifold. Recover the gasket (see illustration).

60 Refitting is a reversal of removal, using a new gasket.

Fuel pressure regulator
Removal

61 The pressure regulator is located at the end of the fuel rail (see illustration).

62 Depressurise the fuel system as described in Section 7, then disconnect the battery negative lead.

63 If desired, to improve access, remove the strengthening bar from the suspension unit turrets (1794 cc/F3P engine), or the inlet air trunking (certain 1721 cc/F3N engines).

64 Disconnect the vacuum hose from the pressure regulator.

65 Where applicable, disconnect the fuel return hose from the pressure regulator. Be prepared for fuel spillage.

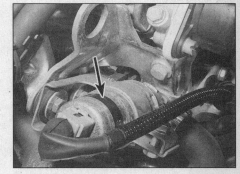

16.51a Idle speed control valve (arrowed) - 1721 cc (F3N) engine

16.51b Idle speed control valve (arrowed) - 1764 cc ((F7P) engine

16.59 Idle speed control valve securing screw (arrowed) - 1794 cc (F3P) engine

16.61 Fuel pressure regulator (arrowed) - 1721 cc (F3N) engine

4B

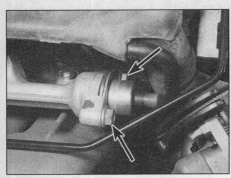

6.66 Fuel pressure regulator securing screws (arrowed) - 1764 cc (F7P) engine

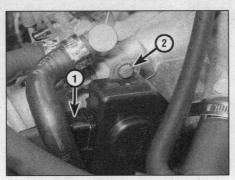

16.69a Throttle position sensor wiring plug (1) and securing screw (2) - 1721 cc (F3N) engine

16.69b Throttle position sensor wiring plug (1) and securing screws (2) - 1764 cc (F7P) engine

66 Remove the securing screws, and withdraw the pressure regulator from the fuel rail or mounting bracket, as applicable **(see illustration)**. Where applicable, recover the gasket.

Refitting

67 Refitting is a reversal of removal, but where applicable, use a new gasket. On completion, check for fuel leaks.

Throttle position sensor
Removal

68 Make alignment marks between the sensor and the throttle housing, for reference when refitting.
69 Disconnect the multi-plug, and remove the two screws which secure the sensor **(see illustrations)**. Remove the sensor.

Refitting

70 Refit by reversing the removal operations. If a new sensor has been fitted, the initial setting of the sensor must be verified using Renault test box XR25.

Computer

71 Refer to the procedure given in Section 14 for single-point injection models.

Manifold pressure (MAP) sensor

72 Refer to the procedure given in Section 14 for single-point injection models.

Road speed sensor

73 Refer to Section 14.

Engine speed/position sensor

74 Refer to Chapter 5C for details.

17 Anti-percolation system - general

All except 1764 cc (F7P) engine models

1 Certain models may be fitted with an anti-percolation system. Its purpose is to reduce the underbonnet fuel temperature when the vehicle is stopped after a run. This prevents fuel percolation (vaporisation due to excess heat) occurring in the fuel rail, so avoiding hot-start problems and fuel vapour emissions.
2 The main components of the system are an electric fan (radiator cooling fan), air ducts leading to the fuel rail, and the control circuitry **(see illustrations)**. A combined temperature switch/timer unit actuates the fan for a set period after switch-off, if the temperature exceeds a certain value.
3 No specific testing or repair procedures for the anti-percolation system were available at the time of writing.

1764 cc (F7P) engine models

4 The principle of operation of the system is similar to that described previously for other engines, but instead of ducting air to the fuel rail, the system operates the main radiator cooling fan and an auxiliary water pump, to lower the overall underbonnet temperature.
5 The anti-percolation system comes into operation only when the engine is stopped and the coolant temperature is 105°C or greater. Under these conditions, the auxiliary water pump and the cooling fan are energised for approximately 8 minutes. Operation continues for the complete period, even when the coolant temperature falls below 105°C.
6 For details of the auxiliary water pump, refer to Chapter 3.

18 Inlet manifold - removal and refitting

1390 cc (C3J) engine

1 The inlet and exhaust manifolds are removed as an assembly.
2 Remove the throttle housing (Section 14).
3 The procedure is now as described in Chapter 4A, Section 16, ignoring the reference to the carburettor. Note that on models fitted with an exhaust gas recirculation system (see Chapter 4C) it will be necessary to disconnect the gas pipe joining the manifolds, before the manifolds can be separated.

1390 cc (E7J) engine

4 Remove the throttle housing (Section 14).
5 Where applicable, disconnect the wiring from the inlet air temperature sensor.
6 The procedure is now as described in Chapter 4A, Section 18, disregarding references to the carburettor and choke cable, and ignoring the reference to draining the cooling system (the manifold is not coolant-heated).

1721 cc (F3N) and 1794 cc (F3P) single-point injection engines

7 Although the inlet and exhaust manifolds are separate, they are retained by the same bolts,

17.2a Anti-percolation ducting-to-radiator shroud securing nuts (arrowed) - 1721 cc (F3N) engine

17.2b Anti-percolation ducting connection to fuel rail (arrowed) - 1721 cc (F3N) engine

since the bolt holes are split between the manifold flanges.

8 Remove the throttle housing (Section 14).

9 The procedure is now as described in Chapter 4A, Section 17, ignoring the reference to the carburettor. Where applicable, also ignore the reference to draining the cooling system (not all models have a coolant-heated manifold). Note that on models fitted with an exhaust gas recirculation system (see Chapter 4C) it will be necessary to disconnect the gas pipe joining the manifolds, before the manifolds can be separated.

1721 cc (F3N) multi-point injection engine

10 Although the inlet and exhaust manifolds are separate, they are retained by the same bolts, since the bolt holes are split between the manifold flanges.

11 Remove the air inlet plenum chamber as described in Section 16.

12 Remove the fuel injectors as described in Section 16.

13 The procedure is now as described in Chapter 4A, Section 17, ignoring the references to the carburettor and draining the cooling system (the manifold is not coolant-heated).

14 Refer to Section 16 when refitting the fuel injectors.

1794 cc (F3P) multi-point injection engine

15 Although the inlet and exhaust manifolds are separate, they are retained by the same bolts, since the bolt holes are split between the manifold flanges.

16 Disconnect the battery negative lead.

17 Disconnect the accelerator cable (Section 3), the electrical wiring plugs, and any breather or vacuum hoses, as applicable, from the throttle housing.

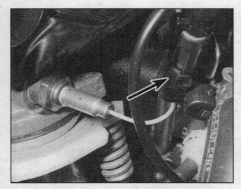

19.2 Oxygen sensor wiring connector (arrowed) - 1390 cc (E7J) engine with manifold-mounted oxygen sensor

18 Loosen the clamp screw, and disconnect the air inlet trunking from the throttle housing.

19 Disconnect the wiring plug and the hose from the idle speed control valve.

20 Disconnect all remaining breather and vacuum hoses from the manifold, noting their locations to aid refitting.

21 Remove the fuel injectors as described in Section 16.

22 The procedure is now as described in Chapter 4A, Section 17, ignoring the references to the carburettor and draining the cooling system (the manifold is not coolant-heated).

23 When refitting, ensure that all hoses are correctly reconnected as noted before removal, and refit the fuel injectors with reference to Section 16.

1764 cc (F7P) engine

Removal

24 Disconnect the battery negative lead.

25 Remove the radiator (Chapter 3).

26 Remove the fuel injectors, and the cold start injector, as described in Section 16.

27 Remove the alternator (Chapter 5A) and the bolts which secure the alternator bracket to the manifold.

28 Loosen the clamp screw, and disconnect the air inlet trunking from the throttle housing.

29 Disconnect the accelerator cable (Section 3), the electrical wiring plugs, and any breather or vacuum hoses, as applicable, from the throttle housing.

30 Disconnect all remaining breather and vacuum hoses and electrical connections from the manifold, noting their locations to aid refitting.

31 Unbolt the manifold bracing struts from the engine and the bottom of the manifold.

32 Make a final check to ensure that all relevant hoses and wiring connections have been disconnected.

33 Unscrew the securing nuts, and withdraw the manifold from the cylinder head.

Refitting

34 Refit by reversing the removal operations, using a new manifold gasket.

35 On completion, tension the alternator drivebelt and refill the cooling system as described in Chapter 1.

19 Exhaust manifold - removal and refitting

1390 cc (C3J) engine

1 The inlet and exhaust manifolds are removed as an assembly. Refer to Section 18.

1390 cc (E7J) engine

2 The procedure is as described in Chapter 4A, Section 19, but on models with an exhaust manifold-mounted oxygen sensor, disconnect the wiring connector before removing the manifold (see illustration).

1721 cc (F3N) and 1794 cc (F3P) engines

3 Although the inlet and exhaust manifolds are separate, they are retained by the same bolts, since the bolt holes are split between the manifold flanges. Refer to Section 18 for details of manifold removal and refitting.

1764 cc (F7P) engine

4 Where applicable, unclip any relevant hoses and wiring, and move it to one side to improve access to the manifold.

5 Unscrew and remove the two nuts, then remove the washers, tension springs and sleeves securing the exhaust front pipe to the manifold. Slide the flange plate off the manifold studs, and separate the joint.

6 Remove the securing nuts, and withdraw the manifold from the cylinder head. Recover the gasket.

7 Refitting is a reversal of removal, using a new gasket.

20 Exhaust system - general information and component renewal

4B

General information

1 Refer to Chapter 4A, noting the information given in the following paragraphs.

2 On models fitted with a catalytic converter, the oxygen sensor may be located in the exhaust front pipe (see Chapter 4C). Where applicable, disconnect the sensor wiring connector before removing the exhaust front section.

3 Where applicable, the catalytic converter is located between the exhaust front pipe and the intermediate section. The catalytic converter is attached to the exhaust front pipe and intermediate section by flange joints.

Component renewal

4 Refer to Chapter 4A, noting the following.

5 The catalytic converter can be removed without disturbing the surrounding exhaust components after unscrewing the flange nuts and bolts. Recover the joint gaskets.

6 When refitting the catalytic converter, use new gaskets.

Notes

Chapter 4 Part C: Emission control systems

Contents

Degrees of difficulty

Easy, suitable for novice with little experience	Fairly easy, suitable for beginner with some experience	Fairly difficult, suitable for competent DIY mechanic	Difficult, suitable for experienced DIY mechanic	Very difficult, suitable for expert DIY or professional

1 General information and precautions

Evaporative emission control

1 The purpose of the evaporative emission control system is to minimise emissions of fuel vapour. The fuel tank filler cap and hoses form part of this system. The rest of the system varies according to model, as follows.

Carburettor engines

2 Certain carburettor models are equipped with a vapour separator (or degassing unit) and a vapour reservoir. Typical pipe runs and connections are shown in Chapter 4A, in connection with the fuel pump.
3 Fuel vapour which forms in the carburettor float chamber when the engine is not running is stored in the vapour reservoir. The vapour separator intercepts vapour formed in the fuel supply line, and returns it to the fuel tank.

Fuel injection engines

4 Fuel vapour which forms when the engine is not running is stored in a charcoal canister located under the right-hand headlight. With the engine running, vapour is drawn into the inlet manifold, and fresh air is drawn into the canister. A solenoid valve and a calibrated bleeding valve control the rate at which this happens (see illustration). On models with the 1390 cc (C3J) and 1721 cc (F3N) single-point injection engines, the system operates in conjunction with a vacuum valve located on the inlet manifold.

Crankcase emission control

5 This system ensures that there is always a partial vacuum in the crankcase, and so prevents pressure which could cause oil contamination, fume emission and oil leakage past seals.
6 The layout of the crankcase ventilation system varies according to model (see illustrations).
7 When the engine is idling, or under partial load conditions, the high depression in the inlet manifold draws the crankcase fumes (diluted by air from the air cleaner side of the throttle valve) through the calibrated restrictor and into the combustion chambers.
8 The crankcase ventilation hoses and restrictors should be periodically cleaned to ensure correct operation of the system.

Exhaust emission control

9 This system is fitted to most fuel injection models. The system comprises an oxygen sensor and a catalytic converter. These components ensure a very low level of toxic emissions in the exhaust gas.
10 The oxygen sensor (also known as a

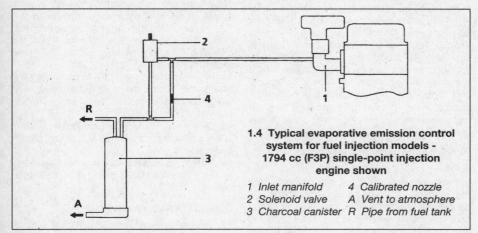

1.4 Typical evaporative emission control system for fuel injection models - 1794 cc (F3P) single-point injection engine shown

1 Inlet manifold	4 Calibrated nozzle
2 Solenoid valve	A Vent to atmosphere
3 Charcoal canister	R Pipe from fuel tank

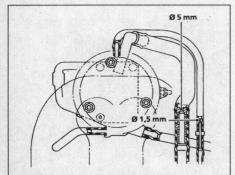

1.6a Crankcase ventilation system for the 1390 cc (E6J) engine located around the carburettor

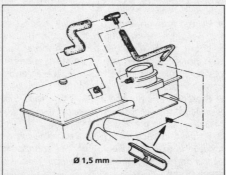

1.6b Crankcase ventilation system for the 1237 cc (C1G) and 1397 cc (C1J) engines

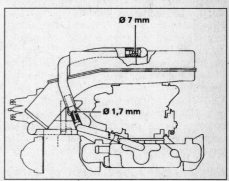

1.6c Crankcase ventilation system for the 1721 cc (F2N) engine

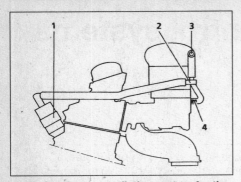

1.6d Crankcase ventilation system for the 1794 cc (F3P) single-point injection engine

1 Oil separator   3 Calibrated nozzle
2 T-piece   4 Calibrated nozzle

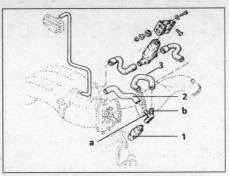

1.6e Crankcase ventilation system for the 1721 cc (F3N) multi-point injection engine

1 Oil separator   a Calibrated nozzle
2 Breather hose   b Calibrated nozzle
3 Breather hose

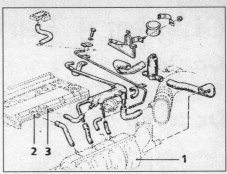

1.6f Crankcase ventilation system for the 1764 cc (F7P) engine

1 Inlet manifold   3 Calibrated nozzle
2 Calibrated nozzle

"lambda" sensor, from the symbol used to indicate air/fuel ratio) is located in the exhaust manifold or front pipe (depending on model). It provides a signal to the injection computer which varies according to the oxygen content of the exhaust gas. The computer uses the varying signal to calculate the amount of fuel which must be injected to ensure efficient combustion and low emission levels.

11 The catalytic converter is located in the exhaust system, at the end of the front section furthest from the manifold. It contains a ceramic honeycomb structure coated with a precious metal compound. This compound acts as a catalyst in the conversion of carbon monoxide (CO) to carbon dioxide (CO_2), and unburned hydrocarbons (HC_x) to water and carbon dioxide (H_2O and CO_2).

Catalytic converter - precautions

12 For long life and satisfactory operation of the catalytic converter, certain precautions must be observed. These are as follows.
13 Only use unleaded fuel. Leaded fuel will poison the catalyst and the oxygen sensor.
14 Do not run the engine for long periods if it is misfiring. Unburnt fuel entering the catalytic converter can cause it to overheat, resulting in permanent damage. For the same reason, do not try to start the engine by pushing or towing the car, nor crank it on the starter motor for long periods.
15 Do not strike or drop the catalytic converter. The ceramic honeycomb which forms part of its internal structure may be damaged.
16 Always renew seals and gaskets upstream of the catalytic converter whenever they are disturbed.
17 Remember that the catalytic converter gets hotter than the rest of the exhaust system. Avoid parking over long grass, undergrowth or similar material which could catch fire or be damaged.

Exhaust gas recirculation system

18 This system is fitted to 1390 cc (C3J) and 1721 cc (F3N) single-point injection engines.
19 Under certain engine running conditions, a vacuum-operated valve located on the inlet manifold allows a small amount of exhaust gas to be recirculated from the exhaust manifold directly into the inlet manifold via a metal pipe.

2 Emission control system components - testing and renewal

Evaporative emission control

Carburettor models

1 There are no specific testing procedures for the carburettor evaporative emission control components. Check periodically that the various hoses are in good condition and securely connected.
2 Should component renewal be necessary, it is simply a case of disconnecting the hoses, and unbolting or unclipping the vapour separator or reservoir. Dispose of the old component safely, bearing in mind that it may contain liquid fuel and/or fuel vapour.

Fuel injection models - testing

3 The operating principle of the system is that the solenoid valve should be open only when the engine is warm and at part-throttle conditions. The following procedure is based on information relating to the 1764 cc (F7P) engine, but it is broadly applicable to the others.
4 Bring the engine to normal operating temperature, then switch it off. Connect a vacuum gauge (range 0 to 1000 mbars) into the hose between the canister and the restrictor. Connect a voltmeter to the solenoid valve terminals.
5 Start the engine and allow it to idle. There should be no vacuum shown on the gauge, and no voltage present at the solenoid.
6 If manifold vacuum is indicated although no voltage is present, check that the restrictor is of the correct size. If it is, the solenoid valve is stuck open.
7 If voltage is present at idle, there is a fault in the wiring or the computer.
8 Depress the accelerator slightly. Voltage should appear momentarily at the solenoid terminals, and manifold vacuum be indicated on the gauge.
9 If vacuum is not indicated even though voltage is present, either there is a leak in the hoses, or the valve is not opening.
10 If no voltage appears, there is a fault in the wiring or the computer.

Fuel injection models - canister renewal

11 The canister is located under the right-hand front wheel arch.
12 Where applicable, remove the wheel arch splash shield for access to the canister.
13 Working in the engine compartment, disconnect the two hoses from the top of the canister, noting their locations **(see illustration)**.
14 Working under the front wing, release the two rubber straps securing the canister, and withdraw the canister from its mounting bracket.
15 Dispose of the old canister safely, bearing in mind that it may contain liquid fuel and/or fuel vapour.
16 Refit by reversing the removal operations. Make sure that the hoses are connected correctly.

Solenoid valve renewal

17 The valve may be mounted on a bracket on the inlet manifold or next to the injection

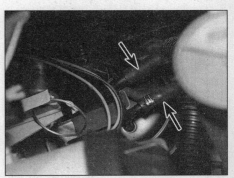

2.13 Carbon canister hoses (arrowed) - viewed from above

2.17a Removing a solenoid valve from the bracket on the inlet manifold - 1390 cc (E7J) engine

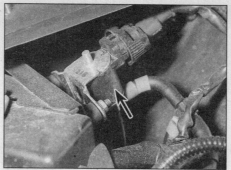

2.17b Solenoid valve location (arrowed) on right-hand body panel - 1764 cc (F7P) engine

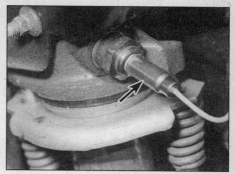

2.31a Oxygen sensor (arrowed) located in exhaust manifold - 1390 cc (E7J) engine

computer, depending on model (see illustrations).

18 Unclip or unbolt (as applicable) the valve from its bracket.

19 Disconnect the hoses from the solenoid valve, marking them if necessary for reference when reassembling.

20 Disconnect the multi-plug from the valve, and withdraw it.

21 Refit by reversing the removal operations. Make sure that the hoses are connected correctly.

Crankcase emission control

Testing

22 There is no specific test procedure for the crankcase emission control system. If problems are suspected (sometimes indicated by oil contamination of the air cleaner element), check that the hoses are clean internally, and that the restrictors are not blocked or missing.

Component renewal

23 This is self-evident. Mark the various hoses before disconnecting them, if there is any possibility of confusion on reassembly.

Exhaust emission control (fuel injection models only)

24 The remainder of this Section only applies to fuel injection models equipped with oxygen sensor and catalyst.

Testing

25 An exhaust gas analyser (CO meter) will be needed. The ignition system must be in good condition, the air cleaner element must be clean, and the engine must be in good mechanical condition.

26 Bring the engine to normal operating temperature, then connect the exhaust gas analyser in accordance with the equipment maker's instructions.

27 Allow the engine to idle, and check the CO level (Chapter 1 Specifications). Repeat the check at 2500 to 3000 rpm. If the CO level is within the specified limits, the system is operating correctly.

28 If the CO level is higher than specified, try

the effect of disconnecting the oxygen sensor wiring. If the CO level rises when the sensor is disconnected, this suggests that the oxygen sensor is OK and that the catalytic converter is faulty. If disconnecting the sensor has no effect, this suggests a fault in the sensor.

29 If a digital voltmeter is available, the oxygen sensor output voltage can be measured (terminal C of the sensor multi-plug, or terminal 35 of the computer multi-plug). Voltage should alternate between 625 to 1100 mV (rich mixture) and 0 to 100 mV (lean mixture).

30 Before renewing either component, run the car using several tankfuls of unleaded fuel, if there is any possibility that leaded fuel has been used in error. Repeat the test to see if the CO level has reduced.

Oxygen sensor - renewal

31 The oxygen sensor may be located in the exhaust manifold or in the exhaust front section, depending on model (see illustrations).

32 Where necessary for access, apply the handbrake, then jack up the front of the vehicle and support securely on axle stands (see "Jacking, towing and wheel changing").

33 Disconnect the sensor wiring plug.

34 Where applicable, unclip the heat shield.

35 Unscrew the sensor from the exhaust manifold or front pipe, as applicable, and remove it.

36 Clean the threads in the exhaust pipe or

manifold, and the threads of the sensor (if it is to be refitted).

37 Note that if the sensor wires are broken, the sensor must be renewed. No attempt should be made to repair them.

38 Apply high-temperature anti-seize compound to the sensor threads. Screw the sensor in by hand, then tighten it fully.

39 Where applicable, refit the heat shield.

40 Reconnect the sensor wiring plug.

Catalytic converter - renewal

41 The catalytic converter is renewed in the same way as any other part of the exhaust system. Refer to Chapter 4B.

Exhaust gas recirculation system

Vacuum valve renewal

42 The valve is located on the rear of the inlet manifold (see illustration).

43 Disconnect the hose from the valve.

44 Unscrew the two securing screws, and withdraw the valve. Recover the gasket.

45 Refit by reversing the removal operations, using a new gasket.

Gas pipe renewal

46 Unscrew the two bolts securing the pipe to the exhaust manifold. Recover the washers and gasket.

47 Unscrew the union from the inlet manifold, and withdraw the pipe.

48 Fit the new pipe using a reversal of the removal procedure. Fit a new gasket.

4C

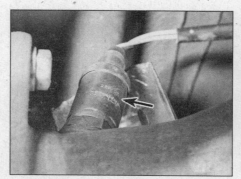

2.31b Oxygen sensor (arrowed) located in exhaust front section (shown with heat shield fitted) - 1764 cc (F7P) engine

2.42 Vacuum valve (arrowed) located on rear of inlet manifold - 1390 cc (C3J) engine

Notes

Chapter 5 Part A:
Starting and charging systems

Contents

Degrees of difficulty

Easy, suitable for novice with little experience	**Fairly easy,** suitable for beginner with some experience	**Fairly difficult,** suitable for competent DIY mechanic	**Difficult,** suitable for experienced DIY mechanic	**Very difficult,** suitable for expert DIY or professional

Specifications

General
Electrical system type . . . .   12-volt negative earth

Battery
Type . . . .   Lead-acid, low-maintenance or "maintenance-free" (sealed-for-life)
Capacity . . . .   35, 50 or 65 Ah, according to model

Alternator
Type . . . .   Paris-Rhone, Valeo or Ducellier
Maximum output at 13.5 volts and 8000 (alternator) rpm . . . .   60, 70, 90 or 110 amps, accordingto model
Regulated voltage . . . .   13.5 to 14.8 volts

Starter motor
Make and type . . . .   Valeo, Paris-Rhone or Bosch pre-engaged

1 General information and precautions

General information

The engine electrical system includes all charging, starting and ignition system components and engine oil sensors. Because of their engine-related functions, these components are covered separately from the body electrical devices such as the lights, instruments, etc (which are covered in Chapter 12).

The electrical system is of the 12-volt negative earth type.

The battery is of the low-maintenance or "maintenance-free" (sealed-for-life) type, and is charged by the alternator, which is belt-driven from a crankshaft-mounted pulley.

The starter motor is of the pre-engaged type, incorporating an integral solenoid. On starting, the solenoid moves the drive pinion into engagement with the flywheel ring gear before the starter motor is energised. Once the engine has started, a one-way clutch prevents the motor armature being driven by the engine until the pinion disengages from the flywheel.

The ignition system is covered in Parts B and C of this Chapter.

Further details of the various systems are given in the relevant Sections of this Chapter. While some repair procedures are given, the usual course of action is to renew the component concerned. The owner whose interest extends beyond mere component renewal should obtain a copy of the *"Automobile Electrical & Electronic Systems Manual"*, available from the publishers of this manual.

Precautions

It is necessary to take extra care when working on the electrical system, to avoid damage to semi-conductor devices (diodes and transistors), and to avoid the risk of personal injury. In addition to the precautions given in *"Safety first!"* at the beginning of this manual, observe the following when working on the system:

Always remove rings, watches, etc before working on the electrical system. Even with the battery disconnected, capacitive discharge could occur if a component's live terminal is earthed through a metal object. This could cause a shock or nasty burn.

Do not reverse the battery connections. Components such as the alternator, ignition system components, or any other components having semi-conductor circuitry could be irreparably damaged.

If the engine is being started using jump leads and a slave battery, connect the batteries *positive-to-positive* and *negative-to-negative* (see *"Booster battery (jump) starting"*). This also applies when connecting a battery charger.

Never disconnect the battery terminals, the alternator, any electrical wiring or any test instruments when the engine is running.

Do not allow the engine to turn the alternator when the alternator is not connected.

Never "test" for alternator output by "flashing" the output lead to earth.

Never use an ohmmeter of the type incorporating a hand-cranked generator for circuit or continuity testing.

Always ensure that the battery negative lead is disconnected when working on the electrical system.

Before using electric-arc welding equipment on the vehicle, disconnect the battery, alternator and components such as the ignition system control module, to protect them from the risk of damage.

In most cases, the radio/cassette unit fitted as standard equipment by Renault is equipped with a built-in security code to deter thieves. If the power source to the unit is cut, the anti-theft system will activate. Even if the power source is immediately reconnected, the radio/cassette unit will not function until the correct security code has been entered. Therefore, if you do not know the correct security code for the radio/cassette unit, *do not* disconnect the battery negative terminal of the battery or remove the radio/cassette unit from the vehicle. Refer to *"Radio/cassette unit anti-theft system precaution"* Section at the beginning of this manual for details of how to enter the security code.

2 Electrical fault finding - general information

Refer to Chapter 12.

3 Battery - testing and charging

Note: *Refer to the precautions given in "Safety first!" and in Section 1 of this Chapter.*

Testing

1 Most vehicles are fitted with a "maintenance-free" (sealed-for-life) battery, in which case the electrolyte level cannot be checked. In this case, refer to the battery manufacturer's recommendations for maintenance and charging procedures.
2 Where a conventional battery is fitted, the electrolyte level of each cell should be checked, and if necessary topped-up with distilled or de-ionised water, at the intervals given in Chapter 1. On some batteries, the case is translucent, and incorporates minimum and maximum level marks.
3 If the vehicle covers a very small annual mileage, it is worthwhile checking the specific gravity of the electrolyte every three months, to determine the state of charge of the battery. Use a hydrometer to make the check, and

compare the results obtained with the following table.

	Normal climates	Tropics
Discharged	1.120	1.080
Half-charged	1.200	1.160
Fully-charged	1.280	1.230

4 If the battery condition is suspect, where possible, first check the specific gravity of the electrolyte in each cell. A variation of 0.040 or more between cells indicates loss of electrolyte, or deterioration of the internal plates.
5 An accurate test of battery condition can be made by a battery specialist, using a heavy-discharge meter. Alternatively, connect a voltmeter across the battery terminals, and earth the coil HT lead with a suitable wire; operate the starter motor with the headlights, heated rear window and heater blower switched on. If the voltmeter reading remains above 9.6 volts, the battery condition is satisfactory. If the voltmeter reading drops below 9.6 volts, and the battery has already been charged, it is faulty.

Charging

6 In normal use, the battery should not require charging from an external source, unless it is discharged accidentally (for instance by leaving the lights on). Charging can also temporarily revive a failing battery, but if frequent recharging is required (and the alternator output is correct), the battery is worn out.
7 Unless the battery manufacturer advises differently, the charging rate in amps should be no more than one-tenth of the battery capacity in amp-hours (for instance, 6.5 amps for a 65 amp-hour battery). Most domestic battery chargers have an output of 5 amps or so, and these can safely be used overnight. Rapid "boost" charging is not recommended; if it is not carefully controlled, it can cause serious damage to the battery plates through overheating.
8 Both battery terminal leads must be disconnected before connecting the charger leads (disconnect the negative lead first). Connect the charger leads *before* switching on at the mains. When charging is complete, switch off at the mains *before* disconnecting the charger. If this procedure is followed, there

is no risk of creating a spark at the battery terminals. Continue to charge the battery until no further rise in specific gravity is noted over a four-hour period, or until vigorous gassing is observed.
9 On completion of charging, check the electrolyte level (if possible) and top-up if necessary, using distilled or de-ionised water.

4 Battery - removal and refitting

Removal

1 The battery is located beneath a plastic cover on the right-hand side of the bulkhead. First check that all electrical components are switched off, in order to avoid a spark occurring as the negative lead is disconnected. Note also that if the radio has a security coding, it will be necessary to insert this code when the battery is re-connected.
2 Remove the plastic cover from over the battery. To do this, first pull up the weatherseal, then remove the screws and lift the cover from the battery. The cover may be stuck to the plastic cover in front of the windscreen, but a sharp pull will release it.
3 Loosen the plastic nut on the negative terminal clamp, then lift the clamp and lead from the terminal and place it on the bulkhead. This is the terminal to disconnect before working on any electrical component on the vehicle. If the terminal is tight, carefully ease it off by moving it from side to side.
4 Loosen the plastic nut on the positive terminal clamp **(see illustration)**, then lift the clamp and lead from the terminal and place it on the bulkhead. If necessary, the nut can be removed completely and the lead disconnected from the clamp.
5 Unscrew the extended clamp bolt, and remove the clamp from the front of the battery **(see illustration)**.
6 Lift the battery from the tray, keeping it upright and taking care not to let it touch your clothing.
7 If necessary, remove the battery tray from the bulkhead.
8 Clean the battery terminal posts, clamps, tray and battery casing. If the bulkhead is rusted as a result of battery acid spillage,

4.4 Disconnecting the positive terminal lead from the battery

4.5 Unscrewing the extended clamp bolt to remove the battery

clean it thoroughly, and re-paint with reference to Chapter 11.

Refitting

9 Refitting is a reversal of removal, but always connect the positive terminal clamp first and the negative terminal clamp last.

5 Charging system - testing

Note: *Refer to the warnings given in "Safety first!" and in Section 1 of this Chapter before starting work.*

1 If the ignition (no-charge) warning light fails to illuminate when the ignition is switched on, first check the security of the alternator wiring connections. If satisfactory, check that the warning light bulb has not blown, and that the bulbholder is secure in its location in the instrument panel. If the light still fails to illuminate, check the continuity of the warning light feed wire from the alternator to the bulbholder. If all is satisfactory, the alternator is at fault, and should be renewed or taken to an auto-electrician for testing and repair.

2 If the ignition warning light illuminates when the engine is running, stop the engine and check that the drivebelt is correctly tensioned (Chapter 1) and that the alternator connections are secure. If all is so far satisfactory, check the alternator brushes and slip rings (see Section 8). If the fault persists, the alternator should be renewed, or taken to an auto-electrician for testing and repair.

3 If the alternator output is suspect even though the warning light functions correctly, the regulated voltage may be checked as follows.

4 Connect a voltmeter across the battery terminals, and start the engine.

5 Increase the engine speed until the voltmeter reading remains steady; the reading should be between 13.5 and 14.8 volts.

6 Switch on as many electrical accessories (headlights, heated rear window, heater blower etc) as possible, and check that the alternator maintains the regulated voltage between 13.5 and 14.8 volts. It may be necessary to increase engine speed slightly.

7 If the regulated voltage is not as stated, the fault may be due to worn brushes, weak brush springs, a faulty voltage regulator, a faulty diode, a severed phase winding, or worn or damaged slip rings. The brushes and slip rings may be checked (see Section 8), but if the fault persists, the alternator should be renewed or taken to an auto-electrician for testing and repair.

6 Auxiliary drivebelts - removal, refitting and adjustment

Refer to Chapter 1.

7 Alternator - removal and refitting

C-type (1237 cc/C1G, 1390 cc/C3J and 1397 cc/C1J/C2J) engines
Removal

1 Disconnect the battery negative lead.

2 Make a note of the electrical lead locations at the rear of the alternator, and disconnect them.

3 Loosen the adjustment bolt on the adjustment link, followed by the pivot bolt on the bottom of the alternator (see illustration).

4 Swivel the alternator towards the engine, then slip the drivebelt off the pulley.

5 Remove the alternator pivot and adjustment bolts, and withdraw the alternator from the engine.

Refitting

6 Refitting is a reversal of removal. Tension the drivebelt with reference to Chapter 1.

E-type (1390 cc/E6J/E7J) engines
Removal

7 Disconnect the battery negative lead.

8 Make a note of the electrical lead locations at the rear of the alternator, and disconnect them (see illustration).

9 Apply the handbrake, then jack up the front right-hand side of the vehicle and support it securely on axle stands (see *"Jacking, towing and wheel changing"*). Remove the roadwheel, then remove the cover plate from inside the wheel arch for improved access.

10 Where applicable, remove the plastic protection cover from the alternator (see illustration).

11 Loosen the bolt securing the alternator to the slotted tensioner bracket, and swivel the alternator towards the engine so that the drivebelt tension is fully released.

12 Slip the drivebelt off the pulley.

13 Disconnect the right-hand steering track rod end from the stub axle carrier, with reference to Chapter 10.

14 Using a parallel pin punch, drive out the double roll pin securing the right-hand inner driveshaft joint yoke to the differential sunwheel stub shaft. Drive out the small inner roll pin first, then drive out the outer roll pin.

15 Unscrew and remove the two bolts securing the right-hand stub axle carrier to the suspension strut. Note that the nuts are on the rear side of the strut.

16 Pull the top of the stub axle carrier outwards until the inner end of the driveshaft is released from the sunwheel stub shaft. Support the driveshaft and stub axle carrier in this position.

17 Working under the vehicle, unscrew the nut from the bottom of the right-hand engine mounting.

18 Using a hoist attached to the engine (or alternatively, a trolley jack and wooden block beneath the engine sump), raise the engine approximately 150 mm. Unbolt the engine mounting from the cylinder block, then lower the engine onto a wooden block interposed between the cylinder block/sump flange and the engine subframe (see illustration).

7.3 Alternator adjustment bolt (arrowed) - 1390 cc (C3J) engine

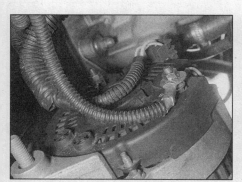

7.8 Electrical lead connections at rear of alternator - 1390 cc (E6J) engine

7.10 Plastic protection cover on the alternator (arrowed) - 1390 cc (E6J) engine

7.18 Engine supported on a wooden block - 1390 cc (E6J) engine

5A

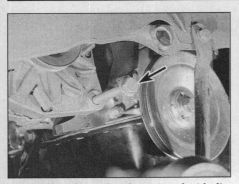

7.19a Removing the alternator pivot bolt (arrowed) - 1390 cc (E6J) engine

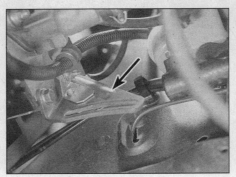

7.19b Alternator mounting bracket (arrowed) - 1390 cc (E6J) engine

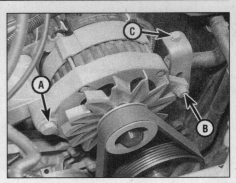

7.23 Alternator mountings on 1721 cc (F2N) engine

A Alternator pivot bolt   C Tensioner bolt
B Tensioner locknut

19 Remove the alternator pivot and adjustment bolts, and withdraw the alternator from the engine. If required, the alternator mounting bracket may be unbolted from the cylinder head at this stage (see illustrations).

Refitting

20 Refitting is a reversal of removal. Tension the drivebelt with reference to Chapter 1.

1721 cc (F2N and F3N) and 1794 cc (F3P) engines

Removal

21 Disconnect the battery negative lead.
22 Make a note of the electrical lead locations at the rear of the alternator, and disconnect them.

7.31a Alternator bracing strut-to-alternator bolt (arrowed) . . .

23 Loosen the alternator pivot nut and bolt, and the tensioner locknut on the adjustment bracket (see illustration).
24 Unscrew the tensioner bolt so that the drivebelt tension is fully released. Remove the drivebelt from the alternator pulley.
25 Remove the alternator pivot bolt and nut, and the adjustment locknut, then withdraw the alternator from the engine.

Refitting

26 Refitting is a reversal of removal. Tension the drivebelt with reference to Chapter 1.

1764 cc (F7P) engine

Removal

27 Disconnect the battery negative lead.
28 Unscrew the retaining screws, and remove the front grille panel.
29 Remove the right-hand headlight, as described in Chapter 12.
30 Release the power-assisted steering fluid reservoir mounting clip(s), and move the reservoir to one side (leave the fluid hoses connected).
31 Unscrew the fixings, and remove the alternator rear bracing strut (see illustrations).
32 Slacken the alternator drivebelt tension adjuster, and remove the drivebelt with reference to Chapter 1.
33 Remove the securing bolts, and withdraw the belt tensioner.
34 Remove the two screws securing the alternator front mounting plate to the inlet manifold (see illustration).

35 Unscrew the alternator pivot nut and the remaining fixings securing the front mounting plate. Note that it is only necessary to loosen the lower front fixing, as the mounting plate is slotted. Withdraw the mounting plate.
36 Withdraw the pivot bolt from the rear of the alternator, then remove the alternator through the headlight aperture.

Refitting

37 Refitting is a reversal of removal, but refit and tension the drivebelt as described in Chapter 1.

8 Alternator brushes and regulator - removal, inspection and refitting

Removal

1 Disconnect the battery negative lead.
2 Note the locations of the wiring connectors and leads at the rear of the alternator, and disconnect them. On certain engines (particularly the 1764 cc/F7P) the alternator must be removed to permit access, as described in Section 7.
3 Note the location of the lead on the B+ terminal, then unscrew and remove the nuts and lead, and remove the plastic rear cover (see illustration).
4 Unscrew the two small screws or nuts

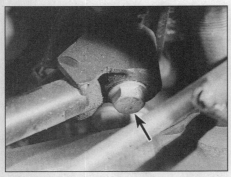

7.31b . . . and bracing strut-to-engine bolt (arrowed) - 1764 cc (F7P) engine

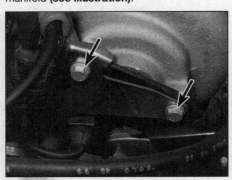

7.34 Alternator front mounting plate-to-inlet manifold screws (arrowed) - 1764 cc (F7P) engine

8.3 Alternator brush and regulator lead to the B+ terminal (arrowed)

securing the regulator and brushbox assembly to the rear of the alternator. Lift off the regulator and brushbox, disconnect the electrical lead(s), noting their locations, then remove the regulator and brushbox assembly from the alternator (see illustrations).

Inspection

5 Measure the length of each brush, from the end of the holder to the top of the brush (see illustration). No dimension is given by Renault, but as a rough guide, 5 mm should be regarded as a minimum. If either brush is worn below this amount, obtain and fit a new brushbox. If the brushes are still serviceable, clean them with a petrol-moistened cloth. Check that the brush spring pressure is equal for both brushes, and gives reasonable tension. If in doubt about the condition of the brushes and springs, compare them with new parts at a Renault parts dealer. The regulator can be separated from the brushbox after removing the cover if necessary.

6 Clean the alternator slip rings with a petrol-moistened cloth, then check for signs of scoring, burning or severe pitting (see illustration). If evident, the slip rings should be attended to by an automobile electrician.

Refitting

7 Refitting is a reversal of removal.

9 Starting system - testing

Note: *Refer to the precautions given in "Safety first!" and in Section 1 of this Chapter before starting work.*

1 If the starter motor fails to operate when the ignition key is turned to the appropriate position, the possible causes are as follows.
  (a) The battery is faulty.
  (b) The electrical connections between the switch, solenoid, battery and starter motor are somewhere failing to pass the necessary current from the battery through the starter to earth.
  (c) The solenoid is faulty.
  (d) The starter motor is mechanically or electrically defective.

2 To check the battery, switch on the headlights. If they dim after a few seconds, this indicates that the battery is discharged - recharge (see Section 3) or renew the battery. If the headlights glow brightly, operate the starter switch and observe the lights. If they dim, then this indicates that current is reaching the starter motor, therefore the fault must lie in the starter motor. If the lights continue to glow brightly (and no clicking sound can be heard from the starter motor solenoid), this indicates that there is a fault in the circuit or solenoid - see the following paragraphs. If the starter motor turns slowly when operated, but the battery is in good condition, then this indicates either that the starter motor is faulty, or there is considerable resistance somewhere in the circuit.

8.4a Unscrew the two small screws (arrowed) . . .

8.4b . . . and remove the regulator and brushbox assembly

8.5 Measuring the length of the alternator brushes

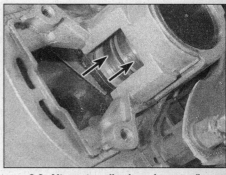
8.6 Alternator slip rings (arrowed)

3 If a fault in the circuit is suspected, disconnect the battery leads (including the earth connection to the body), the starter/solenoid wiring and the engine/transmission earth strap. Thoroughly clean the connections, and reconnect the leads and wiring. Use a voltmeter or test light to check that full battery voltage is available at the battery positive lead connection to the solenoid. Smear petroleum jelly around the battery terminals to prevent corrosion - corroded connections are among the most frequent causes of electrical system faults.

4 If the battery and all connections are in good condition, check the circuit by disconnecting the wire from the solenoid blade terminal. Connect a voltmeter or test light between the wire end and a good earth (such as the battery negative terminal), and check that the wire is live when the ignition switch is turned to the "start" position. If it is, then the circuit is sound - if not, there is a fault in the ignition/starter switch or wiring.

5 The solenoid contacts can be checked by connecting a voltmeter or test light between the battery positive feed connection on the starter side of the solenoid, and earth. When the ignition switch is turned to the "start" position, there should be a reading or lighted bulb, as applicable. If there is no reading or lighted bulb, the solenoid is faulty, and should be renewed.

6 If the circuit and solenoid are proved sound, the fault must lie in the starter motor. Begin

checking the starter motor by removing it (see Section 10), and checking the brushes (see Section 11). If the fault does not lie in the brushes, the motor windings must be faulty. In this event, the starter motor must be renewed, unless an auto-electrical specialist can be found who will overhaul the unit at a cost significantly less than that of a new or exchange starter motor.

10 Starter motor - removal and refitting

C-type (1237 cc/C1G, 1390 cc/C3J and 1397 cc/C1J/C2J) engines
Removal

1 Open the bonnet and disconnect the battery negative lead.

2 For improved access, remove the air cleaner assembly as described in Chapter 4.

3 Where applicable, remove the starter motor heat shield.

4 Disconnect the wiring from the terminals on the starter motor solenoid.

5 Unscrew the bolt securing the starter motor rear support bracket to the cylinder block.

6 Unscrew the three bolts securing the starter motor to the gearbox bellhousing, and withdraw the motor from the engine. Note the locating dowel in the bellhousing bolt hole.

10.12 Starter motor terminals on the solenoid (arrowed) - 1390 cc (E6J) engine

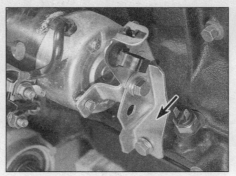

10.13 Starter motor support bracket on the face of the cylinder block (arrowed) - 1390 cc (E6J) engine

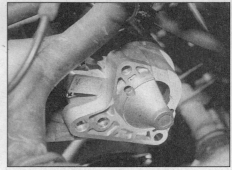

10.14 Withdrawing the starter motor - 1390 cc (E6J) engine

Refitting

7 Refitting is a reversal of removal. Ensure that the locating dowel is correctly positioned in the bellhousing bolt hole, as noted during removal.

E-type (1390 cc/E6J/E7J) engines
Removal

8 Open the bonnet and disconnect the battery negative lead.

9 For improved access, remove the air cleaner assembly as described in Chapter 4.

10 Unscrew the two bolts and the single nut securing the starter motor to the transmission bellhousing.

11 Apply the handbrake, then jack up the front of the vehicle and support it securely on axle stands (see *"Jacking, towing and wheel changing"*).

12 Disconnect the wiring from the terminals on the starter motor solenoid **(see illustration)**.

13 Unscrew the bolt securing the starter motor rear support bracket to the cylinder block, noting that on certain models, the bolt also secures a wiring harness support bracket **(see illustration)**.

14 Carefully withdraw the starter motor sideways from under the right-hand side of the vehicle **(see illustration)**. Note the locating dowel in the bellhousing bolt hole.

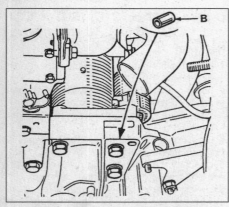

10.22 Starter motor locating dowel (B) in bellhousing bolt hole - F-type engines

Refitting

15 Refitting is a reversal of removal. Ensure that the locating dowel is correctly positioned in the bellhousing bolt hole, as noted during removal.

1721 cc (F2N and F3N) and 1794 cc (F3P) engines
Removal

16 Open the bonnet and disconnect the battery negative lead.

17 For improved access, remove the air cleaner assembly as described in Chapter 4.

18 Unscrew the three bolts securing the starter motor to the transmission bellhousing. Where applicable, note the location of any wiring brackets secured by the bolts.

19 Jack up the front of the vehicle and support it securely on axle stands (see *"Jacking, towing and wheel changing"*). For improved access, remove the front right-hand roadwheel.

20 Unscrew the bolts securing the exhaust heat shield/rear mounting bracket assembly to the cylinder block and the starter motor bracket, and withdraw the assembly.

21 Disconnect the wiring from the terminals on the starter motor solenoid.

22 Working under the vehicle, withdraw the motor from the engine. Note the locating dowel in the bellhousing hole **(see illustration)**.

Refitting

23 Refitting is a reversal of removal, bearing in mind the following points:
  (a) Ensure that the locating dowel is correctly positioned in the bellhousing bolt hole, as noted during removal.
  (b) When reconnecting the wiring to the motor, make sure that the terminal on the end of the wiring is positioned clear of the starter motor body and surrounding components.
  (c) Ensure that the exhaust heat shield is refitted.
  (d) Where applicable, refit any wiring brackets to the starter motor mounting bolts.

1764 cc (F7P) engine
Removal

24 Open the bonnet and disconnect the battery negative lead.

25 Remove the strengthening bar from between the front suspension unit turrets.

26 Unscrew the two securing bolts, and withdraw the starter motor heat shield.

27 Unscrew the three bolts securing the starter motor to the gearbox bellhousing. Where applicable, note the location of any wiring brackets secured by the bolts.

28 Jack up the front of the vehicle and support it securely on axle stands (see *"Jacking, towing and wheel changing"*). Remove the front right-hand roadwheel.

29 Unscrew the two securing bolts, and remove the exhaust manifold-to-cylinder block bracing bracket.

30 Unscrew the bolts securing the rear starter motor mounting bracket assembly to the cylinder block and the starter motor bracket, and withdraw the assembly.

31 Unbolt the starter motor cable mounting.

32 Disconnect the wiring from the terminals on the starter motor solenoid.

33 Working under the vehicle, withdraw the starter motor, manipulating it out along the driveshaft, and removing it from under the right-hand side of the vehicle. Note the locating dowel in the bellhousing hole.

Refitting

34 Refitting is a reversal of removal, bearing in mind the following points:
  (a) Ensure that the locating dowel is correctly positioned in the bellhousing bolt hole, as noted during removal.
  (b) When reconnecting the wiring to the motor, make sure that the terminal on the end of the wiring is positioned clear of the starter motor body and surrounding components.
  (c) Ensure that the starter motor heat shield is refitted.
  (d) Where applicable, refit any wiring brackets to the starter motor mounting bolts.

11 Starter motor - brush renewal

1 With the starter motor removed from the vehicle as described in Section 10, proceed as follows **(see illustration)**.

2 Make alignment marks on the end cover and the motor body.

3 Where applicable, unscrew the two securing nuts, and remove the mounting bracket from the rear of the starter motor **(see illustration)**.

4 Where applicable, unscrew the securing screws, and remove the armature shaft end cap **(see illustration)**.

5 Remove the circlip or the bolt from the end of the armature shaft **(see illustration)**. Recover the washers and spacers, noting their orientation. On motors with a bolt in the end of the shaft, it will be necessary to counterhold the pinion in order to unscrew the bolt.

6 Unscrew the two through-bolts or through-studs, and withdraw the armature end cover, along with the mounting bracket, when fitted. Release the rubber wiring grommet from the end cover as it is removed. Note that on some types of motor, the brush springs are located in the armature end cover **(see illustrations)**.

7 On motors with brush springs located in the armature end cover, the brushes can now be withdrawn from the brush carrier assembly **(see illustration)**.

8 On motors with brushes retained by springs attached to lugs on the brush holder plate, release the springs from the brushes, using a

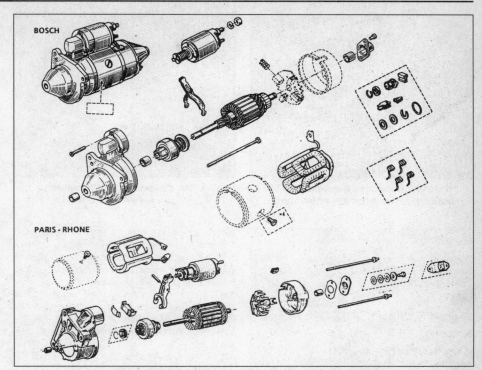

11.1 Exploded views of the Bosch and Paris-Rhone starter motors

screwdriver. Withdraw the brushes from the brush holder.

9 On motors with brushes mounted in clip-on brush holders, unclip the brush holders from

the brush holder plate, and recover the springs.

10 Examine the brushes for wear and damage. If they are damaged, or worn to the

11.3 Removing the mounting bracket - Valeo type starter motor

11.4 Removing the armature shaft end cap - Valeo type starter motor

11.5 Unscrewing the bolt from the end of the armature shaft - Valeo type starter motor

11.6a Unscrewing a starter motor through-bolt - Valeo type starter motor

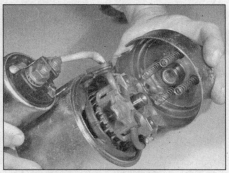

11.6b Removing the armature end cover. Note brush springs in cover - Valeo type starter motor

11.7 Brush (arrowed) withdrawn from brush carrier assembly - Valeo type starter motor

5A

11.18 Disconnecting the wire from the solenoid - Valeo type starter motor

11.19a Unscrew the two securing screws . . .

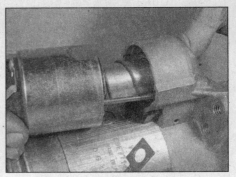

11.19b . . . and remove the solenoid housing - Valeo type starter motor

11.20 Remove the rubber insert from the edge of the pinion end housing - Valeo type starter motor

11.21 Drive the actuating arm pivot pin from the pinion end housing - Valeo type starter motor

extent where the springs are unable to exert sufficient pressure to maintain good contact with the commutator, they should be renewed. If renewal is necessary, unsolder the old brushes, and solder new ones into place.

11 Clean the brush holder assemblies, and wipe the commutator with a petrol-moistened cloth. If the commutator is dirty, it may be cleaned with fine glass paper, then wiped with the cloth.

12 Fit the new brushes using a reversal of the removal procedure, bearing in mind the following points.

13 Ensure that the brushes move freely in their holders.

14 Ensure that the brush springs provide adequate pressure on the brushes, and renew any worn springs.

15 Align the marks made on the end cover and the motor body (paragraph 2).

16 Ensure that the washers and spacers on the end of the armature shaft are fitted as noted before removal.

17 On motors fitted with a bolt in the commutator end of the armature shaft, it will be necessary to proceed as follows in order to counterhold the armature as the bolt is tightened. This is due to the one-way clutch, which will allow the armature to move independently of the drive pinion as the bolt is tightened.

18 Unscrew the nut securing the wire to the solenoid terminal. Recover the washer (see illustration).

19 Unscrew the two securing screws, and remove the solenoid housing from the pinion end housing (see illustrations). Recover the solenoid spring.

20 Remove the rubber insert from the edge of the pinion end housing (see illustration).

21 Using a pin punch, drive out the actuating arm pivot pin from the pinion end housing (see illustration).

22 Withdraw the pinion end housing, then lift the actuating arm and solenoid plunger from the armature shaft (see illustrations).

23 Counterhold the end of the armature shaft, taking care not to damage the surface of the shaft, then tighten the bolt in the commutator end of the shaft (see illustration).

24 Refit the pinion end housing and the solenoid components using a reversal of the removal procedure.

25 Refit the starter motor as described in Section 10.

12 Ignition switch - removal and refitting

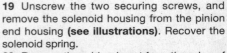

Removal

1 Disconnect the battery negative lead.

2 Unscrew the cross-head screws, and remove the steering column shrouds. Where applicable, also remove the internal cover (see illustrations).

3 Note the routing of the wiring, then

11.22a Withdraw the pinion end housing . . .

11.22b . . . then lift the actuating arm and solenoid plunger from the armature shaft - Valeo type starter motor

11.23 Tightening the armature shaft bolt - Valeo type starter motor

12.2a Remove the screws . . .

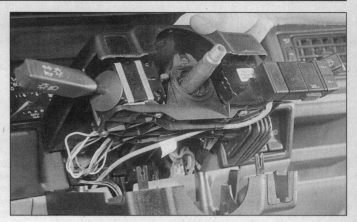

12.2b . . . and withdraw the steering column shrouds

12.2c Removing the ignition switch internal cover

12.4 Unscrewing the ignition switch grub screw

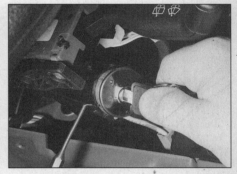

12.6 Depress the retaining lug and withdraw the switch assembly

5A

13.1a Oil pressure warning light switch (arrowed) - 1390 cc (C3J) engine

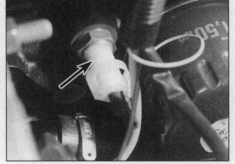

13.1b Oil pressure warning light switch (arrowed) - 1794 cc (F3P) engine

15.0 Oil level sensor (arrowed) - 1794 cc (F3P) engine

disconnect the two ignition switch wiring connectors.

4 Using an angled cross-head screwdriver (or a suitable similar tool to gain access), remove the small grub screw located at the rear, or on the top of, the ignition switch (see illustration).

5 Insert the ignition key, and turn it to the position between "A" and "M".

6 Depress the retaining lug (located under the switch), using a suitable pin punch, and withdraw the switch assembly using the key (see illustration). Feed the wiring through the housing in the steering column.

Refitting

7 Refitting is a reversal of removal, ensuring that the wiring is correctly routed as noted before removal.

13 Oil pressure warning light switch - removal and refitting

Removal

1 The oil pressure warning light switch is located at the front upper left-hand side of the cylinder block on models with C-type (1237 cc/

C1G, 1390 cc/C3J and 1397 cc/C1J/C2J) engines and E-type (1390 cc/E6J/E7J) engines. On models with F-type (1721 cc/F2N/F3N, 1764 cc/F7P and 1794 cc/F3P) engines, the switch is at the lower front right-hand side of the cylinder block **(see illustrations)**.

2 Disconnect the battery negative lead, then release the wiring connector from the switch.

3 Carefully unscrew the switch, and withdraw it from the cylinder block. Be prepared for some oil spillage.

4 Recover the sealing ring, where applicable.

Refitting

5 Refitting is a reversal of removal, but clean the threads of the switch before screwing it into the cylinder block, and where applicable, use a new sealing ring.

14 Oil pressure sensor - removal and refitting

1 The oil pressure sensor operates the oil pressure gauge on the instrument panel, where fitted.

2 The sensor is integral with the oil pressure warning light switch on C-type (1237 cc/C1G, 1390 cc/C3J and 1397 cc/C1J/C2J) engines - see previous Section. On F-type (1721 cc/F2N/F3N, 1764 cc/F7P and 1794 cc/F3P) engines, the sensor is located at the lower rear right-hand side of the cylinder block.

3 Removal and refitting are as described for the oil pressure warning light switch in the previous Section. Note that on F-type engines, access to the sensor is most easily obtained from under the vehicle.

15 Oil level sensor - removal and refitting

Where fitted, the oil level sensor is located in the front lower face of the cylinder block, or in the side of the sump **(see illustration)**. Removal and refitting details are as described for the oil pressure warning light switch in Section 13.

Chapter 5 Part B: Transistor-assisted contact breaker ignition system

Contents

5B

Degrees of difficulty

| **Easy,** suitable for novice with little experience | | **Fairly easy,** suitable for beginner with some experience | | **Fairly difficult,** suitable for competent DIY mechanic | | **Difficult,** suitable for experienced DIY mechanic | | **Very difficult,** suitable for expert DIY or professional | |

Specifications

General

System type	Contact breaker and coil, with electronic assistance in low-tension circuit
Application	1397 cc (C1J) engine
Firing order	1-3-4-2
Location of No 1 cylinder	Transmission end of engine

Distributor

Type	Conventional with contact breaker points and condenser
Direction of rotation	Clockwise

Ignition coil

Primary resistance (typical)	1.5 ohms
Secondary resistance (typical)	5000 ohms

For ignition timing and spark plug specifications, see Chapter 1

1 General information and precautions

General information

This type of ignition system consists of a basic conventional contact breaker ignition system, but with the addition of a transistor assistance unit **(see illustration)**. The transistor assistance unit has two sockets on it. The top one is for normal use, which includes transistor assistance, and the bottom one is for emergency use, which bypasses the transistor unit and converts the system to a conventional contact breaker ignition system. The wiring plug is simply moved from one socket to the other as required. **Note:** *Some models may have a sealed unit without the two socket positions.*

In order that the engine may run correctly, it is necessary for an electrical spark to ignite the fuel/air mixture in the combustion chamber at exactly the right moment in relation to engine speed and load.

Basically, the conventional ignition system functions as follows. Low-tension voltage from the battery is fed to the ignition coil, where it is converted into high-tension voltage. The high-tension voltage is powerful enough to jump the spark plug gap in the cylinder many times a second under high compression pressure, provided that the ignition system is in good working order, and that all adjustments are correct.

The ignition system consists of two individual circuits, known as the low-tension (LT) circuit and high-tension (HT) circuit.

The low-tension circuit (sometimes known as the "primary" circuit) consists of the battery, the lead to the ignition switch, the lead to the low-tension or primary coil windings, and the lead from the low-tension coil windings to the contact breaker points and condenser in the distributor.

The high-tension circuit (sometimes known as the "secondary" circuit) consists of the high-tension or secondary coil winding, the heavily-insulated lead from the centre of the coil to the centre of the distributor cap, the rotor arm, the spark plug leads, and the spark plugs.

The complete ignition system operates as follows. Low-tension voltage from the battery is changed within the ignition coil to high-tension voltage by the opening and closing of the contact breaker points in the low-tension circuit. High-tension voltage is then fed, via a contact in the centre of the distributor cap, to the rotor arm of the distributor. The rotor arm revolves inside the distributor cap. Each time the rotor arm passes one of the four metal segments in the cap, the opening and closing of the contact breaker points causes the high-tension voltage to build up, jump the gap from the rotor arm to the appropriate metal segment and so, via the spark plug lead, to the spark plug. At the spark plug, the voltage

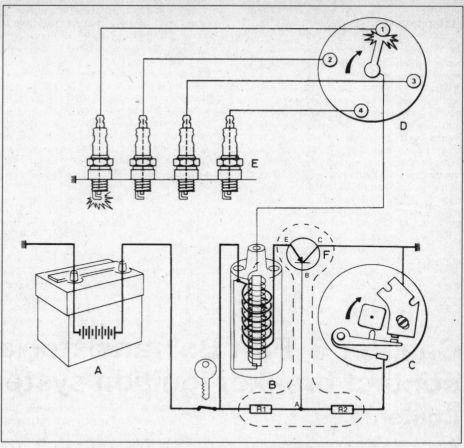

1.1 Layout of the transistor-assisted ignition system

A *Battery*
B *Ignition coil*
C *Distributor body and contact points*

D *Distributor cap*
E *Spark plugs*
F *Transistor and resistances*

finally jumps the gap between the two spark plug electrodes, one being earthed.

The ignition timing is advanced and retarded automatically, to ensure that the spark occurs at just the right instant for the particular load at the prevailing engine speed.

The ignition advance is controlled both mechanically and by a vacuum-operated system. The mechanical governor mechanism consists of two weights, which move out under centrifugal force from the central distributor shaft as the engine speed rises. As they move outwards, they rotate the cam relative to the distributor shaft, and so advance the spark. The weights are held in position by two light springs, and it is the tension of these springs which is largely responsible for correct spark advancement.

The vacuum control consists of a diaphragm, one side of which is connected (via a small-bore tube) to the carburettor; the other side is connected to the contact breaker plate. Depression in the induction manifold and carburettor, which varies with engine speed and throttle opening, causes the diaphragm to move, so rotating the contact breaker plate and advancing or retarding the spark.

The function of the transistor-assistance unit is to relieve the contact points of carrying the full primary current, and therefore extend their service life and provide a more reliable system. The contact points are used to switch a transistor on and off, and it is the transistor which carries the full primary current.

The transistor operates as follows, noting that components mentioned relate to those shown in area F, of illustration 1.1. With the points open, the base (B) and emitter (E) are of the same potential, and therefore no current flows. When the points close, the base (B) becomes negative due to the voltage drop at point (A), and current then flows through the transistor collector (C). The resistances R1 and R2 are incorporated in the circuit to provide a low control voltage; this also greatly increases the life of the contact points, as they only carry a small current. When the points open again, the voltage increases at point (A) and the base (B), and the transistor is switched off.

Precautions

Refer to the precautions given in Parts A and C before carrying out any work on the ignition system.

2 Ignition system - testing

Note: *Refer to the precautions given in Parts A and C before proceeding.*

1 Should a fault occur in the ignition system, first bypass the transistor assistance unit by pulling the connector from the top of the unit and plugging it into the lower socket. (On models without a lower socket, the same effect can be achieved by joining pins 1 and 3 in the connector - see paragraph 9). If the fault disappears, the fault is proved to be in the transistor assistance unit. If the fault remains, check the basic conventional system with reference to the following paragraphs.

2 There are two main symptoms indicating faults in the ignition system. Either the engine will not start or fire, or the engine is difficult to start and misfires. If it is a regular misfire (ie the engine is running on only two or three cylinders), the fault is almost sure to be in the secondary (high-tension) circuit. If the misfiring is intermittent, the fault could be in either the high- or low-tension circuits. If the vehicle stops suddenly, or will not start at all, it is likely that the fault is in the low-tension circuit. Loss of power and overheating, apart from faulty carburation settings, are normally due to faults in the distributor, or to incorrect ignition timing.

Engine fails to start

3 If the engine fails to start and the engine was running normally when it was last used, first check that there is fuel in the fuel tank. If the engine turns normally on the starter motor and the battery is fully charged, then the fault may be in either the high- or low-tension circuits. First check the high-tension circuit. (If the starter motor turns slowly or not at all, this is not an ignition system fault. Refer to Chapter 5.)

4 One of the most common reasons for bad starting is wet or damp spark plug leads and distributor. Remove the distributor cap. If condensation is visible internally, dry the cap with a rag, and also wipe over the leads. Refit the cap. Alternatively, using a moisture-dispersant can be very effective in starting the engine.

5 If the engine still fails to start, check that the current is reaching the plugs, by disconnecting each plug lead in turn at the spark plug end, and holding the end of the cable about 5 mm away from the cylinder block. Hold the lead with rubber-insulated pliers to avoid electric shocks. Spin the engine on the starter motor.

6 Sparking between the end of the cable and the block should be fairly strong with a good, regular blue spark. If current is reaching the plugs, then remove them and check their gaps. When the plugs are refitted, the engine should start - if not, try new plugs.

7 If there is no spark at the plug leads, take off the HT lead from the centre of the distributor cap, and hold it to the block as before. Spin the engine on the starter once more. A rapid succession of blue sparks between the end of

the lead and the block indicates that the coil is in order, and that either the distributor cap is cracked, the rotor arm faulty, or the carbon brush in the distributor cap is not making good contact with the rotor arm.

8 If there are no sparks from the end of the lead from the coil, check the connections at the coil end of the lead. If it is in order, start checking the low-tension circuit.

9 Either transfer the connector to the lower socket on the transistor-assistance unit, or remove the connector and interconnect pins 1 and 3 in the connector, as shown **(see illustration)**. The 5 amp fuse in the illustration protects the Renault diagnostic equipment, and does not need to be fitted if diagnostic equipment is not being used. As a precaution against a faulty condenser at the distributor, a known good condenser should be connected to earth as shown.

10 Use a 12-volt voltmeter, or a 12-volt bulb and two lengths of wire. With the ignition switched on and the points open, test between the low-tension wire to the coil positive (+) terminal and earth. No reading indicates a break in the supply from the ignition switch. Check the connections at the switch to see if any are loose; refit them, and the engine should run.

11 If a reading is indicated but the engine does not run, this shows a faulty coil or condenser, or a broken lead between the coil and the distributor. Take the condenser wire off the points assembly, and with the points open, test between the moving point and earth. If there is now a reading, then the fault is in the condenser. Fit a new one, as described in Chapter 1, and the fault should clear.

12 With no reading from the moving point to earth, take a reading between earth and the coil negative (-) terminal. A reading here shows a broken wire between the coil and distributor. No reading confirms that the coil has failed and must be renewed, after which the engine should run. Remember to refit the condenser wire to the points assembly. For these tests, it is sufficient to separate the points with a piece of paper while testing with the points open.

Engine misfires

13 If the engine misfires regularly, run it at a fast idle speed. Pull off each of the plug caps in turn, and listen to the note of the engine. Hold the plug cap in a dry cloth or with a rubber glove, as additional protection against a shock from the HT supply.

14 No difference in engine running will be noticed when the lead from the defective circuit is removed. Removing the lead from one of the good cylinders will accentuate the misfire.

15 Remove the plug lead from the end of the defective plug, and hold it about 5 mm away from the block. Restart the engine. If the sparking is fairly strong and regular, the fault must lie in the spark plug.

16 The plug may be loose, the insulation may be cracked, or the electrodes may have burnt away, giving too wide a gap for the spark to

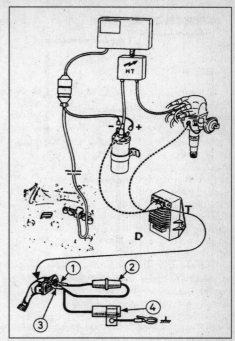

2.9 Testing the transistor-assisted ignition system

1 Terminal 1
2 Fuse (see text)
3 Terminal 2
4 Condenser
D Connector plug
T Transistorised assistance unit

Note that Renault diagnostic equipment is shown in the illustration

jump. Worse still, one of the electrodes may have broken off. Renew the spark plugs in this case.

17 If there is no spark at the end of the plug lead, or if it is weak and intermittent, check the ignition lead from the distributor to the plug. If the insulation is cracked or perished, renew the lead. Check the connections at the distributor cap.

18 If there is still no spark, examine the distributor cap carefully for tracking. This can be recognised by a very thin black line running between two or more electrodes, or between an electrode and some other part of the distributor. These lines are paths which now conduct electricity across the cap, thus letting it run to earth. The only answer is a new distributor cap.

19 Apart from the ignition timing being incorrect, other causes of misfiring have already been dealt with under the section dealing with the failure of the engine to start. To recap, these are that:
(a) The coil may be faulty, giving an intermittent misfire.
(b) There may be a damaged wire or loose connection in the low-tension circuit.
(c) The condenser may be short-circuiting.
(d) There may be a mechanical fault in the distributor (broken driving spindle or contact breaker spring).

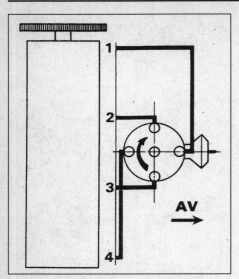

3.14 HT spark plug lead connection diagram

AV Front of vehicle

20 If the ignition is too far retarded, it should be noted that the engine will tend to overheat, and there will be quite a noticeable drop in power. If the engine is overheating and the power is down, and the ignition timing is correct, then the carburettor should be checked, as it is likely that this is where the fault lies.

3 Distributor - removal, overhaul and refitting

Removal

1 Mark the spark plug HT leads to aid refitting, and pull them off the ends of the plugs. Release the distributor cap retaining clips, and place the cap and leads to one side.
2 Remove No 1 spark plug (nearest the transmission end of the engine).
3 Place a finger over the plug hole, and turn the engine in the normal direction of rotation (clockwise from the crankshaft pulley end) until pressure is felt in No 1 cylinder. This indicates that the piston is commencing its compression stroke. The engine can be turned with a socket or spanner on the crankshaft pulley bolt.
4 Continue turning the engine until the mark on the flywheel is aligned with the TDC notch on the clutch bellhousing.
5 Using a dab of paint or a small file, make a reference mark between the distributor base and the cylinder block.
6 Detach the vacuum advance pipe, and disconnect the LT lead at the wiring connector. Release the wiring loom from the support clip on the distributor body.
7 Unscrew the distributor clamp retaining nut, and lift off the clamp. Withdraw the distributor from the engine, and recover the seal.

Overhaul

8 Renewal of the contact breaker assembly, condenser, rotor and distributor cap should be regarded as the limit of overhaul on these units, as few other spares are available separately. Refer to Chapter 1 for these procedures. It is possible to renew the vacuum unit, but this must then be set up to suit the advance curve of the engine by adjustment of the serrated cam on the baseplate; this is best left to a Renault dealer or automotive electrician.
9 When the distributor has seen extended service, and the shaft, bushes and centrifugal mechanism have become worn, it is advisable to purchase a new distributor.

Refitting

10 To refit the distributor, first check that the engine is still at the TDC position with No 1 cylinder on compression. If the engine has been turned while the distributor was removed, return it to the correct position as previously described. Also make sure that the seal is in position on the base of the distributor.
11 With the rotor arm pointing directly away from the engine and the vacuum unit at approximately the 5 o'clock position, slide the distributor into the cylinder block. Turn the rotor arm slightly, until the offset peg on the distributor drive dog positively engages with the drivegear.
12 Align the previously-made reference marks on the distributor base and cylinder block. If a new distributor is being fitted, position the distributor body so that the rotor arm points toward the No 1 spark plug HT lead segment in the cap. With the distributor in this position, refit the clamp, and secure with the retaining nut.
13 Reconnect the LT lead at the connector, refit the vacuum advance pipe, and secure the wiring loom in the support clip.
14 Refit the No 1 spark plug, the distributor cap and the spark plug HT leads **(see illustration)**.
15 Check and if necessary adjust the ignition timing as described in Chapter 1.

4 Ignition coil - removal and refitting

Removal

1 Where fitted, remove the cover from the top of the coil. Disconnect the HT lead from the coil.
2 Identify the LT leads for position, then disconnect them from the terminals on the coil.
3 Loosen the mounting nut, and slide the coil and bracket from the mounting stud.

Refitting

4 Refitting is a reversal of removal, but if necessary, wipe clean the top of the coil to prevent any tracking of the HT current.

5 Transistorised assistance unit - removal and refitting

Removal

1 Disconnect the wiring plug from the transistorised assistance unit located on the bulkhead.
2 Unscrew the mounting nuts and remove the unit.

Refitting

3 Refitting is a reversal of removal.

Chapter 5 Part C: Electronic ignition system

Contents

Degrees of difficulty

Easy, suitable for novice with little experience	**Fairly easy,** suitable for beginner with some experience	**Fairly difficult,** suitable for competent DIY mechanic	**Difficult,** suitable for experienced DIY mechanic	**Very difficult,** suitable for expert DIY or professional

Specifications

General

System type	Fully-electronic, computer-controlled
Application	All engines except 1397 cc (C1J)
Firing order	1-3-4-2
Location of No 1 cylinder	Transmission end of engine

Distributor

Type	Simple body, rotor arm and cap (no advance/retard functions)
Direction of rotation	Anti-clockwise

Ignition coil

Type	Renix, mounted on ignition module
Primary resistance (typical)	0.4 to 0.8 ohms
Secondary resistance (typical)	6500 ohms

Ignition timing is not adjustable. For spark plug specifications, see Chapter 1.

1 General information and precautions

General information

This Part of Chapter 5 deals with the fully-electronic ignition system fitted to most Renault 19 models. The system fitted to carburettor models is known as AEI (Allumage Electronique Intégrale). A modified version of this system is fitted to models with fuel injection, one computer having control over both the injection and the ignition systems.

Operation of both systems is similar. An engine speed/position sensor, bolted to the flywheel housing, provides signals indicating engine speed and crankshaft angular position. A manifold vacuum (MAP) sensor provides a signal varying with inlet manifold vacuum, which is an indication of load. The signals are processed by a computer, and used to determine the moment when ignition must occur. The computer controls an amplifier which drives the ignition coil.

Certain fuel injection models also have a knock sensor, which provides a signal if pre-ignition (pinking) occurs. This enables the

computer to advance ignition timing to the most efficient point, without risking engine damage through pre-ignition. It also means that the system is self-correcting for small variations in fuel octane rating.

High-tension voltage passes from the coil to the distributor rotor arm, and from there to the appropriate spark plug. The distributor has no other function than the distribution of HT; speed- and load-related advance are handled by the computer. There is no means of adjusting ignition timing, short of changing the computer or the sensors.

On carburettor models, the computer, amplifier, ignition coil and vacuum sensor are all mounted together on a single module. The only item which can be renewed separately is the ignition coil.

On fuel injection models, the ignition module consists of the amplifier and the ignition coil, mounted together. The computer is shared with the fuel injection system, and is described in detail in Chapter 4; the same applies to the manifold vacuum (MAP) sensor.

Precautions

The following precautions must be observed, to prevent damage to the ignition

system components, and to reduce risk of personal injury:

  (a) Ensure that the ignition is switched off before disconnecting any of the ignition wiring.
  (b) Ensure that the ignition is switched off before connecting or disconnecting any ignition test equipment, such as a timing light.
  (c) Do not connect a suppression condenser or test light to the ignition coil negative terminal.
  (d) Do not connect any test appliance or stroboscopic timing light requiring a 12-volt supply to the ignition coil positive terminal.
  (e) Do not allow an HT lead to short out or spark against the computer control unit body.
  (f) Do not earth the coil primary or secondary circuits.
  (g) When carrying out welding operations on the vehicle using electric welding equipment, the battery and alternator should be disconnected.
  (h) Although the underbonnet-mounted modules will tolerate normal underbonnet conditions, they can be

adversely affected by excess heat or moisture. If using welding equipment or pressure washing equipment in the vicinity of an electronic module, take care not to direct heat, or jets of water or steam, at the module. If this cannot be avoided, remove the module from the vehicle, and protect its wiring plug with a plastic bag.

(i) Do not attempt to improvise fault diagnosis procedures using a test light or multimeter, as irreparable damage could be caused to the module.

(j) After working on ignition system/engine management system components, ensure that all wiring is correctly reconnected before reconnecting the battery or switching on the ignition.

⚠️ **Warning: The voltages produced by the electronic ignition system are considerably higher than those produced by conventional systems. Extreme care must be taken when working on the system with the ignition switched on. Persons with surgically-implanted cardiac pacemaker devices should keep well clear of the ignition circuits, components and test equipment.**

2 Ignition system - testing

Carburettor models

1 There are two main symptoms indicating faults in the ignition system. Either the engine will not start or fire, or the engine is difficult to start and misfires. Each of these possibilities is covered separately in the following paragraphs.

Engine turns normally, but fails to start

2 First check the HT leads, distributor cap and spark plugs.
3 Remove the two connectors from the bottom of the ignition module, and check the terminals for corrosion. If necessary, remove and refit the connectors several times in order to clean the terminals. If they are very dirty, scrape the terminals with a suitable instrument.
4 Using a voltmeter, and with the ignition switched on, check that the voltage between the coil positive (+) terminal at the interference suppression condenser output and earth, is at least 9.5 volts.
5 Disconnect the supply connector **(see illustration)**, and connect a voltmeter between terminal 1 and earth. Switch on the ignition, and attempt to start the engine. The reading on the voltmeter should be at least 9.5 volts. If not, check the battery voltage, and recharge if necessary. Also check the ignition module supply wiring.
6 With the supply connector (A in illustration 2.5) still disconnected and the ignition switched off, connect an ohmmeter between

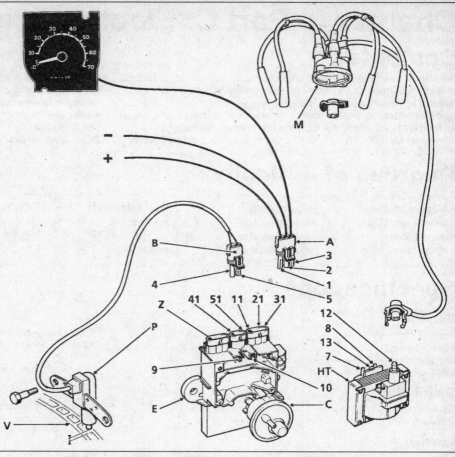

2.5 Electronic ignition system components - carburettor models

1 Positive supply (+)
2 Earth (-)
3 Tachometer connector
4 Engine speed/position sensor terminal
5 Engine speed/position sensor terminal
7 Coil positive (+) and interference suppression terminals
8 Coil negative (-) terminal
9 Coil positive (+) terminal on the control unit
10 Coil negative (-) terminal on the control unit
11 Control unit positive (+) supply
12 Coil HT terminal
13 Coil positive (+) terminal for interference suppression capacitor

21 Control unit negative (-) terminal
31 Tachometer output
41 Engine speed/position signal
51 Engine speed/position signal
A Supply/tachometer connector
B Speed/position signal connector
C Vacuum capsule
E Control unit
HT Ignition coil
M Distributor cap
P Engine speed/position sensor
V Flywheel
Z Socket for temperature-related timing advance (1721 cc/F2N engine)

terminal 2 and the vehicle earth. If the reading is not zero, check the earth wiring from the connector for a possible loose connection.
7 With the supply connector still disconnected and the ignition switched off, connect an ohmmeter between the coil terminal 6 and terminal 11 on the ignition module. If the read is not zero, renew the ignition module.
8 Reconnect the supply connector, and switch on the ignition. Connect a voltmeter between terminal 6 and the vehicle earth. If the reading is not at least 9.5 volts, shake the connector, and observe if the reading increases. If it is still incorrect, check the coil terminal contacts for corrosion. If still incorrect, renew the supply connector.

9 With the ignition switched off, disconnect the engine speed/position sensor signal connector (B in illustration 2.5). Check the resistance of the sensor by connecting an ohmmeter across terminals 4 and 5. The reading should be 200 ± 50 ohms. If the reading is incorrect, renew the sensor.
10 Using a feeler blade, check that the clearance between the end of the sensor (P) and the flywheel (V) is 1.0 ± 0.5 mm (see illustration 2.5). If the clearance is incorrect, renew the sensor.
11 Reconnect both connectors (A and B in illustration 2.5), then remove the ignition coil (Section 4). Connect a 12-volt test light (2 watts maximum) between the coil feed

terminals (8 and 9) on the ignition module. Spin the engine on the starter motor, and check that the test light flashes. If the light does not flash, renew the ignition module.

12 With the ignition coil still removed, connect an ohmmeter between terminals 7 and 12 on the coil to check the resistance of the high-tension windings. The resistance should be between 2000 and 12 000 ohms. Renew the coil if the resistance is incorrect.

13 With the ignition coil still removed, connect an ohmmeter between terminals 6 and 7 on the coil, to check the resistance of the low-tension windings. The resistance should be between 0.4 ohms and 0.8 ohms. Renew the coil if the resistance is incorrect.

14 With the ignition switched off, disconnect the supply connector (A in illustration 2.5) from the ignition module. Check the resistance of the tachometer by connecting an ohmmeter between terminals 2 and 3. The resistance should be at least 20 000 ohms. If the resistance is incorrect, check the wiring for a fault. If the wiring is OK, renew the tachometer.

15 If after making the previous checks there is still no HT spark, renew the ignition module.

Engine misfires

16 First check the HT leads, distributor cap and spark plugs, with reference to Chapter 1.

17 Disconnect the main HT lead from the coil at the distributor cap end, and hold the end of the lead 20 mm away from the cylinder head using a well-insulated pair of pliers. *Do not allow the HT lead to touch the computer control unit.*

18 Spin the engine on the starter motor, and check that there are regular strong HT sparks between the HT lead and the cylinder head. If the sparking is good, but the engine still misfires, check the carburation and the mechanical condition of the engine (valve clearances, valve timing, compression) for possible faults. If there are no sparks, continue with the following checks.

19 Disconnect the supply connector (A in illustration 2.5) and connect a voltmeter between terminal 1 and earth. Switch on the ignition, and attempt to start the engine. The reading on the voltmeter should be at least 9.5 volts. If not, check the battery voltage, and recharge if necessary. Also

check the ignition module supply wiring.

20 With the ignition switched off, disconnect the engine speed/position sensor signal wiring connector (B in illustration 2.5). Check the resistance of the engine speed/position sensor by connecting an ohmmeter across terminals 4 and 5. The reading should be 200 ± 50 ohms. If the reading is incorrect, renew the sensor.

21 Using a feeler blade, check that the clearance between the end of the sensor (P) and the flywheel (V) is 1.0 ± 0.5 mm (see illustration 2.5). If the clearance is incorrect, renew the sensor. If it is correct, remove the sensor, and clean the magnetic end of the sensor of any oil, dirt or grease. Refit the sensor, but if the misfire still persists, renew the sensor.

22 To check the condition of the vacuum capsule on the ignition module, reconnect all plugs, then start the engine and hold its speed steady at 3000 rpm. Pull the vacuum pipe from the capsule, and note if the engine speed falls. If it does, the capsule is operating correctly; if the speed remains constant, check the vacuum pipes. If the misfire still persists, renew the ignition module.

23 On 1721 cc (F2N) engine models, there is an additional connector fitted to the computer control unit at position Z (see illustration 2.5); this is linked to the electric cooling fan switch in the radiator. This connector provides a signal to allow ignition timing correction to protect the engine against pre-ignition ("pinking") under severe operating conditions. When the switch is off (ie at coolant temperatures less than 90°C), there should be no voltage at the connector terminals, and the ignition timing is unaffected. If the coolant temperature is greater than 90°C, there should be 12 volts at the terminals. Under these conditions, the ignition timing is retarded by 3° ± 2°, between engine speeds of 1200 and 4700 rpm and at a manifold vacuum of between 0 to 270 mbars.

Fuel injection models

24 As mentioned in Chapter 4B, there is little that can be done by way of testing the control circuitry on fuel injection models without special test equipment. The following

paragraphs provide suggestions for preliminary checks which can be made without such equipment.

Engine turns normally, but fails to start

25 Check the HT leads, distributor cap and spark plugs as described in Chapter 1.

26 Remove the connectors from the ignition amplifier, and check the terminals for corrosion. If necessary, remove and refit the connectors several times in order to clean the terminals. If they are very dirty, scrape the terminals with a suitable instrument.

27 Check the engine speed/position sensor as described in paragraphs 9 and 10, using an ohmmeter at the sensor connector on top of the gearbox/transmission.

28 Disconnect the coil terminals, and check the resistance of the windings using an ohmmeter. Typical values are given in the Specifications.

Engine misfires

29 Carry out the HT checks as described for carburettor models (paragraphs 16 to 18).

30 Check the engine speed/position sensor as described earlier.

31 If no improvement is produced, consult a Renault dealer or other specialist.

---

3 Distributor - removal, overhaul and refitting

C-type (1237 cc/C1G, 1390 cc/C3J and 1397 cc/C2J) engines

1 Refer to the procedure given for the conventional ignition system in Part B of this Chapter. Note that there is no need to make reference marks on the distributor base and cylinder block, as the distributor can only be fitted in one position (see illustration).

E-type (1390 cc/E6J/E7J) engines
Removal

2 Check that the spark plug leads and distributor cap are marked, to aid correct refitting. Pull the leads off the plugs or distributor cap, as wished. Unscrew the retaining screws, and place the distributor cap and leads to one side (see illustration).

3.1 Distributor clamp bolt (arrowed) - 1390 cc (C3J) engine

3.2 Unscrewing the distributor cap retaining screws - 1390 cc (E6J) engine

3.3a Removing the rotor arm - 1390 cc (E6J) engine

3.3b Distributor mounting bolts (arrowed) - 1390 cc (E6J) engine

3.3c Removing the distributor - 1390 cc (E6J) engine

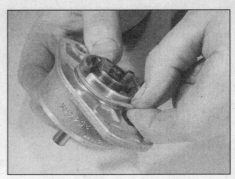

3.3d Removing the seal from the base of the distributor

3 Pull the rotor arm off the distributor shaft and where applicable, remove the plastic shield. Use a Torx key to unscrew the two mounting bolts, and withdraw the distributor from the cylinder head. Note that although the upper mounting bolt hole in the distributor body may be slotted, the lower bolt hole is not slotted, so it is not possible to adjust the position of the distributor. Remove the seal from the base of the distributor **(see illustrations)**.

Overhaul

4 Check the rotor arm and distributor cap as described in Chapter 1, and renew them if necessary. Note that on some models, a cover is fitted to the distributor cap; this should be removed for inspection and cleaning.

5 Check the amount of play between the distributor shaft and body. This should not be excessive unless the engine has covered a high mileage. If it is excessive, the complete distributor should be renewed.

6 Check the condition of the distributor base seal, and renew it if necessary.

Refitting

7 Refitting is a reversal of removal.

1721 cc (F2N/F3N) and 1794 cc (F3P) engines

Removal

8 Proceed as described in paragraph 2 **(see illustration)**.

9 The rotor arm is connected directly to the camshaft. On certain models, it may be attached by a circlip, or alternatively, it may be bonded. To remove the circlip type, carefully prise it off. To remove the bonded type, twist it using a pair of grips - this should break the bond, and enable the arm to be removed. (It is easy to damage the rotor arm when doing this, so a spare should be available.) Remove the plastic shield **(see illustrations)**.

Overhaul

10 Refer to paragraph 4.

Refitting

11 Refitting is a reversal of removal. Do not attempt to bond a rotor arm to a camshaft designed to accept a rotor arm with a circlip.

1764 cc (F7P) engine

12 The procedure is similar to that described previously for the 1721 cc (F2N and F3N) and 1794 cc (F3P) engines. The rotor arm is fitted to the exhaust camshaft.

4 Ignition coil (carburettor models) - removal and refitting

Removal

1 Disconnect the HT wire from the coil.

2 Remove the four screws and withdraw the coil from the computer control unit on the bulkhead, at the same time disconnecting the LT wiring terminals.

Refitting

3 Refitting is a reversal of removal, but make sure that the wires are fitted securely.

5 Ignition module (carburettor models) - removal and refitting

Removal

1 Disconnect the battery negative lead.

2 Disconnect the HT lead from the coil.

3 Disconnect the two or three multi-plugs (according to model) from the bottom of the unit.

4 Disconnect the hose from the vacuum advance capsule **(see illustration)**.

5 Unbolt and remove the ignition module from the bulkhead.

6 The coil is the only part of the module which can be renewed separately (see Section 4). If a fault develops in the computer, the amplifier or the vacuum unit, the complete module must be renewed.

Refitting

7 Refitting is a reversal of removal.

3.8 Unscrewing a distributor cap retaining screw - 1794 cc (F3P) engine

3.9a Removing the rotor arm . . .

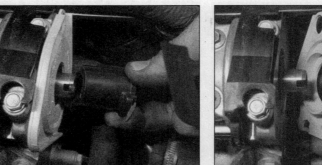

3.9b . . . and the plastic shield - 1794 cc (F3P) engine

5.4 Vacuum advance capsule hose (arrowed) on ignition module

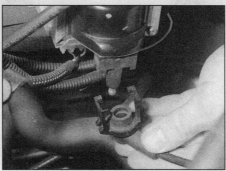

6.1 Disconnecting the HT lead from the coil

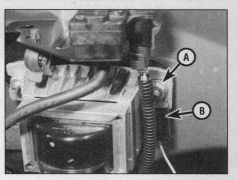

6.3 Ignition module securing nut (A) and suppression condenser (B)

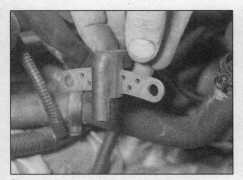

7.3 Removing the speed/position sensor from the top of the transmission bellhousing

8.1a Knock sensor (arrowed) - 1721 cc (F3N) engine

8.1b Knock sensor (arrowed) - 1794 cc (F3P) engine

6 Ignition module (fuel injection models) - removal and refitting

Note: *The ignition coil is not renewable separately on fuel injection models.*

Removal

1 Disconnect the battery negative lead. Release the securing lugs, and disconnect the HT lead from the coil **(see illustration)**.
2 Disconnect the two multi-plugs from the module.
3 Remove the two nuts which secure the module. Note that one of them also secures the radio interference suppression condenser **(see illustration)**.
4 Remove the ignition module.

Refitting

5 Refit by reversing the removal operations.

7 Engine speed/position sensor - removal and refitting

Removal

1 Disconnect the speed/position sensor connector from the bottom of the ignition module or computer, as applicable.

2 Where necessary, for improved access, remove the air cleaner assembly as described in Chapter 4, and unbolt any hose or wiring brackets obscuring the sensor.
3 Unbolt and remove the sensor from the aperture at the top of the transmission bellhousing **(see illustration)**.

Refitting

4 Refitting is a reversal of removal. It is important to use only the special shouldered bolts to attach the sensor to the bellhousing, as these determine the correct clearance from the flywheel.

8 Knock sensor - removal and refitting

Removal

1 The location of the knock sensor varies according to engine type. On the 1390 cc (E7J) engine, it is located at the rear of the engine, below the inlet manifold; access is obtained from below. On the 1721 cc (F3N) and 1794 cc (F3P) engines, the sensor is located at the front of the cylinder head. On the 1764 cc (F7P) engine, the sensor is again located at the front of the cylinder head, but it is obscured by

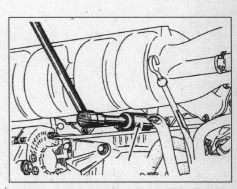

8.2 Knock sensor removal on the 1764 cc (F7P) engine requires a deep socket (arrowed)

5C

the inlet manifold. A deep 24 mm socket will be required to reach it, and it may also be necessary to remove the radiator for access **(see illustrations)**.
2 Disconnect the sensor wiring plug. Unscrew the sensor and remove it **(see illustration)**.

Refitting

3 Refit by reversing the removal operations. Make sure that the wiring plug is securely connected.

Notes

Chapter 6 Clutch

Contents

Degrees of difficulty

Easy, suitable for novice with little experience	**Fairly easy,** suitable for beginner with some experience	**Fairly difficult,** suitable for competent DIY mechanic	**Difficult,** suitable for experienced DIY mechanic	**Very difficult,** suitable for expert DIY or professional

Specifications

General

Clutch type	Single dry plate, diaphragm spring, cable-operated
Adjustment	Automatic

Clutch disc

Diameter:	
1237 cc (C1G), 1390 cc (E6J and E7J) and 1397 cc (C1J and C3J) engines	181.5 mm
1721 cc (F2N and F3N), 1764 cc (F7P) and 1794 cc (F3P) engines	200.0 mm
Lining thickness (new, and in compressed position)	7.7 mm

Torque wrench settings

	Nm	lbf ft
Clutch cover bolts:		
7 mm diameter	18	13
8 mm diameter	25	18

1 General information

All manual gearbox models are equipped with a cable-operated clutch. The unit consists of a steel cover which is dowelled and bolted to the rear face of the flywheel, and contains the pressure plate and diaphragm spring **(see illustration)**.

The clutch disc is free to slide along the gearbox splined input shaft. The disc is held in position between the flywheel and the pressure plate by the pressure of the diaphragm spring. Friction lining material is riveted to the clutch disc, which has a spring-cushioned hub, to absorb transmission shocks and to help ensure a smooth take-up of the drive.

The clutch is actuated by a cable, controlled by the clutch pedal. The clutch release mechanism consists of a release arm and bearing which are in permanent contact with the fingers of the diaphragm spring **(see illustration)**.

Depressing the clutch pedal actuates the release arm by means of the cable. The arm pushes the release bearing against the diaphragm fingers, so moving the centre of the diaphragm spring inwards. As the centre of the spring is pushed in, the outside of the spring pivots out, so moving the pressure plate backwards and disengaging its grip on the clutch disc.

When the pedal is released, the diaphragm spring forces the pressure plate into contact with the friction linings on the clutch disc. The disc is now firmly sandwiched between the pressure plate and the flywheel, thus transmitting engine power to the gearbox.

Wear of the friction material on the clutch disc is automatically compensated for by a self-adjusting mechanism attached to the clutch pedal. The mechanism consists of a serrated quadrant, a notched cam and a tension spring. One end of the clutch cable is attached to the quadrant, which is free to pivot on the pedal, but is kept in tension by a spring. When the pedal is depressed, the notched cam contacts the quadrant, thus locking it and allowing the pedal to pull the cable and operate the clutch. When the pedal is released, the tension spring causes the notched cam to move free of the quadrant; at the same time, tension is maintained on the cable, keeping the release bearing in contact with the diaphragm spring. As the friction material on the disc wears, the self-adjusting quadrant will rotate when the pedal is released, and the pedal free play will be maintained between the notched cam and the quadrant.

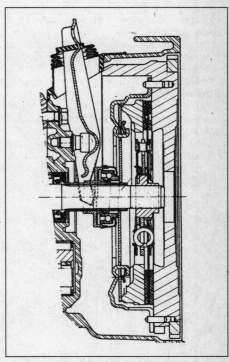

1.1 Cross-section of the clutch components

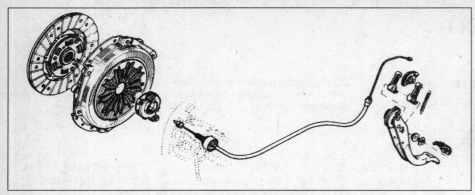

1.3 Clutch cable and pedal components

2.1 Withdrawing the outer cable from the bellhousing bracket

2 Clutch cable - removal and refitting

Removal

1 Working in the engine compartment, disengage the inner cable from the release fork located on the clutch bellhousing, then withdraw the outer cable from the bracket on the bellhousing (see illustration).
2 On certain models, it may be necessary to unclip the trim panel from under the facia, to improve access to the pedal assembly.
3 Press the clutch pedal to the floor, and then release it, and pull the cable end retainer from the quadrant on the pedal assembly (see illustration).
4 Pull the end of the cable down, release it from the quadrant, then manipulate the cable out through the guide at the rear of the pedal (see illustration).
5 Using a screwdriver, release the retaining tangs, and push the cable outer retaining bush from the bulkhead (see illustration).
6 To aid refitting, tie a suitable length of string to the end of the cable.
7 Pull the cable through into the engine compartment, and detach it from the support clips.
8 Untie the string from the end of the cable,

and leave the string in position to aid refitting. Remove the cable from the car.

Refitting

9 To refit the cable, tie the end of the string left in the engine compartment to the end of the cable, then use the string to draw the cable through into the inside of the car. Once the cable is in position, untie the string from the cable end.
10 From inside the vehicle (the aid of an assistant will ease the job), align the cable outer retaining bush with the appropriate locating hole in the bulkhead.
11 Working in the engine compartment, push the retaining bush through the bulkhead until it locks in position.
12 Untie the string from the end of the cable.
13 Ensure that the cable passes through the guide on the rear of the pedal, then lay the cable over the quadrant.
14 Position the cable end in the end of the quadrant, then refit the cable end retainer. Make sure that the self-adjusting cam support arms return to their rest position freely under the tension of the return spring.
15 Working in the engine compartment, slip the other end of the cable through the bellhousing bracket, and connect the inner cable to the release fork. Refit the cable to the support clips.
16 Depress the clutch pedal several times in order to allow the self-adjusting mechanism to set the correct free play.

2.3 Clutch cable end retainer (arrowed) in the quadrant on the self-adjusting mechanism

17 When the self-adjusting mechanism on the clutch pedal is functioning correctly, there should be a minimum of 20.0 mm slack in the cable. To check this dimension, pull out the inner cable near the release fork on the gearbox (see illustration). If there is less than the minimum slack in the cable, the self-adjusting quadrant should be checked for seizure or possible restricted movement.
18 Depress the clutch pedal fully, and check that the total movement at the top of the release fork is as shown (see illustration). This movement ensures that the clutch pedal stroke is correct. If the movement is not correct, make sure that the quadrant and support arms are free to turn on their

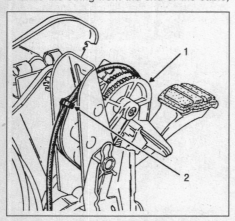

2.4 Clutch cable self-adjusting quadrant (1) and guide (2)

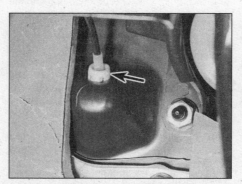

2.5 Clutch cable retaining bush (arrowed) at bulkhead

2.17 Checking the clutch inner cable slack at the release fork end

respective pivots, and that the spring has not lost its tension. If necessary, check the free length of the spring against a new one. Also check that the inner cable is not seizing in the outer cable.

19 Where applicable, refit the trim panel under the facia.

3 Clutch pedal - removal and refitting

Removal

1 Disconnect the cable end from the clutch pedal assembly as described in the previous Section. Note that there is no need to remove the cable from the bulkhead.

2 Working at the left-hand (right-hand-drive models) or right-hand (left-hand-drive models) end of the pedal pivot shaft, remove the retaining spring clip from the end of the shaft.

3 Remove the washer, wave washer, and plastic bush from the end of the pivot shaft.

4 Pull the shaft to the right or left, as applicable, and slide the pedal assembly from the shaft.

5 Recover the remaining plastic bush from the end of the shaft, noting its location (the two bushes either side of the pedal are not the same, and are not interchangeable) **(see illustration)**.

6 If desired, the self-adjuster quadrant return spring can be unhooked and removed, but note the position of all the components to ensure correct refitting.

7 Similarly, remove the bushes and withdraw the self-adjuster support arms and quadrant. Inspect these components, and renew them if worn.

Refitting

8 Apply some multi-purpose grease to the bushes, and to the bearing surfaces or the support arms, quadrant and pivot shaft.

9 Locate the plastic bushes on the pedal, making sure that the thick bush is on the brake pedal side, and ensuring that the lugs on the bushes locate in the cut-outs in the pedal and the self-adjuster support arms. Reconnect the self-adjuster quadrant return spring.

10 To facilitate the refitting procedure, and to hold the bushes and support arms together, it is helpful to assemble the pedal on a dummy shaft. If a suitable shaft is not available, the pedal can still be refitted, but it will be necessary to hold the bushes together until the retaining spring clip is refitted to the end of the pivot shaft.

11 Locate the pedal assembly in the bracket, and push the pedal shaft through the pedal.

12 Refit the wave washer, washer and spring clip to the end of the shaft. Where applicable, make sure that the ends of the clip engage correctly with the cut-out in the pedal bracket, and ensure that the clip engages with the groove in the pivot shaft.

13 Reconnect the clutch cable to the pedal assembly, and check the operation of the self-

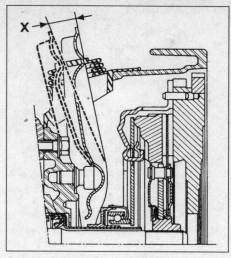

2.18 Checking the clutch release fork movement (X)

X = 17 to 18 mm

adjusting mechanism as described in the previous Section.

4 Clutch assembly - removal, inspection and refitting

⚠️ *Warning: Dust created by clutch wear and deposited on the clutch components may contain asbestos, which is a health hazard. DO NOT blow it out with compressed air, or inhale any of it. DO NOT use petrol or petroleum-based solvents to clean off the dust. Brake system cleaner or methylated spirit should be used to flush the dust into a suitable receptacle. After the clutch components are wiped clean with rags, dispose of the contaminated rags and cleaner in a sealed, marked container.*

Removal

1 Access to the clutch may be gained in one of two ways. Either the gearbox may be removed independently, as described in Chapter 7A, or the engine/gearbox unit may be removed as described in Chapter 2D, and the gearbox separated from the engine on the bench. If the gearbox is being removed independently on the 1721 cc (F2N and F3N), 1764 cc (F7P) and 1794 cc (F3P) engines, it need only be moved to one side for access to the clutch. **Note:** *On 1764 cc (F7P) engines fitted with an aluminium sump, the clutch cannot be removed with the engine in the car; the engine and gearbox must be removed as a unit, and separated.*

2 Having separated the gearbox from the engine, unscrew and remove the clutch cover retaining bolts. Work in a diagonal sequence, and slacken the bolts only a few turns at a time. Hold the flywheel stationary by positioning a screwdriver over the gearbox

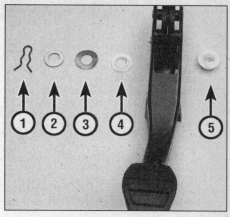

3.5 Clutch pedal components

1 Spring clip	4 Plastic bush
2 Washer	5 Plastic bush
3 Wave washer	

location dowel on the cylinder block, and engaging it with the starter ring gear **(see illustrations)**.

3 Ease the clutch cover off its locating dowels. Be prepared to catch the clutch disc, which will drop out as the cover is removed. Note which way round the disc is fitted **(see illustration)**.

Inspection

4 With the clutch assembly removed, clean off all traces of asbestos dust using a dry cloth.

4.2 Unscrewing the clutch cover retaining bolts, showing a screwdriver (arrowed) engaged with the starter ring gear

4.3 Removing the clutch cover and disc from the flywheel

6

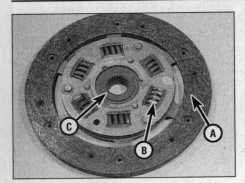

4.5 Inspect the clutch disc linings (A), springs (B) and splines (C)

4.6a Check the machined face of the pressure plate (arrowed) . . .

4.6b . . . and the diaphragm spring, paying particular attention to the tips (arrowed)

This is best done outside or in a well-ventilated area; refer to the warning at the beginning of this Section.

5 Examine the linings of the clutch disc for wear or loose rivets, and the disc rim for distortion, cracks, broken torsion springs, and worn splines (see illustration). The surface of the friction linings may be highly glazed, but as long as the friction material pattern can be clearly seen, this is satisfactory. If there is any sign of oil contamination, indicated by shiny black discoloration, the disc must be renewed, and the source of the contamination traced and rectified. This will be a leaking crankshaft oil seal, gearbox input shaft oil seal, or both. The renewal procedure for the former is given in Chapter 2A, 2B or 2C, as applicable. Renewal of the gearbox input shaft oil seal should be entrusted to a Renault garage, as it involves dismantling the gearbox, and the renewal of the clutch release bearing guide tube using a press. The disc must also be renewed if the linings have worn down to, or just above, the level of the rivet heads.

6 Check the machined faces of the flywheel and pressure plate. If either is grooved, or heavily scored, renewal is necessary. The pressure plate must also be renewed if any cracks are apparent, or if the diaphragm spring is damaged or its pressure suspect (see illustrations).

7 Take the opportunity to check the condition of the release bearing, as described in Section 5.

8 It is good practice to renew the clutch disc, pressure plate and release bearing as an assembly. Renewing the disc alone is not always satisfactory. A clutch repair kit can be obtained containing the new components.

9 Renault clutch kits for the F-type engine contain a special dummy bush, which may be fitted in the crankshaft bore to enable the use of the clutch centring tool also supplied in the kit. To fit this bush, first clean the bore in the end of the crankshaft, and apply locking fluid to the outer surface of the bush. Press the bush fully into the crankshaft using a length of tubing of 38 mm outside diameter, making sure that the open end of the bush faces outwards (see illustration).

Refitting

10 Before commencing the refitting procedure, apply a little high-melting-point grease to the splines of the gearbox input shaft. (A sachet of suitable grease may be supplied with the clutch kit.) Distribute the grease by sliding the clutch disc on and off the splines a few times. Remove the disc, and wipe away any excess grease.

11 It is important that no oil or grease is allowed to come into contact with the friction material of the clutch disc or the pressure plate and flywheel faces. It is advisable to refit the clutch assembly with clean hands, and to wipe the pressure plate and flywheel faces with a clean dry rag before assembly begins.

12 Begin reassembly by placing the clutch disc against the flywheel, with the side having the larger offset facing away from the flywheel (see illustration).

13 Place the clutch cover over the dowels. Refit the retaining bolts and tighten them finger-tight so that the clutch disc is gripped, but can still be moved.

14 The clutch disc must now be centralised so that, when the engine and gearbox are mated, the splines of the gearbox input shaft will pass through the splines in the centre of the clutch disc hub. If this is not done accurately, it will be impossible to refit the gearbox.

15 Centralisation can be carried out quite easily by inserting a round bar through the hole in the centre of the clutch disc, so that the end of the bar rests in the hole in the end of the crankshaft. Note that a plastic centralising tube is supplied with Renault clutch kits, making the use of a bar unnecessary (see illustration).

16 If a bar is being used, move it sideways or up and down until the clutch disc is centralised. Centralisation can be judged by removing the bar, and viewing the clutch disc hub in relation to the bore in the end of the crankshaft. When the bore appears exactly in the centre of the clutch disc hub, all is correct.

17 If a non-Renault clutch is being fitted, an alternative and more accurate method of centralisation is to use a commercially-available clutch-aligning tool obtainable from most accessory shops (see illustration).

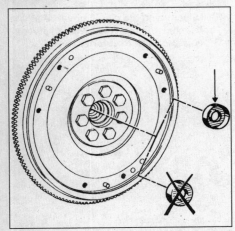

4.9 Fit the dummy bush in the crankshaft bore with the open end facing outwards

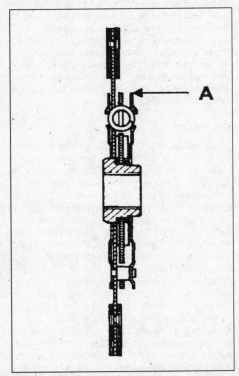

4.12 Clutch disc offset (A) faces away from flywheel

4.15 Centralising the clutch disc using the special tube supplied with Renault clutch kits

4.17 Using a clutch alignment tool to centralise the clutch disc

4.18 Tightening the clutch cover bolts

18 Once the clutch is centralised, progressively tighten the cover bolts in a diagonal sequence to the torque setting given in the Specifications **(see illustration)**. Remove the centralising device.

19 The gearbox can now be refitted to the engine, referring to the appropriate Chapter of this manual.

20 On completion, check the functioning of the clutch pedal as described in Section 2 and Chapter 1.

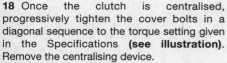

5 Clutch release bearing - removal, inspection and refitting

Removal

1 To gain access to the release bearing, it is necessary to separate the engine and gearbox as described at the beginning of the previous Section.

2 With the gearbox removed from the engine, tilt the release fork, and slide the bearing assembly off the gearbox input shaft guide tube.

3 To remove the release fork, disengage the rubber cover, and then pull the fork off its pivot ball stud.

Inspection

4 Check the bearing for smoothness of operation. Renew it if there is any roughness or harshness as the bearing is spun. It is good practice to renew the bearing as a matter of course during clutch overhaul, regardless of its apparent condition.

Refitting

5 Refitting the release fork and release bearing is the reverse sequence to removal, but note the following points:

(a) Lubricate the release fork pivot ball stud and the release bearing-to-diaphragm spring contact areas sparingly with molybdenum disulphide grease.

(b) Ensure that the clip on the bearing carrier engages with the release fork **(see illustration)**.

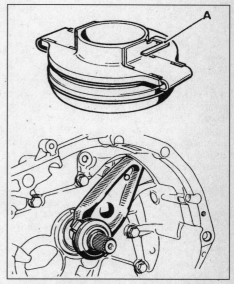

5.5 Clutch release components. Clip (A) on bearing carrier must engage with release fork

Notes

Chapter 7 Part A: Manual gearbox

Contents

Degrees of difficulty

Easy, suitable for novice with little experience		Fairly easy, suitable for beginner with some experience		Fairly difficult, suitable for competent DIY mechanic		Difficult, suitable for experienced DIY mechanic		Very difficult, suitable for expert DIY or professional	

Specifications

Note: *The gearbox code is stamped on a tag attached to one of the upper main housing-to-rear housing bolts.*

General

Type . . . . Four or five forward speeds (all synchromesh) and reverse. Final drive differential integral with main gearbox

Designation:
   Four-speed units . . . . JB0 or JB4
   Five-speed units . . . . JB1, JB3 or JB5

Gear ratios (typical)

JB0 and JB4 gearboxes:
   1st 3.7:1
   2nd 2.1:1
   3rd 1.3:1
   4th 0.9:1
   Reverse 3.6:1
   Final drive . . . . 3.6:1 to 3.9:1, depending on application

JB1, JB3 and JB5 gearboxes:
   1st . . . . 3.7:1 (3.1:1 - 16-valve)
   2nd . . . . 2.1:1 (1.8:1 - 16-valve)
   3rd 1.3:1
   4th 1.0:1
   5th 0.8:1
   Reverse 3.6:1
   Final drive . . . . 3.6:1 to 4.2:1, depending on application

Torque wrench settings

	Nm	lbf ft
Gear lever assembly casing-to-body nuts	15	11
Gearchange link rod clamp nuts and bolts	30	22

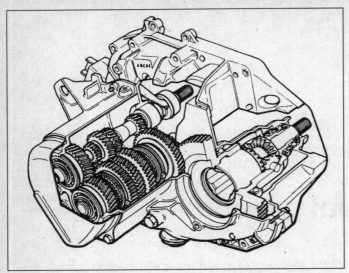

1.1a Cutaway view of the four-speed gearbox

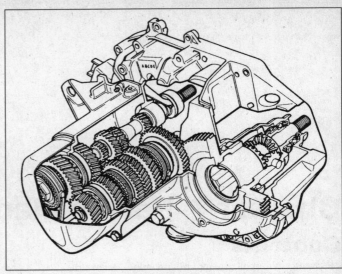

1.1b Cutaway view of the five-speed gearbox

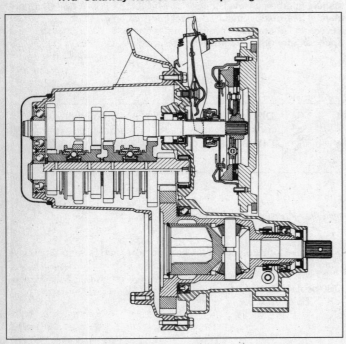

1.1c Sectional view of the four-speed gearbox

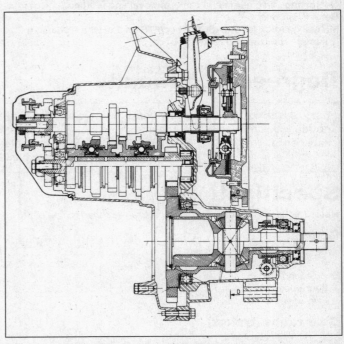

1.1d Sectional view of the five-speed gearbox

1 General information

The manual gearbox is either of four-speed (JB0 or JB4) or five-speed (JB1, JB3 or JB5) type, with one reverse gear (**see illustrations**). Baulk ring synchromesh gear engagement is used on all the forward gears. The final drive (differential) unit is integral with the main gearbox, and is located between the main gearbox casing and the clutch bellhousing. The gearbox and differential both share the same lubricating oil.

Gear selection is by means of a floor-mounted lever, connected by a remote control linkage to the gearbox selector mechanism (**see illustration**).

2 Gearchange linkage/ mechanism - adjustment

1 Apply the handbrake, then jack up the front of the vehicle and support it securely on axle stands (see *"Jacking, towing and wheel changing"*).
2 If desired, to improve access, lower or remove the exhaust system and if necessary the heat shield, with reference to Chapter 4.
3 Select 1st gear on the gearbox by moving the lever to the appropriate position. Renault technicians use a special tool to hold the lever

in position and take up any free play, but a suitable alternative tool can be made from flat metal bar or a piece of wood (**see illustrations**).
4 Using a feeler blade, check that the clearance between the reverse stop-ring on the gear lever and the inclined plane on the right-hand side of the gear lever housing is as shown (**see illustration**).
5 If adjustment is necessary, unhook the return spring from the gear lever end of the link rod, then loosen the clamp bolt at the gearbox end of the link rod so that the rod can be moved on the clevis.
6 Move the gear lever so that the reverse stop-ring is against the inclined plane on the

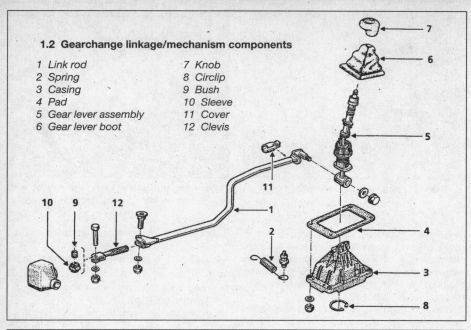

1.2 Gearchange linkage/mechanism components

1 Link rod	7 Knob
2 Spring	8 Circlip
3 Casing	9 Bush
4 Pad	10 Sleeve
5 Gear lever assembly	11 Cover
6 Gear lever boot	12 Clevis

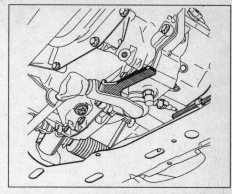

2.3b Using the special Renault tool to hold the gearbox lever in 1st gear position

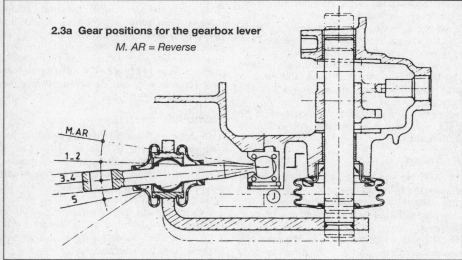

2.3a Gear positions for the gearbox lever

M. AR = Reverse

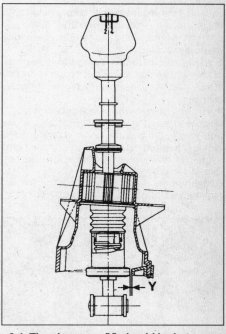

2.4 The clearance (Y) should be between 2 and 5 mm

housing, then insert a 2 mm feeler blade between the ring and plane. Hold the lever in this position, then tighten the clamp bolt **(see illustration)**.

7 Remove the holding tool and refit the return spring.

8 Recheck the clearance in illustration 2.4.

9 Check that all gears can be selected, then lower the vehicle to the ground.

3 Gearchange linkage/mechanism - removal and refitting

Removal

1 Working inside the vehicle, prise the gear lever boot from the centre console **(see illustration)**.

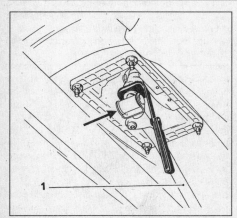

2.6 Adjusting the gearchange linkage using a 2 mm feeler blade

1 Link rod
Arrow indicates direction of pressure

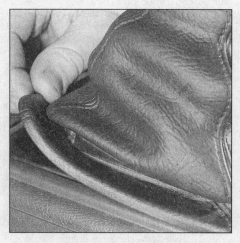

3.1 Removing the gear lever boot from the centre console

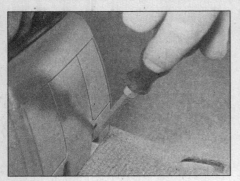

3.2a Remove the centre console rear screws . . .

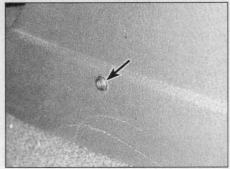

3.2b . . . and side screws (arrowed)

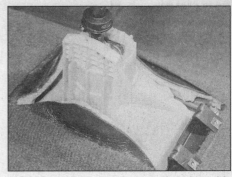

3.2c View of the gear lever and casing with the centre console removed

2 Unscrew the screws and lift off the centre console **(see illustrations)**. Where applicable, disconnect the battery negative lead, and disconnect the wiring plugs from the centre console-mounted switches.

3 Apply the handbrake, then jack up the front of the vehicle and support it securely on axle stands (see *"Jacking, towing and wheel changing"*).

4 Working beneath the vehicle, disconnect the flexible exhaust pipe mountings, and where applicable, remove the screws securing the exhaust heat shield. Ensure that the exhaust system is adequately supported, to prevent damage to the system.

5 Unhook the return spring from the link rod **(see illustration)**.

3.5 Unhook the link rod return spring (arrowed)

6 Pull back the rubber boot from the front end of the link rod. Unscrew and remove the bolt, and disconnect the rod from the gearbox lever. Recover the bush and sleeve. Note that the clevis at the front end of the rod is offset, and must be refitted correctly.

7 Unscrew and remove the nuts securing the gear lever assembly casing to the body, then lower the assembly while carefully pulling the exhaust system to one side.

8 Mark the link rod and gear lever clevis in relation to each other. Unscrew the clamp bolt and remove the rod from the clevis.

9 Grip the gear lever in a vice, then remove the knob and gear lever boot. The knob is bonded to the lever, and may be difficult to remove.

10 Extract the circlip from the bottom of the gear lever, and withdraw the lever and latch from the casing.

Refitting

11 Refitting is a reversal of removal, bearing in mind the following points.

12 Lubricate the pivot points with grease, and use a suitable adhesive to bond the knob to the lever.

13 Make sure that the clevis on the front end of the link rod is fitted with the offset towards the gearbox. If the clevis has been removed, or if a new clevis is being fitted, connect the link rod to the clevis leaving the correct amount of the knurled area showing **(see illustration)**.

This will locate the gear lever in its longitudinal position.

14 Adjust the gearchange mechanism as described in Section 2.

4 Speedometer drive - removal and refitting

Note: *On some later models, the speedometer drive is taken from the right-hand side of the gearbox, just above the driveshaft. It is not possible to remove the drive on this type. The later type can be identified by the plastic cable connection to the gearbox instead of the clip type connection on earlier models (see illustration).*

Removal

1 Disconnect the left-hand driveshaft at the gearbox end - refer to Chapter 8. There is no need to disturb the hub end of the driveshaft; the driveshaft/stub axle carrier assembly can be withdrawn together, as described for engine removal (Chapter 2D).

2 Extract the circlip and thrustwasher, then withdraw the left-hand sunwheel from the differential. The sunwheel also acts as the driveshaft spider housing.

3 Turn the differential until the planet wheels are in a vertical plane, so that the speedometer drivegear is visible **(see illustration)**.

4 Pull out the clip and disconnect the

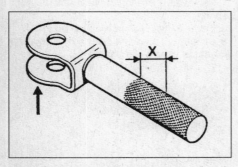

3.13 Link rod offset (arrowed) must face towards gearbox

Knurled area showing (X) = 10 to 12 mm

4. Speedometer drive plastic cable connection (arrowed) on later models

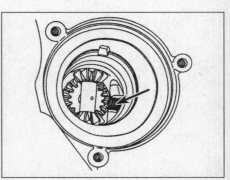

4.3 View of the speedometer drivegear (arrowed) with the differential sunwheel removed

speedometer cable from the outside of the gearbox.

5 Using long-nosed pliers, extract the speedometer drivegear shaft vertically from the outside of the gearbox.

6 Using the same pliers, extract the speedometer drivegear from inside the differential housing, being very careful not to drop it.

7 Examine the drivegear teeth for wear and damage. Renew it if necessary. Note that if the drivegear teeth on the differential are worn or damaged, it will be necessary to dismantle the gearbox - this work should be entrusted to a Renault dealer.

Refitting

8 Using long-nosed pliers, insert the speedometer drivegear into its location.

9 From outside the gearbox, refit the drivegear shaft. Make sure that it engages with the gear location notches correctly **(see illustration)**.

10 Refit the speedometer cable, and secure with the clip.

11 Insert the differential sunwheel, then refit the thrustwasher and circlip.

12 Reconnect the left-hand driveshaft with reference to Chapter 8.

5 Differential output oil seal (right-hand side) - renewal

Note: *New driveshaft-to-differential side gear roll pins will be required on refitting.*

1 Apply the handbrake, then jack up the front of the car and support it on axle stands. Remove the right-hand wheel.

2 Position a suitable container beneath the gearbox, then unscrew the drain plug and allow the oil to drain. (On some models, it may be necessary to remove a splash guard from the bottom of the gearbox first.) When most of the oil has drained, clean and refit the drain plug, tightening it securely.

3 Using a pin punch (5 mm diameter), drive out the double roll pins securing the inner end of the right-hand driveshaft to the differential side gear. New pins will be required when reassembling.

4 Unscrew the nut securing the steering track rod end to the steering arm. Use a balljoint separator tool to separate the balljoint taper.

5 Refer to Chapter 9 and unbolt the brake caliper from the stub axle carrier. Do not disconnect the hydraulic hose from the caliper. Tie the caliper to the suspension coil spring without straining the hydraulic hose.

6 Loosen (but do not remove) the lower bolt securing the stub axle carrier to the bottom of the suspension strut. Unscrew and remove the upper bolt, then tilt the stub axle carrier and disconnect the driveshaft. Take care not to damage the driveshaft rubber bellows.

7 Recover the O-ring from the side gear shaft.

8 Wipe clean the old oil seal, and measure its fitted depth below the casing edge. This is necessary to determine the correct fitted

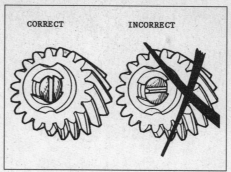
4.9 Notches in the speedometer drivegear engage with the shaft

position of the new oil seal, if the special Renault fitting tool is not being used.

9 Free the old oil seal, using a small drift to tap the outer edge of the seal inwards so that the opposite edge of the seal tilts out of the casing **(see illustration)**. A pair of pliers or grips can then be used to pull out the oil seal. Take care not to damage the splines of the differential side gear.

10 Wipe clean the oil seal seating in the casing.

11 Before fitting the new oil seal, it is necessary to cover the splines on the side gear, to prevent damage to the oil seal lips. Ideally, a close-fitting plastic cap should be located on the splines. If this is not available, wrap some adhesive tape over the splines.

12 Smear a little grease on the lips of the new oil seal and on the protective cap or tape.

13 Carefully locate the new oil seal over the splines of the side gear, and enter it squarely into the casing. Using a piece of metal tube or a socket, tap the oil seal into position to its correct depth, as noted previously **(see illustrations)**. Renault technicians use a special tool to ensure that the oil seal is fitted to the correct depth; it may be possible to hire this tool from a Renault garage or tool hire shop.

13 Remove the plastic cap or adhesive tape, and apply a little grease to the splines of the side gear. Fit a new O-ring to the side gear shaft.

14 Engage the driveshaft with the splines on the side gear, so that the roll pin holes are correctly aligned. Tilt the stub axle carrier, and

5.13a Locate the new differential output oil seal over the side gear splines . . .

5.9 Tap the old differential output oil seal with a small drift to remove it

slide the driveshaft onto the side gear, making sure that it enters the oil seal centrally.

15 With the holes aligned, tap the new roll pins into position. Seal the ends of the roll pins with a suitable sealant.

16 Refit the upper bolt securing the stub axle carrier to the bottom of the suspension strut, then tighten both upper and lower bolts to the specified torque (see Chapter 10).

17 Refit the brake caliper to the stub axle carrier, and tighten the bolts to the specified torque with reference to Chapter 9.

18 Clean the track rod end balljoint taper and the steering arm, then refit the balljoint to the arm and tighten the nut to the specified torque (see Chapter 10).

19 Refill the gearbox with the correct quantity and grade of oil, with reference to Chapter 1. Refit the splash guard where necessary.

20 Refit the roadwheel and lower the car to the ground.

6 Reversing light switch - removal and refitting

Removal

1 Apply the handbrake, then jack up the front of the car and support it on axle stands.

2 Where applicable, unbolt and remove the splash guard from the bottom of the gearbox.

3 Position a suitable container beneath the gearbox, then unscrew the drain plug and allow the oil to drain. When all of the oil has drained, clean and refit the drain plug, tightening it securely.

5.13b . . . and tap it into position with a socket or metal tube

4 The switch is located on the left-hand side of the gearbox, next to the driveshaft (see illustration). Disconnect the wiring from the switch.

5 Unscrew the switch from the gearbox, and remove the washer.

Refitting

6 Clean the location in the gearbox, and the threads of the switch.

7 Insert the switch together with a new washer, and tighten it securely.

8 Reconnect the wiring.

9 Refill the gearbox with the correct quantity and grade of oil, with reference to Chapter 1.

10 Refit the gearbox splash guard, where applicable.

11 Lower the car to the ground.

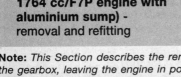

7 Manual gearbox (all except 1764 cc/F7P engine with aluminium sump) - removal and refitting

Note: *This Section describes the removal of the gearbox, leaving the engine in position in the car. However, if an adequate lifting hoist is available, it may be easier to remove both the engine and the gearbox together (as described in Chapter 2D) and then to separate the gearbox from the engine on the bench. Suitable means of supporting both the engine and gearbox will be required during this procedure. A balljoint separator will be required.*

Removal

1 The manual gearbox is removed upwards from the engine compartment after disconnecting it from the engine. Due to the weight of the unit, it will be necessary to have some form of lifting equipment available, such as an engine crane or suitable hoist to enable the unit to be removed in this way.

2 Apply the handbrake, then jack up the front of the vehicle, and support it securely on axle stands (see *"Jacking, towing and wheel changing"*). Remove both the front roadwheels.

3 Where applicable, remove the engine splash guard.

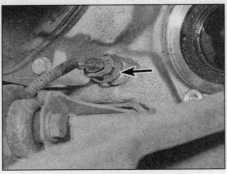

6.4 Reversing light switch (arrowed) viewed with driveshaft removed

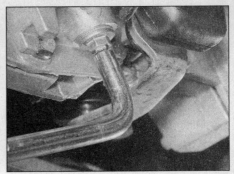

7.4 Unscrewing the gearbox oil drain plug

4 Position a suitable container beneath the gearbox, then unscrew the drain plug and allow the oil to drain (see illustration). When all of the oil has drained, clean and refit the drain plug, tightening it securely.

5 Disconnect the battery negative lead.

6 Unscrew the nut securing the left-hand steering track rod end to the steering arm, then use a balljoint separator tool to separate the balljoint taper.

7 Working in the engine compartment, where applicable, remove the air cleaner assembly and its mounting bracket from their locations above the gearbox bellhousing. Refer to Chapter 4 for further details.

8 Working in the engine compartment, unscrew the three bolts securing the left-hand driveshaft rubber gaiter retaining plate to the gearbox.

9 Refer to Chapter 9 and unbolt the left-hand brake caliper from the stub axle carrier. Do not disconnect the hydraulic hose from the caliper. Tie the caliper to the suspension coil spring, without straining the hydraulic hose.

10 Unbolt the front left-hand inner wing protective cover. The cover is secured by two Torx screws and one self-tapping screw (see illustration).

11 Unscrew and remove the pinch-bolt securing the front suspension lower arm balljoint to the bottom of the stub axle carrier.

12 Support the weight of the stub axle carrier and driveshaft on a trolley jack or an axle stand, then slacken and remove the two nuts and washers from the bolts securing the stub axle carrier to the suspension strut, noting that

the nuts are positioned on the rear side of the strut. Withdraw the bolts, and separate the stub axle carrier from the bottom of the suspension strut.

13 Withdraw the left-hand driveshaft and stub axle carrier assembly from the gearbox. Be prepared for some oil spillage as the driveshaft is withdrawn. Make sure that the rollers on the end of the driveshaft tripod remain in position, otherwise they may fall into the gearbox.

14 Working on the right-hand driveshaft, rotate the driveshaft until the double roll pin, securing the inner constant velocity joint to the sunwheel shaft, is visible. Using a hammer and a 5 mm diameter pin punch, drive out the double roll pin. New roll pins must be used on refitting.

15 Slacken and remove the two nuts and washers from the bolts securing the stub axle carrier to the suspension strut, again noting that the nuts are positioned on the rear side of the strut. Withdraw the upper bolt, but leave the lower bolt in position.

16 Pull the top of the stub axle carrier outwards until the driveshaft inner constant velocity joint splines are released from the sunwheel shaft in the differential. Remove the O-ring from the sunwheel shaft splines.

17 Support the driveshaft to one side, using wire or string attached to a suitable point on the vehicle body - do not allow the driveshaft to hang under its own weight, as this may damage the joints.

18 Where applicable, unscrew and remove the bolts securing the engine-to-gearbox tie-rod bracket to the gearbox (note that the tie-

7.10 Removing the left-hand inner wing protective cover

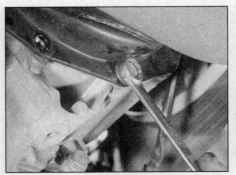

7.18a Remove the bolts securing the tie-rod bracket to the gearbox . . .

7.18b . . . and the engine

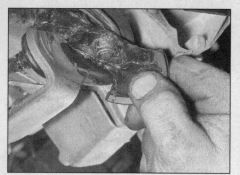

7.20a Pull back the rubber boot . . .

7.20b . . . then disconnect the gear lever rod from the lever on the gearbox

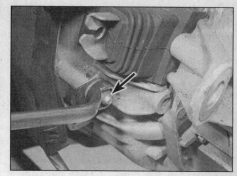

7.27 Unscrewing an engine-to-gearbox nut

rod bracket is fixed to the gearbox bellhousing cover plate). Loosen the tie-rod mounting bolts on the engine, or alternatively remove them and remove the tie-rod completely (see illustrations).

19 Where applicable, if not already done, unbolt the gearbox bellhousing cover plate.

20 Working under the gearbox, cut the plastic tie, and pull back the rubber boot from the gear linkage. Disconnect the gear lever rod from the lever on the gearbox by unscrewing the nut and removing the bolt (see illustrations). Recover the bush from inside the lever.

21 On all models except those with 1390 cc (E6J and E7J) engines, disconnect the wiring from the starter motor.

7.29 Removing the left-hand front engine mounting assembly

22 Disconnect the wiring from the reversing light switch.

23 Where applicable, unbolt and remove the engine speed/position sensor from the aperture at the top of the clutch bellhousing. Ideally, the sensor should be removed completely to avoid the possibility of damage as the gearbox is removed (refer to Chapter 5), but if desired, the sensor can be moved to one side and fastened in a position where it cannot be damaged.

24 Disengage the clutch inner cable from the release fork located on the clutch bellhousing, then withdraw the outer cable from the bracket on the bellhousing.

25 Position the clutch cable to one side, clear of the gearbox.

26 Pull out the clip and disconnect the speedometer cable from the outside of the gearbox.

27 Unscrew and remove the engine-to-gearbox nuts and bolts from around the gearbox and from the starter motor (see illustration). There is no need to remove the starter motor.

28 Connect a suitable hoist to the engine, and lift it slightly. Alternatively, the engine may be supported using a trolley jack and interposed block of wood positioned under the sump, so that the hoist can be used to remove the gearbox.

29 Unbolt the left-hand front engine mounting assembly from the gearbox and from the subframe, and withdraw the assembly (see illustration).

30 Unbolt the earth strap from the body, beneath the left-hand front wing (see illustration).

31 Unscrew the bolts securing the rear engine mounting bracket to the gearbox, and move it to the rear as far as possible. The bracket may be removed completely if necessary, by moving the engine forward and withdrawing the bracket upwards.

32 Slightly raise the gearbox using a trolley jack.

33 The radiator must now be moved to one side, although it is not necessary to drain the coolant or disconnect any of the hoses. First disconnect the wiring from the cooling fan motor and the thermostatic switch. Unscrew the radiator mounting bracket bolts from the body front panel, then remove the brackets, and move the radiator to the right-hand side (see illustration). Use a piece of cardboard to protect the radiator matrix from damage until the radiator is refitted.

34 Remove the gearbox locating studs (using two nuts locked together to unscrew each of them) from their locations on the front and rear of the bellhousing (see illustration). The front stud protrudes to the left-hand side, and the rear stud protrudes to the right-hand side at the rear of the engine (see illustration 4.26 in Chapter 2D).

35 On models with power-assisted steering, remove the two clips securing the fluid hose to the body panel and subframe.

36 Ensure that the weight of the gearbox is supported on the trolley jack. Separate the

7A

7.30 Earth strap (arrowed) beneath the left-hand front wing

7.33 Radiator moved to the right-hand side, to facilitate removal of the gearbox

7.34 Using two nuts locked together to unscrew a gearbox locating stud

gearbox from the engine, while sliding the 5th speed housing between the subframe and the side panel beneath the left-hand front wing. Careful use of a wide-bladed screwdriver may be necessary to free the bellhousing from the locating dowels.

37 Raise the engine slightly and move it to the rear, then turn the gearbox to the front and release it from the engine.

38 Attach a hoist and lifting tackle to the gearbox. Connect one end of the lifting tackle to the clutch cable mounting lug, and connect the other end to a bolt temporarily fitted to the gearbox. Lift the gearbox from the engine compartment (see illustration).

Refitting

39 Refitting is a reversal of removal, noting the following points:

(a) Make sure that the locating studs are correctly positioned in the gearbox. Note that their positions vary for the different engine types.

(b) Apply a little high-melting-point grease to the splines of the gearbox input shaft. Do not apply too much, otherwise there is the possibility of the grease contaminating the clutch friction disc. Make sure the clutch release bearing is correctly located on the release arm.

(c) Fit new roll pins to the right-hand driveshaft, and seal the ends using a suitable sealant.

(d) Refit and tighten the brake caliper mounting bolts with reference to Chapter 9.

(e) Refill the gearbox with oil, and check the level with reference to Chapter 1.

(f) Tighten all nuts and bolts to the specified torque.

8 Manual gearbox (1764 cc/F7P engine with aluminium sump) - removal and refitting

Since approximately April 1991, 1764 cc (F7P) engines have been fitted with an aluminium sump instead of the previous tin (pressed) type.

To accommodate this modification, a modified clutch bellhousing is fitted, preventing the gearbox from being removed independently of the engine.

The engine and gearbox must be removed as an assembly, and then separated, as described in Chapter 2D.

9 Manual gearbox overhaul - general information

Overhauling a manual gearbox is a difficult and involved job for the DIY home mechanic. In addition to dismantling and reassembling many small parts, clearances must be precisely measured and, if necessary, changed by selecting shims and spacers. Gearbox internal components are also often difficult to obtain, and in many instances, extremely expensive. Because of this, if the gearbox develops a fault or becomes noisy, the best course of action is to have the unit overhauled by a specialist repairer, or to obtain a complete exchange reconditioned unit.

Nevertheless, it is not impossible for the more experienced mechanic to overhaul a gearbox, provided the special tools are available, and the job is done in a deliberate step-by-step manner so that nothing is overlooked.

The tools necessary for an overhaul include internal and external circlip pliers, bearing pullers, a slide-hammer, a set of pin punches, a dial test indicator, and possibly a hydraulic press. In addition, a large, sturdy workbench and a vice will be required.

During dismantling of the gearbox, make careful notes of how each component is fitted, to make reassembly easier and more accurate (see illustrations).

Before dismantling the gearbox, it will help if you have some idea of which area is malfunctioning. Certain problems can be closely related to specific areas in the gearbox, which can make component examination and replacement easier. Refer to the "Fault finding" section at the end of this manual for more information.

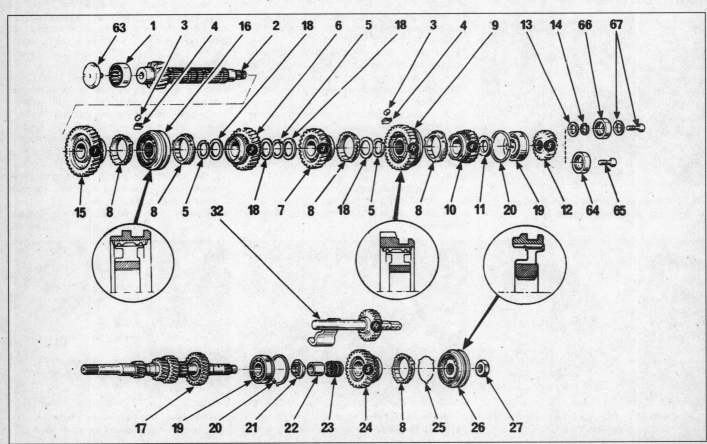

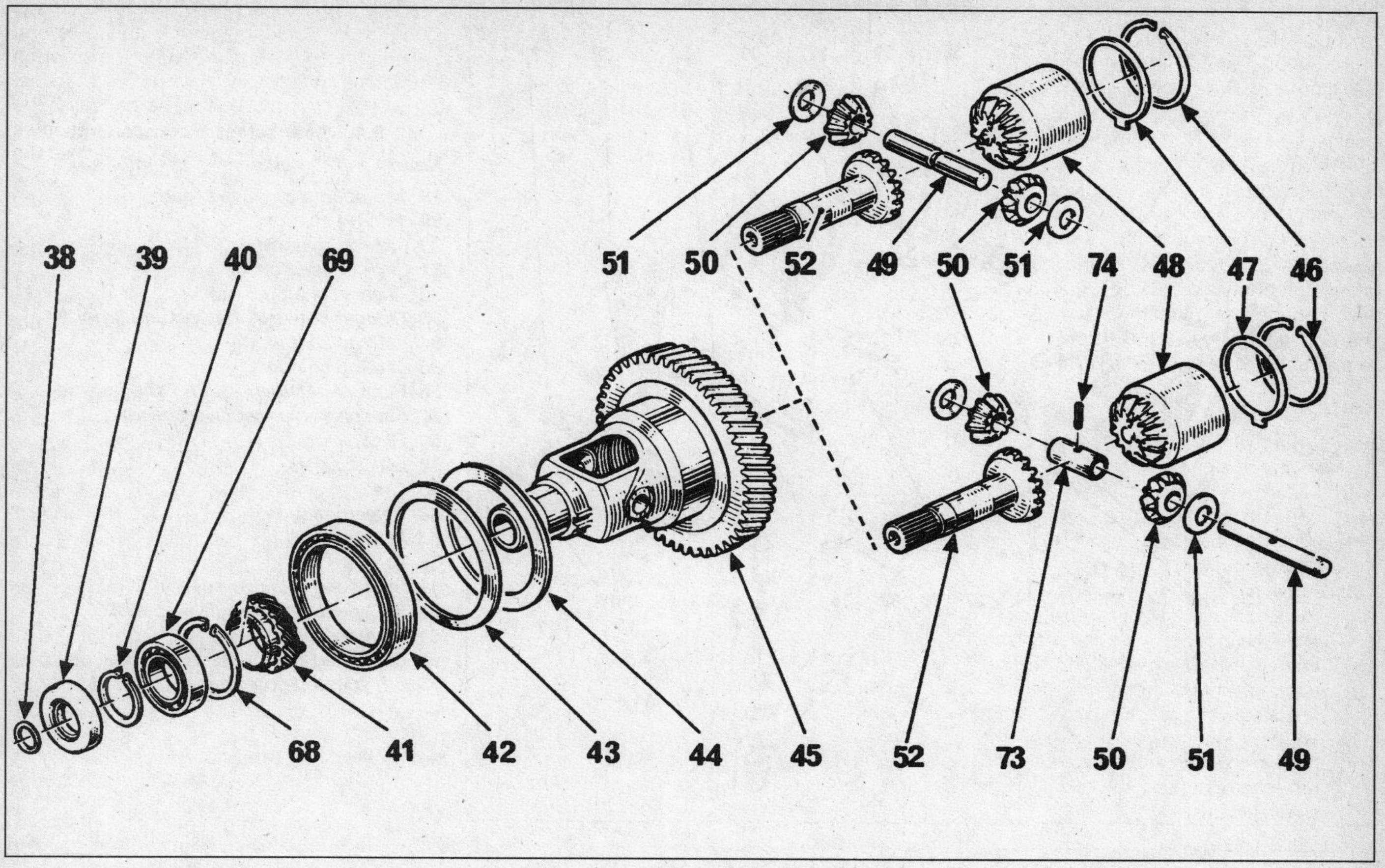

38 39 40 69 51 50 52 49 50 51 74 48 47 46

68 41 42 43 44 45 52 73 50 51 49

9.4b Differential components

38 O-ring
39 Oil seal
40 Circlip
41 Speedometer drivegear
42 Ball race

43 Spacer washer
44 Spring washer
45 Differential housing
46 Circlip
47 Shim

48 Spider-type sun wheel
49 Planet wheel shaft
50 Planet wheels
51 Planet wheel washer
52 Sun wheel with splined shaft

68 Circlip
69 Ball race
73 Sleeve
74 Pin

7A

9.4a Gearbox internal components (5-speed gearbox shown)

1 Roller race
2 Output shaft
3 Roller
4 Spring
5 Circlip
6 2nd speed gear
7 3rd speed gear
8 Synchro-ring
9 3rd/4th gear hub

10 4th speed gear
11 Washer
12 5th speed gear
13 Washer
14 5th speed circlip
15 1st speed gear
16 1st/2nd gear hub
17 Input shaft
18 Splined ring

19 Ball race
20 Circlip
21 Washer
22 5th speed ring
23 Needle race
24 5th speed gear (primary)
25 5th speed spring
26 5th speed gear hub

27 5th speed nut
32 Reverse shaft and gear
63 Oil baffle
64 Thrustwasher
65 5th speed end bolt on output
   shaft
66 Shouldered washer
67 Retaining bolt and washer

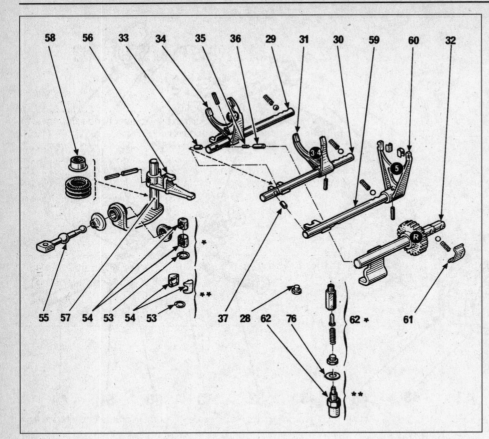

9.4c Gear selector components

*Note: * and ** = alternative assemblies*

28 *Threaded stop (four-speed)*
29 *1st/2nd shift rod*
30 *3rd/4th shift rod*
31 *3rd/4th gear fork*
32 *Reverse shaft*
33 *Plunger between 1st/2nd and 3rd/4th*
34 *1st/2nd shift fork*
35 *1st/2nd plunger*
36 *Plunger between 1st/2nd and reverse*
37 *5th speed plunger (five-speed)*
53 *Circlip*
54 *Link support*
55 *Link*
56 *Selector finger*
57 *Input shaft*
58 *Bush*
59 *5th speed rod (five-speed)*
60 *5th speed shift fork (five-speed)*
61 *Reverse stirrup*
62 *5th speed detent assembly (five-speed)*
76 *5th speed detent shim washer*

Chapter 7 Part B: Automatic transmission

Contents

Degrees of difficulty

Easy, suitable for novice with little experience	Fairly easy, suitable for beginner with some experience	Fairly difficult, suitable for competent DIY mechanic	Difficult, suitable for experienced DIY mechanic 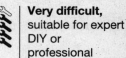	Very difficult, suitable for expert DIY or professional

Specifications

Note: For details of engine identification, refer to *"Buying spare parts and vehicle identification numbers"*.

General

Type:
MB1 and MB3	Three forward speeds and reverse. Final drive differential integral with transmission
AD4	Four forward speeds and reverse. Final drive differential integral with transmission

Application:
1390 cc (E6J and E7J) engines	MB1
1721 cc (F2N) engine	AD4
1721 cc (F3N) engine	MB3 or AD4
1794 cc (F3P) engine	AD4
Transmission fluid type and capacity	See *"Lubricants, fluids and capacities"*

Gear ratios (typical)

MB1 and MB3 transmissions:
1st	2.50:1
2nd	1.50:1
3rd	1.00:1
Reverse	2.00:1

AD4 transmission:
1st	2.71:1
2nd	1.55:1
3rd	1.00:1
4th	0.68:1
Reverse	2.11:1

Final drive

Ratio:
MB1 and MB3 transmissions	3.87:1
AD4 transmission	3.76:1 or 4.12:1
Final drive oil type and capacity	See *"Lubricants, fluids and capacities"*

Torque wrench settings

	Nm	lbf ft
Driveplate-to-torque converter bolts:		
MB1 and MB3 transmissions	25	18
AD4 transmission	15	11
Fluid cooler bolts:		
MB1 and MB3 transmissions	40	30
AD4 transmission	25	18

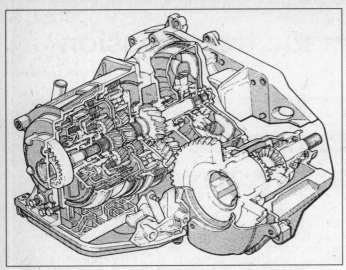

1.1a Cutaway view of the MB1 automatic transmission

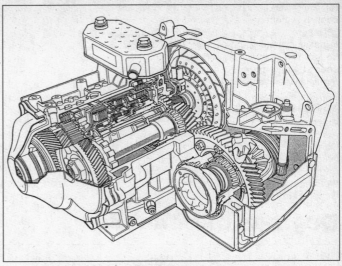

1.1b Cutaway view of the AD4 automatic transmission

1 General information

Automatic transmission is available as an option on 1390 cc (E6J), 1721 cc (F2N and F3N) and 1794 cc (F3P) engines. A three-speed (MB1 or MB3) or 4-speed (AD4) transmission may be fitted, depending on model (see Specifications) **(see illustrations)**.

The transmission consists of a torque converter, an epicyclic geartrain, hydraulically-operated clutches and brakes, and a computer control unit.

The torque converter provides a fluid coupling between engine and transmission, which acts as an automatic clutch, and also provides a degree of torque multiplication when accelerating.

The epicyclic geartrain provides the forward gears or reverse gear, depending on which of its component parts are held stationary or allowed to turn. The components of the geartrain are held or released by brakes and clutches which are activated by a hydraulic control unit. An fluid pump within the transmission provides the necessary hydraulic pressure to operate the brakes and clutches.

Impulses from switches and sensors connected to the transmission throttle and selector linkages are directed to a computer module, which determines the ratio to be selected from the information received **(see illustration)**. The computer activates solenoid valves, which in turn open or close ducts within the hydraulic control unit. This causes the clutches and brakes to hold or release the various components of the geartrain, and provide the correct ratio for the particular engine speed or load. The information from the computer module can be overridden by use of the selector lever, and a particular gear can be held if required, regardless of engine speed.

The automatic transmission fluid is cooled by passing it through a cooler located on the

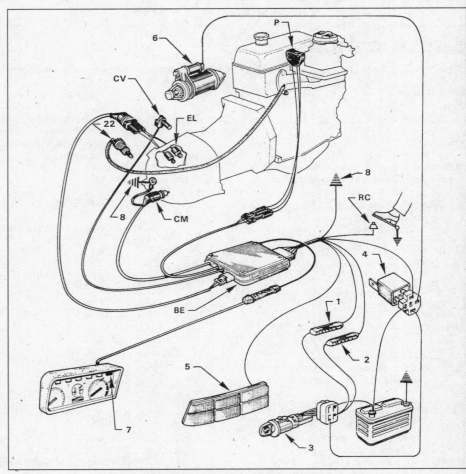

1.5 MB1 automatic transmission electronic control layout

1 Fuse - reversing light (5 amp)	6 Starter	BE Computer module
2 Fuse (1.5 amp)	7 Automatic transmission warning light	CM Multi-function switch
3 Ignition switch	8 Automatic transmission earth	CV Speed sensor
4 Starter relay		EL Solenoid valves
5 Reversing lights	22 Vacuum capsule	RC Kickdown switch
		P Load potentiometer

top of the transmission. Coolant from the cooling system passes through the cooler.

Due to the complexity of the automatic transmission, any repair or overhaul work must be left to a Renault dealer with the necessary special equipment for fault diagnosis and repair. In the event of a fault developing, begin by checking the fluid level (Chapter 1) and the adjustment of the selector mechanism (Section 2 of this Chapter).

Note: *Some of the following Sections dealing with the AD4 transmission require a full-throttle validation setting procedure, using special Renault test equipment. Where this is the case, the work should not be attempted unless the necessary equipment is available, otherwise the transmission will not change gear at the correct speeds. Consult a Renault dealer for more information.*

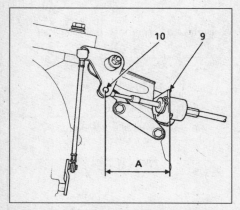

2.5a Selector cable adjustment dimension on the MB1 and MB3 transmissions

A = 131 mm
9 Outer cable location bracket
10 Cable end fitting centre point

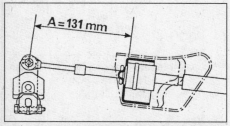

2.5b Selector cable adjustment dimension on the AD4 transmission

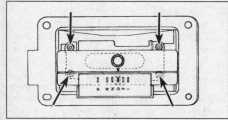

2.6 Control casing on the selector assembly

Adjustment screws arrowed

2 Selector mechanism - adjustment

1 Apply the handbrake, then jack up the front of the car and support it on axle stands (see *"Jacking, towing and wheel changing"*).

2 Move the selector lever inside the car to the "D" position.

3 Working under the car, remove the protective cover from under the selector lever. Disconnect the selector cable end fitting from the lever.

4 Check that the lever on the transmission is in the "D" position, and if necessary move the lever accordingly.

5 Check that the dimension between the cable end fitting and the outer cable location bracket is as shown (see illustrations). If this is not the case, loosen the bracket mounting nut(s) and move the bracket as necessary until the dimension is correct. Tighten the nut(s).

6 Working inside the car, unclip the selector lever surround from the centre console. Loosen the four adjustment screws securing the control casing to the lower assembly (see illustration). Align the selector lever position indicator with the "D" position, then tighten the adjustment screws and refit the selector lever surround.

7 Loosen the outer selector cable cover stop by turning it through a quarter-turn. Check that the cable slides freely.

8 Connect the cable to the bottom of the selector lever, and tighten the cover stop by turning it through a quarter-turn.

9 Refit the protective cover to the selector lever assembly.

10 Check that the selector lever moves freely,

and that the starter motor will only operate with "P" or "N" selected. Also check that the Park function operates correctly. Small adjustments may be made by turning the outer cable cover stop through a quarter-turn, then pulling or pushing the cable as required before tightening the stop again.

11 Lower the car to the ground.

3 Selector mechanism and cable - removal and refitting

Removal

1 Apply the handbrake, then jack up the front of the car and support it on axle stands (see *"Jacking, towing and wheel changing"*).

2 Working inside the car, move the selector lever to position "D".

3 Remove the selector lever by pulling it hard upwards.

4 Working under the car, remove the protective cover from under the selector lever.

5 Disconnect the cable end fittings from the bottom of the selector lever and from the intermediate lever on the transmission (see illustrations).

6 Unscrew the four nuts securing the selector lever assembly to the underbody, then lower the assembly. Disconnect the wiring from the selector lever assembly.

7 Extract the clips, and withdraw the cable from the selector lever assembly and from the transmission.

Refitting

8 Refitting is a reversal of removal, but adjust the cable as described in Section 2.

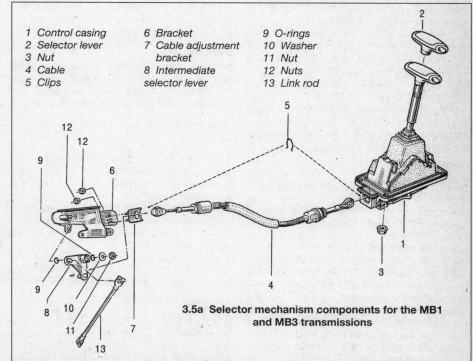

1 Control casing	6 Bracket	9 O-rings
2 Selector lever	7 Cable adjustment	10 Washer
3 Nut	bracket	11 Nut
4 Cable	8 Intermediate	12 Nuts
5 Clips	selector lever	13 Link rod

3.5a Selector mechanism components for the MB1 and MB3 transmissions

7B

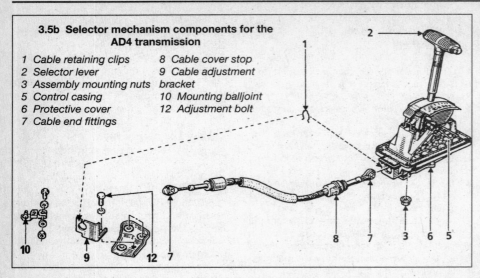

3.5b Selector mechanism components for the AD4 transmission

1 Cable retaining clips
2 Selector lever
3 Assembly mounting nuts
5 Control casing
6 Protective cover
7 Cable end fittings
8 Cable cover stop
9 Cable adjustment bracket
10 Mounting balljoint
12 Adjustment bolt

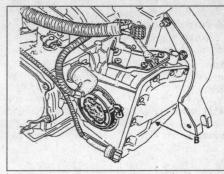

4.6 Remove the final drive housing cover plate (B) - AD4 transmission

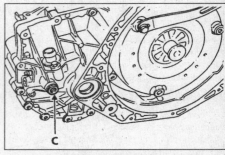

4.8 Final drive filler/level plug (C) - AD4 transmission

4 Speedometer drive - removal and refitting

MB1 and MB3 transmissions
Removal and refitting

1 Refer to Chapter 7A, Section 4.

AD4 transmission
Removal

2 On the AD4 transmission, it is necessary to remove the final drive housing cover plate to permit removal of the speedometer drive pinion.
3 Where necessary, to improve access, remove the air cleaner housing assembly and mounting bracket with reference to Chapter 4.
4 Disconnect the speedometer cable from the transmission by unscrewing the collar.
5 Place a suitable container under the final drive housing, to catch the fluid which will be released as the cover plate is removed.
6 Unscrew the securing bolts, and remove the final drive housing cover plate (see illustration). Recover the gasket.
7 Unscrew the retaining sleeve from the top of the transmission, then unclip the pinion from the sleeve, and withdraw the pinion from inside the final drive housing. Recover the O-ring seal.

Refitting

8 Refitting is a reversal of removal, bearing in mind the following points:
  (a) Examine the condition of the O-ring seal on the retaining sleeve, and renew if necessary.
  (b) Use a new gasket when refitting the final drive housing cover plate.
  (c) On completion, refill the final drive using the correct type of oil (see "Lubricants, fluids and capacities"). Remove the final drive filler/level plug, and fill through the filler/level hole until oil overflows from the hole (see illustration). Refit and tighten the plug, using a new sealing ring on completion.

5 Multi-function switch - removal and refitting

Note: Before working on the AD4 transmission, read the note given in Section 1.

MB1 and MB3 transmissions
Removal

1 On the MB1 and MB3 transmissions, the multi-function switch is originally supplied complete with the computer, and for renewal it is necessary to cut the wiring and obtain a new switch, together with a fitting kit. The switch is located on the left-hand end of the transmission.
2 To remove the switch from the transmission, unscrew the mounting bolt and the earth wire bolt, and pull out the switch.
3 If renewing the switch, cut the wiring and connect the new switch, following the instructions provided with the kit.

Refitting

4 Check that the O-ring seals are in good condition, and renew them if necessary. Insert the switch in the transmission, and tighten the mounting bolt. Insert and tighten the earth bolt.

AD4 transmission
Removal

5 On the AD4 transmission, the multi-function switch is located on the rear of the transmission, above the left-hand driveshaft (see illustration).
6 To remove the switch, first disconnect the switch wiring lead from the computer, located at the left-hand front corner of the engine compartment.
7 Unscrew the mounting bolt and remove the clamp plate. Unscrew the earth wire bolt, then pull the switch out of the transmission.

Refitting

8 Refitting is a reversal of the removal procedure, but before using the car on the road, the computer full-throttle position should be validated using Renault test equipment.

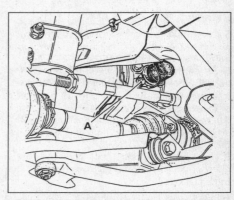

5.5 Multi-function switch location on the AD4 transmission

A Earth wire bolt

6 Kickdown switch - removal and refitting

MB1 and MB3 transmissions

1 The kickdown switch is integral with the load potentiometer. The load potentiometer is mounted on the carburettor or throttle housing (as applicable), and is preset at the factory. No attempt should be made to remove or adjust the switch without the use of the appropriate Renault test equipment. Refer any suspected problems to a Renault dealer.

AD4 transmission

2 The kickdown switch is an integral part of the accelerator cable. Refer to Chapter 4.

7 Vehicle speed sensor - removal and refitting

Note: *Before working on the AD4 transmission, read the note at the end of Section 1.*

MB1 and MB3 transmissions

Removal

1 On the MB1 and MB3 transmissions, the speed sensor is originally supplied complete with the computer. It is necessary to cut the wiring and obtain a new switch, together with a fitting kit.

2 The sensor is located on the front of the transmission. To remove the sensor, unscrew the mounting bolt and remove the clamp, then pull out the sensor.

3 If renewing the sensor, cut the wiring and connect the new sensor, following the instructions provided with the kit.

Refitting

4 Check that the O-ring seal is in good condition, and renew if necessary. Insert the sensor in the transmission, and refit the clamp. Insert and tighten the mounting bolt.

AD4 transmission

Removal

5 On the AD4 transmission, the speed sensor is located on the top left-hand side of the transmission **(see illustration)**.

6 To remove the sensor, first disconnect the appropriate wiring lead from the automatic transmission computer, on the left-hand side of the engine compartment.

7 If necessary, to improve access, remove the air cleaner assembly and mounting bracket, as described in Chapter 4.

8 Unscrew the mounting bolt and remove the clamp plate, then pull the switch out of the transmission.

Refitting

9 Refitting is a reversal of the removal procedure, but before using the car on the road, the computer full-throttle position should be validated using Renault test equipment.

8 Engine speed sensor (AD4 transmission) - removal and refitting

1 Removal and refitting of the engine speed sensor is as described for the engine speed/position sensor in Chapter 5C, but disconnect the appropriate wiring connector from the automatic transmission computer.

2 Note that on certain models, a double sensor is fitted. One sensor supplies data to the fuel injection computer, and the other sensor supplies data to the automatic transmission computer. When removing a

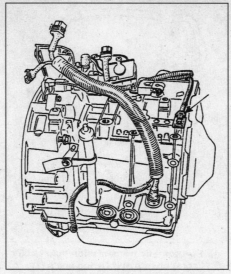

7.5 Speed sensor (arrowed) on the AD4 transmission

double sensor, it will be necessary to disconnect the engine speed/position sensor wiring connector, in addition to disconnecting the appropriate wiring connector from the automatic transmission computer.

9 Load potentiometer - removal and refitting

MB1 and MB3 transmissions

1 The load potentiometer is mounted on the carburettor or throttle housing (as applicable), and is preset at the factory. No attempt should be made to remove or adjust the switch without the use of the appropriate Renault test equipment. Refer any suspected problems to a Renault dealer.

AD4 transmission

2 The load potentiometer is incorporated in the throttle housing. It is preset at the factory, and cannot be repaired or adjusted. No attempt should be made to remove it from the throttle housing.

3 In the event of a fault, the lower half of the throttle housing must be renewed. Refer to Chapter 4 for further information.

10 Computer - removal and refitting

Note: *Before working on the AD4 transmission, read the note at the end of Section 1.*

MB1 and MB3 transmissions

Removal

1 The computer is mounted on the left-hand side of the engine compartment. If the

10.7 AD4 automatic transmission computer location (arrowed)

computer is suspected of having a fault, the car should be taken to a Renault dealer to have the system checked.

2 Note that the computer is originally supplied complete with the vehicle speed sensor and the multi-function switch. In order to remove the computer, first remove the vehicle speed sensor and the multi-function switch, as described in the relevant Sections of this Chapter, ignoring the references to cutting the wiring.

3 Disconnect the battery negative lead, if not already done.

4 Disconnect the remaining wiring connectors from the computer.

5 Release the strap, or remove the securing screws, as applicable, and withdraw the computer from its bracket. Take care not to allow dirt or foreign matter to drop into the wiring sockets.

Refitting

6 Refitting is a reversal of removal, but refit the vehicle speed sensor and the multi-function switch as described in the relevant Sections of this Chapter.

AD4 transmission

Removal

7 The computer is mounted on the left-hand side of the engine compartment **(see illustration)**. If the computer is suspected of having a fault, the car should be taken to a Renault dealer to have the system checked.

8 To remove the computer, first disconnect the battery negative lead, then disconnect the wiring plugs, noting their positions. Release the strap, and withdraw the computer from its bracket. Take care not to allow any dirt or foreign matter to drop into the wiring sockets.

Refitting

9 Refitting is a reversal of the removal procedure, but before using the car on the road, the computer full-throttle position should be validated using Renault test equipment.

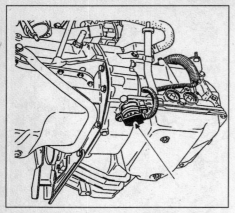

11.1 AD4 automatic transmission line pressure sensor (arrowed)

11 Line pressure sensor (AD4 transmission) - removal and refitting

Note: *Before working on the AD4 transmission, read the note at the end of Section 1.*

Removal

1 The line pressure sensor is mounted on the lower front of the transmission **(see illustration)**.
2 To remove the line pressure sensor, first apply the handbrake, then jack up the front of the car and support on axle stands (see *"Jacking, towing and wheel changing"*).
3 Where applicable, remove the splash guard from under the automatic transmission.
4 Disconnect the appropriate wiring plug from the computer, on the left-hand side of the engine compartment.
5 Unscrew the mounting bolts and withdraw the sensor from the transmission.

Refitting

6 Refitting is a reversal of the removal procedure, but before using the car on the road, the computer full-throttle position should be validated using Renault test equipment.

12 Differential output oil seals - renewal

Right-hand side differential output oil seal (MB1 and MB3 transmissions)

1 Refer to Chapter 7A. The procedure is as described for the manual gearbox.

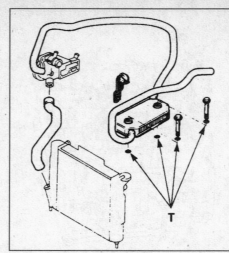

13.1 Automatic transmission fluid cooler components and O-ring seals (T)

Differential output oil seals (AD4 transmission)

2 On the AD4 automatic transmission, access to the differential output oil seals is gained by removing the output flanges. This work should be carried out by a Renault garage, as special tooling is required to overcome the tension of a large spring located behind each of the flanges. Also, it is necessary to validate the full-throttle position using special Renault test equipment.

13 Fluid cooler - removal and refitting

Removal

1 The fluid cooler is located on top of the transmission **(see illustration)**. Where applicable, for improved access, remove the air cleaner and mounting bracket, with reference to Chapter 4.
2 Fit hose clamps, if available, to the coolant hoses each side of the fluid cooler. The alternative method is to drain the cooling system completely, with reference to Chapter 1.
3 Loosen the clips and disconnect the hoses from the fluid cooler.
4 Unscrew the mounting through-bolts, and remove the fluid cooler from the top of the transmission. There will be some loss of fluid, so some clean rags should be placed around the cooler to absorb spillage. Make sure that dirt is prevented from entering the hydraulic system.

5 Remove the through-bolts, and examine the O-ring seals for damage. If necessary, obtain and fit new O-ring seals. Note that O-rings should be fitted to the through-bolts either side of the cooler (ie, top and bottom).

Refitting

6 Refitting is a reversal of the removal procedure, but on completion, check the transmission fluid level with reference to Chapter 1.

14 Automatic transmission - removal and refitting

Note: *Before working on the AD4 transmission, read the note at the end of Section 1.*

The automatic transmission must be removed together with the engine, and then separated on the bench. Refer to Chapter 2D for the removal and refitting procedures. On the AD4 transmission, before using the vehicle on the road, the computer full-throttle position should be validated by a Renault dealer.

15 Automatic transmission overhaul - general information

Note: *Check the transmission fluid level and the selector mechanism adjustment before assuming that a fault exists with the transmission itself.*

In the event of a transmission fault occurring, it is first necessary to determine whether it is of an electrical, mechanical or hydraulic nature, and to do this, special test equipment is required. It is therefore essential to have the work carried out by a Renault dealer if a transmission fault is suspected, or if the transmission warning light on the instrument panel illuminates continuously.

If the warning light flashes when the engine is cold and the external temperature is less than -20°C, the automatic transmission fluid temperature is too low. Continue driving until the light goes out. If it flashes under any other circumstances, the fluid temperature is too high; drive at a lower speed until the light goes out.

Do not remove the transmission from the car for possible repair before professional fault diagnosis has been carried out, since most tests require the transmission to be in the vehicle.

Chapter 8 Driveshafts

Contents

Degrees of difficulty

Easy, suitable for novice with little experience

Fairly easy, suitable for beginner with some experience

Fairly difficult, suitable for competent DIY mechanic

Difficult, suitable for experienced DIY mechanic

Very difficult, suitable for expert DIY or professional

Specifications

General

Driveshaft type . . . . Equal-length solid steel shafts, splined to inner and outer constant velocity joints. Vibration damper fitted on some shafts

Lubricant type/specification . . . . Special grease supplied in sachets with gaiter kits - joints are otherwise pre-packed with grease, and sealed

Torque wrench settings

	Nm	lbf ft
Driveshaft nut*	250	185
Left-hand driveshaft gaiter retaining plate bolts - manual gearbox, and MB1/MB3 automatic transmissions	25	18
Driveshaft-to-transmission flange bolts - AD4 automatic transmission	35	26

*Note: A new nut must be used when refitting.

1 General information

Drive is transmitted from the differential to the front wheels by means of two, equal-length, open driveshafts.

Both driveshafts are fitted with a constant velocity (CV) joint at their outer ends, which may be of the spider-and-yoke type or of the ball-and-cage type. Each joint has an outer member, which is splined at its outer end to accept the wheel hub, and is threaded so that it can be fastened to the hub by a large nut. The joint contains either a spring-loaded plunger or six balls within a cage, which engage with the inner member. The complete assembly is protected by a flexible gaiter secured to the driveshaft and joint outer member **(see illustrations)**.

On vehicles equipped with a manual gearbox or with the three-speed (MB1 or MB3) automatic transmission unit, a different inner constant velocity joint arrangement is fitted to

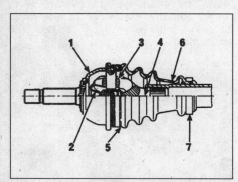

1.2a **Sectional view of the spider-and-yoke type outer constant velocity joint**

1 Outer member
2 Thrust plunger
3 Driveshaft spider
4 Driveshaft
5 Outer retaining clip
6 Gaiter
7 Inner retaining clip

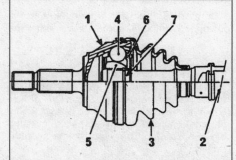

1.2b **Sectional view of the ball-and-cage type outer constant velocity joint**

1 Outer member
2 Driveshaft
3 Gaiter
4 Ball
5 Inner member
6 Ball cage
7 Circlip

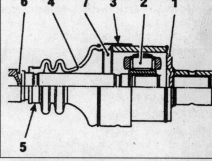

1.3 **Sectional view of a right-hand inner constant velocity joint - RC490 type**

1 Outer member
2 Tripod joint
3 Metal cover
4 Gaiter
5 Inner retaining clip
6 Driveshaft
7 Metal insert

8

each driveshaft. On the right-hand side, the driveshaft is splined to engage with a tripod joint, containing needle roller bearings and cups. The tripod joint is free to slide within the yoke of the joint outer member, which is splined and retained by a roll pin to the differential sunwheel stub shaft. As on the outer joints, a flexible gaiter secured to the driveshaft and outer member protects the complete assembly **(see illustration)**. On the left-hand side, the driveshaft also engages with a tripod joint, but the yoke in which the tripod joint is free to slide is an integral part of the differential sunwheel. On this side, the gaiter is secured to the transmission casing with a retaining plate, and to a ball-bearing on the driveshaft with a retaining clip. The bearing allows the driveshaft to turn within the gaiter, which does not revolve.

On vehicles equipped with the four-speed (AD4) automatic transmission, both the left- and right-hand inner joints are the same. Each joint is secured to the transmission drive flange by six retaining bolts. As with the outer joint, the complete assembly is protected by a flexible gaiter which is secured to the driveshaft and outer member.

2 Driveshaft - removal and refitting

Note: *A new driveshaft nut must be used on refitting. If a new driveshaft is fitted on models with ABS, the ABS wheel sensor reluctor ring must be removed from the old driveshaft, and fitted to the new driveshaft as described in Chapter 9.*

Removal

1 Apply the handbrake, then jack up the front of the vehicle and support it on axle stands. Remove the appropriate front roadwheel.
2 Refit at least two roadwheel bolts to the front hub, and tighten them securely. Have an assistant firmly depress the brake pedal to prevent the front hub from rotating. Using a socket and a long extension bar, slacken and remove the driveshaft retaining nut and washer. This nut is extremely tight **(see illustration)**.

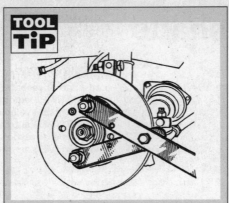

TOOL TiP

To secure the hub, a tool can be fabricated from two lengths of steel strip (one long, one short) and a nut and bolt; the nut and bolt form the pivot of a forked tool. Bolt the tool to the hub using two wheel bolts, and hold the tool to prevent the hub from rotating as the driveshaft retaining nut is undone. Discard the driveshaft nut; a new one should be used on refitting.

3 Unscrew the two bolts securing the brake caliper assembly to the stub axle carrier, and slide the caliper assembly off the disc. Using a piece of wire or string, tie the caliper to the front suspension coil spring, to avoid placing any strain on the hydraulic brake hose.
4 Slacken and remove the nut securing the steering gear track rod end balljoint to the stub axle carrier. Release the balljoint tapered shank using a universal balljoint separator.
5 Slacken and remove the two nuts and washers from the bolts securing the stub axle carrier to the suspension strut, noting that the nuts are positioned on the rear side of the strut **(see illustration)**. Withdraw the upper bolt, but leave the lower bolt in position at this stage. Now proceed as described under the relevant sub-heading.

Left-hand driveshaft - models with manual gearbox, or MB1/MB3 automatic transmissions

6 On models fitted with a manual gearbox, position a suitable container beneath the

2.2 Removing the driveshaft retaining nut and washer

gearbox drain plug, then remove the drain plug and allow the oil to drain from the gearbox. Once the oil has drained, wipe the threads of the drain plug clean, refit it to the gearbox and tighten it securely.
7 On models with automatic transmission, drain the transmission fluid as described in Chapter 1.
8 Slacken and remove the three bolts securing the rubber gaiter retaining plate to the side of the gearbox/transmission **(see illustration)**.
9 Pull the top of the stub axle carrier outwards until the driveshaft tripod joint is released from its yoke; be prepared for some oil spillage as the joint is withdrawn **(see illustration)**. Be careful that the rollers on the end of the tripod do not fall off.
10 Remove the lower bolt securing the stub axle carrier to the suspension strut. Taking care not to damage the driveshaft gaiters, release the outer constant velocity joint from the hub, and remove the driveshaft. Note that locking fluid is applied to the outer constant velocity joint splines during assembly, so it is likely that they will be a tight fit in the hub splines. Use a hammer and a soft metal drift to tap the joint out of the hub, or use an extractor to push the driveshaft out of the hub **(see illustration)**.

2.5 Unscrewing a stub axle carrier-to-suspension strut nut

2.8 Remove the left-hand gaiter retaining plate bolts . . .

2.9 . . . and release the tripod joint from the transmission

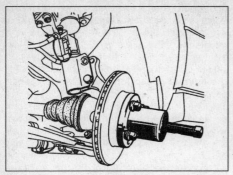

2.10 Using an extractor to press the driveshaft out of the front hub

2.11 Drive out the roll pins with a suitable pin punch

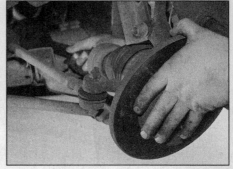

2.12 Pulling out the right-hand driveshaft

Right-hand driveshaft - models with manual gearbox, or MB1/MB3 automatic transmissions

Note: *New roll pins must be used on refitting.*

11 Rotate the driveshaft until the double roll pin, securing the inner constant velocity joint to the sun wheel shaft, is visible. Using a hammer and a 5 mm diameter pin punch, drive out the double roll pin (see illustration). New roll pins must be used on refitting.

12 Pull the top of the stub axle carrier outwards until the inner constant velocity joint splines are released from the sunwheel shaft (see illustration). Remove the O-ring from the sunwheel shaft splines.

13 Remove the driveshaft as described in paragraph 10.

Both driveshafts - models with AD4 automatic transmission

14 Slacken and remove the six bolts and washers securing the driveshaft inner constant velocity joint to the transmission drive flange, rotating the shaft as necessary to gain access to the bolts.

15 Pull the top of the stub axle carrier outwards, and disengage the inner constant velocity joint from the drive flange.

16 Remove the driveshaft as described in paragraph 10.

Refitting

17 All new driveshafts supplied by Renault are equipped with cardboard or plastic

protectors, to prevent damage to the gaiters. Even the slightest knock to the gaiter can puncture it, allowing the entry of water or dirt at a later date, which may lead to the premature failure of the joint. If the original driveshaft is being refitted, it is worthwhile making up some cardboard protectors as a precaution. They can be held in position with elastic bands. The protectors should be left on the driveshafts until the end of the refitting procedure.

Left-hand driveshaft - models with manual gearbox, or MB1/MB3 automatic transmissions

18 Wipe clean the side of the gearbox/transmission. Insert the tripod joint into the sunwheel yoke, keeping the driveshaft horizontal as far as possible.

19 Align the gaiter retaining plate with its bolt holes. Refit the retaining bolts, and tighten them to the specified torque. Ensure that the gaiter is not twisted.

20 Check that the splines on the driveshaft outer constant velocity joint and hub are clean and dry. Apply a coat of locking fluid to the splines.

21 Move the top of the stub axle carrier inwards, at the same time engaging the driveshaft with the hub.

22 Slide the hub fully onto the driveshaft splines, then insert the two suspension strut mounting bolts from the front side of the strut. Refit the washers and nuts to the rear of the

bolts, and tighten them to the specified torque (Chapter 10 Specifications).

23 Slide on the washer, then fit the new driveshaft retaining nut, tightening it by hand only at this stage.

24 Reconnect the steering track rod balljoint to the stub axle carrier, and tighten its retaining nut to the specified torque (Chapter 10 Specifications).

25 Slide the brake caliper assembly into position over the brake disc. Refit the caliper mounting bolts, having first applied a few drops of locking fluid to their threads, and tighten them to the specified torque (Chapter 9 Specifications).

26 Using the method employed during removal to prevent the hub from rotating, tighten a *new* driveshaft retaining nut to the specified torque (see illustration). Check that the hub rotates freely, then remove the protectors from the driveshaft, taking great care not to damage the flexible gaiters.

27 Refit the roadwheel. Lower the car to the ground, and tighten the roadwheel bolts to the specified torque.

28 Refill the gearbox or automatic transmission with oil or fluid; refer to Chapter 1 for details.

Right-hand driveshaft - models with manual gearbox, or MB1/MB3 automatic transmissions

29 Ensure that the inner constant velocity joint and sunwheel shaft splines are clean and

8

2.26 Tighten the driveshaft retaining nut to the specified torque

2.29 Fit the new O-ring onto the sunwheel shaft . . .

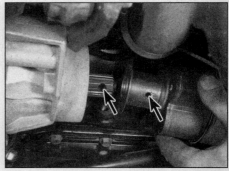

2.30 . . . and engage the driveshaft, ensuring that the roll pin holes (arrowed) are correctly aligned

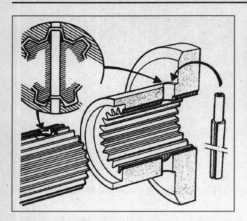

2.31a Right-hand driveshaft inner constant velocity joint roll pin arrangement - models with manual gearbox, or MB1/MB3 automatic transmissions

dry. Apply a smear of molybdenum disulphide grease to the splines. Fit a new O-ring over the end of the sunwheel shaft, and slide the O-ring along the shaft until it abuts the transmission oil seal **(see illustration)**.

30 Engage the driveshaft splines with those of the sunwheel shaft, making sure that the roll pin holes are in alignment **(see illustration)**. Slide the driveshaft onto the sunwheel shaft until the roll pin holes are aligned.

31 Drive in new roll pins with their slots 90° apart, then seal the ends of the pins with sealing compound (Renault CAF 4/60 THIXO paste or equivalent) **(see illustrations)**.

32 Carry out the procedures described in paragraphs 20 to 27.

Both driveshafts - models with AD4 automatic transmission

33 Ensure the inner constant velocity joint and transmission drive flange mating surfaces are clean and dry. Pack the drive flange recess with Molykote BR2 grease (available from your Renault dealer).

34 Engage the driveshaft inner constant velocity joint with the transmission drive flange, then refit the six retaining bolts. Securely tighten the retaining bolts, and wipe off any surplus grease.

35 Carry out the procedures described in paragraphs 20 to 27.

3 Outer constant velocity joint gaiter (models with manual gearbox, or MB1/MB3 automatic transmissions) - renewal

1 Remove the driveshaft as described in Section 2.

2 Cut through the gaiter retaining clip(s) or release the retaining spring and inner collar (as applicable), then slide the gaiter down the shaft to expose the outer constant velocity joint.

3 Scoop out as much grease as possible from the joint, and determine which type of

2.31b Seal the ends of the roll pins with a suitable sealing compound

constant velocity joint is fitted. Proceed as described under the relevant sub-heading.

Ball-and-cage type joint

4 Using circlip pliers, expand the joint internal circlip. At the same time, tap the exposed face of the ball hub with a mallet to separate the joint from the driveshaft. Slide off the gaiter and rubber collar.

5 With the constant velocity joint removed from the driveshaft, clean the joint using paraffin, or a suitable solvent, and dry it thoroughly. Carry out a visual inspection of the joint.

6 Move the inner splined driving member from side to side, to expose each ball in turn at the top of its track. Examine the balls for cracks, flat spots, or signs of surface pitting.

7 Inspect the ball tracks on the inner and outer members. If the tracks have widened, the balls will no longer be a tight fit. At the same time, check the ball cage windows for wear or cracking between the windows.

8 If on inspection any of the constant velocity joint components are found to be worn or damaged, it will be necessary to renew the complete driveshaft assembly, since no components are available separately. If the joint is in satisfactory condition, obtain a repair kit from your Renault dealer consisting of a new gaiter, rubber collar, retaining spring, and the correct type and quantity of grease.

9 Tape over the splines on the end of the

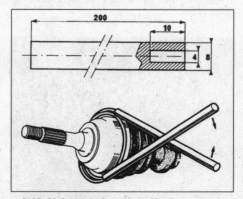

3.12 Using two lengths of hollow metal tubing to install the gaiter retaining spring. Tube dimensions in mm

driveshaft, then slide the rubber collar and gaiter onto the shaft. Locate the inner end of the gaiter on the driveshaft, and secure it in position with the rubber collar.

10 Remove the tape, then slide the constant velocity joint coupling onto the driveshaft until the internal circlip locates in the driveshaft groove.

11 Check that the circlip holds the joint securely on the driveshaft, then pack the joint with the grease supplied. Work the grease well into the ball tracks, and fill the gaiter with any excess.

12 Locate the outer lip of the gaiter in the groove on the joint outer member. With the coupling aligned with the driveshaft, lift the lip of the gaiter to equalise the air pressure. Secure the gaiter in position with the large retaining spring, using two lengths of hollow metal tubing to ease the spring into position **(see illustration)**.

13 Check that the constant velocity joint moves freely in all directions, then refit the driveshaft to the vehicle as described in Section 2.

Spider-and-yoke type joint

14 Remove the inner constant velocity joint, bearing and gaiter (as applicable), as described in Section 4 or 5 of this Chapter.

15 Where a vibration damper is fitted, clearly mark the position of the damper on the driveshaft, then use a puller or press to remove it from the inner end of the driveshaft, noting which way around it is fitted **(see illustration)**. Ensure that the legs of the puller or support plate rest only on the damper inner rubber bush, otherwise the damper will distort and break away from the outer metal housing as it is removed.

16 Slide the outer constant velocity joint gaiter off the inner end of the driveshaft.

17 Clean the outer constant velocity joint using paraffin or a suitable solvent, and dry it thoroughly. Carry out a visual inspection of the joint.

18 Check the driveshaft spider and outer member yoke for signs of wear, pitting or scuffing on their bearing surfaces. Also check that the outer member pivots smoothly and easily, with no traces of roughness.

19 If inspection reveals signs of wear or

3.15 Removing the vibration damper from the driveshaft

3.19 Renault driveshaft gaiter repair kit

3.21 Pack the joint with the grease supplied in the repair kit . . .

3.22 . . . then slide the gaiter into position over the joint

damage, it will be necessary to renew the driveshaft complete, since no components are available separately. If the joint components are in satisfactory condition, obtain a repair kit consisting of a new gaiter, retaining clips, and the correct type and quantity of grease **(see illustration)**.

20 Tape over the splines on the inner end of the driveshaft, then carefully slide the outer gaiter onto the shaft.

21 Pack the joint with the grease supplied in the repair kit. Work the grease well into the joint, and fill the gaiter with any excess **(see illustration)**.

22 Ease the gaiter over the joint, and ensure that the gaiter lips are correctly located in the grooves on the driveshaft and on the joint **(see**

3.23a Fit the large retaining clip . . .

3.23b . . . and the small retaining clip. Note use of pincers to secure the clip

illustration). With the coupling aligned with the driveshaft, lift the lip of the gaiter to equalise the air pressure.

23 Fit the large metal retaining clip to the gaiter. Remove any slack in the gaiter retaining clip by carefully compressing the raised section of the clip. In the absence of the special tool, a pair of pincers may be used. Secure the small retaining clip using the same procedure **(see illustrations)**. Check that the constant velocity joint moves freely in all directions before proceeding further.

24 To refit the vibration damper (when applicable), lubricate the driveshaft with a solution of soapy water. Press or drive the vibration damper along the shaft, using a tubular spacer which bears only on the damper inner bush, until it is aligned with the mark made prior to removal.

25 Refit the inner constant velocity joint components as described in Section 4 or 5 (as applicable), then refit the driveshaft to the vehicle as described in Section 2.

4 Right-hand driveshaft inner gaiter (models with manual gearbox, or MB1/MB3 automatic transmissions) - renewal

1 Remove the driveshaft as described in Section 2.

4.4 Bend up the anti-separation tangs with pliers to release the joint outer member (GI62 type)

2 On these models, two different types of inner constant velocity joint are used on the right-hand driveshaft: type GI62 and type RC490. The joints can be identified by the shape of their outer members. The GI62 joint has a smooth, circular outer member; the RC490 joint has a recessed outer member which appears clover-shaped when viewed end-on. Identify the type of joint fitted, then proceed as described under the relevant sub-heading.

GI62-type joint

3 Release the large retaining spring and the inner retaining collar, then slide the gaiter down the shaft to expose the joint.

4 Using pliers, carefully bend up the anti-separation plate tangs at their corners **(see illustration)**. Slide the outer member off the tripod joint. Be prepared to hold the rollers in place, otherwise they may fall off the tripod ends as the outer member is withdrawn. If necessary, secure the rollers in place using tape after removal of the outer member. The rollers are matched to the tripod joint stems, and it is important that they are not interchanged.

5 Using circlip pliers, extract the circlip securing the tripod joint to the driveshaft **(see illustration)**. Note that on some models, the joint may be staked in position; if so, relieve the staking using a file. Mark the position of the tripod in relation to the driveshaft, using a dab of paint or a punch.

4.5 Remove the circlip . . .

8

4.6 . . . and withdraw the tripod joint from the driveshaft end

6 The tripod joint can now be removed **(see illustration)**. If it is tight, draw the joint off the driveshaft end using a puller. Ensure that the legs of the puller are located behind the joint inner member, and do not contact the joint rollers. Alternatively, support the inner member of the tripod joint, and press the shaft out using a hydraulic press, again ensuring that no load is applied to the joint rollers.

7 With the tripod joint removed, slide the gaiter and inner retaining collar off the end of the driveshaft.

8 Wipe clean the joint components, taking care not to remove the alignment marks made on dismantling. *Do not* use paraffin or other solvents to clean this type of joint.

9 Examine the tripod joint, rollers and outer member for any signs of scoring or wear. Check that the rollers move smoothly on the tripod stems. If wear is evident, the tripod joint and roller assembly can be renewed, but it is not possible to obtain a replacement outer member. Obtain a new gaiter, retaining spring/collar and a quantity of the special lubricating grease. These parts are available in the form of a repair kit from your Renault dealer.

10 Tape over the splines on the end of the driveshaft, then carefully slide the inner retaining collar and gaiter onto the shaft.

11 Remove the tape, then, aligning the marks made on dismantling, engage the tripod joint with the driveshaft splines. Use a hammer and soft metal drift to tap the joint onto the shaft, taking great care not to damage the driveshaft splines or joint rollers. Alternatively, support the driveshaft, and press the joint into position using a hydraulic press and suitable tubular spacer which bears only on the joint inner member.

12 Secure the tripod joint in position with the circlip, ensuring that it is correctly located in the driveshaft groove. Where no circlip is fitted, secure the joint in position by staking the end of the driveshaft in three places, at intervals of 120°, using a hammer and punch.

13 Evenly distribute the grease contained in the repair kit around the tripod joint and inside the outer member. Pack the gaiter with the remainder of the grease.

14 Slide the outer member into position over the tripod joint.

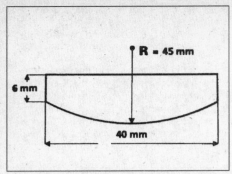

4.15 Support plate dimensions for re-forming the anti-separation plate tangs (GI62-type joint)

15 Using a piece of 2.5 mm thick steel or similar material, make up a support plate to the dimensions shown **(see illustration)**.

16 Position the support plate under each anti-separation plate tang in the outer member in turn, and tap the tang down onto the support plate. Remove the plate when all the tangs have been returned to their original shape.

17 Slide the gaiter up the driveshaft. Locate the gaiter in the grooves on the driveshaft and outer member.

18 Slide the inner retaining collar into place over the inner end of the gaiter.

19 Using a blunt rod, carefully lift the outer lip of the gaiter, to equalise the air pressure. With the rod in position, compress the joint until the dimension from the inner end of the gaiter to the flat end face of the outer member is as shown **(see illustration)**. Hold the outer member in this position, and withdraw the rod.

20 Slip the new retaining spring into place, to secure the outer lip of the gaiter to the outer member. Take care to ensure that the retaining spring is not overstretched during the fitting process.

21 Check that the constant velocity joint moves freely in all directions, then refit the driveshaft as described in Section 2.

RC490-type joint

22 Using a pair of grips, bend up the metal joint cover at the points where it has been staked into the outer member recesses.

23 Using a pair of snips, cut the gaiter inner retaining clip.

24 Using a soft metal drift, tap the metal joint cover off the outer member **(see illustration)**. Slide the outer member off the end of the tripod joint. Be prepared to hold the rollers in place, otherwise they may fall off the tripod ends as the outer member is withdrawn. If necessary, secure the rollers in place using tape after removal of the outer member. The rollers are matched to the tripod joint stems, and it is important that they are not interchanged.

25 Remove the tripod joint and gaiter assembly, and examine the joint components for wear, using the information given in paragraphs 6 to 9 of this Section. Make alignment marks between the spider and the

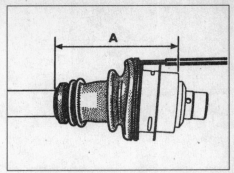

4.19 Fitting dimension for the right-hand driveshaft inner constant velocity joint gaiter - GI62-type joint

A = 153 ± 1 mm

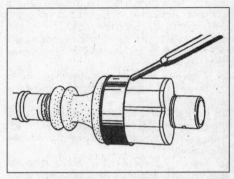

4.24 Removing the metal cover from the right-hand driveshaft inner constant velocity joint - RC490 type

shaft for use when refitting. Obtain a repair kit consisting of a gaiter, retaining clip, metal insert and joint cover, and the correct type and amount of special grease.

26 Fit the metal insert into the inside of the gaiter, then locate the gaiter assembly inside the metal joint cover.

27 Tape over the driveshaft splines, and slide the gaiter and joint cover assembly onto the driveshaft.

28 Refit the tripod joint as described in paragraphs 11 and 12.

29 Evenly distribute the special grease contained in the repair kit around the tripod joint and inside the outer member. Pack the gaiter with the remainder of the grease.

30 Slide the outer member into position over the tripod joint.

31 Slide the metal joint cover onto the outer member until it is flush with the outer member guide panel. Secure the joint cover in position by staking it into the recesses in the outer member, using a hammer and a round-ended punch.

32 Using a blunt rod, carefully lift the inner lip of the gaiter, to equalise the air pressure. With the rod in position, compress the joint until the dimension from the inner end of the gaiter to the flat end face of the outer member is as shown **(see illustration)**. Hold the outer member in this position and withdraw the rod.

33 Fit the small retaining clip to the inner end

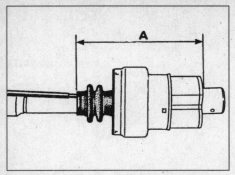

4.32 Fitting dimension for the right-hand driveshaft inner constant velocity joint gaiter - RC490-type joint

A = 156 ± 1 mm

of the gaiter. Remove any slack in the gaiter retaining clip by carefully compressing the raised section of the clip. In the absence of the special tool, a pair of pincers may be used.

34 Check that the constant velocity joint moves freely in all directions, then refit the driveshaft as described in Section 2.

5 Left-hand driveshaft inner gaiter (models with manual gearbox, or MB1/MB3 automatic transmissions) - renewal

1 Remove the driveshaft as described in Section 2.
2 Using circlip pliers, extract the circlip securing the tripod joint to the driveshaft. Note that on some models, the joint may be staked in position; if so, relieve the stakings using a file. Using a dab of paint or a hammer and punch, mark the position of the tripod joint in relation to the driveshaft, to use as a guide to refitting.
3 The tripod joint can now be removed. If it is tight, draw the joint off the driveshaft end using a puller. Ensure that the legs of the puller are located behind the joint inner member, and do not contact the joint rollers. Alternatively, support the inner member of the tripod joint, and press the shaft out of the joint, again ensuring that no load is applied to the joint rollers.
4 The gaiter and bearing assembly is removed in the same way, either by drawing the bearing off the driveshaft, or by pressing the driveshaft out of the bearing. Remove the retaining plate, noting which way round it is fitted.
5 Obtain a new gaiter, which is supplied complete with the small bearing.
6 Owing to the lip-type seal used in the bearing, the bearing and gaiter must be pressed into position. If a hammer and tubular drift are used to drive the assembly onto the driveshaft, there is a risk of distorting the seal.
7 Refit the retaining plate to the driveshaft,

ensuring that it is fitted the correct way around.
8 Support the driveshaft, and press the gaiter bearing onto the shaft, using a tubular spacer which bears only on the bearing inner race. Position the bearing so that the distance from the end of the driveshaft to the inner face of the bearing is as shown **(see illustrations)**.
9 Align the marks made on dismantling, and engage the tripod joint with the driveshaft splines. Use a hammer and soft metal drift to tap the joint onto the shaft, taking care not to damage the driveshaft splines or joint rollers. Alternatively, support the driveshaft, and press the joint into position using a tubular spacer which bears only on the joint inner member.
10 Secure the tripod joint in position with the circlip, ensuring that it is correctly located in the driveshaft groove. Where no circlip is fitted, secure the joint in position by staking the end of the driveshaft in three places, at intervals of 120°, using a hammer and punch.
11 Refit the driveshaft to the vehicle as described in Section 2.

6 Constant velocity joint gaiter renewal (models with AD4 automatic transmission) - general information

1 At the time of writing, no information on driveshaft dismantling was available for these models. If gaiter renewal is necessary, the driveshaft should be removed from the vehicle, as described in Section 2, and taken to a Renault dealer.

7 Driveshaft overhaul - general information

1 If any of the checks described in Chapter 1 reveal wear in a driveshaft joint, first remove the roadwheel trim or centre cap (as appropriate) and check that the driveshaft retaining nut is still correctly tightened; if in doubt, use a torque wrench to check it. Refit the centre cap or trim, and repeat the check on the other driveshaft.
2 Road-test the vehicle, and listen for a metallic clicking from the front as the vehicle is driven slowly in a circle on full-lock. If a clicking noise is heard, this indicates wear in the outer constant velocity joint.
3 If vibration, consistent with road speed, is felt through the vehicle when accelerating, there is a possibility of wear in the inner constant velocity joints.
4 Constant velocity joints can be dismantled and inspected for wear as described in Sections 3, 4 and 5.
5 On models with a manual gearbox, or MB1/MB3 automatic transmissions, wear in the outer constant velocity joint can only be rectified by renewing the driveshaft. This is

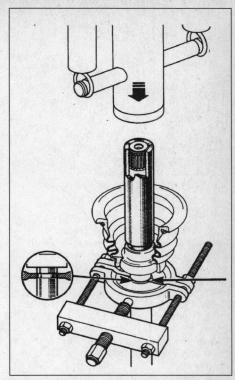

5.8a Pressing the inner bearing/gaiter onto the end of the left-hand driveshaft

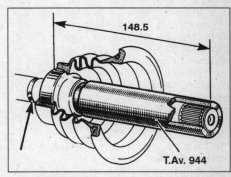

148.5

T.Av. 944

5.8b Fitting dimension (in mm) for the left-hand driveshaft inner bearing/gaiter

T.Av.944 = Renault special tool

necessary since no outer joint components are available separately. For the inner joint, the tripod joint and roller assembly is available separately, but wear in any of the other components will also necessitate driveshaft renewal.
6 On models equipped with the AD4 automatic transmission, wear in either constant velocity joint will necessitate driveshaft renewal; no components for either joint are available separately.
7 On models with ABS, the reluctor ring should be removed from the old driveshaft and fitted to the new one. See Chapter 9.

8

Notes

Chapter 9 Braking system

Contents

Degrees of difficulty

Easy, suitable for novice with little experience	**Fairly easy,** suitable for beginner with some experience	**Fairly difficult,** suitable for competent DIY mechanic	**Difficult,** suitable for experienced DIY mechanic	**Very difficult,** suitable for expert DIY or professional

Specifications

General

System type:

Conventional system	Dual hydraulic circuit, split diagonally, with servo assistance
Bendix ABS	Dual hydraulic circuit, split diagonally, with electric high-pressure pump
Bosch ABS	Dual hydraulic circuit, split diagonally, with servo assistance
Front brakes	Disc, with single-piston sliding caliper
Rear brakes	Self-adjusting drum or disc, according to model
Handbrake	Cable-operated, to rear wheels

Front brakes

Disc diameter:

All except 16-valve models	238.0 mm	
16-valve models	259.0 mm	
Disc thickness:	**New**	**Minimum**
1237 cc, 1390 cc and 1397 cc engine models (except models with ABS)	12.0 mm	10.5 mm
1721 cc and 1794 cc engine models	20.0 mm	18.0 mm
All models with ABS except 1764 cc (16-valve) engine models	20.0 mm	18.0 mm
1764 cc (16-valve) engine models	20.7 mm	17.7 mm
Maximum disc run-out	0.07 mm	
	New	**Minimum**
Brake pad thickness (friction material and backing plate)	18.0 mm	6.0 mm

Rear drum brakes

Drum diameter:

New	180.25 mm	
Maximum diameter after machining	181.25 mm	
	New	**Minimum**
Brake shoe thickness (friction material and shoe)	6.5 mm	2.5 mm

Rear disc brakes

Disc diameter	238.0 mm	
Disc thickness:	**New**	**Minimum**
All models except 1764 cc (16-valve) engine models	12.0 mm	10.5 mm
1764 cc engine (16-valve) models	8.0 mm	7.0 mm
Maximum disc run-out	0.07 mm	
	New	**Minimum**
Brake pad minimum thickness (friction material and backing plate) . . .	11.0 mm	5.0 mm

Anti-lock braking system (ABS)

Wheel sensor-to-reluctor ring clearance:	**Front**	**Rear**
Bendix ABS	0.15 to 1.15 mm	0.20 to 0.81 mm
Bosch ABS	0.21 to 1.03 mm	0.40 to 1.50 mm
Wheel sensor electrical resistance:		
Bendix ABS	No information available at time of writing	
Bosch ABS	1130 ohms (approximately)	

Torque wrench settings

	Nm	lbf ft
Vacuum servo-to-bulkhead nuts	20	15
Brake fluid pipe and hose unions	13	10
Master cylinder-to-servo nuts	13	10
Bendix front brake caliper mounting bolts	100	74
Girling front brake caliper:		
Guide pin bolts*	35	26
Mounting bracket-to-stub axle carrier bolts	100	74
Front brake disc securing screws	25	18
Rear hub nut*	160	118
Rear drum brake backplate	45	33
Fluid bleed screw	7	5
ABS wheel sensor bolts	9	7

*Note: Use a new nut/bolts.

1 General information

The braking system is of the servo-assisted, dual-circuit hydraulic type. The arrangement of the hydraulic system is such that each circuit operates one front and one rear brake, from a tandem master cylinder. Under normal circumstances, both circuits operate in unison. However, in the event of hydraulic failure in one circuit, full braking force will still be available at two wheels **(see illustration)**.

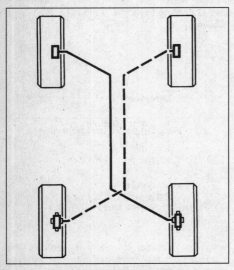

1.1 Diagonally-split brake hydraulic system (rear drum brake model shown)

16-valve models are equipped with disc brakes all round as standard, whereas all other models without an anti-lock braking system (ABS) are fitted with front disc brakes and rear drum brakes. An anti-lock braking system (ABS) is offered as an option on certain models; on models with ABS, disc brakes are fitted both front and rear. (Refer to Section 22 for further information on ABS operation.)

The front disc brakes are actuated by single-piston sliding type calipers, which ensure that equal pressure is applied to each disc pad.

On models with rear drum brakes, the rear brakes incorporate leading and trailing shoes, which are actuated by twin-piston wheel cylinders (one cylinder per drum). The wheel cylinders incorporate integral pressure-regulating valves, which control the hydraulic pressure applied to the rear brakes. The regulating valves help to prevent rear wheel lock-up during emergency braking. As the brake shoe linings wear, footbrake operation automatically operates a self-adjuster mechanism, which effectively lengthens the strut between the shoes, and reduces the lining-to-drum clearance.

On models with rear disc brakes, the brakes are actuated by single-piston sliding calipers which incorporate mechanical handbrake mechanisms. A load-sensitive pressure-regulating valve is connected into the brake lines to the rear calipers. The regulating valve is similar to that fitted to the rear wheel cylinders (on rear drum brake models), and helps to prevent rear wheel lock-up during emergency braking. It does this by varying the

hydraulic pressure applied to the rear calipers in proportion to the load being carried by the vehicle.

On all models, the handbrake provides an independent mechanical means of rear brake application.

Note: *When servicing any part of the system, work carefully and methodically; also observe scrupulous cleanliness when overhauling any part of the hydraulic system. Always renew components (in axle sets, where applicable) if in doubt about their condition, and use only genuine Renault replacement parts, or at least those of known good quality. Note the warnings given in "Safety first!" and at relevant points in this Chapter, concerning the dangers of asbestos dust and hydraulic fluid.*

2 Brake pedal - removal and refitting

Removal

1 Working inside the vehicle, remove the lower facia panel from beneath the steering column for access to the pedal bracket **(see illustration)**.

2 Extract the spring clip, washer and clevis pin securing the vacuum servo unit pushrod to the brake pedal **(see illustrations)**. Note the location of the plastic spacer on the right-hand end of the clevis pin.

3 Remove the clutch pedal, as described in Chapter 6.

4 Slide the remaining spacer from the clutch pedal end of the pedal pivot shaft.

2.1 Removing the lower facia panel

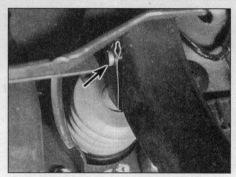

2.2a Clevis pin (arrowed) securing the vacuum servo unit pushrod to the brake pedal

2.2b Removing the spring clip from the clevis pin

5 Slide out the pivot shaft to the right, until the brake pedal can be withdrawn **(see illustration)**.
6 Examine the pivot bushes for wear, and renew them if necessary.

Refitting

7 Refitting is a reversal of removal, but lubricate the bushes, pivot shaft and pushrod clevis pin with molybdenum disulphide grease.
8 Refit the clutch pedal as described in Chapter 6.

3 Vacuum servo unit - testing, removal and refitting

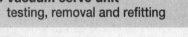

Testing

1 To test the operation of the servo unit, depress the footbrake four or five times to exhaust the vacuum, then start the engine while keeping the footbrake depressed. As the engine starts, there should be a noticeable "give" in the brake pedal as vacuum builds up. Allow the engine to run for at least two minutes, and then switch it off. If the brake pedal is now depressed again, it should be possible to detect a hiss from the servo when the pedal is depressed. After about four or five applications, no further hissing will be heard, and the pedal will feel considerably firmer.

Removal

2 The servo must be removed upwards from the engine compartment. On certain right-hand-drive models, it will be necessary to remove the inlet and/or exhaust manifold assemblies (see Chapter 4) to give sufficient access and clearance for the servo to be removed.
3 Where applicable, unbolt the brackets or release the clips, and move any hoses, pipes or wiring obscuring the servo to one side.
4 Disconnect the battery negative lead.
5 Refer to Section 8 and remove the master cylinder.
6 Disconnect the vacuum hose at the servo non-return valve.

7 Working inside the vehicle, remove the lower facia panel from beneath the steering column.
8 Extract the spring clip, washer and clevis pin securing the servo unit pushrod to the brake pedal.
9 Unscrew the four nuts and remove the washers securing the servo to the bulkhead, then withdraw the unit into the engine compartment.
10 Note that the servo unit cannot be dismantled for repair or overhaul and, if faulty, must be renewed.

Refitting

11 Before refitting the servo unit, check the pushrod and clevis dimensions as shown, and if necessary adjust them **(see illustration)**. Make sure that the locknuts are tight after making an adjustment.
12 Refitting is a reversal of removal, but refit the master cylinder with reference to Section 8, and where applicable, refit the manifold(s) with reference to Chapter 4.

4 Vacuum servo unit non-return valve - removal, testing and refitting

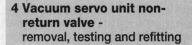

Removal

1 Slacken the clip and disconnect the vacuum pipe from the non-return valve on the front face of the servo unit.
2 Withdraw the valve from its rubber sealing grommet by pulling and twisting. Remove the sealing grommet from the servo unit.

Testing

3 Examine the non-return valve and sealing grommet for damage and signs of deterioration, and renew if necessary. The valve may be tested by blowing through it in both directions - it should only be possible to blow from the servo end to the manifold end.

Refitting

4 Refitting is a reversal of removal.

2.5 Slide out the pedal pivot shaft (arrowed)

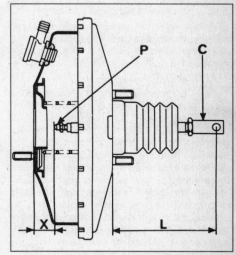

3.11 Vacuum servo unit adjustment dimensions

C Pushrod clevis   L = 117.5 mm
P Pushrod nut   X = 22.3 mm

5 Vacuum servo unit air filter - renewal

1 Working inside the vehicle, remove the lower facia panel from beneath the steering column.
2 Ease the convoluted rubber cover off the

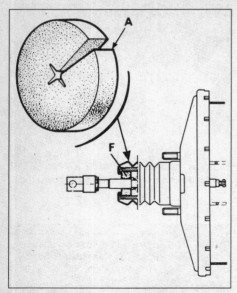

5.4 Vacuum servo unit air filter renewal

A Cut the new filter as shown
F Correct fitted position of filter in servo unit

rear of the servo unit, and move it up the pushrod.

3 Using a screwdriver or scriber, hook out the old air filter, and remove it from the servo.

4 Make a cut in the new filter as shown. Place it over the pushrod and into position in the servo end **(see illustration)**.

5 Refit the rubber cover, then refit the lower facia panel beneath the steering column.

6 Hydraulic system - bleeding

⚠️ *Warning: Hydraulic fluid is poisonous; wash off immediately and thoroughly in the case of skin contact, and seek immediate medical advice if any fluid is swallowed or gets into the eyes. Certain types of hydraulic fluid are inflammable, and may ignite when allowed into contact with hot components; when servicing any hydraulic system, it is safest to assume that the fluid IS inflammable, and to take precautions against the risk of fire as though it is petrol that is being handled. Finally, it is hygroscopic (it absorbs moisture from the air) - old fluid may be contaminated and unfit for further use. When topping-up or renewing the fluid, always use the recommended type (see Chapter 1), and ensure that it comes from a freshly-opened, previously-sealed container.*

Hydraulic fluid is an effective paint stripper, and will attack plastics; if any is spilt, it should be washed off immediately, using copious quantities of fresh water

Note: *On models with ABS, before disconnecting any part of the hydraulic system, the system must be depressurised as described later in this Section. Failure to do so could result in personal injury.*

Non-ABS models

1 The correct operation of any hydraulic system is only possible after removing all air from the components and circuit; this is achieved by bleeding the system.

2 During the bleeding procedure, add only clean, unused hydraulic fluid of the recommended type; never re-use fluid that has already been bled from the system. Ensure that sufficient fluid is available before starting work.

3 If there is any possibility of incorrect fluid being already in the system, the system must be flushed completely with uncontaminated, correct fluid, and new seals should be fitted to the various components.

4 If air has entered the hydraulic system because of a leak, ensure that the fault is cured before proceeding further.

5 Park the vehicle on level ground, switch off the engine, and select first or reverse gear (or "P" on automatic transmission models). Chock the wheels, and release the handbrake.

6 Check that all pipes and hoses are secure, unions tight and bleed screws closed. Clean any dirt from around the bleed screws.

7 Unscrew the fluid reservoir cap, and top the reservoir up to the "MAX" level line; refit the cap loosely. Remember to maintain the fluid level at least above the "MIN" level line throughout the procedure, or there is a risk of further air entering the system.

8 There are a number of one-man, do-it-yourself brake bleeding kits currently available from motor accessory shops. It is recommended that one of these kits is used whenever possible, as they greatly simplify the bleeding operation, and also reduce the risk of expelled air and fluid being drawn back into the system. If such a kit is not available, the basic (two-man) method must be used, which is described in detail below.

9 If a kit is to be used, prepare the vehicle as described previously, and follow the kit manufacturer's instructions. The procedure may vary slightly according to the type of kit being used; general procedures are as outlined below in the relevant sub-section.

10 Whichever method is used, the correct bleeding sequence must be followed, to ensure the removal of all air from the system.

Bleeding sequence

11 If the system has been only partially disconnected, and suitable precautions were taken to minimise fluid loss, it should be necessary only to bleed that part of the system (ie the primary or secondary circuit).

12 If the complete system is to be bled, then it should be done working in the following sequence:
(a) Left-hand rear brake.
(b) Right-hand front brake.
(c) Right-hand rear brake.
(d) Left-hand front brake.

Bleeding - basic (two-man) method

13 Collect a clean glass jar, a suitable length of plastic or rubber tubing which is a tight fit over the bleed screw, and a ring spanner to fit the screw. The help of an assistant will also be required.

14 Remove the dust cap from the first screw in the sequence. Fit the spanner and tube to the screw, place the other end of the tube in the jar, and pour in sufficient fluid to cover the end of the tube.

15 Ensure that the reservoir fluid level is maintained at least above the "MIN" level line throughout the procedure.

16 Have the assistant fully depress the brake pedal several times to build up pressure, then maintain it on the final stroke.

17 While pedal pressure is maintained, unscrew the bleed screw (approximately one turn) and allow the compressed fluid and air to flow into the jar. The assistant should maintain pedal pressure, following it down to the floor if necessary, and should not release it until instructed to do so. When the flow stops, tighten the bleed screw again. Have the assistant release the pedal slowly.

18 Repeat the steps given in paragraphs 16 and 17 until the fluid emerging from the bleed screw is free from air bubbles. Remember to recheck the fluid level in the reservoir every five strokes or so. If the master cylinder has been drained and refilled, and air is being bled from the first screw in the sequence, allow approximately five seconds between strokes for the master cylinder passages to refill.

19 When no more air bubbles appear, tighten the bleed screw securely, remove the tube and spanner, and refit the dust cap. Do not overtighten the bleed screw.

20 Repeat the procedure on the remaining screws in the sequence, until all air is removed from the system, and the brake pedal feels firm.

21 Proceed to paragraph 30.

Bleeding - using a one-way valve kit

22 As their name implies, these kits consist of a length of tubing with a one-way valve fitted, to prevent expelled air and fluid being drawn back into the system; some kits include a translucent container, which can be positioned so that the air bubbles can be more easily seen flowing from the end of the tube **(see illustration)**.

23 The kit is connected to the bleed screw, which is then opened. The user returns to the driver's seat and depresses the brake pedal with a smooth, steady stroke and slowly releases it; this is repeated until the expelled fluid is clear of air bubbles.

24 Note that these kits simplify work so much that it is easy to forget the reservoir fluid level; ensure that this is maintained at least above the "MIN" level line at all times.

25 Proceed to paragraph 30.

Bleeding - using a pressure-bleeding kit

26 These kits are usually operated by the reservoir of pressurised air contained in the spare tyre, although it may be necessary to reduce the pressure to lower than normal; refer to the instructions supplied with the kit.

27 By connecting a pressurised, fluid-filled container to the fluid reservoir, bleeding can be carried out simply by opening each screw in turn (in the specified sequence) and allowing the fluid to flow out until no more air bubbles can be seen in the expelled fluid.

28 This method has the advantage that the large reservoir of fluid provides an additional safeguard against air being drawn into the system during bleeding.

29 Pressure-bleeding is particularly effective when bleeding "difficult" systems, or when bleeding the complete system at the time of routine fluid renewal.

All methods

30 When bleeding is complete, and firm pedal feel is restored, wash off any spilt fluid, tighten the bleed screws securely, and refit their dust caps.

31 Check the hydraulic fluid level, and top-up if necessary (Chapter 1).

32 Discard any hydraulic fluid that has been bled from the system; it will not be fit for re-use.

33 Check the feel of the brake pedal. If it feels at all spongy, air must still be present in the system, and further bleeding is required. Failure to bleed satisfactorily after several repetitions of the bleeding procedure may be due to worn master cylinder seals.

Bendix ABS system

⚠️ *Warning: Before carrying out any work involving disconnection of fluid lines, or loosening of bleed screws, it is essential to depressurise the system as described in the following paragraphs. Failure to observe this could result in personal injury. Due to the complex nature of the ABS, it is recommended that this work is carried out by a Renault dealer.*

Note: *Due to the requirement for special test equipment, and the associated risk of personal injury if the equipment is not available, no procedure is given here for bleeding the braking system on models with Bendix ABS. It is strongly recommended that bleeding of the system is entrusted to a Renault dealer, who will have access to the required specialist knowledge and equipment.*

Depressurising the system

34 Working under the front of the vehicle, slacken the bolt on the underside of the pump unit by one turn. **Note:** *Do not slacken the bolt by more than two turns, otherwise the O-ring seal will be damaged.* Check that the accumulator has emptied by checking the fluid level in the reservoir, which should be level with the upper mark **(see illustrations)**.

6.22 Bleeding a front brake caliper

35 Retighten the bolt on the underside of the pump.

Bleeding the system

36 Bleeding of the system should be entrusted to a Renault dealer, due to the requirement for specialist knowledge and test equipment.

Bosch ABS system

37 At the time of writing, no information was available regarding the Bosch ABS system fitted to certain later models (from 1994 model year). Before attempting to carry out any work on a vehicle fitted with this system, consult a Renault dealer for advice.

7 Hydraulic pipes and hoses - inspection, removal and refitting

⚠️ *Warning: Before attempting to disconnect any fluid pipes or hoses on models with ABS, refer to the information given for depressurising and bleeding the ABS system in Section 6.*

Note: *Before starting work, refer to the warning at the beginning of Section 6 concerning the dangers of hydraulic fluid.*

Inspection

1 The hydraulic pipes, hoses, hose connections and pipe unions should be regularly examined.

2 First check for signs of leakage at the pipe unions, then examine the flexible hoses for signs of cracking, chafing and fraying **(see illustration)**.

3 The brake pipes should be examined carefully for signs of dents, corrosion or other damage. Corrosion should be scraped off, and if the depth of pitting is significant, the pipes renewed. This is particularly likely in those areas underneath the vehicle body where the pipes are exposed and unprotected.

Removal

4 If any pipe or hose is to be renewed, minimise fluid loss by removing the fluid reservoir cap and then tightening it down onto a piece of polythene (taking care not to

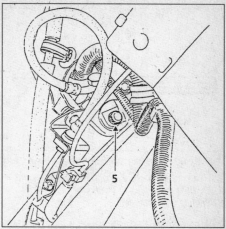

6.34a Slacken the bolt (5) to depressurise the ABS hydraulic system - right-hand-drive models

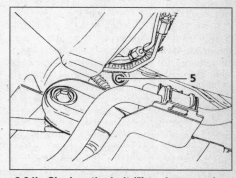

6.34b Slacken the bolt (5) to depressurise the ABS hydraulic system - left-hand-drive models

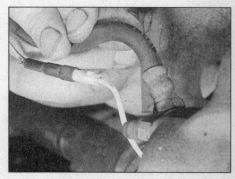

7.2 Checking a brake flexible hose for cracking

damage the level sender unit) to obtain an airtight seal. Alternatively, flexible hoses can be sealed, if required, using a proprietary brake hose clamp; metal brake pipe unions can be plugged (if care is taken not to allow dirt into the system) or capped immediately they are disconnected. Place a wad of rag under any union that is to be disconnected, to catch any spilt fluid. If a section of pipe is to be removed from the master cylinder, the reservoir should be emptied by syphoning out the fluid, or drawing out the fluid with a pipette.

9

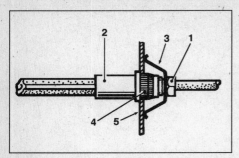

7.5 Brake pipe-to-flexible hose connection

1 Union nut
2 Flexible hose
3 Spring clip support
4 Splined end fitting
5 Bodywork

5 If a flexible hose is to be disconnected, unscrew the brake pipe union nut before removing the spring clip which secures the hose to its mounting bracket **(see illustration)**.
6 To unscrew the union nuts, it is preferable to obtain a brake pipe spanner of the correct size (11 mm/13 mm split ring); these are available from motor accessory shops **(see illustration)**. Failing this, a close-fitting open-ended spanner will be required, though if the nuts are tight or corroded, their flats may be rounded off if the spanner slips. In such a case, a self-locking wrench is often the only way to unscrew a stubborn union, but it follows that the pipe and the damaged nuts must be renewed on reassembly. Always clean a union and the surrounding area before disconnecting it. If disconnecting a component with more than one union, make a careful note of the connections before disturbing any of them.
7 If a brake pipe is to be renewed, it can be obtained, cut to length and with the union nuts and end flares in place, from Renault dealers. All that is then necessary is to bend it to shape, following the line of the original, before fitting it to the vehicle. Alternatively, most motor accessory shops can make up brake pipes from kits, but this requires very careful measurement of the original to ensure that the replacement is of the correct length. The safest answer is usually to take the original to the shop as a pattern.

Refitting

8 On refitting, do not overtighten the union nuts. The specified torque wrench settings (where given) are not high, and it is not necessary to exercise brute force to obtain a sound joint.
9 Ensure that the pipes and hoses are correctly routed, with no kinks, and that they are secured in the clips or brackets provided. In the case of flexible hoses, make sure that they cannot contact other components during movement of the steering and/or suspension assemblies.
10 After fitting, remove the polythene from the reservoir (or remove the plugs or clamps, as applicable), and bleed the hydraulic system as described in Section 6. Wash off any spilt fluid, and check carefully for fluid leaks.

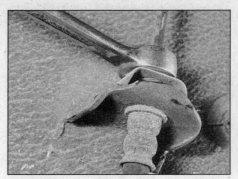

7.6 Using a brake pipe spanner to unscrew a hydraulic union nut

8 Master cylinder (non-ABS models) - removal and refitting

⚠️ *Warning: Before attempting to disconnect any fluid pipes or hoses on models with ABS, refer to the information given for depressurising and bleeding the ABS system in Section 6.*

Note: *A new master cylinder-to-servo seal will be required on refitting.*

Removal

1 Where necessary, remove the air cleaner and ducting from the carburettor or throttle housing, with reference to Chapter 4.
2 Where applicable, unbolt and remove the strengthening bar from between the front suspension turrets.
3 On certain right-hand-drive models, it may be necessary to remove the inlet and/or exhaust manifolds, as described in Chapter 4.
4 Where applicable, unbolt the brackets or release the clips, and move any hoses, pipes or wiring obscuring the master cylinder to one side.
5 Syphon the brake fluid from the reservoir (not by mouth - use an old poultry baster or a pipette). Alternatively, place a container beneath the master cylinder, and cover the surrounding components with rags.
6 On models with a remotely-mounted fluid reservoir, disconnect the hoses leading from the reservoir to the master cylinder, at the master cylinder. Wipe up any fluid spillage immediately.
7 On models where the fluid reservoir is mounted directly on the master cylinder, pull the reservoir from the top of the master cylinder.
8 Identify the brake pipes for position, then unscrew the union nuts and disconnect them. Tape over the pipe ends to prevent the entry of dust and dirt.
9 Unscrew the mounting nuts, and withdraw the master cylinder from the servo unit. Note the position of the vacuum hose support bracket **(see illustration)**.
10 It is not possible to obtain seals or internal components for the master cylinder, therefore

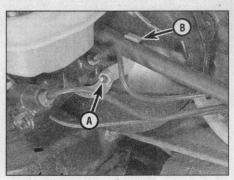

8.9 Master cylinder mounting nut (A) and vacuum hose support bracket (B)

if it is faulty it should be renewed complete. Where applicable, the reservoir locating seals may be renewed if necessary. The seal between the master cylinder and the vacuum servo should be renewed as a matter of course whenever the unit is removed, as a leak at this point will allow atmospheric pressure into the servo unit.

Refitting

11 Before refitting the master cylinder, clean the mounting faces. Check that the distance between the tip of the master cylinder end of the pushrod and the front of the servo unit (dimension "X") is as shown in illustration 3.11. If necessary, adjust by repositioning the pushrod nut "P".
12 Refitting is a reversal of removal, but tighten the securing nuts to the specified torque. Fit a new seal between the master cylinder and the servo, and when offering the master cylinder to the servo, make sure that it is correctly aligned so that the pushrod enters the piston centrally.
13 On completion, bleed the hydraulic system as described in Section 6.

9 Front brake pads - renewal

⚠️ *Warning: Disc brake pads must be renewed on both front wheels at the same time - never renew the pads on only one wheel, as uneven braking may result. Also, the dust created by wear of the pads may contain asbestos, which is a health hazard. Never blow it out with compressed air, and don'tinhale any of it. An approved filtering mask should be worn when working on the brakes. DO NOT use petroleum-based solvents to clean brake parts - use brake cleaner or methylated spirit only.*

1 Apply the handbrake, then jack up the front of the vehicle and support it securely on axle stands (see "Jacking, towing and wheel changing"). Remove the front roadwheels.

Bendix calipers

2 Disconnect the brake pad wear warning sensor wire at the connector.

9.4a Extract the small spring . . .

9.4b . . . and withdraw the pad retaining key (Bendix caliper)

9.5a Removing the outer brake pad . . .

9.5b . . . and the inner brake pad (Bendix caliper)

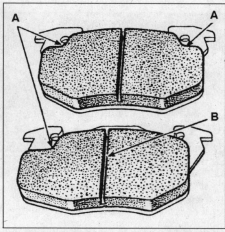

9.8a Bendix caliper symmetrical-lining pad (top) and offset-lining pad (bottom). Offset lining has only a single cut-out (A) and the groove in the friction material (B) is not central

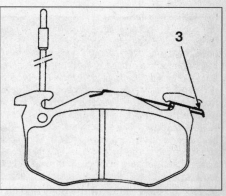

9.8b Anti-rattle spring (3) correctly fitted to Bendix inner brake pad

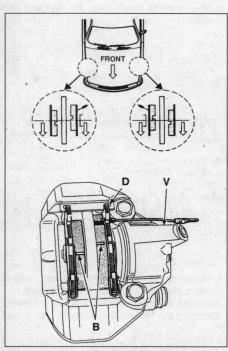

9.8c Correct fitting of Bendix offset lining brake pads

B Grooves
D Pad retaining plate spring clip location
V Bleed screw

9.8d Correct fitted positions of the Bendix offset lining brake pads

3 Push the piston into its bore by pulling the caliper outwards.
4 Extract the small spring clip, and then withdraw the pad retaining key (see illustrations).
5 Using pliers if necessary, withdraw the pads from the caliper, and remove the anti-rattle spring from each pad (see illustrations). If required, the thickness of the pad linings can be checked at this stage, using a steel rule.

6 With the pads removed, check that the caliper is free to slide on the guide sleeves, and that the rubber dust excluders around the piston and guide sleeves are undamaged. If attention to these components is necessary, refer to Section 10.
7 To refit the pads, move the caliper sideways as far as possible towards the centre of the car. Fit the anti-rattle spring to the innermost pad, making sure that this pad is the one with the wear warning sensor wire, then locate the pad in position, with the backing plate against the piston.
8 Note that the pads are of the offset type, having only one cutaway on their outer edge, compared with the two cutaways on the symmetrical type. Looking at the pads from the front of the car, the innermost pad groove must be higher than the outer pad groove. Make sure that the pads are fitted correctly (see illustrations).
9 Move the caliper outwards, then fit the anti-rattle spring to the outer pad, and locate the pad in the caliper.
10 Slide the retaining key into place, and refit the small spring clip at the inner end. It may be necessary to file an entry chamfer on the edge of the retaining key, to enable it to be fitted without difficulty (see illustration).
11 Reconnect the brake pad wear warning sensor wire, then refit the roadwheel and repeat the renewal procedure on the other front brake.

9

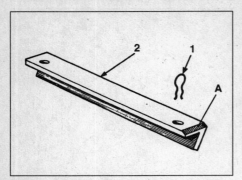

9.10 Bendix disc pad retaining plate (2) and spring clip (1), showing filed chamfer (A)

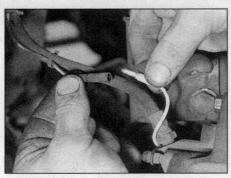

9.14 Disconnecting the brake pad wear warning sensor wiring (Girling caliper)

9.15a On Girling calipers, slacken the guide pin bolts whilst holding the guide pins with an open-ended spanner . . .

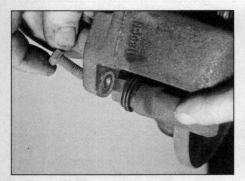

9.15b . . . then withdraw the bolts and lift off the brake caliper

9.17 Removing the outer brake pad from the carrier bracket (Girling caliper)

20 Make sure that the caliper piston is fully retracted in its bore. If not, carefully push it in, preferably using a G-clamp or, alternatively, using a flat bar or screwdriver as a lever.

21 Position the caliper over the pads, then fit the lower guide pin bolt, having first coated its threads with locking fluid. Apply locking fluid to the upper guide pin bolt, press the caliper into position, then fit the bolt. Tighten the bolts to the specified torque, starting with the lower bolt.

22 Reconnect the brake pad wear warning sensor wiring, then refit the roadwheel and repeat the renewal procedure on the other front brake.

23 On completion, check the hydraulic fluid level in the reservoir. Depress the brake pedal two or three times, to bring the pads into contact with the disc. Lower the vehicle to the ground.

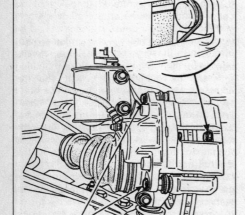

9.19 Girling caliper showing guide pin bolts (7) and correct fitted position of anti-rattle spring

12 On completion, check the hydraulic fluid level in the reservoir. Depress the brake pedal two or three times, to bring the pads into contact with the disc. Lower the vehicle to the ground.

Girling calipers

13 Pull the caliper body outwards, away from the centre of the car. This will push the piston

back into its bore to facilitate removal and refitting of the pads.

14 Disconnect the brake pad wear warning sensor wiring at the connector **(see illustration)**.

15 Unscrew the upper and lower guide pin bolts using a suitable spanner, while holding the guide pins with a second spanner **(see illustrations)**.

16 With the guide pins removed, lift the caliper off the brake pads and carrier bracket, and tie it up in a convenient place under the wheelarch. Do not allow the caliper to hang unsupported on the flexible brake hose.

17 Withdraw the two brake pads from the carrier bracket **(see illustration)**. If required, the thickness of the pads can be checked at this stage, using a steel rule.

18 Before refitting the pads, check that the guide pins are free to slide in the carrier bracket, and check that the rubber dust excluders around the guide pins are undamaged. Brush the dust and dirt from the caliper and piston, but *do not inhale it*, as it is injurious to health. Inspect the dust excluder around the piston for damage, and check the piston for evidence of fluid leaks, corrosion or damage. If attention to any of these components is necessary, refer to Section 10.

19 To refit the pads, place them in position on the carrier bracket, noting that the pad with the warning sensor wire must be nearest to the centre of the car. The anti-rattle springs must be located as shown **(see illustration)**.

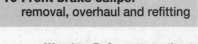

10 Front brake caliper - removal, overhaul and refitting

⚠ *Warning: Before attempting to disconnect any fluid pipes or hoses on models with ABS, refer to the information given for depressurising and bleeding the ABS system in Section 6.*

Note: *Before starting work, refer to the warnings at the beginning of Sections 6 and 9 concerning the dangers of hydraulic fluid and asbestos dust.*

Removal

1 Apply the handbrake, then jack up the front of the vehicle and support it securely on axle stands (see *"Jacking, towing and wheel changing"*). Remove the appropriate roadwheel.

2 Minimise fluid loss by removing the fluid reservoir cap and tightening it down onto a piece of polythene, to obtain an airtight seal (taking care not to damage the sender unit). Alternatively, use a brake hose clamp, a G-clamp, or a similar tool with protected jaws, to clamp the flexible hose.

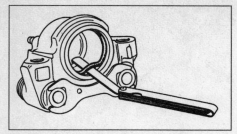

10.11 Using a feeler gauge to remove the piston seal from a Bendix type caliper

Bendix caliper

3 Remove the brake pads as described in Section 9, paragraphs 2 to 5.
4 Clean the area around the union, then loosen the brake hose union nut.
5 Slacken the two bolts securing the caliper assembly to the stub axle carrier, and remove them along with the mounting plate, noting which way round the plate is fitted. Lift the caliper assembly away from the brake disc, and unscrew it from the end of the brake hose.

Girling caliper

6 Clean the area around the hose union, then loosen the brake hose union nut.
7 Slacken and remove the upper and lower caliper guide pin bolts, using a slim open-ended spanner to prevent the guide pin itself from rotating. Discard the guide pin bolts; new bolts must be used on refitting. With the guide pin bolts removed, lift the caliper away from the brake disc, then unscrew the caliper from the end of the brake hose. Note that the brake pads need not be disturbed, and can be left in position in the caliper mounting bracket.

Overhaul

Note: *Ensure that an appropriate overhaul kit can be obtained before dismantling the caliper.*
8 With the caliper on the bench, wipe away all traces of dust and dirt, but *avoid inhaling the dust, as it is injurious to health.*
9 On the Girling caliper, using a small flat-bladed screwdriver, carefully prise the dust seal retaining clip out of the caliper bore.
10 On all calipers, withdraw the partially-ejected piston from the caliper body, and remove the dust seal. The piston can be withdrawn by hand, or if necessary forced out by applying compressed air to the union bolt hole. **Caution:** *The piston may be ejected with some force. Only low pressure should be required, such as is generated by a foot pump.*
11 Extract the piston hydraulic seal using a blunt instrument such as a knitting needle or a feeler gauge, taking care not to damage the caliper bore **(see illustration)**.
12 Withdraw the guide sleeves or pins from the caliper body or mounting bracket (as applicable) and remove the rubber gaiters.
13 Thoroughly clean all components, using only methylated spirit, isopropyl alcohol or clean hydraulic fluid as a cleaning medium. Never use mineral-based solvents, such as petrol or paraffin, which will attack the

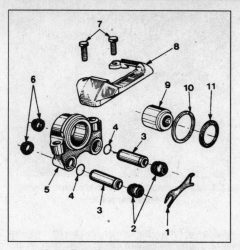

10.14 Bendix type brake caliper components

1 Mounting plate
2 Guide sleeve inner rubber gaiters
3 Guide sleeves
4 Guide sleeve seals
5 Caliper body
6 Guide sleeve outer rubber gaiters
7 Mounting bracket retaining bolts
8 Mounting bracket
9 Piston
10 Piston seal
11 Piston dust seal

hydraulic system rubber components. Dry the components immediately, using compressed air or a clean, lint-free cloth. Use compressed air to blow clear the fluid passages.
14 Check all components, and renew any that are worn or damaged **(see illustration)**. Check particularly the cylinder bore and piston; if they are scratched, worn or corroded in any way, they must be renewed (note that this means the renewal of the complete body assembly). Similarly, check the condition of the guide sleeves or pins and their bores; they should be undamaged and (when cleaned) a reasonably tight sliding fit in the body or mounting bracket bores. If there is any doubt about the condition of a component, renew it.
15 If the assembly is fit for further use, obtain the appropriate repair kit; the components are available from Renault dealers, in various combinations.
16 Renew all rubber seals, dust covers and caps disturbed on dismantling as a matter of course; these should never be re-used.
17 Before commencing reassembly, ensure that all components are absolutely clean and dry.
18 Dip the piston and the new piston (fluid) seal in clean hydraulic fluid. Smear clean fluid on the cylinder bore surface.
19 Fit the new piston (fluid) seal, using only your fingers (no tools) to manipulate it into the cylinder bore groove. Fit the new dust seal to the piston. Refit the piston to the cylinder bore using a twisting motion, ensuring that the piston enters squarely into the bore. Press the

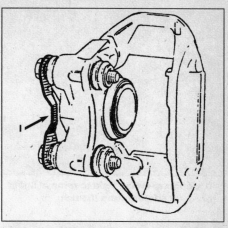

10.22 On Bendix calipers, ensure that the mounting plate (1) is fitted so that its bend curves towards the caliper body

piston fully into the bore, then press the dust seal into the caliper body.
20 On the Girling caliper, install the dust seal retaining clip, ensuring that it is correctly seated in the caliper groove.
21 On all calipers, apply the grease supplied in the repair kit, or a good-quality high-temperature brake grease or anti-seize compound to the guide sleeves or pins. Fit the sleeves or pins to the caliper body or mounting bracket. Fit the new rubber gaiters, ensuring that they are correctly located in the grooves on both the sleeve or pin, and body or mounting bracket (as applicable).

Refitting
Bendix caliper

22 Screw the caliper fully onto the flexible hose union nut. Position the caliper over the brake disc, then refit the two caliper mounting bolts and the mounting plate. Note that the mounting plate must be fitted so that its bend curves towards the caliper body **(see illustration)**; this is necessary to prevent the plate contacting the driveshaft gaiter when the steering is on full-lock. With the plate correctly positioned, tighten the caliper bolts to the specified torque setting.
23 Tighten the brake hose union nut to the specified torque, then refit the brake pads as described in Section 9.
24 Proceed to paragraph 28.

Girling caliper

25 Screw the caliper body fully onto the flexible hose union nut. Check that the brake pads are still correctly fitted in the caliper mounting bracket.
26 Position the caliper over the pads. Coat the threads of the new lower guide pin bolt with locking fluid, and fit the bolt. Apply locking fluid to the new upper guide pin bolt, press the caliper into position, and fit the bolt. Check that the anti-rattle springs are correctly located (see illustration 9.19), then tighten the guide pin bolts to the specified torque, starting with the lower bolt.

9

11.2 Using emery tape to remove light scoring from the disc

11.3 Measuring brake disc thickness with a micrometer

11.4 Checking brake disc run-out with a dial gauge

11.6 Girling brake caliper assembly suspended from the front suspension coil spring (pads removed)

27 Tighten the brake hose union nut to the specified torque.

All calipers

28 Remove the brake hose clamp or polythene, where fitted, and bleed the hydraulic system as described in Section 6. Providing the precautions described were taken to minimise brake fluid loss, it should only be necessary to bleed the relevant front brake.

29 Refit the roadwheel, then lower the vehicle to the ground and tighten the roadwheel bolts to the specified torque.

11 Front brake disc - inspection, removal and refitting

Note: *Before starting work, refer to the warning at the beginning of Section 9 concerning the dangers of asbestos dust. If either disc requires renewal, BOTH should be renewed at the same time, to ensure even and consistent braking. In principle, new pads should be fitted also.*

Inspection

1 Apply the handbrake, then jack up the front of the vehicle and support it securely on axle stands (see *"Jacking, towing and wheel changing"*). Remove the appropriate front roadwheel.

2 Slowly rotate the brake disc so that the full area of both sides can be checked; remove the brake pads, as described in Section 9, if better access is required to the inboard surface. Light scoring is normal in the area swept by the brake pads, and can be removed using emery tape **(see illustration)**. If heavy scoring is found, the disc must be renewed.

3 It is normal to find a lip of rust and brake dust around the disc's perimeter; this can be scraped off if required. If, however, a lip has formed due to wear of the brake pad swept area, the disc thickness must be measured using a micrometer **(see illustration)**. Take measurements at several places around the disc at the inside and outside of the pad swept area; if the disc has worn at any point to the specified minimum thickness or less, it must be renewed.

4 If the disc is thought to be warped, it can be checked for run-out, ideally by using a dial gauge mounted on any convenient fixed point, while the disc is slowly rotated **(see illustration)**. In the absence of a dial gauge, use feeler blades to measure (at several points all around the disc) the clearance between the disc and a fixed point such as the caliper mounting bracket. If the measurements obtained are at the specified maximum or beyond, the disc is excessively warped, and must be renewed; however, it is worth checking first that the hub bearing is in good condition (Chapters 1 and 10). Also try the effect of removing the disc and turning it through 180° to reposition it on the hub; if the run-out is still excessive, the disc must be renewed.

5 Check the disc for cracks (especially around the wheel bolt holes), and for any other wear or damage. Renew the disc if necessary.

Removal

6 Unscrew the two bolts securing the brake caliper assembly to the stub axle carrier, and slide the caliper assembly, complete with pads, off the disc. Using a piece of wire or string, tie the caliper to the front suspension coil spring, to avoid placing any strain on the hydraulic brake hose **(see illustration)**.

7 If the same disc is to be refitted, use chalk or paint to mark the relationship of the disc to

the hub. Remove the two screws securing the brake disc to the hub, and remove the disc. If it is tight, lightly tap its rear face with a hide or plastic mallet.

Refitting

8 Refitting is the reverse of the removal procedure, noting the following points:

    (a) Ensure that the mating surfaces of the disc and hub are clean and flat.

    (b) If applicable, align the marks made on removal.

    (c) Securely tighten the disc retaining screws.

    (d) If a new disc has been fitted, use a suitable solvent to wipe any preservative coating from the disc before refitting the caliper.

    (e) Apply locking fluid to the threads of the brake caliper mounting bolts, and tighten them to the specified torque.

    (f) Refit the roadwheel, then lower the vehicle to the ground and tighten the roadwheel bolts to the specified torque.

    (g) On completion, depress the brake pedal several times, to bring the brake pads into contact with the disc.

12 Rear brake drum - removal, inspection and refitting

Note: *Before starting work, refer to the warning at the beginning of Section 9 concerning the dangers of asbestos dust. If either drum requires renewal or refinishing, BOTH should be dealt with at the same time, to ensure even and consistent braking. In principle, new shoes should be fitted also. A new rear hub nut will be required on refitting.*

Removal

1 Chock the front wheels, engage reverse gear (or "P" on models with automatic transmission) and release the handbrake. Jack up the rear of the vehicle, and support it securely on axle stands (see *"Jacking, towing and wheel changing"*). Remove the appropriate rear wheel.

2 Using a hammer and suitable large flat-bladed screwdriver, carefully tap and prise the

12.2 Prise the cap from the centre of the brake drum . . .

12.3 . . . then remove the rear hub nut and thrustwasher

cap out of the centre of the brake drum **(see illustration)**.

3 Using a socket and long bar, slacken and remove the rear hub nut, and withdraw the thrustwasher **(see illustration)**. Discard the hub nut; a new nut must used on refitting.

4 It should now be possible to withdraw the brake drum and hub bearing assembly from the stub axle by hand. It may be difficult to remove the drum due to the tightness of the hub bearing on the stub axle, or due to the brake shoes binding on the inner circumference of the drum. If the bearing is tight, tap the periphery of the drum using a hide or plastic mallet, or use a universal puller, secured to the drum with the wheel bolts, to pull it off. If the brake shoes are binding, proceed as follows.

5 First ensure that the handbrake is fully off.

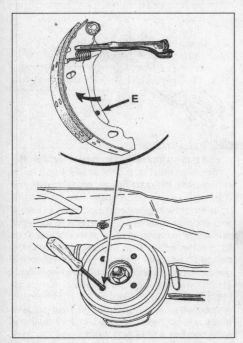

12.6a Using a screwdriver inserted through the brake drum to release the handbrake operating lever

E Handbrake operating lever stop-peg location

From underneath the vehicle, slacken the handbrake cable adjuster locknut, then back off the adjuster nut on the handbrake lever rod. Note that on some models, it will first be necessary to remove the mounting nut(s) and lower the exhaust heat shield to gain access to the adjuster nut.

6 Insert a screwdriver through one of the wheel bolt holes in the brake drum, so that it contacts the handbrake operating lever on the trailing brake shoe **(see illustrations)**. Push the lever until the stop-peg slips behind the brake shoe web, allowing the brake shoes to retract fully. Withdraw the brake drum, and slide the spacer off the stub axle.

Inspection

7 Working carefully, remove all traces of brake dust from the drum, but *avoid inhaling the dust, as it is injurious to health.*

8 Scrub clean the outside of the drum, and check it for obvious signs of wear or damage, such as cracks around the roadwheel bolt holes; renew the drum if necessary.

9 Carefully examine the inside of the drum. Light scoring of the friction surface is normal, but if heavy scoring is found, the drum must be renewed. It is usual to find a lip on the drum's inboard edge which consists of a mixture of rust and brake dust; this should be scraped away, to leave a smooth surface which can be polished with fine (120 to 150 grade) emery paper. If the lip is due to the friction surface being recessed by wear, then the drum must be refinished (within the specified limits) or renewed.

12.6b Releasing the handbrake operating lever using a screwdriver

10 If the drum is thought to be excessively worn or oval, its internal diameter must be measured at several points using an internal micrometer. Take measurements in pairs, the second at right-angles to the first, and compare the two to check for signs of ovality. Minor ovality can be corrected by machining; otherwise, renew the drum.

Refitting

11 If a new brake drum is to be installed, use a suitable solvent to remove any preservative coating that may have been applied to its interior.

12 Ensure that the handbrake lever stop-peg is correctly repositioned against the edge of the brake shoe web **(see illustration)**. Apply a smear of gear oil to the stub axle, and slide on the spacer and brake drum, being careful not to get oil onto the brake shoes or the friction surface of the drum. Fit the thrustwasher and a new hub nut; tighten the nut to the specified torque. Tap the hub cap into place in the centre of the brake drum.

13 Depress the footbrake several times to operate the self-adjusting mechanism.

14 Repeat the above procedure on the remaining rear brake assembly (where necessary), then adjust the handbrake as described in Chapter 1.

15 On completion, refit the roadwheel(s), lower the vehicle to the ground and tighten the wheel bolts to the specified torque.

13 Rear brake shoes - inspection and renewal

⚠ *Warning: Brake shoes must be renewed on BOTH rear wheels at the same time - never renew the shoes on only one wheel, as uneven braking may result. Also, the dust created by wear of the shoes may contain asbestos, which is a health hazard. Never blow it out with compressed air, and don't inhale any of it. An approved filtering mask should be worn when working on the brakes. DO NOT use petroleum-based solvents to clean brake parts - use brake cleaner or methylated spirit only.*

12.12 Ensure that the handbrake lever stop-peg (arrowed) is correctly repositioned against the edge of the brake shoe web

9

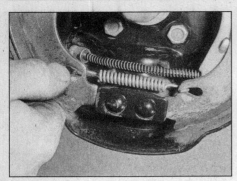

13.7 Ease the shoes out of the lower pivot point, and disconnect the lower return spring - Bendix brakes

13.8a Easing the upper ends of the brake shoes from the wheel cylinder - Bendix brakes

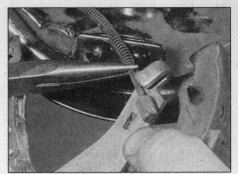

13.8b Disconnecting the handbrake cable from the trailing shoe - Bendix brakes

13.8c Removing the leading shoe and adjuster bolt from the adjuster strut - Bendix rear brakes

13.9a Rear brake trailing shoe and adjuster strut - Bendix rear brakes

13.9b Rear brake leading shoe and adjuster bolt - Bendix rear brakes

Inspection

1 Remove the brake drum as described in Section 12.

2 Working carefully, remove all traces of brake dust from the brake drum, backplate and shoes.

3 Measure the thickness of each brake shoe (friction material and shoe) at several points; if either shoe is worn at any point to the specified minimum thickness or less, all four shoes must be renewed as a set. Also, the shoes should be renewed if any are fouled with oil or grease; there is no satisfactory way of degreasing friction material, once contaminated.

4 If any of the brake shoes are worn unevenly, or fouled with oil or grease, trace and rectify the cause before reassembly.

Renewal

5 The procedure now varies according to which make of brake is fitted.

Bendix brake shoes

6 Using a pair of pliers, remove the shoe retainer spring cups by depressing and turning them through 90° With the cups removed, lift off the springs and withdraw the retainer pins.

7 Ease the shoes out one at a time from the lower pivot point, to release the tension of the return spring, then disconnect the lower return spring from both shoes **(see illustration)**.

8 Ease the upper ends of both shoes out from their wheel cylinder locations, taking care not to damage the wheel cylinder seals, and disconnect the handbrake cable from the trailing shoe. The brake shoe and adjuster strut assembly can then be manoeuvred out of position and away from the backplate **(see illustrations)**. Do not depress the brake pedal until the brakes are reassembled; wrap a strong elastic band around the wheel cylinder pistons to retain them.

9 With the shoe and adjuster strut assembly on the bench, make a note of the correct fitted positions of the springs and adjuster strut, to use as a guide on reassembly **(see illustrations)**. Release the handbrake lever stop-peg (if not already done), then detach the adjuster strut bolt retaining spring from the leading shoe. Disconnect the upper return spring, then detach the leading shoe and return spring from the trailing shoe and strut assembly. Unhook the spring securing the adjuster strut to the trailing shoe, and separate the two.

10 If genuine Renault brake shoes are being installed, it will be necessary to remove the handbrake lever from the original trailing shoe, and fit it to the new shoe. Secure the lever in position with the new retaining clip which is supplied with the brake shoes. All return springs should be renewed, regardless of their apparent condition; spring kits are also available from Renault dealers.

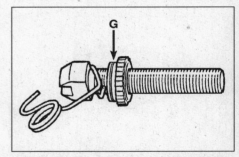

13.11 Bendix rear drum brake left-hand adjuster strut bolt can be identified by groove (G) on adjuster wheel collar

11 Withdraw the adjuster bolt from the strut, and carefully examine the assembly for signs of wear or damage, paying particular attention to the threads of the adjuster bolt and the knurled adjuster wheel, and renew if necessary. Note that left-hand and right-hand struts are not interchangeable - they are marked "G" (gauche/left) and "D" (droit/right) respectively. Also note that the strut adjuster bolts are not interchangeable; the left-hand strut bolt has a left-hand thread, and the right-hand bolt a right-hand thread. The left-hand bolt can be identified by the groove on its adjuster wheel collar **(see illustration)**. The right-hand bolt does not have a groove on the adjuster wheel collar, but the bolt itself is painted.

13.12 Correct fitted position of Bendix adjuster spring components

13.16 Apply a little high-melting point grease to the shoe contact points on the backplate - Bendix brakes

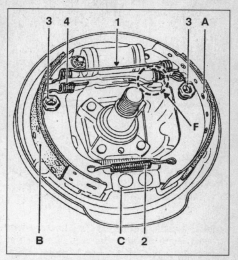

13.19 Correct fitted position of Bendix rear brake components

A Leading shoe
B Trailing shoe
C Lower pivot point
F Adjuster strut mechanism
1 Upper return spring
2 Lower return spring
3 Retaining pin, spring and spring cup
4 Adjuster strut-to-trailing shoe spring

12 Ensure the components on the end of the strut are correctly positioned (see illustration), then apply a little high-melting-point grease to the threads of the adjuster bolt. Screw the adjuster wheel onto the bolt until only a small gap exists between the wheel and the head of the bolt, then install the bolt in the strut.

13 Fit the adjuster strut retaining spring to the trailing shoe, ensuring that the shorter hook of the spring is engaged with the shoe. Attach the adjuster strut to the spring end, then ease the strut into position in its slot in the trailing shoe.

14 Engage the upper return spring with the trailing shoe. Hook the leading shoe onto the other end of the spring, and lever the leading shoe down until the adjuster bolt head is correctly located in its groove. Once the bolt is correctly located, hook its retaining spring into the slot on the leading shoe.

15 Remove the elastic band fitted to the wheel cylinder. Peel back the rubber protective caps, and check the wheel cylinder for fluid leaks or other damage. Also check that both cylinder pistons are free to move easily. Refer to Section 14, if necessary, for information on wheel cylinder renewal.

16 Prior to installation, clean the backplate, and apply a thin smear of high-temperature brake grease or anti-seize compound to all those surfaces of the backplate which bear on the shoes, particularly the wheel cylinder pistons and lower pivot point (see illustration). Do not use too much, and don't allow the lubricant to contaminate the friction material.

17 Ensure that the handbrake lever stop-peg is correctly located against the edge of the trailing shoe.

18 Manoeuvre the shoe and strut assembly into position on the vehicle. Engage the upper ends of both shoes with the wheel cylinder pistons. Attach the handbrake cable to the trailing shoe lever. Fit the lower return spring to both shoes, and ease the shoes into position on the lower pivot point.

19 Centralise the shoes relative to the backplate, by tapping them. Refit the shoe retainer pins and springs, and secure them in position with the spring cups (see illustration).

20 Using a screwdriver, turn the strut adjuster wheel until the diameter of the shoes is between 178.7 and 179.2 mm. This should allow the brake drum to just pass over the shoes.

21 Slide the drum into position over the linings, but do not refit the hub nut yet.

22 Repeat the above procedure on the remaining rear brake.

23 Once both sets of rear shoes have been renewed, adjust the lining-to-drum clearance by repeatedly depressing the brake pedal. Whilst depressing the pedal, have an assistant listen to the rear drums, to check that the adjuster strut is functioning correctly; if this is so, a clicking sound will be emitted by the strut as the pedal is depressed.

24 Remove both the rear drums, and check that the handbrake lever stop-pegs are still correctly located against the edges of the trailing shoes, and that each lever operates smoothly. If all is well, adjust the handbrake cable with the aid of an assistant. When the adjustment is correct, the handbrake lever on each rear brake assembly starts to move as the handbrake is moved between the first and second notch (click) of its ratchet mechanism; ie the stop-pegs should be in contact with the shoes when the handbrake is on the first notch of the ratchet, but not when the handbrake is on the second notch. Once the handbrake adjustment is correct, hold the adjuster nut and securely tighten the locknut. Where necessary, refit the exhaust system heat shield to the vehicle underbody.

25 Refit the brake drums as described in Section 12.

26 On completion, check the hydraulic fluid level as described in Chapter 1.

27 If new shoes have been fitted, full braking efficiency will not be obtained until the linings have bedded-in. Be prepared for longer stopping distances, and avoid harsh braking as far as possible for the first hundred miles or so after fitting new shoes.

Girling brake shoes

28 Make a note of the correct fitted positions of the springs and adjuster strut, to use as a guide on reassembly.

29 Carefully unhook both the upper and lower return springs, and remove them from the brake shoes.

30 Using a pair of pliers, remove the leading shoe retainer spring cup by depressing it and turning through 90°. With the cup removed, lift off the spring, then withdraw the retainer pin and remove the shoe from the backplate. Unhook the adjusting lever spring, and remove it from the leading shoe.

31 Detach the adjuster strut, and remove it from the trailing shoe.

32 Remove the trailing shoe retainer spring cup, spring and pin as described previously, then detach the handbrake cable and remove the shoe from the vehicle. Do not depress the brake pedal until the brakes are reassembled; wrap a strong elastic band around the wheel cylinder pistons to retain them.

33 If genuine Renault brake shoes are being installed, it will be necessary to remove the adjusting lever from the original leading shoe, and install it on the new shoe. All return springs should be renewed, regardless of their apparent condition; spring kits are also available from Renault dealers.

34 Withdraw the forked end from the adjuster strut. Carefully examine the assembly for signs of wear or damage, paying particular attention to the threads and the knurled adjuster wheel, and renew if necessary. Note that left-hand and right-hand struts are not interchangeable; the left-hand fork has a right-hand thread, and the right-hand fork a left-hand thread. The forks can also be identified by their colour: the left-hand fork is silver, and the right-hand fork is gold.

35 Remove the elastic band fitted to the wheel cylinder. Peel back the rubber

9

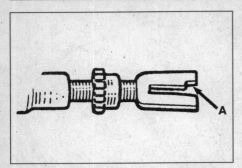

13.39 On Girling rear brakes, adjuster strut fork cut-out (A) must engage with leading shoe adjusting lever on refitting

14.3 Brake hose clamp fitted to the rear brake flexible hose

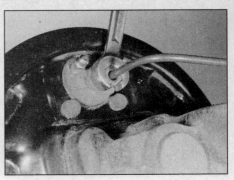

14.4 Unscrewing the union nut from the rear of the wheel cylinder

protective caps, and check the wheel cylinder for fluid leaks or other damage. Check that both cylinder pistons are free to move easily. Refer to Section 14, if necessary, for information on wheel cylinder renewal.

36 Prior to installation, clean the backplate, and apply a thin smear of high-temperature brake grease or anti-seize compound to all those surfaces of the backplate which bear on the shoes, particularly the wheel cylinder pistons and lower pivot point. Do not allow the lubricant to contaminate the friction material.

37 Ensure that the handbrake lever stop-peg is correctly located against the edge of the trailing shoe.

38 Locate the upper end of the trailing shoe in the wheel cylinder piston, then refit the retainer pin and spring, and secure it in position with the spring cup. Connect the handbrake cable to the lever.

39 Screw in the adjuster wheel until the minimum strut length is obtained, then hook the strut into position on the trailing shoe. Rotate the adjuster strut forked end so that the cut-out of the fork will engage with the leading shoe adjusting lever **(see illustration)**.

40 Fit the spring to the leading shoe adjusting lever, so that the shorter hook of the spring engages with the lever.

41 Slide the leading shoe assembly into position, ensuring that it is correctly engaged with the adjuster strut fork, and that the fork cut-out is engaged with the adjusting lever. Engage the upper end of the shoe in the wheel cylinder piston, then secure the shoe in position with the retainer pin, spring and spring cup.

42 Install the upper and lower return springs, then tap the shoes to centralise them on the backplate.

43 Using a screwdriver, turn the strut adjuster wheel until the diameter of the shoes is between 178.7 and 179.2 mm. This should just allow the brake drum to pass over the shoes.

44 Slide the drum into position over the linings, but do not refit the hub nut yet.

45 Repeat the above procedure on the remaining rear brake.

46 Carry out the procedures described previously in paragraphs 23 to 27.

14 Rear wheel cylinder - removal and refitting

Note: *Before starting work, refer to the warnings at the beginning of Sections 6 and 9, concerning the dangers of hydraulic fluid and asbestos dust.*

Removal

1 Remove the brake drum as described in Section 12.

2 Using pliers, carefully unhook the brake shoe upper return spring, and remove it from the brake shoes. Pull the upper ends of the shoes away from the wheel cylinder to disengage them from the pistons.

3 Minimise fluid loss by removing the fluid reservoir cap and tightening it down onto a piece of polythene, to obtain an airtight seal (taking care not to damage the fluid level sender unit). Alternatively, use a brake hose clamp, a G-clamp or a similar tool with protected jaws, to clamp the flexible hose at the nearest convenient point to the wheel cylinder **(see illustration)**.

4 Wipe away all traces of dirt around the brake pipe union at the rear of the wheel cylinder, and unscrew the union nut **(see illustration)**. Carefully ease the pipe out of the wheel cylinder, and plug or tape over its end, to prevent dirt entry. Wipe off any spilt fluid immediately.

5 Unscrew the two wheel cylinder retaining bolts from the rear of the backplate. Remove the cylinder, taking care not to allow hydraulic fluid to contaminate the brake shoe linings.

6 It is not possible to overhaul the cylinder, since no components are available separately. If faulty, the complete wheel cylinder assembly must be renewed.

Refitting

7 Ensure the backplate and wheel cylinder mating surfaces are clean, then spread the brake shoes and manoeuvre the wheel cylinder into position.

8 Engage the brake pipe, and screw in the union nut two or three turns to ensure that the thread has started.

9 Insert the two wheel cylinder retaining bolts,

and tighten them securely. Now fully tighten the brake pipe union nut.

10 Remove the clamp from the brake hose, or the polythene from the fluid reservoir (as applicable).

11 Ensure that the brake shoes are correctly located in the cylinder pistons. Carefully refit the brake shoe upper return spring, using a screwdriver to stretch the spring into position.

12 Refit the brake drum as described in Section 12.

13 Bleed the brake hydraulic system as described in Section 6. Providing suitable precautions were taken to minimise loss of fluid, it should only be necessary to bleed the relevant rear brake.

15 Rear brake pads - inspection and renewal

⚠️ *Warning: Renew BOTH sets of rear brake pads at the same time - never renew the pads on only one wheel, as uneven braking may result. Note that the dust created by wear of the pads may contain asbestos, which is a health hazard. Never blow it out with compressed air, and don't inhale any of it. An approved filtering mask should be worn when working on the brakes. DO NOT use petroleum-based solvents to clean brake parts - use brake cleaner or methylated spirit only.*

Inspection

1 Chock the front wheels, then engage reverse gear (or "P" on models with automatic transmission) and release the handbrake. Jack up the rear of the vehicle and support it securely on axle stands (see *"Jacking, towing and wheel changing"*). Remove the rear wheels.

2 Extract the small spring clip from the pad retaining plate. Slide the plate out of the caliper **(see illustrations)**.

3 Withdraw the inner pad from the caliper, using pliers if necessary. Where applicable, slacken and remove the two outer pad retaining screws, then withdraw the outer pad

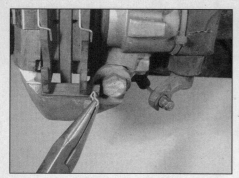

15.2a To remove the rear brake pads, remove the spring clip . . .

15.2b . . . then withdraw the retaining plate from the caliper

15.3a Slide out the inner brake pad . . .

from the caliper **(see illustrations)**. Make a note of the correct fitted position of the anti-rattle springs, and remove the springs from each pad.

4 First measure the thickness of each brake pad (friction material and backing plate). If either pad is worn at any point to the specified minimum thickness or less, all four pads must be renewed. Also, the pads should be renewed if any are contaminated with oil or grease; there is no satisfactory way of degreasing friction material, once contaminated. If any of the brake pads are worn unevenly, or fouled with oil or grease, trace and rectify the cause before reassembly. New brake pads and spring kits are available from Renault dealers.

5 If the brake pads are still serviceable, carefully clean them using a clean, fine wire brush or similar, paying particular attention to the sides and back of the metal backing. Clean out the grooves in the friction material, and pick out any large embedded particles of dirt or debris. Clean the pad locations in the caliper body/mounting bracket.

6 Prior to fitting the pads, check that the guide sleeves are free to slide easily in the caliper body, and that the guide sleeve rubber gaiters are undamaged. Brush the dust and dirt from the caliper and piston, but *do not inhale it, as it is injurious to health.* Inspect the dust seal around the piston for damage, and the piston for evidence of fluid leaks, corrosion or

damage. If attention to any of these components is necessary, refer to Section 16.

Renewal

7 If new brake pads are to be fitted, it will be necessary to retract the piston fully into the caliper bore by rotating it in a clockwise direction. This can be achieved using a suitable square-section bar, such as the shaft of a suitable screwdriver, which locates snugly in the caliper piston slots **(see illustration)**. Provided that the fluid reservoir has not been overfilled with hydraulic fluid, there should be no spillage, but keep a careful watch on the fluid level while retracting the piston. If the fluid level rises above the "MAX" level, the surplus should be syphoned off (not by mouth - use an old poultry baster or a pipette), or ejected via a plastic tube connected to the bleed screw (see Section 16).

8 Position the caliper piston so that the small groove scribed across the piston points in the direction of the caliper bleed screw. This is necessary to ensure that the lug on the inner pad will locate with the caliper piston slot on installation **(see illustration)**.

9 Refit the anti-rattle springs to the pads, so that when the pads are installed in the caliper, the spring end will be located at the opposite end of the pad in relation to the pad retaining plate **(see illustration)**. The brake pad with the lug on its backing plate is the inner pad.

15.3b . . . undo the two retaining screws . .

15.3c . . . and withdraw the outer brake pad

15.7 Retract the piston using a square-section bar

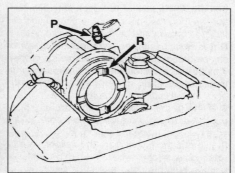

15.8 Prior to installing rear brake pads, align groove on caliper piston (R) with bleed screw (P)

15.9 Inner brake pad can be identified by its locating lug (arrowed). Note correct fitted positions of anti-rattle springs

9

15.13 Ensure inner pad locating lug is correctly located in piston slot (arrowed)

16.6 Remove the caliper mounting bolts, noting which way around the mounting plate is fitted (arrowed)

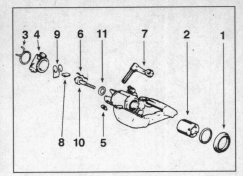

16.12 Exploded view of the rear brake caliper

1 Dust seal
2 Piston
3 Retaining clip
4 Handbrake
  mechanism dust
  cover
5 Circlip

6 Spring washers
7 Handbrake
  operating lever
8 Plunger cam
9 Return spring
10 Adjusting screw
11 Thrustwasher

10 Locate the outer brake pad in the caliper body, ensuring that its friction material is against the brake disc. Where applicable, insert the retaining screws and tighten them securely.

11 Slide the inner pad into position in the caliper, ensuring that the lug on the pad backing plate is aligned with the slot in the caliper piston. Recheck that the anti-rattle spring ends on both pads are at the opposite end of the pad to which the retaining plate is to be inserted.

12 Slide the retaining plate into place, and install the small spring clip at its inner end. It may be necessary to file an entry chamfer on the edge of the retaining key, to enable it to be fitted without difficulty.

13 Depress the brake pedal repeatedly until the pads are pressed into firm contact with the brake disc. Check that the inner pad lug is correctly engaged with one of the caliper piston slots **(see illustration)**.

14 Repeat the procedure on the remaining rear brake caliper.

15 Check the handbrake cable adjustment as described in Chapter 1, then refit the roadwheels and lower the vehicle to the ground. Tighten the roadwheel bolts to the specified torque.

16 Check the hydraulic fluid level as described in Chapter 1.

17 If new pads have been fitted, full braking efficiency will not be obtained until the linings have bedded-in. Be prepared for longer stopping distances, and avoid harsh braking as far as possible for the first hundred miles or so after fitting new pads.

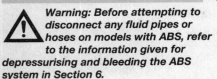

16 Rear brake caliper - removal, overhaul and refitting

⚠ *Warning: Before attempting to disconnect any fluid pipes or hoses on models with ABS, refer to the information given for depressurising and bleeding the ABS system in Section 6.*

Note: *Before starting work, refer to the warnings at the beginning of Sections 6 and 9 concerning the dangers of hydraulic fluid and asbestos dust.*

Removal

1 Chock the front wheels, engage reverse gear (or "P" on models with automatic transmission) and release the handbrake. Jack up the rear of the vehicle and support it securely on axle stands (see *"Jacking, towing and wheel changing"*). Remove the relevant rear wheel.

2 Remove the brake pads as described in paragraphs 2 and 3 of Section 15.

3 Free the handbrake inner cable from the caliper handbrake operating lever, then tap the outer cable out of its bracket on the caliper body.

4 Minimise fluid loss by removing the fluid reservoir cap and tightening it down onto a piece of polythene, to obtain an airtight seal (taking care not to damage the fluid level sender unit). Alternatively, use a brake hose clamp, a G-clamp or a similar tool with protected jaws, to clamp the flexible hose at the nearest convenient point to the brake caliper.

5 Wipe away all traces of dirt around the brake pipe union on the caliper, and unscrew the union nut. Carefully ease the pipe out of position, and plug or tape over its end, to prevent dirt entry. Wipe off any spilt fluid immediately.

6 Slacken the two bolts securing the caliper assembly to the trailing arm, and remove them along with the mounting plate, noting which way around the plate is fitted **(see illustration)**. Lift the caliper assembly away from the brake disc.

Overhaul

Note: *Ensure that an appropriate overhaul kit can be obtained before dismantling the caliper.*

7 With the caliper on the bench, wipe away all traces of dust and dirt, but *avoid inhaling the dust, as it is injurious to health*.

8 Using a small screwdriver, carefully prise out the dust seal from the caliper bore, taking care not to damage the piston.

9 Remove the piston from the caliper bore by rotating it anti-clockwise. This can be achieved using a suitable square-section bar, such as the shaft of a suitable screwdriver, which locates snugly in the caliper piston slots. Once the piston turns freely but does not come out

any further, the piston can be withdrawn by hand, or if necessary forced out by applying compressed air to the union bolt hole.

⚠ *Caution: The piston may be ejected with some force - only low pressure should be required, such as is generated by a foot pump.*

10 Using a blunt instrument such as a knitting needle or a crochet hook, extract the piston hydraulic seal, taking care not to damage the caliper bore.

11 Withdraw the guide sleeves from the caliper body, and remove the guide sleeve gaiters.

12 Inspect the caliper components as described in Section 10, paragraphs 13 to 17 **(see illustration)**. Renew the components as necessary, noting that the inside of the caliper piston *must not* be dismantled. If necessary, the handbrake mechanism can be overhauled as described in the following paragraphs. If it is not wished to overhaul the handbrake mechanism, proceed to paragraph 16.

13 Release the handbrake mechanism dust cover retaining clip, and peel the cover away from the rear of the caliper. Make a note of the correct fitted positions of the relative components, to use as a guide on reassembly. Remove the circlip from the base of the operating lever shaft, then compress the adjusting screw spring washers, and withdraw the operating lever and dust cover from the caliper body. With the lever withdrawn, remove the return spring, plunger cam, adjusting screw, spring washers and thrustwasher from the rear of the caliper body. Using a suitable pin punch, carefully tap the adjusting screw bush out of the caliper body, and remove the O-ring.

14 Clean all the handbrake mechanism components in methylated spirit, and examine them for wear. If there is any sign of wear or damage, the complete handbrake mechanism

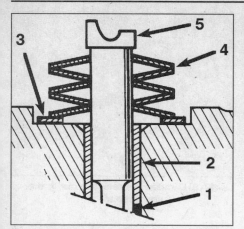

16.15 Correct fitted positions of rear brake caliper handbrake mechanism adjuster screw and associated components

1 O-ring
2 Adjusting screw bush
3 Thrustwasher
4 Correct arrangement of spring washers
5 Adjusting screw

assembly should be renewed; a kit is available from your Renault dealer.

15 Ensure that all components are clean and dry. Install the O-ring, then press the adjusting screw bush into position until its outer edge is flush with the rear of the caliper body; if necessary, tap the bush into position using a suitable tubular drift. Fit the thrustwasher, then install the adjusting screw and spring washers, ensuring that the washers are positioned as shown (see illustration). Locate the plunger cam in the end of the adjusting screw, and position the return spring in the caliper housing. Fit the new dust cover to the operating lever. Compress the adjusting screw spring washers, and insert the lever shaft through the caliper body, ensuring that it is correctly engaged with the return spring and plunger cam. Secure the operating lever in position with the circlip, then release the spring washers and check the operation of the handbrake mechanism. Apply a smear of high-melting point grease to the operating lever shaft and adjusting screw. Slide the dust cover over the caliper body, and secure it in position with a cable tie.

16 Soak the piston and the new piston (fluid) seal in clean hydraulic fluid. Smear clean fluid on the cylinder bore surface.

17 Fit the new piston (fluid) seal, using only the fingers to manipulate it into the cylinder bore groove, and refit the piston assembly. Turn the piston in a clockwise direction, using the method employed on dismantling, until it is fully retracted into the caliper bore.

18 Fit the dust seal to the caliper, ensuring that it is correctly located in the caliper and also the groove on the piston.

19 Apply the grease supplied in the repair kit (or a good-quality high-temperature brake grease or anti-seize compound) to the guide sleeves. Fit the guide sleeves to the caliper body, and fit the new gaiters, ensuring that the gaiters are correctly located in the grooves on both the guide sleeve and caliper body.

16.23 Tap the handbrake outer cable into position using a hammer and punch

Refitting

20 Position the caliper over the brake disc. Refit the two caliper mounting bolts and the mounting plate, noting that the mounting plate must be fitted so that its bend curves towards the caliper body. With the plate correctly positioned, tighten the caliper bolts to the specified torque.

21 Wipe clean the brake pipe union. Refit the pipe to the caliper, and tighten its union nut securely.

22 Remove the clamp from the brake hose, or the polythene from the fluid reservoir (as applicable).

23 Insert the handbrake cable through its bracket on the caliper, and tap the outer cable into position using a hammer and a pin punch (see illustration). Reconnect the inner cable to the caliper operating lever.

24 Refit the brake pads as described in Section 15.

25 Bleed the hydraulic system as described in Section 6. Note that, providing the precautions described were taken to minimise brake fluid loss, it should only be necessary to bleed the relevant rear brake.

26 Repeatedly apply the brake pedal, to bring the pads into contact with the disc. Check and if necessary adjust the handbrake cable as described in Chapter 1.

27 Refit the roadwheel, lower the vehicle to the ground and tighten the wheel bolts to the specified torque.

28 On completion, check the hydraulic fluid level as described in Chapter 1.

17 Rear brake disc - inspection, removal and refitting

Note: Before starting work, refer to the warning at the beginning of Section 16 concerning the dangers of asbestos dust. If either disc requires renewal, BOTH should be renewed at the same time, to ensure even and

17.5 Prising out the rear disc hub cap

consistent braking. A new rear hub nut will be required on refitting.

Inspection

1 Chock the front wheels, engage reverse gear (or "P" on models with automatic transmission) and release the handbrake. Jack up the rear of the vehicle and support it securely on axle stands (see "Jacking, towing and wheel changing"). Remove the appropriate rear roadwheel.

2 Inspect the disc as described in Section 11, paragraphs 2 to 5.

Removal

3 Remove the brake pads as described in paragraphs 2 and 3 of Section 15.

4 Remove the two caliper frame retaining bolts. Remove the frame from the caliper body.

5 Using a hammer and a large flat-bladed screwdriver, carefully tap and prise the cap out of the centre of the brake disc (see illustration).

6 Using a socket and long bar, slacken and remove the rear hub nut, and withdraw the thrustwasher. Discard the hub nut; a new nut must be used on refitting.

7 It should now be possible to withdraw the brake disc and hub bearing assembly from the stub axle by hand. It may be difficult to remove the disc, due to the tightness of the hub bearing on the stub axle. If the bearing is tight, tap the periphery of the disc using a hide or plastic mallet. Alternatively, use a universal puller, secured to the disc with the wheel bolts, to pull it off. Remove the spacer from the rear of the disc, noting which way round it is fitted.

Refitting

8 Prior to refitting the disc, smear the stub axle shaft with gear oil. Be careful not to contaminate the friction surfaces with oil. If a new disc is to be fitted, use a suitable solvent to wipe any preservative coating from its surface.

9 Refit the spacer to the rear of the disc, noting that its slightly bigger protrusion should face the hub bearing. Slide the disc onto the

9

17.9a Refit the spacer to the rear of the brake disc . . .

17.9b . . . and slide the disc onto the stub axle

17.10 Tighten the rear hub nut to the specified torque

stub axle, and tap it into position using a soft-faced mallet **(see illustrations)**.

10 Slide on the thrustwasher, then fit the new rear hub nut and tighten it to the specified torque **(see illustration)**. Tap the cap back into position in the centre of the disc.

11 Apply a few drops of locking fluid to the threads of the caliper frame retaining bolts. Offer up the frame and refit the bolts. Tighten both bolts to the specified torque **(see illustrations)**.

12 Refit the brake pads as described in Section 15.

13 Check the handbrake cable adjustment as described in Chapter 1.

14 Refit the roadwheels and lower the vehicle to the ground. Tighten the roadwheel bolts to the specified torque.

17.11a Apply locking fluid to the retaining bolts, then refit the caliper bracket . . .

17.11b . . . and tighten the bolts

18 Load-sensitive pressure-regulating valve (models with rear disc brakes) - general information

1 On models with rear disc brakes, a load-sensitive pressure-regulating valve is incorporated in the hydraulic circuit. The valve regulates the pressure applied to the rear brakes, and reduces the risk of the rear wheels locking under heavy braking. It is mounted underneath the rear of the vehicle, above the rear axle assembly **(see illustration)**.

2 Removal and refitting of the valve is a straightforward process, but on completion, specialist equipment is required to check and adjust the operation of the valve. Therefore, if the valve is to be removed or if it is thought to be faulty, the work should be entrusted to a Renault dealer, who will have the necessary test equipment.

19 Handbrake lever - removal and refitting

Removal

1 Chock the front wheels, then jack up the rear of the vehicle and support it securely on axle stands (see *"Jacking, towing and wheel changing"*). Fully release the handbrake.

2 Working under the vehicle, unscrew the

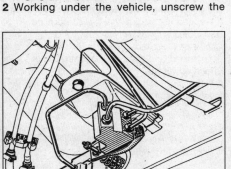
18.1 Load-sensitive pressure-regulating valve - models with rear disc brakes

handbrake cable adjuster locknut and the adjuster nut from the end of the handbrake lever rod. Remove the cable compensator from the handbrake lever rod.

3 Release the handbrake lever rod from the support/guide block.

4 Working inside the vehicle, remove the covers (two screws in each case), then unbolt the two seat belt flexible stalk anchorages.

5 Make a slit in the carpet, just to the rear of the lever assembly, to provide access to the lever mountings.

6 Spread the carpet and disconnect the "handbrake-on" warning light switch wiring.

7 Unscrew the two bolts securing the lever assembly to the floor, and remove the assembly from inside the vehicle **(see illustration)**.

Refitting

8 Refitting is a reversal of removal but, on completion, adjust the handbrake as described in Chapter 1.

20 Handbrake cables - removal and refitting

Removal

1 The handbrake cable consists of two sections, a right- and left-hand section, which are linked to the lever assembly by an equaliser plate. Each section can be removed individually as follows.

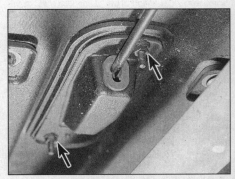
19.7 View of handbrake lever mounting bolts (arrowed) from under the vehicle

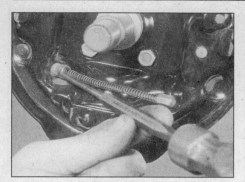

20.5 Tapping the handbrake outer cable from the brake backplate (rear drum brake models)

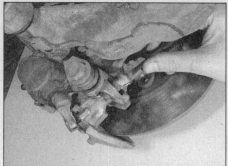

20.6 On rear disc brake models, disconnect the handbrake cable from the brake caliper

20.7 Handbrake cable support clip

2 Chock the front wheels, engage reverse gear (or "P" on models with automatic transmission) and release the handbrake. Jack up the rear of the vehicle and support it securely on axle stands (see *"Jacking, towing and wheel changing"*).

3 Where applicable, working from underneath the vehicle, undo the nut(s) securing the exhaust system heat shield to the vehicle underbody. Lower the rear of the heat shield to gain access to the handbrake cable adjuster nuts. If necessary, disconnect the exhaust system from its rubber mountings to give additional clearance (make sure that the system is not strained).

4 Slacken the cable locknut and adjuster nut, until there is sufficient slack in the inner cable to allow it to be disconnected from the equaliser plate.

5 On models with rear drum brakes, remove the rear brake shoes from the appropriate side as described in Section 13. Using a hammer and pin punch, carefully tap the outer cable from the brake backplate **(see illustration)**.

6 On models with rear disc brakes, disengage the inner cable from the caliper handbrake lever. Using a hammer and pin punch, tap the outer cable out of its mounting bracket on the caliper **(see illustration)**.

7 Working along the length of the cable, remove any retaining bolts and screws, and free the cable from any retaining clips and ties **(see illustration)**. Remove the cable from under the vehicle.

Refitting

8 Refitting is a reversal of removal, but adjust the handbrake as described in Chapter 1. Note that on models with rear drum brakes, the cable is adjusted before the brake drum is refitted.

21 Stop-light switch - removal, refitting and adjustment

Removal

1 The stop-light switch is located on the pedal bracket, beneath the facia **(see illustration)**.

2 To remove the switch, reach up behind the facia, then pull off the wiring plug, and unscrew the switch from the bracket.

Refitting and adjustment

3 Screw the switch back into position in the pedal bracket.

4 Connect a continuity tester (ohmmeter or self-powered test light) across the switch terminals. Screw the switch in until an open-circuit is present between the switch terminals (infinite resistance, or the test light goes out). Gently depress the pedal, and check that continuity exists between the switch terminals (zero resistance, or the test light comes on) after the pedal has travelled approximately 6.0 mm. If necessary, reposition the switch until it operates as specified.

5 In the absence of a continuity tester, the same adjustment can be made by reconnecting the wiring to the switch, and having an assistant observe the stop-lights (ignition on).

6 Once the stop-light switch is correctly adjusted, reconnect the wiring, if not already done, and recheck the operation of the stop-lights.

22 Anti-lock braking system (ABS) - general information

⚠️ *Warning: Before attempting to disconnect any fluid pipes or hoses on models with ABS, refer to the information given for depressurising and bleeding the ABS system in Section 6.*

Bendix ABS

1 ABS is available as an option on certain models. The purpose of the system is to prevent wheel(s) locking during heavy braking. This is achieved by automatic release of the brake on the relevant wheel, followed by reapplication of the brake.

2 The main components of the system are four wheel sensors (one per wheel), a master cylinder/regulator assembly, an electric pump unit (used to return fluid to the reservoir), and the ABS computer **(see illustrations)**.

3 The solenoids are controlled by the

21.1 Stop-light switch and wiring (arrowed)

computer, which receives signals from the wheel sensors. The sensors detect the speed of rotation of a toothed ring, known as a reluctor ring, attached to the wheel hub. By comparing the speed signals from the four wheels, the computer can determine when a wheel is decelerating at an abnormal rate, and can therefore predict when a wheel is about to lock. During normal operation, the system functions in the same way as a non-ABS braking system.

4 If the computer senses that a front wheel is about to lock, the ABS system regulates the fluid pressure supplied to the relevant caliper(s) as follows. The computer operates the relevant solenoid valve(s) in the regulator block. If the computer determines that a rapid pressure release is required, the high-pressure input to the relevant caliper(s) is shut off, and the return to the reservoir is opened. If a slow pressure release is required, the direct return to the reservoir is closed off, so that the fluid has to pass through calibrated holes on its way back to the reservoir. If a wheel picks up speed, the relevant solenoid valve(s) are opened to reapply fluid pressure as required.

5 If the computer senses that a rear wheel is about to lock, the high-pressure input to the calipers is shut off, and the return to the reservoir is opened. At the same time, the pressure differential between the high-pressure side and the return side causes a mechanical valve to close. The fluid pressure to both rear wheels is regulated similarly, and the computer establishes the degree of control

9

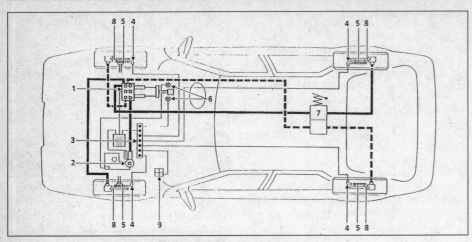

22.2a Bendix ABS components

1 Hydraulic modulator/master
   cylinder unit
2 Electric pump assembly
3 Computer
4 Wheel sensors
5 Sensor reluctor rings
6 Instrument panel warning
   lights
7 Pressure-regulating valve
8 Disc brakes
9 Diagnostic socket

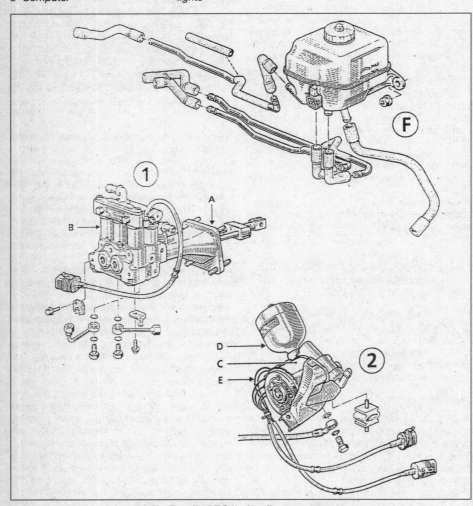

22.2b Bendix ABS hydraulic components

1 Hydraulic modulator/master
   cylinder unit
2 Electric pump assembly
A Master cylinders
B Modulator unit
C Electric pump
D Pressure accumulator
E Pressure switches
F Fluid reservoir assembly

to be applied using information from the rear wheel with the lowest level of grip.

6 If a rear wheel picks up speed, the high-pressure circuit is opened, and the return to the reservoir is closed. The fluid flows through a circuit which is parallel with the mechanical valve (which is still closed), passing through calibrated holes until the pressure differential between the high pressure and return sides falls to zero.

7 The cycling of applying and releasing the brakes can be carried out at up to 10 times a second.

8 The action of the solenoid valves and the electric pump creates pulses in the hydraulic circuit. When the ABS system is functioning, these pulses can be felt through the brake pedal.

9 The operation of the ABS system is entirely dependent on electrical signals. To prevent the system responding to any inaccurate signals, a built-in safety circuit monitors all signals received by the computer. If an inaccurate signal (or low battery voltage) is detected, the ABS system is automatically shut down, and the warning light on the instrument panel is illuminated, to inform the driver that the ABS system is not operational. Normal braking is unaffected, although in some instances, greater pedal pressure may be required to operate the brakes, due to the lack of servo assistance.

10 If a fault does develop in the ABS system, the vehicle must be taken to a Renault dealer for fault diagnosis and repair. Check first, however, that the problem is not due to loose or damaged wiring connections, or badly-routed wiring picking up spurious signals from the ignition system.

Bosch ABS

11 The purpose of the system is to prevent wheel(s) locking during heavy braking. This is achieved by automatic release of the brake on the relevant wheel, followed by reapplication of the brake.

12 The main components of the system are four wheel sensors (one per wheel), and a modulator block which contains the ABS computer, the hydraulic solenoid valves and accumulators, and an electrically-driven return pump **(see illustration)**.

13 The solenoids are controlled by the computer, which receives signals from the wheel sensors. The sensors detect the speed of rotation of a toothed ring, known as a reluctor ring, attached to the wheel hub. By comparing the speed signals from the four wheels, the computer can determine when a wheel is decelerating at an abnormal rate, and can therefore predict when a wheel is about to lock. During normal operation, the system functions in the same way as a non-ABS braking system.

14 If the computer senses that a wheel is about to lock, the ABS system enters the "pressure-maintain" phase. The computer operates the relevant solenoid valve in the modulator block; this isolates the brake caliper on the wheel in question from the master cylinder, effectively sealing-in the hydraulic pressure.

15 If the speed of rotation of the wheel continues to decrease at an abnormal rate, the ABS system then enters the "pressure-decrease" phase. The return pump operates, and pumps the hydraulic fluid back into the master cylinder, releasing pressure on the brake caliper. When the speed of rotation of the wheel returns to an acceptable rate, the pump stops and the solenoid valve opens, allowing hydraulic pressure to return to the caliper and reapply the brake. This cycle can be carried out at up to 10 times a second.

16 The action of the solenoid valves and return pump creates pulses in the hydraulic circuit. When the ABS system is functioning, these pulses can be felt through the brake pedal.

17 The solenoid valves connected to the front calipers operate independently, but the valve connected to the rear calipers, together with the load-sensitive pressure-regulating valve, operates both calipers simultaneously. Since the braking circuit is split diagonally, a separate mechanical plunger valve in the modulator block divides the rear solenoid valve hydraulic outlet into two separate circuits.

18 The operation of the ABS system is entirely dependent on electrical signals. To prevent the system responding to any inaccurate signals, a built-in safety circuit

monitors all signals received by the computer. If an inaccurate signal (or low battery voltage) is detected, the ABS system is automatically shut down, and the warning light on the instrument panel is illuminated, to inform the driver that the ABS system is not operational. Normal braking is unaffected.

19 If a fault does develop in the ABS system, the vehicle must be taken to a Renault dealer for fault diagnosis and repair. Check first, however, that the problem is not due to loose or damaged wiring connections, or badly-routed wiring picking up spurious signals from the ignition system.

23 Anti-lock braking system components (Bendix ABS) - removal and refitting

Front wheel sensor
Removal

1 The front wheel sensors are originally supplied complete with the computer, and for renewal it is necessary to cut the wiring and obtain a new sensor, complete with a fitting kit **(see illustration)**. The sensors are located in the front stub axle carriers.

2 Disconnect the battery negative lead.

3 Apply the handbrake, then jack up the front of the vehicle, and support securely on axle

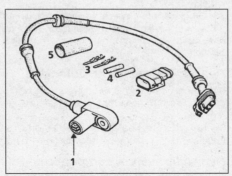

23.1 Bendix ABS front wheel sensor fitting kit

1 Sensor   2 Tab connector   3 Tabs
4 Sleeves containing sealing mastic
5 Heat shrinking cover

stands (see *"Jacking, towing and wheel changing"*). Remove the relevant roadwheel.

4 Remove the sensor securing screw **(see illustration)**.

5 Release the sensor wiring from any clips and brackets, and peel back the plastic sleeving.

6 Cut the wiring at the point where the connector is to be fitted, then remove the sensor.

Refitting

7 Fit the female half of the connector supplied in the fitting kit to the wiring running from the computer. Place the sleeves full of sealing mastic over the wiring, approximately 5.0 mm from the wire apertures in the connector. Fit the heat shrink cover, taking great care to ensure that the connection is absolutely leak-proof.

8 Coat the sensor with light grease, then fit it to the stub axle carrier and tighten the securing screw.

9 Connect the two halves of the wiring connector, and clip the wiring into position.

10 For reference, it is possible to check the air gap between the sensor and the reluctor ring, as follows. Note that the gap cannot be adjusted; the check will merely give an indication as to whether the components (sensor and reluctor ring) are damaged.

11 Turn the wheel hub/brake disc until the crest of one of the reluctor ring teeth is directly opposite the tip of the sensor.

12 Using a feeler gauge, check that the air gap between the reluctor ring tooth and the tip of the sensor is as given in the Specifications.

Rear wheel sensor
Removal

13 The sensors are located in brackets attached to the trailing arms.

14 Disconnect the battery negative lead.

15 Chock the front wheels, engage reverse gear (or "P" on models with automatic transmission) and release the handbrake. Jack up the rear of the vehicle and support it securely on axle stands (see *"Jacking, towing and wheel changing"*). Remove the relevant rear wheel.

16 Remove the sensor securing screw, and withdraw the sensor from its bracket **(see illustration)**.

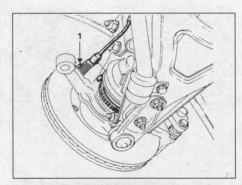

23.4 Bendix ABS front wheel sensor securing screw (1)

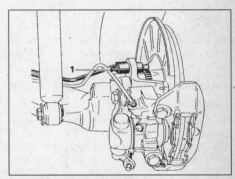

23.16 Bendix ABS rear wheel sensor securing screw (1)

22.12 Bosch ABS components

1 Modulator assembly
2 Master cylinder and servo unit
3 Wheel sensor
4 Sensor reluctor ring
5 Pressure-regulating valve

9

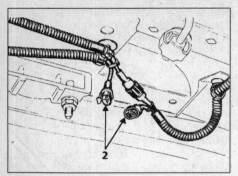

23.17 Bendix ABS rear wheel sensor wiring connector (2)

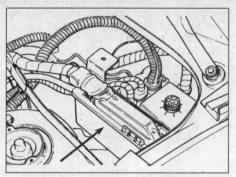

23.20 Bendix ABS computer location (arrowed)

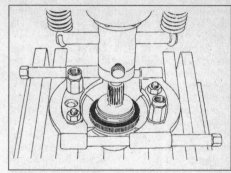

23.29 Pressing the ABS reluctor ring from a driveshaft

17 Unclip the wiring from any support clips and brackets, then separate the two halves of the wiring connector (located near the rear suspension assembly left-hand mounting point) **(see illustration)**.

Refitting

18 Coat the sensor with light grease, then refit it using a reversal of the removal procedure. Ensure that the wiring connector halves are securely reconnected.
19 On completion, using a feeler gauge, check that the air gap between the reluctor ring tooth and the tip of the sensor is as given in the Specifications. Note that the air gap cannot be adjusted; the check will merely give an indication as to whether the components (sensor and reluctor ring) are damaged.

ABS computer

Removal

20 The computer is located in the left-hand corner of the scuttle, in front of the windscreen **(see illustration)**.
21 Disconnect the battery negative lead.
22 Remove the securing screws, and withdraw the plastic cover from in front of the windscreen.
23 Release the securing clip, and disconnect the wiring plug from the computer.
24 Unscrew the three bolts securing the computer mounting plate to the bodyshell, then lift the assembly clear of the scuttle.
25 Remove the three bolts securing the computer to the mounting plate, and withdraw the computer.

Refitting

26 Refitting is a reversal of removal, ensuring that the wiring connector is securely reconnected.

Front wheel sensor reluctor ring

Removal

27 The reluctor ring is attached to the driveshaft.
28 Remove the driveshaft as described in Chapter 8.
29 Support the reluctor ring in a suitable press, then press the driveshaft from the ring **(see illustration)**. Alternatively, use a suitable

three-legged puller to pull the ring from the end of the driveshaft.

Refitting

30 Ensure that the mating faces of the driveshaft and the reluctor ring are absolutely clean.
31 Coat the inner mating face of the reluctor ring with locking compound, then fit it over the end of the driveshaft.
32 Carefully tap the reluctor ring into position on the driveshaft using a soft-faced mallet. Tap evenly around the outside of the ring, making sure that it does not tilt, and ensuring that it seats firmly against the driveshaft shoulder.
33 On completion, check the air gap between the wheel sensor and the reluctor ring, as described in paragraphs 10 to 12 of this Section.

Rear wheel sensor reluctor ring

34 The reluctor ring is an integral part of the brake disc/hub assembly, and cannot be removed.
35 Refer to Section 17 of this Chapter for details of brake disc/hub removal and refitting.

Hydraulic system components

⚠️ **Warning: Before attempting to disconnect any fluid pipes or hoses on models with ABS, refer to the information given for depressurising and bleeding the ABS system in Section 6.**

24.1a Loosening a front wheel sensor securing screw - Bosch ABS

36 After removal and refitting of any of the hydraulic system components, it is necessary to bleed the complete hydraulic system, and test the operation of the system. Due to the requirement for specialist knowledge and equipment to carry out these operations, it is recommended that any tasks involving the removal and refitting of hydraulic system components are entrusted to a Renault dealer.

24 Anti-lock braking system components (Bosch ABS) - removal and refitting

Wheel sensors

1 Refer to the procedure given in the previous Section for models with the Bendix ABS system. The front wheel sensor is connected to the ABS wiring harness using a conventional connector, therefore the references to cutting the wiring, and the use of a fitting kit, can be ignored **(see illustrations)**.

ABS computer

Removal\

2 The computer is located on the ABS modulator unit in the engine compartment.
3 Disconnect the battery negative lead.
4 Slacken the retaining screw, and remove the relay cover from the modulator assembly **(see illustration)**.
5 Disconnect the three wiring connectors from the computer unit **(see illustration)**.

24.1b Removing a front wheel sensor - Bosch ABS

24.1c Checking a front wheel sensor-to-reluctor ring clearance - Bosch ABS

24.4 Slackening the relay cover retaining screw - Bosch ABS

24.5 Disconnect the three wiring connectors (arrowed) . . .

6 Remove the six Torx retaining screws, and lift the computer away from the modulator assembly **(see illustrations)**.

Refitting

7 Refitting is a reversal of removal.

Wheel sensor reluctor rings

8 The procedures are as described for the Bendix ABS in the previous Section.

Hydraulic system components

9 At the time of writing, no information was available for removal and refitting of the Bosch ABS hydraulic system components.

24.6a . . . remove the retaining screws . . .

24.6b . . . and remove the ABS computer from the modulator

9

Notes

Chapter 10 Suspension and steering

Contents

Degrees of difficulty

Easy, suitable for novice with little experience	Fairly easy, suitable for beginner with some experience	Fairly difficult, suitable for competent DIY mechanic	Difficult, suitable for experienced DIY mechanic	Very difficult, suitable for expert DIY or professional

Specifications

Front suspension

Type	Independent by MacPherson struts, with inclined coil springs and integral shock absorbers. Anti-roll bar on certain models
Hub bearing endfloat	0 to 0.05 mm

Rear suspension

Type	Trailing arms, with transverse torsion bars (enclosed- or open-bar type, according to model) and telescopic shock absorbers. Rear anti-roll bar(s) on all models
Hub bearing endfloat	0 to 0.03 mm

Steering

Type	Rack-and-pinion, power-assisted on certain models

Wheel alignment

Front wheel toe-setting (all models - vehicle unladen)	1.0 ± 1.0 mm (0°10' ± 10') toe-out
Rear wheel toe-setting:	
Open-bar type rear suspension	0.5 to 2.5 mm (0°05' to 0°25') toe-in
Enclosed-bar type rear suspension	1.0 to 3.0 mm (0°10' to 0°30') toe-in

Roadwheels

Type	Pressed-steel or alloy (according to model)
Size	5Bx13, 5Jx13, 51/2Bx13, 51/2Jx14 or 61/2Jx15 (depending on model)
Maximum run-out at rim	1.2 mm

Tyres

Size	145 R 13S, 165/70 R 13T, 175/70 R 13T, 175/70 R 13H, 175/65 R 14T, 175/65 R 14H or 195/50 R 15V (depending on model)
Pressures	See *Chapter 1 Specifications*

Torque wrench settings

	Nm	lbf ft
Front suspension		
Lower balljoint-to-stub axle carrier clamp bolt	55	41
Stub axle carrier-to-strut bolts	110	81
Suspension strut upper mounting bolts	25	18
Suspension strut upper mounting nut	60	44
Anti-roll bar mountings	35	26
Lower arm inner pivot bolts	75	55
Balljoint-to-lower arm bolts	75	55
Driveshaft nut	250	185
Rear suspension		
Shock absorber lower mounting bolts	60	44
Shock absorber upper mounting nuts	20	15
Anti-roll bar-to-trailing arm bolts (enclosed-bar rear suspension)	45	33
Trailing arm (rear axle) bearing bracket mounting bolts	80	59
Rear hub nut	160	118
Brake backplate-to-trailing arm bolts	45	33
Steering		
Track rod end-to-stub axle carrier nut	35	26
Track rod end locknut	35	26
Steering wheel mounting nut	40	30
Steering gear mounting bolts	50	37
Intermediate shaft-to-pinion shaft universal joint clamp bolt	30	22
Roadwheels		
Wheel bolts	80	59

1 General information

The independent front suspension is of the MacPherson strut type, incorporating coil springs and integral telescopic shock absorbers. The MacPherson struts are located by transverse lower suspension arms, which utilise rubber inner mounting bushes, and incorporate a balljoint at the outer ends. The front stub axle carriers, which carry the wheel bearings, brake calipers and the hub/disc assemblies, are bolted to the MacPherson struts, and connected to the lower arms via the balljoints. A front anti-roll bar is fitted to all most larger-engined models. The anti-roll bar is rubber-mounted onto the subframe, and connects both the lower suspension arms **(see illustrations)**.

The rear suspension differs according to model. Models with 1237 cc, 1390 cc and 1397 cc engines have an enclosed-bar type rear axle, which consists of two torsion bars within a tubular crossmember which connects both the rear trailing arms. An anti-roll bar is situated just to the rear of the crossmember, and is also connected to both trailing arms **(see illustrations)**.

Models with 1721 cc, 1764 cc and 1794 cc engines are fitted with an open-bar rear axle which consists of two torsion bars, two anti-roll bars, and an L-section metal crossmember which is connected to both the trailing arms. The two torsion bars and two anti-roll bars are connected at the centre with a link, and at their outer ends to the trailing arms **(see illustration)**.

The steering column is connected by a universal joint to an intermediate shaft, which has a second universal joint at its lower end.

The lower universal joint is attached to the steering gear pinion by means of a clamp bolt.

The steering gear is mounted onto the front subframe. It is connected by two track rods and balljoints to steering arms projecting rearwards from the stub axle carriers. The track rod ends are threaded to permit wheel alignment adjustment.

Power-assisted steering is available on most larger-engined models. On 1764 cc (F7P engine) models equipped with air conditioning and power steering, an electric power steering pump is used to power the steering hydraulic system; this is due to lack of space in the engine compartment to house both the air conditioning compressor and a belt-driven pump. All other models equipped with power steering are fitted with a traditional belt-driven pump, which is driven off the crankshaft pulley.

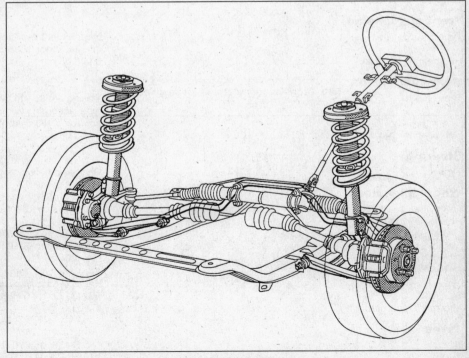

1.1a Front suspension layout

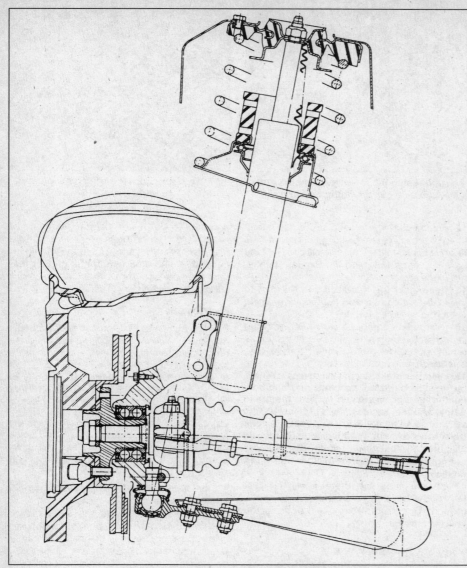

1.1b Cross-section of the front suspension

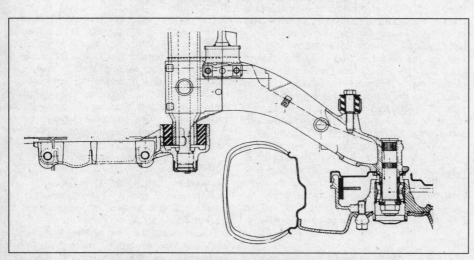

1.2b Cross-section of the enclosed-bar type rear suspension

2 Front stub axle carrier - removal and refitting

Removal

1 Apply the handbrake, then jack up the front of the vehicle and support it securely on axle stands (see *"Jacking, towing and wheel changing"*). Remove the appropriate front roadwheel.

2 Refit at least two roadwheel bolts to the front hub, and tighten them securely. Have an assistant firmly depress the brake pedal to prevent the front hub from rotating. Using a socket and a long extension bar, slacken and remove the driveshaft retaining nut and washer. This nut is extremely tight. Discard the driveshaft nut; a new one should be used on refitting.

> **TOOL TiP** *To secure the hub, a tool can be fabricated from two lengths of steel strip (one long, one short) and a nut and bolt; the nut and bolt form the pivot of a forked tool. Bolt the tool to the hub using two wheel bolts, and hold the tool to prevent the hub from rotating as the driveshaft retaining nut is undone (see illustration).*

3 If the hub bearings are to be disturbed, remove the brake disc as described in Chap-

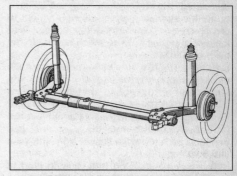

1.2a Enclosed-bar type rear suspension layout (drum brakes shown)

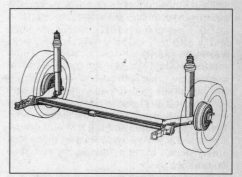

1.3 Open-bar type rear suspension layout (drum brakes shown)

10

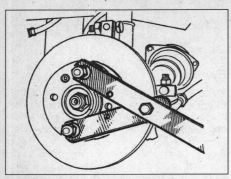

2.2 Using two lengths of metal bar to hold the front hub stationary when unscrewing the driveshaft nut

2.6 Loosening the lower suspension arm-to-stub axle carrier clamp bolt and nut

2.7 Stub axle carrier-to-suspension strut nuts (arrowed)

ter 9. If not, unbolt the brake caliper and move it to one side, as described in Chapter 9. Note that there is no need to disconnect the fluid hose - tie the caliper to the front suspension coil spring, using a piece of wire or string, to avoid straining the brake hose.

4 On models equipped with ABS, undo the retaining bolt and withdraw the front wheel sensor from the stub axle carrier. Tie the sensor to the suspension strut, so that it does not get damaged during the remainder of the removal procedure.

5 Remove the nut securing the track rod end balljoint to the stub axle carrier. Release the balljoint tapered shank using a universal balljoint separator.

6 Remove the nut and clamp bolt securing the lower suspension arm to the stub axle carrier **(see illustration)**. Carefully lever the balljoint out of the stub axle carrier, taking care not to damage the balljoint or driveshaft gaiters. Note the plastic protector plate which is fitted to the balljoint shank.

7 Remove the two nuts and washers from the bolts securing the stub axle carrier to the suspension strut, noting that the nuts are positioned on the rear side of the strut **(see illustration)**. Withdraw the bolts, and support the stub axle carrier assembly.

8 Release the driveshaft joint from the hub, and remove the stub axle carrier assembly from the vehicle. Note that locking fluid is applied to the joint splines during assembly, so it is likely that they will be a tight fit in the hub. Use a hammer and soft metal drift to tap the joint out of the hub, or use a puller to draw the swivel hub assembly off the joint splines.

Refitting

9 Ensure that the driveshaft joint and hub splines are clean and dry, then apply a coat of locking fluid to the joint splines.

10 Engage the joint splines with the hub, and slide the hub fully onto the driveshaft. Insert the two stub axle carrier-to-suspension strut mounting bolts from the front side of the strut, then refit the washers and nuts to the rear of the bolts, and tighten them to the specified torque.

11 Slide on the washer and fit the new driveshaft nut, tightening it by hand only at this stage.

12 Ensure that the plastic protector is still fitted to the lower arm balljoint, then locate the balljoint shank in the stub axle carrier. Refit the balljoint clamp bolt, and tighten its retaining nut to the specified torque.

13 Reconnect the track rod end balljoint to the stub axle carrier, and tighten its retaining nut to the specified torque.

14 On models equipped with ABS, refit the sensor to the stub axle carrier, and tighten its retaining bolt to the specified torque (see Chapter 9).

15 Refit the brake disc (if removed), aligning the marks made on removal, and securely tighten its retaining screw(s). Refit the brake caliper assembly as described in Chapter 9.

16 Insert and tighten two wheel bolts. Tighten the driveshaft nut to the specified torque (Chapter 8), using the method employed during removal to prevent the hub from rotating.

17 Check that the hub rotates freely, then refit the roadwheel and lower the vehicle to the ground. Tighten the roadwheel bolts to the specified torque.

3 Front hub bearings - checking, removal and refitting

Note: *The bearing is a sealed, pre-adjusted and pre-lubricated, double-row roller type, and is intended to last the car's entire service life without maintenance or attention. Do not attempt to remove the bearing unless absolutely necessary, as it will be damaged during the removal operation. Never overtighten the driveshaft nut in an attempt to "adjust" the bearing.*

A press will be required to dismantle and rebuild the assembly; if such a tool is not available, a large bench vice and suitable spacers (such as large sockets) will serve as an adequate substitute. The bearing's inner races are an interference fit on the hub; if the inner race remains on the hub when it is pressed out of the hub carrier, a suitable knife-edged bearing puller will be required to remove it.

Checking

1 Wear in the front hub bearings can be checked by measuring the amount of side play

present. To do this, a dial gauge should be fixed so that its probe is in contact with the disc face of the hub. The play should be between 0 and 0.05 mm. If it is greater than this, the bearings are worn excessively, and should be renewed.

Removal

2 Remove the stub axle carrier as described in Section 2. Where applicable, undo the brake disc shield retaining screws and remove the shield from the stub axle carrier.

3 Support the stub axle carrier securely on blocks or in a vice. Using a suitable tubular spacer which bears only on the inner end of the hub flange, press the hub flange inner out of the bearing. If the bearing outboard inner race remains on the hub, remove it using a suitable bearing puller (see note above), then slide the thrustwasher off the hub flange, noting which way round it is fitted.

4 Extract the bearing retaining circlip from the inner end of the stub axle carrier.

5 Where necessary, refit the inner race in position over the ball cage, and securely support the inner face of the stub axle carrier. Using a suitable tubular spacer which bears only on the inner race, press the complete bearing assembly out of the housing in the stub axle carrier.

6 Thoroughly clean the hub and stub axle carrier, removing all traces of dirt and grease. Polish away any burrs or raised edges which might hinder reassembly. Check for cracks or any other signs of wear or damage, and renew the components if necessary. As noted above, the bearing and its circlip must be renewed whenever they are disturbed. A replacement bearing kit, which consists of the bearing, circlip and thrustwasher, is available from Renault dealers.

Refitting

7 On reassembly, check (if possible) that the new bearing is packed with grease. Apply a light film of oil to the bearing outer race and to the hub flange shaft.

8 Before fitting the new bearing, remove the plastic covers protecting the seals at each end, but leave the inner plastic sleeve in position to hold the inner races together.

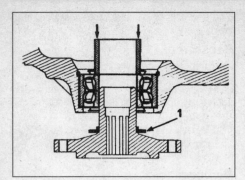

3.12 Refitting the hub flange

1 Thrustwasher

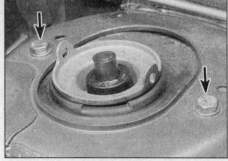

4.3 Front suspension strut upper mounting bolts (arrowed)

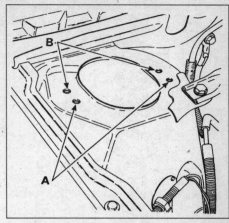

4.7 Front suspension strut upper mounting bolt holes

A Manual steering models
B Power-assisted steering models

9 Securely support the stub axle carrier, and locate the bearing in its housing. Press the bearing into position, ensuring that it enters the housing squarely, using a suitable tubular spacer which bears only on the outer race.

10 Once the bearing is correctly seated, secure it with the new circlip and remove the plastic sleeve. Apply a smear of grease to the oil seal lips.

11 Slide the thrustwasher onto the hub flange, ensuring that its flat surface is facing the flange. Securely support the outer face of the hub flange.

12 Locate the stub axle carrier and the bearing inner race over the end of the hub flange. Press the bearing onto the hub flange, using a tubular spacer which bears only on the inner race, until it seats against the thrustwasher **(see illustration)**. Check that the hub flange rotates freely. Wipe off any excess oil or grease.

13 Where applicable, refit the brake disc shield to the stub axle carrier, and tighten its retaining screws.

14 Refit the stub axle carrier as described in Section 2.

4 Front suspension strut - removal and refitting

Removal

1 Apply the handbrake, then jack up the front of the vehicle and support it securely on axle stands (see *"Jacking, towing and wheel changing"*). Remove the appropriate roadwheel.

2 Remove the two nuts and washers from the bolts securing the stub axle carrier to the suspension strut, noting that the nuts are positioned on the rear side of the strut. Withdraw the bolts, and support the stub axle carrier.

3 From within the engine compartment, unscrew the two bolts securing the strut upper mounting to the turret **(see illustration)**. Note that there are two sets of holes - one for models with manual steering, and the other for models with power-assisted steering.

4 Release the strut from the stub axle carrier, and withdraw it from under the wheel arch,

while pressing on the lower suspension arm to prevent damage to the driveshaft gaiter.

Refitting

5 Manoeuvre the strut assembly into position, taking care not damage the driveshaft gaiter.

6 Insert the two stub axle carrier-to-suspension strut mounting bolts from the front side of the strut. Refit the washers and nuts to the rear of the bolts, and tighten them to the specified torque.

7 Refit the two bolts securing the upper strut mounting to the turret, ensuring that they are fitted to the correct holes in the turret **(see illustration)**. Tighten the bolts to the specified torque.

8 Refit the roadwheel, lower the vehicle to the ground and tighten the roadwheel bolts to the specified torque.

5 Front suspension strut - dismantling, inspection and reassembly

Note: *Before attempting to dismantle the front suspension strut, a tool to hold the coil spring in compression must be obtained. A Renault special tool is used at Renault dealers **(see illustration)**, but careful use of conventional coil spring compressors will prove satisfactory. Any attempt to dismantle the strut without such a tool is likely to result in damage or personal injury.*

Dismantling

1 With the strut removed from the car as described in Section 4, clean away all external dirt, then mount the strut upright in a vice.

2 Fit the spring compressor tool, and compress the coil spring until all tension is relieved from the upper mounting **(see illustration)**.

3 Withdraw the plastic cap over the strut upper mounting nut, hold the strut piston with an Allen key or a hexagon bit, and unscrew the nut with a ring spanner **(see illustration)**.

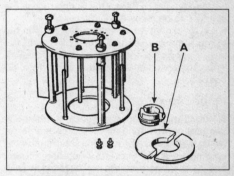

5.0 Renault spring compressor tool

A Thrust cup   *B Retaining shell*

5.2 Using a spring compressor tool to compress the front suspension strut coil spring

5.3 Unscrewing the front suspension strut upper mounting nut while holding the strut piston

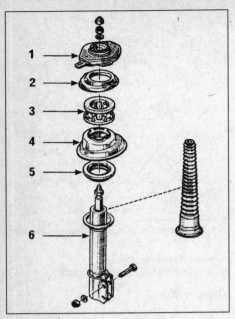

5.8a Exploded view of a front suspension strut - all models except 16-valve

1 Upper mounting   4 Lower spring seat
2 Upper spring seat   5 Bearing
3 Bump stop   6 Strut

4 Lift off the washer, upper mounting, bearing (16-valve models only) and spring seat assembly.

5 Lift off the spring and compressor tool. Do not remove the tool from the spring unless the spring is to be renewed.

6 On all except 16-valve models, remove the bump stop, convoluted dust cover, and the lower spring seat and bearing components.

7 On 16-valve models, remove the convoluted dust cover.

Inspection

8 With the strut assembly now completely dismantled, examine all the components for wear, damage or deformation, and check the bearing for smoothness of operation. Renew any of the components as necessary **(see illustrations)**.

9 Examine the strut for signs of fluid leakage. Check the strut piston for signs of pitting along

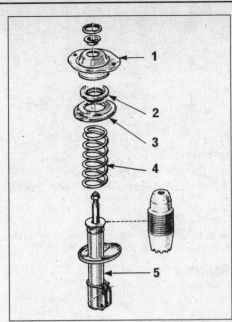

5.8b Exploded view of a front suspension strut - 16-valve models

1 Upper mounting   4 Spring
2 Bearing   5 Strut
3 Upper spring seat

its entire length, and check the strut body for signs of damage or elongation of the mounting bolt holes. Test the operation of the strut, while holding it in an upright position, by moving the piston through a full stroke, and then through short strokes of 50 to 100 mm. In both cases, the resistance felt should be smooth and continuous. If the resistance is jerky, or uneven, or if there is any visible sign of wear or damage to the strut, renewal is necessary.

10 If any doubt exists about the condition of the coil spring, gradually release the spring compressor, and check the spring for distortion and signs of cracking. Since no minimum free length is specified by Renault, the only way to check the tension of the spring is to compare it to a new component. Renew the spring if it is damaged or distorted, or if there is any doubt as to its condition.

11 Inspect all other components for signs of

damage or deterioration, and renew any that are suspect.

Reassembly

12 Reassembly is a reversal of dismantling. Make sure that the spring ends are correctly located in the upper and lower seats, and tighten the upper nut to the specified torque.

6 Front suspension anti-roll bar - removal and refitting

Removal

1 Apply the handbrake, then jack up the front of the vehicle and support it securely on axle stands (see *"Jacking, towing and wheel changing"*). Remove both front roadwheels.

2 Remove the exhaust downpipe as described in Chapter 4.

3 On models fitted with a manual gearbox, disconnect the gearchange mechanism from the gearbox with reference to Chapter 7A.

4 Unscrew the nuts and remove the clamp bolts securing the ends of the anti-roll bar to the lower suspension arms. Remove the clamps.

5 Unscrew the nuts and remove the clamp bolts from the clamps on the subframe **(see illustration)**. Remove the clamps.

6 Lower the anti-roll bar from the rear of the subframe.

7 Check the bar for damage, and the rubber bushes for wear and deterioration. If the bushes are in need of renewal, slide them off the bar. Fit new ones after lubricating them with rubber grease.

Refitting

8 Refitting is a reversal of removal, bearing in mind the following points:

  (a) Do not fully tighten the anti-roll bar mountings until the (unladen) weight of the vehicle is on the suspension (ie, the vehicle is resting on its wheels).

  (b) On models with a manual gearbox, reconnect the gearchange mechanism as described in Chapter 7A.

  (c) Refit the exhaust downpipe as described in Chapter 4.

7 Front suspension lower arm - removal, overhaul and refitting

Removal

1 Apply the handbrake, then jack up the front of the vehicle and support it securely on axle stands (see *"Jacking, towing and wheel changing"*). Remove the appropriate front roadwheel.

2 Unscrew the nuts and remove the clamp bolts holding the ends of the anti-roll bar to the lower arms. Remove the clamps, then loosen the mounting clamp bolts and pull the anti-roll bar downwards.

3 Remove the nut and clamp bolt securing the lower arm balljoint to the stub axle carrier. Note which way round the bolt is fitted.

6.5 Front suspension anti-roll bar mounting clamp on the subframe

7.4 Removing the plastic protector plate from the lower arm balljoint shank

4 Loosen the lower arm inner pivot bolts, then carefully lever the arm down to release the balljoint from the stub axle carrier. Take care not to damage the balljoint or driveshaft gaiters. Remove the plastic protector plate which is fitted to the balljoint shank **(see illustration)**.

5 Unscrew the nuts, and remove the spacers and pivot bolts from the inner end of the lower arm. Withdraw the arm from the subframe.

Overhaul

6 Clean the lower arm and the area around the arm mountings, then check for cracks, distortion or any other signs of damage. Check that the lower arm balljoint moves freely, without any sign of roughness, and that the balljoint gaiter is free from cracks and splits. Examine the shanks of the pivot bolts for signs of wear or scoring. Renew worn components as necessary.

7 Inspect the lower arm pivot bushes. If they are worn, cracked, split or perished, they must be renewed. To renew the bushes, support the lower arm, and press the first bush out using a tubular spacer, such as a socket, which bears only on the hard, outer edge of the bush. Note: *Remove only one bush at a time from the arm, to ensure that each new bush is correctly positioned on installation.* Thoroughly clean the lower arm bore, removing all traces of dirt and grease, and polish away any burrs or raised edges which might hinder reassembly. Apply a smear of a suitable grease to the outer edge of the new bush. Press the bush into position until the distance "A" between the inner edges of the lower arm bushes is as shown **(see illustration)**. Wipe away surplus grease. Repeat the procedure on the remaining bush.

Refitting

8 Refitting is a reversal of removal, bearing in mind the following points:
   (a) Make sure that the plastic protector plate is positioned over the balljoint gaiter.
   (b) Ensure that the balljoint clamp bolt is orientated as noted before removal.
   (c) Do not fully tighten the lower arm pivot bolts or the anti-roll bar fixings until the

(unladen) weight of the vehicle is on the suspension (ie, the vehicle is resting on its wheels).
   (d) Tighten all fixings to the specified torques, where applicable.

8 Front suspension lower arm balljoint - removal, inspection and refitting

Removal

1 Apply the handbrake, then jack up the front of the vehicle and support it securely on axle stands (see *"Jacking, towing and wheel changing"*). Remove the appropriate front roadwheel.

2 Unscrew the nut and remove the clamp bolt securing the lower suspension balljoint to the stub axle carrier.

3 Loosen the lower arm inner pivot bolts, then carefully lever the arm down to release the balljoint from the stub axle carrier. Take care not to damage the balljoint or driveshaft gaiters. Remove the plastic protector plate which is fitted to the balljoint shank.

4 Remove the two nuts and bolts securing the balljoint to the lower arm **(see illustration)**. Remove the balljoint.

Inspection

5 Check that the balljoint moves freely, without any sign of roughness or free play. Examine the balljoint gaiter for signs of damage and deterioration such as cracks or splits. Renew the complete balljoint assembly if damaged; it is not possible to renew the balljoint gaiter separately. The balljoint renewal kit obtainable from Renault dealers contains the balljoint, the plastic protector plate, and all fixings.

Refitting

6 Refitting is a reversal of removal, bearing in mind the following points:
   (a) Do not fully tighten the lower arm inner pivot bolts until the (unladen) weight of the vehicle is on the suspension (ie, the vehicle is resting on its wheels).
   (b) Tighten all fixings to the specified torques.

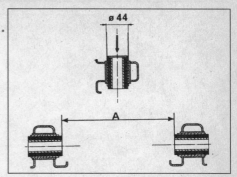

7.7 Front suspension lower arm pivot bush fitting dimension
A = 147. ± 0.5 mm

9 Rear hub bearings - checking, removal and refitting

Note: *The bearing is a sealed, pre-adjusted and pre-lubricated, double-row tapered-roller type, and is intended to last the car's entire service life without maintenance or attention. Never overtighten the hub nut in an attempt to "adjust" the bearings.*

Checking

1 Chock the front wheels and engage reverse gear (or "P" on automatic transmission models). Jack up the rear of the vehicle and support it securely on axle stands (see *"Jacking, towing and wheel changing"*). Remove the appropriate rear roadwheel, and fully release the handbrake.

2 Wear in the rear hub bearings can be checked by measuring the amount of side play present. To do this, a dial test indicator should be fixed so that its probe is in contact with the hub outer face. The play should be between 0 and 0.03 mm. If it is greater than this, the bearings are worn excessively, and should be renewed.

Removal

3 The rear hub bearing is integral with the brake drum/disc (as applicable) **(see illustration)**.

4 Remove the rear brake disc or drum (as applicable), as described in Chapter 9.

5 Using circlip pliers, extract the bearing retaining circlip from the centre of the brake disc or drum **(see illustration)**.

6 Securely support the disc or drum hub. Press or drive the bearing out of the hub, using a tubular drift of suitable diameter inserted through the inside of the hub, and in contact with the bearing outer race **(see illustration)**.

7 Thoroughly clean the hub, removing all traces of dirt and grease. Polish away any burrs or raised edges which might hinder reassembly. Check the hub/drum/disc assembly for cracks or any other signs of damage, and renew if necessary. The bearing and its circlip must be renewed whenever they are disturbed. A replacement bearing kit is

10

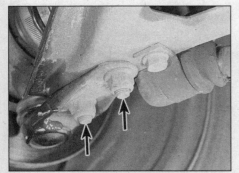

8.4 Front suspension lower arm balljoint-to-lower arm securing nuts (arrowed)

9.3 Exploded view of the rear hub bearing assembly - drum brake model shown

9.5 Extract the circlip . . .

9.6 . . . then drive out the rear hub bearing using a tubular drift

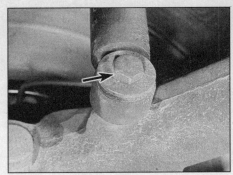

10.2 Rear shock absorber lower mounting bolt (arrowed)

available from Renault dealers, consisting of the bearing, circlip, spacer, thrustwasher, hub nut and grease cap.

Refitting

8 On reassembly, check (if possible) that the new bearing is packed with grease. Apply a light film of gear oil to the bearing outer race, and to the stub axle.

9 Securely support the hub, then press the bearing into position, using a suitable tube in contact with the bearing outer race. Ensure that the bearing enters the hub squarely.

10 Ensure that the bearing is correctly seated against the hub shoulder, and secure it in position with the new circlip. Ensure that the circlip is correctly seated in its groove.

10 Refit the brake disc or drum (as applicable) as described in Chapter 9.

10 Rear shock absorber - removal, inspection and refitting

Removal

1 Chock the front wheels and engage reverse gear (or "P" on models with automatic transmission). Jack up the rear of the vehicle and support it securely on axle stands (see *"Jacking, towing and wheel changing"*). Remove the appropriate rear roadwheel.

2 Using a jack, raise the trailing arm slightly until the shock absorber is slightly compressed. Remove the lower mounting bolt and recover the washer **(see illustration)**.

3 Working inside the luggage compartment, pull off the rubber cover, then unscrew the shock absorber upper mounting nut **(see illustrations)**. If necessary, hold the piston rod stationary using a further spanner.

4 Withdraw the shock absorber from under the vehicle. Recover the mounting rubbers and their seats, if they are loose.

Inspection

5 Examine the shock absorber for signs of fluid leakage. Check the piston for signs of pitting along its visible length, and check the shock absorber body for signs of damage. Test the operation of the shock absorber (mounting it in a vice if necessary), while holding it in an upright position, by moving the piston through a full stroke, and then through short strokes of 59 to 100 mm. In both cases, the resistance felt should be smooth and continuous. If the resistance is jerky, or uneven, or if there is any visible sign of wear or damage to the shock absorber, renewal is necessary. Note that the mounting bushes are not available separately. Inspect the mounting bolt and nut for signs of wear or damage, and renew as necessary.

Refitting

6 Prior to refitting the shock absorber, mount it upright in a vice, and operate it fully through several strokes, in order to prime it. (This is necessary even if a new unit is being fitted, as it may have been stored horizontally, and so need priming). Apply a smear of multi-purpose

grease to the shock absorber mounting bolt and nut.

7 Refitting is a reversal of removal, but delay tightening the mounting bolt and nut until the (unladen) weight of the vehicle is on the suspension (ie, the vehicle is resting on its wheels).

11 Rear suspension anti-roll bar (enclosed-bar rear axle) - removal and refitting

Removal

1 Chock the front wheels and engage reverse gear (or "P" on models with automatic transmission). Jack up the rear of the vehicle and support it securely on axle stands (see *"Jacking, towing and wheel changing"*).

2 Remove the bolts securing the ends of the anti-roll bar to the rear suspension trailing arms, noting the fitted positions of the handbrake cable retaining clips. Recover the anti-roll bar retaining nut plates from the top of the trailing arms.

3 Withdraw the anti-roll bar from under the vehicle.

Refitting

4 Refit the anti-roll bar to the vehicle, noting that the cutaway ends of the anti-roll bar retaining bolt brackets must face towards the front of the vehicle **(see illustration)**.

5 Position the retaining nut plates on the top

10.3a Rear shock absorber upper mounting nut (arrowed) in the luggage compartment

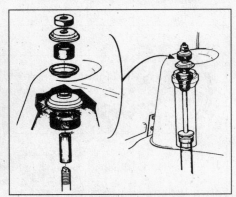

10.3b Exploded view of the rear shock absorber upper mounting

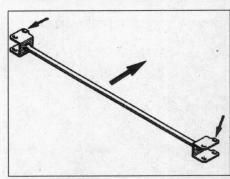

11.4 Cutaway ends of the rear anti-roll bar brackets (small arrows) must face the front of the vehicle (large arrow)

of the trailing arms. Refit the retaining bolts, ensuring that the handbrake cable retaining clips are correctly positioned. Tighten the anti-roll bar retaining bolts to the specified torque.

6 Lower the vehicle to the ground.

12 Steering wheel - removal and refitting

⚠️ **Warning: At the time of writing, no information was available regarding the removal and refitting of the steering wheel on models fitted with an air bag. To avoid any possibility of injury or damage, it is therefore strongly recommended that on models fitted with an air bag, any procedures involving the steering wheel are entrusted to a Renault dealer.**

Removal

1 Set the front wheels in the straight-ahead position, and release the steering lock by inserting the ignition key.

2 Ease off the steering wheel pad to provide access to the retaining nut (see illustration).

3 Using a socket, unscrew and remove the retaining nut.

4 Mark the steering wheel and steering column shaft in relation to each other, and withdraw the wheel from the shaft splines. If it is tight, tap it upwards near the centre, using the palm of your hand, or twist the steering wheel from side-to-side to release it from the splines.

Refitting

5 Refitting is a reversal of removal, but align the previously-made marks, and tighten the retaining nut to the specified torque.

13 Steering column - removal, checking and refitting

Removal

1 Disconnect the battery leads.

2 Remove the steering wheel as described in Section 12.

3 Remove the two securing screws, and

12.2 Steering wheel retaining nut (arrowed)

withdraw the lower facia panel from under the steering wheel.

4 Remove the screws, and withdraw the steering column upper and lower shrouds. Note that on models with a radio/cassette player remote control switch, it will be necessary to loosen the switch clamp screw before the shrouds can be removed (see Chapter 12).

5 Remove the steering column combination switch assembly from the column, with reference to Chapter 12.

6 Disconnect the wiring from the ignition switch.

7 Remove the two screws which secure the facia panel to the steering column.

8 Apply the handbrake, then jack up the front of the vehicle and support it securely on axle stands (see "Jacking, towing and wheel changing").

9 On manual steering models, cut the retaining clip and release the universal joint rubber boot from the steering gear.

10 Mark the relationship between the intermediate shaft universal joint and the steering gear drive pinion, using a hammer and punch, white paint or similar. Remove the nut and clamp bolt securing the joint to the pinion.

11 Unscrew the two bolts and two nuts securing the steering column to the bulkhead (see illustration).

12 Remove the lower facia fastening, the lower heater control cover, and the facia mounting nuts and bolts, with reference to Chapter 11.

13 Slightly lift the facia, in order to release it

13.11 Steering column-to-bulkhead securing nuts and bolts (arrowed)

from the clip on the steering column (see illustration).

14 Withdraw the steering column from inside the vehicle. On power-assisted steering models, it will be necessary to release the rubber boot from the scuttle when withdrawing the steering column.

Checking

15 The intermediate shaft attached to the bottom of the steering column incorporates a telescopic safety feature. In the event of a front-end crash, the shaft collapses and prevents the steering wheel injuring the driver. Before refitting the steering column, the length of the intermediate shaft must be checked. Make sure that the applicable length is as given (see illustration). If the length is shorter than specified, the complete steering column must be renewed. Damage to the intermediate shaft is also implied if it is found that the clamp bolt at its base cannot be inserted freely when refitting the column.

16 Check the steering shaft for signs of free play in the column bushes, and check the universal joints for signs of damage or roughness in the joint bearings. If damage or wear is found on the steering shaft universal joints or shaft bushes, the column must be renewed as an assembly.

Refitting

17 Refitting is a reversal of removal, bearing in mind the following points:

(a) Align the marks made on the intermediate shaft and the steering gear pinion shaft before removal.

10

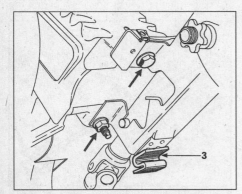

13.13 Steering column-to-bulkhead securing nut and bolt (arrowed) and facia-to-steering column clip (3)

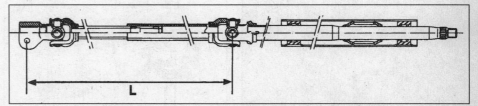

13.15 Steering column intermediate shaft checking dimension (L)

Right-hand-drive models with manual steering - 406. ± 1. mm
Right-hand-drive models with power steering - 354.5 ± 1. mm
Left-hand-drive models with manual steering - 408. ± 1. mm
Left-hand-drive models with power steering - 355.5 ± 1. mm

(b) Before tightening the steering column mounting bolts, check that there is a clearance between the direction indicator return finger, and the lighting multi-function switch mounting.

(c) On manual steering models, use a new cable tie to secure the universal joint rubber boot to the steering gear.

(d) On models with a height-adjustable steering column, check that the locking lever operates freely, and is easily accessible. If the lever is partially concealed and/or difficult to operate, it can be adjusted by removing the lever clamp nut and fully lowering the column. Lock the column by tightening the adjuster nut using the locking lever. Position the locking lever a distance of 30 mm from the steering column support bracket, then refit the lever clamp nut **(see illustration)**. Refit the steering column shrouds, and check that the lever is accessible - if not, increase or reduce (as necessary) the dimension between the locking lever and the steering column support bracket by 10 mm.

(e) Tighten all fixings to the specified torque.

14 Steering gear rubber gaiter - renewal

1 Remove the track rod end balljoint as described in Section 20.

2 Mark the fitted position of the gaiter on the track rod. Release the retaining clips, and slide the gaiter off the steering gear housing and track rod end.

3 Thoroughly clean the track rod and the steering gear housing. Use fine abrasive paper to polish off any corrosion, burrs or sharp edges, which might damage the sealing lips of the new gaiter on installation.

4 Recover the grease from inside the old gaiter. If it is uncontaminated with dirt or grit, apply it to the track rod inner balljoint. If the old grease is contaminated, or it is suspected that some has been lost, apply some new molybdenum disulphide grease.

5 Grease the inside of the new gaiter. Carefully slide the gaiter onto the track rod,

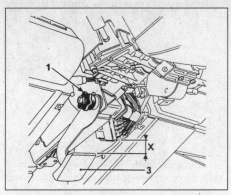

13.17 Checking the position of the height-adjustable steering column lever

1 Lever clamp nut   *X = 30. mm*
3 Locking lever

and locate it on the steering gear housing. Align the outer edge of the gaiter with the mark made on the track rod prior to removal, then secure it in position with new retaining clips.

6 Refit the track rod balljoint as described in Section 20.

15 Steering gear (manual steering) - removal, overhaul and refitting

Removal

1 Apply the handbrake, then jack up the front of the vehicle and support it securely on axle stands (see *"Jacking, towing and wheel changing"*). Remove both front roadwheels.

2 Working on both sides of the vehicle, remove the nuts securing the track rod end balljoints to the stub axle carriers. Release the balljoint tapered shanks using a universal balljoint separator.

3 Working from underneath the vehicle, cut the retaining clip, then fold the rubber boot back from the steering gear to gain access to the intermediate shaft universal joint clamp bolt **(see illustrations)**.

4 Mark the relationship between the intermediate shaft universal joint and the steering gear drive pinion, using a hammer and punch, white paint or similar. Remove the nut and clamp bolt securing the joint to the pinion.

5 Remove the two nuts and bolts securing the steering gear assembly to the rear of the subframe. Release the steering gear pinion from the universal joint, and manoeuvre the assembly sideways out of position **(see illustration)**.

Overhaul

General

6 Renewal procedures for the gaiters, the track rod end balljoints and the track rods (complete with inner balljoints) are given in Sections 14, 20 and 21 respectively.

7 Examine the steering gear assembly for signs of wear or damage. Check that the rack moves freely over the full length of its travel, with no signs of roughness or excessive free play between the steering gear pinion and rack. Internal wear or damage can only be cured by renewing the steering gear assembly, but note the points in the following paragraphs.

Thrust plunger adjustment

8 If there is excessive free play of the rack in the steering gear housing, accompanied by a knocking noise, it may be possible to correct this by adjusting the rack thrust plunger. Relieve the staking on the plunger adjusting nut. Using a 10 mm Allen key, tighten the adjusting nut until the free play disappears (but by no more than three flats). Check that the rack still moves freely over its full travel, then secure the adjusting nut by staking it **(see illustration)**.

Anti-noise bush

9 If a grating noise has been noticed from the steering assembly whilst the steering wheel is being turned, this is probably due to the anti-noise bush being dry. To lubricate this bush, first obtain a sachet of the specified grease (Molykote BR2) and a steering gear gaiter retaining clip, from your Renault dealer. Cut the clip securing the gaiter to the opposite end of the steering gear from the pinion housing (ie the left-hand end on right-hand drive models, right-hand end on left-hand drive models). Peel the gaiter back from the housing. Move the steering rack so that its exposed end is fully extended, then smear the grease over the steering rack surface. Refit the gaiter to the housing, and secure it in position with the new retaining clip.

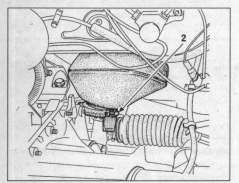

15.3a Cut the retaining clip (2), and fold back the rubber boot . . .

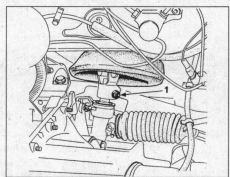

15.3b . . . for access to the universal joint clamp bolt (1) - manual steering gear

15.5 Manual steering gear mounting nut (arrowed)

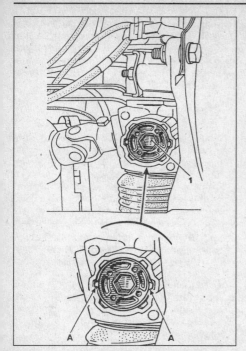

15.8 Manual steering rack thrust plunger adjustment

1 Adjusting nut   A Staking points

10 The anti-noise bush can be renewed if necessary. After removing the track rod on the side concerned, prise the old bush out using a screwdriver. Fit the new bush, making sure that its lugs engage in the slots in the rack housing **(see illustration)**. Lubricate the bush as described previously.

Refitting

11 Manoeuvre the steering gear assembly into position. Engage the universal joint with the steering gear pinion splines, aligning the marks made prior to removal.
12 Insert the steering gear mounting bolts from the rear of the subframe. Refit the nuts and tighten them to the specified torque.
13 Refit the universal joint clamp bolt and nut, and tighten to the specified torque. Relocate the rubber boot on the steering gear, and secure it in position with a new cable tie.
14 Reconnect the track rod balljoints to the stub axle carriers, and tighten their retaining nuts to the specified torque.
15 Refit the roadwheels, lower the vehicle to the ground and tighten the wheel bolts to the specified torque.
16 Check the front wheel toe setting as described in Section 22.

16 Steering gear (power-assisted steering) - removal, overhaul and refitting

Removal

1 Apply the handbrake, then jack up the front of the vehicle and support it securely on axle stands (see *"Jacking, towing and wheel*

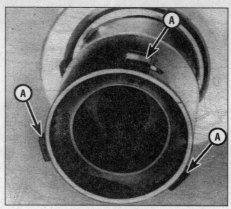

15.10 Manual steering rack anti-noise bush. Lugs (A) must engage in slots

changing"). Remove both front roadwheels.
2 Working on both sides of the vehicle, remove the nuts securing the track rod end balljoints to the stub axle carriers. Release the balljoint tapered shanks using a universal balljoint separator.
3 Mark the relationship between the intermediate shaft universal joint and the steering gear drive pinion, using a hammer and punch, white paint or similar. Remove the nut and clamp bolt securing the joint to the pinion.
4 Using brake hose clamps, clamp both the supply and return hoses near the fluid reservoir. This will prevent unnecessary loss of fluid during subsequent operations.
5 Remove the air cleaner assembly as described in Chapter 4.
6 Unscrew the union nuts for the hydraulic fluid supply and return lines at the steering gear. Mark the pipe unions to ensure that they are correctly positioned on reassembly. Also unbolt the fluid line mounting brackets. Be prepared for some loss of fluid by placing a suitable container beneath the line unions. Plug the pipe ends and the steering gear orifices, to prevent dirt ingress and excessive fluid leakage. The spilt fluid must be disposed of.
7 Loosen the clips, then disconnect the short length of hose from the low-pressure return line. Completely remove the low-pressure line.
8 Where necessary, for improved access, remove the exhaust downpipe with reference to Chapter 4.
9 With the container in place beneath the steering gear, unscrew the union nuts connecting the secondary pipes to the rack-and-pinion housing. To prevent dirt and dust entering the hydraulic circuit, fit plugs to the apertures in the steering gear and in the ends of the pipes.
10 Unscrew and remove the mounting bolts, then release the steering gear pinion from the universal joint, and manoeuvre the steering gear sideways out of position.

Overhaul

11 Examine the steering gear for signs of wear or damage **(see illustration)**. Check that the rack moves freely over the full length of its

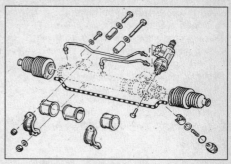

16.11 Power-assisted steering gear components

travel, with no signs of roughness or excessive free play between the pinion and rack. The steering gear must be renewed as an assembly if internal wear or damage is present. Track rod, track rod balljoint and steering gear gaiter renewal procedures are given in Sections 21, 20 and 14 respectively. Note that it is also possible to renew the pinion housing assembly, but it is recommended that this task be entrusted to a Renault dealer.
12 Inspect the steering gear fluid unions for signs of leakage.
13 Examine the steering gear mounting rubbers for signs of damage and deterioration; renew as necessary.

Refitting

14 Manoeuvre the steering gear assembly into position. Aligning the marks made prior to removal, engage the universal joint with the steering gear pinion splines.
15 Locate the mounting brackets and clamps on the steering gear mounting rubbers, then insert the four steering gear mounting bolts from the rear of the subframe. Refit the nuts and tighten the mounting bolts to the specified torque.
16 Refit the universal joint clamp bolt and nut, and tighten to the specified torque.
17 Remove the plugs from the secondary hydraulic fluid pipes and the rack-and-pinion housing, and wipe the unions clean. Reconnect the pipes to the steering gear, and tighten the union nuts.
18 Where applicable, refit the exhaust downpipe as described in Chapter 4.
19 Reconnect the low-pressure fluid return line, and secure with the clips.
20 Wipe clean the fluid supply and return pipe unions, then reconnect them to their respective positions on the steering gear. Tighten the union nuts. Refit the fluid line mounting brackets.
21 Refit the air cleaner assembly, as described in Chapter 4.
22 Reconnect the track rod balljoints to the stub axle carriers. Tighten their retaining nuts to the specified torque.
23 Refit the roadwheels, lower the vehicle to the ground and tighten the wheel bolts to the specified torque.
24 Remove the hose clamps from the reservoir hoses. Top-up the reservoir, and

10

bleed the power steering hydraulic system as described in Section 19.

25 On completion, check the front wheel toe setting as described in Section 22.

17 Mechanical power steering pump - removal and refitting

E-type (1390 cc/E6J/E7J) engines
Removal

1 Remove the power steering pump drivebelt, as described in Chapter 1.

2 Where applicable, unbolt the drivebelt tensioner strut from the pump.

3 Using a brake hose clamp, clamp the fluid supply hose to the pump. This will prevent unnecessary loss of fluid during subsequent operations. Also position a suitable container beneath the pump to catch spilled fluid.

4 Unscrew the union nut, and disconnect the high-pressure fluid line from the pump. Recover the sealing washer.

5 Unscrew the pump mounting bolts, and withdraw the pump from its bracket **(see illustration)**.

6 If desired, the pulley can be unbolted from the front of the pump.

Refitting

7 Refitting is a reversal of removal, bearing in mind the following points:

- (a) Use a new sealing washer when reconnecting the high-pressure fluid line.
- (b) Refit and tension the power steering pump drivebelt as described in Chapter 1.
- (c) On completion, top-up and bleed the fluid circuit, as described in Section 19.

1721 cc (F2N and F3N) and 1794 cc (F3P) engines
Removal

8 Remove the auxiliary drivebelt, as described in Chapter 1.

9 Remove the alternator, as described in Chapter 5.

10 Using brake hose clamps, clamp both the supply and return hoses leading from the fluid reservoir. This will prevent unnecessary loss of fluid during subsequent operations. Also position a suitable container beneath the pump to catch spilled fluid.

11 Remove the drivebelt tensioner support bracket.

12 Where applicable, disconnect the wiring plug from the fluid pressure switch, then unbolt the high-pressure line support bracket.

13 Disconnect the supply hose from the pump. Be prepared for fluid spillage.

14 Unscrew the union nut, and disconnect the high-pressure line from the pump. Recover the sealing washer.

15 Unscrew the four bolts securing the pump bracket to the engine, then remove the bracket and pump assembly **(see illustration)**.

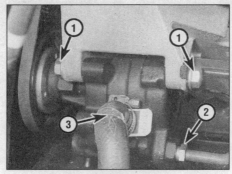

17.5 Power steering pump mounting details - 1390 cc (E7J) engine

1 Pump mounting bolts
2 High-pressure fluid line
3 Fluid supply hose

16 To remove the pulley, or separate the pump from the bracket, proceed as follows.

17 Measure the dimension from the end of the shaft to the pulley, to ensure correct refitting, then use a puller or press to remove the pulley from the shaft.

18 Unbolt the bracket from the pump.

Refitting

19 Refitting is a reversal of removal, bearing in mind the following points:

- (a) Ensure that the pump bracket has been refitted before refitting the pulley. Fit the pulley in the position noted before removal.
- (b) Use a new sealing washer when reconnecting the high-pressure fluid line.
- (c) Refit and tension the auxiliary drivebelt as described in Chapter 1.
- (d) On completion, top-up and bleed the fluid circuit, as described in Section 19.

1764 cc (F7P) engine
Removal

20 Proceed as described in paragraphs 8 to 14, ignoring the reference to removing the drivebelt tensioner support bracket.

21 Remove the three pump securing bolts, then withdraw the pump.

22 If desired, the pump pulley can be removed using a puller. Measure the dimension from the end of the shaft to the pulley, to ensure correct refitting.

Refitting

23 Refer to paragraph 19, ignoring the reference to refitting the pump bracket.

18 Electric power steering pump (1764 cc/F7P engine models with air conditioning) - general information, removal and refitting

General information

1 On 1764 cc (F7P) engine models equipped with air conditioning, an electric power steering pump is used. This is because there is

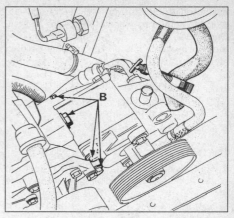

17.15 Power steering pump bracket securing bolts (B) - 1721 cc (F2N and F3N) and 1794 cc (F3P) engines

not sufficient space in the engine compartment to mount a conventional belt-driven pump; the air conditioning compressor is situated where the power steering pump would normally be.

2 Operation of the system is complex. If any fault develops, the vehicle should be taken to a Renault dealer for the fault to be diagnosed.

Removal and refitting

3 At the time of writing, no information was available for the removal and refitting of the electric power steering pump.

19 Power steering system - bleeding

1 This procedure will only be necessary when any part of the hydraulic system has been disconnected, or if air has entered because of leakage.

2 Remove the fluid reservoir filler cap, and top-up the fluid level to the maximum mark, using only the specified fluid. Refer to Chapter 1 "Lubricants, fluids and capacities" for fluid specifications, and to Chapter 1 for details of the different types of fluid reservoir markings.

3 With the engine stopped, slowly move the steering from lock-to-lock several times to expel trapped air, then top-up the level in the fluid reservoir. Repeat this procedure until the fluid level in the reservoir does not drop any further.

4 Start the engine. Slowly move the steering from lock-to-lock several times, to expel any air remaining in the system. Repeat this procedure until bubbles cease to appear in the fluid reservoir.

5 If, when turning the steering, an abnormal noise is heard from the fluid pipes, it indicates that there is still air in the system. Check this by turning the wheels to the straight-ahead position and switching off the engine. If fluid level in the reservoir rises, air is still present in the system, and further bleeding is necessary.

6 Once all traces of air have been removed, stop the engine and allow the system to cool. Once cool, check that the fluid level is up to the maximum mark on the power steering fluid reservoir; top-up if necessary.

20 Track rod end balljoint - removal and refitting

Removal

1 Apply the handbrake, then jack up the front of the vehicle and support it securely on axle stands (see *"Jacking, towing and wheel changing"*). Remove the appropriate front roadwheel.
2 If the balljoint is to be re-used, use a straight-edge and a scriber, or similar, to mark its relationship to the track rod.
3 Holding the balljoint, unscrew its locknut by one quarter of a turn **(see illustration)**. Do not move the locknut from this position, as it will serve as a reference mark on refitting.
4 Remove the nut securing the track rod balljoint to the stub axle carrier. Release the balljoint tapered shank using a universal balljoint separator. If the balljoint is to be re-used, protect the threaded end of the shank by screwing the nut back on a few turns before using the separator **(see illustration)**.
5 Counting the *exact number* of turns necessary to do so, unscrew the balljoint from the track rod end.
6 Count the number of exposed threads between the end of the balljoint and the locknut, and record this figure. If a new balljoint is to be fitted, unscrew the locknut from the old balljoint.
7 Carefully clean the balljoint and the threads. Renew the balljoint if its movement is sloppy or if it is too stiff, if it is excessively worn, or if it is damaged in any way. Carefully check the shank taper and threads. If the balljoint gaiter is damaged, the complete balljoint must be renewed; it is not possible to obtain the gaiter separately.

Refitting

8 If applicable, screw the locknut onto the new balljoint, and position it so that the same number of exposed threads are visible, as noted prior to removal.
9 Screw the balljoint into the track rod by the number of turns noted on removal. This should bring the balljoint locknut to within a quarter of a turn of the end of the track rod, with the alignment marks that were made on removal (if applicable) lined up.
10 Refit the balljoint shank to the stub axle carrier, and tighten the retaining nut to the specified torque. If difficulty is experienced due to the balljoint shank rotating, jam it by exerting pressure on the underside of the balljoint, using a tyre lever or a jack.
11 Refit the roadwheel, lower the vehicle to the ground and tighten the roadwheel bolts to the specified torque.

20.3 Track rod end balljoint locknut (arrowed)

12 Check the front wheel toe setting as described in Section 22, then tighten the balljoint locknut.

21 Track rod and inner balljoint - removal and refitting

Removal

1 Remove the track rod end balljoint as described in Section 20.
2 Cut the retaining clips, and slide the steering gear gaiter off the track rod.
3 Using a suitable pair of grips, unscrew the track rod inner balljoint from the steering rack end. Prevent the steering rack from turning by holding the balljoint lockwasher with a second pair of grips. Take care not to mark the surfaces of the rack and balljoint.
4 Remove the track rod/inner balljoint assembly, and discard the lockwasher; a new one must be used on refitting.
5 Examine the inner balljoint for signs of slackness or tight spots. Check that the track rod itself is straight, and free from damage. If necessary, renew the track rod/inner balljoint; the new one will be supplied complete with a new lockwasher and a new end balljoint. It is also recommended that the steering gear gaiter is renewed.

Refitting

6 If a new track rod is being installed, remove the outer balljoint from the track rod end.
7 Locate the new lockwasher assembly on the end of the steering rack, ensuring that its locating tabs are correctly located with the flats on the rack end **(see illustration)**.
8 Apply a few drops of locking fluid to the inner balljoint threads. Screw the balljoint into the steering rack, and tighten it securely. Again, take care not to damage or mark the balljoint or steering rack.
9 Slide the new gaiter onto the track rod end, and locate it on the steering gear housing. Turn the steering from lock-to-lock to check that the gaiter is correctly positioned, then secure it with new retaining clips.
10 Refit the track rod end balljoint as described in Section 20.

20.4 Releasing the track rod end balljoint tapered shank from the stub axle carrier using a balljoint separator tool

22 Wheel alignment and steering angles

General information

1 A vehicle's steering and suspension geometry is defined in four basic settings **(see illustration)**. For this purpose, all angles are expressed in degrees (toe settings are also expressed as a measurement of length). The steering axis is defined as an imaginary line drawn through the axis of the suspension strut, extended where necessary to contact the ground.
2 *Camber* is the angle between each roadwheel and a vertical line drawn through its centre and tyre contact patch, when viewed from the front or rear of the car. Positive camber is when the roadwheels are tilted outwards from the vertical at the top; negative camber is when they are tilted inwards.
3 Camber is not adjustable.
4 *Castor* is the angle between the steering axis and a vertical line drawn through each roadwheel's centre and tyre contact patch, when viewed from the side of the car. Positive castor is when the steering axis is tilted so that it contacts the ground ahead of the vertical; negative castor is when it contacts the ground behind the vertical.
5 Castor is not adjustable.
6 *Steering axis inclination/SAI* - also known as *kingpin inclination/KPI* - is the angle between the steering axis and a vertical line drawn

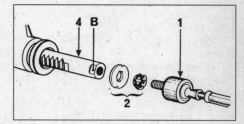

21.7 Track rod inner balljoint components

1 Inner balljoint
2 Lockwasher assembly
4 Steering rack
B Lockwasher locating flats

10

through each roadwheel's centre and tyre contact patch, when viewed from the front or rear of the car.

7 SAI/KPI is not adjustable.

8 *Toe* is a measurement of the amount by which the distance between the front inside edges of the roadwheels differs from that between the rear inside edges, when measured at hub height (the amount by which the roadwheels point inwards or outwards when viewed from above). If the distance between the front edges is less than at the rear, the wheels are said to "toe-in". If it is greater than at the rear, the wheels are said to "toe-out". The value for toe can be expressed as an angle (taking the centre-line of the car as zero), or as a measurement of length (taking measurements between the inside rims of the wheels at hub height).

9 The front wheel toe setting is adjusted by screwing the balljoints in or out of their track rods to alter the effective length of the track rod assemblies.

10 Rear wheel toe setting is not adjustable.

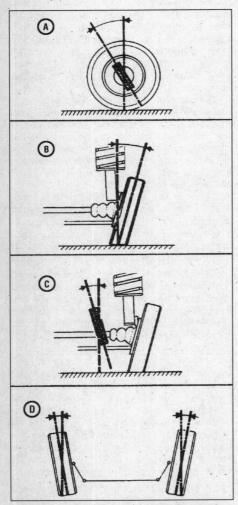

22.1 Wheel alignment and steering angles

A Castor
B Camber
C Steering axis inclination
D Toe

Checking - general

11 Due to the special measuring equipment necessary to check the wheel alignment, and the skill required to use it properly, the checking and adjustment of these settings is best left to a Renault dealer or similar expert. Most tyre-fitting shops now possess sophisticated checking equipment.

12 For accurate checking, the vehicle must be at the kerb weight specified in *"General dimensions and weights"*.

13 Before starting work, check first that the tyre sizes and types are as specified, then check tyre pressures and tread wear. Also check roadwheel run-out, the condition of the hub bearings, the steering wheel free play and the condition of the front suspension components (Chapter 1). Correct any faults found.

14 Park the vehicle on level ground, with the front roadwheels in the straight-ahead position. Rock the rear and front ends to settle the suspension. Release the handbrake, and roll the vehicle backwards approximately 1 metre (3 feet), then forwards again, to relieve any stresses in the steering and suspension components.

Toe setting - checking and adjusting

Front wheels - checking

15 Two methods are available to the home mechanic for checking the front wheel toe setting. One method is to use a gauge to measure the distance between the front and rear inside edges of the roadwheels. The other method is to use a scuff plate, in which each front wheel is rolled across a movable plate which records any deviation, or "scuff", of the tyre from the straight-ahead position as it moves across the plate. Such gauges are available in relatively-inexpensive form from accessory outlets. It is up to the owner to decide whether the expense is justified, in view of the small amount of use such equipment would normally receive.

16 Prepare the vehicle as described in paragraphs 12 to 14 above.

17 If the measurement procedure is being used, carefully measure the distance between the front edges of the roadwheel rims and the rear edges of the rims. Subtract the rear measurement from the front measurement, and check that the result is within the specified range. If not, adjust the toe setting as described in paragraph 19.

18 If scuff plates are to be used, roll the vehicle backwards, check that the roadwheels are in the straight-ahead position, then roll it across the scuff plates so that each front roadwheel passes squarely over the centre of its respective plate. Note the angle recorded by the scuff plates. To ensure accuracy, repeat the check three times, and take the average of the three readings. If the roadwheels are running parallel, there will of course be no angle recorded; if a deviation value is shown

on the scuff plates, compare the reading obtained for each wheel with that specified. If the value recorded is outside the specified tolerance, the toe setting is incorrect, and must be adjusted as follows.

Front wheels - adjusting

19 Apply the handbrake, then jack up the front of the vehicle and support it securely on axle stands (see *"Jacking, towing and wheel changing"*). Turn the steering wheel onto full-left lock, and record the number of exposed threads on the right-hand track rod end. Now turn the steering onto full-right lock, and record the number of threads on the left-hand side. If there are the same number of threads visible on both sides, then subsequent adjustment should be made equally on both sides. If there are more threads visible on one side than the other, it will be necessary to compensate for this during adjustment. **Note:** *It is important to ensure that, after adjustment, the same number of threads are visible on each track rod end.*

20 First clean the track rod threads; if they are corroded, apply penetrating fluid before starting adjustment. Release the rubber gaiter outboard clips, then peel back the gaiters and apply a smear of grease inside the end of the gaiters, so that both gaiters are free, and will not be twisted or strained as their respective track rods are rotated.

21 Use a straight-edge and a scriber (or similar) to mark the relationship of each track rod to its balljoint. Holding each track rod in turn, unscrew its locknut fully.

22 Alter the length of the track rods, bearing in mind the note in paragraph 19, by screwing them into or out of the balljoints. Rotate the track rod using an open-ended spanner fitted to the flats provided. Shortening the track rods (screwing them onto their balljoints) will reduce toe-in and increase toe-out.

23 When the setting is correct, hold the track rods and securely tighten the balljoint locknuts. Check that the balljoints are seated correctly in their sockets, and count the exposed threads. If the number of threads exposed is not the same on both sides, then the adjustment has not been made equally, and problems will be encountered with tyre scrubbing in turns; also, the steering wheel spokes will no longer be horizontal when the wheels are in the straight-ahead position.

24 When the track rod lengths are the same, lower the vehicle to the ground and re-check the toe setting; readjust if necessary. When the setting is correct, tighten the track rod balljoint locknuts. Ensure that the rubber gaiters are seated correctly and are not twisted or strained, then secure them in position with new retaining clips.

Rear wheel toe setting

25 The procedure for checking the rear toe setting is same as described for the front in paragraph 17. However, no adjustment is possible.

Chapter 11 Bodywork and fittings

Contents

Degrees of difficulty

Easy, suitable for novice with little experience	**Fairly easy,** suitable for beginner with some experience	**Fairly difficult,** suitable for competent DIY mechanic	**Difficult,** suitable for experienced DIY mechanic	**Very difficult,** suitable for expert DIY or professional

Specifications

Torque wrench setting	Nm	lbf ft
Seat belt anchorages	20	15

1 General information

The bodyshell and underframe are of all-steel welded construction, incorporating progressive crumple zones at the front and rear, and a rigid centre safety cell. The assembly and welding of the main body unit is completed by computer-controlled robots, and is checked for dimensional accuracy using computer and laser technology. All major body panels are protected with an electrolytic zinc coating, and are given a zinc phosphate bath.

The front and rear bumpers are of collapsible cellular construction to minimise minor accident damage, and the front wings are bolted in position to facilitate accident damage repair. The plastic side panels are also designed to absorb light impact without damage.

4-door Saloon, 3- and 5-door Hatchback, 2-door Cabriolet, and 3-door Van body styles are available.

In the Spring of 1992, the "Phase 2" models were introduced, incorporating subtle styling changes to the front grille and the light clusters.

2 Maintenance - bodywork and underframe

The general condition of a vehicle's bodywork is the one thing that significantly affects its value. Maintenance is easy, but needs to be regular. Neglect, particularly after minor damage, can lead quickly to further deterioration and costly repair bills. It is important also to keep watch on those parts of the vehicle not immediately visible, for instance the underside, inside all the wheel arches, and the lower part of the engine compartment.

The basic maintenance routine for the bodywork is washing - preferably with a lot of water, from a hose. This will remove all the loose solids which may have stuck to the vehicle. It is important to flush these off in such a way as to prevent grit from scratching the finish. The wheel arches and underframe need washing in the same way, to remove any accumulated mud, which will retain moisture and tend to encourage rust. Paradoxically enough, the best time to clean the underframe and wheel arches is in wet weather, when the mud is thoroughly wet and soft. In very wet weather, the underframe is usually cleaned of large accumulations automatically, and this is a good time for inspection.

Periodically, except on vehicles with a wax-based underbody protective coating, it is a good idea to have the whole of the underframe of the vehicle steam-cleaned, engine compartment included, so that a thorough inspection can be carried out to see what minor repairs and renovations are necessary. Steam-cleaning is available at many garages, and is necessary for the removal of the accumulation of oily grime, which sometimes is allowed to become thick in certain areas. If steam-cleaning facilities are not available, there are some excellent grease solvents available which can be brush-applied; the dirt can then be simply hosed off. Note that these methods should not be used on vehicles with wax-based underbody protective coating, or the coating will be removed. Such vehicles should be inspected annually, preferably just prior to Winter, when the underbody should be washed down, and any damage to the wax coating repaired. Ideally, a completely fresh coat should be applied. It would also be worth considering the use of such wax-based protection for injection into door panels, sills, box sections, etc, as an additional safeguard against rust damage, where such protection is not provided by the vehicle manufacturer.

After washing paintwork, wipe off with a chamois leather to give an unspotted clear finish. A coat of clear protective wax polish will give added protection against chemical pollutants in the air. If the paintwork sheen has dulled or oxidised, use a cleaner/polisher combination to restore the brilliance of the shine. This requires a little effort, but such dulling is usually caused because regular washing has been neglected. Care needs to be taken with metallic paintwork, as special non-abrasive cleaner/polisher is required to avoid damage to the finish. Always check that the door and ventilator opening drain holes and pipes are completely clear, so that water can be drained out. Brightwork should be treated in the same way as paintwork. Windscreens and windows can be kept clear of the smeary film which often appears, by the use of proprietary glass cleaner. Never use any form of wax or other body or chromium polish on glass.

3 Maintenance - upholstery and carpets

Mats and carpets should be brushed or vacuum-cleaned regularly, to keep them free of grit. If they are badly stained, remove them from the vehicle for scrubbing or sponging, and make quite sure they are dry before refitting. Seats and interior trim panels can be kept clean by wiping with a damp cloth. If they do become stained (which can be more apparent on light-coloured upholstery), use a little liquid detergent and a soft nail brush to scour the grime out of the grain of the material. Do not forget to keep the headlining clean in the same way as the upholstery. When using liquid cleaners inside the vehicle, do not over-wet the surfaces being cleaned. Excessive damp could get into the seams and padded interior, causing stains, offensive odours or even rot.

HAYNES HiNT *If the inside of the vehicle gets wet accidentally, it is worthwhile taking some trouble to dry it out properly, particularly where carpets are involved. Do not leave oil or electric heaters inside the vehicle for this purpose.*

4 Minor body damage - repair

Note: *For more detailed information about bodywork repair, Haynes Publishing produce a book by Lindsay Porter called "The Car Bodywork Repair Manual". This incorporates information on such aspects as rust treatment, painting and glass-fibre repairs, as well as details on more ambitious repairs involving welding and panel beating.*

Repairs of minor scratches in bodywork

If the scratch is very superficial, and does not penetrate to the metal of the bodywork, repair is very simple. Lightly rub the area of the scratch with a paintwork renovator, or a very fine cutting paste, to remove loose paint from the scratch, and to clear the surrounding bodywork of wax polish. Rinse the area with clean water.

Apply touch-up paint to the scratch using a fine paint brush; continue to apply fine layers of paint until the surface of the paint in the scratch is level with the surrounding paintwork. Allow the new paint at least two weeks to harden, then blend it into the surrounding paintwork by rubbing the scratch area with a paintwork renovator or a very fine cutting paste. Finally, apply wax polish.

Where the scratch has penetrated right through to the metal of the bodywork, causing the metal to rust, a different repair technique is required. Remove any loose rust from the bottom of the scratch with a penknife, then apply rust-inhibiting paint to prevent the formation of rust in the future. Using a rubber or nylon applicator, fill the scratch with bodystopper paste. If required, this paste can be mixed with cellulose thinners to provide a very thin paste which is ideal for filling narrow scratches. Before the stopper-paste in the scratch hardens, wrap a piece of smooth cotton rag around the top of a finger. Dip the finger in cellulose thinners, and quickly sweep it across the surface of the stopper-paste in the scratch; this will ensure that the surface of the stopper-paste is slightly hollowed. The scratch can now be painted over as described earlier in this Section.

Repairs of dents in bodywork

When deep denting of the vehicle's bodywork has taken place, the first task is to pull the dent out, until the affected bodywork almost attains its original shape. There is little point in trying to restore the original shape completely, as the metal in the damaged area will have stretched on impact, and cannot be reshaped fully to its original contour. It is better to bring the level of the dent up to a point which is about 3 mm below the level of the surrounding bodywork. In cases where the dent is very shallow anyway, it is not worth trying to pull it out at all. If the underside of the dent is accessible, it can be hammered out gently from behind, using a mallet with a wooden or plastic head. Whilst doing this, hold a suitable block of wood firmly against the outside of the panel, to absorb the impact from the hammer blows and thus prevent a large area of the bodywork from being "belled-out".

Should the dent be in a section of the bodywork which has a double skin, or some other factor making it inaccessible from behind, a different technique is called for. Drill several small holes through the metal inside

the area - particularly in the deeper section. Then screw long self-tapping screws into the holes, just sufficiently for them to gain a good purchase in the metal. Now the dent can be pulled out by pulling on the protruding heads of the screws with a pair of pliers.

The next stage of the repair is the removal of the paint from the damaged area, and from an inch or so of the surrounding "sound" bodywork. This is accomplished most easily by using a wire brush or abrasive pad on a power drill, although it can be done just as effectively by hand, using sheets of abrasive paper. To complete the preparation for filling, score the surface of the bare metal with a screwdriver or the tang of a file, or alternatively, drill small holes in the affected area. This will provide a really good "key" for the filler paste.

To complete the repair, see the Section on filling and respraying.

Repairs of rust holes or gashes in bodywork

Remove all paint from the affected area, and from an inch or so of the surrounding "sound" bodywork, using an abrasive pad or a wire brush on a power drill. If these are not available, a few sheets of abrasive paper will do the job most effectively. With the paint removed, you will be able to judge the severity of the corrosion, and therefore decide whether to renew the whole panel (if this is possible) or to repair the affected area. New body panels are not as expensive as most people think, and it is often quicker and more satisfactory to fit a new panel than to attempt to repair large areas of corrosion.

Remove all fittings from the affected area, except those which will act as a guide to the original shape of the damaged bodywork (eg headlight shells etc). Then, using tin snips or a hacksaw blade, remove all loose metal and any other metal badly affected by corrosion. Hammer the edges of the hole inwards, in order to create a slight depression for the filler paste.

Wire-brush the affected area to remove the powdery rust from the surface of the remaining metal. Paint the affected area with rust-inhibiting paint, if the back of the rusted area is accessible, treat this also.

Before filling can take place, it will be necessary to block the hole in some way. This can be achieved by the use of aluminium or plastic mesh, or aluminium tape.

Aluminium or plastic mesh, or glass-fibre matting, is probably the best material to use for a large hole. Cut a piece to the approximate size and shape of the hole to be filled, then position it in the hole so that its edges are below the level of the surrounding bodywork. It can be retained in position by several blobs of filler paste around its periphery.

Aluminium tape should be used for small or very narrow holes. Pull a piece off the roll, trim it to the approximate size and shape required, then pull off the backing paper (if used) and stick the tape over the hole; it can be overlapped if the thickness of one piece is insufficient. Burnish down the edges of the tape with the handle of a screwdriver or similar, to ensure that the tape is securely attached to the metal underneath.

Bodywork repairs - filling and respraying

Before using this Section, see the Sections on dent, deep scratch, rust holes and gash repairs.

Many types of bodyfiller are available, but generally speaking, those proprietary kits which contain a tin of filler paste and a tube of resin hardener are best for this type of repair. A wide, flexible plastic or nylon applicator will be found invaluable for imparting a smooth and well-contoured finish to the surface of the filler.

Mix up a little filler on a clean piece of card or board - measure the hardener carefully (follow the maker's instructions on the pack), otherwise the filler will set too rapidly or too slowly. Using the applicator, apply the filler paste to the prepared area; draw the applicator across the surface of the filler to achieve the correct contour and to level the surface. As soon as a contour that approximates to the correct one is achieved, stop working the paste - if you carry on too long, the paste will become sticky and begin to "pick-up" on the applicator. Continue to add thin layers of filler paste at 20-minute intervals, until the level of the filler is just proud of the surrounding bodywork.

Once the filler has hardened, the excess can be removed using a metal plane or file. From then on, progressively-finer grades of abrasive paper should be used, starting with a 40-grade production paper, and finishing with a 400-grade wet-and-dry paper. Always wrap the abrasive paper around a flat rubber, cork, or wooden block - otherwise the surface of the filler will not be completely flat. During the smoothing of the filler surface, the wet-and-dry paper should be periodically rinsed in water. This will ensure that a very smooth finish is imparted to the filler at the final stage.

At this stage, the "dent" should be surrounded by a ring of bare metal, which in turn should be encircled by the finely "feathered" edge of the good paintwork. Rinse the repair area with clean water, until all of the dust produced by the rubbing-down operation has gone.

Spray the whole area with a light coat of primer - this will show up any imperfections in the surface of the filler. Repair these imperfections with fresh filler paste or bodystopper, and once more smooth the surface with abrasive paper. Repeat this spray-and-repair procedure until you are satisfied that the surface of the filler, and the feathered edge of the paintwork, are perfect. Clean the repair area with clean water, and allow to dry fully.

 If bodystopper is used, it can be mixed with cellulose thinners, to form a really thin paste which is ideal for filling small holes

The repair area is now ready for final spraying. Paint spraying must be carried out in a warm, dry, windless and dust-free atmosphere. This condition can be created artificially if you have access to a large indoor working area, but if you are forced to work in the open, you will have to pick your day very carefully. If you are working indoors, dousing the floor in the work area with water will help to settle the dust which would otherwise be in the atmosphere. If the repair area is confined to one body panel, mask off the surrounding panels; this will help to minimise the effects of a slight mis-match in paint colours. Bodywork fittings (eg chrome strips, door handles etc) will also need to be masked off. Use genuine masking tape, and several thicknesses of newspaper, for the masking operations.

Before commencing to spray, agitate the aerosol can thoroughly, then spray a test area (an old tin, or similar) until the technique is mastered. Cover the repair area with a thick coat of primer; the thickness should be built up using several thin layers of paint, rather than one thick one. Using 400-grade wet-and-dry paper, rub down the surface of the primer until it is really smooth. While doing this, the work area should be thoroughly doused with water, and the wet-and-dry paper periodically rinsed in water. Allow to dry before spraying on more paint.

Spray on the top coat, again building up the thickness by using several thin layers of paint. Start spraying at one edge of the repair area, and then, using a side-to-side motion, work until the whole repair area and about 2 inches of the surrounding original paintwork is covered. Remove all masking material 10 to 15 minutes after spraying on the final coat of paint.

Allow the new paint at least two weeks to harden, then, using a paintwork renovator, or a very fine cutting paste, blend the edges of the paint into the existing paintwork. Finally, apply wax polish.

Plastic components

With the use of more and more plastic body components by the vehicle manufacturers (eg bumpers, spoilers, and in some cases major body panels), rectification of more serious damage to such items has become a matter of either entrusting repair work to a specialist in this field, or renewing complete components. Repair of such damage by the DIY owner is not really feasible, owing to the cost of the equipment and materials required for effecting such repairs. The basic technique involves making a groove along the line of the crack in the plastic, using a rotary burr in a power drill. The damaged part is then welded back together, using a hot-air gun to heat up and fuse a plastic filler rod into the groove. Any

excess plastic is then removed, and the area rubbed down to a smooth finish. It is important that a filler rod of the correct plastic is used, as body components can be made of a variety of different types (eg polycarbonate, ABS, polypropylene).

Damage of a less serious nature (abrasions, minor cracks etc) can be repaired by the DIY owner using a two-part epoxy filler repair material. Once mixed in equal proportions, this is used in similar fashion to the bodywork filler used on metal panels. The filler is usually cured in twenty to thirty minutes, ready for sanding and painting.

If the owner is renewing a complete component himself, or if he has repaired it with epoxy filler, he will be left with the problem of finding a suitable paint for finishing which is compatible with the type of plastic used. At one time, the use of a universal paint was not possible, owing to the complex range of plastics encountered in body component applications. Standard paints, generally speaking, will not bond to plastic or rubber satisfactorily. However, it is now possible to obtain a plastic body parts finishing kit which consists of a pre-primer treatment, a primer and coloured top coat. Full instructions are normally supplied with a kit, but basically, the method of use is to first apply the pre-primer to the component concerned, and allow it to dry for up to 30 minutes. Then the primer is applied, and left to dry for about an hour before finally applying the special-coloured top coat. The result is a correctly-coloured component, where the paint will flex with the plastic or rubber, a property that standard paint does not normally posses.

5 Major body damage - repair

Where serious damage has occurred, or large areas need renewal due to neglect, it means that complete new panels will need welding-in; this is best left to professionals. If the damage is due to impact, it will also be necessary to check the alignment of the bodyshell; this can only be carried out accurately by a Renault dealer using special jigs. If the body is misaligned, it is dangerous, as the vehicle will not handle properly. In addition, uneven stresses will be imposed on the steering, suspension and possibly transmission, causing abnormal wear or complete failure, particularly of items such as the tyres.

6 Front and rear bumpers - removal and refitting

11

Front bumper - "Phase 1" models
Removal
1 Apply the handbrake, then jack up the front of the vehicle and support it securely on axle stands (see *"Jacking, towing and wheel changing"*).

6.2 Foglight wiring plug (5) and front bumper front mounting bolt (6) (arrowed) - "Phase 1" models

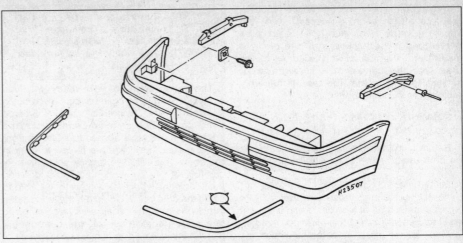

6.5 Front bumper components - "Phase 1" models

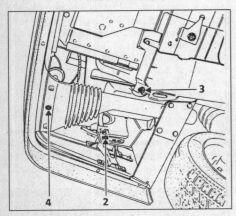

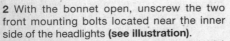

6.6 Front bumper side mounting bolt (2), bumper-to-subframe bolts (3), and air intake duct rivet (4) - "Phase 1" 16-valve models

2 With the bonnet open, unscrew the two front mounting bolts located near the inner side of the headlights **(see illustration)**.
3 Remove the screws (two on each side) securing the sides of the bumper to the wheelarch shields.

6.14 Unscrewing a front bumper upper securing bolts - "Phase 2" model

4 Unscrew the two bolts securing the bumper to the front subframe.
5 Unscrew the two side mounting bolts **(see illustration)**.
6 On 16-valve models, drill out the rivets (one on each side) securing the air intake ducts to the bumper **(see illustration)**.
7 Where applicable, disconnect the foglight wiring plug (after disconnecting the battery negative lead), which is located in front of the radiator.
8 Carefully release the wheel arch shields

from the edges of the bumper, and withdraw the bumper from the vehicle.
9 If necessary, unbolt and remove the mounting brackets, and where applicable, unbolt the spoiler extension from the bottom of the bumper.

Refitting

10 Refitting is a reversal of removal. On 16-valve models, use new rivets to secure the air intake ducts to the lower edge of the bumper.

Front bumper - "Phase 2" models
Removal

11 Remove the front grille panels, with reference to Section 24.
12 Where applicable, disconnect the foglight wiring connector(s) (after disconnecting the battery negative lead).
13 Remove the relevant securing screws and clips, and detach the front edges of the wheel arch shields from the bumper.
14 Working in the grille panel aperture, remove the two upper bumper mounting bolts **(see illustration)**.
15 Working in the engine compartment, remove the two side bumper securing screws (one each side), securing the bumper to the wings **(see illustration)**.

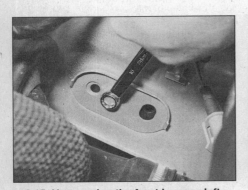

6.15 Unscrewing the front bumper left-hand side securing screw - "Phase 2" model

6.16a Front bumper lower securing bolt (arrowed) - "Phase 2" model

6.16b Front bumper securing rivet (arrowed) - "Phase 2" model

6.19a Withdraw the container carrier . . .

6.19b . . . for access to the rear bumper left-hand side mounting bolt

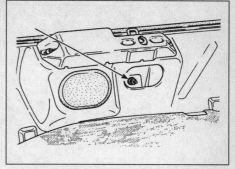

6.20 Rear bumper centre retaining nut (arrowed)

16 Working under the front of the vehicle, support the bumper, then remove the two lower bumper mounting bolts, and drill out the centre rivet **(see illustrations)**. Where applicable, drill out the rivets securing the brake cooling ducts to the bumper.

17 Withdraw the bumper from the vehicle.

Refitting

18 Refitting is a reversal of removal, but use a new rivet to secure the lower edge of the bumper to the body, and where applicable, use new rivets to secure the brake cooling ducts to the bumper.

Rear bumper

Removal

19 Working inside the rear luggage compartment, remove the securing screws, and withdraw the container carrier on the left-hand side for access to the bumper side mounting bolt. Unscrew and remove the bolt **(see illustrations)**.

20 For access to the centre bumper retaining nut, prise out the grommet from the centre of the rear luggage compartment panel, or remove the screw and withdraw the lock trim panel, as applicable. Unscrew and remove the centre retaining nut **(see illustration)**.

21 On models with the number plate lights mounted in the bumper, disconnect the battery negative lead, then prise the number plate lights from the bumper, and disconnect the wiring plugs.

22 Chock the front wheels, then jack up the rear of the vehicle and support it securely on axle stands (see *"Jacking, towing and wheel changing"*).

23 Working beneath the vehicle, unscrew the two bolts securing the bumper to the crossmember. Also unscrew the right-hand mounting bolt **(see illustration)**.

24 Remove the screws and/or clips securing the rear wheel arch liners to the bumper, then withdraw the bumper from the vehicle.

Refitting

25 Refitting is a reversal of removal.

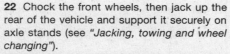

7 Bonnet - removal, refitting and adjustment

Removal

1 Open the bonnet, and support it in the open position using the stay.

2 Disconnect the windscreen washer hose by first prising out the rubber grommet on the right-hand corner. Pull the T-connector from the access hole, and disconnect the right-hand hose **(see illustrations)**.

3 Mark the outline of the hinges with a soft pencil, then loosen the four mounting screws using a Torx key **(see illustration)**.

4 With the help of an assistant, remove the stay, unscrew the four screws, and lift the bonnet from the car **(see illustration)**.

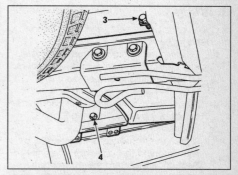

6.23 Rear bumper-to-crossmember bolt (3) and right-hand mounting bolt (4)

7.2a Prise out the windscreen washer rubber grommet . . .

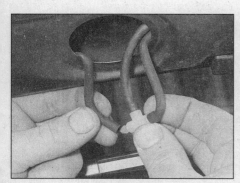

7.2b . . . and disconnect the hose

7.3 Bonnet mounting screws (arrowed)

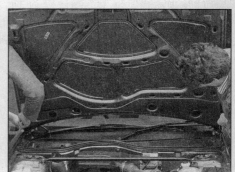

7.4 Removing the bonnet

11

7.5 Bonnet front support rubber buffer

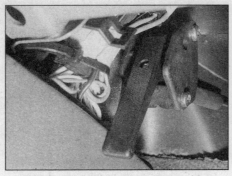

8.6a Bonnet release lever assembly securing bolts - early model

8.6b Removing the bonnet release lever assembly - later model

Refitting

5 Refitting is a reversal of removal, bearing in mind the following points:

(a) Position the bonnet hinges within the outline marks made during removal, but alter its position as necessary to provide a uniform gap all round.

(b) Adjust the rear height of the bonnet as necessary by repositioning it on the hinges.

(c) Adjust the front height if necessary by repositioning the lock with reference to Section 9, then turn the rubber buffers on the engine compartment front cross panel up or down to support the bonnet (see illustration).

8 Bonnet release cable - removal and refitting

Removal

1 The bonnet release lever may be located on the driver's or the passenger's side of the vehicle, depending on model.

2 Open the bonnet.

3 On "Phase 2" models, remove the front grille panels, as described in Section 24.

4 Unclip the cable outer from the lock assembly, then manipulate the end of the cable from the lock lever.

5 Working under the facia (if necessary, for access) remove the glovebox with reference to Section 32.

6 Remove the bolt(s) securing the release lever assembly to the side of the facia (see illustrations).

7 Note the routing of the cable within the engine compartment, then withdraw the cable through the bulkhead into the vehicle interior. To aid refitting, a length of string can be tied to the end of the cable before removal. Untie the string from the end of the cable, and leave it in position when the cable is removed; tie the end of the string to the new cable, and use it to pull the cable into position.

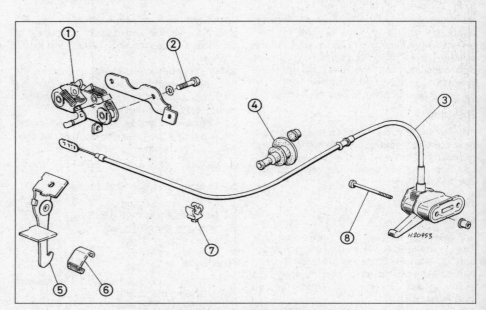

9.3 Bonnet lock and release cable components

1 Lock	4 Grommet	7 Clip
2 Lock mounting bolt	5 Safety catch and striker	8 Handle mounting bolt
3 Cable and handle assembly	6 Guide	

Refitting

8 Refitting is a reversal of removal, ensuring that the cable is routed as noted before removal.

9 Bonnet lock - removal and refitting

Removal

1 Open the bonnet.

2 On "Phase 2" models, remove the front grille panels, as described in Section 24.

3 Unclip the cable outer from the lock assembly, then manipulate the end of the cable from the lock lever (see illustration).

4 Unscrew the two retaining bolts, and remove the lock from the vehicle.

Refitting

5 Refitting is a reversal of removal, but adjust the lock height so that the bonnet line is flush with the front wings, and shuts securely without force. If necessary, adjust the lock laterally so that the striker enters the lock recess correctly; it may also be necessary to reposition the striker itself (see illustration).

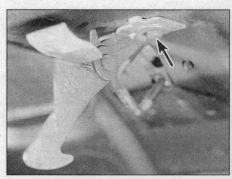

9.5 Bonnet lock striker securing bolt (arrowed)

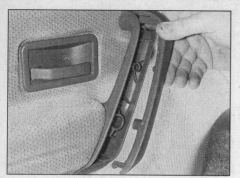

10.1 Removing the plastic insert from the door grip

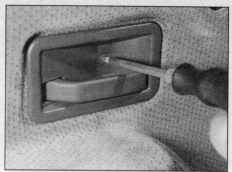

10.2a Remove the screw . . .

10.2b . . . and remove the interior door handle finger plate

10 Door inner trim panel - removal and refitting

Front door
Removal

1 Using a screwdriver, prise the plastic insert from the door grip **(see illustration)**. Unscrew the screws and remove the grip from the inner trim panel.

2 Remove the screw from the interior door handle finger plate. Pull the plate out, and disconnect it from the pull rod **(see illustrations)**.

3 Turn the loudspeaker cover anti-clockwise, and remove it. Remove the screws and withdraw the loudspeaker, then disconnect the wiring **(see illustrations)**.

4 Remove the screws, and withdraw the loudspeaker holder and side pocket from the trim panel **(see illustrations)**.

5 Remove the screw, then remove the exterior mirror inner plastic cover, taking care not to damage the plastic retaining posts **(see illustration)**.

6 Where applicable, remove the window regulator handle, but first note its position with the window fully shut. If necessary, use a tool similar to that shown, together with a piece of cloth **(see illustration)**.

7 The trim panel is clipped in place, and

10.3a Removing the loudspeaker cover . . .

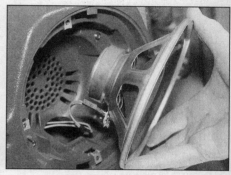

10.3b . . . and loudspeaker

10.4a Remove the front mounting screws (arrowed) . . .

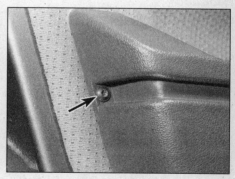

10.4b . . . and rear mounting screws . . .

10.4c . . . and remove the loudspeaker holder and side pocket

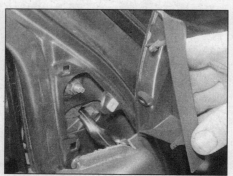

10.5 Removing the exterior mirror inner plastic cover

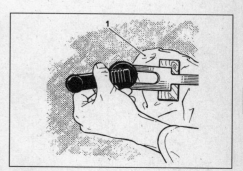

10.6 Using a special tool to remove the window regulator handle

1 Protective cloth

11

10.12 Removing the window regulator handle

10.13 Removing the ashtray holder

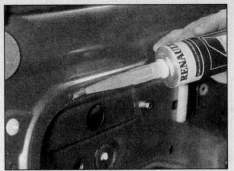

10.15 Applying mastic to the rear inner door panel

sealed with mastic. If the mastic has hardened, it may be necessary to cut it free using a knife or small saw. Try prising the panel from the door carefully with a wide-bladed screwdriver before cutting the mastic. Prise the panel by inserting the screwdriver under the retaining clips, to avoid tearing the inner surface of the panel.

8 Where applicable, disconnect the wiring from the electric window switch.

Refitting

9 Refitting is a reversal of removal, but apply suitable mastic to the inner door panel before fitting the trim panel. Check the retaining clips for breakage, and renew them if necessary.

Rear door

Removal

10 Using a screwdriver, prise the plastic insert from the door grip. Unscrew the screws, and remove the grip from the inner trim panel.

11 Remove the screw from the interior door handle finger plate. Pull the plate out, and disconnect it from the pull rod.

12 Check that the window is fully shut, then note the position of the regulator handle. Pull the handle direct from the splines, and remove the bezel - the handle is only a press fit on the splines **(see illustration)**.

13 Remove the ashtray, then remove the screws and withdraw the ashtray holder from the trim panel **(see illustration)**.

14 The trim panel is clipped in place, and

sealed with mastic. If the mastic has hardened, it may be necessary to cut it free using a knife or small saw. Try prising the panel from the door carefully with a wide-bladed screwdriver before cutting the mastic. Prise the panel by inserting the screwdriver under the retaining clips, to avoid tearing the inner surface of the panel.

Refitting

15 Refer to paragraph 9 **(see illustration)**.

11 Door window glass and regulator - removal and refitting

Front door window glass and regulator - all models except Cabriolet

Removal

1 Remove the door inner trim panel as described in Section 10.

2 Remove the lower rubbing strip.

3 Disconnect the lifter from the bottom of the window glass by pulling the fastener sharply from the plate pin **(see illustration)**. With the window free from the pin, lower the plate into the bottom of the door.

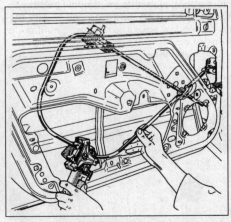

11.7 Removing the front door window regulator and electric motor

4 Release the pad on the rear edge of the window glass from its slide channel, then push the window forwards and lift it out from the outside.

5 Where applicable, reach inside the door, and disconnect the wiring plug from the winder motor.

6 Unscrew the bolts and nuts securing the regulator assembly to the inner door panel **(see illustration)**.

7 Tilt the assembly so that the motor/regulator is at the bottom, then withdraw the assembly through the aperture **(see illustration)**.

8 The electric window control cable may be renewed if necessary. On four-and five-door models, cut the cable to the required length before fitting it **(see illustration)**.

Refitting

9 Refitting is a reversal of removal.

11.3 Front door window lifter (arrowed)

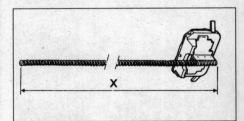

11.8 Front door electric window control cable length for four- and five-door models

X = 1013 ± 5 mm

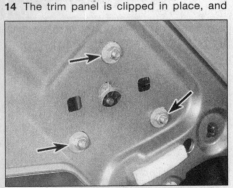

11.6 Front door window regulator mounting nuts (arrowed)

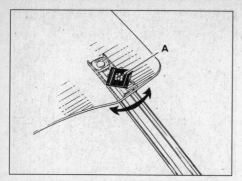

11.12 Clip (A) securing front door glass to guide rail - Cabriolet models

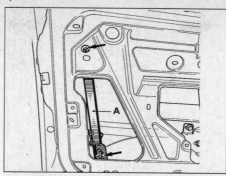

11.13 Rear window guide rail (A) securing bolts (arrowed) - Cabriolet models

11.14 Front door window securing bolts (arrowed) - Cabriolet models

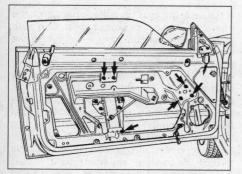

11.17 Front door window regulator assembly fixings (arrowed) - Cabriolet models

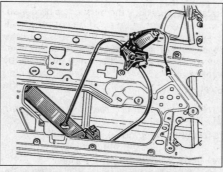

11.18 Manipulating the front door window regulator mechanism out from the door - Cabriolet models

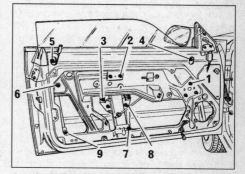

11.19 Tighten the front door window regulator mechanism fixings in the order shown - Cabriolet models

Front door window glass and regulator - Cabriolet models

Removal

10 Ensure that the window is in the fully-raised position, then remove the door inner trim panel, as described in Section 10.

11 Pull the weather strips from the lower edge of the window aperture.

12 Reach up inside the door, and remove the clip securing the glass to the guide rail, by turning it through a quarter of a turn **(see illustration)**.

13 Unscrew the two securing bolts, and withdraw the rear window guide rail through the aperture in the door **(see illustration)**.

14 Lower the window to gain access to the window securing bolts **(see illustration)**.

15 Unscrew the window securing bolts, and withdraw the window from the door.

16 To remove the regulator assembly, first disconnect the battery negative lead.

17 Unscrew the securing nuts and screws, or drill out the rivets (as applicable) securing the assembly to the door **(see illustration)**.

18 Disconnect the wiring plug from the motor, then manipulate the assembly out through the aperture in the door as shown **(see illustration)**.

Refitting

19 Refitting is a reversal of removal, but tighten the fixings in the order shown **(see illustration)**. Note that the window height can be adjusted using screws 4 and 5, and the lateral window adjustment is carried out using fixings 7 and 9.

Rear door window regulator

Removal

20 Remove the door inner trim panel as described in Section 10.

21 Lower the window glass so that the lifter is visible, then unscrew the two screws securing the lifter to the bottom of the window **(see illustration)**. Fully raise the window, and hold it in this position using a block of wood (or alternatively, by using wide adhesive tape).

22 Unscrew the bolts securing the regulator assembly to the inner door panel **(see illustrations)**.

23 Tilt the assembly, taking care not to catch it in the internal locking rod, then withdraw it through the aperture.

11.21 Rear door window regulator-to-glass securing screws (arrowed)

11.22a Rear door window regulator front mounting bolts (arrowed) . . .

11.22b . . . rear upper mounting bolt (arrowed) . . .

11

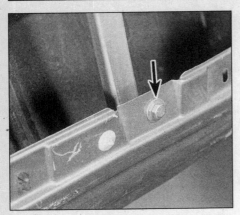

11.22c . . . and rear lower mounting bolt (arrowed)

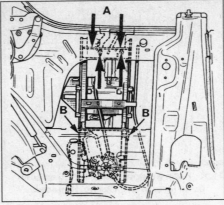

11.45 Rear quarter window regulator fastenings (A and B) - Cabriolet models

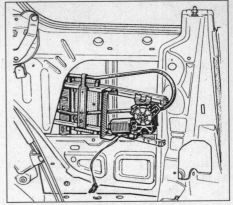

11.46 Manipulating the quarter window regulator mechanism from the body - Cabriolet models

Refitting

24 Refitting is a reversal of removal.

Rear door window glass

Removal

25 Remove the door inner trim panel as described in Section 10.
26 Remove the inner and outer rubbing strips.
27 Lower the window so that the lifter is visible, unscrew the lifter screws, then lower the window to the bottom of the door.
28 Unscrew the rear guide mounting bolts located at the top and bottom of the guide, then remove the guide.
29 Raise the window and remove it from the inside of the door.

Refitting

30 Refitting is a reversal of removal, but before tightening the lifter screws, have the window 25 to 50 mm open, and press it firmly into the rear guide. This will align the window correctly. The lifter screws are accessed through the small hole in the inner door panel with the window in this position.

Rear door fixed window

Removal

31 Remove the main window glass as described previously.
32 Pull the fixed window forwards, and withdraw it from the door.
33 Remove the lower stop from inside the door.

Refitting

34 Refitting is a reversal of removal.

Rear quarter window glass - Cabriolet models

Removal

35 Remove the quarter trim panel with reference to Section 26.
36 Pull the weatherstrips from the lower edge of the window aperture.
37 Fully lower the window.

38 Working through the aperture in the door, remove the securing screws and withdraw the window.

Refitting

39 Refitting is a reversal of removal, but adjust the position of the window in the body as follows.
40 Adjust the height of the window using the two upper securing screws. Adjust the lateral position of the window using the screws at the bottom of the regulator mechanism.

Rear quarter window regulator - Cabriolet models

Removal

41 Remove the quarter trim panel with reference to Section 26.
42 If the mechanism has failed with the window in the lowered position, proceed to paragraph 47.
43 Remove the window glass as described in previously in this Section.
44 Disconnect the battery negative lead, then disconnect the wiring plug from the motor.
45 Remove the fastenings "A" and "B" as shown (see illustration).
46 Manipulate the mechanism out through the aperture in the body as shown (see illustration).
47 If the mechanism fails with the window in the lowered position, proceed as follows.

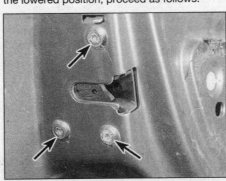

12.3 Door lock mounting screws (arrowed)

48 Remove the two accessible window securing screws.
49 Remove the regulator mechanism fastenings with reference to illustration 11.45.
50 Swing the window glass round in the body to gain access to the remaining fastening.
51 Withdraw the window glass and the regulator mechanism.

Refitting

52 Refitting is a reversal of removal, but refit the window glass as described previously in this Section.

12 Door lock, lock cylinder and handles - removal and refitting

Door lock

Removal

1 Remove the door inner trim panel as described in Section 10.
2 Reach inside the door, and disconnect the exterior handle control rod and the locking rod from the lock.
3 Unscrew the lock mounting screws from the rear edge of the door (see illustration).
4 Where applicable, disconnect the wiring from the central locking motor (see illustration).

12.4 Disconnect the wiring (arrowed) from the central locking motor

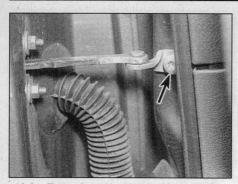

13.2a Front door check link-to-door pillar securing screw (arrowed)

13.2b Front door check link (arrowed) viewed from inside door

13.7 Door striker

5 Disconnect the interior handle operating rod, then withdraw the lock through the aperture in the door inner panel.
6 Where applicable, the motor may be removed from the lock by unscrewing the single retaining screw.

Refitting

7 Refitting is a reversal of removal.

Lock cylinder

Removal

8 Remove the door inner trim panel as described in Section 10.
9 Reach inside the door, and disconnect the operating rod.
10 Pull out the retaining clip, then withdraw the lock cylinder from the outside of the car.

Refitting

11 Refitting is a reversal of removal.

Interior handle

Removal

12 Remove the door inner trim panel as described in Section 10.
13 Remove the screw from inside the handle finger plate, withdraw the handle, and disconnect it from the operating rod.

Refitting

14 Refitting is a reversal of removal.

Exterior handle

Removal

15 Remove the door inner trim panel as described in Section 10.
16 Disconnect the operating rods from the lock.
17 Insert a screwdriver through the hole in the inner door panel, unscrew the mounting screw, then withdraw the handle from inside the door.

Refitting

18 Refitting is a reversal of removal.

13 Door - removal, refitting and adjustment

Removal

1 Where applicable, disconnect the battery negative lead, then remove the door trim panel as described in Section 10. Disconnect the wiring plugs from any electrical components mounted in the door. Note the routing of the wiring to aid refitting, then pass the wiring harness through the front edge of the door.
2 Disconnect the door check link by unscrewing the Torx screw on the door pillar. If necessary, the link may be unbolted from the door **(see illustrations)**.
3 Support the door on blocks of wood.

4 Prise off the caps covering each hinge pin.
5 Using a cranked metal rod of suitable diameter as a drift, drive out the upper and lower hinge pins.
6 Lift the door from the hinges.

Refitting and adjustment

7 Refitting is a reversal of removal, but check that the door is correctly aligned with the surrounding bodywork, with an equal clearance around its edge. Adjustment is made by loosening the Torx screws and moving the door within the elongated mounting holes. A shim is fitted between the hinge plates and door for vertical alignment with the rear pillar. Check that the striker enters the lock centrally when the door is closed, and if necessary loosen it with a Torx key, re-position and re-tighten it **(see illustration)**.

14 Exterior mirror and glass - removal and refitting

Mirror glass

Removal

1 There are two types of mirror glass fitted - one is retained with a wire spring, and the other by plastic clips. The former type is identified by having a small tab located under the bottom edge of the mirror.
2 To remove the wire spring type, use a small screwdriver to push the tab outwards, then withdraw the mirror and disconnect the heater wiring from the rear of the mirror (where applicable) **(see illustrations)**.
3 To remove the plastic clip type, it is recommended that a suction pad is used to pull it out, together with a small screwdriver to release the clips **(see illustration)**.

Refitting

4 Before refitting the wire spring type, refit the clip, then press the mirror into position. To refit the plastic clip type, press the mirror inwards until the clips snap into place.

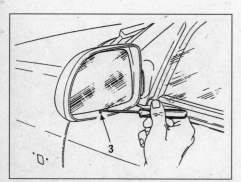

14.2a Pushing the tab (3) outwards to remove the wire spring-retained exterior mirror glass

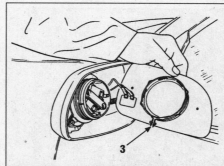

14.2b Inside view of the tab (3) on the wire spring type exterior mirror glass

11

14.3 Removing the plastic clip type exterior mirror glass

14.7 Removing the exterior mirror

15.1 Hinge mounting on the boot lid

Mirror assembly

Removal

5 Remove the mirror trim panel, or the door inner trim panel (Section 10), as applicable.
6 Where applicable, disconnect the wiring plug.
7 Unscrew the three nuts, and withdraw the mirror assembly from the door, feeding the wiring harness (where applicable) through the rubber grommet **(see illustration)**.

Refitting

8 Refitting is a reversal of removal.

15 Boot lid - removal, refitting and adjustment

Removal

1 Open the boot lid, and mark the position of the bolts on the hinges with a pencil **(see illustration)**. Where applicable, disconnect the wiring for the central locking.
2 Place cloth rags beneath each corner of the boot lid, to prevent damage to the paintwork.
3 Disconnect the strut(s) by prising out the retainer with a small screwdriver and pulling the strut from the boot lid ball.
4 With the help of an assistant, unscrew the mounting bolts and lift the boot lid from the car.
5 If necessary, the boot lid hinges may be unbolted from the body.

Refitting and adjustment

6 Refitting is a reversal of removal, but check that the boot lid is correctly aligned with the surrounding bodywork, with an equal clearance around its edge. Adjustment is made by loosening the mounting bolts and moving the boot lid within the elongated mounting holes. Check that the lock enters the striker centrally when the boot lid is closed, and if necessary adjust the positions within the elongated holes.

16 Boot lid support strut - removal and refitting

Removal

1 Support the boot lid in its open position.
2 Disconnect each end of the support strut by prising out the retainers with a small screwdriver and pulling the strut from the ball mountings **(see illustration)**.

Refitting

3 Refitting is a reversal of removal, but note that the piston end of the strut faces downwards.

17 Boot lid lock and cylinder - removal and refitting

Lock

Removal

1 Open the boot lid, then disconnect the operating rod from the lock by reaching through the aperture.
2 Using a Torx key, unscrew the lock mounting bolts, and withdraw the lock from the boot lid.

Refitting

3 Refitting is a reversal of removal, but check that the striker enters the lock centrally when

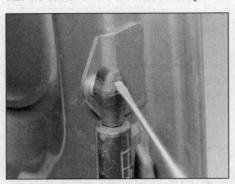

16.2 Prising the retainer from the boot lid upper strut mounting

the boot lid is closed, and if necessary reposition the striker by loosening the mounting screws.

Lock cylinder

Removal

4 Open the boot lid, then disconnect the operating rods for the lock and central locking unit (where applicable) by reaching through the aperture **(see illustration)**.
5 Using a pair of pliers, pull out the retaining clip, then withdraw the lock cylinder from the boot lid.

Refitting

6 Refitting is a reversal of removal.

18 Tailgate - removal, refitting and adjustment

Removal

1 Open the tailgate, and support it in the open position, either with the aid of an assistant, or with a suitable piece of wood.
2 Remove the screws and hooks, and unclip the trim panel from the tailgate. Disconnect the rear window washer tube **(see illustrations)**. Where applicable, also disconnect the wiring for the tailgate wiper motor and the central locking.
3 Unclip and remove the headlining rear cover strip.

17.4 Boot lid lock operating rod (arrowed)

18.2a Remove the screws and hooks . . .

18.2b . . . and unclip the trim panel from the tailgate

18.4 Disconnecting the strut from the tailgate

4 Ensure that the tailgate is adequately supported, then disconnect the struts by prising out the spring clip retainers **(see illustration)**.

5 With the help of an assistant, unscrew the mounting nuts and lift the tailgate from the rear of the vehicle.

6 If necessary, the hinge can be removed from the tailgate by driving out the pin with a suitable drift.

Refitting and adjustment

7 Refitting is a reversal of removal, but check that the tailgate is correctly aligned with the surrounding bodywork, with an equal clearance around its edge. Adjustment is made by loosening the mounting bolts and moving the tailgate within the elongated mounting holes. Check that the striker enters the lock centrally when the tailgate is closed, and if necessary adjust the position of the striker within the elongated holes. The striker position also determines the rear height of the tailgate.

19 Tailgate support strut - removal and refitting

Removal

1 Support the tailgate in its open position.

2 Disconnect each end of the support strut by prising out the spring clip retainers with a small screwdriver, and pulling the strut from the ball mountings.

Refitting

3 Refitting is a reversal of removal, but note that the piston

end of the strut faces downwards.

20 Tailgate lock and lock cylinder - removal and refitting

Lock

Removal

1 Open the tailgate, then remove the screws and hooks, and unclip the inner trim panel.

2 Using a Torx key, unscrew and remove the lock mounting bolts.

3 Pull out the lock, and at the same time turn it to release the operating rod from the cylinder assembly. If necessary, also remove the central locking unit **(see illustrations)**.

Refitting

4 Refitting is a reversal of removal. When refitting the lock, check that the striker enters the lock centrally when the tailgate is closed, and if necessary re-position the striker by loosening the mounting screws **(see illustration)**.

Lock cylinder

Removal

5 Open the tailgate, then disconnect the operating rods for the lock and central locking unit (where applicable) by reaching through the aperture **(see illustrations)**.

20.3a Removing the tailgate lock . . .

20.3b . . . and central locking unit

20.4 Tailgate lock striker mounting screws (arrowed)

20.5a Central locking unit operating rod (arrowed) on the tailgate lock cylinder

20.5b Disconnecting the lock operating rod from the tailgate lock cylinder

11

20.6 Removing the lock cylinder from the tailgate

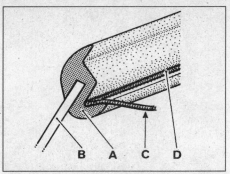

21.5 Cross-section of the rear side window (three-door Hatchback) with cord inserted for refitting

A Weatherseal   C Refitting cord
B Window glass   D Groove

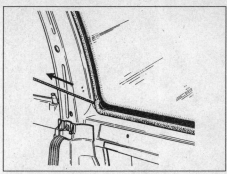

21.7 Pull the cord to locate the lip of the weatherseal over the aperture

6 Using a pair of pliers, pull out the retaining clip, then withdraw the lock cylinder from the tailgate (see illustration).

Refitting

7 Refitting is a reversal of removal.

21 Rear side window (three-door Hatchback) - removal and refitting

Removal

1 Working inside the vehicle, on the appropriate side, remove the rear side shelf, side panel trim, pillar upper trim, and rear quarter panel trim.
2 Using a blunt-ended instrument, push the inner lip of the weatherseal beneath the window frame, starting at the top. Support the window on the outside during this operation.
3 With the weatherseal free, withdraw the window from the body.

Refitting

4 Clean the window and aperture in the body.
5 Fit the weatherseal on the window, then insert a cord in the weatherseal groove so that the ends project from the bottom of the window, and are overlapped by approximately 200 mm (see illustration).
6 Locate the window on the aperture in the body, and pass the ends of the cord inside the vehicle. Have an assistant hold the window in position.

7 Slowly pull one end of the cord so that the lip of the weatherseal goes over the aperture; at the same time, have the assistant press firmly on the outside of the window (see illustration). When the cord reaches the middle top of the window, pull the remaining length of cord to position the other half of the weatherseal.
8 Refit the trim panels in reverse order.

22 Windscreen and rear window/tailgate glass - general information

The windscreen and rear window/tailgate glass are bonded in place with special mastic. Special tools are required to cut free the old units and fit replacements, together with cleaning solutions and primers. It is therefore recommended that this work is entrusted to a Renault dealer or windscreen replacement specialist.

23 Body exterior fittings/ exterior trim panels - general information

The front wing side protection strip can be removed by partially removing the plastic wheelarch, then removing the clip or metal nut from inside the wing. Using a screwdriver, lift

the front of the strip to free the pin from the hole, then push the strip to the rear. The strip is refitted by pressing it until the clip engages.

The door protection strips can be removed by removing the mounting screws from inside the door, then pushing the strip forwards. Align the clips when refitting the strips.

The sill protection strips can be removed by prising up their end covers and unscrewing the retaining screws, then pulling the strip forwards. The clips may be removed from the sill by turning them through 90° with a pair of pliers.

24 Front grille panels ("Phase 2" models) - removal and refitting

Removal

1 Open the bonnet.
2 Remove the securing screws and clips, and withdraw the two radiator shield panels. Each panel is secured by one screw and a plastic clip, which must be turned to release it (see illustrations).
3 Slacken the upper grille panel securing screw (there is no need to remove it) (see illustration).
4 Remove the two lower grille panel securing screws (see illustration).
5 Working in the grille panel aperture, remove the two screws securing the grille panel to the inside of the headlights (see illustration).

24.2a Remove the securing screw . . .

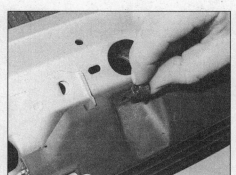

24.2b . . . and the plastic clip . . .

24.2c . . . to release the radiator shield panel

24.3 Slackening the upper grille panel securing screw

24.4 Removing a lower grille panel securing screw

24.5 Removing an inner grille panel-to-headlight securing screw

6 Remove the front indicator lights as described in Chapter 12.
7 Remove the single screw on each side securing the grille panel to the body bracket **(see illustration)**.
8 Withdraw the grille panel from the vehicle **(see illustration)**.

Refitting

9 Refitting is a reversal of removal.

25 Seats - removal and refitting

Front seat

Removal

1 Working under the vehicle, unscrew the four nuts securing the seat runners to the floor. Lift the seat out from inside the vehicle. Note the location of the spacers between the runners and the floor **(see illustrations)**.
2 If desired, the seat can be separated from the runners, after removing the seat side trim panels (where applicable) and unscrewing the seat-to-runner securing bolts **(see illustration)**.

Refitting

3 Refitting is a reversal of removal.

Rear seat

Removal

4 Fold the rear seat backrest forwards, then raise the two levers on the hinges and remove the backrest from the vehicle **(see illustration)**.
5 To remove the seat cushion, tilt the cushion forwards, then release the two brackets from the location holes and remove the cushion from the vehicle.

Refitting

6 Refitting is a reversal of removal.

24.7 Removing a grille panel-to-body bracket securing screw

24.8 Removing the front grille panel

25.1a Seat runner mounting nut viewed from under the vehicle

25.1b Removing a seat. Note the spacer (arrowed)

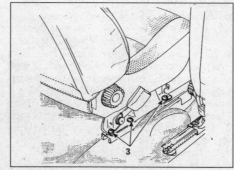

25.2 Seat-to-runner securing bolts (3) on inner side of seat

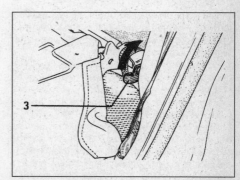

25.4 Rear seat backrest securing lever (3)

11

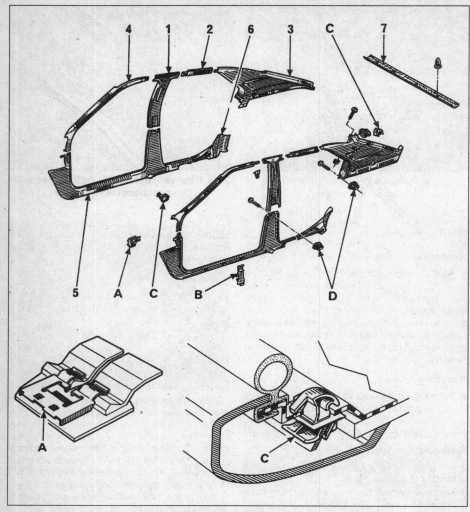

26.2 Removing the coat hanger

26.3 Side lower trim top securing screw (arrowed)

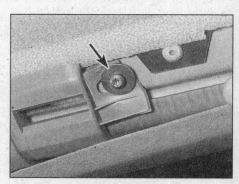

26.5 Rear quarter panel trim front securing screw (arrowed)

26.1 Interior trim panels and plastic clips

A, B, C and D - Plastic clips
1 Centre pillar upper trim
2 Upper door trim
3 Rear quarter panel trim
4 Front pillar upper trim
5 Side lower trim
6 Rear lower trim
7 Headlining rear panel

26 Interior trim panels - general information

1 The interior trim panels shown are retained with plastic clips, which may easily break on removal (see illustration). It is recommended that any broken clips are renewed after removal to ensure secure fitting.

2 To remove the centre pillar upper trim, first remove the coat hanger, seat belt mounting and height adjustment pushrod, then release the trim and seals and remove the sliding cover (see illustration).

3 To remove the side lower trim, first remove the centre pillar upper trim, then remove the screws and the lower belt mounting. Release the rear and front ends, then remove the trim from the rear of the vehicle (see illustration).

4 To remove the front pillar upper trim, first remove the centre pillar upper trim, then

remove the screws and withdraw the trim downwards and rearwards.

5 To remove the rear quarter panel trim on all except Cabriolet models, first remove the centre pillar upper trim, rear door upper and lower trim, and the headlining rear trim. Remove the seal from the luggage compartment aperture frame, the side shelf, and the two upper screws. Release the trim starting at the door seal end (see illustration).

6 To remove the rear quarter panel trim panel on Cabriolet models, lower the hood, and tilt the rear seat cushion forwards. Remove the seat belt lower anchor bolt, and the hood latch handle. Remove the securing nut (see illustration), then release the securing clips and manipulate the panel from the window weatherstrips.

7 To remove the rear side shelf, first remove the centre shelf, then disconnect the wiring from the loudspeaker and remove the five mounting screws.

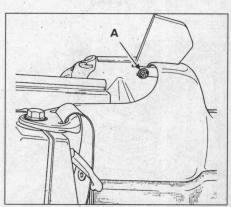

26.6 Rear quarter panel trim securing nut (A) - Cabriolet models

27.2 Front seat belt bottom anchor bolt

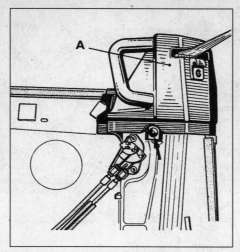
27.5 Centre pillar trim upper section (A) - Cabriolet models

27.8 Rear seat belt inertia reel viewed with trim panel removed

27 Seat belts - removal and refitting
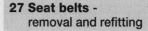

Warning: Certain later models may be fitted with a seat belt pretensioning system, which pretensions the front seat belts in the event of a severe frontal impact. Where this system is fitted, DO NOT attempt to carry out any work involving the front seat belt stalks. If the system is activated unintentionally, personal injury could result. If the vehicle is involved in an accident, have the system checked by a Renault dealer.

Front seat belt - all models except Cabriolet
Removal

1 To remove a front seat belt stalk, move the seat to the rear and, where applicable, remove the trim panel covering the stalk mounting. Unscrew the mounting bolt, and remove the stalk from the seat.
2 To remove a front seat belt inertia reel and belt, first unbolt the bottom anchor from the

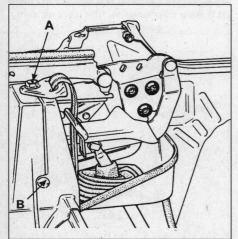
27.11 Rear seat belt upper securing bolt (A) and trim panel (B) - Cabriolet models

inner sill **(see illustration)**. Remove the trim panels, and unbolt the inertia reel and upper sliding mounting from the centre pillar. On three-door models, unbolt the rail from the inner sill.

Refitting

3 Refitting is a reversal of removal, but tighten the anchorages to the specified torque.

Front seat belt - Cabriolet models
Removal

4 Remove the rear quarter trim panel, with reference to Section 26.
5 Remove the centre pillar trim panels **(see illustration)**.
6 Remove the upper belt anchor bolt, and the inertia reel, and withdraw the seat belt from the vehicle.

Refitting

7 Refitting is a reversal of removal, but tighten the anchorages to the specified torque.

Rear seat belt - all except Cabriolet models
Removal

8 To remove the rear seat belts, first remove the rear seat backrest and cushion. Prise off the plastic caps, and unbolt the seat belts from the body. To remove the inertia reel, it will first be necessary to remove the trim panels **(see illustration)**.

Refitting

9 Refitting is a reversal of removal, but tighten the anchorages to the specified torque.

Rear seat belt - Cabriolet models
Removal

10 Remove the rear seat back.
11 Unbolt the upper and lower anchor bolts **(see illustration)**.

12 Unclip the seat belt trim panel, then remove the inertia reel securing bolt and withdraw the belt.

Refitting

13 Refitting is a reversal of removal, but tighten the anchorages to the specified torque.

28 Hood (Cabriolet models) - general information

The hood fitted to Cabriolet models is manually-operated. To avoid damage, the correct sequence must be followed when raising or lowering the hood. If the correct sequence (described in the manufacturer's vehicle handbook) is not followed, an alarm will sound. If this happens, stop the procedure to avoid the possibility of damage.

Due to the fact that the hood components are easily damaged, and the requirement for accurate alignment and adjustment, it is recommended that removal and refitting of the hood assembly and components is entrusted to a Renault dealer **(see illustration)**.

29 Sunroof components - removal and refitting

Note: *The sunroof is a complex piece of equipment, consisting of a large number of components. It is strongly recommended that the sunroof mechanism is not disturbed unless absolutely necessary. If the sunroof mechanism is faulty, or requires overhaul, consult a Renault dealer for advice.*

Glass panel
Removal

1 Raise the glass to the tilted position.
2 Remove the four Torx-type glass panel securing screws (two on each side) **(see illustration)**.
3 Tilt the glass slightly rearwards, and withdraw it forwards from outside the vehicle.

11

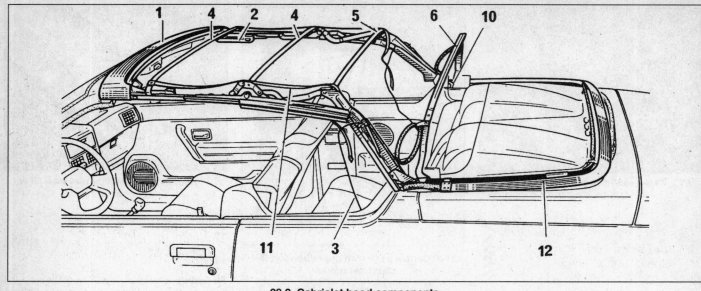

28.2 Cabriolet hood components

1 Hood front crossmember	*4 Front and centre stretchers*	*10 Pivot bearing*
2 Front latch handle	*5 Main stretcher*	*11 Tensioner straps*
3 Hood tensioner cable	*6 Angle stretcher*	*12 Hood rear frame*

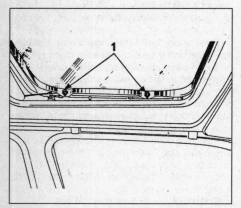

29.2 Two of the sunroof glass panel securing screws (1)

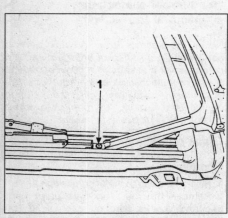

29.9 Sunroof air deflector securing rivet (1)

Refitting and adjustment

4 Lower the glass panel into position, and refit the four securing screws - do not fully tighten them at this stage.

5 Close the sunroof, and adjust the position of the glass panel to bring it flush with the roof.

6 Tighten the securing screws.

7 Open and close the sunroof several times, to ensure that it remains flush with the roof, and if necessary re-adjust as described previously.

Air deflector

Removal

8 Open the sunroof.

9 Carefully drill out the two pop-rivets securing the deflector mountings **(see illustration)**.

10 Remove the deflector by pulling it forwards.

Refitting

11 Refitting is a reversal of removal, using new pop-rivets.

Crank mechanism and motor

12 For access to these components, it is necessary to remove the headlining, which is clipped and glued to the roof. To remove the headlining, it is necessary to remove the surrounding trim panels. Due to the complicated nature of this procedure, and the risk of damage, it is recommended that any work on the sunroof crank mechanism and motor is entrusted to a Renault dealer.

30 Centre console - removal and refitting

Removal

1 Working inside the vehicle, on manual gearbox models, prise the gear lever boot from the centre console; on automatic transmission models, remove the selector lever. Refer to Chapter 7 if necessary.

2 Remove the mounting screws, and lift the centre console from the car. Where applicable, disconnect the wiring from the switches **(see illustrations)**.

Refitting

3 Refitting is a reversal of removal.

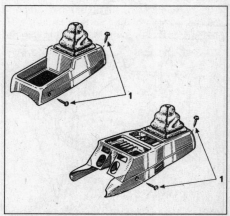

30.2a Alternative types of centre console and securing screws (1)

30.2b Switch and cigarette lighter wiring at rear of centre console

31.7 Facia-to-steering column securing screw (arrowed)

31.12a Remove the screws . . .

31 Facia - removal and refitting

Removal

1 Disconnect the battery negative lead.
2 Remove the centre console with reference to Section 30.
3 Remove the front left-hand and right-hand pillar upper and lower trim, with reference to Section 26.
4 Remove the steering wheel with reference to Chapter 10, noting the warning given for models fitted with air bags.
5 Remove the steering column upper and lower shrouds. Note that, on models with a radio/cassette player remote control switch, it will be necessary to loosen the switch clamp screw before the shrouds can be removed (see Chapter 12).
6 Remove the combination switch from the steering column, with reference to Chapter 12.
7 Unscrew and remove the two screws securing the facia to the top of the steering column, then remove the moulding and disconnect the ignition switch **(see illustration)**.
8 On models with a non-adjustable steering column, unscrew and remove the steering column mounting nuts and bolts (see Chapter 10), and lower the column away from the facia.
9 On models with an adjustable steering column, set the steering wheel in its lowest position, then remove the adjusting locknut

and control lever. The steering column mountings do not have to be removed.
10 Where applicable, remove the screw securing the choke control knob to the facia, then disconnect the warning light wiring, and push the knob back into the facia.
11 Disconnect the speedometer cable.
12 Remove the screws from the heater control panel and lower cover, disconnect the wiring, and push the panel inside the facia **(see illustrations)**.
13 Remove the screws securing the heater unit to the facia, and the screws securing the moulding on the heater unit. Release the wiring harness for the centre console.
14 Disconnect the wiring connectors on the left- and right-hand A-pillars.
15 Unscrew the earth cable mounting bolts.
16 Remove the courtesy light switches from the A-pillars. Disconnect the wiring plugs located in the pillars.
17 On the left-hand side of the engine compartment, remove the cover and disconnect the engine wiring harness.
18 Remove the plastic shield from the left-hand wheelarch, then unclip the engine wiring harness. Pass the harness inside the car.
19 Remove the scuttle grille from the right-hand side.
20 Disconnect the wiring harness from the windscreen wiper, the battery positive terminal, and the heater matrix motor.
21 Using a screwdriver, prise off the facia mounting nut covers from the left and right-hand lower corners **(see illustration)**.

Unscrew and remove the two nuts.
22 Prise the two upper covers from the left and right-hand speaker locations on the facia, then remove the two nuts from the facia upper mountings.
23 With the help of an assistant, release the facia from the bulkhead, and withdraw it from one side of the vehicle, noting the routing of the wiring harness.

Refitting

24 Refitting is a reversal of removal, but note the following points:
  (a) Check that the plastic centring lug is in position on the top of the bulkhead.
  (b) Ensure that the wiring harness is routed as noted before removal.
  (c) Tighten all nuts and bolts securely.
  (d) Before re-connecting the battery leads, switch off the ignition and all electrical switches. After re-connecting the leads, check that all electrical components are operating correctly.

32 Glovebox - removal and refitting

Removal

1 With the glovebox open, pull out the hinge pins and withdraw the glovebox from the facia.
2 If necessary, the lock may be removed from the glovebox lid and the facia.

Refitting

3 Refitting is a reversal of removal.

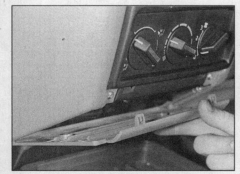

31.12b . . . and remove the heater panel lower cover

31.12c Removing the heater control panel

31.21 Removing a lower facia mounting nut cover

11

Notes

Chapter 12 Body electrical systems

Contents

Degrees of difficulty

Easy, suitable for novice with little experience		Fairly easy, suitable for beginner with some experience		Fairly difficult, suitable for competent DIY mechanic		Difficult, suitable for experienced DIY mechanic		Very difficult, suitable for expert DIY or professional	

Specifications

Fuses (main fusebox) - all models except Cabriolet

Fuse No	Rating (amps)	Circuit(s) protected
1	30	Left-hand electric window
2	30	Right-hand electric window
3	10	Left-hand side and rear lights
4	10	Right-hand side and rear lights, lights-on buzzer, switch lighting
5	10	Rear foglight
6	10	Flasher
7	30	Air conditioning
8	20	Engine electric cooling fan
9	30	Air conditioning
10	5	Seat belt pre-tensioning system
11	20	Protected engine functions
12	5	Automatic transmission
13	15	Anti-lock brakes
14	20	Sunroof, trip computer, heated rear screen, heated mirrors, anti-theft switch
15	5	Alarm
16	-	Not used
17	10	Clock, radio, trip computer, alarm
18	20	Heater blower
19	30	Headlight washers
20	10	Windscreen wiper timer
21	30	Central door locking, anti-theft switch
22	20	Heated rear screen
23	15	Radio, interior lights, luggage compartment light
24	30	Accessories cut-off (cuts off power to interior lights, clock, etc, when cranking)
25	15	Clock, trip computer, alarm, rear view mirrors
26	15	Windscreen wiper, windscreen washers
27	10	Heated seats
28	15	Rear screen wiper, cigarette lighter, reversing lights
29	10	Stop-lights

12

Fuses (main fusebox) - Cabriolet models

Fuse No	Rating (amps)	Circuit(s) protected
1	30	Rear left-hand electric window
2	30	Front left-hand electric window
3	30	Front right-hand electric window
4	10	Left-hand side and tail lights
5	10	Right-hand side and tail lights, lights-on buzzer, switch lighting
6	10	Rear foglight
7	10	Flasher unit
8	30	Air conditioning
9	20	Engine electric cooling fan
10	30	Air conditioning
11	5	Seat belt pre-tensioning system
12	20	Protected engine functions
13	5	Automatic transmission
14	15	Anti-lock braking system
15	20	Heated rear view mirrors
16	5	Alarm
17	-	Not used
18	10	Clock, radio, alarm, aerial amplifier
19	20	Heater blower
20	-	Not used
21	30	Rear right-hand electric window
22	10	Windscreen wiper "park" function
23	30	Door locks
24	20	Heated rear window
25	15	Radio, interior lights, luggage compartment lights
26	30	Accessories cut-off (cuts off power to interior lights, clock, etc, when cranking)
27	15	Clock, hood alarm, electric rear view mirrors
28	15	Windscreen washer
29	-	Not used
30	15	Cigarette lighter, reversing lights
31	10	Stop-lights

Fuses (auxiliary fusebox) - "Phase 2" models

Fuse No	Rating (amps)	Circuit(s) protected
1	70	Pre-heating circuit (Diesel)
2	40	Cooling fan
3	2	Fuel injection computer
4	30	Fuel pump
5	15	Engine functions
6	25	Cooling fan

Bulbs

	Wattage		Wattage
Headlight	60/55	Rear direction indicator	21
Front sidelight:		Reversing light	21
Single headlights	5	Stop-light	21
Dual headlights	3	Rear foglight	21
Front foglight	21	Number plate light	5
Front direction indicator	21	Interior lights	10
Direction indicator side repeater	5	Instrument panel lights	1.2 or 2
Tail light	5		

1 General information and precautions

General information

The body electrical system consists of all lights, wash/wipe equipment, interior electrical equipment, and associated switches and wiring.

The electrical system is of the 12-volt negative earth type. Power to the body electrical system is provided by a 12-volt battery, which is charged by the alternator (see Chapter 5).

The engine electrical system (battery, alternator, starter motor, ignition system, etc) is covered separately in Chapter 5.

Precautions

Refer to the precautions given in Chapter 5A before carrying out any work on the body electrical system. In particular, take note of the precautions to be observed before disconnecting the battery on a vehicle equipped with a security-coded radio/cassette unit.

2 Electrical fault-finding - general information

Note: *Refer to the precautions given in "Safety first!" and in Chapter 5A before starting work. The following tests relate to testing of the main electrical circuits, and should not be used to test delicate electronic circuits (such as engine management systems, anti-lock braking systems, etc), particularly where an electronic control module is used. Refer to Chapter 5C for precautions to be observed when working on models fitted with electronic control units.*

General

1 A typical electrical circuit consists of an electrical component, any switches, relays, motors, fuses, fusible links or circuit breakers related to that component, and the wiring and connectors which link the component to both the battery and the chassis. To help to pinpoint a problem in an electrical circuit, wiring diagrams are included at the end of this manual.

2 Before attempting to diagnose an electrical fault, first study the appropriate wiring diagram, to obtain a complete understanding of the components included in the particular circuit concerned. The possible sources of a fault can be narrowed down by noting if other components related to the circuit are operating properly. If several components or circuits fail at one time, the problem is likely to be related to a shared fuse or earth connection.

3 Electrical problems usually stem from simple causes, such as loose or corroded connections, a faulty earth connection, a blown fuse, a melted fusible link, or a faulty relay (refer to Section 3 for details of testing relays). Visually inspect the condition of all fuses, wires and connections in a problem circuit before testing the components. Use the wiring diagrams to determine which terminal connections will need to be checked in order to pinpoint the troublespot.

4 The basic tools required for electrical fault-finding include a circuit tester or voltmeter (a 12-volt bulb with a set of test leads can also be used for certain tests); a self-powered test light (sometimes known as a continuity tester); an ohmmeter (to measure resistance); a battery and set of test leads; and a jumper wire, preferably with a circuit breaker or fuse incorporated, which can be used to bypass suspect wires or electrical components. Before attempting to locate a problem with test instruments, use the wiring diagram to determine where to make the connections.

5 To find the source of an intermittent wiring fault (usually due to a poor or dirty connection, or damaged wiring insulation), a "wiggle" test can be performed on the wiring. This involves wiggling the wiring by hand to see if the fault occurs as the wiring is moved. It should be possible to narrow down the source of the fault to a particular section of wiring. This method of testing can be used in conjunction with any of the tests described in the following sub-Sections.

6 Apart from problems due to poor connections, two basic types of fault can occur in an electrical circuit - open-circuit, or short-circuit.

7 Open-circuit faults are caused by a break somewhere in the circuit, which prevents current from flowing. An open-circuit fault will prevent a component from working, but will not cause the relevant circuit fuse to blow.

8 Short-circuit faults are caused by a "short" somewhere in the circuit, which allows the current flowing in the circuit to "escape" along an alternative route, usually to earth. Short-circuit faults are normally caused by a breakdown in wiring insulation, which allows a feed wire to touch either another wire, or an earthed component such as the bodyshell. A short-circuit fault will normally cause the relevant circuit fuse to blow.

Finding an open-circuit

9 To check for an open-circuit, connect one lead of a circuit tester or voltmeter to either the negative battery terminal or a known good earth.

10 Connect the other lead to a connector in the circuit being tested, preferably nearest to the battery or fuse.

11 Switch on the circuit, bearing in mind that some circuits are live only when the ignition switch is moved to a particular position.

12 If voltage is present (indicated either by the tester bulb lighting or a voltmeter reading, as applicable), this means that the section of the circuit between the relevant connector and the battery is problem-free.

13 Continue to check the remainder of the circuit in the same fashion.

14 When a point is reached at which no voltage is present, the problem must lie between that point and the previous test point with voltage. Most problems can be traced to a broken, corroded or loose connection.

Finding a short-circuit

15 To check for a short-circuit, first disconnect the load(s) from the circuit (loads are the components which draw current from a circuit, such as bulbs, motors, heating elements, etc).

16 Remove the relevant fuse from the circuit, and connect a circuit tester or voltmeter to the fuse connections.

17 Switch on the circuit, bearing in mind that some circuits are live only when the ignition switch is moved to a particular position.

18 If voltage is present (indicated either by the tester bulb lighting or a voltmeter reading, as applicable), this means that there is a short-circuit.

19 If no voltage is present, but the fuse still blows with the load(s) connected, this indicates an internal fault in the load(s).

Finding an earth fault

20 The battery negative terminal is connected to "earth" - the metal of the engine/transmission unit and the car body - and most systems are wired so that they only receive a positive feed, the current returning via the metal of the car body. This means that the component mounting and the body form part of that circuit. Loose or corroded mountings can therefore cause a range of electrical faults, ranging from total failure of a circuit, to a puzzling partial fault. In particular, lights may shine dimly (especially when another circuit sharing the same earth point is in operation), motors (eg wiper motors or the radiator cooling fan motor) may run slowly, and the operation of one circuit may have an apparently-unrelated effect on another. Note that, on many vehicles, earth straps are used between certain components, such as the engine/transmission and the body, usually where there is no metal-to-metal contact between components due to flexible rubber mountings, etc.

21 To check whether a component is properly earthed, disconnect the battery, and connect one lead of an ohmmeter to a known good earth point. Connect the other lead to the wire or earth connection being tested. The resistance reading should be zero; if not, check the connection as follows.

22 If an earth connection is thought to be faulty, dismantle the connection, and clean back to bare metal both the bodyshell and the wire terminal or the component earth connection mating surface. Be careful to remove all traces of dirt and corrosion, then use a knife to trim away any paint, so that a clean metal-to-metal joint is made. On reassembly, tighten the joint fasteners securely; if a wire terminal is being refitted, use serrated washers between the terminal and the bodyshell, to ensure a clean and secure connection. When the connection is remade, prevent the onset of corrosion in the future by applying a coat of petroleum jelly or silicone-based grease. Alternatively, at regular intervals, spray on a proprietary ignition sealer, or a water-dispersant lubricant.

3 Fuses and relays - general information

Fuses

1 Fuses are designed to break a circuit when a predetermined current is reached, in order to protect components and wiring which could be damaged by excessive current flow. Any excessive current flow will be due to a fault in the circuit, usually a short-circuit (see Section 2).

2 The main fuses are located in the fusebox, under the facia/glovebox on the passenger's side (see illustrations).

3 For access to the fuses, turn the two fasteners through a quarter-turn, then lower the fusebox panel from the facia. The circuits protected by the fuses are marked on a sticker at the bottom of the fusebox panel.

4 On "Phase 2" models, additional fuses may be located in an auxiliary fusebox under the bonnet, on the left-hand side of the engine compartment. For access to these fuses, unclip the auxiliary fusebox lid. The circuits protected by the fuses are marked on a sticker under the fusebox lid (see illustrations).

5 The fuse for the radio/cassette player is mounted on the rear of the unit.

6 A blown fuse can be recognised from its melted or broken wire (see illustration).

7 To remove a fuse, first ensure that the relevant circuit is switched off.

8 Using the plastic tool provided in the

12

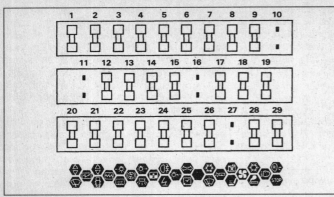

3.2a Fuse location chart (main fusebox) - "Phase 1" models (for fuse identification see Specifications)

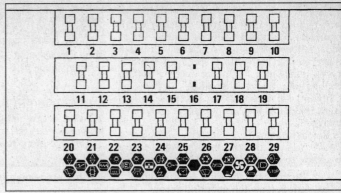

3.2b Fuse location chart (main fusebox) - "Phase 2" models except Cabriolet (for fuse identification see Specifications)

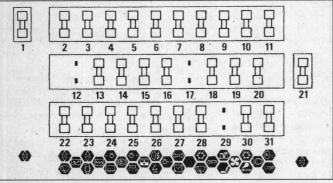

3.2c Fuse location chart (main fusebox) - "Phase 2" Cabriolet models (for fuse identification see Specifications)

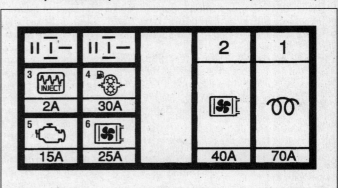

3.4a Fuse location chart (auxiliary fusebox) - "Phase 2" models (for fuse identification see Specifications)

3.4b Auxiliary fusebox with cover removed

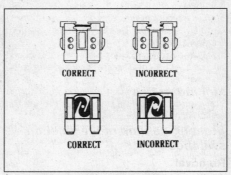

3.6 Identifying a blown fuse
Left OK   Right Blown

3.8 Removing a fuse using the tool provided

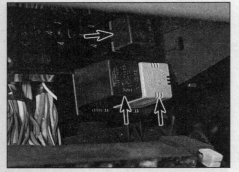

3.13a Relays (arrowed) located in the main fusebox - "Phase 1" models

3.13b Relay location chart (main fusebox)

A Front foglight shunt
B Front foglight shunt
C Front foglight relay
D & E Not used

F Trip computer lighting rheostat relay
G Not used
H Heated rear window relay
J Door locking timer

K Not used
L Flasher unit
M Lights "on" warning buzzer
S Diagnostic plug
T Windscreen wiper timer

4.4a Removing a steering column multi-function switch securing screw

4.4b Removing the wash/wipe switch . . .

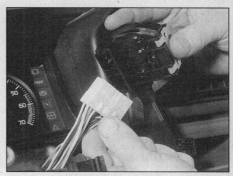

4.4c . . . and disconnecting the wiring plug

fusebox, pull the fuse from its location (see illustration).

9 Spare fuses are provided at the right-hand side of the main fusebox.

10 Before renewing a blown fuse, trace and rectify the cause, and always use a fuse of the correct rating. Never substitute a fuse of a higher rating, or make temporary repairs using wire or metal foil; more serious damage, or even fire, could result.

11 Note that the fuses are colour-coded as follows. Refer to the Specifications for details of the fuse ratings and the circuits protected.

Colour	Rating
Orange	5A
Red	10A
Blue	15A
Yellow	20A
Clear or white	25A
Green	30A

Relays

12 A relay is an electrically-operated switch, which is used for the following reasons:
(a) A relay can switch a heavy current remotely from the circuit in which the current is flowing, therefore allowing the use of lighter-gauge wiring and switch contacts.
(b) A relay can receive more than one control input, unlike a mechanical switch.
(c) A relay can have a "timer" function - for example, the intermittent wiper relay.

13 Most of the relays are located in the main and auxiliary fuseboxes (see previous sub-Section) (see illustrations).

14 If a circuit controlled by a relay develops a fault, and the relay is suspect, operate the circuit. If the relay is functioning, it should be possible to hear the relay click as it is energised. If this is the case, the fault lies with the components or wiring in the system. If the relay is not being energised, then either the relay is not receiving a switching voltage, or the relay itself is faulty (do not overlook the relay socket terminals when tracing faults). Testing is by the substitution of a known good unit, but be careful; while some relays are identical in appearance and in operation, others look similar, but perform different functions.

4 Switches - removal and refitting

Ignition switch

1 Refer to Chapter 5A.

Steering column multi-function switches

Removal

2 Disconnect the battery negative lead.
3 Remove the securing screws and withdraw

the steering column shrouds. Note that it may be necessary to loosen the radio/cassette player remote control switch clamp screw (see later in this Section), before the shrouds can be removed. Where applicable, also remove the internal cover.

4 Unscrew the mounting screws, withdraw the switch from the steering column, and disconnect the wiring plug (see illustrations).

Refitting

5 Refitting is a reversal of removal.

Facia switches (except for headlight aim adjustment switch)

Removal

6 Disconnect the battery negative lead.
7 Prise the switch from the facia using a small screwdriver (see illustration).
8 Disconnect the wiring plug.

Refitting

9 Refitting is a reversal of removal.

Door and centre console switches

10 Proceed as described previously for the facia switches (see illustrations).

Courtesy light switches

Removal

11 Disconnect the battery negative lead.
12 With the door open, prise the switch from

4.7 Prising out a facia switch

4.10a Prising out a door switch . . .

4.10b . . . for access to the wiring plug

4.12 Removing a courtesy light switch

4.16 Prising out the instrument panel rheostat . . .

4.17 . . . and disconnecting the wiring plug

the door pillar using a small screwdriver **(see illustration)**. Pull out the wiring slightly, and tie a piece of string to it, to prevent it dropping back into the door pillar.
13 Disconnect the wiring from the switch.

Refitting

14 Refitting is a reversal of removal.

Instrument panel rheostat

Removal

15 Disconnect the battery negative lead.
16 Prise the rheostat from the steering column shroud using a small screwdriver **(see illustration)**.
17 Disconnect the wiring plug **(see illustration)**.

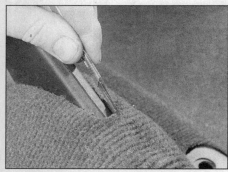

4.20 Make a slit in the carpet with a knife . . .

Refitting

18 Refitting is a reversal of removal.

Handbrake warning light switch

Removal

19 Disconnect the battery negative lead.
20 Make a slit in the carpet just to the rear of the handbrake lever **(see illustration)**.
21 Disconnect the wiring from the switch **(see illustration)**.
22 Unscrew the mounting bolt and remove the switch.

Refitting

23 Refitting is a reversal of removal.

Map reading and front courtesy light switch

Removal

24 Using a small ,screwdriver prise off the lens and cover panel.
25 Release the switch assembly from the headlining by depressing the plastic tabs at each end of the switch **(see illustration)**.
26 Disconnect the wiring and remove the switch **(see illustration)**.

Refitting

27 Refitting is a reversal of removal.

Radio/cassette player remote control switch

Removal

28 Disconnect the battery negative lead.

29 Remove the radio/cassette player, as described in Section 18.
30 Disconnect the remote control switch wiring from the rear of the radio/cassette unit.
31 Slide the cover from the switch to reveal the switch clamp screw. Loosen, but do not remove the screw.
32 Remove the steering column shrouds.
33 Slide the switch from its bracket, then feed the wiring through from behind the facia, noting its routing.

Refitting

34 Refitting is a reversal of removal, noting the following points:
   (a) Refit the radio/cassette player as described in Section 18.
   (b) Ensure that the wiring is routed as noted before removal.
   (c) Do not fully tighten the switch clamp screw until the steering column shrouds have been refitted.

Headlight aim adjustment switch

35 No details were available at the time of writing.

5 Bulbs (exterior lights) - renewal

Headlight

1 Disconnect the battery negative lead.
2 On "Phase 1" models, turn the headlight

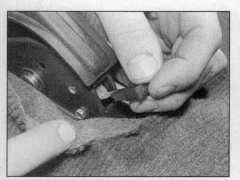

4.21 . . . and disconnect the wiring plug

4.25 Depress the plastic tabs to release the switch

4.26 Wiring plug (arrowed) on the rear of the map reading and front courtesy light switch

5.5 Removing a headlight bulb - "Phase 1" model

5.8 Removing a front sidelight bulb - "Phase 1" model

5.12 Removing a front direction indicator bulb

plastic rear cover through 90° to remove it. On "Phase 2" models, release the retaining tabs, and pull the cover from the rear of the headlight.

3 Pull the wiring connector from the rear of the headlight bulb.

4 Release the spring clip, and pivot the clip clear.

5 Withdraw the bulb from its location in the headlight (see illustration).

> **HAYNES HiNT** *Take care not to touch the headlight bulb glass with your fingers - if touched, clean the bulb with methylated spirit.*

6 Fit the new bulb using a reversal of the removal procedure, but make sure that the tabs on the bulb support are correctly located in cut-outs in the lens assembly.

Front sidelight

7 Proceed as described in paragraphs 1 to 3 inclusive.

8 On "Phase 1" models, pull the bulbholder from the light unit. On "Phase 2" models, twist the bulbholder anti-clockwise to remove it (see illustration).

9 The bulb is a push-fit in the bulbholder.

10 Fit the new bulb using a reversal of the removal procedure.

Front direction indicator

Front wing-mounted assembly

11 Disconnect the battery negative lead.

12 Twist the bulbholder anti-clockwise to remove it from the rear of the light unit (see illustration).

13 The bulb is a bayonet fit in the bulbholder.

14 Fit the new bulb using a reversal of the removal procedure.

Bumper-mounted assembly

15 Disconnect the battery negative lead.

16 Push one side of the light unit inwards, then insert a screwdriver behind the light unit, and lever it out.

17 Release the retaining clips, and remove the lens from the light unit.

18 The bulb is a bayonet fit in the light unit.

19 Fit the new bulb using a reversal of the removal procedure.

Front direction indicator repeater

20 Disconnect the battery negative lead.

21 Carefully prise the light from the front wing, taking care not to damage the paintwork.

22 On "Phase 1" models, pull out the bulbholder and wiring.

23 On "Phase 2" models, twist the bulbholder anti-clockwise and withdraw it from the rear of the light unit.

24 The bulb is a push fit in the bulbholder (see illustration).

25 Fit the new bulb using a reversal of the removal procedure.

Front foglight

"Phase 1" models

26 Disconnect the battery negative lead.

27 Unscrew the two screws, and pull the lens unit forward.

28 Disconnect the two halves of the wiring connector, and remove the lens unit.

29 Pull off the rubber cover, or twist the bulbholder and remove it from the lens unit, as applicable.

30 Depress and twist the bulb to remove it, or release the spring clip and lift out the bulb, as applicable (see illustration).

31 Hold the new bulb in a piece of paper or cloth, then fit it in the bulbholder.

32 Refit the bulbholder/cover using a reversal of the removal procedure. On completion, if necessary adjust the light beam alignment using the adjusting screw at the top corner of the light.

"Phase 2" models

33 Disconnect the battery negative lead.

34 Unclip the trim plate from the inside edge of the light unit, to reveal the light unit securing screw (see illustration).

35 Remove the securing screw, and withdraw the light unit from the front of the bumper (see illustration).

36 Disconnect the two wires.

37 Twist the rear cover to remove it from the rear of the light unit.

38 Release the spring clip, and pivot the clip clear.

5.24 Removing a front direction indicator repeater bulb - "Phase 1" model

5.30 Removing a front foglight bulb - "Phase 1" model

5.34 Front foglight trim plate (2) and beam adjustment screw (1) - "Phase 2" models

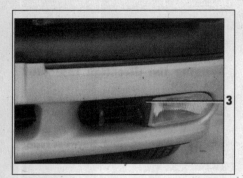

5.35 Front foglight securing screw (3) - "Phase 2" models

5.42 Releasing the rear light cluster bulbholder assembly - Saloon model

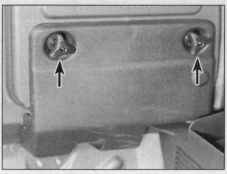

5.46 Rear light cluster cover securing nuts (arrowed) - Hatchback model

5.47 Disconnecting the rear light cluster wiring plug - Hatchback model

5.49 Removing a rear light cluster bulbholder - Hatchback model

39 Withdraw the bulb.
40 Hold the new bulb in a piece of paper or cloth, then fit it using a reversal of the removal procedure.

Rear light cluster

Saloon models

41 Disconnect the battery negative lead.
42 Working in the rear of the luggage compartment, release the securing clips, and release the bulbholder assembly from the rear of the light unit (see illustration).
43 The bulbs are a bayonet fit in the bulbholder.
44 Fit the new bulb using a reversal of the removal procedure.

Hatchback and Cabriolet models
45 Disconnect the battery negative lead.
46 Working in the rear of the luggage compartment, unscrew the two plastic nuts and, where applicable, release the securing clip, and withdraw the cover from the rear of the light unit (see illustration).
47 Disconnect the wiring plug, and, where applicable, remove the inner cover (see illustrations).
48 Withdraw the light cluster from outside the vehicle.
49 Squeeze together the two tabs, and withdraw the bulbholder from the rear of the light cluster (see illustration).

50 The bulbs are a bayonet fit in the bulbholder (see illustration).
51 Fit the new bulb using a reversal of the removal procedure.

Tailgate/boot lid-mounted rear foglights - "Phase 2" models

52 Disconnect the battery negative lead.
53 Open the tailgate, and unclip the cover from the rear of the light unit.
54 Twist the bulbholder anti-clockwise to release it from the rear of the light unit.
55 The bulb is a bayonet fit in the bulbholder.
56 Fit the new bulb using a reversal of the removal procedure.

Number plate lights

57 Disconnect the battery negative lead.
58 Prise the number plate light from the rear bumper using a small screwdriver (see illustration).
59 Disconnect the wiring plug from the light.
60 Remove the lens cover, then release the festoon-type bulb from the spring contacts (see illustration).
61 Fit the new bulb using a reversal of the removal procedure, but check the tension of the spring contacts, and if necessary bend them so that they firmly contact the bulb end caps.

5.50 Removing a bulb from a rear light cluster bulbholder

5.58 Prising out a number plate light - "Phase 1" model

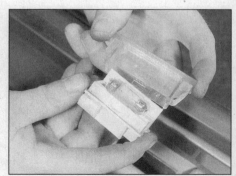

5.60 Removing a number plate light lens cover

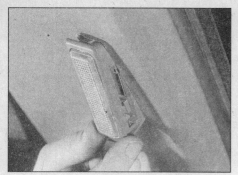

6.2a Removing a courtesy light

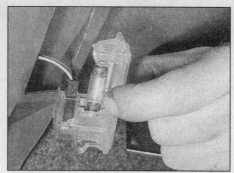

6.2b Removing the luggage compartment light - Hatchback model

6.6 Prising the lens and cover panel from a map reading and front courtesy light

6 Bulbs (interior lights) - renewal

Courtesy lights and luggage compartment light

1 Disconnect the battery negative lead.
2 Prise out the light using a small screwdriver (see illustrations).
3 Release the festoon-type bulb from the spring contacts.
4 Fit the new bulb using a reversal of the removal procedure, but check the tension of the spring contacts, and if necessary bend them so that they firmly contact the bulb end caps.

Map reading and front courtesy light

5 Disconnect the battery negative lead.
6 Using a small screwdriver, prise off the lens and cover panel (see illustration).
7 The remainder of the procedure is as described previously for the courtesy lights.

Instrument panel lights

8 Remove the instrument panel as described in Section 8.
9 Turn the bulbholder a quarter-turn to align the shoulders with the slots, then remove it.

10 The bulbs are a push fit in the bulbholders (see illustration).
11 Fit the new bulb in reverse order.

Automatic transmission selector illumination

12 Disconnect the battery negative lead.
13 Prise out the lever surround, then pull the bulbholder from under the selector lever position indicator, and remove the bulb.
14 Fit the new bulb in reverse order.

Glovebox light

15 Open the glovebox, then proceed as described previously for the courtesy lights (see illustration).

7 Exterior light units - removal and refitting

Headlight unit

"Phase 1" models

1 Disconnect the battery negative lead.
2 Turn the headlight plastic rear cover through 90° to remove it.
3 Pull off the wiring connectors.
4 Remove the direction indicator assembly as described later in this Section.

6.10 Removing an instrument panel bulb

5 Unscrew the four mounting nuts from the rear of the headlight.
6 Unscrew the screws located on the inner side of the headlight.
7 Withdraw the headlight forwards, and at the same time, release the lug so that the hidden mounting screw can be removed (see illustration).
8 Remove the headlight from its location (see illustration).
9 Refitting is a reversal of removal, but before tightening the front inner screw, align the outer edge of the direction indicator in relation to the front wing.
10 On completion, check the headlight aim as described in Chapter 1.

6.15 Removing the glovebox light

7.7 Headlight retaining screw location (arrowed) - "Phase 1" model

7.8 Removing the headlight - "Phase 1" model

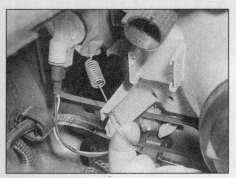

7.22 Unhooking the front direction indicator retaining spring - "Phase 1" model

7.36 Disconnecting the front foglight wiring connector

7.45 Rear light cluster securing nuts (arrowed) - Saloon model

"Phase 2" models

11 Disconnect the battery negative lead.
12 Remove the front grille panels as described in Chapter 11.
13 Remove the direction indicator assembly as described later in this Section.
14 Unclip the cover from the rear of the headlight, and disconnect the wiring plugs.
15 Where applicable, disconnect the wiring plug from the headlight aim adjuster motor.
16 Unscrew the two upper headlight securing bolts.
17 Remove the lower securing bolt, located at the inside edge of the headlight, and the securing nut, located at the outside edge.
18 Withdraw the headlight unit.
19 Refitting is a reversal of removal.
20 On completion, check the headlight beam alignment as described in Chapter 1.

Front direction indicator

Front wing-mounted assembly

21 Disconnect the battery negative lead.
22 Unhook the retaining spring from the rear of the headlight unit **(see illustration)**.
23 Move the direction indicator unit forwards in order to release it.
24 Turn the bulbholder, and release it from the rear of the direction indicator unit.
25 Remove the direction indicator unit from the vehicle.
26 Refitting is a reversal of removal.

Bumper-mounted assembly

27 Disconnect the battery negative lead.

28 Push one side of the light unit inwards, then insert a screwdriver behind the light unit, and lever it out.
29 Disconnect the wiring plug, and withdraw the light unit.
30 Refitting is a reversal of removal.

Front direction indicator repeater

31 Disconnect the battery negative lead.
32 Carefully prise the light from the front wing, taking care not to damage the paintwork.
33 Pull out the bulbholder and wiring, then remove the light.
34 Refitting is a reversal of removal.

Front foglights

"Phase 1" models

35 Disconnect the battery negative lead.
36 Unscrew the two securing screws, withdraw the foglight unit from the bumper, and disconnect the two halves of the wiring connector **(see illustration)**.
37 Refitting is a reversal of removal, but if necessary adjust the foglight by turning the adjustment screw located on the upper corner of the foglight.

"Phase 2" models

38 Disconnect the battery negative lead.
39 Unclip the trim plate from the inside edge of the light unit, to reveal the light unit securing screw.
40 Remove the securing screw, and withdraw the light unit from the front of the bumper.

41 Disconnect the two wires.
42 Refitting is a reversal of removal, but if necessary adjust the foglight by turning the adjustment screw located on the upper corner of the foglight.

Rear light cluster

Saloon models

43 Disconnect the battery negative lead.
44 Working in the rear luggage compartment, release the securing clips, and withdraw the bulbholder assembly from the rear of the light unit.
45 Unscrew the securing nuts from inside the luggage compartment, then withdraw the light unit from outside the vehicle **(see illustration)**.
46 Refitting is a reversal of removal.

Hatchback and Cabriolet models

47 Disconnect the battery negative lead.
48 Working in the rear luggage compartment, unscrew the two plastic nuts, and unclip the cover from the rear of the light cluster.
49 Disconnect the wiring plug and, where applicable, remove the inner cover.
50 Withdraw the light unit from outside the vehicle.
51 Refitting is a reversal of removal.

Number plate lights

52 Prise the number plate light from the rear bumper using a small screwdriver, then disconnect the wiring plug **(see illustration)**.
53 Refitting is a reversal of removal.

---

8 Instrument panel - removal and refitting

"Phase 1" models

Removal

1 Disconnect the battery negative lead.
2 Remove the steering wheel as described in Chapter 10.
3 Remove the securing screws, and remove the steering column shrouds. Note that it may be necessary to loosen the radio/cassette player remote control switch clamp screw (see Section 4) before the shrouds can be removed. Where applicable, also remove the internal cover.

7.52 Disconnecting the number plate light wiring plug - "Phase 1" model

8.4 Unscrewing one of the top instrument panel visor securing screws - "Phase 1" model

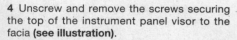

8.5a Unscrewing an instrument panel visor lower securing screw (arrowed) - "Phase 1" model

8.5b Removing the instrument panel visor - "Phase 1" model

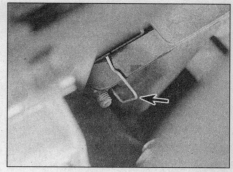

8.6 Speedometer cable retaining spring (arrowed) at the transmission end

4 Unscrew and remove the screws securing the top of the instrument panel visor to the facia **(see illustration)**.
5 Unscrew and remove the screws securing the bottom of the instrument panel visor to the facia, and remove the visor. The screws are located on each side of the steering column **(see illustrations)**.
6 Working in the engine compartment, pull out the spring clip and disconnect the speedometer cable from the transmission **(see illustration)**. Release the cable from the support clips in the engine compartment.
7 Unscrew the screws securing the top of the instrument panel to the facia, then pull out the panel until there is sufficient room to reach behind it and disconnect the speedometer cable **(see illustrations)**.
8 Note the location of all the wiring connectors, then disconnect them from the rear of the instrument panel. Withdraw the instrument panel from the facia.

Refitting

9 Refitting is a reversal of removal. On completion, check the function of all electrical components.

"Phase 2" models
Removal

10 Proceed as described in paragraphs 1 to 3 inclusive.
11 Remove the two securing screws, and withdraw the instrument panel visor **(see illustration)**.
12 Unscrew the securing screws, and remove the facia panel from below the steering column.
13 Remove the two upper instrument panel securing screws **(see illustration)**.
14 For access to the lower right-hand instrument panel securing bolt, it is necessary to move the ignition switch wiring connector mounting. Remove the mounting by pulling it towards the steering column, before sliding it along its retaining runner.
15 Remove the two lower instrument panel securing screws.
16 Working in the engine compartment, release the securing clip(s) and disconnect the speedometer cable from the transmission.

8.7a Remove the securing screws . . .

8.7b . . . and pull out the instrument panel - "Phase 1" models

17 Tilt the instrument panel for access to the speedometer cable and wiring connections.
18 Disconnect the wiring connectors and the speedometer cable from the rear of the instrument panel, then withdraw the panel from the facia.

Refitting

19 Refitting is a reversal of removal, but ensure that all wiring connectors and the speedometer cable are securely reconnected.

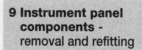
9 Instrument panel components - removal and refitting

Note: *Various different instrument panel layouts may be encountered, depending on model. Although the details may differ from those described, the following paragraphs can be used as a guide for all models.*

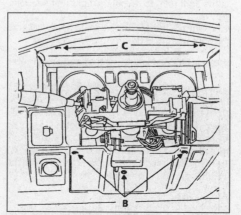

8.11 Facia panel securing screws (B) and instrument panel visor securing screws (C) - "Phase 2" models

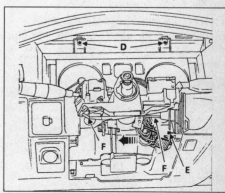

8.13 Upper instrument panel securing screws (D), lower securing bolts (F), and wiring connector mounting (E) - "Phase 2" models

12

11.2 Prising the clock from the facia

12.1 Typical horn location (viewed from front of vehicle)

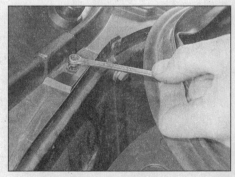

13.5 Correct position of the speedometer cable retaining clip in the rear engine mounting bracket

Removal

1 Remove the instrument panel as described in Section 8.
2 Prise the plastic hooks outwards, and remove the front cover.
3 To remove the speedometer, extract the two screws from the front and rear of the unit.
4 To remove the coolant temperature gauge, extract the printed circuit nuts and the two retaining screws.
5 To remove the fuel gauge, extract the printed circuit nuts and the two retaining screws.
6 To remove the tachometer, extract the single rear screw and the two front screws.
7 To remove the oil level gauge, first remove the tachometer, then extract the printed circuit nuts and the two retaining screws.

Refitting

8 Refitting is a reversal of removal.

10 Cigarette lighter - removal and refitting

Removal

1 Disconnect the battery negative lead.
2 Pull out the ashtray.
3 Push the cigar lighter out of its location, and disconnect the wiring.
4 To remove the fixed metal section of the cigar lighter, push from behind the main body while releasing the two tabs. Also remove the plastic cover.

Refitting

5 Refitting is a reversal of removal.

11 Clock - removal and refitting

Removal

1 Disconnect the battery negative lead.
2 Carefully prise the clock from the facia, and disconnect the wiring plug **(see illustration)**. The clock is retained by plastic clips which are pushed aside as the clock is removed.

Refitting

3 Refitting is a reversal of removal.

12 Horn - removal and refitting

Removal

1 The horn(s) is/are located on the body front valance behind the front bumper **(see illustration)**.
2 To remove a horn, first apply the handbrake, then jack up the front of the vehicle and support it securely on axle stands (see *"Jacking, towing and wheel changing"*).
3 Disconnect the battery negative lead, then reach up and disconnect the horn supply lead.
4 Unscrew the nut securing the horn to the mounting bracket, and remove the horn from the vehicle.

Refitting

5 Refitting is a reversal of removal.

13 Speedometer drive cable - removal and refitting

Removal

1 Refer to Section 8, and remove the instrument panel sufficiently to allow the speedometer cable to be disconnected.
2 Where a trip computer is fitted, disconnect the sender unit from the upper and lower cable sections.
3 Working in the engine compartment, unclip or unscrew the end of the speedometer cable from the transmission. Where applicable, note how the securing clip locates on the transmission, as several types of clip are used.
4 Withdraw the speedometer drive cable into the passenger compartment through the bulkhead, noting its routing.

Refitting

5 Refitting is a reversal of removal, bearing in mind the following points:
   (a) On models where the speedometer cable is secured to the transmission by a wire clip, ensure that the clip is located as shown (see illustration).
   (b) Make sure that the cable is routed as noted before removal, and be careful not to kink or twist the cable between the bulkhead and the rear of the instrument panel.

14 Windscreen wiper motor and linkage - removal and refitting

Removal

1 Switch the wipers on, then switch off so that they (and the wiper motor) return to their "parked" position.
2 Disconnect the battery negative lead.
3 Remove the windscreen wiper arms with reference to Chapter 1.
4 Remove the battery as described in Chapter 5A.
5 Unbolt and remove the plastic cover from the plenum chamber just in front of the windscreen **(see illustration)**.
6 Unscrew the nuts from the wiper spindles protruding through the windscreen valance **(see illustration)**.
7 Unscrew and remove the mounting bolts **(see illustration)**.
8 Disconnect the wiring plug **(see illustration)**.
9 Withdraw the wiper motor and linkage assembly from the bulkhead.

14.5 Unbolting the plastic cover from the plenum chamber

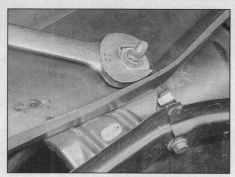

14.6 Unscrewing a wiper spindle nut

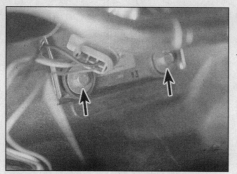

14.7 Windscreen wiper motor mounting bolts (arrowed)

14.8 Disconnecting the wiper motor wiring plug

10 If necessary, the linkage may be separated from the motor by removing the cranked arm and unbolting the linkage.

Refitting

11 Refitting is a reversal of removal.

15 Tailgate wiper motor and linkage - removal and refitting

Removal

1 Operate the wiper, then switch it off so that it returns to its "parked" position. Note that the wiper motor will only operate with the tailgate shut, as the spring-tensioned connector pins on the tailgate must be in contact with the contact plates.
2 Disconnect the battery negative lead.
3 Remove the wiper arm with reference to Chapter 1.
4 Unscrew the nut from the spindle housing protruding through the tailgate.
5 Remove the trim panel from inside the tailgate.
6 Disconnect the wiring plug, then unbolt and remove the wiper motor/linkage assembly from inside the tailgate (**see illustrations**).
7 If necessary, the connector pin assembly and connector plate assembly may be removed and the wiring disconnected (**see illustrations**).

Refitting

8 Refitting is a reversal of removal.

16 Rear window wiper motor and linkage (Saloon models) - removal and refitting

Removal

1 Disconnect the battery negative lead.
2 Remove the wiper arm with reference to Chapter 1.
3 Remove the cover from the spindle nut, then unscrew the nut.
4 Remove the plastic washer and the metal cup from the spindle.
5 Pull the rubber grommet from the window, taking care not to damage the glass.
6 Gently pull the washer jet free.
7 Working inside the vehicle, remove the two securing screws and withdraw the cover from the motor.
8 Disconnect the wiring plug.
9 Remove the two screws securing the motor mounting bracket, taking care not to damage the heated rear window with the screwdriver.
10 Lift the motor and its mounting bracket, free the left-hand side of the bracket, and pass it over the wiring harness. Take care not to break the washer jet positioning lug (**see illustration**).
11 Free the spindle from the hole in the rear

15.6a Disconnect the wiring plug . . .

15.6b . . . then unbolt and remove the wiper motor/linkage assembly

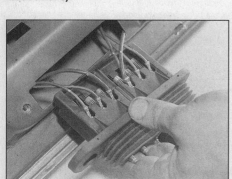

15.7a Removing the tailgate connector pin assembly . . .

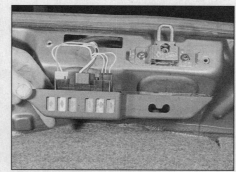

15.7b . . . and tailgate connector plate assembly

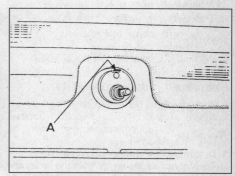

16.10 Rear washer jet positioning lug (A) - Saloon models

12

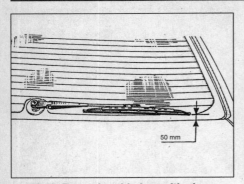

**16.19 Rear wiper blade positioning -
Saloon models**

**18.2 Using the U-shaped rods to remove
the radio/cassette player**

**18.3 Aerial lead and wiring plugs on rear of
radio/cassette player**

window, pivot the assembly, and withdraw it to the right. Remove the assembly carefully, as the washer tube is connected to the motor spacer.

Refitting

12 Manipulate the motor back into position, ensuring that the wiring harness and washer tube are not trapped by the motor bracket.
13 Refit, but do not yet fully tighten, the motor bracket securing screws.
14 Clean the area around the motor spindle on the window glass, then refit the following components in the order given.
   (a) A new rubber grommet.
   (b) Washer jet.
   (c) Metal cup.
   (d) Plastic washer.
15 Tighten the motor spindle nut. Note that the motor spindle does not locate in the centre of the hole in the rear window.
16 Working inside the vehicle, tighten the two motor bracket securing screws, again taking care not to damage the heated rear window.
17 Refit the motor cover.
18 Refit the cover to the spindle nut.
19 Ensure that the motor is in its "parked" position, then refit the wiper arm, positioning the end of the wiper arm 50 mm away from the edge of the rear window seal **(see illustration)**.
20 Check that the wiper operates correctly, and if necessary adjust the washer jet.

17 Windscreen/rear window/headlight washer system components - removal and refitting

Removal

1 Disconnect the battery negative lead.
2 Where applicable, to improve access, remove the fuel injection computer, as described in Chapter 4B.
3 To remove the washer reservoir and pump, unscrew the mounting screw(s) and lift the reservoir from the front right-hand corner of the engine compartment. Where applicable, the front washer reservoir also supplies the

rear window washer, by means of a tube running along the right-hand lower edge of the floor area and up the right-hand rear corner pillar.
4 Disconnect the wiring from the pump, then disconnect the plastic tubing from the reservoir.
5 Empty the reservoir of any remaining fluid, then pull the pump from the rubber grommet.
6 Disconnect the tubing from the pump, and remove the grommet from the reservoir.

Refitting

7 Refitting is a reversal of removal.

18 Radio/cassette player - removal and refitting

Removal

1 Disconnect the battery negative lead. If the radio/cassette player has a security code, make sure this is known before disconnecting the battery (refer to *"Radio/cassette unit anti-theft system"* at the front of this manual).
2 In order to release the retaining clips, two U-shaped rods must be inserted into the special holes on each side of the unit **(see illustration)**. If possible, it is preferable to obtain purpose-made rods from an audio specialist, as these have cut-outs which snap firmly into the clips so that the radio can be pulled out. (These tools are often supplied with the vehicle when new, where the radio is original equipment.)
3 Withdraw the unit sufficiently to disconnect the wiring plugs and aerial lead **(see illustration)**.

Refitting

4 Refitting is a reversal of removal.

19 Speakers - removal and refitting

Removal

1 To remove a front speaker located on the top of the facia panel, where applicable, remove the securing screws, then prise out the

speaker grille panel. Remove the speaker securing screws, then lift out the speaker and disconnect the wiring.
2 Access to the rear speakers is gained by opening the rear tailgate/boot lid. Disconnect the wiring, then remove the screws and withdraw the speaker.
3 To remove a door speaker, first remove the speaker cover. On "Phase 1" models, turn the speaker cover anti-clockwise and remove it. On "Phase 2" models, remove the screws, then pull the speaker cover from the door. Remove the screws and withdraw the speaker, then disconnect the wiring.

Refitting

4 Refitting is a reversal of removal.

20 Radio aerial - removal and refitting

Removal

1 Remove the map reading and front courtesy light switch assembly, with reference to Section 4.
2 Unscrew the nut from the bottom of the aerial, disconnect the lead, then remove the aerial from the outside of the vehicle **(see illustration)**.

Refitting

3 Refitting is a reversal of removal.

20.2 Radio aerial lead connection to the aerial (arrowed)

21 Remote control central door locking system - general

1 The ignition key incorporates an infra-red remote control door locking transmitter. The transmitter signal is decoded by a receiver mounted on the roof console, and this activates the electro-mechanical system to lock or unlock the doors.
2 The transmitter is powered by two 1.5 volt alkaline type batteries, which have a life of approximately 12 months. The batteries can be renewed after unscrewing the transmitter case screw and opening the case to gain access **(see illustrations)**.
3 In the event of a fault occurring in the system, it is recommended that you seek the advice of a Renault dealer, as specialist knowledge and equipment are necessary for accurate fault diagnosis.

22 Headlight aim adjustment motor - removal and refitting

Removal

1 Disconnect the battery negative lead.
2 Working at the rear of the headlight, disconnect the motor wiring plug.
3 Pull the motor securing clip down to release it, then twist the motor clockwise.
4 Pull the motor sharply from the rear of the light to release the adjuster balljoint **(see illustration)**. Take care, as it is easy to break the balljoint.

Refitting

5 Refitting is a reversal of removal, but hold the rear of the headlight reflector when pushing the motor balljoint into position.

23 Anti-theft alarm system - general

Certain models are fitted with an anti-theft alarm and/or engine immobiliser system as standard or optional equipment.

Various systems may be fitted, some operating in conjunction with the remote control central door locking system.

Some systems have a self-diagnosis function, which can be used to detect faults in conjunction with Renault dedicated test equipment.

21.2a Remove the screw from the remote control door locking transmitter . . .

21.2b . . . and separate the covers

Where the alarm incorporates an engine immobiliser function, it is worth bearing in mind, should any puzzling starting problems be encountered which cannot be attributed to other causes.

No specific details were available for the anti-theft systems at the time of writing. Consult a Renault dealer for further information.

24 Air bag - general information and precautions

General information

Certain models are fitted with a driver's side air bag, located in the steering wheel boss.

The system consists of the air bag unit, a gas cartridge, an electronic unit, two batteries, and a warning light, all incorporated in the steering wheel.

In the event of a severe frontal impact, the air bag inflates (in approximately 30 milliseconds), softening the impact of the driver's head with the steering wheel. The air bag then deflates.

The warning light incorporated in the steering wheel illuminates to indicate that the air bag battery charge is low, or when there is a fault with the system.

Precautions

The following precautions *must* be observed when working on models equipped with an air bag.

Do not, under any circumstances, attempt to carry out any work on the steering wheel or

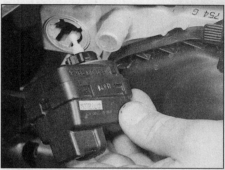
22.4 Removing a headlight aim adjustment motor

the air bag system itself. There is a risk of personal injury if the air bag is accidentally triggered. Consult a Renault dealer if any work involving the steering wheel is to be carried out.

Do not cover the steering wheel hub.

If the air bag warning light illuminates, take the vehicle to a Renault dealer as soon as possible, to have the system checked.

If the vehicle is involved in an accident, have the air bag system checked by a Renault dealer as soon as possible.

In the event of the vehicle being scrapped, contact a Renault dealer first, to have the gas cartridge removed from the steering wheel.

If the vehicle has been stolen, or an attempt has been made to steal the vehicle, have the air bag system checked by a Renault dealer as a precaution.

If you sell the vehicle, inform the new owner that an air bag system is fitted.

12

NOTES

1. All diagrams are divided into numbered circuits depending on function e.g. Diagram 2: Exterior lighting.
2. Items are arranged in relation to a plan view of the vehicle.
3. Items may appear on more than one diagram so are found using a grid reference e.g. 2/A1 denotes an item on diagram 2 grid location A1.

4. Complex items appear on the diagrams as blocks and are expanded on the internal connections page.
5. Brackets show how the circuit may be connected in more than one way.
6. Not all items are fitted to all models.
7. All earth wires are coloured black.

INTERNAL CONNECTION DETAILS

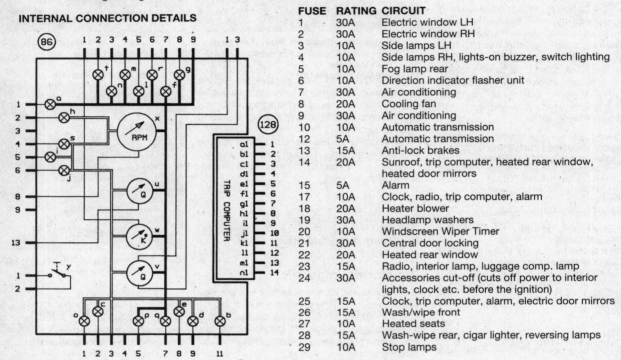

FUSE	RATING	CIRCUIT
1	30A	Electric window LH
2	30A	Electric window RH
3	10A	Side lamps LH
4	10A	Side lamps RH, lights-on buzzer, switch lighting
5	10A	Fog lamp rear
6	10A	Direction indicator flasher unit
7	30A	Air conditioning
8	20A	Cooling fan
9	30A	Air conditioning
10	10A	Automatic transmission
12	5A	Automatic transmission
13	15A	Anti-lock brakes
14	20A	Sunroof, trip computer, heated rear window, heated door mirrors
15	5A	Alarm
17	10A	Clock, radio, trip computer, alarm
18	20A	Heater blower
19	30A	Headlamp washers
20	10A	Windscreen Wiper Timer
21	30A	Central door locking
22	20A	Heated rear window
23	15A	Radio, interior lamp, luggage comp. lamp
24	30A	Accessories cut-off (cuts off power to interior lights, clock etc. before the ignition)
25	15A	Clock, trip computer, alarm, electric door mirrors
26	15A	Wash/wipe front
27	10A	Heated seats
28	15A	Wash-wipe rear, cigar lighter, reversing lamps
29	10A	Stop lamps

KEY TO INSTRUMENT CLUSTER (ITEM 86)

a = Hazard Warning Lamp
b = No Charge Warning Lamp
c = Oil Pressure Warning Lamp
d = Brake System Warning Lamp
e = High Temp. Warning Lamp
f = Rear Foglamp Warning Lamp
g = Heated Rear Window Warning Lamp
h = Brake Pad Wear Warning Lamp
i = Choke Warning Lamp
j = Electronic incident Warning Lamp
k = Pre Heater Warning Lamp
l = Sidelamp Warning Lamp
m = Dipped Beam Warning Lamp
n = Main Beam Warning Lamp
o = Low Fuel Warning Lamp
p = Direction indicator LH
q = Direction indicator RH
r = Front Foglamp Warning Lamp
s = ABS Warning Lamp
t = Instrument Illumination
u = Fuel Gauge
v = Oil Level Gauge
w = Coolant Temp. Gauge
x = Tachometer
y = Trip Computer Zero Switch

KEY TO TRIP COMPUTER (ITEM 128)

a1 = Electronic Earth
b1 = Battery Feed
c1 = Ignition Feed
d1 = Speed Data
e1 = Fuel Flow Data
f1 = Fuel Level Data
g1 = Temp. Data
h1 = Side Lamp Feed
i1 = Lighting Via Dimmer
j1 = Temp. Sensor Earth
k1 = Fuel Sender Unit Earth
l1 = Low Fuel Warning
m1 = Trip Comp. Zero
n1 = Trip Comp. Run Through

WIRE COLOURS

Ba	White	No	Black
Be	Blue	Or	Orange
Bj	Beige	Rg	Red
Cy	Clear	Sa	Pink
Gr	Grey	Ve	Green
Ja	Yellow	Vi	Mauve
Ma	Brown		

KEY TO SYMBOLS

PLUG-IN CONNECTOR
PLUG
SOCKET
EARTH
BULB
DIODE
VARIABLE RESISTOR
MOTOR/PUMP
PRESSURE ACTUATED
TEMPERATURE ACTUATED
LEVEL ACTUATED
LINE CONNECTORS
FUSE/FUSIBLE LINK

Notes, internal connection details, key to symbols and wire colours

ITEM	DESCRIPTION	DIAGRAM/GRID REF.
1	ABS ECU	4a/A6
2	ABS Pressure Warning Relay	4a/G6
3	ABS Pump Relay	4a/G5
4	ABS Safety Relay	4a/H6
5	ABS Starter Shut-Off Relay	4a/H6
6	Air Temp. Sensor	1b/B6, 1c/B3
7	Alternator	1/C2, 1a/B2
8	Auto. Trans. ECU	1a/C1
9	Auto. Trans. Starter Relay	1a/B8
10	Ballast Coil Relay	1b/D8, 1c/D8
11	Battery	1/E1, 1a/E1, 1b/H1, 1c/H1, 2/E1, 2a/E1, 2b/C1, 2c/D1, 2d/C1, 3/D1, 3a/C1, 3b/B1, 4/B1, 4a/E1
12	Brake Pad Wear Sensor	1/C1, 1/C8
13	Central Locking Actuator LH Front	3b/J8
14	Central Locking Actuator LH Rear	3b/M8
15	Central Locking Actuator RH Front	3b/J1
16	Central Locking Actuator RH Rear	3b/M1
17	Central Locking Actuator Tailgate	3b/M4
18	Central Locking infra-red - Signal Receiver	3b/K4
19	Central Locking Master Switch	2b/H5, 3b/F4
20	Central Locking Timer Relay	3b/B7
21	Choke Switch	1/L2
22	Cigar Lighter	2b/L5
23	Clock - Analogue	2c/J7
24	Clock - Digital	2c/K7
25	Combination Switch - Lighting, Direction indicators And Horn	2/K4, 2a/J2, 2b/K3, 2c/J3, 2d/G3, 3/J6
26	Combination Switch - Wash/Wipe	3/J2, 4/H5
27	Cold Start Injector	1c/F4
28	Contact Breaker	1a/E4
29	Coolant Temp. Gauge Sender Unit	1/E6
30	Coolant Temp. Sensor	1b/B5, 1c/C6
31	Cooling Fan Motor	1/A4
32	Cooling Fan Switch	1/A6
33	Dim/Dip Relay	2/J6
34	Dim/Dip Resistor	2/K7
35	Direction indicator Flasher Relay	2/F7
36	Direction indicator LH Front	2a/A8
37	Direction indicator LH Side Repeater	2a/C8
38	Direction indicator RH Front	2a/A1
39	Direction indicator RH Side Repeater	2a/C1
40	Distributor	1a/D4, 1a/E7, 1b/H4, 1c/G3
41	Earth Shunt	2/F1, 2b/C7, 2c/E7, 2d/C7, 3a/E7, 3b/C7
42	EGR Solenoid	1b/G2
43	Electric Mirror Control Switch	3a/H2
44	Electric Mirror LH	3a/J8
45	Electric Mirror RH	3a/J2, 4/H1
46	Electric Window Motor LH Front	3b/G8
47	Electric Window Motor RH Front	3b/G1
48	Electric Window Switch LH Front	2b/H6, 3b/F5
49	Electric Window Switch RH Front	2b/H6, 3b/F4
50	Foglamp Front	2/A3, 2/A6
51	Foglamp Relay Front	2/D5
52	Foglamp Relay Rear	2/D7
53	Foglamp Shunt Front	2/D7
54	Foglamp Switch Front	2/K1, 2b/H1
55	Foglamp Switch Rear	2/J3, 2b/H2
56	Fuel Flow Meter	4/A3
57	Fuel Gauge Sender Unit	1/M4, 4/M4
58	Fuel Injection ECU	1b/D1, 1c/D1
59	Fuel Injectors	1b/F5, 1c/G5
60	Fuel Pump	1b/M4, 1c/M4
61	Fuel Pump Ballast Resistor	1b/E7, 1c/E7
62	Fuel Pump Relay	1b/H8, 1c/J8
63	Glove Box Lamp	2b/H8
64	Glove Box Lamp Switch	2b/H8
65	Handbrake Warning Switch	1/L4, 4a/L5
66	Hazard Warning Lamp Switch	2a/J5, 2b/G4
67	Headlamp Unit LH	2/A8
68	Headlamp Unit RH	2/A1
69	Heated Rear Window	3a/M5
70	Heated Rear Window Relay	2a/D5, 3a/B6
71	Heated Rear Window Switch	2b/G4, 3a/H5
72	Heated Blower Motor	2c/H6
73	Heater Blower Motor Speed Controller	2c/H6, 3a/J5
74	Horn	3/A4
75	Idle Speed Regulator	1b/F5, 1c/C4
76	Idle Speed Regulator Solenoid	1c/E4
77	Ignition Coil	1a/D4
78	Ignition Module	1a/F4, 1a/G7
79	Ignition Switch	1/H1, 1a/H1, 1b/K1, 1c/L1, 2/H1, 2a/H1, 2b/F1, 2c/G1, 3/H2, 3a/F1, 3b/F1, 4/F1, 4a/K1
80	Injection Power Module	1b/H5, 1c/H4
81	Injection Locking Relay	1b/F8, 1c/G8
82	Inlet Manifold Heater	1/F4
83	Inlet Manifold Heater Relay	1/B8
84	Inlet Manifold Heater Switch	1/F6
85	Inlet Manifold Pressure Sensor	1b/H6, 1c/H5
86	Instrument Cluster	1/H4, 1a/J4, 1b/K5, 1c/K4, 2/F4, 2a/G3, 2b/E4, 2c/E3, 3a/E4, 4/D4, 4a/K4
87	Instrument Illumination Control	2c/J5
88	Interior Lamp Door Switch LH Front	2d/F8
89	Interior Lamp Door Switch LH Rear	2d/J8
90	Interior Lamp Door Switch RH Front	2d/F1
91	Interior Lamp Door Switch RH Rear	2d/J2
92	Interior Lamp Front	2d/J4
93	Interior Lamp Front/Map Reading Lamp	2d/J5, 3b/J5
94	Interior Lamp LH Rear	2d/L7
95	Interior Lamp RH Rear	2d/L2
96	Knock Sensor	1b/F4, 1c/A5
97	Lambda Sensor	1b/F3, 1c/F3
98	Lamp Cluster LH Rear	2/M7, 2a/M7
99	Lamp Cluster RH Rear	2/M2, 2a/M2
100	Lights-On Buzzer	2d/B6
101	Low Brake Fluid Sender Unit	1/E3, 4a/D2
102	Luggage Comp. Lamp	2d/L4
103	Number Plate Lamp	2/M4, 2/M5
104	Oil Level Sender Unit	1/E4
105	Oil Pressure Switch	1/D6
106	Power Steering Pressostat	1c/B1
107	Radio/Cassette Unit	4/K6
108	Resistor	4a/D7
109	Reversing Lamp Switch	2a/C6
110	Rheostat Relay	2c/C6
111	Side And Rear Lamp Shunt	2/F7, 2b/C7, 2c/E7, 2d/D8
112	Spark Plugs	1a/D5, 1a/D7, 1b/H3, 1c/G3
113	Speaker LH Front (Dashboard)	4/G8
114	Speaker LH Front (Door)	4/J8
115	Speaker LH Rear	4/L8
116	Speaker RH Front (Dashboard)	4/G1
117	Speaker RH Front (Door)	4/J1
118	Speaker RH Rear	4/L1
119	Speed Sensor	1b/C7, 1c/B5, 4/B4
120	Starter Motor	1/C6
121	Stop-Lamp Switch	2a/E3
122	Sunroof Motor	4/L3
123	Sunroof Switch	4/L4
124	Tailgate Switch	2d/M4, 3/M4
125	TDC Sensor	1a/F7, 1c/D4
126	Throttle Position Switch	1b/B3
127	Throttle Potentiometer	1c/A6
128	Trip Computer	2c/E3, 4/E3
129	Washer Pump Front	3/B2
130	Washer Pump Rear	3/B1
131	Wheel Sensor LH Front	4a/A8
132	Wheel Sensor LH Rear	4a/M8
133	Wheel Sensor RH Front	4a/A1
134	Wheel Sensor RH Rear	4a/M1
135	Wiper Motor Front	3/D3
136	Wiper Motor Rear	3/M4
137	Wiper Relay	3/D6

Key to wiring diagrams

WD

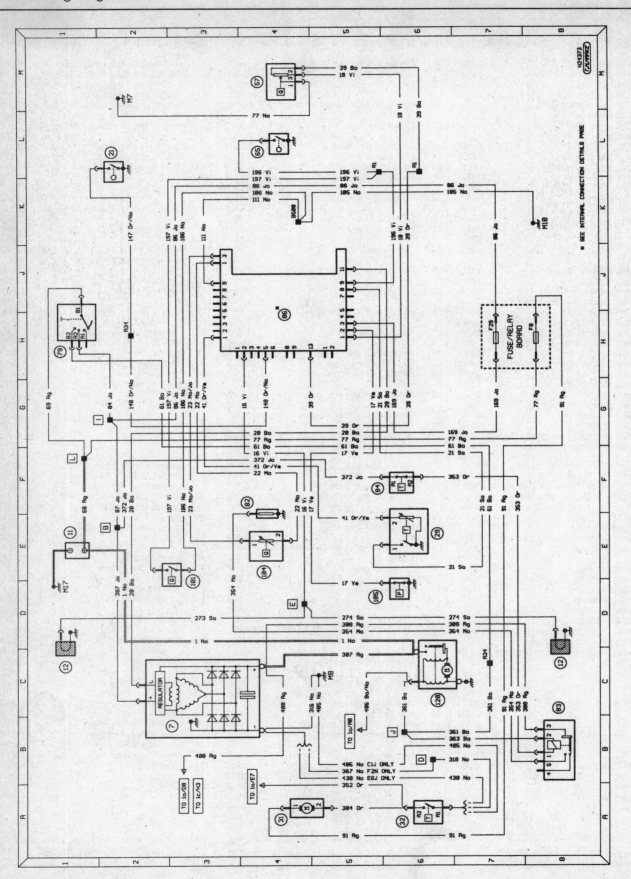

Diagram 1: Typical starting, charging, cooling fan, warning lights and gauges

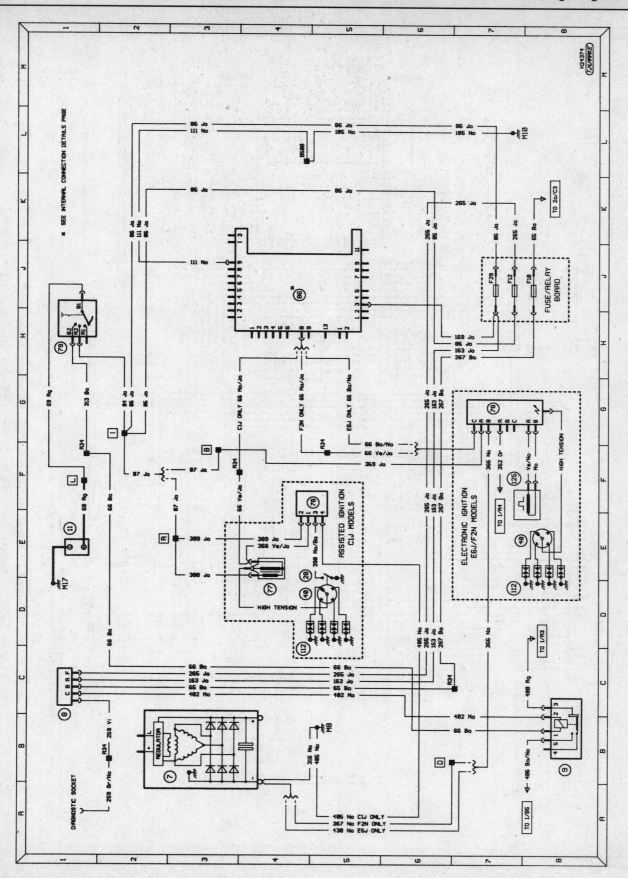

Diagram 1a: Automatic transmission and ignition systems (all models)

WD

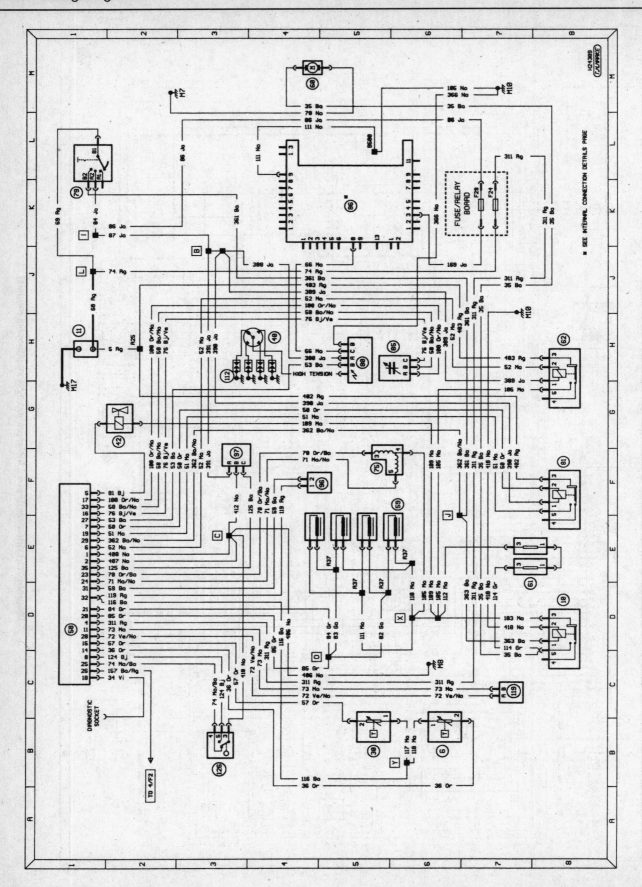

Diagram 1b: Typical multi-point fuel injection system (8-valve models)

For single-point fuel injection systems, refer to supplementary diagram on last page of wiring diagrams

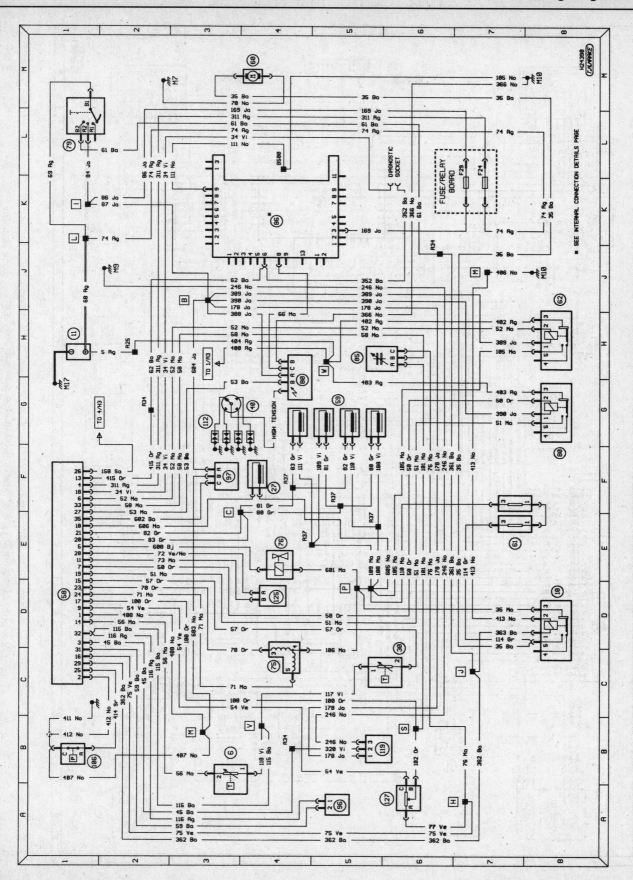

Diagram 1c: Typical multi-point fuel injection system (16-valve models)

WD

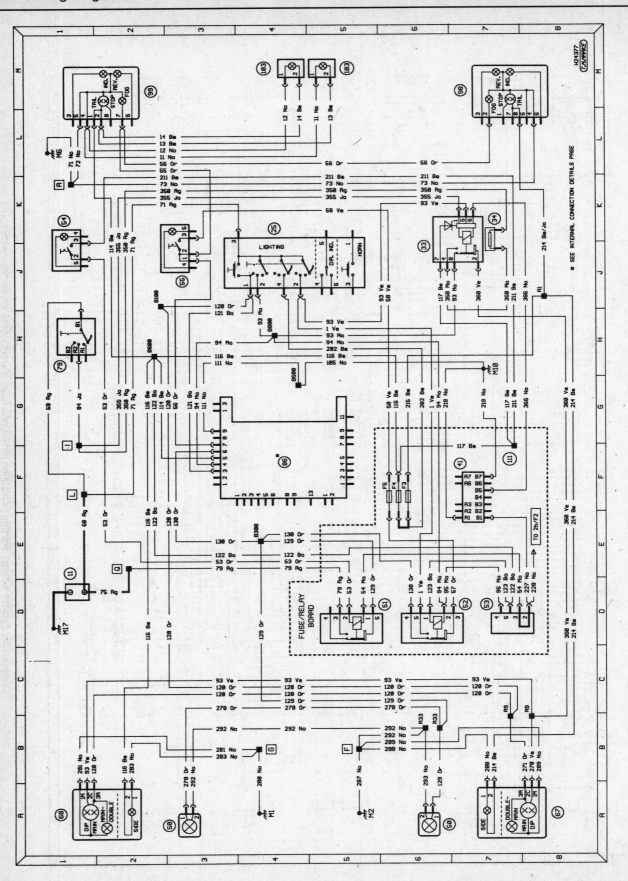

Diagram 2: Typical exterior lighting - fog, side and headlights

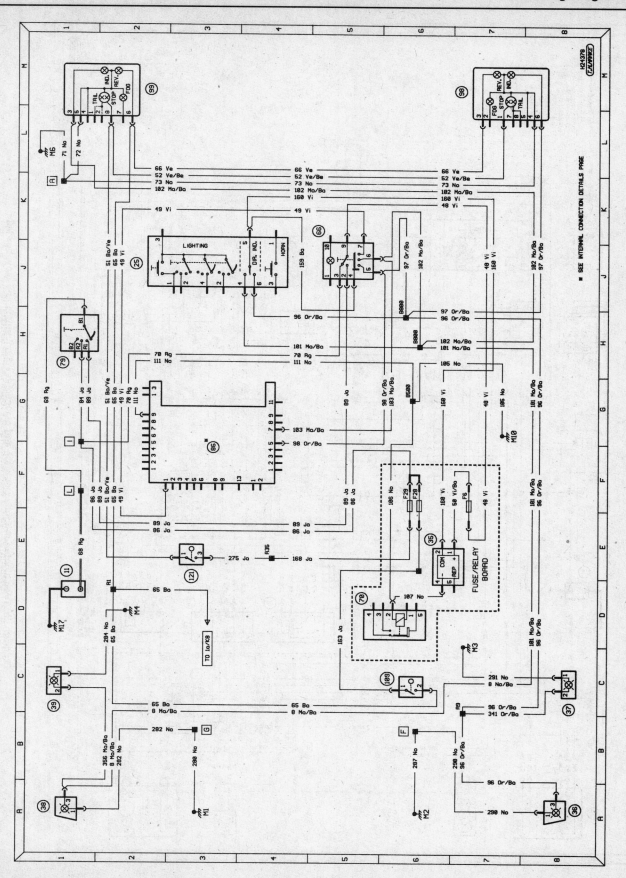

Diagram 2a: Typical exterior lighting – direction indicators, hazard warning, stop and reversing lights

WD

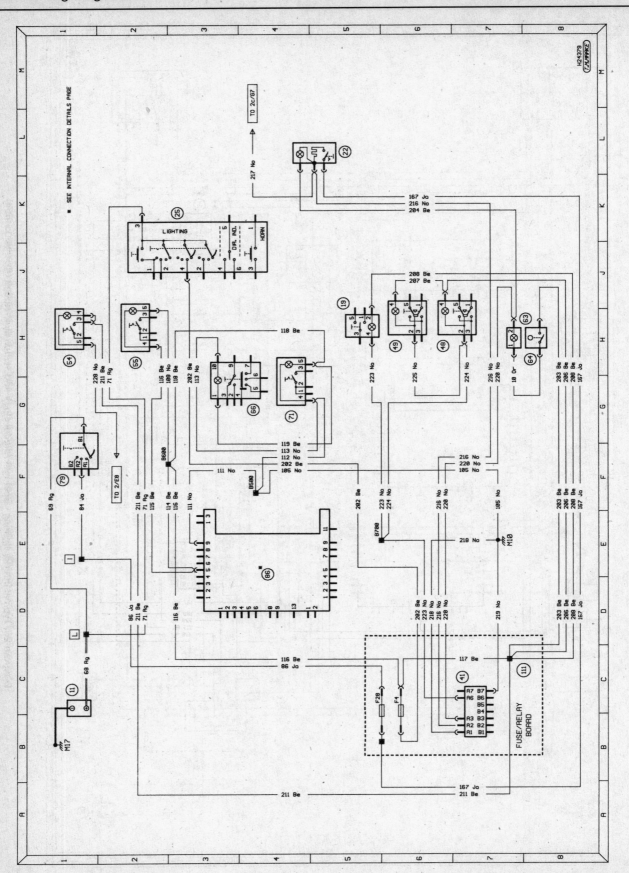

Diagram 2b: Typical interior lighting - switch and cigar lighter illumination, and glovebox light

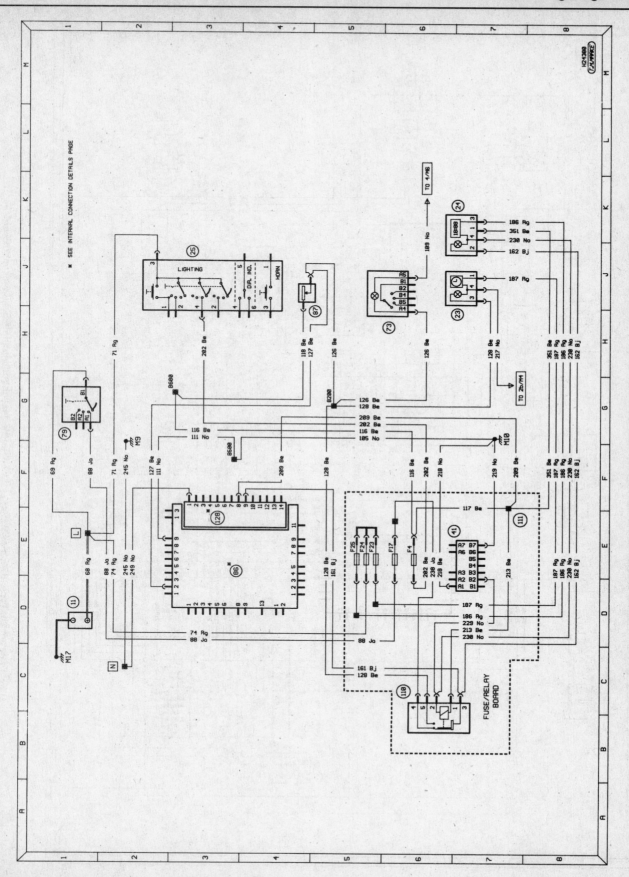

Diagram 2c: Typical interior lighting - analogue/digital clock and switch illumination (dimmer circuit)

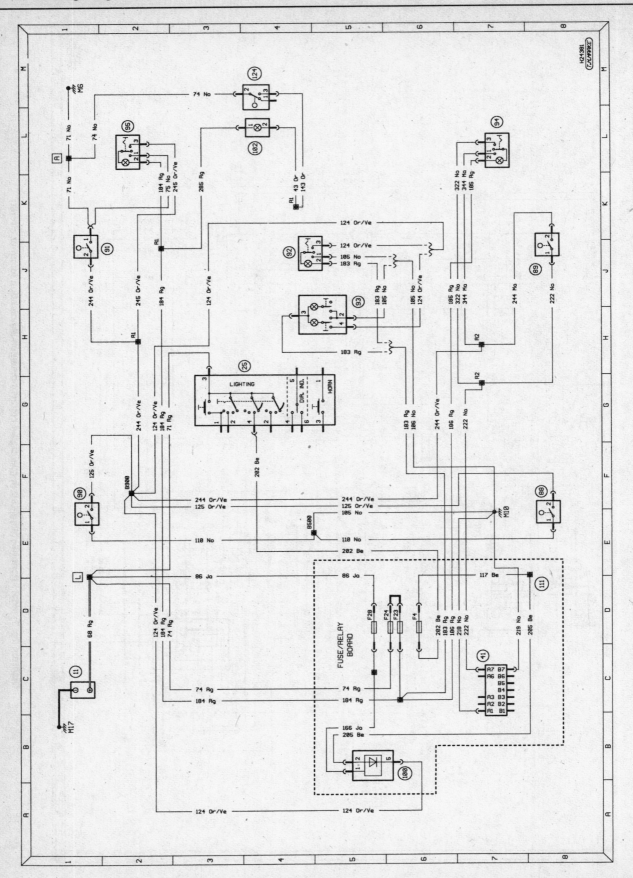

Diagram 2d: Typical interior lighting – "lights-on" buzzer, luggage compartment and interior lights

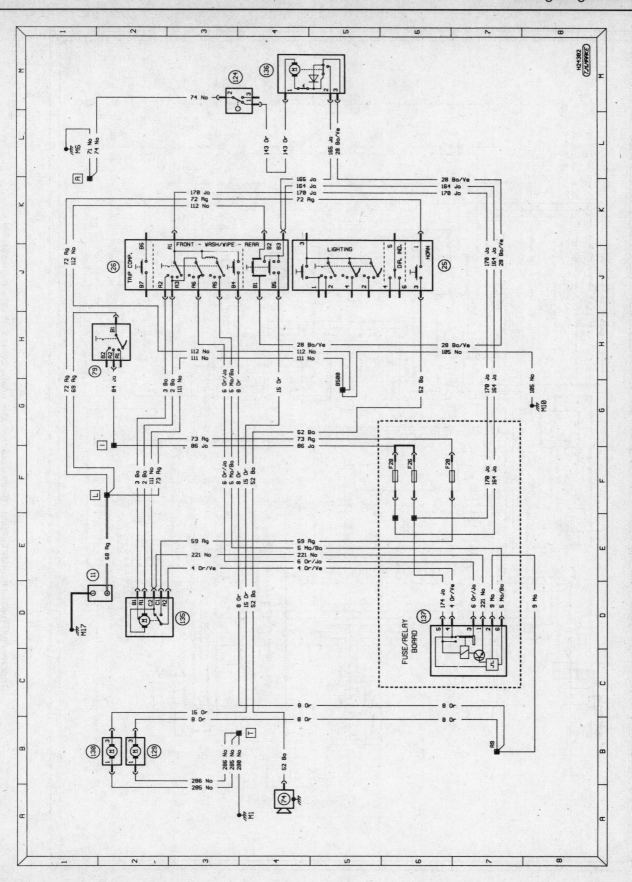

Diagram 3: Typical ancillary circuits - wash/wipe and horn

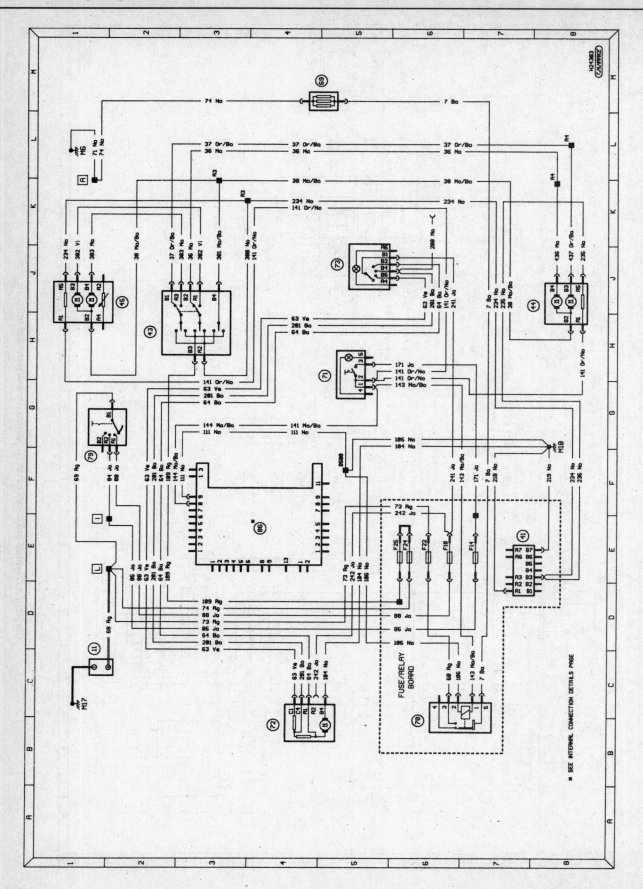

Diagram 3a: Typical ancillary circuits - heated rear window, heater blower and electric door mirrors

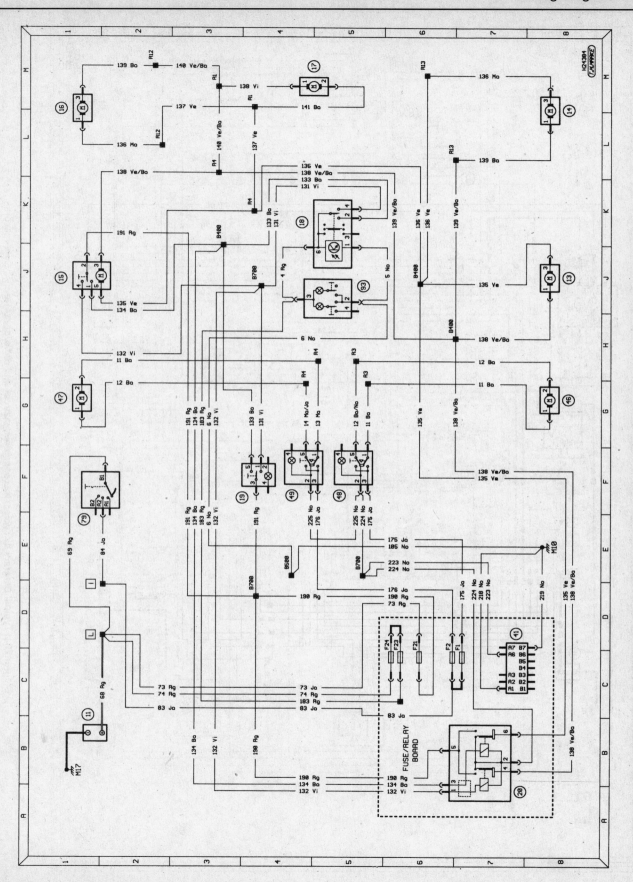

Diagram 3b: Typical ancillary circuits - electric windows and central door locking

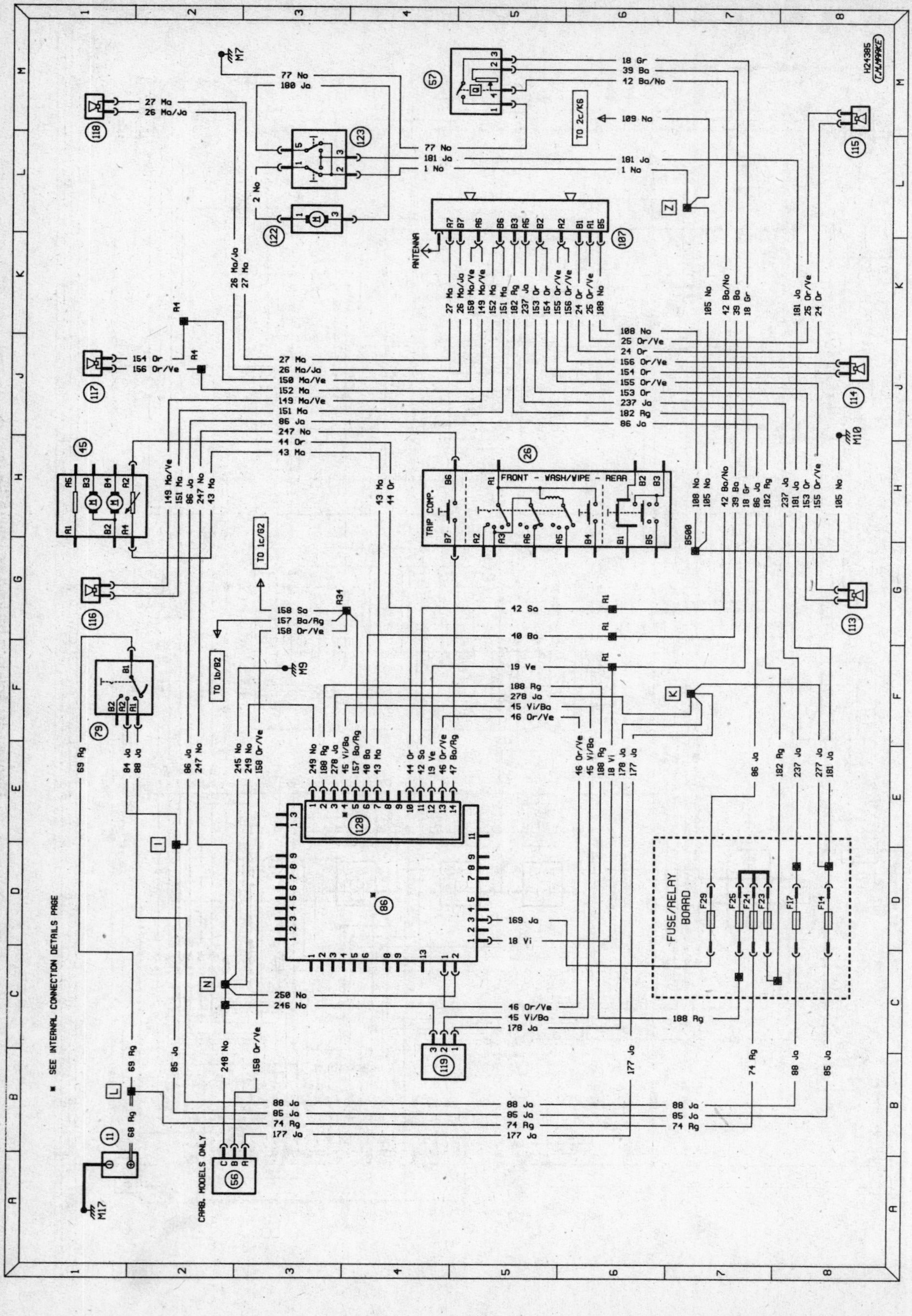

Diagram 4: Typical trip computer, sunroof and radio/cassette

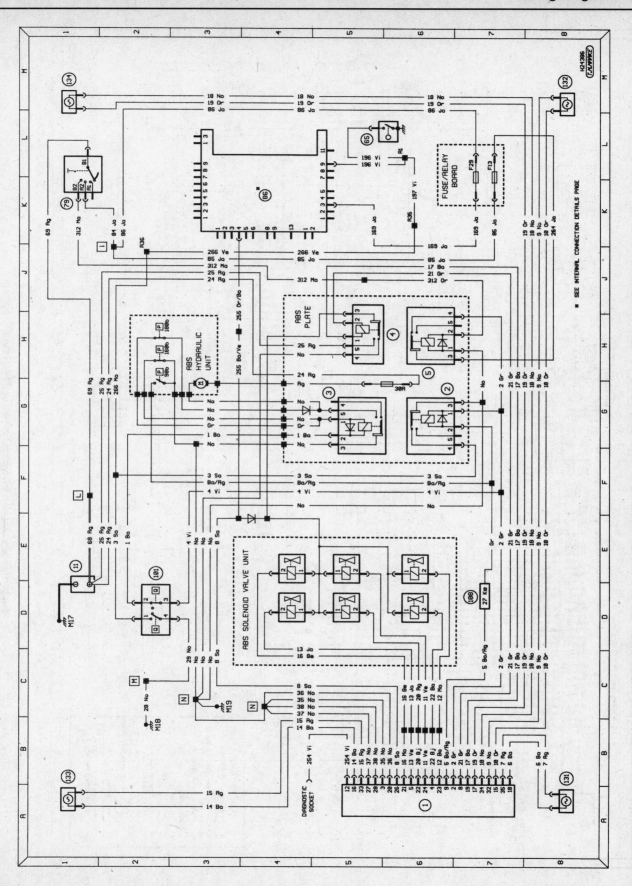

Diagram 4a: Anti-lock braking system (ABS)

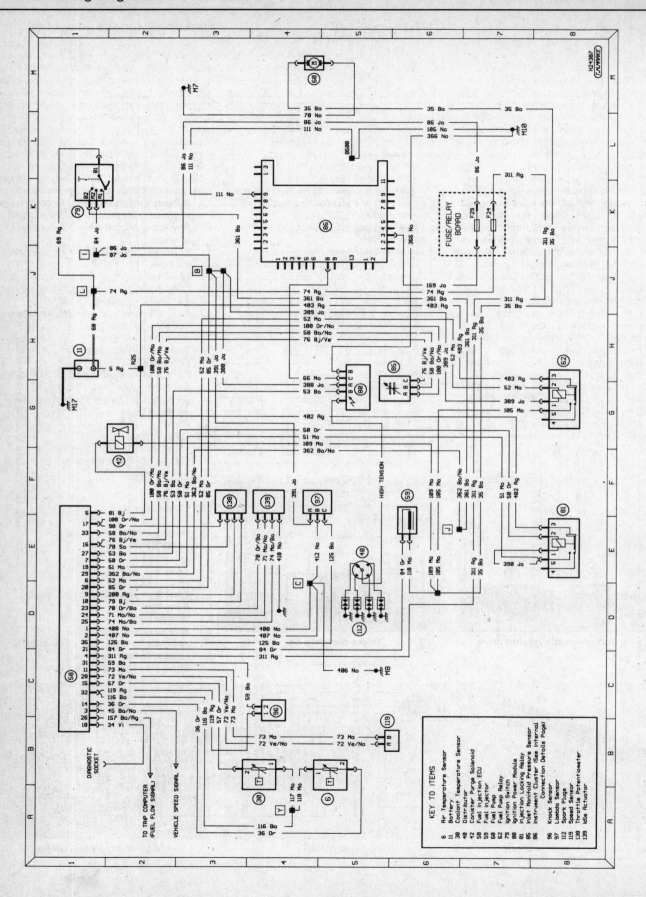

Supplementary diagram for typical single-point fuel injection system

Introduction

A selection of good tools is a fundamental requirement for anyone contemplating the maintenance and repair of a motor vehicle. For the owner who does not possess any, their purchase will prove a considerable expense, offsetting some of the savings made by doing-it-yourself. However, provided that the tools purchased meet the relevant national safety standards and are of good quality, they will last for many years and prove an extremely worthwhile investment.

To help the average owner to decide which tools are needed to carry out the various tasks detailed in this manual, we have compiled three lists of tools under the following headings: *Maintenance and minor repair, Repair and overhaul*, and *Special*. Newcomers to practical mechanics should start off with the *Maintenance and minor repair* tool kit, and confine themselves to the simpler jobs around the vehicle. Then, as confidence and experience grow, more difficult tasks can be undertaken, with extra tools being purchased as, and when, they are needed. In this way, a *Maintenance and minor repair* tool kit can be built up into a *Repair and overhaul* tool kit over a considerable period of time, without any major cash outlays. The experienced do-it-yourselfer will have a tool kit good enough for most repair and overhaul procedures, and will add tools from the *Special* category when it is felt that the expense is justified by the amount of use to which these tools will be put.

Maintenance and minor repair tool kit

The tools given in this list should be considered as a minimum requirement if routine maintenance, servicing and minor repair operations are to be undertaken. We recommend the purchase of combination spanners (ring one end, open-ended the other); although more expensive than open-ended ones, they do give the advantages of both types of spanner.

- [ ] *Combination spanners:*
  Metric - 8 to 19 mm inclusive
- [ ] *Adjustable spanner - 35 mm jaw (approx.)*
- [ ] *Spark plug spanner (with rubber insert) - petrol models*
- [ ] *Spark plug gap adjustment tool - petrol models*
- [ ] *Set of feeler gauges*
- [ ] *Brake bleed nipple spanner*
- [ ] *Screwdrivers:*
  Flat blade - 100 mm long x 6 mm dia
  Cross blade - 100 mm long x 6 mm dia
  Torx - various sizes (not all vehicles)
- [ ] *Combination pliers*
- [ ] *Hacksaw (junior)*
- [ ] *Tyre pump*
- [ ] *Tyre pressure gauge*
- [ ] *Oil can*
- [ ] *Oil filter removal tool*
- [ ] *Fine emery cloth*
- [ ] *Wire brush (small)*
- [ ] *Funnel (medium size)*
- [ ] *Sump drain plug key (not all vehicles)*

Repair and overhaul tool kit

These tools are virtually essential for anyone undertaking any major repairs to a motor vehicle, and are additional to those given in the *Maintenance and minor repair* list. Included in this list is a comprehensive set of sockets. Although these are expensive, they will be found invaluable as they are so versatile - particularly if various drives are included in the set. We recommend the half-inch square-drive type, as this can be used with most proprietary torque wrenches.

The tools in this list will sometimes need to be supplemented by tools from the *Special* list:

- [ ] *Sockets (or box spanners) to cover range in previous list (including Torx sockets)*
- [ ] *Reversible ratchet drive (for use with sockets)*
- [ ] *Extension piece, 250 mm (for use with sockets)*
- [ ] *Universal joint (for use with sockets)*
- [ ] *Flexible handle or sliding T "breaker bar" (for use with sockets)*
- [ ] *Torque wrench (for use with sockets)*
- [ ] *Self-locking grips*
- [ ] *Ball pein hammer*
- [ ] *Soft-faced mallet (plastic or rubber)*
- [ ] *Screwdrivers:*
  Flat blade - long & sturdy, short (chubby), and narrow (electrician's) types
  Cross blade – long & sturdy, and short (chubby) types
- [ ] *Pliers:*
  Long-nosed
  Side cutters (electrician's)
  Circlip (internal and external)
- [ ] *Cold chisel - 25 mm*
- [ ] *Scriber*
- [ ] *Scraper*
- [ ] *Centre-punch*
- [ ] *Pin punch*
- [ ] *Hacksaw*
- [ ] *Brake hose clamp*
- [ ] *Brake/clutch bleeding kit*
- [ ] *Selection of twist drills*
- [ ] *Steel rule/straight-edge*
- [ ] *Allen keys (inc. splined/Torx type)*
- [ ] *Selection of files*
- [ ] *Wire brush*
- [ ] *Axle stands*
- [ ] *Jack (strong trolley or hydraulic type)*
- [ ] *Light with extension lead*
- [ ] *Universal electrical multi-meter*

Sockets and reversible ratchet drive

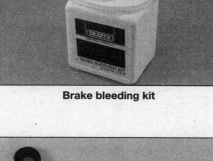

Brake bleeding kit

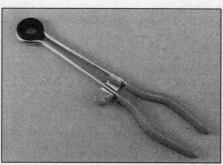

Torx key, socket and bit

Hose clamp

Angular-tightening gauge

Tools and Working Facilities

Special tools

The tools in this list are those which are not used regularly, are expensive to buy, or which need to be used in accordance with their manufacturers' instructions. Unless relatively difficult mechanical jobs are undertaken frequently, it will not be economic to buy many of these tools. Where this is the case, you could consider clubbing together with friends (or joining a motorists' club) to make a joint purchase, or borrowing the tools against a deposit from a local garage or tool hire specialist. It is worth noting that many of the larger DIY superstores now carry a large range of special tools for hire at modest rates.

The following list contains only those tools and instruments freely available to the public, and not those special tools produced by the vehicle manufacturer specifically for its dealer network. You will find occasional references to these manufacturers' special tools in the text of this manual. Generally, an alternative method of doing the job without the vehicle manufacturers' special tool is given. However, sometimes there is no alternative to using them. Where this is the case and the relevant tool cannot be bought or borrowed, you will have to entrust the work to a dealer.

- [ ] *Angular-tightening gauge*
- [ ] *Valve spring compressor*
- [ ] *Valve grinding tool*
- [ ] *Piston ring compressor*
- [ ] *Piston ring removal/installation tool*
- [ ] *Cylinder bore hone*
- [ ] *Balljoint separator*
- [ ] *Coil spring compressors (where applicable)*
- [ ] *Two/three-legged hub and bearing puller*
- [ ] *Impact screwdriver*
- [ ] *Micrometer and/or vernier calipers*
- [ ] *Dial gauge*
- [ ] *Stroboscopic timing light*
- [ ] *Dwell angle meter/tachometer*
- [ ] *Fault code reader*
- [ ] *Cylinder compression gauge*
- [ ] *Hand-operated vacuum pump and gauge*
- [ ] *Clutch plate alignment set*
- [ ] *Brake shoe steady spring cup removal tool*
- [ ] *Bush and bearing removal/installation set*
- [ ] *Stud extractors*
- [ ] *Tap and die set*
- [ ] *Lifting tackle*
- [ ] *Trolley jack*

Buying tools

Reputable motor accessory shops and superstores often offer excellent quality tools at discount prices, so it pays to shop around.

Remember, you don't have to buy the most expensive items on the shelf, but it is always advisable to steer clear of the very cheap tools. Beware of 'bargains' offered on market stalls or at car boot sales. There are plenty of good tools around at reasonable prices, but always aim to purchase items which meet the relevant national safety standards. If in doubt, ask the proprietor or manager of the shop for advice before making a purchase.

Care and maintenance of tools

Having purchased a reasonable tool kit, it is necessary to keep the tools in a clean and serviceable condition. After use, always wipe off any dirt, grease and metal particles using a clean, dry cloth, before putting the tools away. Never leave them lying around after they have been used. A simple tool rack on the garage or workshop wall for items such as screwdrivers and pliers is a good idea. Store all normal spanners and sockets in a metal box. Any measuring instruments, gauges, meters, etc, must be carefully stored where they cannot be damaged or become rusty.

Take a little care when tools are used. Hammer heads inevitably become marked, and screwdrivers lose the keen edge on their blades from time to time. A little timely attention with emery cloth or a file will soon restore items like this to a good finish.

Working facilities

Not to be forgotten when discussing tools is the workshop itself. If anything more than routine maintenance is to be carried out, a suitable working area becomes essential.

It is appreciated that many an owner-mechanic is forced by circumstances to remove an engine or similar item without the benefit of a garage or workshop. Having done this, any repairs should always be done under the cover of a roof.

Wherever possible, any dismantling should be done on a clean, flat workbench or table at a suitable working height.

Any workbench needs a vice; one with a jaw opening of 100 mm is suitable for most jobs. As mentioned previously, some clean dry storage space is also required for tools, as well as for any lubricants, cleaning fluids, touch-up paints etc, which become necessary.

Another item which may be required, and which has a much more general usage, is an electric drill with a chuck capacity of at least 8 mm. This, together with a good range of twist drills, is virtually essential for fitting accessories.

Last, but not least, always keep a supply of old newspapers and clean, lint-free rags available, and try to keep any working area as clean as possible.

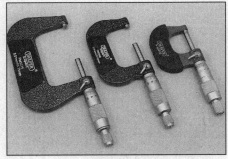
Micrometers

Dial test indicator ("dial gauge")

Strap wrench

Compression tester

Fault code reader

Length (distance)

Inches (in)	X 25.4	= Millimetres (mm)	X 0.0394	= Inches (in)
Feet (ft)	X 0.305	= Metres (m)	X 3.281	= Feet (ft)
Miles	X 1.609	= Kilometres (km)	X 0.621	= Miles

Volume (capacity)

Cubic inches (cu in; in3)	X 16.387	= Cubic centimetres (cc; cm3)	X 0.061	= Cubic inches (cu in; in3)
Imperial pints (Imp pt)	X 0.568	= Litres (l)	X 1.76	= Imperial pints (Imp pt)
Imperial quarts (Imp qt)	X 1.137	= Litres (l)	X 0.88	= Imperial quarts (Imp qt)
Imperial quarts (Imp qt)	X 1.201	= US quarts (US qt)	X 0.833	= Imperial quarts (Imp qt)
US quarts (US qt)	X 0.946	= Litres (l)	X 1.057	= US quarts (US qt)
Imperial gallons (Imp gal)	X 4.546	= Litres (l)	X 0.22	= Imperial gallons (Imp gal)
Imperial gallons (Imp gal)	X 1.201	= US gallons (US gal)	X 0.833	= Imperial gallons (Imp gal)
US gallons (US gal)	X 3.785	= Litres (l)	X 0.264	= US gallons (US gal)

Mass (weight)

Ounces (oz)	X 28.35	= Grams (g)	X 0.035	= Ounces (oz)
Pounds (lb)	X 0.454	= Kilograms (kg)	X 2.205	= Pounds (lb)

Force

Ounces-force (ozf; oz)	X 0.278	= Newtons (N)	X 3.6	= Ounces-force (ozf; oz)
Pounds-force (lbf; lb)	X 4.448	= Newtons (N)	X 0.225	= Pounds-force (lbf; lb)
Newtons (N)	X 0.1	= Kilograms-force (kgf; kg)	X 9.81	= Newtons (N)

Pressure

Pounds-force per square inch (psi; lbf/in²; lb/in²)	X 0.070	= Kilograms-force per square centimetre (kgf/cm²; kg/cm²)	X 14.223	= Pounds-force per square inch (psi; lbf/in²; lb/in²)
Pounds-force per square inch (psi; lbf/in²; lb/in²)	X 0.068	= Atmospheres (atm)	X 14.696	= Pounds-force per square inch (psi; lbf/in²; lb/in²)
Pounds-force per square inch (psi; lbf/in²; lb/in²)	X 0.069	= Bars	X 14.5	= Pounds-force per square inch (psi; lbf/in²; lb/in²)
Pounds-force per square inch (psi; lbf/in²; lb/in²)	X 6.895	= Kilopascals (kPa)	X 0.145	= Pounds-force per square inch (psi; lbf/in²; lb/in²)
Kilopascals (kPa)	X 0.01	= Kilograms-force per square centimetre (kgf/cm²; kg/cm²)	X 98.1	= Kilopascals (kPa)
Millibar (mbar)	X 100	= Pascals (Pa)	X 0.01	= Millibar (mbar)
Millibar (mbar)	X 0.0145	= Pounds-force per square inch (psi; lbf/in²; lb/in²)	X 68.947	= Millibar (mbar)
Millibar (mbar)	X 0.75	= Millimetres of mercury (mmHg)	X 1.333	= Millibar (mbar)
Millibar (mbar)	X 0.401	= Inches of water (inH₂O)	X 2.491	= Millibar (mbar)
Millimetres of mercury (mmHg)	X 0.535	= Inches of water (inH₂O)	X 1.868	= Millimetres of mercury (mmHg)
Inches of water (inH₂O)	X 0.036	= Pounds-force per square inch (psi; lbf/in²; lb/in²)	X 27.68	= Inches of water (inH₂O)

Torque (moment of force)

Pounds-force inches (lbf in; lb in)	X 1.152	= Kilograms-force centimetre (kgf cm; kg cm)	X 0.868	= Pounds-force inches (lbf in; lb in)
Pounds-force inches (lbf in; lb in)	X 0.113	= Newton metres (Nm)	X 8.85	= Pounds-force inches (lbf in; lb in)
Pounds-force inches (lbf in; lb in)	X 0.083	= Pounds-force feet (lbf ft; lb ft)	X 12	= Pounds-force inches (lbf in; lb in)
Pounds-force feet (lbf ft; lb ft)	X 0.138	= Kilograms-force metres (kgf m; kg m)	X 7.233	= Pounds-force feet (lbf ft; lb ft)
Pounds-force feet (lbf ft; lb ft)	X 1.356	= Newton metres (Nm)	X 0.738	= Pounds-force feet (lbf ft; lb ft)
Newton metres (Nm)	X 0.102	= Kilograms-force metres (kgf m; kg m)	X 9.804	= Newton metres (Nm)

Power

Horsepower (hp)	X 745.7	= Watts (W)	X 0.0013	= Horsepower (hp)

Velocity (speed)

Miles per hour (miles/hr; mph)	X 1.609	= Kilometres per hour (km/hr; kph)	X 0.621	= Miles per hour (miles/hr; mph)

Fuel consumption*

Miles per gallon, Imperial (mpg)	X 0.354	= Kilometres per litre (km/l)	X 2.825	= Miles per gallon, Imperial (mpg)
Miles per gallon, US (mpg)	X 0.425	= Kilometres per litre (km/l)	X 2.352	= Miles per gallon, US (mpg)

Temperature

Degrees Fahrenheit = (°C x 1.8) + 32

Degrees Celsius (Degrees Centigrade; °C) = (°F - 32) x 0.56

It is common practice to convert from miles per gallon (mpg) to litres/100 kilometres (l/100km), where mpg (Imperial) x l/100 km = 282 and mpg (US) x l/100 km = 235

Contents

Introduction

The vehicle owner who does his or her own maintenance according to the recommended service schedules should not have to use this section of the manual very often. Modern component reliability is such that, provided those items subject to wear or deterioration are inspected or renewed at the specified intervals, sudden failure is comparatively rare. Faults do not usually just happen as a result of sudden failure, but develop over a period of time. Major mechanical failures in particular are usually preceded by characteristic symptoms over hundreds or even thousands of miles. Those components which do occasionally fail without warning are often small and easily carried in the vehicle.

With any fault-finding, the first step is to decide where to begin investigations. Sometimes this is obvious, but on other occasions, a little detective work will be necessary. The owner who makes half a dozen haphazard adjustments or replacements may be successful in curing a fault (or its symptoms), but will be none the wiser if the fault recurs, and ultimately may have spent more time and money than was necessary. A calm and logical approach will

be found to be more satisfactory in the long run. Always take into account any warning signs or abnormalities that may have been noticed in the period preceding the fault - power loss, high or low gauge readings, unusual smells, etc - and remember that failure of components such as fuses or spark plugs may only be pointers to some underlying fault.

The pages which follow provide an easy reference guide to the more common problems which may occur during the operation of the vehicle. These problems and their possible causes are grouped under headings denoting various components or systems, such as Engine, Cooling system, etc. The Chapter and/or Section which deals with the problem is also shown in brackets. Whatever the fault, certain basic principles apply. These are as follows:

Verify the fault. This is simply a matter of being sure that you know what the symptoms are before starting work. This is particularly important if you are investigating a fault for someone else, who may not have described it very accurately.

Don't overlook the obvious. For example, if

the vehicle won't start, is there petrol in the tank? (Don't take anyone else's word on this particular point, and don't trust the fuel gauge either!) If an electrical fault is indicated, look for loose or broken wires before digging out the test gear.

Cure the disease, not the symptom. Substituting a flat battery with a fully-charged one will get you off the hard shoulder, but if the underlying cause is not attended to, the new battery will go the same way. Similarly, changing oil-fouled spark plugs for a new set will get you moving again, but remember that the reason for the fouling (if it wasn't simply an incorrect grade of plug) will have to be established and corrected.

Don't take anything for granted. Particularly, don't forget that a "new" component may itself be defective (especially if it's been rattling around in the boot for months), and don't leave components out of a fault diagnosis sequence just because they are new or recently fitted. When you do finally diagnose a difficult fault, you'll probably realise that all the evidence was there from the start.

1 Engine

Engine fails to rotate when attempting to start

Battery terminal connections loose or corroded (Chapter 1).
Battery discharged or faulty (Chapter 5A).
Broken, loose or disconnected wiring in the starting circuit (Chapter 5A).
Defective starter solenoid or switch (Chapter 5A).
Defective starter motor (Chapter 5A).
Starter pinion or flywheel ring gear teeth loose or broken (Chapter, 5A or Chapter 2A, 2B or 2C).
Engine earth strap broken or disconnected (Chapter 5A).
Automatic transmission not in Park/Neutral position, or starter inhibitor switch faulty (Chapter 7B).

Engine rotates, but will not start

Fuel tank empty.
Battery discharged (engine rotates slowly) (Chapter 5A).
Battery terminal connections loose or corroded (Chapter 1).
Ignition components damp or damaged (Chapters 1 and 5).
Broken, loose or disconnected wiring in the ignition circuit (Chapters 1 and 5).
Worn, faulty or incorrectly-gapped spark plugs (Chapter 1).
Choke mechanism sticking, incorrectly adjusted, or faulty - carburettor models only (Chapter 4A).
Fuel injection system fault (Chapter 4B).
Major mechanical failure (eg camshaft drive) (Chapter 2A, 2B or 2C).

Engine difficult to start when cold

Battery discharged (Chapter 5A).
Battery terminal connections loose or corroded (Chapter 1).
Worn, faulty or incorrectly-gapped spark plugs (Chapter 1).
Choke mechanism sticking, incorrectly adjusted, or faulty - carburettor models only (Chapter 4A).
Fuel injection system fault (Chapter 4B).
Other ignition system fault (Chapters 1 and 5).
Low cylinder compressions (Chapter 2A, 2B or 2C).

Engine difficult to start when hot

Air filter element dirty or clogged (Chapter 1).
Choke mechanism sticking, incorrectly adjusted, or faulty - carburettor models only (Chapter 4A).
Carburettor float chamber flooding (Chapter 4A).
Fuel injection system fault (Chapter 4B).
Low cylinder compressions (Chapter 2A, 2B or 2C).

Starter motor noisy or excessively-rough in engagement

Starter pinion or flywheel ring gear teeth loose or broken (Chapter 5A, or Chapter 2A, 2B or 2C).
Starter motor mounting bolts loose or missing (Chapter 5A).
Starter motor internal components worn or damaged (Chapter 5A).

Engine starts, but stops immediately

Insufficient fuel reaching carburettor (Chapter 4A).
Loose or faulty electrical connections in the ignition circuit (Chapters 1 and 5).
Vacuum leak at the carburettor/throttle housing or inlet manifold (Chapter 4A or 4B).
Blocked carburettor jet(s) or internal passages (Chapter 4A).
Fuel injection system fault (Chapter 4B).

Engine idles erratically

Incorrectly-adjusted idle speed and/or mixture settings (Chapter 1).
Air filter element clogged (Chapter 1).
Vacuum leak at the carburettor/throttle housing, inlet manifold or associated hoses (Chapter 4A or 4B).
Worn, faulty or incorrectly-gapped spark plugs (Chapter 1).
Incorrectly-adjusted valve clearances (Chapter 2A, 2B or 2C).
Uneven or low cylinder compressions (Chapter 2A, 2B or 2C).
Camshaft lobes worn (Chapter 2A, 2B, 2C or 2D).
Timing belt/chain incorrectly tensioned (Chapter 2A, 2B or 2C).
Fuel injection system fault (Chapter 4B).

Engine misfires at idle speed

Worn, faulty or incorrectly-gapped spark plugs (Chapter 1).
Faulty spark plug HT leads (Chapter 1).
Incorrectly-adjusted idle mixture settings (Chapter 1).
Incorrect ignition timing (Chapter 1).
Vacuum leak at the carburettor/throttle housing, inlet manifold or associated hoses (Chapter 4A or 4B).
Distributor cap cracked or tracking internally (Chapter 1).
Incorrectly-adjusted valve clearances (Chapter 2A, 2B or 2C).
Uneven or low cylinder compressions (Chapter 2A, 2B or 2C).
Disconnected, leaking or perished crankcase ventilation hoses (Chapter 4C).
Fuel injection system fault (Chapter 4B).

Engine misfires throughout the driving speed range

Blocked carburettor jet(s) or internal passages (Chapter 4A).
Carburettor worn or incorrectly adjusted (Chapters 1 and 4A).

Fuel filter choked (Chapter 1).
Fuel pump faulty or delivery pressure low (Chapter 4A or 4B).
Fuel tank vent blocked or fuel pipes restricted (Chapter 4A or 4B).
Vacuum leak at the carburettor/throttle housing, inlet manifold or associated hoses (Chapter 4A or 4B).
Worn, faulty or incorrectly-gapped spark plugs (Chapter 1).
Faulty spark plug HT leads (Chapter 1).
Distributor cap cracked or tracking internally (Chapter 1).
Faulty ignition coil (Chapter 5).
Uneven or low cylinder compressions (Chapter 2A, 2B or 2C).
Fuel injection system fault (Chapter 4B).

Engine hesitates on acceleration

Worn, faulty or incorrectly-gapped spark plugs (Chapter 1).
Carburettor accelerator pump faulty (Chapter 4A).
Blocked carburettor jets or internal passages (Chapter 4A).
Vacuum leak at the carburettor/throttle housing, inlet manifold or associated hoses (Chapter 4A or 4B).
Carburettor worn or incorrectly adjusted (Chapters 1 and 4A).
Fuel injection system fault (Chapter 4B).

Engine stalls

Incorrectly-adjusted idle speed and/or mixture settings (Chapter 1).
Blocked carburettor jet(s) or internal passages (Chapter 4A).
Vacuum leak at the carburettor/throttle housing, inlet manifold or associated hoses (Chapter 4A or 4B).
Fuel filter choked (Chapter 1).
Fuel pump faulty or delivery pressure low (Chapter 4A and 4B).
Fuel tank vent blocked or fuel pipes restricted (Chapter 4A and 4B).
Fuel injection system fault (Chapter 4B).

Engine lacks power

Incorrect ignition timing (Chapter 1).
Carburettor worn or incorrectly adjusted (Chapters 1 and 4A).
Timing belt/chain incorrectly fitted or tensioned (Chapter 2A, 2B or 2C).
Fuel filter choked (Chapter 1).
Fuel pump faulty or delivery pressure low (Chapter 4A or 4B).
Uneven or low cylinder compressions (Chapter 2A, 2B or 2C).
Worn, faulty or incorrectly-gapped spark plugs (Chapter 1).
Vacuum leak at the carburettor/throttle housing, inlet manifold or associated hoses (Chapter 4A or 4B).
Brakes binding (Chapters 1 and 9).
Clutch slipping (Chapter 6).
Automatic transmission fluid level incorrect (Chapter 1).
Fuel injection system fault (Chapter 4B).

Engine backfires

Ignition timing incorrect (Chapter 1).
Timing belt/chain incorrectly fitted or tensioned (Chapter 2A, 2B or 2C).
Carburettor worn or incorrectly adjusted (Chapters 1 and 4A).
Vacuum leak at the carburettor/throttle housing, inlet manifold or associated hoses (Chapter 4A or 4B).
Fuel injection system fault (Chapter 4B).

Oil pressure warning light illuminated with engine running

Low oil level or incorrect grade (Chapter 1).
Faulty oil pressure sensor (Chapter 5).
Worn engine bearings and/or oil pump (Chapter 2D).
High engine operating temperature (Chapter 3).
Oil pressure relief valve defective (Chapter 2A, 2B or 2C).
Oil pick-up strainer clogged (Chapter 2A, 2B or 2C).

Engine runs-on after switching off

Idle speed excessively high (Chapter 1).
Excessive carbon build-up in engine (Chapter 2D).
High engine operating temperature (Chapter 3).
Carburettor fault (Chapter 4A).
Fuel injection system fault (Chapter 4B).

Engine noises

Pre-ignition (pinking) or knocking during acceleration or under load

Ignition timing incorrect (Chapter 1).
Incorrect grade of fuel (Chapters 1 and 4).
Vacuum leak at the carburettor/throttle housing, inlet manifold or associated hoses (Chapter 4A or 4B).
Excessive carbon build-up in engine (Chapter 2D).
Worn or damaged distributor or other ignition system component (Chapter 5).
Carburettor worn or incorrectly adjusted (Chapters 1 and 4A).
Fuel injection system fault (Chapter 4B).

Whistling or wheezing noises

Leaking inlet manifold or carburettor/throttle housing gasket (Chapter 4A or 4B).
Leaking exhaust manifold gasket or pipe-to-manifold joint (Chapter 4A or 4B).
Leaking vacuum hose (Chapter 4A, 4B, 4C, 5, or 9).
Blowing cylinder head gasket (Chapter 2A, 2B or 2C).

Tapping or rattling noises

Incorrect valve clearances (Chapter 2A, 2B or 2C).
Worn valve gear or camshaft (Chapter 2A, 2B or 2C).
Worn timing chain or tensioner (Chapter 2B).

Ancillary component fault (water pump, alternator, etc) (Chapter 3, 5 or 10).

Knocking or thumping noises

Worn big-end bearings (regular heavy knocking, perhaps less under load) (Chapter 2D).
Worn main bearings (rumbling and knocking, perhaps worsening under load) (Chapter 2D).
Piston slap (most noticeable when cold) (Chapter 2D).
Ancillary component fault (alternator, water pump, etc) (Chapter 3, 5 or 10).

2 Cooling system

Overheating

Insufficient coolant in system (Chapter 1).
Thermostat faulty (Chapter 3).
Radiator core blocked, or grille restricted (Chapter 3).
Electric cooling fan or thermoswitch faulty (Chapter 3).
Pressure cap faulty (Chapter 3).
Water pump drivebelt worn, or incorrectly adjusted (Chapter 1 and/or 2C).
Ignition timing incorrect (Chapter 1).
Inaccurate temperature gauge sender unit (Chapter 3).
Air-lock in cooling system (Chapter 1).

Overcooling

Thermostat faulty (Chapter 3).
Inaccurate temperature gauge sender unit (Chapter 3).

External coolant leakage

Deteriorated or damaged hoses or hose clips (Chapter 1).
Radiator core or heater matrix leaking (Chapter 3).
Pressure cap faulty (Chapter 3).
Water pump seal leaking (Chapter 3).
Boiling due to overheating (Chapter 3).
Core plug leaking (Chapter 2D).

Internal coolant leakage

Leaking cylinder head gasket (Chapter 2A, 2B or 2C).
Cracked cylinder head or cylinder bore (Chapter 2A, 2B, 2C or 2D).

Corrosion

Infrequent draining and flushing (Chapter 1).
Incorrect antifreeze mixture or inappropriate type (Chapter 1).

3 Fuel and exhaust systems

Excessive fuel consumption

Air filter element dirty or clogged (Chapter 1).
Carburettor worn or incorrectly adjusted (Chapter 4A).

Choke cable incorrectly adjusted, or choke sticking - carburettor models only (Chapter 4A).
Fuel injection system fault (Chapter 4B).
Ignition timing incorrect (Chapter 1).
Tyres under-inflated (Chapter 1).

Fuel leakage and/or fuel odour

Damaged or corroded fuel tank, pipes or connections (Chapter 4A or 4B).
Carburettor float chamber flooding (Chapter 4A).
Fuel injection system fault (Chapter 4B).

Excessive noise or fumes from exhaust system

Leaking exhaust system or manifold joints (Chapter 1, 4A or 4B).
Leaking, corroded or damaged silencers or pipe (Chapter 1, 4A or 4B).
Broken mountings causing body or suspension contact (Chapter 1).

4 Clutch

Pedal travels to floor - no pressure or very little resistance

Broken clutch cable (Chapter 6).
Incorrect clutch adjustment (Chapter 6).
Faulty clutch pedal self-adjust mechanism (Chapter 6).
Broken clutch release bearing or fork (Chapter 6).
Broken diaphragm spring in clutch pressure plate (Chapter 6).

Clutch fails to disengage (unable to select gears)

Incorrect clutch adjustment (Chapter 6).
Faulty clutch pedal self-adjust mechanism (Chapter 6).
Clutch disc sticking on gearbox input shaft splines (Chapter 6).
Clutch disc sticking to flywheel or pressure plate (Chapter 6).
Faulty pressure plate assembly (Chapter 6).
Clutch release mechanism worn or incorrectly assembled (Chapter 6).

Clutch slips (engine speed increases, with no increase in vehicle speed)

Incorrect clutch adjustment (Chapter 6).
Faulty clutch pedal self-adjust mechanism (Chapter 6).
Clutch disc linings excessively worn (Chapter 6).
Clutch disc linings contaminated with oil or grease (Chapter 6).
Faulty pressure plate or weak diaphragm spring (Chapter 6).

Judder as clutch is engaged

Clutch disc linings contaminated with oil or grease (Chapter 6).

Fault Finding REF•7

Clutch disc linings excessively worn (Chapter 6).
Clutch cable sticking or frayed (Chapter 6).
Faulty or distorted pressure plate or diaphragm spring (Chapter 6).
Worn or loose engine or gearbox mountings (Chapter 2A).
Clutch disc hub or gearbox input shaft splines worn (Chapter 6).

Noise when depressing or releasing clutch pedal

Worn clutch release bearing (Chapter 6).
Worn or dry clutch pedal bushes (Chapter 6).
Faulty pressure plate assembly (Chapter 6).
Pressure plate diaphragm spring broken (Chapter 6).
Broken clutch disc cushioning springs (Chapter 6).

5 Manual gearbox

Noisy in neutral with engine running

Input shaft bearings worn (noise apparent with clutch pedal released, but not when depressed) (Chapter 7A).*
Clutch release bearing worn (noise apparent with clutch pedal depressed, possibly less when released) (Chapter 6).

Noisy in one particular gear

Worn, damaged or chipped gear teeth (Chapter 7A).*

Difficulty engaging gears

Clutch fault (Chapter 6).
Worn or damaged gear linkage (Chapter 7A).
Incorrectly-adjusted gear linkage (Chapter 7A).
Worn synchroniser units (Chapter 7A).*

Jumps out of gear

Worn or damaged gear linkage (Chapter 7A).
Incorrectly-adjusted gear linkage (Chapter 7A).
Worn synchroniser units (Chapter 7A).*
Worn selector forks (Chapter 7A).*

Vibration

Lack of oil (Chapter 1).
Worn bearings (Chapter 7A).*

Lubricant leaks

Leaking differential output oil seal (Chapter 7A).
Leaking housing joint (Chapter 7A).*
Leaking input shaft oil seal (Chapter 7A).*
*Although the corrective action necessary to remedy the symptoms described is beyond the scope of the home mechanic, the above information should be helpful in isolating the cause of the condition, so that the owner can communicate clearly with a professional mechanic.

6 Automatic transmission

Note: *Due to the complexity of the automatic transmission, it is difficult for the home mechanic to properly diagnose and service this unit. For problems other than the following, the vehicle should be taken to a dealer service department or automatic transmission specialist.*

Fluid leakage

Automatic transmission fluid is usually deep red in colour. Fluid leaks should not be confused with engine oil, which can easily be blown onto the transmission by airflow.
To determine the source of a leak, first remove all built-up dirt and grime from the transmission housing and surrounding areas, using a degreasing agent, or by steam-cleaning. Drive the vehicle at low speed, so airflow will not blow the leak far from its source. Raise and support the vehicle, and determine where the leak is coming from. The following are common areas of leakage:
(a) Transmission fluid pan (Chapter 1).
(b) Dipstick tube (Chapters 1 and 7B).
(c) Transmission-to-fluid cooler fluid pipes/unions (Chapter 7B).

Transmission fluid brown, or has burned smell

Transmission fluid level low, or fluid in need of renewal (Chapter 1).

General gear selection problems

Chapter 7B deals with checking and adjusting the selector linkage on automatic transmissions. The following are common problems which may be caused by a poorly-adjusted linkage:
(a) Engine starting in gears other than Park or Neutral.
(b) Indicator on gear selector lever pointing to a gear other than the one actually being used.
(c) Vehicle moves when in Park or Neutral.
(d) Poor gearshift quality or erratic gear changes.
Refer to Chapter 7B for the selector linkage adjustment procedure.

Transmission will not downshift (kickdown) with accelerator pedal fully depressed

Low transmission fluid level (Chapter 1).
Incorrect selector mechanism adjustment (Chapter 7B).

Engine will not start in any gear, or starts in gears other than Park or Neutral

Incorrect starter/inhibitor switch adjustment (Chapter 7B).
Incorrect selector mechanism adjustment (Chapter 7B).

Transmission slips, shifts roughly, is noisy, or has no drive in forward or reverse gears

There are many probable causes for the above problems, but the home mechanic should be concerned with only one possibility - fluid level. Before taking the vehicle to a dealer or transmission specialist, check the fluid level and condition of the fluid as described in Chapter 1. Correct the fluid level as necessary or change the fluid and filter if needed. If the problem persists, professional help will be necessary.

7 Driveshafts

Clicking or knocking noise on turns (at slow speed on full-lock)

Lack of constant velocity joint lubricant (Chapter 8).
Worn outer constant velocity joint (Chapter 8).

Vibration when accelerating or decelerating

Worn inner constant velocity joint (Chapter 8).
Bent or distorted driveshaft (Chapter 8).

8 Braking system

Note: *Before assuming that a brake problem exists, make sure that the tyres are in good condition and correctly inflated, that the front wheel alignment is correct, and that the vehicle is not loaded with weight in an unequal manner. Apart from checking the condition of all pipe and hose connections, any faults occurring on the anti-lock braking system should be referred to a Renault dealer for diagnosis.*

Vehicle pulls to one side under braking

Worn, defective, damaged or contaminated front or rear brake pads/shoes on one side (Chapter 1).
Seized or partially-seized front or rear brake caliper/wheel cylinder piston (Chapter 9).
A mixture of brake pad/shoe lining materials fitted between sides (Chapter 1).
Brake caliper mounting bolts loose (Chapter 9).
Rear brake backplate mounting bolts loose (Chapter 9).
Worn or damaged steering or suspension components (Chapters 1 and 10).

Noise (grinding or high-pitched squeal) when brakes applied

Brake pad or shoe friction lining material worn down to metal backing (Chapter 1).
Excessive corrosion of brake disc or drum. (May be apparent after the vehicle has been standing for some time (Chapters 1 and 9).

Foreign object (stone chipping etc) trapped between brake disc and splash shield (Chapters 1 and 9).

Excessive brake pedal travel

Inoperative rear brake self-adjust mechanism (Chapters 1 and 9).
Faulty master cylinder (Chapter 9).
Air in hydraulic system (Chapters 1 and 9).
Faulty vacuum servo unit (Chapter 9).

Brake pedal feels spongy when depressed

Air in hydraulic system (Chapters 1 and 9).
Deteriorated flexible rubber brake hoses (Chapters 1 and 9).
Master cylinder mounting nuts loose (Chapter 9).
Faulty master cylinder (Chapter 9).

Excessive brake pedal effort required to stop vehicle

Faulty vacuum servo unit (Chapter 9).
Disconnected, damaged or insecure brake servo vacuum hose (Chapter 9).
Primary or secondary hydraulic circuit failure (Chapter 9).
Seized brake caliper or wheel cylinder piston(s) (Chapter 9).
Brake pads or brake shoes incorrectly fitted (Chapter 1).
Incorrect grade of brake pads or brake shoes fitted (Chapter 1).
Brake pads or brake shoe linings contaminated (Chapter 1).

Judder felt through brake pedal or steering wheel when braking

Excessive run-out or distortion of front discs or rear drums (Chapter 9).
Brake pad or brake shoe linings worn (Chapter 1).
Brake caliper or rear brake backplate mounting bolts loose (Chapter 9).
Wear in suspension or steering components or mountings (Chapters 1 and 10).

Brakes binding

Seized brake caliper or wheel cylinder piston(s) (Chapter 9).
Incorrectly-adjusted handbrake mechanism or linkage (Chapter 1).
Faulty master cylinder (Chapter 9).

Rear wheels locking under normal braking

Rear brake shoe linings contaminated (Chapter 1).
Faulty brake pressure regulator (Chapter 9).

9 Suspension and steering systems

Note: *Before diagnosing suspension or steering faults, be sure that the trouble is not due to incorrect tyre pressures, mixtures of tyre types or binding brakes.*

Vehicle pulls to one side

Defective tyre (Chapter 1).
Excessive wear in suspension or steering components (Chapters 1 and 10).
Incorrect front wheel alignment (Chapter 10).
Accident damage to steering or suspension components (Chapter 1).

Wheel wobble and vibration

Front roadwheels out of balance (vibration felt mainly through the steering wheel) (Chapters 1 and 10).
Rear roadwheels out of balance (vibration felt throughout the vehicle) (Chapters 1 and 10).
Roadwheels damaged or distorted (Chapters 1 and 10).
Faulty or damaged tyre (Chapter 1).
Worn steering or suspension joints, bushes or components (Chapters 1 and 10).
Wheel bolts loose (Chapters 1 and 10).

Excessive pitching and/or rolling around corners or during braking

Defective shock absorbers (Chapters 1 and 10).
Broken or weak coil spring and/or suspension component (Chapters 1 and 10).
Worn or damaged anti-roll bar or mountings (Chapter 10).

Wandering or general instability

Incorrect front wheel alignment (Chapter 10).
Worn steering or suspension joints, bushes or components (Chapters 1 and 10).
Roadwheels out of balance (Chapters 1 and 10).
Faulty or damaged tyre (Chapter 1).
Wheel bolts loose (Chapters 1 and 10).
Defective shock absorbers (Chapters 1 and 10).

Excessively-stiff steering

Lack of steering gear lubricant (Chapter 10).
Seized tie-rod end balljoint or suspension balljoint (Chapters 1 and 10).
Broken or incorrectly-adjusted power steering pump drivebelt (Chapter 1).
Incorrect front wheel alignment (Chapter 10).
Steering rack or column bent or damaged (Chapter 10).

Excessive play in steering

Worn steering column universal joint(s) or intermediate coupling (Chapter 10).
Worn steering tie-rod end balljoints (Chapters 1 and 10).
Worn rack and pinion steering gear (Chapter 10).
Worn steering or suspension joints, bushes or components (Chapters 1 and 10).

Lack of power assistance

Broken or incorrectly-adjusted power steering pump drivebelt (Chapter 1).
Incorrect power steering fluid level (Chapter 1).
Restriction in power steering fluid hoses (Chapter 1).

Faulty power steering pump (Chapter 10).
Faulty rack-and-pinion steering gear (Chapter 10).

Tyre wear excessive

Tyres worn on inside or outside edges

Tyres under-inflated (wear on both edges) (Chapter 1).
Incorrect camber or castor angles (wear on one edge only) (Chapter 10).
Worn steering or suspension joints, bushes or components (Chapters 1 and 10).
Excessively hard cornering.
Accident damage.

Tyre treads exhibit feathered edges

Incorrect toe setting (Chapter 10).

Tyres worn in centre of tread

Tyres over-inflated (Chapter 1).

Tyres worn on inside and outside edges

Tyres under-inflated (Chapter 1).

Tyres worn unevenly

Tyres out of balance (Chapter 1).
Excessive wheel or tyre run-out (Chapter 1).
Worn shock absorbers (Chapters 1 and 10).
Faulty tyre (Chapter 1).

10 Electrical system

Note: *For problems associated with the starting system, refer to the faults listed under "Engine" earlier in this Section.*

Battery will not hold a charge for more than a few days

Battery defective internally (Chapter 5A).
Battery electrolyte level low (Chapter 1).
Battery terminal connections loose or corroded (Chapter 1).
Alternator drivebelt worn or incorrectly adjusted (Chapter 1).
Alternator not charging at correct output (Chapter 5A).
Alternator or voltage regulator faulty (Chapter 5A).
Short-circuit causing continual battery drain (Chapter 5A).

Ignition (no-charge) warning light remains illuminated with engine running

Alternator drivebelt broken, worn, or incorrectly adjusted (Chapter 1).
Alternator brushes worn, sticking, or dirty (Chapter 5A).
Alternator brush springs weak or broken (Chapter 5A).
Internal fault in alternator or voltage regulator (Chapter 5A).
Broken, disconnected, or loose wiring in charging circuit (Chapter 5A).

Ignition (no-charge) warning light fails to come on

Warning light bulb blown (Chapter 12).
Broken, disconnected, or loose wiring in warning light circuit (Chapter 12).
Alternator faulty (Chapter 5A).

Lights inoperative

Bulb blown (Chapter 12).
Corrosion of bulb or bulbholder contacts (Chapter 12).
Blown fuse (Chapter 12).
Faulty relay (Chapter 12).
Broken, loose, or disconnected wiring (Chapter 12).
Faulty switch (Chapter 12).

Instrument readings inaccurate or erratic

Instrument readings increase with engine speed

Faulty voltage regulator (Chapter 12).

Fuel or temperature gauges give no reading

Faulty gauge sender unit (Chapters 3, 4A or 4B).
Wiring open-circuit (Chapter 12).
Faulty gauge (Chapter 12).

Fuel or temperature gauges give continuous maximum reading

Faulty gauge sender unit (Chapters 3, 4A or 4B).
Wiring short-circuit (Chapter 12).
Faulty gauge (Chapter 12).

Horn inoperative, or unsatisfactory in operation

Horn operates all the time

Horn push either earthed or stuck down (Chapter 12).
Horn cable-to-horn push earthed (Chapter 12).

Horn fails to operate

Blown fuse (Chapter 12).
Cable or cable connections loose, broken or disconnected (Chapter 12).
Faulty horn (Chapter 12).

Horn emits intermittent or unsatisfactory sound

Cable connections loose (Chapter 12).
Horn mountings loose (Chapter 12).
Faulty horn (Chapter 12).

Windscreen/tailgate wipers inoperative, or unsatisfactory in operation

Wipers fail to operate, or operate very slowly

Wiper blades stuck to screen, or linkage seized or binding (Chapters 1 and 12).
Blown fuse (Chapter 12).
Cable or cable connections loose, broken or disconnected (Chapter 12).
Faulty relay (Chapter 12).
Faulty wiper motor (Chapter 12).

Wiper blades sweep over too large or too small an area of the glass

Wiper arms incorrectly positioned on spindles (Chapter 1).
Excessive wear of wiper linkage (Chapter 1).
Wiper motor or linkage mountings loose or insecure (Chapter 12).

Wiper blades fail to clean the glass effectively

Wiper blade rubbers worn or perished (Chapter 1).
Wiper arm tension springs broken, or arm pivots seized (Chapter 1).
Insufficient windscreen washer additive to adequately remove road film (Chapter 1).

Windscreen/tailgate washers inoperative, or unsatisfactory in operation

One or more washer jets inoperative

Blocked washer jet (Chapter 1).
Disconnected, kinked or restricted fluid hose (Chapter 12).
Insufficient fluid in washer reservoir (Chapter 1).

Washer pump fails to operate

Broken or disconnected wiring or connections (Chapter 12).
Blown fuse (Chapter 12).
Faulty washer switch (Chapter 12).
Faulty washer pump (Chapter 12).

Washer pump runs for some time before fluid is emitted from jets

Faulty one-way valve in fluid supply hose (Chapter 12).

Electric windows inoperative, or unsatisfactory in operation

Window glass will only move in one direction

Faulty switch (Chapter 12)

Window glass slow to move

Incorrectly-adjusted door glass guide channels (Chapter 11).
Regulator seized or damaged, or in need of lubrication (Chapter 11).
Door internal components or trim fouling regulator (Chapter 11).
Faulty motor (Chapter 11).

Window glass fails to move

Incorrectly-adjusted door glass guide channels (Chapter 11).
Blown fuse (Chapter 12).
Faulty relay (Chapter 12).
Broken or disconnected wiring or connections (Chapter 12).
Faulty motor (Chapter 11).

Central locking system inoperative, or unsatisfactory in operation

Complete system failure

Blown fuse (Chapter 12).
Faulty relay (Chapter 12).
Broken or disconnected wiring or connections (Chapter 12).

Latch locks but will not unlock, or unlocks but will not lock

Faulty master switch (Chapter 12).
Broken or disconnected latch operating rods or levers (Chapter 11).
Faulty relay (Chapter 12).

One solenoid/motor fails to operate

Broken or disconnected wiring or connections (Chapter 12).
Faulty solenoid/motor (Chapter 11).
Broken, binding or disconnected latch operating rods or levers (Chapter 11).
Fault in door latch (Chapter 11).

Buying Spare Parts

Spare parts are available from many sources; for example, Renault garages, other garages and accessory shops, and motor factors. Our advice regarding spare part sources is as follows.

Officially-appointed Renault garages - This is the best source for parts which are peculiar to your car, and are not generally available (eg complete cylinder heads, internal gearbox components, badges, interior trim etc). It is also the only place at which you should buy parts if the vehicle is still under warranty. To be sure of obtaining the correct parts, it will be necessary to give the storeman your car's vehicle identification number, and if possible, take the old parts along for positive identification. Many parts are available under a factory exchange scheme - any parts returned should always be clean. It obviously makes good sense to go straight to the specialists on your car for this type of part, as they are best equipped to supply you.

Other garages and accessory shops - These are often very good places to buy materials and components needed for the maintenance of your car (eg oil filters, spark plugs, bulbs, drivebelts, oils and greases, touch-up paint, filler paste, etc). They also sell general accessories, usually have convenient opening hours, charge lower prices and can often be found not far from home.

Motor factors - Good factors will stock all the more important components which wear out comparatively quickly (eg exhaust systems, brake pads, seals and hydraulic parts, clutch components, bearing shells, pistons, valves etc). Motor factors will often provide new or reconditioned components on a part exchange basis - this can save a considerable amount of money.

Vehicle Identification Numbers

Modifications are a continuing and unpublicised process in vehicle manufacture, quite apart from major model changes. Spare parts manuals and lists are compiled upon a numerical basis, the individual vehicle identification numbers being essential to correct identification of the component concerned.

When ordering spare parts, always give as much information as possible. Quote the car model, year of manufacture, body and engine numbers, as appropriate.

The *vehicle identification number (VIN)* is stamped on the VIN plate located under the bonnet, and is also stamped into the top of the right-hand front suspension turret. On early models, the plate is located on the right-hand suspension turret - two separate plates may be fitted, or all the information may be on a single plate. On later models, the plate is located on the body front panel, at the front right-hand side of the engine compartment - all information is incorporated on a single plate (see illustrations).

The *chassis number* appears on the VIN plate (as described previously), and is also stamped into the top of the right-hand front suspension strut turret, directly after the VIN number (see illustration).

The *paint code number* is stamped on the VIN plate.

The *engine number* is stamped on a plate riveted to the engine. The location of the plate varies according to engine type (see illustrations).

VIN plate – early models

VIN plate (alternative type) - early models
A - Oval plate   C - Manufacturer's plate

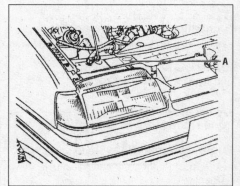

VIN plate (A) - later models

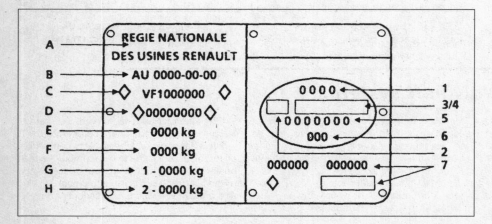

VIN plate codes

A Manufacturer's name
B EEC official approval number
C VIN number
D Chassis number
E Gross vehicle weight
F Gross train weight
G Maximum permissible front axle weight
H Maximum permissible rear axle weight
1 Vehicle model code
2 Special features of vehicle
3 Country of origin
4 Equipment number and options
5 Factory and fabrication number
6 Paint code
7 Additional marking

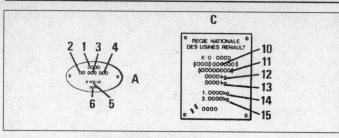

Alternative VIN plate codes

A Oval plate
C Manufacturer's plate
1 Vehicle model code
2 Special features of vehicle
3 Country of origin
4 Equipment number and
   options
5 Factory and fabrication
   number

6 Paint code
10 VIN number
11 Chassis number
12 Gross vehicle weight
13 Gross train weight
14 Maximum permissible front
    axle weight
15 Maximum permissible rear
    axle weight

VIN number and chassis number stamped on suspension turret

Engine Identification

The engine type can be identified from the engine number, located on a plate, as described previously ("Vehicle identification numbers").

Full details of engine codes can be found in the Specifications Section of the relevant engine Chapter (2A, 2B, or 2C, as applicable).

Throughout this manual, engines are referred to by type, or type code, as follows:

C-type: 1237 cc (C1G), 1390 cc (C3J) and 1397 cc (C1J and C2J)
E-type: 1390 cc (E6J and E7J)
F-type: 1721 cc (F2N and F3N), 1764 cc (F7P) and 1794 cc (F3P)

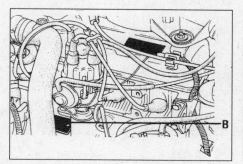

Engine number location (B) - C-type engines

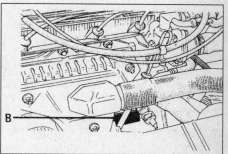

Engine number location (B) - E-type engines

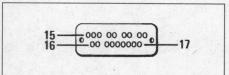

Engine plate codes

15 Engine type   17 Engine number
16 Engine type suffix

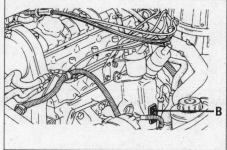

Engine number location (B) - F-type engines (except 16-valve - 1764 cc/F7P)

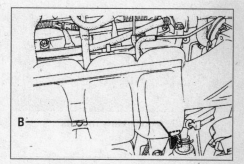

Engine number location (B) - 16-valve 1764 cc (F7P) engine

Radio/cassette unit anti-theft system

The radio/cassette unit fitted as standard equipment by Renault may be equipped with a built-in security code, to deter thieves. If the power source to the unit is cut, the anti-theft system will activate. Even if the power source is immediately reconnected, the radio/cassette unit will not function until the correct security code has been entered.

Therefore, if you do not know the correct security code for the radio/cassette unit, do not disconnect the battery negative terminal of the battery, or remove the radio/cassette unit from the vehicle.

To enter the correct security code, follow the instructions provided with the radio/cassette player handbook.

If an incorrect code is entered, the unit will become locked, and cannot be operated.

If this happens, or if the security code is lost or forgotten, seek the advice of your Renault dealer. On presentation of proof of ownership, a Renault dealer will be able to unlock the unit and provide you with a new security code.

Notes

Note: *References throughout this index relate to Chapter•page number*

Preserving Our Motoring Heritage

< The Model J Duesenberg Derham Tourster. Only eight of these magnificent cars were ever built – this is the only example to be found outside the United States of America

Almost every car you've ever loved, loathed or desired is gathered under one roof at the Haynes Motor Museum. Over 300 immaculately presented cars and motorbikes represent every aspect of our motoring heritage, from elegant reminders of bygone days, such as the superb Model J Duesenberg to curiosities like the bug-eyed BMW Isetta. There are also many old friends and flames. Perhaps you remember the 1959 Ford Popular that you did your courting in? The magnificent 'Red Collection' is a spectacle of classic sports cars including AC, Alfa Romeo, Austin Healey, Ferrari, Lamborghini, Maserati, MG, Riley, Porsche and Triumph.

A Perfect Day Out

Each and every vehicle at the Haynes Motor Museum has played its part in the history and culture of Motoring. Today, they make a wonderful spectacle and a great day out for all the family. Bring the kids, bring Mum and Dad, but above all bring your camera to capture those golden memories for ever. You will also find an impressive array of motoring memorabilia, a comfortable 70 seat video cinema and one of the most extensive transport book shops in Britain. The Pit Stop Cafe serves everything from a cup of tea to wholesome, home-made meals or, if you prefer, you can enjoy the large picnic area nestled in the beautiful rural surroundings of Somerset.

-> John Haynes O.B.E., Founder and Chairman of the museum at the wheel of a Haynes Light 12.

< Graham Hill's Lola Cosworth Formula 1 car next to a 1934 Riley Sports.

The Museum is situated on the A359 Yeovil to Frome road at Sparkford, just off the A303 in Somerset. It is about 40 miles south of Bristol, and 25 minutes drive from the M5 intersection at Taunton.
Open 9.30am - 5.30pm (10.00am - 4.00pm Winter) 7 days a week, *except Christmas Day, Boxing Day and New Years Day*
Special rates available for schools, coach parties and outings Charitable Trust No. 292048